Praise for Susan Butler's

ROOSEVELT AND STALIN

"Franklin Roosevelt's relationship with Joseph Stalin has been well plumbed by historians, but Butler brings intimacy and texture to the topic. . . . Few will deny the pleasure her book provides."
—*Foreign Affairs*

"A rigorous study of one of the twentieth century's unlikeliest alliances. Throughout her excellent book, Butler shows how the leaders of the capitalist and communist worlds had not a grudging marriage of convenience but a willing friendship, one founded on and motivated by a shared vision: to defeat Hitler and create a lasting postwar peace. . . . Her attention to detail . . . keeps us gripped. . . . The result is a rewarding read about a meeting of disparate minds."
—*Minneapolis Star Tribune*

"This painstaking examination of Roosevelt and Stalin's complicated relationship centers on two face-to-face meetings—in Tehran in 1943 and in Yalta in 1945—as they argued over wartime strategy and postwar planning. Butler relays entertaining details (when Stalin doodled, he drew Siberian wolves), and emphasizes Roosevelt's unwavering resolve to keep Stalin 'inside the tent,' in order to establish the United Nations. Particularly compelling is her account of F.D.R.'s death."
—*The New Yorker*

"Absorbing, provocative. . . . Likely to energize considerable debate."
—*Booklist*

"Butler effectively demonstrates that there was no greater mediator and champion of peace than Roosevelt, whose sudden death in the final months of WWII robbed the world of perhaps the man who could have averted the Cold War."
—*Publishers Weekly*

"Comprehensive. . . . Meticulous. . . . Striking. . . . A thorough account of the alliance between two very different leaders."
—*Kirkus Reviews*

"[Susan Butler's book is] the most detailed account available of the relationship between these two extraordinary men. . . . Answers the question, as definitively as counterfactuals *can* be answered, of just how much of a difference Roosevelt's death made. . . . An essential recounting of how the initial alliance between Stalin and FDR and its subsequent dissolution under Truman shaped the postwar world and our own." —Marilyn B. Young,
author of *The Vietnam Wars 1945–1990*

"Well written, richly detailed, and well considered. A significant narrative of a historically critical relationship and possibly, a lost opportunity to head off the arms race and the Cold War."
—Evan Thomas, author of
Ike's Bluff: President Eisenhower's Secret Battle to Save the World

"The most complete study to date of FDR's relationship with Stalin." —Frank Costigliola, author of *Roosevelt's Lost Alliances: How Personal Politics Helped Start the Cold War*

"Susan Butler's brilliantly readable book firmly places FDR where he belongs, as the American president engaged most directly in diplomacy and strategy, who not only had an ambitious plan for the postwar world, but had the strength, ambition and personal charm to overcome Churchill's reluctance and Stalin's suspicion to bring about what was, in effect, an *American* peace, and to avoid the disastrous consequences that followed the botched peace of Versailles in 1919. It is at once a long overdue tribute to FDR and his vision, and a serious work of history that reads like a novel. I would rank it next to Margaret MacMillan's *Paris 1919*, and it casts new light on the character and war aims of Stalin, Churchill and FDR himself. *Brava!*" —Michael Korda,
author of *Ike: An American Hero*

Susan Butler

ROOSEVELT AND STALIN

Susan Butler grew up in New York and received her MA from Columbia University. She is the author of *East to the Dawn* and the editor of *My Dear Mr. Stalin*. She lives in Lake Wales, Florida.

www.susanbutler.org

ALSO BY SUSAN BUTLER

My Dear Mr. Stalin

East to the Dawn

ROOSEVELT AND STALIN

ROOSEVELT AND STALIN

Portrait of a Partnership

SUSAN BUTLER

Vintage Books
A Division of Penguin Random House LLC
New York

FIRST VINTAGE BOOKS EDITION, MARCH 2016

Copyright © 2015 by Susan Butler

All rights reserved. Published in the United States by Vintage Books, a division of Penguin Random House LLC, New York, and distributed in Canada by Random House of Canada, a division of Penguin Random House Canada Ltd., Toronto. Originally published in hardcover in the United States by Alfred A. Knopf, a division of Penguin Random House LLC, New York, in 2015.

Vintage and colophon are registered trademarks of Penguin Random House LLC.

The Library of Congress has cataloged the Knopf edition as follows:
Butler, Susan.
Roosevelt and Stalin : Portrait of a Partnership by Susan Butler. — First edition.
pages cm
1. World War, 1939–1945—Diplomatic history.
2. Roosevelt, Franklin D. (Franklin Delano), 1882–1945.
3. Stalin, Joseph, 1879–1953.
4. United States—Foreign relations—Soviet Union.
5. Soviet Union—Foreign relations—United States.   I. Title.
D753.B83 2015   940.53'2—DC23   2014011723

Vintage Books Trade Paperback ISBN: 978-0-307-74181-3
eBook ISBN: 978-1-101-87462-2

Author photograph © Michael Potthast
Book design by Iris Weinstein

www.vintagebooks.com

Printed in the United States of America
10 9 8 7 6 5 4 3 2 1

To the 405,000 Americans and the 27,000,000 Russians
who died in World War II

CONTENTS

ROOSEVELT AND STALIN

I

CROSSING THE ATLANTIC
IN WARTIME

On Thursday morning, November 11, 1943, the twenty-fifth anniversary of the armistice that ended World War I, President Roosevelt left the White House in an open convertible and swept through the capital, the Stars and Stripes and the presidential flag flying from the front of the car. He was on his way to pay homage at the Tomb of the Unknown Soldier at Arlington National Cemetery. There was a holiday air in the city: flags were on display, and banks were closed for the day. As the president's car reached the cemetery and proceeded to the tomb, a twenty-one-gun salute, fired from the latest antitank guns, boomed out across the Potomac valley.

At eleven o'clock, the exact hour the armistice had been signed, Roosevelt stood bareheaded between General Edwin "Pa" Watson, his military aide, and Vice Admiral Wilson Brown, his naval aide, in front of the tomb. The day was chilly and raw, the trees almost bare; there was a cold wind. Over the president's shoulders was the dark navy dress cape he frequently wore on short trips from the White House. An army bugler flanked the group on one side; a soldier holding a big wreath of yellow and russet chrysanthemums stood on the other. An army band struck up "The Star-Spangled Banner," after which there was the customary moment of silence. Admiral Brown then took the wreath and laid it on the tomb for the president. Four ruffles of muffled drums were heard, and the bugler blew taps.

Following the brief ceremony, the sounds of a second twenty-one-gun salute boomed out across the valley as the president's car wound its way out of the cemetery.

The House of Representatives marked the day with commemorative speeches, most of which voiced the sentiment that ways must be found to make the coming peace more durable than the last. The Senate was not in session.

Roosevelt was in the tenth year of his presidency, the country almost two years into World War II. As darkness fell and rain started, the president again left the White House by car, but unlike in the morning he slipped out unobtrusively. He was on his way to the marine base at Quantico, Virginia, where the USS *Potomac,* the sleek white 165-foot presidential yacht, a Coast Guard cutter to which an upper deck and a cabin had been added, awaited. It would take him on the first leg of the 17,442-mile trip through submarine-infested waters to Tehran, Iran, more than halfway around the world. There, for the first time, he would meet Joseph Stalin, the supreme leader of the Soviet Union, the renegade. It would be a momentous occasion for both of them and for the world.

With Roosevelt was his closest adviser, Harry Hopkins, in charge of the Lend-Lease program providing the massive aid flowing to the Soviet Union; his chief of staff, Admiral William Leahy; his personal physician, Vice Admiral Dr. Ross McIntire; Admiral Brown; General Watson; and his physical therapist, Lieutenant Commander George Fox. The president's car arrived at a dark, seemingly deserted dock far away from intrusive eyes, where the *Potomac* awaited. Aboard the *Potomac* all was in readiness.

Exactly six minutes after the presidential party stepped onto the ship, it headed down the Potomac River bound for Cherry Point, Virginia, in the Chesapeake Bay, sixty-three miles distant, where it anchored for the night.

A little after 9:00 the next morning the *Potomac* approached the USS *Iowa,* anchored out in the bay in deeper water. It drew up alongside, and in the very light, cool morning air Roosevelt was placed in a sort of bosun's chair rigged from the rear sundeck of the *Potomac* and swung aboard the *Iowa*'s main deck just abreast of number three turret. When the transfer of the rest of the party was completed, the *Potomac* vanished into the distance, ordered to cruise out of sight and away from its well-known home berth for the next week, to create the impression, in case any journalist noticed the president's absence, that he was off on another private pleasure cruise aboard what some called the Floating White House because of the large amount of time he spent on it.

Roosevelt had always loved the sea. As a young boy at Campobello Island in Canada, where he summered, he had learned to sail his father's sailboat the *Half Moon,* a forty-six-foot cutter, taking it out every chance he got and handling it with ease. After he contracted polio at thirty-nine and lost the use of his legs, he had invested in a houseboat that he kept in Florida waters and lived on for months at a time.

Now he was looking forward to the voyage of the *Iowa,* the navy's newest, largest, fastest battleship. It had been specially fitted out for him: an elevator installed, ramps built over the coamings and deck obstructions to accommodate his wheelchair. As in all places where FDR lived, in the bathroom there was a tub with metal railings that FDR could grasp to raise himself up, a toilet bowl exactly the height of his wheelchair, and a mirror low enough so he could shave sitting down. His favorite leather-upholstered reclining chair was also in his quarters.

Half an hour after he was swung aboard, the big ship was under way. Waiting to greet FDR were all the top brass of the U.S. Armed Forces: General George C. Marshall, chief of staff of the U.S. Army; H. H. "Hap" Arnold, commanding general of the U.S. Army Air Forces; General Brehon B. Somervell, chief of Army Service Forces; Admiral Ernest J. King, commander in chief of the U.S. Fleet; and Admiral William Leahy, the president's chief of staff; plus four other generals, three more admirals, and about fifty staff officers of subordinate rank. At Roosevelt's request, no honors were rendered as he came aboard, and because of wartime restrictions his flag was not flown. Also aboard were the eight Secret Service men who always guarded the president.

So began Roosevelt's trip to meet Joseph Stalin, a meeting he had been trying to arrange for two years and had gone to extraordinary lengths to bring about.

He and Churchill had chosen Casablanca as a meeting place the previous January because they thought there was a good chance Stalin would agree to meet them there. "We are trying to get Stalin to come," Roosevelt had confided to Mike Reilly, supervising Secret Service agent at the White House, as he briefed him on the trip, firmly adding, "I won't go any further than Casablanca to meet him." But in the face of

Stalin's objections to every location he suggested, the president's resolve had crumbled: now he was going thousands of miles farther.

The Tehran meeting had been planned to promote Roosevelt's dearest objective, the establishment of an international organization, a more effective version of the League of Nations, of which every nation would be a member. Such an organization, he believed, was the best, indeed the only, way to maintain a peaceful world. It would supply a forum where any member nation could state its grievance and where all nations could converse. In certain situations it would also have the authority to act. Roosevelt planned that there would be four superpowers—the United States, the Soviet Union, Great Britain, and China—that would act as the world's four policemen. These four, with greater powers than other nations, would enforce order after the war was won.

Stalin was critical to the president's plan. The war had changed nations in unforeseen ways. Postwar, only two superpowers would remain: America and Russia. Without the membership and support of the Soviet Union, Roosevelt realized, there would be no international organization. With it, the United Nations, as Roosevelt had named the proposed organization, would start out as the first true government of the world.

Roosevelt expected to be challenged at his first meeting with the Soviet ruler, and he fully intended to be equal to the task. He planned to impress Stalin with his intelligence, his steadiness of character, and above all his power. In that way he would make the world's most paranoid ruler feel secure. He had to make Stalin comfortable with his ideas of how the world should be run when the war was over: Russia had to take part.

FDR read everything he could about Stalin, who was a Georgian, a bit more than two years older than he, born on the southern rim of Russia to an impoverished, alcoholic father and a mother who, recognizing his intelligence, had persuaded the clergy to educate him in church schools. Stalin had become a rebel, changing his name from Djugashvili to Stalin (steel), and caught the eye of Lenin, whose successor he became. He was, like FDR, physically disabled: two toes on his left foot were fused, giving him a slight rolling gait, and he held and used his left arm awkwardly, the result of being knocked down by a horse and carriage when he was a child.

FDR received conflicting descriptions. He queried the few people he knew who had met him. One, Anna Louise Strong, a founder of the *Moscow News,* a weekly newspaper for Americans, remembered that FDR was particularly, almost obsessively, interested in Stalin's personality. (Contrary to many people's experience, she had found Stalin "the easiest person to talk to I ever met.") FDR knew of his violent background, that he was ruthless, that he imprisoned or killed anyone who stood in his way. In 1930 he had compared Stalin to Mussolini. In 1940, speaking to a group of students gathered at the White House, he had famously said that Stalin's dictatorship was "as absolute as any other dictatorship in the world," that he was guilty of "the indiscriminate killings of thousands of innocent victims." He was under no illusion as to the nature of the Soviet ruler, nor had he any thought of meddling in the Soviet Union's internal affairs. He needed Stalin, and, FDR expected, Stalin needed *him* as much or even more. As Roosevelt said to his personal physician, Vice Admiral Ross McIntire, aboard the *Iowa,* "I bank on his realism. He must be tired of sitting on bayonets."

He had arranged an Egyptian prelude: a four-day round of conferences in Cairo with Winston Churchill and Chiang Kai-shek and, he hoped, Vyacheslav Molotov, the Soviet commissar of foreign affairs, the second most powerful man in the Soviet Union, together with their respective military staffs. After that, he, Churchill, and Molotov would make the short hop by plane to Iran to meet with Stalin. The Cairo Conference was to be the place where the four countries, in concert, would begin to formulate strategic plans—"begin their work," as Roosevelt presented it to Stalin. The meeting would underline Roosevelt's insistence that China be accepted as the fourth great power in the world, even though its power was latent and the country was both in the midst of a civil war and fighting a Japanese invasion. However, when Stalin found out the Chinese leader would be in Cairo, he canceled Molotov's trip, as well as that of the Russian military representative, because he was afraid that if Japan learned that Molotov had met with Generalissimo Chiang Kai-shek, the Japanese might close the port of Vladivostok, so crucial to the Soviet war effort, or worse, unleash the Kwantung army on the Manchurian border. By the time Roosevelt learned of the cancellation, he was already on the high seas.

It was a setback for Roosevelt, but not crucial, because Cairo was important mainly from a public relations standpoint. Roosevelt was the most publicity conscious of presidents. The Russian absence would not take away from the positive publicity that would ensue from Roosevelt's public embrace of Chiang Kai-shek in such an exotic place.

He was haunted by memories of the League of Nations that had failed so miserably. President Wilson had had the dream and the will but neither the public relations skills nor the political savvy needed to make it happen. As assistant secretary of the navy, Roosevelt had been in Paris winding down the U.S. naval presence in France while the Versailles conference was taking place. He watched as Wilson was forced to agree to the vengeful clauses insisted on by his allies: their price to join the League of Nations. He had sailed for the United States on the *George Washington* with Wilson. At lunch in Wilson's cabin, he listened as the president loftily said, "The United States must go in or it would break the heart of the world." Roosevelt was personally persuaded of the crucial importance of the league, but he knew that Wilson was going home to inform the U.S. Senate of what membership in the league entailed and that key Republican senators, excluded from the peace process by Wilson, indeed entirely ignored, were lying in wait for him.

Wilson was attacked in the Senate and took his battle to the country. As Wilson futilely battled on, Roosevelt watched his health break down.

The dream of a world government stayed with Roosevelt. He and the State Department started roughing out the plans for a world organization in 1939, as Hitler began his assault on Europe. FDR would leave no stone unturned in his quest to succeed. What he took away— what he had learned firsthand from Wilson's failure—was that it wasn't enough to have laudable goals, nor sufficient for a president to proclaim them to an enthusiastic, listening planet; after all, Wilson's Fourteen Points had electrified the world. It was necessary to win the backing of his allies and of the U.S. Senate, and it had to be done before the war was over.

FDR kept a portrait of Wilson over the mantelpiece in the Cabinet Room, which he used as a venue to work over speeches with his speechwriters. He would look up at it as he sat working on a speech, remembered the speechwriter, FDR biographer, and friend Robert E. Sherwood: "The tragedy of Wilson was always somewhere within the rim of his consciousness. Roosevelt could never forget Wilson's mistakes."

Roosevelt identified in advance the key groups he had to win over, then built consensus within each group by pointing out the practical advantages that would accrue by following his lead. Before any group was ready to make policy, Roosevelt was there, leading the way.

He had taken to heart the advice given him by A. Lawrence Lowell, president of Harvard, from whom he had taken Government 1 his freshman year at college. The occasion was the Harvard Club annual dinner in New York in January 1933, honoring Roosevelt, when Roosevelt, as president-elect, was putting together his cabinet and top staff. Lowell, the keynote speaker, turning to face Roosevelt directly, had said that the most important principle for the chief executive was that he must always take and hold the initiative in his dealings with Congress, with his cabinet, and generally with the public. Lowell affirmed that if Roosevelt always applied this principle, he would succeed. Roosevelt, according to his Harvard classmate Louis Wehle, who had worked with him on the *Crimson,* was following Lowell's remarks "with absorbed attention and . . . at their end he was deeply thoughtful."

Two days before he left for Tehran, Roosevelt had presided over an elaborate ceremony in the East Room of the White House at which he and representatives of forty-four countries sat around a long table and signed the agreement that set up the United Nations Relief and Rehabilitation Administration (UNRRA). He had waited until Armistice Day, when it would get maximum exposure, to announce the establishment of this first unit of the United Nations. UNRRA, funded by the contribution of 1 percent of each nation's national income, would help clothe, feed, and house the people in the world's population centers that war destroyed. Its director, Herbert Lehman, the governor of New York State, according to a *New York Times* article that day, had just been chosen by four countries, the United States, Great Britain, the Soviet Union, and China. The Russians were behind the founding of UNRRA—an internationally controlled, staffed, and operated relief organization. It had been their idea, a way to put war-torn countries back on their feet. After Stalin learned that Roosevelt expected these four countries to run the postwar world, he had backed the idea that they would form the executive committee of UNRRA.

The mention of the four countries was of the utmost importance to Roosevelt. He wanted to familiarize the world with the concept, for he was planning that "the four policemen" were going to be the core countries of the United Nations, the organization of nations he had brought into existence on January 1, 1942. On that first day of the New Year, only three weeks after Pearl Harbor, Roosevelt had gathered in his White House study Winston Churchill, who was staying at the White House and represented Great Britain, Ambassador Maxim Litvinov for the Soviet Union, and Foreign Minister T. V. Soong for China to sign the UN Declaration. He signed the document himself for the United States. This first United Nations document was the initial step in Roosevelt's grand design. It bound each country to "defend life, liberty, independence, and religious freedom," declared "that they are now engaged in a common struggle against savage and brutal forces seeking to subjugate the world," and agreed that "each Government pledges itself . . . not to make a separate armistice or peace with the enemies." The remaining twenty-two signatories signed the next day, in alphabetical order.

The name of the organization had come to Roosevelt one night when Churchill was staying at the White House. He and Churchill had been considering and discarding various titles. They had worked over the thing until late one evening, finally quitting on a phrase about countries united in fighting aggression. Then Roosevelt had gone to bed with the word "united" in his mind as he fell asleep. Early the next morning he woke up with the solution: the United Nations.

So impatient had he been to test the name on his houseguest that, not waiting for breakfast, Roosevelt called for his man to wheel him to Churchill's door. The prime minister was on the same floor, down the hall in the Rose Suite. FDR knocked. Churchill called out to him to come in but said that he was taking a bath. A few moments later, the prime minister suddenly stepped out of the bathroom into the sitting room, the walls of which were decorated with scenes from Victorian England, with "not a stripe on him." He looked, according to Roosevelt, like "a pink cherub."

Roosevelt recounted that he said, "Winston, I have it: 'the United Nations.'"

"*Good!*" said Churchill.

AT CAIRO, Roosevelt planned to meet with Generalissimo Chiang Kai-shek, head of the Chinese Nationalist government, to discuss China's participation in the war against Japan. Things were going so badly in China that FDR was afraid the Chinese would fall out of the war. "Chiang's troops aren't fighting at all—despite the reports that get printed in the papers," he confided to his son Elliott. He wanted to reinvigorate the generalissimo and stiffen his backbone. But equally important was the publicity their meeting would generate, showcasing China as the fourth great nation in the United Nations—the fourth policeman. Roosevelt's instincts and sense of the future called for a co-equal Asian presence in the United Nations in order for it to fully represent the world. He knew that neither Churchill nor Stalin felt as he did. Their acceptance of China came only at his insistence.

Nevertheless, the president would probably not have gone to Cairo, except for the prospect of a Tehran meeting with Stalin. Chiang Kai-shek could have been summoned to Washington; Madame Chiang had been a White House guest the previous spring. Churchill had visited him many times in the United States. Roosevelt had arranged to meet with Churchill and Chiang Kai-shek in Cairo only after Secretary of State Cordell Hull had wired him a few weeks earlier from Moscow after meeting Stalin and informed him that the marshal was being accommodating, that a meeting with him in the Near East would probably take place, and, most important, that Stalin had told him to tell Roosevelt that "immediately after the end of the war in Europe . . . it [the Soviet Union] will come out against Japan." Cairo was a good place to break up the trip to Tehran.

All high-level meetings during the war were given code names. The code name for Tehran was Eureka, especially apt from Roosevelt's point of view because Archimedes was supposed to have triumphantly exclaimed "Eureka" as he exited his bathtub, having just discovered the basic law of nature regarding volume. And this meeting *was* a triumph for Roosevelt; he had been trying to set it up for more than a year. He had been carrying on a correspondence with Stalin and lacing his messages—they had exchanged well over one hundred so far, mostly concerned with U.S. and British war plans, the progress of the shipment of guns, food, planes, tanks, gasoline, plus raw matériel for Soviet factories, and lately the surrender terms for Italy—with suggestions as to where and when they could rendezvous. Stalin had continually put him off, always on the basis that as the supreme commander of Soviet forces and head of the State Defense Committee as well as head of the supreme general staff, he had to be in constant touch with his general staff, available to work with them to make decisions on a minute-to-minute, day-to-day basis. Therefore he couldn't leave the country.

That was perfectly true, particularly in the beginning of the war, when Russia was in mortal peril. Stalin conferred daily with Marshal Alexander Vasilevsky, chief of the Soviet general staff, and with General Georgi Zhukov, deputy supreme commander, the brave, gifted leader who had defended Moscow and Leningrad. Stalin hadn't started out with great military skills, but he had learned to listen to his generals and absorb a great deal of information, to pore over battle plans. An "outstanding organizer," he "displayed his ability as Supremo starting with Stalingrad . . . mastered the technique of organizing front operations . . . and guided them with skill, thoroughly understanding complicated strategic questions," Zhukov would write of Stalin.

Now, though, as 1943 drew to a close, there was less of a sense of urgency in the Soviet Union. Leningrad was still under siege, but the Red Army had regained two-thirds of the territory seized by the Germans, had triumphed at Stalingrad in February, vanquishing and trapping ninety-two thousand ill-clad, underfed German soldiers, the last remnants of the attacking army, and in July had won back Kursk, southwest of Moscow, in an epic battle fought by two million men, six thousand tanks, and four thousand planes. After Kursk the German army was no longer on the offensive. By the fall of 1943 the Russians spoke of the year about to end as *perelom,* the turning point.

The most tangible sign of this change was that finally in September Stalin decided that the time had come when he could travel, leaving his generals in charge, and could meet Roosevelt face-to-face. Even so, he accepted Roosevelt's plan for the meeting only the day before FDR left Washington. Over the year the two leaders had discussed various possible meeting places. Roosevelt had thrown out a number of dates and locations where they might conceivably get together. Among his suggestions had been Iceland, southern Algeria, Khartoum, the Bering Strait, Fairbanks, Cairo, and Basra. (In proposing the Bering Strait, the president exhibited an imperial streak, writing, "I suggest that we could meet either on your side or my side of Bering Straits.")

Stalin had rejected them all. In one of the rare drafts written in his own hand, received by FDR on August 8, he first unhelpfully suggested

Archangel, in the far north of Russia on the White Sea, or Astrakhan, in southern Russia, then wrote, "Should this proposal be inconvenient for you personally, in that case, you may send to one of the above-mentioned points your responsible and fully trusted person ... As I have already told Mr. Davies, I do not have any objections to the presence of Mr. Churchill at this meeting." Finally, in September, Stalin wrote that he *could* leave for a meeting, but "the exact date of the meeting has to be defined later taking into consideration the situation on the Soviet-German front," and suggested Tehran. Roosevelt had responded that Tehran was very difficult for him, citing constitutional obligations: "I cannot assume the delays attending flights in both directions into the saucer over the mountains in which Tehran lies. Therefore, with much regret I must tell you that I cannot go to Tehran and in this my cabinet members and the Legislative leaders are in complete agreement." It was then that Roosevelt suggested Basra and Baghdad in Iraq, or Ankara, Turkey, closing, "Do not fail me in this crisis."

Stalin had taken two weeks to reply, at which time he informed Roosevelt that Tehran was the only option: "For myself as Supreme Commander the possibility of traveling farther than Tehran is excluded."

Reluctantly, Roosevelt decided he had to fly over the mountains to Tehran. Three days later, on November 8, he wrote Stalin that he would meet him there.

Roosevelt, so media sensitive, so aware how important this meeting was in terms of public opinion, used its role as a talking point, appealing to Stalin's ego: "The whole world is watching for this meeting of the three of us."

With his usual ebullient optimism, FDR went full steam ahead with his travel plans. If he had any doubts that Stalin would actually appear, he kept them to himself. Stalin had chosen a country far from American shores, but it was a country run by Americans and was not as arbitrary a choice as it first appeared. So huge was the passage of Lend-Lease shipments through Iran that an American general had been made chief of staff of the Iranian army, a top U.S. policeman was adviser to the Iranian gendarmerie, and another American was the Iranian government's chief financial adviser. In addition, the Persian Gulf Service Command, consisting of some thirty thousand American soldiers, was bivouacked in two camps on the outskirts of Tehran.

FDR loved to travel—by car, by train, but most especially by ship. So worries aside, *any* ocean voyage on a state-of-the-art warship would have buoyed his spirits.

Harry Hopkins was the only nonmilitary adviser aboard. FDR was wary of State Department career diplomats, many of whom were conservative Republicans. The strongly anti-Soviet Eastern European Division had been dismantled, but the vast majority of State Department career officers had been against his recognition of the Soviet Union in 1933, and although major changes had been made in the department, the ingrained antagonism to him and his policies ran deep. It hadn't helped that when he had sent Hopkins to Europe expressly to check on the foreign service, Hopkins found many U.S. embassies and legations still displaying photographs of Hoover on their walls instead of FDR. (George Kennan, then a young foreign service officer, later to become famous as the author of the policy of containment, was fairly typical in his comment against Roosevelt's recognition of the Soviet Union in 1933: "We should have no relationship at all with them . . . Never— neither then nor at any later date—did I consider the Soviet Union a fit ally or associate, actual or potential, for this country.") "You should go through the experience of trying to get any changes in the thinking, policy and action of the career diplomats and then you'd know what a real problem it was," FDR said to the Federal Reserve Board chair, Marriner Eccles. Other quick minds also thought foreign service officers were stuffy beyond measure. "Communicating through the State Department is like making love through a blanket," quipped the British economist John Maynard Keynes.

Nor did it help that Secretary of the Treasury Henry Morgenthau accused State Department officials of deliberately using "gross procrastination" as a means of condoning Hitler's extermination of the Jews.

On top of all that was FDR's belief in personal diplomacy and his confidence in his own powers of persuasion. He thought he was America's best diplomat. He knew the outcome he was seeking: he wanted to form strong ties with Russia. He looked forward to initiating exploratory conversations with Stalin on the feasibility of a world government and, while they were still allies in arms, to hammering out a consensus: "reach a large measure of general agreement on objectives." He was convinced that this was the necessary first step in the creation of a world government, that such a government would ensure the end of world wars, and that only a world leader—himself—could handle the negotiations.

The absence aboard of State Department personnel served to point up how unique Hopkins was in the president's inner circle. Hopkins, fifty-three, had many desirable qualities: he was charming, intelligent, intuitive, capable, and a bottomless well of news and gossip. Some people called him the assistant president. His ascent was based as much on his ability to judge Roosevelt's moods and needs as on his unquestioned competence. If the president was feeling low, Hopkins gathered people around; if the president needed diversion, he could sense it; if the president wanted companionship—and he often did, for he hated to be alone—Hopkins was there. If there was an important problem that needed dealing with, Roosevelt put Hopkins in charge of finding a solution.

Born in Iowa, a graduate of Grinnell College, Hopkins had become a social worker. He was a superb administrator. Roosevelt, as governor of New York in 1929, had created the first statewide work relief program to deal with the millions out of work in the Depression. Hopkins ran the program so efficiently that Roosevelt brought him to Washington to help shape and run the New Deal work relief programs. With the advent of war, FDR made him head of the Munitions Assignment Board, which allocated all munitions to the Allies and to the U.S. Armed Forces. He was also in charge of directing the massive aid America was sending to the Soviet Union.

He dressed atrociously. "Deplorably untidy; his clothes looked as though he was in the habit of sleeping in them, and his hat as though he made a point of sitting on it," observed Winston Churchill's chief of staff, General Sir Hastings Ismay. A *New Yorker* profile likened his appearance to "an animated piece of Shredded Wheat." He was bedeviled by serious digestive problems that kept him very thin. His health was not good. Surgery was done in 1937, and although the operation helped, he remained prone to severe stomach problems, for which he was periodically hospitalized.

On May 10, 1940, the day the German army invaded Holland and Belgium and Churchill became prime minister, Roosevelt invited Hopkins to dine at the White House. Hopkins had been so helpful assessing the situation and working out actions to take that as the hour grew late, FDR asked him to spend the night. Hopkins borrowed a pair of pajamas, went to sleep in one of the many bedrooms, and never returned to his home. He was given the Lincoln suite, where Abraham Lincoln had signed the Emancipation Proclamation. The suite, on the second floor, the "family floor," two doors away from the president's rooms, consisted of a large, high-ceilinged bedroom with a fireplace facing the South Lawn and the Washington Monument, a smaller sitting room, and a large bathroom. His desk was a card table. In July 1942, when Hopkins married Louise Macy, the former Paris editor of *Harper's Bazaar,* the ceremony took place in Roosevelt's study, in front of the fireplace specially banked with greens for the occasion. Louise Hopkins now moved into the Lincoln suite. Eleanor Roosevelt had initially been dubious about the addition of Louise, but Roosevelt had been firm, telling her "it was absolutely necessary for Harry to be in the house." Nobody was ever as close to Roosevelt as was Hopkins. Still, Roosevelt kept him at a slight distance. Hopkins called him Mr. President, not Franklin, as Eleanor and Prime Minister Churchill did, or Frank, as did the Supreme Court justice Felix Frankfurter.

Andrei Gromyko, Soviet ambassador to the United States during the war years, remembered that Roosevelt "would advise me . . . to see Harry Hopkins about this tricky question. He may not have the answer to every question, but he'll do his best, and he'll give me an accurate account afterwards." Many people called Hopkins Roosevelt's eyes and ears; Gromyko observed that he was Roosevelt's feet as well.

Hopkins was there in place of Cordell Hull. A Tennessean, a much-revered figure, tall, white-haired, dignified, and imposing, Hull was the all-important bridge that linked conservative southern Democratic senators, whose votes were needed to pass New Deal legislation, to Roosevelt. Hull was unique in the cabinet because of his power in Congress, which, observed the president, made him "the only member who brings me any political strength I don't have in my own right."

"Remember how Wilson lost the League of Nations," he once said to his secretary of labor, Frances Perkins, the first female member of a president's cabinet, "lost the opportunity for the United States to take part in the most important international undertaking ever conceived. He lost it by not getting Congress to participate." After a long career in the House, Hull had been elected to the Senate in 1930, resigning his Senate seat when Roosevelt asked him to be secretary of state. The president relied on Hull to keep his southern Senate colleagues in line.

Roosevelt was ever mindful that the Senate had voted down member-ship in the League of Nations. Hull would see to it that the Senate did not vote down the United Nations.

Roosevelt massaged him in public and ignored him in private, annoying Hull beyond measure, but he remained loyal. FDR not only made his own foreign policy decisions; sometimes Hull didn't even know what FDR's next move would be. The respected senior foreign service officer Loy Henderson said FDR "made up the rules as he played. It was impossible, therefore, for Mr. Hull to make decisions on many occa-sions." Some thought personal bias caused Roosevelt to treat Hull as he did, for Hull *was* a bit ponderous and he did have a bit of a judge's manner (his wife always addressed him as "Judge"). It was hypothesized that Roosevelt, quick and intuitive, easily bored, sidelined him because of his slow, deliberate manner, and that was certainly a contributing factor. Hull also had a slight lisp, which people knew grated on FDR's ear. After the United States entered the war, Roosevelt erected a Chinese wall between foreign and military policy and excluded Hull from all conversations touching upon military affairs. As wounding as his exclu-sion was, Hull lived with it—and much more. "I learned from other sources than the President what had occurred at the Casablanca, Cairo, and Tehran conferences," he would admit.

The war broadened Roosevelt's role. After Pearl Harbor, he placed himself at the apex of military as well as civilian planning, quickly set-tling into his new role and title: commander in chief. He loved the title; he was "in his element," as his old friend Louis Wehle put it. Hull had no choice but to notice it. "Please try to address me as Commander-in-Chief, not as President," Roosevelt ordered Hull, on the verge of proposing a toast to him at a cabinet dinner a year into the war.

Hull did attend the Moscow Conference of foreign ministers in October 1943; it was the high point of his career. During the confer-ence he laid the groundwork for the Tehran Conference that Roosevelt was on his way to now. In Moscow the foreign ministers had agreed on the necessity of establishing a universal organization for the support of international peace and security.

At the Moscow Conference, in his only meeting with Stalin, Hull and his delegation had done brilliantly. In what could only be viewed as a most promising development, Hull had prevailed on the Soviet dele-gation to agree to something Stalin had told Roosevelt he wouldn't even have on the agenda: the participation of China. A few weeks before the conference, Stalin had written to Roosevelt, "If I understood you correctly, at the Moscow Conference will be discussed questions concerning only our three countries, and thus, it can be considered as agreed upon, that the question of the declaration of the four nations is not included in the agenda of the conference." Roosevelt simply ignored this statement. Instead, he wrote to Stalin about Italian issues, problems with the French, and the series of places where their meeting might take place.

Hull fought hard for Roosevelt. He succeeded not only in bringing the issue of China up for discussion at the conference but in having the Chinese ambassador in Moscow, Foo Ping-sheung, sign the Joint Four-Nation Declaration along with Molotov, Anthony Eden, the foreign secretary of Great Britain, and himself. Molotov, presumably following the orders he had been given by Stalin, had attempted to derail this turn of events. He grudgingly agreed that he would have no objection if the Chinese signed later, but he continued to insist on the idea of a three-power declaration. Hull suddenly dug in his heels and told Molotov that if the Soviets did not agree to the inclusion of China in the original document, he, the secretary, would pack his bags and return to Washington. Molotov, thereupon, had scratched off a message to Stalin, and the meeting was resumed. In order to hold the point in discussion without a vote, the secretary took the floor and in a sense "filibustered" the meeting until the reply from Stalin was received. Molotov opened the note, smiled broadly, and said, "The Soviet Government welcomes the inclusion of China in the 4-power declaration." The British interpreter, A. H. Birse, watching, observed that as the conference progressed, Stalin seemed to be hovering behind the scenes all the time.

The declaration provided for united action against the enemy, unanimity on terms of surrender, and the creation of an international peacekeeping organization "based on the principle of the sovereign equality of all peace-loving states." This was the first instance of Stalin's bending to Roosevelt's wishes.

It was closely followed by another victory. The Senate passed the Connally resolution that provided for postwar international collaboration and the establishment of a general international organization. This bill, a senatorial green light for the United Nations, immeasurably added to FDR's peace of mind. The president had been so pleased with the passage of the resolution, as well as the outcome of the Moscow Conference, that he was at Washington's National Airport to greet Hull as he stepped off the big army cargo plane that brought him home. It was a huge and unexpected honor. "We'll give you the keys to the city," the *New York Times* reporter covering the scene quoted the president as saying to Hull.

Harry Hopkins took Cordell Hull's place on the trip to Tehran. Roosevelt knew that he could count on Hull's loyalty and that Hull was not physically up to another long trip so close on the heels of the first one.

Eleanor Roosevelt, inveterate traveler that she was, had wanted to go to Tehran, in fact pleaded with the president to take her. Roosevelt refused. Absolutely no women, he decreed. Their daughter, Anna Boettiger, who was present at the conversation, reported to her husband, John, "The OM [old man] sat all over her, and hurt her feelings." Anna, too, asked to go. For Anna he had a ready answer: no women were allowed on shipboard. Anna was furious, particularly because two of her brothers, Elliott, a colonel in the army, and Franklin, a lieutenant in the navy, were invited. ("OM is a stinker in his treatment of the female members of his family," Anna wrote to her husband, who also would join the presidential party in Cairo.)

So, journeying to meet Joseph Stalin to coordinate the war strategy of the three nations and to plan for the postwar world, Roosevelt brought along his generals, admirals, personal staff of cooks, stewards, and valets, and his capable friend Harry.

There was one other nonmilitary foreign policy adviser in addition to Hopkins, Averell Harriman, with whom Roosevelt was close, who would be at Tehran. Roosevelt had sent Harriman to London to set up the initial Lend-Lease program with Churchill and then to Moscow in October 1941 to work out Soviet needs with Stalin and Molotov. Harriman, who had become ambassador to Russia the month before, in time to take part in the Moscow Conference, was waiting in Cairo. Energetic, peripatetic, aristocratic, handsome, even among diplomats, as *The New Yorker* described him, Harriman was slim, six feet one inch tall, with dark hair, deep-set brown eyes, and clean-cut features. He spoke no foreign languages. "My French is excellent," Harriman once said, "except for the verbs," which was the closest anyone ever heard him come to making a joke. He was enormously wealthy, a partner of

Brown Brothers Harriman, and chairman of the board of the Union Pacific Railroad. He was as well a star athlete who had been an eight-goal polo player in his younger days, ranked fourth in the nation.

Like the president, he had gone to Groton, but he then chose Yale, where he had become a member of the legendary secret society Skull and Bones. His family also had a Hudson River estate, Arden House, on the west side of the Hudson, upriver from Roosevelt's Springwood. Unusually for his class and business career, he was a Democrat. Because Roosevelt had raised taxes, established Social Security, and put into place a minimum wage, all of which addressed the needs of the working class, and had then created the Securities and Exchange Commission to regulate the stock market, the vast majority of wealthy, conservative Americans despised him, calling him "a traitor to his class." When the news filtered out to his Wall Street friends that Harriman had gone to work for Roosevelt, they were horrified. "The hate-Roosevelt sentiment ran strong. When I walked down Wall Street, men I had known all my life crossed to the other side so they would not have to shake my hand," Harriman recalled.

Harriman, who in common with Roosevelt had an impatience with details and a dislike of going through channels, was perfectly comfortable circumventing the State Department bureaucracy and his nominal boss, Hull, taking it as normal that on the president's orders he reported directly to him. He was a year younger than Hopkins, and they were great friends. Hopkins had proposed to his wife in Harriman's suite at the Mayflower Hotel in Washington as he and Louise were about to go out for dinner with Harriman and his wife, Marie. On weekends, at Harriman's house in Sands Point, Long Island, whenever they could, the two men locked horns over croquet, at which Harriman was superb.

Safety precautions on the president's voyage were extreme. Nine destroyers and one aircraft carrier took turns guarding the *Iowa*, which itself had 157 guns, two catapults, and three observation scout planes. At all times six destroyers operated as antisubmarine screens. Other ships, including the aircraft carrier *Santee*, were part of a task force that stood twenty-five miles to the north. Fighter planes kept watch, flying sorties over the ship. The *Iowa* steamed at an average of twenty-three knots at Readiness Three, which meant that one-third of its crew was on watch at battle stations at all times. Once at sea the *Iowa* could receive messages but not send. Dispatches to Washington were relayed from the

Iowa by the destroyers, which would drop away before they made radio contact with the outside world. Messages were kept to an absolute minimum, because Roosevelt's safety depended on keeping his whereabouts unknown. One message the *Iowa* did receive had to do with Churchill's wish to change the scene of the conference from Cairo to Malta. Because there seemed to be no reason for the change, the security staff viewed it as "one of the Prime Minister's fits of whimsy." So did Roosevelt. When apprised of the message, he immediately replied, "No change in my plans as to Cairo. Repeat no change in my plans as to Cairo."

The only serious incident, and one that came uncomfortably close to killing the president, happened on the second day out when the *William D. Porter,* the antisubmarine destroyer stationed to starboard, laying on a special exhibition of gunnery for the commander in chief, inexplicably and incredibly launched a torpedo straight at the *Iowa.* According to Roosevelt's notes on the incident, "The destroyer in the escort was holding torpedo drill, using the Iowa as the spotting target. The firing charge was left in the torpedo tube, contrary to regulations. The torpedo was fired and the aim was luckily bad. Admiral King was of course much upset and will I fear take rather drastic disciplinary action. We fired the secondary battery to try to divert the torpedo. Finally we saw it explode a mile or two astern."

An observant young assistant navigator, John Driscoll, recorded the incident. On what he called an amethystine sea, in balmy weather,

> while the President was sitting on the Promenade deck, portside, wearing a maroon polo shirt, gray flannel pants, white fisherman's hat and sunglasses, and Admiral King, Marshall, Leahy et al. were on the bridge walkways watching an exhibition of balloon shooting the *William D. Porter* signaled EMERG. I could hear the Captain roaring "Right Full Rudder" into the conning tower and we began to turn and vibrate mightily. Coming at us, at not more than 5 knots, was a broaching "fish." I glanced down at the port promenade deck below me where the President was sitting. As the ship kept swinging to starboard the torpedo seemed to veer aft as though it would strike us in our port quarter. My eyes came back to the President, Hopkins and Prettyman [Arthur Prettyman, the president's valet]. Hopkins was leaning far out over the lifeline following the course of the torpedo aft. Prettyman had whirled the

President's armless wheelchair aft ["Take me to the starboard rail," FDR had called out] and he too was facing the rear of the ship, his right hand flung out, grasped a life-line at his side, his head was held high, intent, curious and fearless. It was an awe-inspiring picture, the spell broken in me only when I heard a detonation and felt a jar that seemed to come from our port quarter. Then General Quarters was sounded and I hurried to my battle station in the chart-house wondering if we had been hit . . . Word came to the bridge that the ship had not been hit in the port quarter but the torpedo had exploded in the great wake churned up by our turning track probably detonated by the port quarter batteries which were firing at last.

Navy records show the torpedo was traveling at 46 knots; the *Iowa*'s maximum speed was 33.5 knots. According to sailors on the ship, the commanding officer, Captain John L. McCrea, "practically turned the *Iowa* on her ear to avoid the torpedo."

Countermanding Admiral King, Roosevelt ordered that no punishment be meted out to the sailors at fault. He was merely being practical. The enormity of the gaffe was such that he was afraid that had the skipper of the destroyer become aware that Admiral King, General Marshall, all the top brass of the U.S. military establishment, plus the president were on board, he might have "plunged himself to the bottom of the sea rather than face the awful consequences."

Most days the sea was smooth, the temperature usually seventy degrees, allowing the president to be on deck and take the air, which he loved to do. "All goes well and a very comfortable trip so far. Weather good and warm enough to sit with only a sweater over an old pair of trousers and a fishing shirt," he wrote to Eleanor. In the evenings after dinner there were usually movies in the president's quarters.

"This will be another Odyssey—much further afield & afloat than the hardy Trojan whose name I used to take at Groton when I was competing for school prizes," wrote Roosevelt in a diary he began while on the trip.

During the days, the Joint Chiefs of Staff held strategy conferences among themselves, as well as meetings with the president. At the meeting on November 19 in the president's cabin, when General Marshall asked about postwar Germany, Roosevelt replied, "There would definitely be a race for Berlin . . . United States should have Berlin." Roosevelt sketched on a National Geographic map the American zone he wanted—the northwestern part of Germany—which would meet the Russian zone to the east in Berlin.

The Joint Chiefs of Staff anticipated trouble with Churchill. They wanted to make sure Roosevelt didn't accept Churchill's arguments to delay Overlord, the code name for the cross-channel attack, particularly now, when he was on his way to meet Stalin, to whom he had been promising a "second front," as the Russians referred to it, for well over a year. Roosevelt had caved in to Churchill's delaying tactics on the invasion before, and now all concerned, from Hopkins to Marshall to Leahy, were worried it might happen again. Secretary of War Henry L. Stimson, fifteen years older than FDR and highly respected by him as an open-minded, patriotic Republican, had had Hopkins to lunch in his office at the Pentagon the day before he left for Tehran expressly to explore how they could stiffen the president's resolve. "We took up first the question of OVERLORD which we both agreed was the most important problem now before the world and about which we are both anxious owing to the very doubtful attitude of the British Prime Minister. My object was to cheer up Harry and give him my ideas as to how he was to hold the president in line if he could . . . I have no doubt of the British people doing it. It's merely that their Prime Minister is balking," Stimson wrote in his diary.

Churchill's delaying tactics took the form of pressing for a continued push to divert troops to capture the Dodecanese islands in the Mediterranean and mount diversionary battles in Italy. Realizing that the conflict with their British counterparts would be over the question of unified command over all European operations, Leahy, Marshall, and King decided that their strategy would be to insist on the immediate naming of one overall commander, an American, who could veto an operation before it reached the planning stage. Their shipboard meeting resulted in unanimity that "this command should be vested in a single commander, and he should exercise command over the Allied force commanders in the Mediterranean, in northwest Europe, and of the strategic air forces."

While the *Iowa* was at sea, the radio room was notified that the Germans were using their new glide torpedoes at the entrance to the Strait of Gibraltar. These torpedoes, which magnetically locked onto their targets when dropped into the water, were wreaking havoc on Allied ships in the narrow passage. The *Iowa* had to pass through the strait to reach its destination, Oran, Algeria, in the Mediterranean. A message went out to the *Iowa* to be prepared to change course for Dakar, Senegal. An hour after the message was sent, it was learned that there was a strong concentration of German submarines off Dakar, at which point it was decided to adhere to the original schedule and head for Oran. Orders went out to Admiral Kent Hewitt, commander of the U.S. Northwest Africa Naval Forces, to assemble planes, submarines, "everything he could," to clear the strait and keep it clear. He did. A U.S. plane saw and sank one German sub; there were no others. Blacked out, the *Iowa* went through the strait at night. Authorities on Gibraltar contributed a final tense moment by silhouetting the *Iowa* in the beams of their searchlights as it passed into the Mediterranean.

After the eight-day voyage, the *Iowa* docked at the naval anchorage near Oran on a clear, bright Saturday morning. Two of Roosevelt's sons, Elliott and Franklin, waited. They saw him being lowered into the *Iowa*'s motorized whaleboat. Coming ashore a few moments later, Roosevelt gave his sons a big hello and a healthy, sea-tanned grin. Then father and sons immediately drove, with General Eisenhower, commander of Operation Torch, the invasion of French North Africa, who was waiting with his car, to the nearby airport, where they boarded the president's plane, a four-engine Douglas C-54. They would land first in Tunis to refuel for the long flight to Cairo, and after the meetings there FDR would fly on to Tehran to meet the elusive premier Stalin.

2

TRAVELING TO TEHRAN

Escorted by fighters, Major Otis Bryan flew the presidential party on the 650-mile flight to Tunis, tracing the North African coastline. Hopkins's son Sergeant Robert Hopkins, a Signal Corps photographer, was waiting to greet them at the airfield.

The plan had been that Roosevelt would spend the night in General Eisenhower's guest villa located just beyond the ruins of Carthage on the shore of the Gulf of Tunis. Before Eisenhower, the villa had been Field Marshal Erwin Rommel's residence until he was routed by General Bernard Montgomery's Eighth Army earlier in the year. In the morning FDR was scheduled to fly to Cairo, but the flight was delayed until late the next evening. The official explanation for the change was that flying at night was safer because the Germans still held the island of Crete. But it was also true that FDR was in no hurry to get to Cairo, no hurry to see Churchill, and if he stayed in Tunis, he could use the time getting to know General Eisenhower. The president had told everyone Marshall was going to command D-day, but he had actually not yet made up his mind. He used the day to tour battle sites with Eisenhower. Their car was driven by the general's attractive young driver, Kay Summersby, who had been an ambulance driver during the London Blitz and, as a member of the British Mechanized Transport Corps, had been assigned to Eisenhower in 1942. Breaking for a picnic lunch near a grove of trees Roosevelt spotted, the three sat and talked. They were not exactly alone: three trucks and eight motorcycles manned by military police ringed the car at a distance, plus the usual Secret Service personnel. As the three inside relaxed and ate chicken sandwiches, FDR, remembered

Summersby, told them stories and asked and answered questions: he was checking out the general.

At 10:40 that night, accompanied by generals, admirals, Secret Service men, Hopkins, Leahy, McIntire, and his valet, Arthur Prettyman, the president took off in the Douglas C-54 bound for Cairo, a flight of 1,851 miles. A rigged-up bed awaited him on the plane: a rubber mattress stretched across two seats from which the backs had been removed, closed off by a green curtain so that the president could sleep.

A clear, beautiful dawn was breaking as they approached the Egyptian coastline. Roosevelt had asked Bryan to detour southward, and Reilly to wake him at dawn, so that as it became daylight, he could follow the course of the Nile to Cairo and see the southernmost pyramids, the monuments, and the Sphinx. Reilly called him at 7:00 a.m. As the spectacle of the river unfolded and the monuments came into view, Major Bryan circled so that Roosevelt could get his fill of the majestic panorama. Commented Roosevelt after looking at the Pyramids, "Man's desire to be remembered is colossal."

It didn't seem to bother him that because of his sightseeing proclivities the plane was more than two hours off schedule and the two groups of P-39s ordered to rendezvous with and guard his plane never found it. He was not overly concerned with physical danger.

It was said the only thing he was afraid of was fire. He had had plenty of exposure. As a child of three, he had been at his grandfather Delano's house, Algonac, in Newburgh, New York, down the Hudson from Hyde Park, when his mother's youngest sister, Laura, curling her hair too close to an oil lamp, flew down the steps and out onto the lawn, wrapped in a robe that was aflame. The family saw her and tried to help her, but it was too late, she couldn't be saved. At the age of seventeen FDR helped the farm superintendent at Springwood tear up part of the floor in the parlor and throw water on the cellar beams, which were on fire. That same winter at Groton he was in the bucket brigade that tried to save a stable full of horses and remembered "a horrible scene . . . the poor horses . . . lying under the debris with their hide entirely burned off." He was at Harvard when the top two floors of Trinity Hall burned. As editor of the *Crimson,* he fought for the installation of dormitory fire escapes. In 1915, when Springwood was rebuilt, he insisted that the walls be fireproof. At Shangri-La, the president's wartime retreat in Catoctin Mountain Park in Maryland, he had an escape hatch built into the outer wall of his lodge near his bedroom door. It was hinged at the bottom to open outward, forming a ramp he could either be wheeled down and out or crawl down and out.

ROOSEVELT WAS TYPICALLY a curious traveler, always interested in seeing the places of which he had such detailed geographic knowledge. His deep, continuing interest in stamps, which he had started collecting when he was ten years old, both arose from and fueled his interest in geography. He now had more than a million stamps, collected in 150 matching volumes, which he worked on whenever he had a chance. Several volumes, always the heaviest items in his luggage, went with him wherever he went. The previous January when flying from Bathurst, Gambia, to Casablanca, he had ordered a detour so that he could look at Dakar, the seaport on the westernmost tip of Africa that jutted out into the Atlantic and dominated the North and South Atlantic shipping lanes, so crucial to the Allied cause, that had caused such anguish until taken during Operation Torch.

In Cairo, FDR was lodged at a villa on a canal near the base of the Great Pyramid and the Sphinx belonging to Alexander Kirk, the American ambassador to Egypt. Churchill's villa was a half mile distant. Because Cairo was filled with Axis spies and the city was seething with unrest, security was extreme. Reilly set up barbed-wire entanglements patrolled by troops twenty-four hours a day around both residences, closed down the tour guides and their camels at the Pyramids, and replaced the household servants at both villas with American and British mess staff.

Winston Churchill, Chiang Kai-shek (this would be his first meeting with the president), and Madame Chiang were waiting impatiently for FDR in Cairo. All three were looking forward to conferring with Roosevelt as well as his principal advisers, General Marshall, Admiral King, General Arnold, Admiral Leahy, and, of course, Hopkins. But if the meetings were of first importance to them, they were of secondary importance to Roosevelt, now that Molotov would not be present.

The Cairo Conference had been scheduled for a variety of reasons: to publicize the importance of China to the war effort, to allow Churchill and the British military to confer with Roosevelt and the American military establishment, and to give Molotov a taste of what was to come in Tehran. But another reason was the inescapable fact that it provided a cover for Tehran—a valid excuse for a long ocean voyage by the president in case Stalin did not show. Without the Russian presence, Robert E. Sherwood would later write, "aside from the declaration assuring the freedom and independence of Korea, the effect of these meetings on the progress of the war or on history was negligible."

Churchill was pleased Molotov would not be present in Cairo. It was his view that the combined American and British chiefs of staff should decide on tactics and strategy before meeting the Russians. He was, therefore, planning on "many meetings" between the two staffs during the four days in Cairo, particularly because the Combined Chiefs had not met in more than three months. He wanted, in essence, to erect a wall, with the president and himself on one side and Stalin on the other. That was exactly what Roosevelt did not want. He had warned the prime minister politely a few days prior to the meeting that he was going to limit discussions as to strategy as much as possible, because "it would be a terrible mistake if U.J. [Roosevelt and Churchill sometimes referred to Stalin as Uncle Joe between themselves] thought we had ganged up on him on military action." Roosevelt was carefully, but systematically, limiting the ties, not of friendship, but of partnership, with Churchill; the prime minister fought against it, as did the British foreign secretary, Anthony Eden.

In Roosevelt's mind Great Britain was on a par with his other two allies, China and Russia: he was supreme. He therefore avoided having the opening Cairo Conference be a joint Anglo-American meeting by the simple expedient of inviting Chiang Kai-shek to attend. He also instructed Marshall, Leahy, and King that he wanted their meeting with Chiang to be separate from and precede any meeting with the British. Anthony Eden later painfully described the situation to the British War Cabinet: "It was unfortunate from our point of view that the Conference in Cairo opened with a discussion of the Japanese war on account of the presence of Chiang Kai-shek."

Roosevelt conferred with Chiang at length. (Britain still had extraterritorial rights to Shanghai, Canton, and Hong Kong; Chiang wanted British warships out of Chinese ports after the war; FDR promised him "that's what will happen.") Chinese matters, Churchill later complained, "lengthy, complicated and minor . . . occupied first instead of last place at Cairo." So devious was Roosevelt that the U.S. staff floated comments that led the British to believe, remembered Lord Ismay, Churchill's chief of staff, that the Chinese had arrived before they were meant to, which was not the case. "The American chiefs of staff, so far from upset by the premature arrival of the Chinese delegation, seemed positively pleased to have a chaperone," Ismay observed.

IT WAS NO SECRET to any member of the American military staff that Churchill did not favor Operation Overlord, the invasion of France, or that Roosevelt relied almost exclusively on Marshall's advice, and that the central tenet of Marshall's European war plan was Operation Overlord. Roosevelt had chosen Marshall in April 1939 because he was smart, like himself an independent thinker, and had a reputation, dating from World War I, for speaking his mind. Without consulting anyone, even his then secretary of war, Harry Woodring, Roosevelt decided to jump Marshall over the four generals who outranked him and make him chief of staff.

Roosevelt liked to meet with his Sunday and evening visitors in his oval study on the second floor of the White House. He used the room a great deal; it was convenient and easy for him, because his bedroom was next door. The room was handsome and informal, with books piled high on some tables, models of famous sailboats resting on others. Besides his desk there was a scattering of comfortable chairs and a big leather sofa where FDR sat when he had company. In front of the sofa was a tiger rug. Prints and paintings of the great sailing vessels of the nineteenth and early twentieth centuries lined the walls—a small part of his collection of more than twelve hundred naval prints and paintings. It was the room of someone who loved the sea. Behind the desk was a sheaf of roll-out maps, set so that Roosevelt could pull them out. The two women who bookended his life were also present: the portraits of his wife and his mother faced each other on opposite walls.

On a Sunday in April 1939, Roosevelt summoned Marshall to the room to tell him he was making him chairman of the Joint Chiefs of Staff. Marshall, a rather stiff, formal man, said he replied that he "wanted the right to say what I think and it would often be unpleasing. 'Is that all right?' He said, 'Yes.'"

From Roosevelt's point of view Marshall was ideal for the job: he was not only independent but indefatigable, efficient, and dedicated.

His word was rarely questioned because it was conceded that he was always right. The announcement of his appointment was made on September 1, 1939, the day Germany invaded Poland.

Marshall was sure that the way to beat Hitler was to build up Allied forces in England, ferry them across the channel, invade France, and march on to Berlin. It was the shortest route and would result in the fewest casualties. Secretary of War Henry Stimson agreed. Roosevelt fully backed the plan, code-named Overlord, which had been in the planning stages for two years. Stalin had been led to believe that it would take place in 1942 or 1943.

Churchill, by contrast, could be said to be lukewarm at best on the cross-channel operation; he wanted to attack through the Balkans. He also, according to his doctor, who was his confidant, was haunted by memories of the Battle of the Somme in World War I, during which so many British soldiers had died.

When the Combined Chiefs finally sat down together without the president and the prime minister at Cairo, the subject of their talks was almost exclusively the war in Asia. General Ismay complained that "there was no time left to reach agreement as to the exact line which should be taken with the Russians about a Second Front in Europe." That was Roosevelt's plan. Roosevelt's circle had learned this technique from their chief. The president used it when he wanted to stifle debate without seeming to and reach consensus where there was contention. At a meeting he would simply preempt the conversation or perhaps introduce a new subject, dawdle along, talking about various things, or even tell stories, in order to compress the decision into the final moments of a meeting. Then, for lack of time, the decision he wanted, even if unpopular or unexpected, could not be challenged.

Churchill attempted to hide his lack of enthusiasm for the cross-channel invasion from Hopkins, but he wasn't subtle enough. "Winston said he was a hundred per cent for OVERLORD. But it was very important to capture Rome, and then we ought to take Rhodes," Hopkins noted mockingly, two days before they were due to arrive in Tehran.

Hopkins would probably not have been surprised to learn that the British plan, according to Major General Sir John Kennedy, assistant chief of the imperial general staff, was "to continue the offensive in Italy, to increase the flow of supplies to partisans in the Balkans, to bring about an upheaval by inducing the Balkan powers to break away from

Germany, to induce Turkey to enter the war, and to accept a postponement of OVERLORD." (Kennedy would also write, "Had we had our
way, I think there can be little doubt that the invasion of France would
not have been done in 1944.")

Churchill had been arguing incessantly and obdurately against
Overlord for another reason: he mistrusted Stalin. As he had explained
to Averell Harriman earlier in the year, "Stalin's unrelenting pressure for
a second front in 1943 sprang from his designs on the Balkans. What
better way to keep the Western Allies from landing in the Balkans than
to tie them down in a long and costly battle for Western Europe?"

He had been very effective thus far in postponing Overlord. His
dogged pursuit of divergent war plans was actually a tactic: to engage in
battles that would tie up Allied troops and the crucial landing craft—
basically anywhere—so they wouldn't be available for the cross-channel
invasion.

Roosevelt, used to arguing with Churchill, left Cairo in high good
humor but on guard, as is apparent in the note he wrote to his secretary,
Grace Tully, the day after Thanksgiving: "The Conference goes fairly
well—my role is that of peacemaker. I've seen the Pyramids & made
close friends with the Sphinx. Congress should know her."

All of this set the stage for Tehran.

The president wasn't sure where he was going to live in Tehran
or how long he would stay: both things depended on Stalin. He was
going beyond caution in being so accommodating so that Stalin would
have no excuse to back out. The morning he arrived in Cairo, Monday, November 22, Roosevelt had sent Stalin a message that he would
reach Tehran on November 29 and would "remain for two to four days
depending upon how long you can find it possible to be away from
your compelling responsibilities." He had then asked that Stalin let him
know "what day you wish to set for our meeting" and commented that
the Soviet legation and the British legation in Tehran were situated near
each other "whereas my legation is some distance away," which would
mean driving to and fro and thus "taking unnecessary risks." At the end
of the message Roosevelt had posed a seemingly casual but sharp question, fishing for an invitation to stay at the Russian embassy as Stalin's
guest. "Where do you think we should live?" he asked.

This was a charmingly audacious strategy: to show his confidence
in Stalin by putting himself in Stalin's hands, hoping to win his trust

as quickly as possible. He could, of course, have stayed at the British embassy if it was merely a matter of security considerations. Churchill had already asked him to do just that and would have been thrilled if he had agreed. But because FDR intended to present himself to Stalin as a unique and trustworthy leader, and America as the major force in the world, he wanted to make sure that he was perceived as standing alone: he had refused. He didn't want the prime minister of Great Britain, the former secretary in charge of the colonies of the greatest colonial empire in the world, wound round his neck like a millstone. That was why Roosevelt had started the "distancing" in Cairo, serving notice on the British there that he expected to have a free hand in Tehran—behavior that was causing Churchill considerable anguish.

THE PRESIDENTIAL PARTY drove to the Cairo West Airport, waited until a light fog lifted, and took off a little after 7:00 a.m. Major Bryan then flew the thirteen hundred miles east to Tehran over the Suez Canal and circled twice at a low altitude over Jerusalem while FDR pointed out prominent landmarks. They flew over Bethlehem, Jericho, the river Jordan, the Dead Sea, flew over the desert that was Palestine, flew east, and descended again over the Tigris and Euphrates Rivers. Then Bryan turned northeast, circled Baghdad, and headed for Iran. Once in Iranian airspace they saw below them the U.S.-staffed freight trains on the Trans-Iranian Railroad carrying Lend-Lease supplies, as well as American and British convoys carrying more American Lend-Lease supplies over the Abadan–Tehran highway that ran from Basra on the Persian Gulf to Tehran. More than a hundred thousand tons a month were moving to Russia through Iran.

Tehran, the capital of Iran, lies in the southern foothills of the Alborz Mountains, which run parallel to the Caspian Sea and rise to almost nineteen thousand feet.

The previous January, about to fly over the Atlas Mountains on the way to the Casablanca Conference, Ross McIntire had wanted Roosevelt, who suffered from chronic sinusitis, to put on his oxygen mask, but fearing that if he asked him to, the president would refuse, McIntire had resorted to trickery: he enlisted the aid of Admiral McCrea, asking him to put on *his* face mask, after which he would put on his own, explaining, "If I suggest it to him, he probably won't do it. However if he sees us with ours on, he'll probably follow suit." The subterfuge had worked, FDR had reached for his oxygen mask, "and away we went over the mountains."

Now, as they approached Tehran and saw the mountains encircling the city, McIntire was ready to reach for an oxygen mask, but the perfect visibility enabled Bryan to stay under six thousand feet and successfully snake his plane through the twisting mountain passes.

The plane landed at the Russian army field, Gale Morghe, five miles south of the city, on Saturday, November 27, 1943, at 3:00 p.m. Exiting the plane, the presidential party saw that the field was "covered" with newly arrived U.S. Lend-Lease planes, each sporting a huge, shiny red Soviet star. The airfield was ringed with Iranian soldiers, but in the interests of security Major General D. H. Connolly, commanding general of the Persian Gulf Service Command, stood alone on the tarmac to greet the president's plane and usher him and his party into a car for the ride to the American legation.

The American legation was fully prepared, expecting to house FDR and his party. The American diplomatic community, including Louis G. Dreyfus, the U.S. minister to Iran, had been kept in the dark as to the upcoming conference until the very last moment. Dreyfus had returned from a trip to find soldiers installing a new telephone system in the complex and army tents on the legation lawn. He had then been told the president was coming, that the president would stay at the legation, and that he had to move out.

Roosevelt made the long, dangerous trip to Tehran to get to know Stalin, and for that plan to work, it was important to distance himself from Churchill and retain the uniquely positive impression the Russians had of him. As the New Deal president, Roosevelt had won the approval of *Pravda,* and of Stalin, from the start of his presidency. FDR had ignored the anti-Communist sentiment endemic in America and forced the recognition of the Soviet Union by the United States the year he took office. Stalin had been waiting fourteen years for that to happen. Now FDR was intent on clearly and painstakingly demonstrating to Stalin that the United States was on its own path and that he was playing his own hand. For that, he knew instinctively, details were important. Given the paranoid, suspicious personality he was dealing with, in retrospect it seems remarkably clever that Roosevelt went to such great lengths to start off the relationship on the right foot.

Roosevelt had sent Stalin the cable asking him where he should stay—essentially fishing for an invitation—only five days before he was due to arrive. It had gone out from the Map Room in Washington at 2:55 p.m. on November 22. The embassy delivered the cable to the Kremlin, which dated it as received on November 24 (no hour). It was then translated and delivered to Stalin, but two days had passed since it was sent. By that time Stalin was well on his way by train to Tehran, and the train was having serious communications problems.

In the meantime, Andrei Vyshinsky, the first assistant commissar for foreign affairs, called on the president and, possibly after a few hints, invited him to stay at the Russian embassy in Tehran. Vyshinsky, however, a small man with bright black eyes, horn-rimmed glasses, thinning reddish hair, and a mustache, had presided over the infamous Moscow show trials in 1936–38 and was notorious as "cringingly sycophantic" to his seniors. State Department and presidential records are silent as to their appraisal of him in Cairo, but it was obvious that the invitation did not have Stalin's approval or the stamp of an official invitation. Nevertheless, the day after that, the twenty-fourth, Reilly had walked through the Russian embassy as well as the British and U.S. embassies to check security issues and suitability. The Russian and British embassies not only were in the center of Tehran but had gardens back-to-back across the street from each other. Therefore, with a fence thrown up across the street, the two embassies could be connected. The American legation, a mile away, was pronounced "adequate" by Reilly. He said the route to the other embassies presented no security problems, although distance would later be cited as the main reason that Roosevelt stayed in the Russian compound. (The traffic in Tehran was indeed horrendous. The streets were thronged with people, cars, and horse-drawn droshkies, slowing traffic to a crawl.) "We have made no commitments as to a residence for the president," Reilly stated. "He can stay at the U.S., the British, or the Russian embassy, if invited."

The British embassy would probably have been the least comfortable of the three, judging by Lord Ismay's description of it as "a ramshackle house built by the Indian Public Works Department."

Major General Patrick Hurley, former secretary of war, distinguished looking, a smooth talker, whom Roosevelt had appointed minister to New Zealand, was in Tehran as Roosevelt's personal representative. He cabled FDR on Friday morning, November 26, to say that the Russian chargé d'affaires, Mikhail Maximov, had actually come through with a formal invitation to stay: "The Russian Government cordially invites you to be its guest at its embassy while here." However, as the invitation still lacked Stalin's imprimatur, it was refused.

Upon inspection, Hurley found that the conference location and Roosevelt's possible living quarters were both located in the main embassy building of the Soviet compound, which included several smaller buildings. It was a large, handsome, square building, built of light brown stone, fronted by a wide portico with white Doric columns. It stood in the center of a large park that contained a lake, fountains, flower beds, and a network of walking paths. Hurley pronounced it as ideal a place for Roosevelt to stay as could be found in Tehran. It had the additional attribute of being the only building heated by steam in the entire city; portable oil stoves served for all other buildings. This was an important consideration because the days were mild but the nights cold. It had a pleasant vista, with windows fronting on the cedars, willows, and ponds of the embassy gardens that surrounded it. The quarters earmarked for the president consisted of a large bedroom, a sitting room next to the conference room that would be the main venue for the meetings, a large dining room, a kitchen deemed adequate for the Filipino mess boys from Shangri-La who prepared the president's meals, plus a few smaller bedrooms.

The Russians, in fact, had gone to a great deal of trouble fixing up the residence for FDR. All Soviet personnel who worked in the office buildings and lived in the apartments on the grounds had been ordered to take their belongings and move to other quarters in the city by the evening of November 17. Worried that Roosevelt's wheelchair would not fit through ordinary doorways, they had torn out and widened all the door openings where Roosevelt might pass. The bathroom was undergoing major changes, Hurley saw. The bathtub, toilets, and sinks had been ripped out; new ones, in evidence, were waiting to be installed. If Roosevelt had known earlier in the month of the work that had been going on, of the meticulous preparations that had started the first of the month and gone into high gear by mid-November, he would have been less worried.

Hurley reported, "From the standpoint of your convenience and comfort, from the standpoint of conference communications and security, these quarters are far more desirable than your own legation." He gave the Russians a list of the furnishings FDR would need. However, even though the Russians, as he told the president, "still most cordially solicit your acceptance of their invitation," he advised the Russians that Roosevelt planned to stay in the American legation. The rooms weren't ready. There was no word from Stalin.

ROOSEVELT AND HIS PARTY proceeded directly to the American legation, where Minister Dreyfus and Hurley awaited. In the afternoon Admiral Brown and Dreyfus went to the Soviet embassy, where they were met by the chargé d'affaires, Maximov, who told them that he himself had not yet heard from the marshal. With all the Russians virtually paralyzed by Stalin's lack of input, Brown and Dreyfus retreated, saying that Roosevelt would stay at his own legation. When told that Stalin had finally arrived, Roosevelt took the initiative. Seemingly confident that Stalin intended no slight in not responding to his wish to stay at the Russian embassy, he proceeded, through Harriman, to invite him to dinner; the marshal declined on the grounds that he had had a "strenuous" day and that it would be better to stay with the original plan and meet the following afternoon.

Roosevelt had, to borrow a phrase from John Maynard Keynes, the gift of instinctive judgment, and he was exhibiting it now.

STALIN HAD INDEED had a difficult trip. If he had not been interested in the shape of the postwar world and Russia's place in it, which he expected to work out with Roosevelt, he would not have subjected himself to the ordeal: he hated to travel.

He had journeyed to Stockholm, London, and Berlin for party congresses as a young revolutionary, but his last trip outside the Soviet Union had been in 1913, when he had joined Lenin in Vienna. He had only visited the front once, although he intimated to Roosevelt and Churchill that he went often. Stalin rarely traveled beyond his dacha at Kuntsevo, about five and a half miles from the Kremlin, except to go to his dacha at Sochi, the showplace village perched in the foothills of the snow-peaked Caucasus Mountains on the edge of the Black Sea. Stalin had his winter vacation house there because of its famous sulfur baths. He was a hypochondriac, but he also suffered at various times from psoriasis, tonsillitis, occasionally from nephritis, pleurisy, and asthma, and, from his years of exile in Siberia, rheumatism. It was to deal with all his ailments that he spent so much time at Sochi: he was sure the Sochi waters and climate had a restorative effect on him. (It is possible that one reason he insisted on Tehran was that it would be a relief from snowbound Moscow.)

He left Moscow on the evening of November 22 in a special train camouflaged to look like an ordinary supply train. The long "saloon carriages" in which his party traveled were interspersed between freight cars carrying sand and gravel. Stalin's carriage, a green armored bulletproof car that reputedly weighed ninety tons, consisted of his bedroom/study paneled in mahogany, with bed, desk, chair, and a mirror, a bathroom, three two-passenger bedrooms, a conference room, and a kitchen with an electric stove.

The advisers he had chosen to bring with him to the conference numbered exactly two—in startling contrast to the large numbers accompanying Roosevelt and Churchill.

The first was Vyacheslav Molotov, the second most important man in the Soviet Union, with whom he could discuss strategy and policy. Molotov was his most intimate adviser, usually with him in the Kremlin for hours each day, the only person with whom he used the familiar *ty* the equivalent of the French *tu*. Born Vyacheslav Mikhailovich Skriabin, following a practice common at the time, he adopted the name Molotov, "hammer" in Russian: people called him Stalin's hammer.

Molotov had been at college in St. Petersburg when the revolution began; as order broke down, he became a bomb-making revolutionary. He had been arrested by the Okhrana, the tsar's secret police, almost as many times as Stalin.

Molotov was deputy chairman of the State Defense Committee and commissar of foreign affairs. Stalin relied on him, but not to the extent Roosevelt relied on Hopkins. Molotov did not have the authority that Hopkins did to speak for his boss. Stalin never hesitated to overrule Molotov. "I always agree with Marshal Stalin," said Molotov quickly to Eric Johnston, head of the U.S. Chamber of Commerce, after Stalin overruled Molotov in Johnston's presence and said correspondents could visit the front. "Mr. Molotov always agrees with me," Stalin said, with a slight grin. As Sir Stafford Cripps, Britain's ambassador to the Soviet Union in 1941, noted, Molotov wouldn't even offer an opinion if he had not discussed it beforehand with Stalin: "We had a very unenlightening talk as always, as M will not commit himself without consultation even on matters of opinion . . . It really isn't worth going to see him unless one sends a note beforehand so that he can get directions on it."

Molotov and Stalin met putting out the first issues of the Bolshevik newspaper *Pravda* (*Truth*) in St. Petersburg in 1912. Stalin had been its first editor in chief. Molotov, only twenty-two, upon meeting him, had been bowled over. "He's astonishing; he possesses internal revolutionary beauty, a Bolshevik to the marrow, clever, cunning as a conspirator," he told a friend. He never lost his awe.

Molotov's Kremlin office was near Stalin's; his three-room apartment in the Kremlin was next door to Stalin's. Stocky, with dark brown hair, brown eyes, rimless, round pince-nez, a mustache, and a square face, he always dressed in a neat dark suit, white shirt, and dark tie. Like Stalin, he was short. He rarely smiled. He was a workaholic, with the reputation of being the Politburo's best filing clerk. George Kennan would write that he was the nearest thing known to a human machine. Churchill thought him Machiavellian because "he had lived and thrived in a society where ever-varying intrigue was accompanied by the constant menace of personal liquidation . . . He was above all men fitted to be the agent and instrument of the policy of an incalculable machine." All agreed that he was reserved and hardworking. He spoke in a dull, stammering monotone, the stammer becoming more pronounced when Stalin was listening. Vladimir Pavlov, the interpreter Stalin most often used, preferred working for Stalin to Molotov: "It was easier . . . Stalin valued people who understood the issues under discussion, but simultaneously, were modest and did not try to distinguish themselves with their knowledge." More important, according to Pavlov, was that not only did Molotov seem to enjoy dressing down his associates, but when one was denounced by the NKVD, he never attempted to defend the person, always immediately agreeing to an arrest. Still, at Stalin's funeral, Molotov was the only pallbearer who cried. Communism was his religion, as it was Stalin's. He had been in charge of the collectivization of the kulaks—Russian farmers who owned their land—who were offered a pittance for their crops. In protest, many resorted to burning their produce. ("The Kulaks are the most beastly, rude and wild exploiters. More than once in the history of other countries they have restored the power of the landowners, Tsars and corrupt priests," Lenin had written.) Molotov had carried out and justified their annihilation and that of other resisting Russian and Ukrainian farmers whom Communist doctrine viewed as a capitalist class that had to be liquidated for the good of society. Once the farmers had been removed, they were replaced by party workers ignorant of farming techniques, which caused output to fall even more precipitously, putting even seed crops in short supply. The result of this experiment in social engineering had been the death from starvation of so many millions of Russians and Ukrainians that even Stalin had been appalled. "The Collective Farm policy was a terrible struggle . . . Ten millions . . . It was fearful. Four years it lasted; four years Molotov oversaw it. It was absolutely necessary for Russia, if we were to avoid periodic famines, to plough the land with tractors," Stalin famously explained to Churchill. Collectivization finally did become more productive and dependable than traditional farming, but the toll had been huge.

In only one thing was Molotov unusual and vulnerable: his wife, who was slender, fashionable, and Jewish. Polina Zhemchuzhina, a lavish hostess before the war, had run the Soviet trust that manufactured and distributed cosmetics and toilet articles. Her job had been to show Russian women how to wear makeup. "My husband works on their souls, I on their faces," she once said. (Just before he died, Stalin had Polina arrested and thrown in prison along with other Jews he suspected of Zionism; Molotov's position did not change.)

The second conference adviser he had brought with him was Marshal Kliment E. Voroshilov, blond, blue-eyed, a genial and swaggering ex-cavalryman who sported an elegant mustache. A hero of the Russian Civil War and president of the Council of People's Commissars, he had long been in Stalin's good graces—he had roomed with Stalin in Stockholm in 1906—but he was more friend than adviser: "a good fellow but he is no military man," as Stalin described him. There was no question of his loyalty, and Stalin felt comfortable in his company; he was one of the few surviving original members of the Politburo, the tight group of eight men and five alternates that ruled Russia. But he was no longer respected: Voroshilov had been commissar of defense when the Soviet Union invaded Finland in 1939. The Finns had acquitted themselves so brilliantly and the Red Army so miserably that he was removed from that post. After Hitler's invasion Stalin made him commander in chief of the northwestern front, in charge of the defense of Leningrad.

He was not up to that task, either. At one point, believing the future of the city looked hopeless, he was on the verge of surrendering, sure defeat was imminent.

Stalin had replaced him with Georgi Zhukov, who immediately took the necessary heroic measures. Zhukov, a brilliant general, stripped the guns off the Russian warships in the Baltic and repositioned them to help defend the city, energized the starving inhabitants, deployed the city's defenses and resources, and finally saved Leningrad. The siege was lifted in January 1944. After Leningrad, Stalin cut the order "sending Comrade Voroshilov to do war work in the rear." He would be dropped from the State Defense Committee later in 1944.

Voroshilov's saving grace was probably his especially good singing voice. In the late nights when Stalin was in his cups, he loved to unwind by singing with Voroshilov and Molotov, who not only had a good voice but played the violin, the mandolin, and the piano. The three had been harmonizing until the early hours of mornings for years. Molotov was as essential to Stalin as Hopkins was to Roosevelt, but Voroshilov was the loyal court jester.

Also on the train was Lavrenti Beria, people's commissar of internal affairs, better known as the head of the NKVD. He would take no part in the conference but bore the responsibility for Stalin's personal security. Beria was an unsavory character. He was unattractive physically, "somewhat plump, greenish pale, and with soft damp hands" was one description. Averell Harriman's daughter Kathleen wrote he was "little and fat with thick lenses which give him a sinister look." Stalin's daughter, Svetlana Alliluyeva, loathed him, as had her mother; while her mother was alive, Beria was not allowed in their house.

Also aboard the train were General Alexander Golovanov, the pilot who was to fly Stalin from Baku to Tehran; General Sergei Matveevich Shtemenko, later director of operations for the general staff, whose job it was to keep Stalin informed of all battle news; and Stalin's physician, Professor Vinogradov.

Churchill and Roosevelt would be bringing the best of their country's military staffs and civilian minds to Tehran. Except for Molotov, Stalin had left his in Russia. Stalin would explain this during the conference by saying that he had not expected military questions to be discussed, and therefore he had not brought his military experts with him, but "nevertheless Marshal Voroshilov would do his best." Except for the plenary sessions, which were large, formal affairs, he would often be missing.

Fighter planes hovered over Stalin's train during the journey. Three hours into the trip, having covered only fifty-four miles, the train stopped briefly at Golutvin station near the town of Ryazan', where three men were discovered sitting on the train's tender. They were apprehended, their identities were checked, and it was ascertained that they were common criminals hoping to hitch a ride in the darkness and had no knowledge of Stalin's presence.

The train proceeded very slowly southward because there were constant problems. The rail equipment itself was in a terrible state; bearings kept melting down and the axle boxes burned; there was also the necessity of watching out for and repairing damaged rails as they crept through the devastated, war-torn landscape. The train crew had great difficulty keeping to the schedule. As the train stopped at Gryaz near the city of Lipetsk, German bombers suddenly emerged in the night sky. Soviet fighter pilots waited at their planes, ready to scramble, and anti-aircraft squads stood by their guns waiting to fire, as the bombers flew off into the distance.

Communications aboard the train were a major problem. As well as breaks in the rails, there were breaks in the telegraph wires, the result of warm, wet weather suddenly freezing into "glazed frost" that broke the wires, so that the secret telephone communication lines—the Kremlevka lines—gave only spotty service after Ryazan'. As the train proceeded south and approached Stalingrad, now reduced to rubble, where the fighting had been so violent and the devastation so widespread that 500,000 Russians and 200,000 Germans died, the train lost all contact with headquarters. Beria was so enraged he wanted to punish the "guilty" parties. The train arrived at Kilyazi station, fifty miles from Baku, on the Caspian Sea, the morning of the twenty-sixth. Stalin and his group immediately left for the airport. There, four American C-47s waited to fly them the 335 miles to Tehran. Stalin started walking to the plane designated for him, next to which his pilot, General Golovanov, stood, but as he walked, he changed direction, turning toward Beria's plane. Beria's pilot was a colonel, and "generals don't often pilot aircraft, we'd better go with the Colonel," Stalin said in explanation to Golovanov. "Don't take it badly."

It was a classic demonstration of Stalin's paranoia: that it was safer to go with the pilot who flew all the time and safer also to change plans at the last moment to confound any possible conspirators.

The route, an hour by plane from Baku to Tehran, was over the shore of the Caspian Sea, then over the brown expanse of Azerbaijan, then over Tabriz with its scattered little mud houses. But Stalin did not, like Roosevelt, accommodate himself to plane travel. It is doubtful if he even looked out the window at the passing landscape, although he undoubtedly checked out the three formations of fighters, one to the left, one to the right, one above, because the flight was bumpy and Stalin was seriously uncomfortable. The plane dropped periodically into air pockets, and when it did, "he had clung to his armrests with an expression of utter terror on his face."

Stalin arrived at Gale Morghe airfield at noon. Before exiting the plane, he chatted with the pilots; by way of thanks he sent each of them the new-style uniforms with epaulets marking their rank that he had ordered for the upper echelons of the Red Army earlier in the year. He wanted his air force pilots to look smart and well dressed.

Upon landing, he, too, would have seen the rows of P-39s that American Lend-Lease had given the Soviet Union, all sporting red stars. It is not known what kind of car awaited the marshal at the airport, but of the ten cars reserved for his use in Tehran, three were American: a special armored Packard, a special armored Lincoln, and a special armored Cadillac.

American technology was inescapable.

3

TEHRAN

S tretching from the foothills of the Alborz Mountains in the north to the edges of the Dasht-e Kavir desert in the south, Tehran was the largest city in the Middle East. The mountain range, with snowcapped Mount Damavand, the highest mountain in Iran, at its center, dominated the view. From the air the city looked as modern as a Western city, with broad paved avenues lined with trees. Mosques and minarets could be seen, and low white and brown buildings, many with green walled-in gardens. It had relatively modern hospitals, a university, museums, and a working telephone system. But Tehran was a study in contrasts. The streets were paved, but because the sidewalks were not, the air was dusty. The water supply was primitive. It came down from the mountains and ran in open streams alongside the principal streets. Because the streams were the city's sole water supply, people had no choice but to use the water for washing as well as drinking: typhoid was rampant.

Under the circumstances the British, Russian, and U.S. embassies sent tank trucks up into the mountains to siphon water directly from mountain springs. Among the many precautions taken by the Russians during the conference was to change the procedure of accessing this water; each day their tank trucks went up into the mountains to unannounced destinations.

By 7:00 p.m. on Saturday, November 27, Harriman and Molotov were working on the conference schedule. It is of particular note that implicit in this first meeting was the assumption that Roosevelt's wishes would be followed as to timing and discussion points. Harriman gave Molotov Roosevelt's plan for the first day: Stalin to call on him at

3:00 p.m.; the first plenary session to commence at 4:00 p.m.; Stalin, Molotov, Churchill, Eden, the British ambassador, Archibald Clark Kerr, Hopkins, Harriman, plus the three interpreters to dine with him at 7:30 p.m.

Harriman then relayed to Molotov FDR's conceptual outlook for the conference so that Stalin would be alerted. Roosevelt, said Harriman, "had not come with Churchill with fixed ideas, but was prepared to lay before the Marshal the various strategic plans . . . The principal question would be the influence of prompt action in the Mediterranean as against earlier or later OVERLORD." Roosevelt's message was clear: the cross-channel invasion was now within Stalin's grasp—if he faced down Churchill. Harriman and Molotov parted.

Well past midnight Harriman and Clark Kerr received calls from Molotov asking them to come over to the Russian embassy immediately. When they arrived, Molotov announced that Soviet sources had just learned that there were German agents in Tehran who knew of Roosevelt's presence, an assassination attempt was possible, the safest place for him under the circumstances was inside the Soviet compound. Driving through the city to visit each other was dangerous. Roosevelt, Molotov declared, should move.

His story was plausible. Several years earlier when the Iranian ruler had been Shah Reza, who was pro-Fascist and a great admirer of Hitler's, there had been hundreds of German agents in Tehran, leading many to fear that Germany might assume control. To stop it from falling into Hitler's hands, the Soviet Union and Great Britain had jointly invaded Iran, forced the shah to abdicate, and installed his twenty-one-year-old son, Mohammad Reza Pahlavi, on the throne. In the two-year interim, however, known suspicious Germans had been deported.

Molotov was firm on the necessity of Roosevelt's moving to the Soviet embassy and continued to maintain the existence of a possible German assassination plan as the rationale for the late invitation. Quite possibly Stalin, finally taking charge of the situation upon arrival at the embassy, had ordered Molotov to invite Roosevelt to move in even if the quarters were not finished. Possibly to give the story additional authority, General Artikov, Mike Reilly's opposite number in the NKVD, later told Reilly that thirty-eight German parachutists had been dropped on the outskirts of Tehran a few weeks earlier and that six were still at large.

After Molotov declared that Roosevelt should move, late though it was, he took Harriman and Clark Kerr on a tour of the proposed presidential quarters, which were in the central building in the compound, next to the conference room that would be used for the plenary sessions. The tour provided at least a partial answer to the question of why Molotov was just now extending an invitation for the president to stay at the embassy: the apartment was still not finished. Although it was well past midnight, workmen were in the bathroom finishing the installation of the bathtub. In fact, the delay in asking Roosevelt to stay at the embassy had to have been caused by the delay in finishing the rooms. But it little mattered whether the danger was real or imagined. Danger cleared the air for all concerned. Roosevelt was free to accept; not even his severest critics—the rabid right wing in America who thought he was a Communist sympathizer—would be able to fault his choice of residence.

The following morning, obviously delighted at the prospect, FDR announced he would move at 2:30 p.m. and that the U.S. Navy Filipino mess crew who cooked for him at Shangri-La, whom he had brought, would prepare his meals. As all foodstuffs consumed by the U.S. forces were shipped in, and nothing bought locally, the supply of food for the presidential party was not a problem.

Reilly, taking no chances, mindful of the NKVD report and the president's safety, laid on protective measures for the president's move to the embassy, which would be by limousine. Early in the afternoon he assembled a motorcade, with armed jeeps at the head and rear, stationed Secret Service men armed with tommy guns on the running boards of the president's car, and lined the streets of the route with U.S. soldiers standing shoulder to shoulder. As the motorcade moved slowly, majestically past, the Iranians cheered. But inside the car sat a Secret Service agent posing as Roosevelt. After the motorcade was on its way, Reilly whisked FDR, Leahy, and Hopkins into an inconspicuous car. The car, preceded by a jeep, then went through backstreets to the Russian embassy at a brisk pace, arriving before the motorcade. "The Boss, as always, was vastly amused by the dummy cavalcade trip," Reilly remembered. Chief of Staff Leahy and, of course, Hopkins moved in with the president.

Stalin stayed in one of the smaller houses in the parklike Russian compound; Molotov and Voroshilov stayed in yet another.

In moving into the embassy, Roosevelt would have been well aware that his rooms would be bugged by the Russians, that every word he said, every word said to him, would be overheard. But U.S. government personnel and Roosevelt himself had assumed for years that every important building, hotel, and embassy in the Soviet Union was bugged. In 1934, Roosevelt had sent William Bullitt, America's first ambassador to the Soviet Union, with the following advice: "You will, of course, warn all the members of the staff of both Embassy and Consulate in Russia that they will be spied upon constantly." In 1936 a man was discovered in the attic of Spaso House, the ambassador's residence in Moscow, dangling a microphone over a spot roughly above Ambassador Joseph E. Davies's desk. The film *Mission to Moscow*, which Davies had brought to Moscow in the spring of 1943 and shown to Stalin and the assembled Politburo, had in it a scene making fun of the ubiquitous bugging of diplomats by the Soviet government. Roosevelt would have assumed that everything he and his staff said was reported to Stalin, and he would have adjusted all conversation accordingly, even though there was no bugging equipment visible. Indeed, the microphones were so state-of-the-art small, the NKVD's head, Lavrenti Beria, boasted, that it was "impossible" to spot them. Being such a good actor, the president probably enjoyed exercising his talents.

Stalin set great store in listening to the taped conversations, according to Beria, who briefed Stalin each morning at 8:00 as to what he had heard in the president's quarters. Stalin "even went so far as to ask for details of the tone of the conversations: did he say that with conviction or without enthusiasm? How did Roosevelt react? Did he say that resolutely? . . . What do you think, do they know we are listening . . . ? Roosevelt always expressed a high opinion of Stalin." Stalin once remarked, seemingly puzzled, "They know that we can hear them and yet they speak openly! . . . It's bizarre. They say everything, in fullest detail . . . I was able to establish from my eavesdropping that Roosevelt felt great respect and sympathy for Stalin. Admiral Leahy tried several times to persuade him to be firmer with Stalin. Every time he received the reply from Roosevelt: 'That doesn't matter. Do you think you can see further than I can? I am pursuing this policy because I think it is more advantageous. We are not going to pull the chestnuts out of the fire for the British.'"

Nothing underlines Stalin's obsessive and thorough nature quite as clearly as his daily analysis of Roosevelt's supposedly private words and attitudes. Nothing underlines Roosevelt's ability to size people up correctly, and his talents as an actor, more than his pursuit of the invitation to stay in the Russian embassy and his conduct while there. Stalin learned only what Roosevelt wanted him to learn. Roosevelt would have been tickled pink to know that Stalin didn't dream Roosevelt knew his conversations were being picked up by hidden microphones.

Roosevelt's living arrangements brought out paranoia in the British. "Plainly it is convenient to him [Stalin] to have the President under his eye, where he cannot spend his time plotting with the British Prime Minister," observed Churchill's doctor, Lord Moran, voicing the general underestimation of Roosevelt's intelligence that was endemic among the British at the conference.

Intimidatingly fit members of the NKVD wearing pistols took the place of servants in the president's rooms. One look at the men who made their beds and cleaned their rooms made this clear. Remembered Reilly, "Everywhere you went you would see a brute of a man in a lackey's white coat busily polishing immaculate glass or dusting dustless furniture. As their arms swung to dust or polish, the clear, cold outline of a Luger automatic could be seen on every hip." Commander William Rigdon, assistant naval aide, left to wind up things after the presidential party had left, was startled to see that a number of the servants, shedding their white coats, were in reality Russian officers, with uniforms and insignia indicating ranks up to general. Brute Soviet soldiers were, in fact, everywhere. Two hundred soldiers armed with submachine guns ringed the embassy grounds. More soldiers, "all of them really big men[,] [n]othing under six feet two," ringed Roosevelt's particular building. There seemed to be a Soviet guard behind every tree in the park as well. The street between the Russian and the British embassies was turned into a passage by the placement of high walls from embassy to embassy. The Russian embassy park itself was surrounded by a stone wall. And each morning Lavrenti Beria, the collar of his overcoat turned up, his felt hat pulled down over his eyes, cruised the embassy park in a Buick with darkly tinted windows.

The president probably never felt safer. Discussing the living arrangements later, Roosevelt always left out that he had asked Stalin's advice as to where he should stay. He told Frances Perkins a half-truth, that at no time did he believe there had been any plot. But he also told her that it was clear to him that Stalin wanted him at the Russian embassy, and, he went on, embroidering his story, the move distressed

him because, to make it possible, Stalin had to move out to a small cottage on the embassy grounds.

No one, with the single exception of Hopkins, knew about Roosevelt's original query to Stalin asking where he should live until years
later when their full correspondence was published. Churchill would
have been stunned if he had known. But Stalin knew, and Molotov, and
that was the whole point. Roosevelt wanted Stalin to see the lengths he
had gone to to lay the groundwork for their meeting. It was "a small
thing to do to please them . . . If we could woo them in this way, perhaps it was the cheapest thing we could do . . . It was a matter of exhibiting my trust in them, my complete confidence in them. And it did
please them, no question about it," he said later to Perkins.

Roosevelt did it because he wanted Stalin to sign on to a full political agenda. There were the military considerations: he had to set a firm
date for Overlord, the Allied invasion—the second front, as the Russians called it. And although Stalin had told Cordell Hull in Moscow in
October that the Soviet Union would join America in the war against
Japan, Roosevelt needed to hear such a commitment from Stalin's lips.
Soviet military plans had to be coordinated with Overlord.

But what was of supreme importance to Roosevelt was the end-
game, the structure of the peace, and for that he needed Stalin's full
cooperation. Versailles—the horror and futility of that postwar peace
conference—was always on his mind. Only at a conference of the vic-
tors, held while still fighting shoulder to shoulder, still in need of each
other, did he feel he could shape the postwar world.

How many times did Roosevelt suggest a meeting to Stalin? Countless. By spring 1943, no nearer a meeting, FDR was beginning to feel
really anxious: the tide of war was changing in favor of the Allies, and
he still had no meeting scheduled. He decided to try new tactics. He
proposed a meeting without Churchill because, as he told the Canadian
prime minister, Mackenzie King, with whom he had been friends since
Harvard, who was visiting the White House, "I have a hunch that Stalin
does not want to see the two of us together, at least at the outset, and
that he would like to talk with me alone." FDR envisioned this meeting as taking place in Alaska, possibly in Nome, in August. He had it
all worked out in his mind: he would meet up with Mackenzie King
in Ottawa, the two of them would drive north on the Alcan Highway
(FDR had ordered its construction in 1942, the Army Corps of Engi-

neers had finished it against all odds eight months later; he was dying to see it), then he would continue alone to Alaska to meet Stalin.

King, who knew Churchill at least as well as FDR did, told FDR he foresaw no objection from the prime minister, because Churchill had been in Russia "and seen Stalin there." But King was wrong—Churchill minded a great deal—and Roosevelt would later in June deny to Churchill that he had written to Stalin asking him for a private meeting. It had been Stalin's idea, Roosevelt wrote: "I did not suggest to UJ that we meet alone but he told Davies that he assumed (a) that we would meet alone and (b) that he agreed that we should not bring staffs to what would be a preliminary meeting."

To underline the importance of a meeting of just the two of them to Stalin, the president had Joseph E. Davies deliver his message in person. Davies, his good friend, who had established a good relationship with Stalin when he had been American ambassador to the Soviet Union from 1936 to 1938, arrived in Moscow in late May 1943.

In his letter Roosevelt demonstrated his fine geographic knowledge:

> My Dear Mr. Stalin: I am sending this personal note to you by
> the hands of my old friend . . . It relates solely to one subject
> which I think it is easier for us to talk over through a mutual
> friend . . . I want to get away from the difficulties of large Staff
> conferences . . . Africa is almost out of the question in summer,
> and Khartoum is British territory, Iceland I do not like because
> for both you and me it involves rather difficult flights, and in
> addition would make it, quite frankly, difficult not to invite
> Prime Minister Churchill at the same time. Therefore I suggest
> we meet either on your side or our side of the Bering Straits.

Roosevelt hoped to cut through Stalin's anger and disappointment at the lack of concrete plans for the second front, which he had led Molotov to believe was going to happen that summer.

Stalin accorded Davies a special welcome when he arrived in Moscow in 1943. He met with him for two and a half hours on May 20 and three days later threw him a formal dinner in the Kremlin. Virtually all of the Politburo were at the dinner, at the conclusion of which *Mission to Moscow* was shown. The movie, produced by Warner Brothers, based on Davies's book of the same title, was essentially a Hollywood

propaganda film designed to whip up sympathy for the hard-pressed
Russians. It purported to give "the facts as I [Ambassador Davies] saw
them." The all-star cast featured Walter Huston, Roosevelt's "favorite
of favorites" actor, as Davies, Ann Harding as his wife, Marjorie Mer-
riwether Post Davies, and Oskar Homolka as Maxim Litvinov. Other
actors played Joseph Stalin, Winston Churchill, and the British foreign
secretary Anthony Eden. The film was a great paean to Soviet courage,
to Soviet grit, and to the heroic struggle by Soviet civilians and soldiers
against the onslaught of the German army. The movie suggested that
Soviet workers who fulfilled their factory quotas and were rewarded
with extra rubles had a great deal in common with American workers.
Collective farms were depicted as producing mountains of food. There
were dramatic photographs of sabotaged Russian factories being blown
up, as justification for the Moscow show trials of 1936–38. That was
followed by a dramatization of a show trial during which high Soviet
officials confessed to taking orders from the traitor Leon Trotsky, who,
aided by the German government, was seeking to overthrow the Soviet
government. The movie couldn't have been more laudatory to the Soviet
cause if it had been directed by the Kremlin.

When it was over, after the lights were turned on, after the clap-
ping, everyone turned to see Stalin's reaction. He looked quite stunned,
remembered a British diplomat, who reported that at length he said,
"Let's all get a drink." Pleasantly amazed as he must have been by the
enthusiastic, simplistic portrayal, he decreed that it could be shown all
over the Soviet Union. (It pleased him so much that in later years it
became one of the films he most enjoyed watching.)

Davies thought Stalin had agreed to a meeting with FDR. "As to the
particular mission I was engaged upon, I believe that the result thereof
has been completely successful," he advised Roosevelt. Stalin cabled
FDR that he thought they could meet in July or August, saying he
would give the president two weeks' prior notice of the exact date: "I
agree with you that such a meeting is necessary and that it should not
be postponed." But he also warned that "the summer months will be
extremely serious for our Soviet armies." Unusually, this message closed
with Stalin's writing, "With sincere respect."

Then, on June 11, 1943, Stalin wrote to Roosevelt to tell him of his
disappointment in learning that at the Trident Conference just concluded in Washington, "you and Mr. Churchill made the decision, post-

poning the British-American invasion of Western Europe until Spring of 1944 . . . This decision creates exceptional difficulties for the Soviet Union."

Roosevelt did not directly respond to this. Instead, he wrote that he was stepping up the shipments of aluminum that the Soviet Union so desperately needed, and "in addition to our new protocol agreement I have directed that six hundred additional fighters be sent to you during the balance of 1943 . . . the most maneuverable fighter we have . . . I have also directed the shipment of seventy eight additional B-25s."

Stalin sent another angry message regarding the postponement of the invasion to the president on June 24, in the form of relaying the message he had sent to Churchill:

> You write to me that you fully understand my disappointment. I have to tell you that this is not simply [a] matter of disappointment of the Soviet Government, but a matter of preservation of its confidence in the Allies which confidence is subjected to hard trials.
>
> One must not forget, that it is a question of preservation of millions of lives in occupied regions of Western Europe and Russia, and reduction of the tremendous sacrifices of the Soviet armies in comparison with which the sacrifices of the Anglo-American forces constitute a small quantity.

Two days later, however, certainly influenced by a laudatory message Roosevelt sent him on the second anniversary of Hitler's invasion of the Soviet Union (which took two days to get to him), in which the president mentioned the "act of treachery," the "history-making exploits of the armed forces of the Soviet Union," the "almost incredible sacrifices which the Russian people are so heroically making," and "approaching the challenging tasks of peace which victory will present to the world," Stalin sent the president a friendly message that expressed his mind-set at the time, ascertainable because, unusually, he took the trouble to cross out the original "vrajeskiy" as describing the Germans and replace it with "zatvernik," which translates as "brigands":

> I thank you for the high evaluation of the determination and courage of the Soviet people and of their armed forces in their struggle against the German brigands.

As a result of the two-year struggle of the Soviet Union against Hitlerite Germany and her vassals and as a result of the serious blows which have been delivered by the Allies to the Italian-German armies in North Africa the conditions for the final destruction of our common enemy have been created.

In July, Roosevelt impatiently reminded Stalin that he was still waiting for a firm meeting date. But the German counterattack that Stalin had been waiting for had finally begun. Hitler had amassed huge numbers of tanks and guns in preparation for a battle at Kursk, southwest of Moscow, counting on the German army's winning a decisive victory there that would fire up the world. The battle involved four thousand planes, six thousand tanks, and more than two million soldiers. The Red Army fought the Germans to a standstill, then gradually pushed them back and overwhelmed them. By the fifth day the battle was finished; the Red Army was in control. It was a decisive time: the end of Hitler's penetration of the Soviet Union. Almost immediately the Red Army regrouped and began marching, quickly retaking Orel and Belgorod, then advancing in force toward the Dnieper River and beyond.

On August 8, Stalin finally responded to Roosevelt's message. He explained that he couldn't take a long journey: "The battles are in full swing . . . the Soviet Armies repelled the July offensive, recaptured Orel and Belgorod and now is putting the further pressure upon the enemy . . . I . . . shall not be able, unfortunately, during this summer and autumn to keep my promise given to you through Mr. Davies." Unless, he continued, Roosevelt came all the way to him: "Under the present military situation, it could be arranged either in Astrakhan or in Archangel."

As to Roosevelt's suggestion that they meet à deux, Stalin seemed to think it was a trick: "I do not have any objections to the presence of Mr. Churchill at this meeting, hoping you will not have any objections to this." Although there was no way for Roosevelt to know it, Stalin had taken great care with this message; it is one of the few written in his own hand.

Roosevelt took this as a cue that Stalin wanted Churchill present, and his next two cables asking for a meeting were co-signed by Churchill. He followed these up with another on September 4 mentioning Churchill as the third conferee. "I personally could arrange to meet in a place as far as North Africa." Finally, on September 8, Stalin agreed he could now take the time to meet, but he dismissed North Africa as a location: he would only travel as far as Iran.

Roosevelt didn't want to go there with good reason. As he wrote to Stalin on October 14, Tehran presented a problem because the U.S. Constitution stipulated that "new laws and resolutions must be acted on by me after their receipt and must be returned to Congress physically before ten days have elapsed. . . . The possibility of delay in getting over the mountain—first, east bound and then west bound—is insurmountable."

Stalin replied, "Unfortunately, not one of the places proposed instead of Tehran by you for the meeting is suitable for me."

The end of October found Roosevelt as upset as he ever got because of Stalin's insistence on Tehran. In a long, impassioned message, he pulled out all the stops, writing, "I would gladly go ten times the distance to meet you were it not for the fact that I must carry on a constitutional government more than one hundred and fifty years old . . . It would be regarded as a tragedy by future generations if you and I and Mr. Churchill failed today because of a few hundred miles . . . I repeat that I would gladly go to Tehran were I not prevented from doing so because of limitations over which I have no control . . . Please do not fail me in this crisis."

His message was timed so that Hull, in Moscow for the conference of foreign ministers, could personally deliver it to Stalin. The strain of not knowing and keeping up appearances was telling on the president. He came down with the flu on October 19, running a temperature that went as high as 104 degrees for days.

On October 25, Hull, accompanied by Harriman, met with Stalin in the Kremlin, where Stalin had his office in the yellow palace, the stunning yellow and white palace built by Tsar Nicholas I along the Moscow River. They walked through the long green-carpeted corridors to Stalin's large and simply furnished office on the second floor overlooking the river. The windows were lined with heavy drapes and the walls with Russian stoves, both testaments to the bitter cold of the Russian winters that Stalin felt so acutely. On the floor was a thick red carpet. Portraits of Lenin, Marx, and Engels stared down from the walls. In one corner in a glass case was a white death mask of Lenin.

As Hull and Harriman sat across the large conference table from

Stalin in hard, uncomfortable chairs, Hull emphasized how important the still unscheduled meeting was to FDR. Stalin said that he was unable to understand why a delay of two days in the delivery of state papers should be so vital a matter as to preclude Roosevelt's presence in Tehran, whereas a false step in military operations might cost tens of thousands of lives. Hull tried to explain, and while suspicious of Stalin's sincerity he was at least reassured by Stalin's remark that he was not against the meeting "in principle" and his further explanation that he had put off the meeting because he couldn't miss the present opportunity to aid in the decisive defeat of the Germans, "an opportunity which might occur only once in fifty years."

Three more days passed. Hearing nothing from Stalin, on October 28 Roosevelt cabled Hull that he should suggest to Stalin that he fly "as far as Basra even for one day," that the rest of the time Molotov could sit in with Churchill and him. Hull cabled back that such an arrangement was "doubtful." Another day passed with no meeting set up. Sufficiently recovered from the flu to hold a press conference, FDR found himself pressured by reporters about the Moscow Conference. One reporter asked, "You are now confident of Russia's willingness to cooperate with us in maintaining peace?" Roosevelt answered, "I wouldn't put it that way. I always have been personally. This confirms my belief."

> Q: "It has been confirmed—strengthened?"
> ROOSEVELT: "Yes, yes."

Later that day Roosevelt called his good friend Daisy Suckley, who was home in Rhinebeck, New York, and vented his frustration to her. "Things are 'in a mess,'" he complained.

"I can't ask questions over the phone," she wrote in her diary, "He 'expects' to go on the Long Trip, 'thinks' it will go through, but it is not entirely certain, yet."

Suckley, ten years younger than the president, was Roosevelt's sixth cousin and his closest companion during the war years. Her important role in Roosevelt's life is little known because it was only after she died in 1991 that her diary, thousands of pages long, her letters to the president, and thirty-eight handwritten letters to her from him were discovered in a suitcase under her bed. Her diary was published as *Closest Companion,*

edited by Geoffrey Ward, in 1995. She had first laid eyes on Roosevelt
at a New Year's Eve ball when she was an impressionable eighteen and
he twenty-eight. She never forgot the sight of him, she told a confidant, "tall and laughing as he whirled one partner after another around
and around the dance floor." He was the love of her life. She lived at
Wilderstein, her family's large but run-down five-story turreted Queen
Anne Hudson River mansion that was upriver from Springwood, the
Roosevelt compound in Hyde Park built by FDR's father and rebuilt by
him, which FDR considered his real home. She was smart, well-read,
and thoughtful. At this point in the president's life, she was probably
his best friend. She spent more leisure time with him than anyone else.
In addition, she was working with him, using her intimate knowledge
of FDR's life, to arrange the large photograph collection in his new
presidential library, the first presidential library in the country, which
he had built on the grounds of his Hyde Park estate and had given to
the nation.

Suckley was slender, prim looking, always dressed in slightly old-
fashioned clothes. Whether they ever had an affair is not known,
although *something* happened one day when they were at Top Cottage,
the president's strictly private getaway cottage that he had designed and
built on his property in Hyde Park. Whatever it was, it sufficed for
Daisy, binding her to Roosevelt through thick and thin.

She managed to be the most nonthreatening of the women that the
president surrounded himself with and was accepted resignedly by Eleanor, who told her friend and biographer Joseph P. Lash that Franklin's
eye had wandered from the very beginning—while they were on their
honeymoon: "There always was a Martha for relaxation and for the
non-ending pleasure of having an admiring audience for every breath."
Daisy gave Roosevelt Fala, the black Scottie that became famous after
the president, responding to a Republican charge that he had wasted
taxpayer dollars on transportation for Fala (which he showed was
untrue), made the brilliant countercharge that, as low as it was to attack
him, attacking a dog that couldn't defend itself was beyond the pale:
"His Scottish soul was furious. He has not been the same dog since." He
must have been half in love with her himself, for he kept *her* letters to
him with him always, secreting them among the volumes of his stamp
collection that traveled with him wherever he went.

Roosevelt arrived at Hyde Park on October 29 still unable to shake the flu, according to Daisy's diary entry: "He is preparing for the Long Trip—Hopes he won't have to go to Teheran, which is full of disease, and involves a flight over the mountains of up to 15,000 feet. He dreads both things for himself and his whole party." The worst of it was that he still didn't know if the meeting was even going to take place, as he wrote to Mackenzie King on November 1: "I still hope that we can see 'Uncle Joe.' Apparently, however, my constitutional problems weigh lightly with him though I have tried a dozen times to explain to him that while my Congress is in session I must be in a position to receive bills, act on them, and get them back to Congress physically within ten days."

Another cable came from Stalin: "The possibility of traveling farther than Tehran is excluded. My colleagues in the Government consider . . . that my traveling beyond the borders of the USSR at the present time is impossible . . . I could be successfully substituted at this meeting by Mr. V. M. Molotov."

That same day Roosevelt also received some good news: the Senate overwhelmingly, 85 to 5, passed a measure dear to his heart, the Connally resolution approving of the United Nations: "That the Senate recognizes the necessity of there being established at the earliest practicable date a general international organization, based on the principle of the sovereign equality of all peace-loving states, and open to membership by all such states, large and small, for the maintenance of international peace and security." He had jumped the first hurdle—a hurdle Wilson had failed to clear: he had the backing of the legislative branch of government. The Senate would be behind him for his postwar organization for peace.

The next morning Roosevelt had breakfast with Sumner Welles, until very recently, as undersecretary of state, the second-ranking person in the State Department, who had headed the prewar State Department planning group working on the international peace organization. It was a warm gray November day, recalled Welles. Roosevelt was propped up in bed amid a pile of papers, a dark blue cape over his shoulders, smoking a cigarette through his long, uptilted ivory holder, the windows half-open in spite of air heavy with mist. They talked for two hours on the general nature of the organization that he would present to Stalin when they finally met. "We won't get any strong international organization unless we can find the way by which the Soviet Union and the United States can work together to build it up as the years go by," FDR told him. "That to him was the key issue," Welles would write. Later in the morning the president set off for Shangri-La, taking along, for distraction, the Supreme Court justice William O. Douglas and his wife, Mr. and Mrs. Nelson Rockefeller—and Daisy.

The next afternoon, according to her diary, when Daisy walked onto the enclosed porch of the cottage, Roosevelt greeted her with his latest thoughts about Stalin, saying that because he was commander of the Russian forces he "cannot be away from Moscow beyond a certain number of hours . . . The P. suggested that Stalin may be suffering from an inferiority complex . . . It has to do with his 'strategy' toward the outside world—Russia is now so big, and so strong, that she can impose her will, and must be treated at least as an equal—this is such a change from, shall we say, ten years ago, that Stalin may be self conscious about it."

It was never far from Roosevelt's thoughts that the time to make postwar plans was before the fighting ended. He had a private fear that that might be sooner than anyone expected. "It was quite possible Germany might crumple up at any moment," he had said to Mackenzie King the previous December, as Zhukov began tightening the noose around Stalingrad, explaining that he had been getting many reports from Germans "as to the shortage of food, as to the discontent of the people." He *had* to get a meeting scheduled.

Observant Daisy noticed that his hands were shaking more than usual, which he attributed to drinking too much coffee, but his ankles were swollen, which he couldn't explain away—even appearing, Daisy wrote, "a little worried about swelling in his ankles which comes when he is tired. Fox [Lieutenant Commander George Fox, the president's physical therapist] rubs them before dinner and he puts an electric vibrator on them at bedtime."

FDR had presented his travel problem to Attorney General Francis Biddle, a product, as he was, of Groton and Harvard, who solved it by writing up a memo emphasizing that wherever the president might be, he had ten days excepting Sundays, which were not counted, to return a bill to Congress *from the time it had been presented to him.* That problem solved, he decided to go. On Monday, FDR cabled a message to the U.S. embassy in Moscow for Harriman to deliver to Stalin. Stalin, however, was not available; Molotov received the message. Molotov told him that the premier had a light case of the flu and could not receive him, whereupon Harriman had the message translated for Molotov so that, as he explained, in case there were any questions, he could clarify them. "I have worked out a method so that if I get word that a bill requiring my veto has been passed by the Congress . . . I will fly to Tunis to meet it and then return," wrote FDR. Roosevelt's message continued, "It is my thought that the Staffs begin their work in Cairo on November 22, and I hope Mr. Molotov and your military representative, who I hope can speak English, will come there at that time."

Molotov queried Harriman as to what was involved in the preliminary negotiations in Cairo, because he would be the Soviet representative. Harriman admitted he did not know, at which point Molotov frostily asked whether the president had taken note of Marshal Stalin's comment in his November 5 cable that the marshal's colleagues "consider it generally impossible for him to travel outside the borders of the USSR." Harriman answered that he would inform the president about that but that the president "is assigning high priority to this meeting."

THE CABLES BACK AND FORTH to Stalin and to Churchill as well had a huge effect on Stalin. No longer did the world hold him and his nation at arm's length. Now, realizing that FDR and Churchill were treating him as an equal, he began concentrating on grooming the Soviet Union for its coming postwar status as a major world power. Even before Tehran he made systemic changes. The same weekend that the president was at Shangri-La with Daisy fretting about whether or not he would go to Tehran, Stalin was giving his annual Revolution Day peroration. For the first time he introduced a note of praise and accommodation for his allies: "The fighting in Southern Europe is not the Second Front, but, all the same, it is something like the Second Front . . . Naturally, only a real Second Front—which is now not so far away—will greatly speed up victory over Nazi Germany, consolidate still further the comradeship-in-arms of the Allied States." He had admitted only the week before at the Moscow Conference that "the *threat* of a Second Front in Northern France had, in the summer of 1943, pinned down some twenty-five German divisions in the west."

Stalin, a great student of history, particularly liked to think of himself as a ruler following in the steps of Ivan the Terrible, who had made Russia great. When the foreign minister of Lithuania had walked the halls of the Kremlin with him late one night in 1940, Stalin said to him, "Here Ivan the Terrible used to walk." Now, in 1943, he ordered the gifted Soviet film director Sergei Eisenstein to make *Ivan the Terrible*. The film, written and directed by Eisenstein, was an extravaganza that portrayed Ivan as a cruel but wise state builder who united the country, and showed Russia as barbaric, splendid, and strong. Ivan, as portrayed, was "the obvious forerunner" of himself, noted Alexander Werth, correspondent for the BBC and the London *Sunday Times* during the war. Alexis Tolstoy, author of a play about another legendary tsar, Peter the Great, also had to edit his work to make Peter resemble Stalin: "The 'father of the people' revised the history of Russia. Peter the Great became, without my knowing it, 'the proletarian tsar' and the prototype of our Josif!"

Stalin had been thinking for a long time about dissolving the Comintern, an organization specifically charged with fomenting revolution in other countries: he thought it had outlived its usefulness. As early as April 1941, he had gone on record as saying that the Communist parties in other countries, instead of being members of the Comintern, should be transformed into national parties: "Membership in the Comintern makes it easier for the bourgeoisie to persecute the Communist parties." Barbarossa, code name for the German invasion of Russia, had stopped the implementation of the idea. Now Stalin had the time and the platform. Molotov informed Georgi Dimitrov, the head of the Comintern, that the organization would cease to exist. On May 21, at a meeting of the Politburo in Stalin's office in the yellow palace, Molotov read the following resolution:

> When we created the CI and thought we could direct the movement in all countries, we were overestimating our forces. That was our error. The further existence of the CI would discredit the idea of the international, something we do not wish to see . . . There is also another motive for the dissolution . . . And that is the fact that the CPs that belong in the CI are falsely accused of being the agents of a foreign state . . . By dissolving the CI we are knocking this ace out of the enemies' hand.

The dissolution was more than cosmetic but less than total. Molotov told Dimitrov that the Comintern's various operations and functions would be divided up among other agencies. Roosevelt, cynically, thought of it as a hopeful step, a gesture of friendship, a step in the right direction. In point of fact it did not entirely cease to function, but it was no longer centrally controlled: its networks were merged into NKVD networks.

The dissolution clearly exposed past Soviet duplicity. The Soviet government had always maintained that the Comintern was independent of the Soviet government. In fact Stalin steered the activities of the Comintern; for years his letters to Molotov contained advice on what the Comintern should and should not do. The fictional independence of the Comintern was now fully exposed. The dissolution was well on its way when Joseph E. Davies had appeared in Moscow to set up the meeting between Stalin and Roosevelt. Stalin saw the chance of a public relations coup: announce it while Davies was in Moscow. "We ought to rush with the publication," the premier urged Dimitrov. Dimitrov got to work, and the dissolution was announced the day before Stalin's dinner for Davies and the showing of *Mission to Moscow*. Davies had been thrilled at the action. He remarked at the dinner "that when he was ambassador in Moscow, he used to say to Litvinov that the Comintern—the stick with which everybody beat the Soviet Union— was the real source of all the trouble."

Stalin got as much mileage as he could from the act. Harold King, Reuters correspondent in Moscow, asked him what the dissolution meant. On May 28, Stalin replied, "It exposes the lie of the Hitlerites to the effect that 'Moscow' allegedly intends to intervene in the life of other nations and to 'Bolshevize' them. From now on an end is put to this lie."

In keeping with Stalin's new vision, fostered by FDR, that Russia would emerge from the war as a world power rather than the embattled proletarian pariah it had been before the war, Stalin realized that Russia needed a professional, elite officer corps that could deal as equals with those of other countries. As he would say to the English interpreter A. H. Birse, "We have good generals in the Soviet Army. Only ours lack breeding, and their manners are bad. Our people have a long way to go." In August 1943 nine Suvorov Military Schools were established, named after Alexander Suvorov, the great eighteenth-century Russian general who never lost a battle. The schools were closely modeled on the prerevolutionary Cadet Corps in order to create an officer caste such as had existed before the revolution. The young men would get a military education and a secondary school education that would include worldly touches, foreign languages, and social skills such as fine manners and ballroom dancing. They would emerge smart, sophisticated, and cultured. They would also look smart: student uniforms were modeled on Red Army uniforms, with epaulets and other markings. In sum, the next generation of Soviet soldiers would be on a par with the militaries of Britain, France, and America and be respected at home.

Army officers' uniforms themselves underwent a startling transformation earlier in 1943 as the Red Army began to beat back German soldiers. In the middle of the Battle of Stalingrad, indeed at its height, as the Soviet forces gained the upper hand, gold braid and epaulets—imported from England—appeared on officers' uniforms. It wouldn't have been accepted before—epaulets had been torn off the shoulders of the tsar's officers in 1917—but after Stalingrad, officers were seen as proud professionals. "Fine uniforms would have looked all wrong in retreat," as Werth noted, but as the embattled Red soldiers clawed their way back and made the Wehrmacht give way at Stalingrad, officers as a class regained the respect they had been missing in Russia because the anger unleashed in the revolution had leveled all class distinctions. Outstanding officers were singled out and awarded new orders named after Russia's pre-Communist great warriors: the orders of Alexander Suvorov; Mikhail Kutuzov, who defeated Napoleon; Fedor Ushakov, who served under Catherine the Great; Prince Alexander Nevsky, hero of the thirteenth century who ousted the Teutons. Officers above a certain rank were given a new code of conduct to set them off from the rank and file: they could not travel by public transport; they could not do anything as undignified as carrying paper parcels. If a general went to the theater in Moscow, he had to sit in one of the first fifteen rows of the orchestra; if those seats were sold out, he couldn't attend. Enlisted men had to sit in the balcony.

Another, even more profound change in the lives of army officers was instituted, although later it would be countermanded: political commissars, whose job it was to oversee and spy on the officers as well as to ensure political correctness, which had the effect of dissipating officers' prestige, were abolished. For the first time, officers had the sole responsibility for military decisions.

The diplomatic corps was also spruced up. New outfits for diplomats suddenly appeared: dove-gray suits with gold-plated buttons, set off by a peaked cap, vest, black silk socks, white shirt with stiff collar, pearl cuff links, white kid gloves, and a small dagger at the belt.

But Stalin made the biggest change, pushed by FDR, on religion. Two months before Tehran, Stalin officially rescinded his antireligion policy. He knew the Soviet Union's negative attitude toward religion was a constant concern to Roosevelt. The president knew it gave fodder to enemies of the Soviet Union in America, particularly the Catholic Church, but it also offended him personally. Only those very close to Roosevelt were aware of his deep religious streak. Rexford Tugwell, friend and member of the Columbia University brain trust that developed the early policy recommendations for Roosevelt's presidency, remembered that when FDR was about to institute something new, he would first ask all his colleagues to accompany him in asking for divine blessing on what they were about to do. The speechwriter Robert Sherwood believed "his religious faith was the strongest and most mysterious force that was in him."

Roosevelt had pushed for religious freedom in the Soviet Union every chance he got. The day following Hitler's invasion in June 1941, he had notified Stalin that American help and religious freedom went hand in hand: "Freedom to worship God as their consciences dictate is the great and fundamental right of all peoples . . . To the people of the United States this and other principles and doctrines of communistic dictatorship are as intolerable and as alien to our own beliefs, as are the principles and doctrines of Nazi dictatorship. *Neither kind of imposed overlordship can have, or will have, any support or any sway in the mode of life, or in the system of Government, of the American people.*"

In the fall of 1941, as the German army closed in on Moscow, as Averell Harriman and Lord Beaverbrook, press baron and minister of supply, were about to leave for Moscow to work out what supplies their countries could ship to the Soviet Union, FDR had seized the moment to advocate religious freedom in the Soviet Union. Stalin was desperate: FDR knew there would never be a better time. "I believe there is a real possibility that Russia may as a result of this present conflict recognize freedom of religion in Russia," wrote Roosevelt in early September. He took three actions. The first was that he called in Constantine Oumansky, the Soviet ambassador in Washington, to the White House to tell him that it was going to be extremely difficult to get Congress to authorize the aid he knew Russia desperately needed because of the great deal of hostility in Congress toward his country. He then suggested, "If Moscow could get some publicity back to this country regarding the freedom of religion during the next few days without waiting for the Harriman mission to reach Moscow, it might have a very fine educational effect before the next Lend-Lease bill comes up in Congress." Oumansky agreed to attend to the matter. On September 30, FDR held a press conference during which he instructed reporters to read article 124 of the Russian Constitution that granted freedom of conscience and freedom of religion—and publicize the information. (After the press duly reported the information, Roosevelt's archenemy, Hamilton Fish, the Republican congressman from Roosevelt's district, Hyde Park, sarcastically suggested the president invite Stalin to the White House "so that he might be baptized in the White House swimming pool," following which they could both "join the White House Sunday school.")

Roosevelt next instructed Harriman, about to go to Moscow, to raise the issue of freedom of worship with Stalin. Remembered Harriman, "The President wanted me to impress on Stalin how important it was to ease restrictions on religion. Roosevelt was concerned about possible opposition from religious groups . . . In addition he sincerely wanted to use our wartime collaboration to modify Soviet antagonism toward religion." Harriman raised the subject with Stalin, in a context Stalin would relate to: that the political situation and negative public opinion in America regarding Russia would improve if "the Soviets were willing to allow freedom of worship not only in letter but in fact." As Harriman recounted, when he explained this, Stalin "nodded his head and indicated what I understood to mean a willingness to see that something was done."

Harriman also pursued the subject with Molotov, who revealed he didn't believe Roosevelt was being honest. "Molotov expressed to me with great sincerity the high regard that he and the others had for the President . . . At one point . . . he asked me whether the President being such an intelligent man really was as religious as he appeared, or whether his professions were for political purposes," Harriman recalled. It was an understandable Russian reaction. Oumansky might have reported that Roosevelt never went to Sunday services at the National Cathedral, the Episcopal church where presidents and the upper-crust Episcopalians in Washington traditionally attended services (although occasionally he went to St. John's in Lafayette Square). Oumansky couldn't possibly have known FDR stayed away from the National Cathedral because he couldn't stand the presiding Episcopal bishop of Washington, James Freeman. FDR had visited the National Cathedral in 1934 for a special service in celebration of the first anniversary of his inauguration at the invitation of Bishop Freeman. After the service the bishop, who was walking beside FDR as he was wheeled to his car, suggested to the president that he make plans to be buried in the cathedral crypt, as President Wilson and Admiral Dewey had done. Freeman had then suggested to Roosevelt that he dictate a memorandum, "expressing his wish to be buried here." Roosevelt, furious, didn't answer. Once out of the bishop's clutches and safely ensconced in his car, however, Roosevelt kept muttering, "The old body snatcher, the old body snatcher." A bit later, reminded of the bishop's suggestion, Roosevelt dictated a memorandum—to his heirs—directing that he be buried at Hyde Park. He never attended another service at the National Cathedral.

Harriman made nothing more than a dent. Solomon A. Lozovsky, assistant people's commissar for foreign affairs, waited until the day Harriman left Moscow to call a press conference; he read the following: "Public opinion of the Soviet Union learned with great interest of the press conference statement of President Roosevelt concerning freedom of worship in the USSR . . . Freedom of worship and freedom of anti-religious propaganda are recognized for all citizens." But, he said, the Soviet state "did not meddle with religion"; religion was a "private matter." And Lozovsky ended by warning Russian Orthodox Church leaders, many still in jail, "Freedom for any religion presupposes that the religion, church or community will not be used for the overthrow of the existing authority which is recognized in the country." Furthermore, the only newspaper in Russia that ran the item was the *Moscow News,* the English-language newspaper that only Americans read; *Pravda* and *Izvestia* ignored Lozovsky's comments. Roosevelt wasn't happy; he had expected more, remembered Harriman: "He made me feel that it was not enough and took me to task . . . [H]e was critical of my failure to get more."

A few weeks later, after reading a late State Department draft of the United Nations Declaration that all nations at war were to sign on January 1, 1942, FDR had told Hull to get religious freedom into the document: "I believe Litvinov can be induced to agree." When the Soviet

ambassador Litvinov, who had just replaced Oumansky, had objected
to the inclusion of the words concerning religion, Roosevelt spun the
words around, changing "freedom of religion" to "religious freedom."
This alteration, while slight and meaningless, allowed Litvinov to truth-
fully report to Moscow that he had had enough clout to make Roosevelt
alter the document, thus satisfying Stalin.

In November 1942, the first crack came in the Soviet government's
antireligion stance: Nikolas, metropolitan of Kiev, one of the three metropolitans who led the Russian Orthodox Church, was made a member
of the Extraordinary State Commission for Ascertaining Offenses of
the German Fascists. Now, two months before Tehran, there was a big
payoff for Roosevelt. Stalin, who had been a party to the closing and/
or destruction of so many churches, the liquidation of 637 of Russia's
1,026 monasteries and convents, began seeing religion not through the
narrow doctrinaire lens of Communism but as an ally. This was made
easier, of course, by the fact that the Church was no longer a hotbed of
resistance against his regime. It had joined forces with the government
in opposing the Germans; the government and the Church were now
both defenders of Mother Russia.

On September 4, 1943, in the late afternoon, Stalin summoned to
his Kuntsevo dacha G. G. Karpov, chairman of the Council of Russian
Orthodox Church Affairs; Georgy Malenkov, a member of the GKO,
the State Defense Committee; and Lavrenti Beria. After discussing the
friendly role the Church was already playing in the war and the stronger
role it might play in the future, Stalin announced that he had decided
to immediately restore the patriarchate, which he had dissolved in 1925,
and open churches and seminaries throughout the Soviet Union. Later
that same evening, the metropolitans Sergei, Nikolas, and Alexius were
summoned to the Kremlin and informed by Stalin of the momentous
changes he had decided upon. Stalin talked with them until 3:00 in the
morning, undoubtedly probing to make sure that they no longer harbored thoughts of undermining the Soviet regime. The discussion was
fruitful and probably friendly. Stalin respected members of the clergy,
even though he no longer believed in God, probably because his early
education had been at the hands of priests.

The following day *Pravda* announced that the metropolitan Sergei, a great churchman who had opposed Rasputin at the court of Tsar
Nicholas, had spent the intervening twenty-five years in Bolshevik pris-

ons, and believed the Church should make peace with the Soviets, was now free and would be permitted to convene the Council of Bishops to elect a new patriarch. In addition, licenses would be issued for the opening and restoration of religious institutions, and the Church would be allowed to resume publication of its journal. *Pravda* gave Stalin a pat on the back, to make crystal clear that it *was* Stalin behind the new policy: "The head of government, Comrade I. V. Stalin, was sympathetic to these proposals and stated that the government would not stand in the way." Within a short time the Church was a part of the establishment upholding Stalin's right to rule.

Stalin, who had a baritone voice and loved to sing, at this time also decided that the Soviet national anthem was not up to international standards: it too needed sprucing up. He had sung in the choir in his Gori church school as a little boy and continued singing as he grew older in the seminary in Tiflis, in fact, until the seminary expelled him for revolutionary activities, he had earned his spending money by being choir leader. Oddly, all his life Stalin would while away nights singing hymns, usually with Molotov and Voroshilov, including orthodox liturgical chants and Russian folk songs that all Russians knew from their childhood. Perhaps because of this, he decided that, with help, he was fit to upgrade the national anthem. He decreed that there would be a competition for a new national anthem, that he would be the judge, that he would listen to all contestant entries, and that the contest would be at Beethoven Hall in Moscow on November 1, 1943. The day of the competition he, flanked by Molotov, Beria, and Voroshilov, arrived at 9:00 a.m. at the concert hall—one of the rare times that Stalin, a notorious night owl, is noted as being at a morning function. The group sat for four hours listening to the forty renditions, after which Stalin decided that only the lyrics of the anthem needed to be changed. After a great deal of discussion lyrics were chosen of which Stalin approved but which he insisted on endlessly changing. "You can leave the verses," he told the lyricists at one point, "but rewrite the refrains. 'Country of Soviets'—if it's not a problem, change it to 'country of socialism,'" then, an afterthought, he wanted to add "the Motherland." He then approved the insertion of his own name in one of the verses: "The great Lenin lighted our path, Stalin reared us faithful to the people; Inspired us for work and great deeds." Perhaps that had been his aim all along. The famed composers Dmitri Shostakovich and Sergei Prokofiev, obedient Soviet citizens, were put to work orchestrating the music to fit the new words. Stalin loved the result, going so far as to say that the new anthem "parts the sky and heaven like a boundless wave."

Stalin's desire to change the face his government put to the world continued. Sunday, November 7, 1943, the twenty-sixth anniversary of the revolution, was a day of celebration in Moscow. In the evening the celebration continued in the form of a grand party, Polina and Vyacheslav Molotov were the official hosts. The two stood under a huge crystal chandelier in the Spiridonovka Palace, an imposing Gothic mansion from tsarist times, greeting the guests. Harriman and the British ambassador, Sir Archibald Clark Kerr, attended, plus the rest of the diplomatic community. Generals, admirals, famous writers, artists, musicians—including Shostakovich in full evening dress—came to the party. The buffet, extraordinarily lavish, stretched out over twelve rooms. Many of the toasts were in English—so many that Harriman and Clark Kerr, obliged to drain their glasses at each toast, felt that Molotov had decided to make the two of them drunk. One important member of the Politburo, Lazar Kaganovich, who drank too much, began loudly sounding off about how ineffective assistance from the Americans and the British had been and suggested it was time for them to carry out their obligations: "Only a mere two percent—two percent—of what we needed arrived in time . . . How are you running this war? Only one full-time shift. The Red Army is working its shift. But the British and Americans are only working part time . . . What you need are pile drivers." He was hurried into his coat and fur hat and bundled out of the room so quickly Harriman never even noticed him.

4

FIRST IMPRESSIONS

Roosevelt was famous for his extreme loquaciousness. Virtually everyone who knew him well had an anecdote to tell about the president's propensity for talk. Roosevelt was aware of it. He even told the story on himself that once, when he informed his family that he wanted a short cabinet meeting, they said, "Well, you know how you can get it. You can just stop your own talking." Many important people had trouble getting a word in edgewise. Hull admitted that when he was asked by the president to come to lunch conferences, he would "get a little bite to eat first myself so that I could talk while he was eating."

Cabinet meetings were, according to one cabinet member, "a solo performance of the President interspersed with some questions and very few debates." After months in India, Undersecretary of State William Phillips traveled to Washington to explain to FDR what was happening there: "I had much to tell him . . . but he was in one of his talkative moods and had as much to tell me as I had to tell him." Phillips ended up writing him a memo. Secretary of War Henry Stimson learned to be patient but firm. He wrote in his diary of a typical meeting he had with the president: "I should say on a generous allowance I got forty percent of the time to talk in while he talked in the other sixty percent, but that is usual and I have gotten accustomed to it. I had a list of five points which I took up with him in succession and he was very good about letting me break him off from some of his reminiscences and I got them all through by the time I got finished." John Gunther, an acute observer, journalist, and Roosevelt biographer, thought that Roosevelt talked so much because he couldn't walk: "Conversation was his golf, his tennis, his badminton."

SCARCELY HAD THE PRESIDENT arrived at the Russian embassy on Sunday, November 28, when, at 3:15 p.m., Stalin paid him a call.

The president was, at last, face-to-face with the most elusive quarry he had ever sought. Would Stalin go along with what he would propose? Stick to an agreement when the present emergency was over? Three years earlier Hitler had wanted to arrange a meeting with Stalin, or at least he had voiced such a desire to Molotov. Yet within the year German troops had invaded Russia. The thought must have crossed Stalin's ever-suspicious mind that possibly through this meeting that Roosevelt had gone to such great lengths to arrange, even he might be trying to blunt the vigilance of the Soviet government.

Roosevelt was the first person he had met since Lenin who was more powerful than he: a president elected to an unprecedented third term, running what had become the most productive industrial engine in the world, which was now the main support of the Soviet Union. This man, this cripple who did not look or act like a cripple, whose clothes hung on him so well that he appeared, seated on the couch, not just physically normal but elegant, had traveled thousands of miles to meet with him. He was now housed, almost entirely because of his own initiative, in Stalin's own embassy. Clearly, Stalin had to think, this president was made of strong stuff.

It was a beautiful Sunday afternoon, gold and blue, mild and sunny, when the two leaders finally met in Roosevelt's sitting room. In spite of his most strenuous efforts to be included, Churchill was not there. Roosevelt had been resting in his bedroom, having just arrived at the embassy, when he was told Stalin was on his way over. Nevertheless, he managed to be seated waiting on the couch in the sitting room when Stalin made his appearance. "With a most engaging grin on his face," according to Mike Reilly, "he walked toward the Boss very slowly . . . sort of ambled across the room toward Roosevelt, grinning, and reached down to shake FDR's hand for the first time. As they shook hands the Boss grinned too and said, 'It's good to see you, Marshal,' and the Marshal burst into a very gay laugh."

Stalin sat down. Then, recalled Roosevelt, "I caught him looking curiously at my legs and ankles."

Roosevelt wore a navy blue business suit, white shirt, and a conservative tie, with a handkerchief in his vest pocket. He had a frank, clear gaze and a welcoming smile that could light up a room. He now turned it on Stalin.

Roosevelt was famous for his charm and manner: "He could make a casual visitor believe that nothing was so important to him that day as this particular visit, and that he had been waiting all day for this hour to arrive. He inspired an intense loyalty nearly everywhere in his administration. Young and ardent idealists, old and tired politicians, professors, even businessmen who joined up with him were ready to work at all hours of the day or night to carry out his bidding." Harold Ickes confessed, "I never had contact with a man who was loved as he is." He also had a special way of throwing his head up, which seemed a gesture of courage. It attracted people.

Unlike when he had seen him in the summer of 1941, when Hopkins had noted Stalin's rather baggy trousers, lack of medals, and simple but well-cut gray jacket, Stalin now wore one of the smart new Soviet military uniforms, a mustard-colored marshal's jacket with red epaulets and white stars on the shoulders and knife-edged trousers with broad red stripes. The star of the Order of Lenin hung from his neck. Instead of the worn boots Hopkins had seen him in, elegant, shining, soft Caucasian boots were now on his feet.

Stalin didn't look the way people expected. He was smaller. He was short, only five feet four, although many people, including Roosevelt, would comment that he seemed bigger, probably because his body was so thickset and powerful. Hopkins, too, who met him when he was under great pressure in July 1941, when Moscow was under siege from the German army, had come away with the distinct impression that he was a bigger man, "about five feet six . . . He's built close to the ground . . . like a football coach's dream of a tackle. His hands are huge, as hard as his mind."

He had a thick mustache, dark hair, heavy eyebrows, a low forehead, and what many people said were Oriental, honey-colored eyes. Although his Russian was correct in every respect, he had a Georgian accent, an accent as distinct from the ordinary Russian as a Scottish burr is to the English language. Also, surprisingly, he spoke in a low, controlled voice that he sometimes pitched so low it seemed as if he were talking to himself.

He also surprised people because he looked less "grand" than his pictures, which must have been retouched before they were released. His face was pockmarked from the smallpox he had suffered as a child, his teeth broken and stained. Additionally, when he filled his pipe with tobacco (he alternated between smoking cigarettes and a pipe), it could be seen that the motion of his left arm was slightly awkward, the result of a childhood accident.

Another surprise was his manner. Although he was tough, arbitrary, stern, and cold, he came across to newcomers as avuncular and patient, less threatening than they expected. General John Deane, the U.S. coordinator of Lend-Lease and military affairs, stationed in Moscow in 1943 as head of the military mission, who came to know just how obstinate and tough he was, nevertheless wrote that upon meeting him, "I was struck most of all by the kindly expression on his deeply wrinkled, sallow face." Lord Beaverbrook, who with Harriman went to Moscow in October 1941 to arrange the initial flow of aid, thought he was "a kindly man . . . practically never shows any impatience at all." One of Stalin's trusted associates wrote that it was hard to imagine such a man could deceive you, his reactions were so natural, without the slightest sense of him posing. He even impressed Cordell Hull, who wrote, "Any American having Stalin's personality and approach might well reach high public office in my own country." Clinton Olson, Moscow military attaché, described him as a "quiet-looking little man, until you looked at his eyes. Then you could feel that here was a powerful person." Admiral Leahy was in the minority in thinking he was "sinister in appearance."

In spite of the havoc he wreaked on his enemies, or those he imagined might become his enemies, Stalin was also known for his charm, according to his biographer Simon Sebag Montefiore. To his inner circle he was very approachable and very thoughtful. "The foundation of Stalin's power in the Party," Montefiore wrote, "was not fear: it was charm . . . He was what is now known as a 'people person.' While incapable of true empathy on the one hand, he was a master of friendships on the other. He constantly lost his temper, but when he set his mind to charming a man, he was irresistible." His associates called him Soso, his childhood name, or Koba, the name of a brave Georgian he admired as a teenager, or used the informal version of "you." A person, meeting him, was eager to see him again; "he created a sense that there was now a bond that linked them forever."

He was also utterly domineering: he ran the lives of his associates down to the smallest detail. He chose where they lived: for Lavrenti Beria, head of the NKVD, he selected a sumptuous nobleman's mansion near the Kremlin; for Nikita Khrushchev, a favored younger man, he allotted a palatial apartment in the pink granite Granovsky block near the Kremlin; for other members of his inner circle, he decided on an apartment like the one he himself lived in, inside the Kremlin. He chose the cars his associates used, dispensed money to them periodically, and gave them and usually their children thoughtful presents.

He was a workaholic. He found time to view many new Soviet movies, most newspaper editorials and news articles, and all manner of directives issued by the commissariats that controlled Soviet Russia, all of which were funneled first through Molotov's office. On his desk was a bronze cup full of thick-pointed blue and red pencils. When he approved of a movie, an editorial, an article, a directive, he scrawled his initials, JS, across the document with a thick blue pencil. When he did not approve of a document, he scribbled on it with a red pencil. Such occasions profoundly upset Molotov.

Good Communist that Stalin was, he cared little for elegant trappings. He divided his time between a simple apartment in the Kremlin, where his daughter, Svetlana, lived, and a dacha he built in 1934 called Blizhnyaya in Kuntsevo, five and a half miles from the Kremlin, where he usually spent the night, traveling there after dinner. The dacha had, behind thick walls, several bedrooms and reception rooms, a billiard room, halls lined with maps, and a movie theater. Although the house was surrounded by guards, the property surrounded by impenetrable fences, no one but Stalin stayed in the house at night: he was alone after his dinner guests left.

Both Stalin and FDR understood power, how to get it and how to keep it. Stalin had been ruling the Soviet Union since Lenin's death in 1924; Roosevelt had been in power since his inauguration in 1933.

Both were highly intelligent and had excellent memories, although of a different sort. Roosevelt's speechwriter Sam Rosenman wrote, "I had never met anybody who could grasp the facts of a complicated problem as quickly and as thoroughly as he. He could listen attentively to a brief statement of the facts, and then dictate them into a speech, then and there, walk onto a platform or rise at a banquet table and talk about them before an audience as though he had a lifelong familiarity with them." Arthur Schlesinger talked of Roosevelt's "instinct for the basic general issue, his flypaper mastery of detail, his capacity to carry a large variety of problems in his mind, his ability to shift with speed from one problem to another."

Stalin, too, had the ability to grasp and retain information and had the additional gift of a photographic memory. At meetings he worked "with no papers, no notes," "missed nothing"; he had a "memory like a computer," according to Andrei Gromyko, later to be Soviet ambassador to the United States. Beria said that Stalin "dominated his entourage with his intelligence."

Those observers of human nature who spent time in Roosevelt's company saw that he was a consummate actor. Raymond Moley, a member of the Columbia University brain trust, Roosevelt's pool of brilliant idea men who advised him and coined the term "New Deal," spoke of his "deliberately crafted public persona . . . It was a lifetime part that he was playing." Peggy Bacon commented that he had a bright, direct look, "the frank clear gaze of craft, clever as hell but so innocent . . . a grand old actor." Roosevelt even remarked to Orson Welles, "You know, Orson, you and I are the two best actors in America." Once, after he had seen himself in a newsreel, he grinned and said, "That was the Garbo in me."

Stalin on the other hand was famous for his sphinxlike inscrutability.

This meeting would be the first of three to be held without Churchill. The fact that the meetings took place is the best indication of exactly how dominant Roosevelt was, for the prime minister fumed at the very thought of being left out. He knew of the meetings, knew he was not invited, and at least once vented his fury on his doctor, who happened to be handy. He felt strongly about being left out. In point of fact in 1942 the prime minister himself had had not just one but a series of meetings with Stalin in Moscow, with Averell Harriman usually, but not always, present. The purpose had been to inform Stalin that Overlord was not going to take place as scheduled. "My journey to Moscow with Averell in August 1942 was on altogether a lower level" was his rationale.

The three meetings are remarkable. The two men listened to each other, took each other's measure, and probed. They spoke of their greatest desires and their greatest fears. The meetings were unprecedented:

two men, discussing how they were going to lay out the postwar world. Two men, seeking a formula to end war. Two men, seeking peace for their time.

In the histories of the period, these meetings are often overlooked, even though notes were kept by Charles Bohlen. Even Robert E. Sherwood's landmark biography, *Roosevelt and Hopkins,* based on Hopkins's papers, gives them short shrift, probably because Hopkins was not present at any of the meetings. Harriman's book *Special Envoy to Churchill and Stalin,* often taken as the best description of Tehran, hardly mentions them; he was only present at the last one. The meetings are also overlooked because they caused the master historian of the period, Winston Churchill, so much pain that he couldn't bear to even think of them, much less write about them, and it is Churchill, the spellbinding storyteller, to whom historians most often turn. He was right to be afraid of their private discussions, for it was as they met and exchanged words face-to-face that Roosevelt and Stalin found out how much they had in common.

This first historic meeting in Roosevelt's sitting room that sunny Sunday lasted forty minutes, half of which were taken up with translating. Roosevelt spoke first. The meeting is notable for the lack of preliminary small talk, its directness, the ease with which they answered each other's questions, and the remarkable similarity of attitudes between the two. Also notable is the fact that it is Roosevelt who set the agenda and steered the conversation. He would continue to do so at all the meetings.

Roosevelt had been worried that Stalin would ask him exactly how many German divisions could be taken off the Soviet western front immediately. To forestall the question, he now said "he wished that it were within his power to bring about the removal of 30 or 40 German divisions from the Eastern front."

Stalin replied, "It would be of great value."

Roosevelt next offered up "the possibility that after the war a part of the American-British merchant fleet which would be more than either nation could possibly utilize, be made available to the Soviet Union." He said this, knowing that America was going to have the largest merchant marine in the world after the war.

Stalin couched his answer diplomatically in terms of an enhanced merchant fleet allowing the expansion of trade between their two countries, "that if equipment were sent . . . a plentiful supply of raw materials . . . could be made available to the United States."

The president gave a brief overview of the situation in China, reporting that America was now supplying and training thirty Chinese divisions, that the Joint Chiefs were proposing to continue the same process for thirty additional divisions, and that there was a new prospect of an offensive operation through northern Burma.

Stalin observed that the Chinese leaders were responsible for the bad showing of their soldiers.

Stalin then inquired about the situation in Lebanon, a French colonial possession. Roosevelt gave a brief description of the events leading up to the violent unrest that was shaking Lebanon, concluding, "It had been entirely due to the attitude of the French Committee and General de Gaulle."

Lebanon had voted on November 8 to end the French mandate. Three days later the French Committee of National Liberation headed by Charles de Gaulle arrested the Lebanese president and decreed the suspension of the Lebanese Constitution and government. The result was riots in the streets. The United States, acting in tandem with Great Britain, was seeking to force de Gaulle to release the president. Roosevelt wired Hull from the *Iowa* on the way over to "back up the British position in Lebanon and try to make it even more positive," Hull followed directions, forcing de Gaulle to finally give in. Hull had issued a press release two days earlier noting with approval the French remedial action.

As they talked about France, Roosevelt and Stalin discovered they shared a dislike of both the country and its leaders, most particularly Charles de Gaulle.

Stalin described the posturing of de Gaulle. He "did not know General de Gaulle personally, but frankly . . . he was very unreal in his political activities . . . Whereas the real physical France [was] engaged under Pétain in helping our common enemy Germany by making available French ports, materials, machines, etc., for the German war effort . . . the trouble with de Gaulle was that his movement had no communication with the physical France, which should be punished for its attitude during this war. De Gaulle acts as though he were the head of a great state, whereas, in fact, it actually commands little power," Stalin concluded.

Roosevelt, who was resisting de Gaulle's efforts to be recognized as speaking for France, agreed, saying, "No Frenchman over forty, and particularly no Frenchman who had ever taken part in the present French Government, should be allowed to return to positions in the future."

Both vented their anger at the people of France. Stalin expatiated on the French ruling classes: "They should not be entitled to share in any of the benefits of the peace, in view of their past record of collaboration with Germany." Roosevelt took this as an opportunity to point out that Churchill "was of the opinion that France would be very quickly reconstructed as a strong nation but that he did not personally share this view since he felt that many years of honest labor would be necessary before France would be re-established. He said that the first necessity for the French, not only for the Government, but the people as well, was to become honest citizens." Marshal Stalin agreed.

Both then expressed remarkably similar views on Indochina, as Vietnam was then called, and found they agreed on the damage that France had inflicted on the country, as well as the pernicious effect that colonialism had on *all* subject countries.

Stalin declared that he did not propose to have the Allies shed blood to restore Indochina to the old French colonial rule. He said that the recent events in Lebanon made public service the first step toward the independence of people who had formerly been colonial subjects. He repeated the thought that France should not get back Indochina and that the French must pay for their criminal collaboration with Germany.

The president said he was 100 percent in agreement and remarked that after a century of French rule in Indochina, the inhabitants were worse off than they had been before. He said that Chiang Kai-shek had told him China had no designs on Indochina, but the people of Indochina were not yet ready for independence. Roosevelt said he had replied to the generalissimo that when the United States acquired the Philippines, the inhabitants were not ready for independence either, but it would be granted without qualification upon the end of the war against Japan. He added that he had discussed with Chiang Kai-shek the possibility of a system of trusteeship for Indochina that would prepare the people for independence within a definite period of time, perhaps twenty or thirty years.

Marshal Stalin completely agreed with this view.

Roosevelt then mentioned Hull's introduction of the idea at the

Moscow Conference of an international committee that would visit all colonies "and through use of instrumentalities of public opinion correct any abuse they find."

Stalin said he saw merit in the idea.

The conversation continued with Roosevelt dwelling on the problems inherent in colonial possessions. Roosevelt then threw in what Stalin might have taken as merely another dig at Churchill, saying, after continuing on the subject of colonial possessions, he felt it would be better not to discuss India with Mr. Churchill, since the latter had no solution of that question, and merely proposed to defer it to the end of the war.

Marshal Stalin agreed that this was a sore spot with the British.

The President said that at some future date he would like to talk with Marshal Stalin on the question of India; that he felt that the best solution would be reform from the bottom, somewhat on the Soviet line.

This comment was possibly made by Roosevelt with the thought of ingratiating himself with Stalin: certainly Roosevelt knew the history of Lenin's rise to power; he had lived through it. Charles Bohlen, interpreting, was horrified by the comment; "a striking example of Roosevelt's ignorance about the Soviet Union . . . He did not realize that the Bolsheviks were a minority who seized power during the period of anarchy," he would write. (In spite of his occasional disparaging comments about the president, Bohlen wrote, "He clearly was the dominating figure at the Conference.")

Sometimes Roosevelt was devious, sometimes ingenuous; sometimes he just said something to see what the response would be. The latter was probably his objective this time. "Marshal Stalin replied that the India question was a complicated one, with different levels of culture and the absence of relationship in the castes. He added that reform from the bottom would mean revolution."

Roosevelt did not answer.

Although it is missing from the Bohlen minutes, Roosevelt later told Forrest Davis, the world-famous journalist to whom he gave an extended interview, that he brought up the Good Neighbor Policy during this conversation (a policy that repudiated the traditional U.S. policy of armed intervention in Latin American affairs), which the president would have spoken of in the context of India and self-determination, and that he then had gone on to explain the U.S. federal system. He was evidently trying to clear up Stalin's misconception of the relationship of the executive and the legislative branches of government, as well as why he had to respond to congressional bills within a stated period, which had been at the root of his worries about a meeting in Tehran.

In essence, then, in this initial short talk, Roosevelt pointed out his desire to take pressure off the Red Army immediately, emphasized his less than binding relationship with Churchill, offered postwar aid in the form of a merchant navy, and indicated his administration's lack of interest in becoming a colonial power. Stalin, for his part, expressed his desire to become a postwar trading partner with the United States and Russia's lack of interest in becoming a colonial power.

The two great subjects on both of their minds, the second front and the organization of the postwar world, were left for later.

They scheduled their next private meeting for the following afternoon, to take place at 2:45, again in Roosevelt's sitting room.

The first plenary meeting—that is to say, the first meeting with Winston Churchill—followed after their private meeting was over.

The president, the marshal, the prime minister, and their staffs entered the spacious and handsome high-ceilinged boardroom next door to the president's sitting room. A large round table covered with green baize, surrounded by armchairs with mahogany armrests upholstered in striped silk, stood in the center of the room. On the table, in front of each chair, were notebooks and sharpened pencils. A wooden stand holding the flags of the United States, Great Britain, and the Soviet Union stood as the centerpiece. There were tapestries on the walls; the windows were festooned with draperies. On the balcony overlooking the room, Soviet guards quietly patrolled.

The three chiefs, each attended by three of his countrymen, sat down around the table. Roosevelt was seated between Harriman on his right and his interpreter, Charles Bohlen, on his left, with Hopkins on Bohlen's left. With Stalin were Marshal Kliment Voroshilov, Vyacheslav Molotov, and the interpreter, Vladimir Pavlov. Anthony Eden, British foreign minister; Lord Ismay, deputy secretary to the War Cabinet; and Churchill's interpreter, Major Birse, attended the prime minister. Behind this first circle of chairs were rows of chairs for the other conference participants.

This plenary session, and subsequent ones, were completely different in character from the meetings between Roosevelt and Stalin. Instead of policy considerations, the subjects under discussion were campaign decisions, combat problems, and tactics. Usually, Churchill took one side, Roosevelt and Stalin the other.

The character of the meetings was set by Roosevelt, who dominated the proceedings, although, unusually, he spoke very little. By tacit agreement he opened each meeting. He hadn't wanted a formal agenda, so there was none. He (in most cases) decided the subject matter. When he spoke, he frequently took off his pince-nez, which he waved to emphasize a point.

He began this first meeting by saying gracefully that it was his privilege, as the youngest of the three present, to welcome his elders.

"We are sitting around this table for the first time as a family, with the one object of winning the war," were his first words. Then he spoke of the many things they had to discuss, "to achieve constructive accord in order that we may maintain close touch throughout the war and after the war." He then added an interesting cautionary note: "If anyone of us does not want to talk about any particular subject . . . we do not have to."

Diplomat that he was (turning not, as he should have, to the host, Stalin, but to Churchill), Roosevelt said that before they discussed military matters, "Perhaps the Prime Minister would like to say something about matters pertaining to the years to come."

The prime minister responded eloquently: "In our hands we have . . . the future of mankind. I pray that we may be worthy of this God-given opportunity."

Stalin, whom Roosevelt then asked to speak, welcomed the assemblage and said, "I think that history will show that this opportunity has been of tremendous import . . . Now let us get down to business."

Roosevelt then launched into a general survey of the war in the Pacific, where the United States was "bearing a major part of the Pacific war" and where "we believe we are sinking many Jap ships, both naval and merchant—more than they can possibly replace . . . On the west of Japan it is necessary to keep China in the war. Hence, we have arranged plans for operations through North Burma and into the Yunnan Province" that would be accomplished by opening the road to China. "We must definitely keep China actively in the war."

The president then said he would turn to the most important theater of the war—Europe—and brought up the second front. He started out with a nod to Churchill, saying that "he wished to emphasize that for over one year and a half in the last two or three conferences at Casablanca, Washington and Quebec . . . the major part of our plans were involved in consideration of an expedition against the Axis across the English Channel."

He then touched on the problems of such an operation: "Largely because of transportation difficulties we were not able to set a definite date. Not only do we want to get across the English Channel but once we are across, we intend to proceed inland into Germany. It would be impossible to launch such an operation before about 1 May 1944." Then he mentioned possible Anglo-American battle plans in the Mediterranean, Adriatic, and Aegean Seas, but in such a way that he flagged "any large expedition in the Mediterranean" as a danger to Russia, because if such an expedition were undertaken, "it would be necessary to give up this important cross-Channel operation, and certain contemplated operations in the Mediterranean might result in a delay in OVERLORD for one month or two or three."

He then threw the lead to Stalin, stating that the purpose of Anglo-American military strategy was to come to the aid of the Soviet Union and that the decisions made in the Mediterranean were up to Stalin, thus opening the way for Stalin to demand what he wanted: "I pray in this military Conference to have the benefit of the opinion of the two Soviet Marshals and that they will inform us how in their opinion we can be of most help to the U.S.S.R." (Roosevelt was referring to Voroshilov as the other marshal, whom, in fact, Stalin never bothered to confer with or pay any attention to.)

Churchill spoke next, making a statement that, with the benefit of hindsight, appears transparently self-serving. Whereas Roosevelt had used "we" as he referred to joint Anglo-American military operations, Churchill used it to imply that Roosevelt was speaking for both of them, that they were a team. Thus the prime minister said, "We would like to know what we can do that would most greatly help that which the Soviets are doing on their Western Front . . . We have tried to outline matters in the simplest terms. There are no differences between Great Britain and the United States in point of view except as regards 'ways and means.'"

Stalin knew this was not true. The month before, at the Moscow

Conference, Churchill had instructed Foreign Secretary Anthony Eden to "make it clear" to Stalin "that the assurances you have given about [the month of] May OVERLORD subject to the specified conditions must be modified by the exigencies of battle in Italy. I am taking the matter up with President Roosevelt, but nothing will alter my determination not to throw away the battle in Italy at this juncture." General Geroge Marshall, who had been expecting just such a development, immediately had the U.S. Joint Chiefs send a message to Stalin stating that they did not think there was *any* chance of having Overlord delayed, let alone abandoned.

Stalin had been doodling with a red pencil on a notepad. Now, ignoring Churchill, in a casual way he offered Soviet involvement in the war against Japan, saying in a low voice only audible to the interpreter Pavlov, sitting by his side, "Once Germany was finally defeated, it would then be possible to send the necessary reinforcements to Siberia and then we shall be able by our common front to beat Japan."

Hopkins was present. "Then," he observed, Stalin "went on doodling as if nothing had happened." He was drawing wolves.

As a young man in revolutionary Russia, Stalin had been arrested by the Okhrana, the tsar's secret police, nine times. He escaped eight times, on each occasion exiled to a town in Siberia. For one escape, from Solvychegodsk, a Siberian fur-trading outpost, he dressed as a woman. In the nine years following his first arrest in 1908, he was at liberty for only a year and a half. During one of these times, working stealthily from the shadows in St. Petersburg, he became a founder and the first editor of *Pravda*. After the first issue came out, the Okhrana once again found him and exiled him to Siberia. Upon his last arrest he was sent to Kureika, a remote Siberian hamlet at the edge of the Arctic Circle. The Okhrana had settled on Kureika because each time it put him in a more normal prison milieu, he had bribed his guards or used his own wiliness and escaped. Kureika was an extreme environment, and ringed as the tiny village was by tundra wolf packs, no escape was possible. Only the fall of the tsar's government in 1917 resulted in his release.

Stalin couldn't forget the wolves. For the rest of his life when he doodled, the images were of wolves. (He did this normally, but mention of "Siberia" made him start doodling at that moment.)

Following the short silence that ensued after he stated his country's commitment to enter the war against Japan, he spoke of military developments on the Soviet-German front. He stated that "the successes they had achieved this summer and autumn had far exceeded their expectations." Then he gave an overview of German strength—the number of German divisions and non-German divisions (Hungarian, Finnish, Romanian) facing the Soviet armies—and commented that the Red Army had numerical superiority over the Germans and that "one of the great difficulties encountered by the Soviet armies in advancing was the question of supply since the Germans destroyed literally everything in their retreat." He dismissed the Allied Italian campaigns as unproductive strategy and said Soviet military leaders believed "Hitler was endeavoring to retain as many allied Divisions as possible in Italy, where no decision could be reached, and that the best method in Soviet opinion was getting at the heart of Germany with an attack through northern or northwestern France and even through southern France."

Following the marshal, Churchill spoke. He began by stating that "the United States and Great Britain had long agreed as to the necessity of the Cross-channel operation, that at the present time this operation, which is known as OVERLORD was absorbing most of our combined resources and efforts." Then he went into a detailed discussion of the operations of British and American soldiers in North Africa, in Italy, and in the Mediterranean, mentioning that Rome had to be captured, which would happen in January, with Overlord six months later, "if we take Rome and smash up the German armies." The prime minister dwelled—at length—on the possibility and desirability of gaining Turkey's entrance into the war, which would entail sending it the means: "it was proposed to send 20 squadrons of fighters and several anti-aircraft regiments"; he added that the preparations to send these forces to Turkey "were already far advanced." He concluded by inquiring "whether any of the possible operations in the Mediterranean were of sufficient interest to the Soviet Union if these operations involved a two or three months delay in OVERLORD" and said that "he and the President could not make any decision until they knew the Soviet views on the subject and therefore had drawn up no definite plans."

Roosevelt tried to head Churchill off (and possibly appeal to Stalin at the same time) by suggesting "a possible operation at the head of the Adriatic to make a junction with the Partisans under Tito and then to operate northeast into Rumania in conjunction with the Soviet advance from the region of Odessa." This statement so worried Hopkins that he hastily wrote a note to Admiral King: "Who's promoting that Adriatic business?" King replied, "As far as I know it is his own idea."

Stalin said nothing. Churchill, unperturbed, resumed speaking. He continued to push his favorite battle plan, "if we take Rome and smash up the German armies there."

Stalin replied, "It would be better to take OVERLORD as the basis for all 1944 operations; that after the capture of Rome the troops thus relieved might be sent to southern France."

Roosevelt noted that eight or nine French divisions were available for an operation against southern France.

Churchill brought up Turkey again.

Stalin repeated, "These operations would be worthwhile only if Turkey entered the war." He again repeated he did not believe this would happen. (A few days later, in Cairo, Stalin was proven right; Turkey's president, İsmet İnönü, arrived there at Churchill's invitation, and even with Roosevelt's help Churchill could not persuade him to enter the war.)

Churchill now, again, made the case for a strong Mediterranean campaign. He touched on the six months after the capture of Rome, during which "both he and the President were most anxious that their troops should not remain idle since if they were fighting, the British and American governments would not be exposed to the criticism that they were letting the Soviet Union bear the brunt of the war."

Stalin would have none of it. He suggested the invasion of southern France two months before Overlord and postponing the capture of Rome.

Churchill made another argument for the capture of Rome, after which Roosevelt stepped in, with both feet, saying "he personally felt that nothing should be done to delay the carrying out of OVERLORD which might be necessary if any operations in the eastern Mediterranean were undertaken." He proposed, therefore, "that the staffs work out tomorrow morning a plan of operations for striking at southern France."

Churchill grudgingly fell in with the idea but once more spoke of the possibility of Turkey's entering the war. Roosevelt, in agreement with Stalin, said this was not going to happen ("if he were in the Turkish President's place he would demand such a high price in planes, tanks and equipment that to grant the request would indefinitely postpone OVERLORD").

Stalin added that the Turks had already replied negatively to the suggestion.

The prime minister remarked that in his opinion the Turks were crazy.

Marshal Stalin said there were some people who apparently preferred to remain crazy.

The lines were fairly drawn.

The meeting adjourned at 7:20 p.m.

Churchill's doctor, Lord Moran, saw the prime minister right after the meeting broke up: "He seemed so dispirited that I departed from my prudent habit and asked him outright whether anything had gone wrong.

"He answered shortly: 'A bloody lot has gone wrong.' He did not wish to talk about it."

Field Marshal Alan Brooke, the British chief of staff and Britain's senior soldier, thought Roosevelt singularly unhelpful, calling his opening remarks "a poor and not very helpful speech."

Brooke was right, in that the session had developed into a wrangle, but wrong in his characterization of the president's opening remarks as being poor. Roosevelt had begun by pointing out that large-scale Mediterranean actions would delay the second front. He was intentionally unhelpful. It was obvious that Roosevelt had deliberately not come to Churchill's defense and that, as a result, the first plenary session had ended with Churchill in a foul mood and Stalin pleased.

The conference was going as Roosevelt had hoped it would. It was as much about what went unsaid as what was said. There had occurred an implicit meeting of the minds between himself and Stalin. Churchill was left stubbornly trying to persuade Roosevelt and Stalin on a course of action that clearly, in retrospect, neither of them wanted. Churchill was bitterly disappointed. "The Anglo-American plans not having been agreed, we were placed in the unfortunate position of having to discuss matters with the Americans in front of the Russians," he would later tell his War Cabinet.

At some point the president asked Stalin to be photographed with him and Churchill: Stalin with a pipe, Roosevelt with a cigarette holder, and Churchill with a cigar. Stalin refused the request; Roosevelt later said, "I think he felt it might introduce a non-serious note."

In the hour left before dinner Roosevelt signed four congressional bills and worked on his mail.

THE DINNER

At 8:30 p.m., Roosevelt hosted a dinner for the prime minister and the marshal and their staffs prepared by the Filipino sailors he had brought with him. But first he served cocktails, mixing them himself, as he usually did when he was home. This night he served his standard martini: lots of vermouth, both sweet and dry, smaller amounts of gin, all poured into a pitcher full of ice, then stirred. Asked by Roosevelt whether he had enjoyed his cocktail, Stalin answered, "All right, but it is cold on the stomach." (It was generally hazarded that Roosevelt made his martinis with Argentine vermouth and substandard gin and that they were "pretty terrible." No one ever dared complain, for fear of ruining Roosevelt's favorite ritual.)

The dinner was simple, symbolic American fare: steak and baked potatoes, and in place of vodka the toasts were drunk with bourbon.

Roosevelt was wheeled into the dining room in his armless wheelchair ahead of the other guests and was seated at the table by the time the others came in. Present at the dinner were Stalin, Molotov, Churchill, Eden, Clark Kerr, Hopkins, Harriman, and the three interpreters. Marshal Voroshilov was absent. After Stalin took his seat on Roosevelt's right, he turned to his interpreter and told him, "Tell the President that I now understand what it has meant for him to make the effort to come on such a long journey—Tell him that the next time I will go to him."

Roosevelt said that would probably mean going to Alaska, and there began a discussion concerning where they would meet next and when such a meeting should be held. There was apparent agreement on Fairbanks, Alaska, which Stalin said was a "possibility."

Following that, Stalin vented his deep disgust with France and its leaders. His fury at France had deep roots. France had done everything in its power to prevent the Soviet takeover of Russia. It had sent in troops in 1918 to fight on the side of the White Army against the Bolsheviks, had masterminded an economic blockade designed to starve the Bolshevik government into submission, and had, in the mid-1930s, as the menace of Hitler confronted Europe, evaded signing a treaty with the Soviet Union, which not only forced the Soviet Union to make a treaty with Hitler in an effort to stave off war with Germany but permitted Hitler to begin his conquest of Europe unopposed. Great Britain had been France's partner in these events, but the British had redeemed themselves by their heroic defense of their homeland under Churchill. They had stopped Hitler in his tracks, while France had committed the unpardonable sin of collapsing. It was this final coup de grâce that infuriated Stalin: the French people had been so cowardly as to be overrun by the German army in five weeks.

Stalin, speaking now, said that "the entire French ruling class was rotten to the core, and had delivered over France to the Germans and that, in fact, France was now actively helping our enemies." He said that it would be "dangerous to leave in French hands any important strategic points after the war."

Roosevelt replied that he agreed, "in part," and that it was for that reason that he thought anyone over the age of forty should be kept out of any future French government. He mentioned Dakar, Senegal, a French colony that was the westernmost point on the African continent, "a direct threat to the Americas," and New Caledonia, just fortified by the U.S. Navy because it was so situated that it was a threat to Australia and New Zealand. Both colonies, he suggested, should be placed under international trusteeship, and echoing Stalin, said, "It would be not only unjust but dangerous to leave in French hands any important strategic points after the war."

Churchill had very different thoughts about France and changed the subject, announcing that Great Britain "did not desire and did not expect to acquire any additional territories." This statement probably served to remind Roosevelt and Stalin of the great territory England still controlled.

However, Stalin was not finished talking about France. The country could not be trusted with any strategic possessions outside its own border, he said. Churchill protested that France had been a defeated nation and suffered the horrors of occupation. "On the contrary," said Stalin, "their leaders had surrendered the country and 'opened up a front' to the German armies."

Roosevelt switched the conversation to a subject they had not yet

FDR signing the document founding the United Nations Relief and
Rehabilitation Administration on Armistice Day, 1943

Generalissimo Chiang Kai-shek, FDR, and Prime Minister Winston Churchill,
Cairo, November 25, 1943

FDR, Prime Minister Mackenzie King of Canada, and Churchill at the Citadel in Quebec, September 1944. FDR and King were close friends from their days together at Harvard.

An RAF officer presenting the Sword of Stalingrad, a gift of King George VI, to Stalin at Tehran

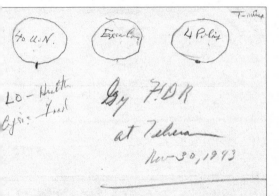

LEFT: FDR drew this sketch showing his conception of the United Nations organization during the Tehran Conference.

BELOW: General George C. Marshall, Sir Archibald Clark Kerr, Harry Hopkins, Charles Bohlen, Stalin, and Marshal Kliment E. Voroshilov at Tehran

Svetlana Alliluyeva sitting on the lap of Lavrenti Beria, head of the NKVD; Stalin in the background, reading.

Stalin and FDR, Tehran, November 29, 1943

touched upon: Germany. He wanted, he said, the concept of the Reich erased from the German mind, "the very word . . . stricken from the language."

Stalin responded in a like vein but said that it was not enough to eliminate the word "Reich": "The very Reich itself must be rendered impotent ever again to plunge the world into war . . . Unless the victorious Allies retained in their hands the strategic positions necessary to prevent any recrudescence of German militarism, they would have failed in their duty."

Stalin next brought up the subject of Poland's borders, stating that he wanted to help the Poles obtain a frontier on the Oder.

Roosevelt, not ready to discuss borders with Stalin, changed the subject to something advantageous to the Soviet Union: the matter of assuring the approaches to the Baltic Sea. He put forth the idea that an international state should be created to ensure free navigation through the Kiel Canal, which the Versailles Treaty had internationalized but put under German supervision. Only 61 miles long, the canal saved ships from having to travel the 250-mile-long rough passage around Denmark. Hitler had closed it to other countries.

Because of a translation error, Stalin heard not "Baltic Sea" but "Baltic States" and immediately took umbrage: "He replied categorically that the Baltic States had by an expression of the will of the people voted to join the Soviet Union and that this question was not therefore one for discussion." When the error was cleared up, he agreed with the president.

Roosevelt returned to the subject of outlying possessions. Trusteeship of colonial territories was one of his root concerns. He now threw out "a concept which had never been developed in past history": that these erstwhile possessions should be administered by "a collective body such as the United Nations."

Before he could amplify, he suddenly turned green and great drops of sweat began to bead off his face; he put a shaky hand to his forehead. Hopkins had the president wheeled to his room. There he was examined by his doctor, Vice Admiral Ross McIntire, who for a moment, until he examined him, thought the president might have been poisoned but quickly saw that the incident wasn't serious and the president was merely suffering from a mild attack of indigestion. McIntire thereupon returned to the dinner and informed Stalin that FDR would be available at ten the next morning. Relations between Stalin and Churchill, without FDR's presence, rapidly degenerated. Stalin cocked an eye at the prime minister and said, "Well, I'm glad that there is somebody here who knows when it is time to go home." Churchill then said something to Stalin. When Stalin's answer was translated, according to Mike Reilly, "Winston burst out so loudly and angrily it was quite easy for everybody to hear him. Facing Stalin, and waving a finger, Churchill said, 'But you won't let me get up to your front and I want to get there!' Stalin smiled very calmly, and answered, 'Maybe it can be arranged sometime, Mr. Prime Minister. Perhaps when you have a front that I can visit, too.'"

After this reminder that there was still no second front, Stalin and Churchill launched into the subject of the treatment of Germany after the war, about which they continued to disagree.

Churchill wanted to make sure Germany would emerge from the war strong enough to balance Russia in Europe: strong but, as he sought to soothingly explain, not dangerous.

Stalin, concerned as he always was about the resurgence of a militant Germany, was not satisfied with the measures Churchill suggested, such as constant supervision of its factories and territorial dismemberment. Such measures were "insufficient to prevent the rebirth of German militarism." He added, although it was a non sequitur, that he had personally questioned German prisoners in the Soviet Union as to why they had burst into Russian homes, killed Russian women, and so forth, and that the only reply he had received was they had been ordered to do so.

Taking full advantage of Roosevelt's absence, Churchill asked Stalin if "it would be possible to discuss the question of Poland." Reluctantly, Stalin agreed. After some discussion, Churchill said that he would like to see Poland moved westward in the same manner as soldiers at drill execute the drill "left close" and illustrated his point with three matches representing the Soviet Union, Poland, and Germany.

Stalin said it would be necessary to look into the matter further.

Stalin brought up, in the president's absence, his concern that the unconditional surrender principle with no definition of the exact terms "might serve to unite the German people." He had agreed to it at the Moscow Conference in October, as he had agreed to the inclusion of China as the fourth policeman, reluctantly: Hull had had to make polite threats about diverting aid from Russia to China to bring Molotov around to agreeing that China would be the fourth signatory, as well as that the four countries would fight until Germany and Japan "laid down their arms on the basis of unconditional surrender."

Because Bohlen continued taking down their conversation even after Roosevelt retired, Stalin and Churchill knew that he would submit their comments to the president. It seems safe to assume that Stalin phrased his concerns about unconditional surrender in this way to be certain the president had no doubts about his position on the issue.

Churchill attempted to see Roosevelt alone the next day before the plenary meeting. He sent the president a note suggesting lunch. Roosevelt "politely" refused. Harry Hopkins, acting as Roosevelt's intermediary, trying to soften the blow to the prime minister's pride, explained that he should view the refusal as part of Roosevelt's campaign to gain Stalin's trust, a campaign that would, if successful, make it easier to deal with Stalin in the future: with that in mind, Churchill should try to understand. But the prime minister continued to be hurt by the distancing Roosevelt had put into place. Lord Moran, his doctor, who saw him a short while after he received the note, remembered that Churchill looked "plainly put out" as he murmured, "It is not like him."

5

A MEETING OF MINDS

The next morning, November 29, Roosevelt worked on his mail and lunched quietly with his household.

Stalin, accompanied by Molotov, arrived in Roosevelt's sitting room punctually at 2:45 p.m. for their second conference. FDR was, as before, seated on the couch. The two Russians drew up chairs in front of him. Elliott Roosevelt, who had just flown in from Egypt, was also present. Stalin offered the president and Elliott each a Russian cigarette protruding from the end of a two-inch cardboard holder. Each accepted a cigarette, politely took a few puffs, and put it down.

Roosevelt had documents next to him that he handed to Marshal Stalin. The first was an Office of Strategic Services (OSS) report concerning Major Linn Farish, OSS liaison to Josip Broz Tito, the Communist Yugoslav leader, who was locating and spiriting out of the country downed American pilots. Farish, who parachuted into Yugoslavia several times, had just returned from his latest mission. His information on the work of Tito's partisans in rescuing hundreds of U.S. airmen helped win U.S. support for Tito.

FDR next handed the marshal a proposal to make air bases in the Ukraine available to U.S. planes. American air attacks on Berlin had already begun and were devastating. Newspapers were reporting, "In anticipation of new Allied air attacks the major part of the Reich administrative machinery is now being moved from Berlin." If the bombers that were taking off from bases in Italy and England to bomb Axis targets could land in the Ukraine to refuel—and take on more bombs—

they could be even more effective. This shuttle bombing could wreak even more damage.

Roosevelt next handed Stalin two papers prepared by the U.S. chiefs of staff built around drawing Russia into the war against Japan. At the same time he told the marshal "how happy he would be to hear his word in regard to the defeat of Japanese forces." One document concerned the planned coordination of air operations, the other the planned coordination of naval operations between their respective countries in the upcoming war against Japan. Stalin scanned the first document and agreed to the planned coordination. But he stalled on navy operations. "Mr. President," he said, "you tell me you frequently have to consult with your Government before making decisions. You must remember that I also have a Government and cannot always act without reference to Moscow." Roosevelt accepted this partial promise of cooperation.

Roosevelt next zeroed in on his favorite subject: organizing a peaceful postwar world. He had been looking forward, he said, to the chance to talk these matters over—informally—with Stalin. When Molotov, a year earlier, had flown to Washington for the express purpose of discussing the opening of the second front, so dear to the Soviet heart, Roosevelt had begun their talk with a discussion of the postwar world. Molotov had kept Stalin apprised of their talks by nightly cables. Stalin had appeared amenable to the idea of a strong international organization.

Roosevelt had been gratified by Stalin and Molotov's positive response, but that interchange had taken place when the Soviet Union was in grave peril, when German troops were still seizing, plundering, and destroying great swaths of Russia, a time when Stalin had been a supplicant, desperate for American aid. Stalin would have agreed to anything remotely reasonable that desperate summer of 1942 if he thought it would speed up the launching of a second front that would draw German troops out of Russia. Circumstances were different now. Now, face-to-face with Stalin, Roosevelt again outlined the proposed international body: "There would be a large, worldwide organization of some thirty-five members of the United Nations which would meet periodically at different places, discuss and make recommendations to a smaller body."

There would be an executive committee, Roosevelt continued, to deal with nonmilitary matters—such matters as agriculture, food, health, and economic questions. This committee, numbering ten, would consist of the Soviet Union, the United States, the United Kingdom, China, two additional European states, one South American state, one Near Eastern state, one Far Eastern country, and one British dominion. This group would meet in various places. (At this point the president observed that "Mr. Churchill did not like this proposal for the reason that the British Empire only had two votes.")

Stalin asked whether the recommendations of this body would be binding on the nations of the world.

Roosevelt replied, "Yes and no," but then in his amplification the answer was clearly no, for, as he admitted, he didn't think Congress would agree to be so bound.

Power would reside in the third body, the president went on, consisting of the four policemen: the Soviet Union, the United States, Great Britain, and China. "This organization," he explained, "would have the power to deal immediately with any threat to the peace and any sudden emergency which requires this action." Had such an organization existed in 1935, he went on, it could have closed the Suez Canal, thereby preventing Italy from attacking and destroying Ethiopia.

Stalin immediately pointed out a problem: "A European state would probably resent China having the right to apply certain machinery to it." He suggested, as a possible alternative, the creation of a European or a Far Eastern committee and a European or a worldwide organization, further suggesting that the European Commission might consist of the United States, Great Britain, the Soviet Union, and "possibly one other European state."

The idea of regional spheres of influence was exactly what Roosevelt was trying to stay away from: they hadn't stopped either world war from starting. Roosevelt replied that Churchill had had a similar idea: regional committees, one for Europe, one for the Far East, and one for the Americas, with the further thought that the United States be a member of the European Commission. The president then dismissed the idea as not feasible, saying he "doubted if the United States Congress would agree to U.S. participation in an exclusively European Committee which might be able to force the dispatch of American troops to Europe."

Stalin pointed out that the world organization Roosevelt suggested, and in particular the idea of the four policemen, might also require sending American troops to Europe. Roosevelt replied that he had only envisaged sending U.S. planes and ships to Europe, "that England and the Soviet Union would have to handle the land armies." He added that if the Japanese had not attacked the United States, he doubted if it would have been possible to send *any* U.S. forces to Europe.

The president continued with the idea of the four policemen. The four would have two methods of dealing with possible aggression: if it were the threat of a revolution or developments in a small country, "it might be possible to apply the quarantine method—closing the frontiers of the countries in question and imposing embargoes." If that didn't work, he went on, if the threat was more serious, the four powers, acting as policemen, would send an ultimatum, and if that was refused, "it would result in the immediate bombardment and possible invasion of that country."

The fact that this did not seem to surprise Stalin must have gratified Roosevelt, because it showed that the premier had been paying attention to what he had explained to Molotov in 1942 in Washington. (Roosevelt didn't know for sure how intimately involved Stalin had been in his conversations with Molotov. He had, after all, no direct knowledge that Molotov was cabling the day's discussions to Stalin each evening and that Molotov's positions each day heavily depended upon Stalin's guidance, although he might have suspected it.)

Stalin now brought up *his* major worry: the future containment of Germany. Stalin had written to a *New York Times* reporter six months earlier that the Germans were not only the greatest danger to future peace but also Russia's "chief enemy." He said to Edvard Beneš, president of Czechoslovakia, at the Bolshoi Theatre the week after Tehran, "You will not change the Germans in a short time. There will be another war with them." He also advised Roosevelt that here he and Churchill differed—that the prime minister did not believe that Germany would rise again to menace Europe.

This alerted Roosevelt that to win Stalin's support, the planned international organization had to have as its highest priority the power to deal with a resurgent Germany. It also indicated that *if* Stalin were sufficiently reassured that such an organization could be created, he would probably welcome it. As the conversation continued, however,

Stalin's comments indicated that he didn't think the world security body, as Roosevelt had presented it, would be strong enough. ("I hate the Germans," Stalin would tell a Czech delegation in March 1945. "But that must not cloud one's judgement of the Germans. The Germans are a great people. Very good technicians and organisers. Good, naturally brave soldiers. It is impossible to get rid of the Germans, they will remain . . . We Slavs must be prepared for the Germans to rise again against us.")

Stalin now told FDR that he personally thought that unless prevented, Germany would completely recover within fifteen to twenty years, and that, therefore, "we must have something more serious than the type of organization proposed by the President . . . The first German aggression had occurred in 1870 and then forty-four years later in the First World War, whereas only twenty-one years elapsed between the end of the last war and the beginning of the present." He added that he did not believe the period before the revival of German strength would be any longer in the future.

There should be control of certain strategic physical points, either within Germany, along German borders, or even farther away, Stalin continued, to ensure that Germany would not embark on another course of aggression. He mentioned specifically Dakar, the westernmost point on the African continent, adding that the same strategy should be applied in the case of Japan and that the islands in the vicinity of Japan should remain under strong control to prevent Japan's embarking on a similar course of aggression.

The president said that he agreed with Marshal Stalin 100 percent. In point of fact Roosevelt, too, had a deep antipathy to Germans, formed in his childhood. As a boy, he had spent many summers in Germany with his mother and father while his father took the baths in Bad Nauheim in a continuing effort to regain his health. James and Sara Roosevelt hired a German tutor for Franklin to teach him the language, and for a while they sent him daily to a *Volksschule*. His German was good enough for him to converse with Albert Einstein in German. His dislike of Germans, usually hidden, was surprisingly intense. He once said to his secretary of the Treasury, Henry Morgenthau, "We have got to be tough with Germany and I mean the German people not just the Nazis. We either have to castrate the German people or you have got to treat them in such manner so they can't just go on reproducing people who want to continue the way they have in the past." Another time he said that the first requisite of the peace had to be that no German should ever again be permitted to wear a uniform.

STALIN NOW VOICED DOUBTS about the question of Chinese participation.

Roosevelt answered that he recognized China's weakness. (No one knew better than he just how unstable China was, or how weak Chiang's government. In 1938, Roosevelt had arranged to give Chiang a $100 million loan because his government had run out of money. Things had not improved; at Cairo, Chiang had just asked him for a $1 billion gold loan.) FDR was concerned that if he pushed Chiang too hard, and didn't give him enough support, the generalissimo might make a deal with Japan. (He wasn't worried that the Chinese Communists would ever surrender.)

But it was the future of the United Nations—always uppermost in his mind—that most worried him, for if the United Nations was to work, it *needed* China. As Roosevelt wrote, "I really feel that it is a triumph to have got the four hundred and twenty-five million Chinese in on the Allied side. This will be very useful 25 or 50 years hence, even though China cannot contribute much military or naval support for the moment." He now told Stalin he was thinking of the already astoundingly large Chinese population, whose sheer numbers would ensure it a major role no matter what its government: "After all China was a nation of 400 million people, and it was better to have them as friends rather than as a potential source of trouble." Roosevelt guided the discussion back to the four policemen as the best deterrent to a resurgent Germany. Addressing himself to Stalin's comments of the previous night (obviously later reported to him) of the ease with which German furniture factories could be transformed into airplane factories, and watch factories could make fuses into shells, he said that "a strong and effective organization of the four powers could move swiftly when the first signs arose of the beginning of the conversion of such factories for warlike purposes."

The Germans had shown great ability at concealing such beginnings, Stalin replied. Roosevelt agreed that that was true and that the strategic positions should be at the disposal of some world organization that could monitor and prevent Germany and Japan from rearming.

Stalin had demonstrated that he believed containing Germany was the single most important task before them—that Germany was and would continue to be the major threat to world peace. It was also obvious, as a result of Stalin's questions, that Roosevelt would have to rethink the world government he was setting out to create.

Elliott Roosevelt was quietly present at the meeting. He wrote down comments that Bohlen left out. Bohlen had a difficult job because he was at once the interpreter and the writer of the minutes of the private conversations. Plus, occasionally showing his loyalty to his State Department pro-British diplomatic background, he sometimes left matters out of the minutes that he considered unimportant or irrelevant or that he hoped would disappear. Elliott reported that his father again dwelled on the divergence between America's goals and England's, particularly in regard to colonial possessions. According to Elliott, Roosevelt pointed out that in the postwar world each of their three countries would have to act separately as well as together. He told Stalin that Chiang had told him at Cairo how important it was for China to end irrevocably Britain's extraterritorial rights in Shanghai, Hong Kong, and Canton and that Chiang also emphasized that Russia had to respect the Manchurian frontier.

Stalin had replied that world recognition of the sovereignty of the Soviet Union was a cardinal principle and that therefore "most certainly he would respect, in turn, the sovereignty of their countries, large or small."

Roosevelt touched on other subjects he had discussed with Chiang, most notably that there had been a promise that Chinese Communists would be taken into the government before there were national elections and that elections would take place as soon as possible after the war. As he talked, after waiting for each thought to be translated, Stalin nodded, seeming to be in complete agreement. General John Deane, head of Lend-Lease in Moscow, formerly liaison between the American and the British chiefs of staff, an observer at Tehran, later wrote that Stalin's position "coincided with that of the American Chiefs of Staff, and every word he said strengthened the support they might expect from President Roosevelt in the ultimate decision."

Just shy of half past three General Pa Watson poked his head in the door and said that everything was ready for the second plenary session.

But first Churchill had prepared a grand event: an honor guard composed of Russian and British soldiers awaited in the great hall, where a drama was about to unfold. As Roosevelt sat in the great hall, with Stalin and Churchill standing on either side, twenty British soldiers marched in with fixed bayonets, followed by a like number of Soviet soldiers bearing tommy guns. A Russian army band played "The Internationale," followed by "God Save the King." The soldiers lined up facing each other against opposite walls. Then Churchill, stout and round shouldered though he was, looking splendid, dressed for the occasion in the blue dress uniform of a high-ranking RAF officer complete with pilot's wings, said that on behalf of the king he was presenting Stalin with the Sword of Stalingrad. He read the inscription on the sword: "To the steel-hearted citizens of Stalingrad, a gift from King George VI as a token of the homage of the British people." The sword was over four feet long with a silver hilt etched with leopard heads, sheathed in a scarlet lambskin scabbard. Stalin was quite moved. He raised the sword to his lips and kissed it. There were tears in his eyes. He offered the sword to Voroshilov, who managed to drop it. This embarrassing moment over, Stalin and the prime minister offered Roosevelt the sword for *his* inspection. While the prime minister held the scabbard, the president pulled out the sword, all fifty inches of tempered steel. He held it straight up. "Truly they had hearts of steel," he is supposed to have appropriately murmured.

Immediately afterward the three adjourned to the portico for a picture-taking session. With that over, the second plenary meeting began. Present with Roosevelt were eleven in staff, including Hopkins, Harriman, Admiral Leahy, General Marshall, Admiral King, General Arnold, Major General Deane, Captain Royal, Captain Ware, and General Somervell. Accompanying Churchill were ten in staff, including Foreign Secretary Anthony Eden, Sir Archibald Clark Kerr, Field Marshal John Greer Dill, General Alan Francis Brooke, Admiral of the Fleet Andrew Cunningham, Air Lieutenant Marshal Charles Portal, Lieutenant General Hastings Ismay, Lieutenant General Gifford Martel, and Brigadier General William Hollis. In contrast to the others, as at all the plenary meetings, Stalin brought Molotov and Marshal Voroshilov.

Roosevelt again opened the meeting, and stating that there was no agenda, he asked for a report from the military staffs that had met in the morning.

General Brooke, General Marshall, and Marshal Voroshilov spoke about the various aspects of Overlord. General Brooke went over the pros and cons of the Mediterranean campaign, of fighting up the leg of Italy, of the advantages of Turkey's participation in the war. General Marshall emphasized that the question of adequate landing craft and suitable airfields was of first importance and that production of landing craft had been stepped up. Marshal Voroshilov said that the answers to his questions had been confirmed.

Stalin weighed in. "Who," he asked, "will command OVERLORD?"

Roosevelt said that had not yet been decided.

Stalin, rather abruptly, then said, "Then nothing will come out of these operations."

"That old Bolshevik is trying to force me to give him the name of the Supreme Commander . . . I have not yet made up my mind," Roosevelt whispered to Leahy.

Roosevelt assured Stalin that the names of all the commanders except the supreme commander had been decided upon.

Stalin replied, "The Supreme Commander might not think that everything necessary had been accomplished by the Chief of Staff. There must be one person in charge."

Roosevelt, unwilling to have Stalin realize that he was still undecided, in a clever stroke gave the prime minister the floor. Then he sat back and listened, never interrupting, as Churchill proceeded to hang himself.

Churchill said his piece, which was long. The prime minister began by declaring that all assistance should be given to Overlord, but, as Harry Hopkins noted later to Churchill's doctor, and as the record bears out, "with this preface he proceeded to traverse systematically the northern coast of the Mediterranean." Although Churchill later wrote that he had only spoken "for about ten minutes," the official account of what he said has him going on for pages. He brought up again the desirability of taking Rhodes; of capturing the German army now in Italy; of Turkey's entrance into the war, which he stated the British were going to force by Christmas; of its effect on the Balkans; of aid to Tito; of the problem of landing craft; of other ancillary Mediterranean operations.

Stalin answered him point by point. (Brooke would later admit, "I rapidly grew to appreciate the fact that he had a military brain of the very highest caliber. Never once in any of his statements did he make any strategic error.") He corrected the prime minister's figures on the number of German divisions in the Balkans, reiterated that "Turkey will not enter the war," called the attention of those present to the importance of not creating diversions from the most important operation in order to carry out secondary operations, and ended with his belief that until a commander had been decided on, no success from Overlord could be expected.

Finally, Roosevelt stepped back in, winding up the discussion with a nod to Churchill's continuing caveats, saying, "If we are all agreed on OVERLORD, the next question would be regarding the timing." He went on to point out the dangers of operations in the eastern Mediterranean, saying that to do it right would probably delay Overlord.

When Stalin said that there were twenty-five German divisions in France, Roosevelt replied, "We should therefore work out plans to contain these German divisions . . . on such a scale as not to divert means from doing OVERLORD at the agreed time."

Which drove Stalin to say, repeating himself, "You are right—You are right."

Now came the moment when Roosevelt joined Stalin in forcing Churchill into a corner.

The president said, "It would be good for OVERLORD to take place about 1 May, or certainly not later than 15 May, or 20 May, if possible."

The prime minister said that he "could not agree to that."

Stalin said he had observed at the conference the day before that "nothing will come out of these proposed diversions."

Churchill, even in the face of such strong disapproval, wouldn't give up: "The many great possibilities in the Mediterranean should [not] be ruthlessly cast aside as valueless merely on the question of a month's delay in OVERLORD."

Stalin repeated, "All Mediterranean operations are diversions, aside from that into Southern France." He added he had "no interest in any other operations other than those into Southern France."

Lord Moran said of Churchill that it was his handling of words that made him unique: "Without that feeling for words he might have made little enough of life. For in judgment, in skill, in administration, in knowledge of human nature, he does not excel."

Churchill was proving Moran's judgments, eloquently. He appeared to think that only Stalin was truly against him, that he still had a chance to change Roosevelt's mind, which was far from the truth. Wrong in his assessment of both men, the prime minister went meticulously over the same points, about using the British army in the Mediterranean, about working toward the defeat of Germany in Italy, and how action in the eastern Mediterranean would contain significant German divisions, and he again brought up Turkey.

Stalin betrayed no impatience. He doodled on his notepad (undoubtedly wolf heads) and smoked cigarettes.

The spoken words do not convey Churchill's frustration and anger or the extent of Stalin's implicit dismissal of what he said, for at some point in this conversation, wrote Admiral King, "Mr. Churchill became so angry that he got on his feet and told Stalin that he could not talk to him, or any other Britisher, in that manner, and proceeded to stump up and down the room for a few minutes until Mr. Eden rose and spoke with him in a low tone, after which Mr. Churchill resumed his seat and appeared somewhat calmer."

Charles Bohlen would write that Roosevelt should have come to Churchill's defense because "he was really being put upon by Stalin," a statement revealing where Bohlen's sympathies lay, given that, as Bohlen admitted, "it was true that Roosevelt was arguing on the same side Stalin was, so in effect this anti-Churchill attitude was justified."

Roosevelt sat back, watching history being made. The last thing he planned to do was interfere. He had no intention of propping up the British Empire: he wanted it dismantled. So Churchill's plan, to attack through the Balkans, the soft underbelly of Europe, which would have isolated the Soviet Union, came to naught.

Stalin had dismissed the Mediterranean campaign as of secondary importance the day before, commenting that the great value of the Italian campaign was the freeing of the Mediterranean for Allied shipping, that Italy was not a suitable place from which to attempt to attack Germany proper, that the Alps constituted an almost insuperable barrier, as the famous Russian general Suvorov had discovered in his time.

Now, in the face of Churchill's obstinacy, Stalin said it again: "The best method in the Soviet opinion, was getting at the heart of Germany with an attack through northern or northwestern France and even through southern France." After that, finally, he asked the president how many more days the conference was going to continue; he said that he had to leave on the first, that he "might" stay to the second, but then he must go away.

Churchill said he would stay forever if necessary.

Stalin took his curved pipe out of his tunic pocket, opened a box of Herzegovina Flor cigarettes, took out several, broke them up slowly, shook the tobacco into his pipe, then lit the pipe and took a few puffs. That done, he looked around.

Roosevelt, trying to bridge the gap between the two men, suggested that the matter go again to the chiefs of staff, who could, in view of the fact that they had been "confronted with every suggestion made at this afternoon's meeting," give the ad hoc committee the substance of the afternoon's conference, then the staff would definitely have only one directive.

Stalin would not yield. The ad hoc committee was unnecessary, he said; "all that was necessary to be solved was the selection of the commander for OVERLORD, the date for OVERLORD, and the matter of supporting operations."

Roosevelt then proposed a more pointed directive for the ad hoc committee—one that succinctly stated his preference, Stalin's preference, but provided a fig leaf for Churchill: (1) the committee assumes Overlord the dominating operation; (2) the committee recommends that subsidiary operation(s) be included in the Mediterranean, taking into consideration that *any delay not affect* Overlord.

Stalin then noted that there was no mention of a date. He pointed out that the Soviet Union had to know the exact date so it could help, "in order that the Soviets could prepare the blow on their side."

Roosevelt then reminded them that the date had been set at Quebec earlier that summer "and that only some much more important matter could possibly affect that date." At least that was his view.

Remarkably, Churchill again weighed in, again trying to muddy the waters. "It was not clear to him what the President's plans were . . . He had questions for Stalin . . . He believed that the Ad Hoc committee should recommend what subsidiary operations should be carried out . . . He believed we should take more time in drawing up a proper directive to the Ad Hoc committee."

Roosevelt again tried to find common ground. Would it not be possible for the ad hoc committee "to go ahead with their deliberations without any further directive and to produce an answer by tomorrow morning"?

Stalin replied, "What can such a committee do? We Chiefs of State have more power and more authority than a committee. General Brooke cannot force our opinions."

And he then asked "if the British are thinking seriously of OVERLORD only in order to satisfy the USSR."

Because this was in point of fact the truth, Churchill sidestepped it—eloquently.

"If the conditions specified at Moscow regarding OVERLORD should exist, he firmly believed it would be England's duty to hurl every ounce of strength she had across the Channel at the Germans."

They broke up, on the understanding that the military staffs, the ad hoc committee, and the foreign ministers (which meant Hopkins, Molotov, and Eden) would talk the next day.

Stalin's last words: "Then at four o'clock tomorrow afternoon we will have our conference again." He was obviously getting restless. He had good reason. Roosevelt closed the meeting with the suggestion that the chiefs of staff meet for lunch at 1:30 p.m. the following day.

It was just after seven when the meeting broke up. Roosevelt admitted to Elliott, who was waiting for him back in his room, that he was tired. He lay down for a moment, then rubbed his eyes, sat up, and started talking to Elliott about Stalin. As Elliott later remembered his father's comments, he said, "It's a pleasure working with him. There's nothing devious. He outlines the subject he wants discussed, and he sticks to it."

"OVERLORD?" questioned Elliott. Roosevelt replied,

That's what he was talking about. And what we were talking about . . . Winston is talking about two operations at once. I guess he knows there's no use trying to argue against the western invasion anymore. Marshall has got to the point where he just looks at the P.M. as though he can't believe his ears . . . If there's one

American general that Winston can't abide, it's General Marshall. And needless to say, it's because Marshall's right . . . I see no reason for putting the lives of American soldiers in jeopardy in order to protect real or fancied British interests on the European continent. We're at war, and our job is to win it as fast as possible and without adventures . . . It was quite obvious to everyone in the room what he [Churchill] really meant. That he was above all else anxious to knife up into central Europe, in order to keep the Red Army out of Austria and Rumania, even Hungary . . . Stalin knew, I knew it, everybody knew it . . . And Uncle Joe, when he argued the military advantages of invasion from the west . . . he was always conscious of the political implications, too.

Father and son talked for a while longer. Then Roosevelt had a bath. Elliott asked him if he wanted a cocktail before the dinner. He did: "But a weak one, Elliott . . . all those toasts coming up!"

IT WAS STALIN'S TURN to give the dinner, which took place in a room off the great hall near Roosevelt's quarters in the Soviet embassy.

The list of invitees included Churchill, Eden, Clark Kerr, Stalin, Molotov, the president, Hopkins, and Harriman, plus the ever-present interpreters.

Elliott received a last-minute invitation to join them when Stalin noticed him standing at the door to the dinner; he pulled him into the room and seated him between Eden and Harriman.

There was "an unbelievable quantity of food" and a lot to drink, as was usual at formal Russian dinners. The dinner began with cold hors d'oeuvres and progressed to hot borscht, fish, various meat dishes, salads, compote, and fruits; course followed course "in greatest profusion." Each accompanied by copious amounts of vodka and wine and, following all the courses, liqueurs.

Stalin's favorite drink, according to Molotov, was champagne, which he sometimes drank at dinners instead of vodka; this night, however, he appeared to be drinking vodka, as Elliott Roosevelt discovered when the marshal poured some from the private bottle at his elbow into Elliott's glass.

In the Russian fashion, most of the talking came through the medium of proposing a toast: as toasts were made, everyone rose to his feet, drained his glass, and sat down—until the next toast. Toasts were cordial, occasionally vapid, but sometimes a means of letting off steam in a controlled environment.

The day had left its mark on Stalin. During the long plenary session he had pushed Churchill to abandon his embrace of the Mediterranean campaign and accept Overlord without qualifying conditions. Churchill had finally, grudgingly, agreed to go along with his two allies, but with such bad grace that it was apparent he agreed only because he had no other choice, not because he was convinced of the rightness of their battle plans.

Roosevelt rarely took umbrage at opposition because he was used to it in the give-and-take of political life. Indeed, overcoming opposition was one of his great enjoyments; he thrived on it. Because he now had consensus on Overlord, he was in high good humor. Stalin, though, was not used to opposition. In his circle his word was law; he expected people to fall into line. Churchill, however, had stubbornly and futilely opposed him, and now he took pleasure in showing his annoyance at the prime minister by riding him. Charles Bohlen wrote that he "lost no opportunity to get in a dig at Mr. Churchill. Almost every remark that he addressed to the prime minister contained some sharp edge." But he wielded his stiletto with great care. "The Marshal's manner was entirely friendly," Bohlen, no fan of the premier's, had to admit. Stalin also issued what amounted to a word of warning: "Just because Russians are a simple people, it was a mistake to believe that they were blind and could not see what was before their eyes." On a more substantive level he accused Churchill of favoring a soft peace for Germany—or worse, of harboring a secret liking for Germany.

Roosevelt, far from defending Churchill, watched. He knew that what Stalin said was indeed fact. He knew something of what was going through Churchill's head—that he wished for a strong Germany to balance the Soviet Union in Europe. "What are we going to have between the white snows of Russia and the white cliffs of Dover?" Churchill had exploded to the president during a meeting in Quebec the previous summer. Roosevelt didn't know that Churchill imagined Russia as even mightier than it was—that in the prime minister's mind he had boosted its population from 165 million to 200 million.

For a brief period the atmosphere among the principals was cordial, and Stalin seemed to relax, at which point Hopkins, with his sure touch, made a respectful toast to the Red Army. Thus complimented, Stalin spoke frankly about the Soviet army. He said that as a result of the winter war against Finland in 1940, in which the army had given such a poor showing, the entire army had been reorganized, which it needed, and had continued to improve as it fought the Germans. Just about then Hopkins, who had not felt well to start with, excused himself.

Later, toward the end of the dinner, Stalin got to his feet to propose his "umpteenth" toast (Elliott Roosevelt would later write, "I had been trying to keep count, but by then I was hopelessly lost"). Elliott remembered Stalin's toast, on the subject of Germany, as "I propose a salute to the swiftest possible justice for all Germany's war criminals—justice before a firing squad. I drink to our unity in dispatching them as fast as we capture them, all of them, and there must be at least fifty thousand of them." Bohlen thought that Stalin made it in a "quasi-jocular fashion." If so, it would have been entirely in character.

Stalin knew firsthand just how vile was the conduct of German soldiers toward all Slavs. The war Hitler waged against the Soviet Union and Poland (the Aryans against the Slavic nations) was brutally different from the war he had waged in Western Europe (Aryans against Aryans).

Hitler believed Slavs were an inferior race. After conquest he planned to turn Russia and Poland into slave nations, their populations to be deprived of basic rights. He boasted of it. "The conflict," he had announced, "will be very different from the conflict in the west." As the Wehrmacht marched into Poland, the führer's policies of ethnic deportation and resettlement were put into place. Members of the intelligentsia were herded into extermination camps, and ordinary Poles were shunted off to areas where they died from starvation and disease, as Richard J. Evans documents in *The Third Reich at War*. Medical aid was withheld so the sickly would die; schools for the children were closed.

Poland was the only country outside the fatherland where death camps were constructed. This was because Hitler planned to exterminate the entire Polish nation. Hitler was planning to institute the same policy in the Soviet Union: start by killing the intellectuals and the Jews, finish off the remaining indigenous population, rebuild the infrastructure, and, finally, repopulate choice areas and remaining towns with German farmers and burghers.

Therefore, to serve a dual purpose, there were three death camps,

Sobibor, Majdanek, and Belzec, that were built virtually on the Polish-Russian border. Hitler framed the Ukraine he envisaged under German rule on the British Empire's subjugation and remodeling of India and Africa. Between 80 and 85 percent of the Poles, 64 percent of the Ukrainians, and 75 percent of the Belorussians were to be forced farther east. That made a grand total of between thirty-one and forty-five million people that Hitler planned to uproot from Eastern Europe, to be replaced by millions of Germans—"colonists"—who would live on handsome, spacious farms, tilling Slav land with the latest agricultural machinery and producing bounteous harvests of food for the growing German nation. Jews were singled out as a group to be exterminated wherever they were found. "In a hundred years our language will be the language of Europe," the führer promised.

Given this mind-set, it followed that all Russian soldiers taken prisoner were routinely brutalized, treated like animals, penned into open fields in the dead of winter, sometimes given minimum rations, sometimes starved to death if death by exposure hadn't killed enough of them. Other prisoners—tens of thousands—were shot by firing squads; still others were shipped to labor camps and extermination camps in Germany. In December 1941, an official German report stated that between 25 and 70 percent of Russian prisoners died en route to camps. By the end of the war 3.3 million Red Army prisoners—more than half of all those captured—had perished. In all cases, captured soldiers were treated as racial and ideological enemies of the Third Reich. The Geneva Conventions simply didn't apply.

The full horror of Hitler's plan for the racial subjugation and extermination of Eastern Europe would never have been believed in the context of Tehran. Neither Roosevelt nor Churchill knew the full extent of the brutal German treatment of Soviet prisoners. Against this background, Stalin's toast was not unreasonable. Even Americans had begun to hear atrocity stories and were feeling vengeful. At the Moscow Conference a few weeks earlier Cordell Hull had said, "If I had my way, I would take Hitler and Mussolini and Tojo and their arch accomplices and bring them before a drumhead court-martial. And at sunrise on the following day there would occur an historic incident."

During the plenary sessions Stalin had repeatedly slighted Churchill. As Harriman remembered, "When the president spoke Stalin listened closely with deference, whereas he did not hesitate to interrupt or stick a knife into Churchill whenever he had the chance." Now, after Stalin's toast, Churchill finally blew up. He growled that the British people would never stand for such mass murder. He *might* have thought that he had a chance to paint Stalin as a boorish, unprincipled, uncivilized tyrant. Or he *might* simply have been so drunk that his gut fear of the idea that Germany might emerge from the war prostrate, not powerful enough to face off Russia, suddenly came out in the open.

He then said, according to Elliott, "Any such attitude is wholly contrary to our British sense of justice. I take this opportunity to say that I feel most strongly that no one, Nazi or no, shall be summarily dealt with, before a firing squad, without proper legal trial, no matter what the known facts and proven evidence against him!"

So ran Elliott Roosevelt's recollection. Churchill's own recounting of this incident has him pronouncing, "The British Parliament and people will never tolerate mass executions. Even if in war passion they allowed them to begin, they would turn violently against those responsible after the first butchery had taken place. The Soviets must be under no delusion on this point."

Stalin, observed Elliott Roosevelt, kept a straight face, but his eyes twinkled. He turned to President Roosevelt, who, Elliott noticed, was hiding a smile, and asked his opinion.

"As usual," Roosevelt said, "it seems to be my function to mediate this dispute. Clearly there must be some sort of compromise between your position, Mr. Stalin, and that of my good friend the Prime Minister. Perhaps we could say that, instead of summarily executing fifty thousand war criminals, we should settle on a smaller number. Shall we say forty-nine thousand five hundred?" (Roosevelt himself had once remarked of the Germans in a cabinet meeting, "There's got to be severe treatment, but I wouldn't make too much of it . . . Just a few drumhead trials in the field and have it over quick." Secretary of the Treasury Henry Morgenthau thought a list should be made of the German arch criminals and that upon capture these men should be shot at once.)

Churchill, usually known for his amazing capacity for liquor, had been drinking brandy steadily all evening, and on this evening he stepped over the edge. His face and neck were flushed red. Now, abruptly, in a fury, he rose from his chair, in the process managing to knock over his brandy glass, and turning on Stalin and Roosevelt, the brandy spreading across the table, he growled that war criminals must pay for their crimes, must stand trial, that he was against executions for political purposes, and further, in a dig at Roosevelt, that he was against great-power control of strategic points, which Roosevelt had advocated earlier in the conference. He added, in another dig at FDR, that Britain would hold fast to its territories and bases and no one would take them away from it without going to war. He mentioned in particular Hong Kong and Singapore. Great Britain might grant eventual independence, he ranted on, but "this would be done entirely by Great Britain herself in accordance with her own moral precepts."

Stalin was enjoying himself. He now proceeded in his most affable manner to walk around the table asking each person for his opinion as to how many Germans he thought should be shot. Eden and Clark Kerr, being diplomats, diplomatically backed off without answering the question, instead commenting to the effect that the subject required more study. Harriman's answer went unrecorded. But when it came to Elliott's turn, he remembered getting to his feet and saying, "Russian, American, and British soldiers will settle the issue for most of those fifty thousand, in battle, and I hope that not only those fifty thousand war criminals will be taken care of, but many hundreds of thousands more Nazis as well."

Before Elliott had a chance to sit down, Stalin was around the table, had flung his arm around his shoulders, and was saying, "An excellent answer! A toast to your health."

That was too much for Churchill. He exploded at Elliott: "Do you know what you are saying? How can you dare say such a thing?" He got up and stamped off into a cloakroom next door that was in semidarkness. Stalin, in a gesture of apology, followed him to make amends.

Wrote Churchill of the incident, putting his own gloss on it for the history books, "I had not been there a minute before hands were clapped upon my shoulders from behind, and there was Stalin, with Molotov at his side, both grinning broadly, and eagerly declaring that they were only playing . . . Stalin has a very captivating manner when he chooses to use it, and I never saw him do so to such an extent as at this moment . . . I consented to return, and the rest of the evening passed pleasantly."

They returned together, Stalin with a broad grin on his face.

Conversation recommenced. Churchill puffed away harder than usual at his cigar.

Roosevelt changed the subject to something he hoped was neutral, saying that bases and strategic points in the vicinity of Germany and Japan should be held under trusteeship.

Stalin agreed.

Churchill was still in a pugnacious state. In the War Room in London, where Churchill and his top military personnel planned British strategy and watched the battles unfold, he sat squarely facing three walls, all covered with huge maps. The maps on the left and center walls showed the progress of the battles on land and sea all over the globe. But always in Churchill's line of sight was the equally large map on the right wall: the map, in majestic red, of the British Empire. From 1905 to 1908 Churchill had been undersecretary of state for the colonies, and secretary of state for the colonies in 1921 and 1922. The empire was never far from his thoughts.

Now, still out of control, he took another jab at Roosevelt, announcing that Britain did not desire to acquire new territory or bases "but intended to hold on to what they had . . . Nothing would be taken away from England without a war."

Roosevelt remained silent. Stalin stepped in, with the conciliatory comment that England had fought well in the war and that he personally favored an increase in the British Empire, "particularly the area around Gibraltar," then under Franco's control.

Churchill, mistakenly thinking he saw a chance to expose Russia's postwar territorial interests, inquired as to what Russia's territorial interests would be. Stalin wouldn't give him the satisfaction of an answer, replying, "When the time comes, we will speak."

They parted. If Roosevelt had any closing words, they have not come down to us.

Bohlen later noted that when he glanced into the now almost deserted dining room, the white-jacketed, enormous Russian, six feet four or five inches tall and built to scale, whom he had noticed standing in back of Stalin all evening and whom he had taken to be a butler, had removed his jacket to reveal the uniform of a major general.

Elliott was worried about the explosion he had caused. After dinner he tried to apologize to his father for precipitating what he feared was an incident between allies, but Roosevelt told him he thought the incident had been amusing. He reassured Elliott: "What you said was perfectly all right. It was fine. Winston just lost his head when everybody refused to take the subject seriously. Uncle Joe . . . the way he was needling him, he was going to take offense at what anybody said, specially if what was said pleased Uncle Joe." He obviously felt no twinge of regret that he had not intervened.

Still later in the evening, to make sure that Churchill went along with the date for Overlord, Hopkins paid a visit to the British embassy to give the prime minister a message: give up trying to delay Overlord; both the United States and the Soviet Union are set on it; yield with grace. It is not clear whether Hopkins went on his own initiative or at the behest of the president, but given the close relationship between the two, the visit was probably made after he and Roosevelt discussed the matter.

Churchill never forgave Elliott Roosevelt. Elliott had been a frequent visitor to Chequers, Churchill's country estate, and had been on such good terms with him that Churchill had treated him with the informality of a son. Once, at the end of a weekend, Elliott had been summoned to Churchill's room to say his good-byes. "He was," remembered Elliott, "stalking about the room, clad only in a cigar." That was finished. To Elliott's regret he was never again invited to Chequers.

WHEN THE COMBINED CHIEFS OF STAFF—that is, the top American and British military—met the next morning, Tuesday, November 30, even Sir Alan Brooke, chief of the imperial general staff, having been given his marching orders by Churchill, had withdrawn opposition to the agreed-upon date of Overlord. The Combined Chiefs unanimously recommended "to the President and Prime Minister respectively that we should inform Marshal Stalin that we will launch OVERLORD during May, in conjunction with a supporting operation against the South of France on the largest scale that is permitted by the landing craft available at that time."

Yet there is evidence there was a fight to the very end; the draft actually gave the date of Overlord as June 1; Roosevelt crossed that out and, in his unmistakable hand, scrawled "May" in its place.

Roosevelt spent part of the morning visiting the branch post exchange that had been set up in the Russian embassy for American personnel shopping for Persian gifts. From among the knives, daggers, rugs, and other objects, he selected a bowl "of some antiquity" as his birthday gift for Churchill. He would present it to him later at dinner.

Roosevelt, Churchill, Stalin, and their interpreters, over lunch in Roosevelt's quarters in the embassy, discussed upcoming plans in some detail. Roosevelt informed Stalin that the Combined Chiefs of Staff had agreed Overlord would be launched by June 1 and that at the same time there would be a supporting operation in southern France. Stalin expressed "his great satisfaction" and said that the Red Army would at the same time mount offensive operations and demonstrate by its actions the value it placed on the decision.

But his question of the previous day had not been answered, so Stalin asked it again: "When would the Commander in Chief be named?"

Roosevelt was still trying to decide between General Marshall and General Eisenhower. In response to Stalin's question, he replied that he needed a few more days to decide. Roosevelt turned to the question of the approaches to the Baltic, a subject he had begun to touch upon the first evening just before taking sick. He said he "liked the idea of establishing . . . Bremen, Hamburg and Lubeck into some sort of free zone, with the Kiel Canal put under international control and guaranty, with freedom of passage for the world's commerce." Some months earlier in the Soviet Union a Foreign Ministry commission on peace treaties and the postwar order had been formed to consider just such questions. The commission, chaired by Maxim Litvinov, envisioned Russia gaining strategic strongholds and the internationalization of the Kiel Canal.

Stalin responded, "That was a good idea." Then he asked, bluntly, "What could be done for Russia in the Far East?"

Churchill took the opportunity to probe, never something Stalin liked. He was, Churchill said, "interested to find out the views of the Soviet government on the Far East."

Certainly the timing of Churchill's question was bad, but also, crucially, Stalin was really not interested in hearing from Churchill: *his* question was aimed at what Roosevelt had in mind. Stalin, therefore, replied to the prime minister that the Russians had their views but that it would be better to await the time when the Russians would be taking an active participation in the Far Eastern war. He added that all the ports in the Far East were closed off from Soviet use, because Vladivostok was only partly ice-free and was subject to closure by the Japanese.

Roosevelt then stepped in to answer Stalin's question: "The idea of a free port might be applied to the Far East . . . Dairen . . . a possibility."

Stalin queried the president as to China's view of such an idea: he didn't think the Chinese would like such a scheme.

Roosevelt, had, of course, just come from the Cairo Conference, where he had spoken with Chiang Kai-shek, so underlying his words was information, couched in diplomatic doublespeak: he thought China would like the idea of a free port under international guaranty. Stalin answered, "That would not be bad." He pointed out that Russia had the ice-free port of Kamchatka but no rail connections there. "There was only one ice-free port to serve the country, that of Murmansk."

Churchill then said that the nations that would govern the postwar world "should be satisfied and have no territorial or other ambitions . . . Hungry nations and ambitious nations are dangerous."

This was well received. Roosevelt and Stalin agreed with Churchill, both probably reflecting that these were lofty, high-sounding, but easy words for the head of the British Empire, still the greatest colonial power in the world, to speak. Churchill had a different problem from protecting borderlands: holding on to the empire.

During the morning, following his visit to the post exchange, Roosevelt met with the young shah of Iran, Mohammad Reza Pahlavi, in his study at the embassy. During their conversation the shah had brought up the subject of Britain's viselike grip on the oil and mineral wealth of his country. Roosevelt listened sympathetically, according to Elliott, who was present, agreeing that something should be done to protect Iran's natural resources. When he left, Roosevelt told Elliott to find Patrick Hurley and give him instructions to work up a statement which he, Stalin, and Churchill could sign that would guarantee Iran independence and the right of self-determination of its economic interests.

Following the meetings, Hurley and Roosevelt worked over Hurley's draft of what would become the Iran Declaration. Hurley shared with Roosevelt the view that British policy in Iran was imperialistic but that nevertheless it was vital that the British navy, floating as it did on Iranian oil, which Churchill called "a prize from fairyland beyond our wildest dreams," continue to be so supplied.

Ordinarily, such a draft would have been worked up by a State Department officer, but Roosevelt had such a low opinion of foreign service officers that there were none present except Charles Bohlen, who was there as interpreter. Roosevelt was not above referring to foreign service officers as "State Department striped-pants boys," saying to his son Elliott some time after Tehran, "Any number of them are convinced that the way for America to conduct its foreign policy is to find out what the British are doing and then copy that." Hopkins also disliked foreign service officers, describing the ones he had encountered cuttingly: "cookie pushers, pansies—and usually isolationists to boot."

Many of the foreign service officers had trained under Robert F. Kelley, the strongly anti-Soviet chief of the State Department's Division of Eastern European Affairs, and were unquestionably biased against both the New Deal and its foreign policy of rapprochement with Russia. Roosevelt had given to Undersecretary of State Sumner Welles, a quick and decisive executive, the job of reorganizing the department and running day-to-day State Department operations. FDR had known Welles, like himself a Groton and Harvard renegade Democrat, since his wedding in 1905, when the twelve-year-old Welles had carried Eleanor's train. Welles, with the president's blessing, proceeded to oust Kelley and merge Eastern European Affairs into the Department of Western European Affairs. Nevertheless, the foreign service's anti-Soviet culture still ran deep. Most foreign service officers were against aid to Russia even after Hitler invaded the Soviet Union. Nor did they try to understand Stalin's view of the West. Thus Charles Bohlen would write of the foreign service officers, noticeably including himself in the comment, that their assessment of Stalin was so off the mark during the war years that "there had been a question among many of us involved in Soviet affairs whether the Soviet Union would seriously contemplate joining a world organization such as the United Nations . . . When the draft of the proposal was first put before the Soviets, we awaited their reaction with some trepidation." More than Kelley was at work: most of them (although there were exceptions) came from conservative, wealthy, socially prominent eastern establishment families that were bitterly anti–New Deal. Even Bohlen, whose views became modified after exposure to Harry Hopkins and FDR, fitted that mold. Bohlen, typically, had attended St. Paul's and Harvard, where he had been admitted to the Porcellian Club, the most snobbish of all the Harvard clubs. As it happened, FDR, whose father had been a member, had not been accepted by the Porcellian Club, which had been the most shocking setback in his young life before he contracted polio. (Bohlen certainly knew, as every Porcellian knew, that FDR had not been "punched," as Porcellians called it, because it was a timeless piece of club news and was undoubtedly the basis for the tinge of superiority that occasionally crept into Bohlen's remarks about the president. On the other hand, the president probably did not know that his new interpreter was a Porcellian.)

Roosevelt wanted men—and occasionally women—who understood what he wanted done and did it without question. Hurley fitted into that category.

Ever since Roosevelt had declared Iran eligible for Lend-Lease supplies in March 1942, the United States had begun to exert considerable authority over the country. By the time of the Tehran Conference, U.S. personnel controlled the nation's key activities such as finance, the police force, and rationing; the United States was also reorganizing the Iranian army. Roosevelt wanted a simple, straightforward declaration that would assure the Iranians that America respected and would maintain Iran's territorial integrity and would leave after the war was ended, and one that stressed Russia and Britain would abide by their agreements as well. Hurley, who had been largely responsible for the position of influence the United States enjoyed in Iran, would know how to state the declaration.

Because this was essentially a restatement of the Atlantic Charter, the promise, specifically, of "the maintenance of the independence, sovereignty and territorial integrity of Iran" was one that neither Stalin nor Churchill could quarrel with. But because both of their nations had a history of agreements with Iran that they routinely disregarded, in all probability neither Churchill nor Stalin gave the statement a second thought: public relations was public relations. (In fact, neither did abide by his agreement. At Yalta, when Anthony Eden suggested that the declaration be reaffirmed, Molotov refused. Great Britain, whose dominance of the southern half of the country, where the Anglo-Iranian Oil Company refinery and valuable oil wells were located, paid lip service to the declaration, but it continued the practice of taking the lion's share of Anglo-Iranian Oil Company profits, housing its Iranian employees in slums, and refusing to hire or train Iranians for managerial positions, thus setting the stage for later turmoil and revolution.)

After Hurley had left, Roosevelt said to Elliott, "I wish I had more men like Pat, on whom I could depend."

Roosevelt continued to be concerned about Iran. Considering the short period of time he was there, he had absorbed a great deal. A few weeks after he returned to the United States, Roosevelt sent a memo to Hull, giving his impressions of the country: "Iran is definitely a very, very backward nation. It consists really of a series of tribes, and 99 percent of the population is, in effect, in bondage to the other 1 percent. The 99 percent do not own their land and cannot keep their own production or convert it into money or property."

IT WAS CHURCHILL'S BIRTHDAY—his sixty-ninth—and he made the most of it. During the day British troops, Indian troops, and employees of the Anglo-Iranian Oil Company mustered up a small parade in his honor. He claimed the night as his to host a dinner by right of his birthday and invited FDR and Stalin, the top military and foreign policy advisers of the three countries, his children Randolph and Sarah, and Elliott Roosevelt to his birthday dinner at the British embassy.

It was a lovely evening. The day had been warm, but at dusk a pleasant coolness had descended. For security (and for the drama of their attire as well) the British assigned Sikhs to stand at the entrance doors of the ornate white building. They also installed ramps on the entrance porch so that Roosevelt in his wheelchair could be rolled in and out.

Not trusting British thoroughness, Beria took security precautions prior to Stalin's entrance. NKVD personnel searched the building from top to bottom, looking not just behind every door but behind every cushion on every chair, and even interrogated embassy servants, according to an irritated Churchill; during the evening Russian guards stood near every door and window as well as on the roof.

By the time the dinner started, however, Churchill, his daughter Sarah at his side, was cheerfully smiling and puffing happily away on a cigar as he received his guests, most of whom came with presents. Roosevelt noted that when Churchill introduced Sarah to Stalin, Stalin bowed from the hips, "took her hand and kissed it in the old-fashioned, elegant European manner."

Roosevelt's gift to the prime minister was the Persian bowl. Stalin gave him an astrakhan hat and a large china sculpture depicting Russian folktales. Churchill was dressed in a tuxedo, but Roosevelt, who didn't like and habitually avoided changing into a dinner jacket, wore, as he often did when formal clothes were called for, a dark navy blue suit with a faintly visible pinstripe and a black bow tie; Stalin was in uniform.

The assemblage moved into the elegant dining room, the walls of which were mirrored tiles, the windows framed by red drapes. The long tables were set with crystal and silver that gleamed in the candlelight; the liveried servants wore gloves. Churchill seated his guests so that Roosevelt was on his right and Stalin on his left.

Churchill's "vast" birthday cake, atop of which sixty-nine candles would glow, towered prominently on a table.

There were enough knives and forks and spoons at each place setting to make Stalin turn to the British interpreter, A. H. Birse, seated next to him, and say, "This is a fine collection of cutlery. It is a problem which to use. You will have to tell me, and also when I can begin to eat. I am unused to your customs."

The dinner fare was actually quite simple and restrained, particularly by Soviet standards. In keeping with British custom, the menu was written out and placed on the table in front of each diner: oxtail *clair,* fillet of sole meunière with sauce mousseline, *dinde* farci garni, *salade de saison, asperges* sauce vinaigrette, *tarte aux pommes,* fruits.

There were a great many toasts back and forth. After each toast custom dictated that all rise (Roosevelt, of course, excepted). Stalin had his own custom: he would go up to the person to whom a toast had been offered and clink glasses with him. Churchill did the same. So, recalled the Russian interpreter Valentin Berezhkov, "there were the two of them, wandering slowly around the room with glasses in their hands." Churchill was happy enough to dance "a gay and abandoned hornpipe."

Roosevelt proposed a toast to Sarah Churchill's health, after which Stalin, as was his habit, walked round the table to clink glasses with her. Sarah remembered that, although he was "a frightening figure with his slit, bear eyes, he was in a jovial mood. Specks of light danced in his eyes like cold sunshine on dark waters." Following clinking glasses with Stalin, Sarah went over to thank the president, who said to her, in a rare comment on his condition, "I would have come to you, my dear, but I cannot."

Two interchanges between Stalin and Churchill were memorable. During one toast Stalin referred to both Roosevelt and Churchill as his "fighting friends" or "comrades in arms," then he paused and said, "If it is possible for me to consider Mr. Churchill my friend." At another moment Churchill said that the world was changing. He remarked in this connection that the complexion of Great Britain was becoming "pinker," at which point Stalin interjected, "That is a sign of health." Churchill replied that he agreed provided the process was not carried so far as to induce congestion. There was another quite different and chilling moment, when Stalin, replying to complimentary toasts to him and to the Russian people, said that "the Red Army had fought heroically, but that the Russian people would have tolerated no other quality from their armed forces . . . [E]ven persons of medium courage—and even cowards—became heroes in Russia. Those who didn't were killed."

At some point Roosevelt raised his glass and toasted Sir Alan Brooke, the British chief of staff. Stalin said he wanted to add something to FDR's toast and proceeded to say he regretted that Sir Alan had adopted a grim and distrustful attitude toward the Russians and that he drank to the general's health in the hope that Sir Alan "would come to know us better and find we are not so bad after all."

The result of this was disastrous. The dinner until then had been quite convivial. Sir Alan Brooke respected Stalin. But he didn't like him. Now, undoubtedly under the influence of too much alcohol, Brooke tapped his knife against his glass and in his toast declared, in effect, that the British had suffered more, lost more, and fought more in the war than either of the other nations.

In the face of this appalling remark that everyone in the room knew to be untrue—the Russians had lost millions more soldiers and civilians than had the British and killed many more Germans—"Stalin became gloomy," observed Berezhkov. "He looked as though a storm was about to burst." But, controlling himself, he calmly said,

I want to tell you, from the Russian point of view, what the President and the United States have done to win the war. The most important things in this war are machines. The United States has proven that it can turn out from 8,000 to 10,000 airplanes per month. Russia can only turn out, at most, 3,000 airplanes a month. England turns out 3,000 to 3,500, which are principally heavy bombers. The United States, therefore, is a country of machines. Without the use of these machines, through Lend-Lease, we would lose this war.

Later the U.S. press noted that Stalin had paid a significant compliment to Roosevelt, coming as it did from the leader of the greatest Communist country in the world to the leader of the greatest capitalist country in the world. It was also a masterly subject change.

Roosevelt, of course, had to respond, and in his response he took the opportunity to emphasize their great achievement in Tehran: they had taken the first steps ever to uniting nations. ("Even here, as he had done in the conference hall, Roosevelt considered it essential to speak of the postwar world and the importance of maintaining the unity and cooperation of the great powers not just then, but in the future also," noted Berezhkov.)

> We have differing customs and philosophies and ways of life. Each of us works out our scheme of things according to the desires and ideas of our own peoples.
>
> But we have proved here at Tehran that the varying ideals of our nations can come together in a harmonious whole, moving unitedly for the common good of ourselves and of the world.
>
> So as we leave this historic gathering, we can see in the sky for the first time, that traditional symbol of hope, the rainbow.

At that point, the dinner was over.

6

CEMENTING THE ALLIANCE

Roosevelt had planned to stay in Tehran through Thursday, December 2, but the weather was taking a turn for the worse; snow was falling in the mountains. He decided to leave late Wednesday and notified everyone.

He spent the last morning catching up with official, time-sensitive mail that had to be dispatched. The plenary session with Stalin and Churchill would begin at noon in the conference room, continue through lunch in the president's quarters, and resume in the conference room in the afternoon, and into the evening as well if necessary, until all issues had been resolved.

FDR certainly didn't know how obsessively Stalin monitored his private conversations, but he did know that Stalin had developed a habit of dropping by his rooms to make sure he was being well taken care of. William Rigdon, FDR's press secretary, and Zoya Vasilyevna Zarubina, a Soviet intelligence officer who spoke English and was charged with watching out for FDR's well-being, both attest that Stalin quite a few times took it upon himself to arrive, unannounced, at FDR's quarters. According to Rigdon, sometimes Stalin arrived with Pavlov, once asking "if we had everything we needed," and through Pavlov he explained the Russian knickknacks on FDR's desk, "all the while smiling and showing great deference for his guest . . . Stalin would insist that the President go right ahead with whatever he was doing. 'Don't let me interfere with your work,' he'd say through Pavlov."

Zarubina remembered that she saw Stalin for the first time one morning when he was somewhere near FDR's suite and obviously intent on visiting the president. She translated as Stalin asked, "May I come in?" Roosevelt said, "Welcome."

"The conversation began with Stalin's simple questions to Roosevelt: 'How are you? Did you have a good sleep?' The President replied, 'Yes, I had a good sleep. I like it here; however, the frogs kept croaking in the pond and I could not fall asleep.' I turned around, looking at Stalin, and in agitation I forgot what was the Russian for 'a frog.' I said, 'Iosif Vissarionovich, those little yellow animals croaking in the pond did not let the President of the USA sleep.' I always begin my recollections with that moment, for it was a kind of shock and failure." (According to the Russian account, all the frogs were killed so FDR's sleep would not again be disturbed.)

Now, on the last morning, after disposing of his mail, Roosevelt decided to approach Stalin as informally as Stalin had, in private, approached him. If he could draw him out, he believed, have a meeting of minds, Stalin might begin to rely on him. FDR felt he needed that intimacy to make Stalin accept his plans, which included an acceptance of power restraints. The United Nations that Roosevelt envisaged, able to enforce peace and face down rogue nations, would draw power from its constituent members. That meant *some* measure of power had to be ceded by each nation to the overall organization. Ceding power was going to be hard to sell to Stalin. FDR needed his full cooperation in setting up the UN; anything less would spell defeat. He went about getting it in his own peculiar way.

This day Roosevelt was at his most devious. He had a propensity for playing games with people's minds—which he got away with because he was so sharp and such an uncanny judge of character. He played, for instance, with General Douglas MacArthur, whom he viewed as a talented general but a dangerous prima donna who needed to be kept off balance: he baffled and stroked him at the same time, as noted by MacArthur's biographer William Manchester. Roosevelt once stated that he viewed the general as one of the two most dangerous men in the country. (The other was Governor Huey Long of Louisiana, an unprincipled demagogue who was assassinated in 1935. These two men had in common the fact that they were both possible presidential contenders.)

MacArthur had done the unforgivable thing for a soldier: he had disobeyed orders. Instead of dispersing the Bonus Army, the assembled penniless World War I soldiers camped with their families near Washington in the summer of 1932, as he had been ordered to do, he torched their encampment. Innocent people—children—died. As president, Roosevelt would give him his dues as a general but otherwise treated him as a bellwether of conservative political thought.

During a White House dinner some years later, MacArthur asked Roosevelt, "Why is it, Mr. President, that you frequently inquire my opinion regarding the social reforms under consideration . . . but pay little attention to my views on the military?" Roosevelt had answered, with Machiavellian honesty, "Douglas, I don't bring these questions up for your advice but for your reactions. To me, you are the symbol of the conscience of the American people."

Now, faced with Joseph Stalin, whose reserve he wanted to break down, he put into operation one of his games. As Roosevelt later told Frances Perkins, he felt drastic measures were called for, because otherwise "what we were doing could have been done by the foreign ministers."

His campaign to get personal with Stalin, done at Churchill's expense, commenced just before the last plenary session began. Churchill *was* in a bad mood. As they entered the conference room, FDR recounted, "I had just a moment to say to him, 'Winston, I hope you won't be sore at me for what I am going to do.'" Churchill's reaction had been to shift his cigar in his mouth and grunt. As soon as they were seated around the table, Roosevelt recounted to Perkins,

I talked privately with Stalin. I didn't say anything that I hadn't said before, but it appeared quite chummy and confidential, enough so that the other Russians joined us to listen. Still no smile from Stalin.

Then I said, lifting my hand up to cover a whisper (which of course had to be interpreted), "Winston is cranky this morning, he got up on the wrong side of the bed."

A vague smile passed over Stalin's eyes, and I decided I was on the right track . . . I began to tease Churchill about his Britishness, about John Bull, about his cigars, about his habits. It began to register with Stalin. Winston got red and scowled, and the more he did so, the more Stalin smiled. Finally Stalin broke out into a deep, hearty guffaw, and for the first time in three days I saw light. I kept it up until Stalin was laughing with me, and it was then that I called him "Uncle Joe." He would have thought me fresh the day before, but that day he laughed and came over and shook my hand.

From that time on our relations were personal, and Stalin himself indulged in an occasional witticism. The ice was broken and we talked like men and brothers.

Roosevelt's teasing of Churchill was undoubtedly meant to show Stalin that he now felt as comfortable and intimate with Stalin as he did with the prime minister. If nothing else, he had put Stalin and certainly himself in a better mood. In June, Litvinov had reported that Roosevelt "was entirely convinced in the need of opening a second front as soon as possible, and surely in Western Europe," but that he was "gradually deviated from this conviction by his military advisers, and, particularly by Churchill . . . It is possible to suppose, without the fear of making a mistake, that as far as the military policy is concerned, Churchill is towing Roosevelt."

Davies had told FDR at roughly the same time that Stalin had accused FDR of supporting "the classic British foreign policy of walling Russia in, closing the Dardanelles, and building a countervailing balance of power against Russia."

If Stalin still had doubts about Roosevelt's foreign policy goals, Roosevelt wanted to put them to rest.

THE PLENARY SESSION BEGAN. Hopkins and Harriman sat on either side of the president, Eden and the British ambassador Clark Kerr sat on either side of Churchill; Molotov sat with Stalin. Roosevelt opened the meeting on the subject of what it would take to induce Turkey's president, İsmet İnönü, to enter the war. Both the Joint Chiefs of Staff and Roosevelt himself thought Turkey's entry basically inadvisable because it would be too costly, involving compensation to the Turks in war matériel and supplies, particularly landing craft, already earmarked for Overlord. Churchill, however, knowing it would sabotage Overlord, argued that a motivated Turkey, supplied with landing craft, could make a successful assault on Rhodes, which he still considered strategically important. He suggested moving landing craft from the Pacific. Hopkins said firmly that there were no landing craft available.

Roosevelt called it "absolutely impossible" to pull landing craft from anywhere. Stalin downplayed the disagreement, because the subject had been dismissed.

Discussion continued during the lunch, which was served in Roosevelt's quarters by the Filipino staff.

Roosevelt next brought up the subject of Finland. He had been furious at Stalin's invasion of Finland in 1939, calling it "this dreadful rape" in a letter. At a cabinet meeting following the invasion, FDR had decreed that no supplies or munitions be sent to the Soviet Union. Since then the situation had, of course, drastically changed: Finnish troops were now part of the German forces ringing Leningrad. Roosevelt thought he knew what was on Stalin's mind now: Litvinov had told Hopkins in June 1942 that Stalin had decided to keep his hands off Finland. Roosevelt hoped that Litvinov had reported Stalin's mind-set correctly, but he wasn't counting on it: he was ready for anything. As he had gloomily written to Cardinal Spellman, New York's archbishop, in September, he thought there was a good chance Stalin would claim Poland, the Baltic States, Bessarabia, and Finland, " 'so better give them gracefully . . . What can we do about it?' Within ten or twenty years . . . 'European influence would bring the Russians to become less barbarian.' "

Now Stalin reassured the president. He began by criticizing Finland, pointing out that there were twenty-one Finnish divisions fighting on the Soviet front and that for the twenty-seven months Leningrad had been under siege, Finnish troops had been serving with the German soldiers. But he next stated that Russia had "no designs" on the independence of Finland. Roosevelt had to have been extremely pleased.

The conversation then turned to the specifics of Russian territorial demands in Finland. Stalin said he wanted one of two ports: Hangö on the south coast of Finland or Petsamo in the far north: "If the cession of Hangö presents a difficulty I am willing to take Petsamo." Roosevelt, relieved, had no objection. "A fair exchange," he volunteered.

The meeting broke up.

Roosevelt had asked Stalin to meet him without Churchill one last time.

Stalin arrived at Roosevelt's quarters at 3:20 p.m., accompanied by Molotov; Harriman was with the president.

As always, Roosevelt set the agenda. Two subjects were on his mind as he and Stalin sat across from each other. The first was Poland.

Roosevelt was prepared to accept the Soviet Union's control of Poland as long as it was peaceful and its institutions preserved. Roosevelt entertained a notable lack of enthusiasm for the Polish government in exile in London, even though the United States as well as Britain recognized it as the official government of Poland. He thought as a group they were not representative of their country, were unrealistic in their expectations, and, even more important, were strongly anti-Russian. Just before he left for Tehran, he had vented his feelings to a young English friend of Eleanor Roosevelt's, saying, "I am sick and tired of these people. The Polish Ambassador came to see me a while ago about this question." He then mimicked the ambassador's request for help in dealing with the Russians and continued, "I said [to him], do you think they will just stop to please you, or us for that matter? Do you expect us and Great Britain to declare war on Joe Stalin if they cross your precious frontier?"

Harriman also had serious reservations about the Polish government in exile. He described them as a group of aristocrats who expected the Americans and the British to restore their position and their landed properties, which were extensive, and prop up the feudalistic system that had existed in Poland earlier in the century.

Now Roosevelt, talking to Stalin, brought up none of these issues. He made clear that he viewed the future of Poland through the lens of the next presidential election: if the war was still in progress in 1944, he would run for a fourth term, and if he ran, which he had not yet announced he would do, he needed the votes of the six to seven million Americans of Polish extraction. (It should be noted that FDR grossly exaggerated the Polish population in America. According to the 1940 U.S. census, there were just under a million native-born Poles in the United States, just under two million citizens of Polish extraction.) FDR then underlined that he would take no part in any discussion of Poland's borders because of his need for the Polish vote but that he agreed with Stalin that Poland's eastern border should be moved to the west and the western border moved to the Oder River. Such a westward move would at one and the same time give the Soviet Union what it wanted in the way of Polish territory—regained Russian territory—and enlarge Poland at the expense of Germany.

Stalin replied that now that the president had explained, he understood.

Roosevelt next brought up for discussion the Baltic States, Lithuania, Latvia, and Estonia, which lay between the Soviet Union and the Baltic Sea. They had been provinces of Russia until Germany seized them during the Bolshevik Revolution, had been freed as a result of World War I, and were admitted to the League of Nations in 1939. In 1940, Stalin had sent in the Red Army and claimed them by force—reclaimed them, in his eyes. Roosevelt had been furious at this action, complaining to Sumner Welles of Moscow's "downright rudeness . . . [He] honestly wonders whether the Soviet Government considers it worthwhile to continue diplomatic relations." He had been so furious he had almost broken off relations and closed all Soviet consulates and finally took the less drastic step of freezing Soviet assets. Hitler's invasion had, of course, wiped out all other considerations, and good relations had immediately been restored.

Roosevelt still thought the Baltic States should be free. The previous March he had told Anthony Eden that he didn't like the idea of turning the Baltic States back to Russia, that the Soviet Union would lose "a great deal of public opinion if she insisted," and that "the old plebiscite was probably a fake." In October, FDR told Hull he intended to appeal on grounds of high morality to Stalin and point out to him that from the viewpoint of Russia's position in the world it would be a good thing if the Soviet Union would agree to hold plebiscites in Latvia, Lithuania, and Estonia two years after the war was over. But by the time November rolled around, FDR's position had changed to one of resigned acceptance. "All those Baltic republics are as good as Russian," he had told Eleanor's friend Lieutenant Miles.

Roosevelt now delicately approached the subject. In what Bohlen described as a joking manner, he said that although there were Lithuanians, Latvians, and Estonians in America (who also voted), "when the Soviet armies re-occupied these areas, he did not intend to go to war with the Soviet Union on this point." Because this was no joking matter, one must conclude that Roosevelt was uncomfortable, indeed embarrassed, at having to cede such a point to Stalin. Reduced to explaining the importance of appearances, he spoke to Stalin of the role of public opinion in the United States, explaining that the big issue would be the question of referendum and the right to self-determination for these three countries and that "world opinion would want some expression of the will of the people, perhaps not immediately after their re-occupation by Soviet forces, but some day."

Stalin already knew that FDR did not feel strongly about the status of the Baltic States but that he *was* interested in appearances, because Litvinov had told him exactly that the previous summer. "The USA does not have even a slight economic or foreign policy interest in the problem of the Baltics or in the controversial border issues between us and Poland . . . [However,] Roosevelt, in view of the forthcoming presidential election campaign, has to court the votes of the descendants from the Baltics and Poland, as well as American Catholics, and for this reason he is unwilling to support our demands publicly," he had reported.

Therefore, as he stood up to Roosevelt, Stalin knew he was on firm ground. He stated that the three countries had had no autonomy under the last tsar, that no one then had raised the question of public opinion, and that he did not see why it was being raised now. He added that he would not agree to any form of international control. He suggested that some propaganda work be done.

Roosevelt pushed; he said that "it would be helpful for him personally if some public declaration in regard to the future elections to which the Marshal had referred, could be made."

Stalin replied, "There would be plenty of opportunities for such an expression of the will of the people."

It goes without saying that in Roosevelt's eyes Stalin had no right to rule the Baltic States. But Roosevelt was having a similar problem with Churchill on the subject of England's right to rule India. Roosevelt had forced Churchill to let India sign the United Nations charter on January 1, 1942, as a separate country, like Canada, something the prime minister had had no intention of letting happen ("Churchill instantly reacted against it, shrugged his shoulders and held back," FDR had observed), but he was making no progress on loosening Britain's grip on India, even though Indians were on the point of rebellion and British policies were causing millions of Indians to die of starvation. As strongly as Roosevelt felt in both cases, there was a point beyond which he could not go. He knew if he pushed Stalin further now, he might materially jeopardize their relationship.

He brought the conversation back to the United Nations, intent on converting Stalin to his idea of an organization truly international in character and form. Roosevelt felt strongly that regional blocs would not work. In 1942, when he had broached the subject to Molotov in Washington, Stalin had directed Molotov to advocate regional blocs; he was still toying with this concept. Churchill also favored an organization shaped into spheres of influence. Intent on convincing Stalin of the rightness of *his* worldwide organizational plan without hectoring, FDR now said he "felt that it was premature to consider them here with Mr. Churchill."

He explained that the UN would be three separate organizations under one umbrella. First, a large assembly of all the member nations. Second, an executive committee that would deal with nonmilitary matters composed of Russia, the United States, Great Britain, China, two additional European states, one South American, one Near Eastern, one Far Eastern country, and one British dominion. Third, the four policemen.

He put the emphasis "particularly" on the four great nations, the United States, Great Britain, the Soviet Union, and China, policing the world in the postwar period, adding that "it was just an idea, the exact form would require further study." Roosevelt was indicating that he wanted input from Stalin, but he was also indicating that he and Stalin, America and Russia, would be the two most powerful policemen.

Once Roosevelt had tried to discuss the problem of an annual wage for workmen with Henry Ford. Roosevelt described how he edged him up to the subject, and when Ford saw what he was leading up to, he would draw back, then FDR would work him up to it from another angle and Ford would draw back, and he said he spent a whole luncheon hour playing chess with "Uncle Henry," as he called him, trying to get him up to the subject. But, Roosevelt said, "I never got him to it." He was doing the same now with Stalin, but with better results.

His argument was that an organization so constituted would have the best chance of enforcing world peace. Stalin, listening, obviously grasped the ramifications.

Molotov certainly did. In a rare interjection he noted that at the Moscow Conference they had agreed to discuss how to assure the continued dominance, "the leading role," of the four great powers.

Stalin replied that "after thinking over the question of the world organization as outlined by the president, he had come to agree with the president that it would be world-wide and not regional."

Their meeting ended on that note.

Roosevelt took "tremendous" encouragement, according to Harriman, who was present, from this statement by Stalin. As Sumner Welles observed, nothing, for Roosevelt, was more important than getting the United Nations and Russia's place in it right: "To Franklin Roosevelt a firm agreement with the Soviet Union was the indispensable foundation for peace in the future." Ceding the Baltic States to the Soviet Union was a small price to pay for a peaceful postwar world, particularly because there were really only two options: to agree gracefully or ungracefully.

Stalin, too, was encouraged by the thrust of the conversations. He believed he was setting the Soviet Union on a new, uncharted course, one that even Lenin could never have envisioned. Lenin, he would tell a Yugoslav Communist later, believed that "everyone would attack us . . . whereas it turns out that one group of the bourgeoisie was against us but the other with us. Lenin did not think it would be possible to ally with one wing of the bourgeoisie. But we managed it."

At 6:00 p.m., Roosevelt, Stalin, and Churchill sat, for the last time, in the silk armchairs around the green baize table in the conference room under the eyes of the Soviet guards on the balcony above. Roosevelt opened this final plenary session by stating that there were two questions still to be discussed, the question of Poland and the treatment of Germany.

Molotov spoke next, however, on a subject that had not yet come up: the Soviet Union's expectation that it was going to receive a portion of the captured Italian fleet. The fleet consisted of a large number of merchant ships and a smaller number of warships. Molotov said the Soviet Union needed and could use the ships right away, "in the common cause until the end of the war," after which they could be divided up. Stalin said he felt the Soviet request was moderate. Churchill suggested the possibility of mutiny in the Italian fleet that could lead to the scuttling of ships, if the ships were suddenly transferred to Russia. After a short discussion it was agreed that the Soviet Union would get the ships "around the end of January."

Roosevelt then turned the conversation to Poland. The Soviet Union had broken off relations with the Polish government in exile in London the previous April, when the latter tried to investigate German charges that the Soviet Union in 1940 had murdered thousands of Polish officers who had been prisoners of war. It was a situation fraught with problems because the charges were true: as part of the centuries-old conflict between the two countries, Stalin, it would later be revealed, had concurred in the execution of the officers, who were considered pro-German, and they had been buried in a mass grave in the Katyn Forest near Smolensk. Roosevelt refused to be concerned with the probability that the Soviets had executed the officers or to be drawn into any sort of investigation. Stalin was his ally, and investigation could do nothing except roil their relationship; under the circumstances, guilt or innocence was irrelevant. He simply voiced his expectation that the Soviet Union would reestablish relations with the Polish government in exile, for then the questions at issue "would facilitate any decisions." However, Stalin continued to make a distinction between the Polish government in exile that was "closely connected with the Germans" and the Polish Provisional Government that the Soviet Union backed.

It was a stalemate. Churchill turned the conversation to the less confrontational question of Poland's borders.

Stalin again said that Russia was in favor of the reconstitution and expansion of Poland, "at the expense of Germany," a position Churchill and Roosevelt could both agree with. The Curzon Line, the exact location of which was ascertained on a map supplied by Bohlen, was informally agreed upon. Stalin marked up the map with a red pencil to show the areas east of the 1941 Soviet-Polish frontier and west of the Curzon Line that he expected would go back to Poland, which he stated was agreeable to him as long as the Soviet Union was given the Prussian ports of Königsberg and Tilsit.

Roosevelt then brought the conversation back to Germany; the question, as he saw it: whether or not to split it up.

Stalin replied unequivocally that Russia was in favor of its dismemberment.

Churchill, who looked forward to the reemergence of Germany as a viable power able to balance the Soviet Union on the Continent, said he was more interested in seeing Prussia, "the evil core of German militarism," separated out but that the southern states could become part of a Danubian confederation.

Roosevelt then presented his plan, which divided Germany into five autonomous parts: (1) Prussia rendered as small and weak as possible; (2) Hannover and the northwest section; (3) Saxony and Leipzig; (4) Hesse-Darmstadt; (5) Bavaria, Baden, and Würtemberg. The Kiel Canal and Hamburg, the Ruhr and the Saar, were to be under United Nations control.

Stalin liked Roosevelt's plan better than Churchill's because it was tougher on Germany but thought that neither went far enough. Stalin said that it would be the job of "any international organization" to neutralize the tendency of Germany to reunite and that the victorious nations "must have the strength to beat the Germans if they ever start on the path to a new war." This statement elicited from Churchill the question, reflecting his deep mistrust of Stalin, "whether Marshal Stalin contemplated a Europe composed of little states, disjoined, separated and weak." Stalin answered, not Europe, only Germany.

Churchill didn't believe him. He was firmly convinced that Stalin was out to weaken and perhaps occupy Western Europe. He would write to Anthony Eden within the month, "Although I have tried in every way to put myself in sympathy with these Communist leaders, I cannot feel the slightest trust or confidence in them."

Roosevelt, in contrast, did not doubt that Stalin's true aim in this case was, as he said, to weaken Germany but leave the rest of Western Europe as it was. In fact, he was correct: Stalin had no military designs on Western Europe. In contrast to German and Japanese racial pronouncements, Stalin did not believe that the Slavs were a master race destined to rule the world. He believed Communism was the economic model of the future and that eventually Communism would be adopted by the West because it was a more efficient form of government, but the task at hand was to win the war and secure the Soviet Union's borders, and that meant controlling Germany.

So obsessed was Stalin with the future of Germany that after he returned to Moscow, he meticulously edited the Russian part of the Tehran discussion to reflect what he said, marking changes in his own hand. The final Soviet document reads as follows: "Comrade Stalin declared that in relation to the aim of weakening Germany, the Soviet government preferred to dismember her. Comrade Stalin positively favoured Roosevelt's plan but without predetermining the number of states into which Germany is to be split. He came out against Churchill's plan for the creation after the splitting up of Germany of a new, unsustainable state like the Danubian Federation."

As the discussion wound down, Roosevelt threw in the hardly neutral information, given the discussion of dismemberment, that when Germany had been made up of 107 provinces, it had been less dangerous to civilization. Churchill confined himself to the response that he "hoped for larger units."

Winding up the session, following a statement from Churchill that the matter of Polish borders should be absolutely settled, Stalin once more declared that if Russia was given the northern part of East Prussia, running along the left bank of the Neman River and including Tilsit and Königsberg, he would accept the Curzon Line as the Polish-Soviet border.

They disbanded, to meet again at dinner. Roosevelt had asked to host the dinner because he knew he could rely on his efficient Filipino staff to make short work of it; Stalin and Churchill agreed.

At this last dinner, the final draft of the Iran Declaration proclaiming their goals was presented to them to read. The declaration on Iran that Roosevelt had insisted upon, drawn up by Hurley, which acknowledged Tehran's contribution to the Allied cause and its future right to be independent, was also presented. The three leaders studied the documents.

At the Moscow Conference a few weeks earlier, Stalin had opposed the issuance of any statement regarding policy toward Iran. Now, after a request for a proposal by the Iranians themselves, plus a personal appeal from the president, Stalin changed his mind and agreed to just such a statement.

All the arguments and changes had evidently been a strain on Stalin. As this last dinner drew to a close, Bohlen observed that he looked exhausted. As Stalin was reading the Russian text of a document, Bohlen briskly approached him from behind with a message from FDR. Stalin turned and snapped in irritation, "For God's sake let us finish this work." When he saw it was Bohlen, "for the first and only time he showed embarrassment."

The signing of the declaration on Iran provides an interesting glimpse into Stalin's reliance on Roosevelt. The official text for the three to sign was ready only in English. Harriman presented it to Stalin and asked him if he wanted it to be translated. Stalin indicated that that wasn't necessary and asked Pavlov to verbally translate it to him. After listening to Pavlov's translation, according to Harriman, "in my presence and Mr. Bohlen's [he] said that he approved the Declaration" and that because of the shortness of time he would agree to sign the English text. But he insisted Churchill sign first. Nor would he be second to sign.

"He said he would do so after the president. I then took the Declaration to the president, who signed it. Thereupon Stalin signed it forthwith."

That Churchill and Stalin signed it at all must have given the Iranians great hope for the future, because it called for "the maintenance of the independence, sovereignty and territorial integrity of Iran," which both Great Britain and the Soviet Union had been ignoring for years. When the two countries had invaded Iran in August 1941, just two months after Barbarossa, the code name for the German invasion of Russia, the shah had cabled FDR asking for his help. FDR had waited until the invasion was a fait accompli and then had soothed the shah with statements to the effect that the invasion was a temporary wartime measure designed to forestall seizure of the country by Hitler. He had then pushed Britain and Russia to make a statement (which they had done) that they would leave after Hitler was beaten. Iran then became eligible for Lend-Lease, which was liberally dispensed. The country was now relying on the United States for administrative as well as economic aid. The president took home from Tehran a carpet from the grateful shah and had it laid in his study.

The dinner broke up promptly at 10:30, by which time the evening had turned cold. Roosevelt was wheeled out onto the porch in his wheelchair and put into a car. The president undoubtedly left Tehran as he had come, in a nondescript limousine following a nondescript jeep, his destination Camp Amirabad, in the desert on the outskirts of Tehran, where American troops of the Persian Gulf Service Command were bivouacked. He and Hopkins spent the night there as guests of General Donald Connolly, an old friend of Hopkins's.

Of the final day, Roosevelt wrote in his diary, "The conferences have been going well—tho' I found I had to go along with the Russians on military plans. This morning the British came along, too, to my great relief."

The next morning Roosevelt toured the desert camp and gave rousing speeches to the sun-scorched troops and the soldiers in the post hospital:

> I have had conferences with Marshal Stalin and Mr. Churchill during the past four days—very successful too—laying military plans for cooperation between the three nations looking toward the winning of the war just as fast as we possibly can . . .

The other purpose was to talk over world conditions after the war—to try to plan a world for us and for our children when the war would cease to be a necessity. We have made great progress in that also.

At the Soviet legation at roughly the same time in the morning as FDR was addressing the soldiers, Valentin Berezhkov witnessed what he thought was Roosevelt's very dramatic leave-taking. He wrote that clad in a black cape and hat, wearing his pince-nez, smoking a cigarette in a long holder, "he," possibly the same Secret Service agent as before, was lifted into a waiting jeep. As the car began moving, continued Berezhkov's narrative, four detectives leaped onto the running boards, then two pulled submachine guns out of their jackets and lay on the front wings of the car. Berezhkov commented disapprovingly, "It seemed to me that the deliberate demonstration put on by the detectives could only attract the attention of any malefactors."

If Mike Reilly had known he had fooled someone as knowledgeable as Berezhkov, he would have been pleased.

Stalin and his party drove to Gale Morghe airport later in the morning, where two twin-engine passenger planes waited to take him and his party to Baku. Stalin left in the second plane. Upon arrival in Baku, he changed out of his smart marshal's outfit and into an ordinary soldier's greatcoat and cap with no markings or badges of rank. Within a short time a file of limousines appeared at the airport. Stalin got into the second car and sat next to the driver, his personal bodyguard got into the backseat, and the cortege sped off to the railroad station. There Stalin's special train, with its long saloon cars, waited to take him back to Moscow.

Stalin made one stop, to see for himself the unbelievable devastation of Stalingrad: lumps that had been walls, piles of rubble, isolated chimneys, charred ground, pockmarked holes—cellars—that marked where a building had stood; the remains of what had once been a thriving city. The train arrived back in Moscow the morning of the fourth day.

Stalin had to have been gratified by the conference. It was the first time since the revolution that he had attended an international conference outside the Soviet Union. Ten years earlier, Roosevelt's recognition of the Soviet Union had changed his pariah government into a legitimate, recognized member of the international community. Now he sat with Roosevelt and Churchill as an equal discussing the future of the world.

And he had found himself on the same wavelength with the president on a number of issues, something that he could not have anticipated. Roosevelt felt as he did that the dismemberment of Germany was necessary, that France should be stripped of its colonies, and that the Polish borders should shift westward to roughly the Curzon Line, in the process taking territory from Germany. Roosevelt's United Nations organization, as envisioned, with power residing in the four policemen, would make the Soviet Union one of the great powers of the world. It amounted to a new world order. Plus Overlord was about to be a reality.

AFTER ARRIVING IN CAIRO, Roosevelt sent two friendly cables to Stalin to thank him for his hospitality: "The conference, I consider, was a great success and I feel sure that it was an historic event in the assurance not only of our ability to wage war together but to work for the peace to come in the utmost harmony. I enjoyed very much our personal talks together."

Stalin cabled back to the president an unusually expansive message: "I agree with you . . . that our personal meetings were, in many respects, extremely important . . . Now there is confidence that our peoples will harmoniously act together during the present time as well as after the war is over . . . I also hope that our meeting in Tehran should not be regarded as the last one, and we shall meet again."

Roosevelt had told Stalin that he would make the appointment of the supreme commander of Overlord within three or four days or immediately after he and Churchill returned to Cairo.

Marshall, in Cairo, waiting expectantly to be named commander, cabled Secretary of War Stimson, one of his champions, on Friday that he was "probably going to take command very soon."

General Dwight David Eisenhower, Ike, as he was known, had been jumped by Marshall the year before over 366 officers to command the Anglo-U.S. forces in North Africa and Italy. During the time they spent together touring the battlefields, Roosevelt had made an intriguingly ambiguous statement: "You and I know who was the Chief of Staff during the last years of the Civil War but practically no one else knows . . . I hate to think that fifty years from now practically nobody will know who George Marshall was. That is one of the reasons why I want George to have the big Command—he is entitled to establish his place in history as a great General."

When he had decided to appoint Marshall chief of staff, FDR had asked advice of no one. Now he proceeded to ask everyone. Among those he consulted were General Pershing, hero of World War I, Admiral Leahy, Admiral King, General Arnold, Henry Stimson, and Harry Hopkins. The first four so respected General Marshall's effectiveness as leader of the competing Allied forces and services and his handling of the complexities of command that they thought he should stay doing just that instead of running Overlord. Hopkins and Stimson, on the other hand, wanted him to have the command. So did Stalin and Churchill.

Roosevelt, without explicitly saying so, had decided against it. According to Stimson, the matter came down to Roosevelt's wanting to appoint Marshall as commander while keeping him as chief of staff, simply detailing another man to work in Washington pro tem, therefore addressing the concerns of Leahy, King, and others. But Marshall insisted that if he took command, he would resign, on the grounds that the position of chief of staff "must be full and permanent in fairness to the man so chosen."

FDR decided to put the decision to Marshall. He sent Harry Hopkins to do the deed. Hopkins went to see Marshall before dinner the day after their arrival in Cairo. Wrote Marshall, Hopkins

> told me the President was in some concern of mind over my appointment . . . I merely endeavored to make it clear that I would go along wholeheartedly with whatever decision the President made . . . I declined to state my opinion. The next day the President had me call at his villa . . . In response to his questions, I recalled saying that I would not attempt to estimate my capabilities; the President would have to do that; I merely wished to make clear that whatever the decision, I would go along with it wholeheartedly . . . The President stated in completing our conversation, "I feel I could not sleep at night with you out of the country."

Roosevelt's cable to Stalin of his selection of Eisenhower as commander of Overlord went as usual via the Map Room in Washington, where it was coded and sent to the American embassy in Moscow, where it was decoded and retyped. Realizing its importance, Harriman, taking Bohlen with him so he could translate the message immediately, personally delivered it to Molotov at the Kremlin. As Harriman listened, Molotov called Stalin to tell him the news. After Stalin hung up, Molotov put down the receiver and announced to Harriman rather stiffly, "Marshal Stalin is satisfied with this decision. He considers Eisenhower a general of experience, especially in directing large forces and amphibious operations."

In fact, Stalin was so pleased that the final piece in the puzzle—the commander of the second front—had finally been decided upon that he edited the cable that went out to Roosevelt, writing, in his own hand, "I welcome the appointment of General Eisenhower."

The final night in Cairo, Elliott wrote, the only thing his father wanted to talk about was the cornerstone accomplishment of his month away from home: the United Nations: "People at home, congressmen, editorial writers, talk about the United Nations as something which exists only on account of war. The tendency is to snipe at it by saying that only because we are forced into unity by war are we unified. But war isn't the real force to unity. Peace is the real force. After the war— then is when I'm going to be able to make sure the United Nations are really the United Nations."

On the way home the president took pen to paper to write to Daisy Suckley: "The trip was almost completely satisfactory, specially the Russians." Another satisfaction was that during the trip forty-four congressional bills had been presented to Roosevelt for his signature. He had vetoed two. All had been returned to Congress within the stipulated time. When Roosevelt saw Stimson, who had been so worried that Churchill might talk him into delaying Overlord, he told him, "I have thus brought OVERLORD back to home safe and sound on the ways for accomplishment." Stimson, as a result, told journalists at a press conference that having just read the minutes of the conference, he was thrilled at what had been accomplished: "While of course, the nature and details of those decisions cannot be made public, I can say that the presence of Premier Stalin and of his companion at the conference, Marshal Voroshilov, has contributed mightily to the success of the conference. Marshal Stalin's power of lucid analysis and the fairness of his attitude contributed strongly to the solution of several long-standing problems."

Stimson almost always agreed with Roosevelt's decisions, although he could never figure out how the president ever reached a correct decision because his mental procedure was intuitive rather than logical. In addition, Stimson was not a politician; he did not understand the subtleties of Roosevelt's handling of people. His diary, therefore, is full of criticism of the process by which Roosevelt got from A to B, even though B was usually the result Stimson had hoped he would reach.

After reading the minutes of everything that had taken place in Cairo and in Tehran, Stimson missed the fact that Roosevelt had let Churchill go on at such length because it suited his purpose of exposing Churchill's strong anti-Soviet bias. Thus Stimson wrote,

> I thank the Lord Stalin was there. In my opinion he saved the day. He was direct and strong and he brushed away the diversionary attempts of the Prime Minister with a vigor which rejoiced my soul. Up to the time of his arrival, our side were at a disadvantage. First, because of the president's rather haphazard grasp of the situation and, second, because Marshall, who has been bearing the whole burden of it, has now been insistent about keeping himself more or less aloof because he feels he is an interested party. Therefore the first meeting before Stalin came in was shown by the minutes to have been a rather discouraging one without any very strong coordinated results being put forwards by our people. But when Stalin came in with his General Voroshilov they completely changed the situation and took the offensive for OVERLORD. They favored a supporting attack in the south of France and they strongly opposed the diversionary attacks in the eastern Mediterranean. In the end Stalin carried the day and I was delighted with it.

Stimson's worry over Roosevelt's casualness and seeming lack of direction, reflected in his diary entries, was a rather common complaint among those who worked for the president. But then, no one could ever quite follow the seeming vagaries of Roosevelt's mind.

Ambassador Harriman learned that in the aftermath of the meeting the Soviet government went to great pains to explain the importance of the conference conclusions to ordinary workers who might not otherwise learn of Russia's new world role and its new allies. The Yugoslav ambassador told him a factory worker described to him how "every brigade in the factory had been called together and a 'political' had explained the declaration and its significance. The workers had been encouraged to ask questions."

Groups of Americans wrote to FDR to register their enthusiasm. "Stupendous task you, our President, Prime Minister Winston Churchill, and Premier Stalin have undertaken to obviate the Fascist powers . . . will be immortalized in the future pages of history," wrote the crew of the USS *George Woodward.* Local 155 of the United Electrical, Radio, and Machine Workers wrote, "We greet with joy the decisions of that conference which spells quick and decisive victory."

The Big Three achievements at Tehran were front-page news all over America.

"A coordinated three-power multi-front attack designed to attain the Allies' first war aim, the destruction of the German Army, and the organization of peace after the war seemed one step nearer tonight after the Roosevelt-Churchill-Stalin meeting at Teheran," wrote James Reston in *The New York Times* on December 6. The previous January, *Time* magazine had anointed Stalin Man of the Year. If it had not been for Stalin, "Hitler would have been undisputed master of Europe." Of Stalin now *Time* magazine wrote, "Over the dead bodies of thousands of Germans he had guided the Soviet armies to the reconquest of some 325 thousands of square miles of Russian ruins since the winter offensive began in November 1942. His shadow spread longer over Eastern and Southern Europe. But no longer was Stalin the lone winner he had been in 1942. He now sought and acknowledged partnership with the other great powers."

Stalin's comment the night of Churchill's dinner regarding the might of American machines made it into the headlines of American papers even before Roosevelt had returned. "The greatest tribute possibly ever paid American industrial production came from Premier Stalin . . . in a toast . . . Without American machines the United Nations never could have won the war," enthused *The New York Times* on the second anniversary of Pearl Harbor.

The Soviet press gave wide and favorable publicity to the conference. *Izvestia* said the decisions taken had "historical importance for the fate of the entire world." *Pravda* called the Tehran Declaration "the harbinger not only of victory but of a long and stable peace." Stalin, an inveterate micromanager, not satisfied with the Tass headline "Conference of the Heads of the Governments of the Soviet Union, USA and Great Britain," changed it to "Conference of the Leaders of the Three Allied Powers."

Tass also published comments from the London *Times*, although after heavy editing by Molotov, who cut out signs of discord: "The road to this meeting for the three leaders was not an easy one. But have parted temporarily as real friends in spirit and in their goals."

Dr. Edvard Beneš, president of Czechoslovakia, who was in Moscow to sign a mutual assistance and defense treaty with Stalin when he returned from Tehran, told Ambassador Harriman that Stalin was "transformed" from the person he had last seen in 1935. Harriman transmitted Beneš's impressions in a cable to Washington:

> Modesty and calm have taken the place of the previous aggressiveness and excitability of the Soviets . . . There has emerged a vigorous nationalism, linked with Russia's past—Russia for the Russians, and not a base for international revolution. The Bolshevizing of other countries had been replaced as an objective by the determination to participate as a powerful nation in world affairs. Great satisfaction in the new relationships . . . was expressed by Stalin, who had been much impressed with the president and who felt that complete agreement on all questions, not of course in detail, but in approach, had been reached with him at Tehran.

U.S. embassy personnel in Moscow reported there was an almost "revolutionary change" in attitude toward America and Great Britain and that the papers almost daily mentioned the historic decisions taken. *Tass* gave prominent space to British Reuters: "Stalin's signature that signifies his complete approval of the English and American plans of cooperation in the military operations from the west and south, drives the final nail into the coffin of the German hopes to sow discord between the three great powers in the matter of waging war." Observed Harriman, "The new association with the United States and Great Britain has been woven into the fabric of the people's consciousness as a basic policy of the Soviet government."

To Marshal Georgi Zhukov, deputy supreme commander of the Red Army, Stalin commented, "Roosevelt has given his word that large-scale action will be mounted in France in 1944. I believe he will keep his word." He added, though, quite in character, "But even if he doesn't we have enough of our own forces to complete the rout of Nazi Germany."

ROOSEVELT'S SEVENTEEN-THOUSAND-MILE journey finally drew to an end on December 16, when the *Potomac* met the *Iowa* in Chesapeake Bay. As he wrote in his diary on that day, "The little *Potomac* has loomed 6 miles ahead at the mouth of the River and at 4:30 I will transfer to her . . . And tomorrow we should get to the Navy Yard in Washington at 9:30 & soon afterwards I will be at the W.H. & using the telephone. So will end a new Odyssey."

Later in the afternoon, aboard the *Potomac* and going through the mail pouch delivered by the Map Room watch officer, Lieutenant R. H. Myers of the U.S. Naval Reserve, he came upon a most intriguing item: up-to-the-minute blueprints of the German fortifications on the French coast. SIS, the acronym for the U.S. Signals Intelligence Service, was responsible for this brilliant coup. In 1940, SIS cryptanalysts had broken the Japanese diplomatic code. U.S. intelligence had been reading the Japanese diplomatic mail ever since. Of particular importance were the cables sent by Ōshima Hiroshi, the Japanese ambassador to Germany, who was a friend of Adolf Hitler's and various members of Hitler's circle and who carefully cabled home everything he heard in Berlin. Ōshima, son of a Japanese minister of war and a graduate of the Japanese military academy, who wanted the Japanese military establishment to join the war against the Soviet Union, regularly transmitted what he had learned about German war plans and military operations to Tokyo.

The detailed information Ōshima sent was transmitted in a Japanese code given the code name Purple by U.S. cryptanalysts. Frank B. Rowlett, a brilliant former schoolteacher, was in charge of the SIS team at Arlington Hall, Virginia, that broke the code after eighteen months of intense work on the Japanese machine cipher. Even though this seemed like a long time, Rowlett's boss, Major General Joseph Mauborgne, the head of SIS, so impressed that Rowlett and his team had pulled it off at all, began referring to the group as "magicians." As a result, Magic became the code word by which the decrypts were known.

Through Ōshima's cables a wealth of information was uncovered. Not only was Ōshima privy to the latest German war plans as told to him by the German high command, but he frequently inspected German military installations, and he always sent his government everything he had learned. General Marshall relied on Ōshima's reports as one of his main sources of information for learning of Hitler's plans.

Fortuitously for Roosevelt and the Allied cause, Ambassador Ōshima had toured the German defense installations on the French coast in October, discussed defense preparations with Field Marshal Gerd von Rundstedt and other high-ranking German officers, and written up the information for his superiors in Tokyo: the order of battle of all German armies engaged in coastal defense, the details of German defense installations from the Netherlands to the French Mediterranean coast. He sent it all.

The cable went on for pages. One section began,

All the German fortifications on the French coast are very close to the shore and it is quite clear that the Germans plan to smash any enemy attempt to land as close to the edge of the water as possible . . . Even the smallest forts are invested so that they can hold out independently for a very long time . . . This overall scheme is similar to defenses evident at the West Wall behind the Franco-German border, but the quality of the Atlantic Wall fortifications is ever so much better . . . The Strait of Dover area is given first place in the German Army's fortification scheme and troop dispositions, and Normandy and the Brittany peninsula come next.

Roosevelt read the detailed cable and sent it on to the Joint Chiefs of Staff. Just what they needed.

Having the blueprint was an incredible strategic and psychological asset; it virtually guaranteed the success of Overlord. If Roosevelt had had this information in hand at Tehran, he would have had an easier task demolishing Churchill's negative vibes, but still, to have it at all, to be able to lay plans with certainty, was a great triumph for the Allied cause. Churchill, too, was given access to Ōshima's material, and it made him more optimistic for the success of Overlord.

Also in the pouch was a communication from Churchill informing the president that the prime minister was in Carthage, sick, which Roosevelt promptly answered: "I am distressed about the pneumonia, and both Harry and I plead with you to be good and throw it off rapidly. I have just left the *Iowa* and am on my way up the Potomac."

The *Potomac* docked at Quantico the next morning. When Roosevelt appeared at the White House at 9:35, he was met by the entire cabinet, the heads of most of the alphabet agencies, Democratic congressional leaders, and a sprinkling of Republicans, all of whom were waiting in the diplomatic reception room.

FDR was dressed in a gray suit, sweater, and plaid shirt. "I would have dressed for the occasion if I had known [about] this," he quipped on viewing the large crowd.

"I do not remember ever seeing the president look more satisfied and pleased than he did that morning," recalled Sam Rosenman, speechwriter, good friend, and biographer. "He believed intensely that he had accomplished what he had set out to do—to bring Russia into co-operation with the Western powers in a formidable organization for the maintenance of peace—and he was glad . . . He was indeed the champ come back with the prize."

Roosevelt met with congressional leaders as his first order of business. He discussed his agenda with them—the major speech he was planning that would be his report to the American people on the conference. Not surprisingly, they suggested he make his report to a joint session of Congress. Roosevelt, so media conscious, so aware that not just America but the world would be listening to him, wanting to gather support for his vision of the postwar world, did not commit himself. By noon he had decided that he would not address Congress, that he would get maximum clout by giving a speech in the form of a fireside chat.

But that took a bit of planning; he could hold a press conference immediately to generate interest and support, and later in the day he did just that. By the time reporters saw him, he had changed into a gray tweed suit, green four-in-hand tie, and white shirt. As the journalists, more than a hundred strong, crowded around his desk in the Oval Office, Roosevelt opened his remarks by saying, "The discussions I hope will have definite and very beneficial effects for the postwar period, based on the general thought that when we win the war we don't want to have another one as long as this generation is alive."

He was smoking a cigarette "in the inevitable long holder," a journalist noted.

Asked what he thought of Stalin, Roosevelt answered, "I would call him something like me. He is a realist."

Asked whether Stalin shared the president's hope of preventing another war in this generation, Roosevelt answered, "Very definitely, if the people who want that objective will back it up."

Asked by May Craig, a reporter for some Maine newspapers, if he could tell them something more about Stalin, Roosevelt replied, "May, I don't write no social column," which elicited much laughter.

The press conference ended on a light note, with a reporter asking how he had withstood all the toasts at the dinners. Roosevelt replied, "We had one banquet where we had dinner in the Russian style. Very good dinner, too. Russian style means a number of toasts, and I counted up to three hundred and sixty-five toasts. And we all went away sober. It's remarkable what you can do, if you try."

Roosevelt chose to give his "summing up" speech as a fireside chat on the afternoon of Christmas Eve. That way he could tie in the objective—permanent peace—with the natural message of Christmas: peace on earth, goodwill to men.

He decided quite abruptly to give the speech at Hyde Park. It was the first Christmas in eleven years that the Roosevelts spent at Hyde Park. But on December 21, Harry Hopkins and his wife, Louise, moved out of the White House and into a town house at Thirty-Third and N Street in Georgetown. Losing Hopkins was a blow to Roosevelt, even though his daughter, Anna Boettiger, would within a short while move into the Lincoln suite in place of the Hopkinses.

Louise Hopkins at first had been enchanted to be so intimate with the Roosevelts, so at the center of things, but as the reality of living in such a small space sank in—all she and Harry had with them were books, a radio-phonograph, a bit of glassware, and a cocktail shaker that stood on top of a bookcase—her nesting instincts came to the fore. She also wanted more time with her husband.

She was jealous at the way FDR preempted her husband at all hours of the day, starting with breakfast and continuing on through dinner in the evening. Hopkins seemed happy to leave. "It is the first time I have had Christmas in my own house for years, and Louise made it the pleasantest that I think I ever had in my life," he wrote to his son Stephen, a marine in the South Pacific. (Sadly, within a few weeks Hopkins collapsed and spent the next year being treated for his stomach problems in various hospitals.)

Roosevelt acted impulsively but never by chance: it was the combination of Hopkins's departure from the White House and the added emotional value he perceived might be gained in delivering a speech from his true home that moved him to return to Hyde Park in the freezing twenty-degree weather.

This Christmas Eve speech was one that the president took extra care with. Robert E. Sherwood, Sam Rosenman, and Hopkins were the chief contributors. After the usual six or seven drafts, Roosevelt might say, according to another speechwriter, John Gunther, "We're getting along fine now. Let's go back to the beginning and start all over." This Christmas Eve speech went through eight drafts, remembered Rosenman; it took intense work.

Roosevelt gave the speech sitting at his desk in his study, a small, cluttered room off the back hall that had been his schoolroom as a boy. Cameras with accompanying klieg lights faced the president from every direction, microphones and telephones covered his desk, wires for everything snaked all over the floor. Watching, crowded into one corner of the study, were his sons Franklin and John, who had secured leave from their units, various grandchildren, neighbors including Henry Morgenthau and his wife, Elinor, and Daisy Suckley. Eleanor Roosevelt found a space on the floor behind the desk with her daughter, Anna. Newsreels of the speech would be shown that week in movie theaters across the country.

Precisely at 3:00 p.m., Roosevelt began. He underlined the milestones reached during his recent trip:

> To use an American and somewhat ungrammatical colloquialism, I may say that I "got along fine" with Marshal Stalin. He is a man who combines a tremendous, relentless determination with a stalwart good humor. I believe he is truly representative of the heart and soul of Russia; and I believe that we are going to get along very well with him and the Russian people—very well indeed.

Then he introduced his concept of the four policemen:

> Britain, Russia, China, and the United States and their allies represent more than three-quarters of the total population of the earth. As long as these four Nations with great military power stick

together in determination to keep the peace there will be no possibility of an aggressor Nation arising to start another world war.

But those four powers must be united with and cooperate with all the freedom-loving peoples of Europe, and Asia, and Africa, and the Americas. The rights of every Nation, large or small, must be respected and guarded as jealously as are the rights of every individual within our own Republic.

The Cairo and Teheran Conferences, however, gave me my first opportunity to meet the Generalissimo, Chiang Kai-shek, and Marshal Stalin—and to sit down at the table with these unconquerable men and talk with them face to face. We had planned to talk to each other across the table at Cairo and Teheran; but we soon found that we were all on the same side of the table. We came to the Conferences with faith in each other. But we needed the personal contact. And now we have supplemented faith with definite knowledge.

Nor did he forget the prime minister:

Of course, as you all know, Mr. Churchill and I have happily met many times before, and we know and understand each other very well. Indeed, Mr. Churchill has become known and beloved by many millions of Americans.

For the first time he tempered his "unconditional surrender" ultimatum, as *The New York Times* noticed, saying,

We wish them [the German people] to have a normal chance to develop, in peace, as useful and respectable members of the European family. But we most certainly emphasize the word "respectable" for we intend to rid them once and for all of Nazism and Prussian militarism and the fantastic and disastrous notion that they constitute the "master race."

In private he was not quite so optimistic. He admitted to Hopkins that he had found Stalin tougher than he expected, although, coining a word, he said he was "getatable." Bill Hassett, Roosevelt's assistant secretary, a discreet ex-newspaperman, asked him what impression of Stalin he would permanently retain. He replied, "A man hewn out of granite."

As Roosevelt was aware, Stalin had accommodated him on three important issues before the meeting was even scheduled: religion, the Comintern, and China. His about-face on China, at the Moscow Conference, agreeing that it could be the fourth policeman, had been particularly gratifying because Stalin had written specifically to Roosevelt before it began, "It can be considered as agreed upon, that the question of the declaration of the four nations is not included in the agenda of the conference."

Hopkins had told Andrei Gromyko, when he was Soviet chargé d'affaires in Washington, that Roosevelt had had reservations about Stalin and the future of Soviet-American relations. Roosevelt expected to size up the Soviet leader at Tehran and explore the possibilities of coexistence: "It depends on many factors—the main one being the stance the USSR adopts as a great world power." Then Hopkins had assured Gromyko that "he [FDR] obviously believes that the USA ought to do everything possible to lay the foundations of good future relations with the USSR."

Roosevelt's comment to Eleanor Roosevelt afterward suggests that he wasn't actually sure he had succeeded: "My husband told me that he felt there was a great distrust on the part of Marshal Stalin when they first met, and he had no idea, on leaving, whether he had been able to dissipate any of it or not. He added that he intended to see that we kept our promises to the letter."

Roosevelt continued to worry whether Stalin remained convinced. Did Stalin really believe that Roosevelt's insistence on an international basis for United Nations actions was the best solution? He feared that Stalin might fall back to his original position, similar to Churchill's regional plan. He confided to Senator Tom Connally that neither Stalin nor Churchill was entirely convinced of the rightness of his vision. "I'll have to work on both of them," he advised the senator.

But to Frances Perkins, secretary of labor, FDR had been more upbeat. "You know," he said to her, "I really think the Russians will go along with me about having no spheres of influence and about agreements for free ports all over the world . . . ports which can be used freely at all times by all the allies. I think that is going to be the solution." He thought with her wide range of labor and business acquaintances she could provide input: "I don't know a good Russian from a bad Russian. I can tell a good Frenchman from a bad Frenchman. I can tell a good Italian from a bad Italian. I know a good Greek when I see one. But I don't understand the Russians. I just don't know what makes them tick . . . find out all you can and tell me from time to time."

Roosevelt held another press conference on December 28 in which he summed up the years before the war and the danger of retreating back into isolationism. Interestingly, his imagery was of a country finally standing on its own two feet, something he must have psychologically talked himself into believing he too did on his own. "Old Dr. New Deal" dealt with internal problems such as saving the banks, aiding the farmers, putting in unemployment insurance. Then it was time for "Dr. Win-the-War." Now "the result is that the patient is back on his feet. He has given up his crutches. He isn't wholly well yet, and he won't be until he wins the war. And when victory comes, the program of the past, of course, has got to be carried on, in my judgment, with what is going on in other countries—postwar program—because it will pay. We can't go into an economic isolationism, any more than it would pay to go into a military isolationism."

Clearly the job now was to work out the steps necessary to structure the postwar world. But the time wasn't ripe nor the plans sufficiently jelled for Roosevelt to discuss them yet with the American people.

Stalin rarely gave speeches. Mikhail Kalinen, president of the Soviet Union, gave a celebratory New Year's Day speech. He called the Tehran Conference "in reality, the greatest event of our times, a historical landmark in the struggle with the German aggressor. All effort of the Germans to separate freedom loving nations failed. The leaders of the three great powers reached full agreement on questions of war and peace."

Certainly he felt reassured by Roosevelt. In fact, from Stalin's point of view, Roosevelt was the dream American president. Actually, he always had been. What Stalin saw was that he was offering the Soviet Union a partnership. Russia, so lately the sick man of Europe, was going to emerge from the war "a powerful nation in world affairs." That made him one of the two most powerful men in the world.

Some weeks after Tehran, Roosevelt chatted up Andrei Gromyko when they met. Here is Roosevelt, as recorded by Gromyko, very aware of his words, once again carefully distancing himself from Churchill: "He began by emphasizing the good terms he was on with Stalin. He then summarized how the conference had gone, and finally he told me: 'To achieve agreement, it was often necessary to put pressure on Churchill. He turns towards compromise rather slowly, I'm afraid. But turn he did, and we reached some pretty useful understandings.'" As he talked about Churchill, Gromyko noted, "the President bestowed on me one of his charming 'Roosevelt' smiles and made it plain that the British prime minister was a partner who gave him plenty of trouble."

In early February there was a flurry of worry in Washington when suddenly *Pravda* made a savage attack on Wendell Willkie, FDR's Republican opponent in the 1940 election. Willkie was on a campaign swing through the western states in search of the Republican nomination for 1944, which was getting quite a bit of media attention. The *Pravda* attack didn't have much to go on, except that when Willkie and Stalin had met the previous year, they had discussed Eastern Europe. Now *Pravda* harrumphed, "It is high time it was understood that the question of the Baltic States is an internal Soviet matter which is none of Mr. Willkie's business." Willkie had been stunned by the attack, according to Clark Kerr, the British ambassador, who had talked to him during a visit to the United States, because he had always been a strong supporter of Soviet aid and the *Pravda* article made him look "ridiculous." However, calm was restored after Clark Kerr informed Harriman that when he told Stalin of Willkie's reaction, Stalin had remarked that he "liked Willkie, regretted the incident and would send him a cable," possibly saying in the cable, "I like you but I don't want you to be President." His popularity had evidently worried Stalin.

Churchill, continuing in his effort to postpone D-day, also needed dealing with. Writing from Marrakesh, Morocco, he had a fistful of new reasons to postpone Overlord. He wrote FDR that to be on the safe side, the initial cross-channel assault should be made with heavier forces, and because it would take more time to assemble them, he wasn't alone in thinking the operation should be delayed. Churchill continued, "The Commanders feel they would have a better chance . . . The ground will be drier for U.J.'s great operations."

Roosevelt answered him very coolly: "In Teheran U.J. was given a promise that OVERLORD be launched during May and supported by the strongest possible Anvil at about the same time and that he agreed to plan for simultaneous Russian attack."

7

STALIN SEARCHES FOR AN ALLY

Lenin had his eye on America from the very beginning of his accession to power, before, even, that power was consolidated—when the Red Army was still fighting White Russian forces, Allied armies were maintaining a blockade, and famine was pervasive. The Council of People's Commissars, the highest government council, on the first day of 1919, pondered how to establish diplomatic relations with the United States. Lenin, chairman of the council, and Stalin, his faithful shadow in those early years, viewed America as a possible ally in an otherwise hostile world, as a country that could shield them from European aggression, at least until they could stand on their own two feet. On January 1, 1919, therefore, the Council of People's Commissars issued a remarkable document:

> On the problem of our relationships with the United States. The Soviet Russia should set herself free out of the iron circle she has been surrounded with. Otherwise, she will perish . . . It is only the United States of America that may help the Soviet Government since they need friendship with the Republican Russia in the interests of their domestic and foreign politics. They need: first, markets for the products of their industry; second, opportunities for profitable investment of their capitals; third to weaken English influence in Europe . . . The relations between the United States and Japan are not sincere . . . The war between them is inevitable . . . It is first of all necessary to enter into relationship with the United States . . . Entering into relationship with the United States

is the issue of paramount national importance and *the fate of Soviet Russia depends on its successful resolution.*

The hope was that recognition by America was achievable because the United States needed Soviet markets, and it feared, as did the Soviet Union, Japanese expansion. Commerce, always the first step, would pave the way to diplomatic relations. Lenin's view never changed. The statement America is "the principal force in the world. All possible means will have to be employed, somehow or other to come to an understanding with the United States," appeared in *Izvestia* two years later.

Lenin died on January 21, 1924. Stalin was by then general secretary of the Central Committee and head of the government. He too wanted to establish a dialogue with America, particularly after the European countries, one by one, and finally Great Britain granted recognition. But America remained out of reach: Harding, Coolidge, and Hoover would have nothing to do with the Soviet Union. By 1930, Stalin, fed up with his lack of progress in gaining recognition, vented his annoyance to the *New York Times* Moscow correspondent Walter Duranty: "America knows where we stand . . . We have done what we could, but we won't hang on their necks. We still are willing to do what I said before: get the debt question settled by the payment of an extra percentage on credits or a loan and resume normal relations, as we have done with the rest of the great powers." He went on, "A debt settlement with America—that is easy enough; it is a comparatively small matter, anyway."

Stalin watched for every new blip in American foreign relations that might involve Russia and might jump-start trade between the two countries. The year 1931 came and went. He was told, "The major issue is the issue of our tactics for the coming year, the latter looks like to be no less difficult than the previous . . . The banks of Morgan . . . the DuPont group—refused to engage in any talks . . . the time for Russian affairs has not come."

Roosevelt, when still governor of New York, called in Walter Duranty, one of the few Americans who knew anything about Soviet Russia, and quizzed him about the Soviet economy, particularly about its gold production and capacity to pay for goods it might buy. Four months after taking office, he decided to pursue recognition. It wasn't that he admired Stalin.

Stalin, age forty; Vladimir Lenin; and Mikhail Kalinen, president of the Soviet Union, March 1919

Alexander Troyanovsky, Russian ambassador to the United States, and Constantine Oumansky, who would succeed him as ambassador, flank Grover Whalen, president of the 1939 World's Fair, to finalize Russia's participation at the fair.

Reich foreign minister Joachim von Ribbentrop and Stalin look on as Vyacheslav Molotov examines the Nonaggression Pact allying Germany and the Soviet Union. Ambassador Friedrich-Werner von der Schulenberg is at the extreme right.

Von Ribbentrop (on Stalin's right) and Stalin both smile as Molotov signs the Nonaggression Pact, August 23, 1939.

Von Ribbentrop flew back to Berlin and went directly from the airport to Hitler. Hermann Göring, commander-in-chief of the Luftwaffe, looks on.

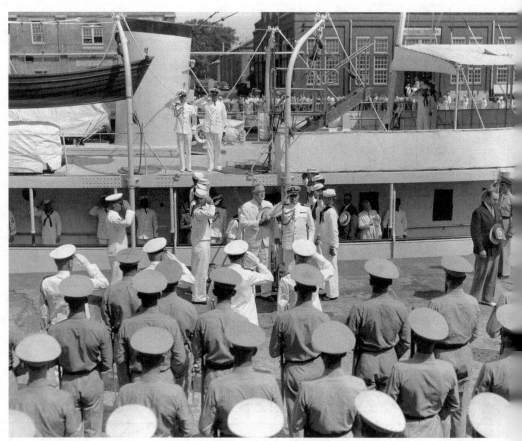

Preparing for war. FDR at Norfolk, Virginia, Navy Yard, July 29, 1940.

America, in the depths of the Depression, badly needed markets for its farmers and its factories; in addition, Japan was pressing into China. The U.S. ambassador to Japan, Joseph C. Grew, saw how quickly FDR had grasped that recognition would address both problems. "He said not a word about Manchuria but started building up the fleet and recognized Soviet Russia." FDR accepted that Stalin was a dictator, as he made clear to Henry Goddard Leach, editor of the magazine *The Forum,* in 1930, when Leach wanted him to step in and take control of New York's cities. FDR wrote to him, "I go along with you 100% in the thought that something must be done, but the answer is not State control or Federal control. That is moral cowardice and leads the country straight for the type of government now in effect in Russia and Italy. The editor of the *Forum* in the year 2030 will recognize that Mussolini and Stalin were not mere distant relatives, but were blood brothers."

By June 1933, the idea of recognizing the Soviet Union had gone mainstream. The U.S. Board of Trade, the dean of the Harvard Business School, and the Foreign Policy Association, among others, backed the reestablishment of diplomatic ties with Russia. Many of the important U.S. newspapers as well were in favor of such a move. Commented Roy Howard, chairman of the board of the Scripps Howard Newspapers, "I think the menace of Bolshevism in the United States is about as great as the menace of sunstroke in Greenland or chilblains in the Sahara."

Because most of the State Department's foreign service officers were so opposed to the move, Roosevelt simply bypassed the department and in August 1933 put Henry Morgenthau, his neighbor and friend, whom he was about to name secretary of the Treasury, in charge of the first step: putting out trade feelers. At lunch one day with FDR, Morgenthau was unburdening himself about the problems he was running into caused on the one hand by the lack of authority on the part of the Russians he was dealing with and on the other by the roadblocks put up by the Reconstruction Finance Corporation that would need to finance loans to the Russians. If he could work out a deal, Morgenthau worriedly remarked to the president, he would be a hero, but if he couldn't, he would have to leave Washington. Roosevelt replied, "Well, of course, you know that I stand back of you in these negotiations, and if you have to leave Washington I will leave with you."

Nevertheless, realizing that Morgenthau's effort was not working, and undoubtedly by this time having apprised members of the State Department that negotiations, however preliminary, were at last beginning, he turned to them for help. With Hull, he crafted a letter to Mikhail Kalinin, president and nominal head of the Soviet Union, asking him to send a representative to Washington to work out the opening of diplomatic relations between their two countries. When it was received in the Soviet Union, it was huge news and incredibly welcome. Radio broadcasts in the Soviet Union had an enormous impact; every home, no matter how humble, had a radio, a radio with only one channel—the government channel. (For this reason radios didn't look like Western radios; there was no dial: a radio was either on or off. Radio was the ideal medium for a totalitarian government to use to educate its populace.) Now Soviet radio, a political tool of the government that reached every home, blasted out the news.

Russians across the land were thrilled by Roosevelt's letter: there was a sense of exhilaration. It was to Soviet citizens as if the Soviet Union had finally arrived. Even the lowliest workers felt it. Charles Thayer, a West Point graduate in Moscow studying to be a foreign service officer, remembered being "awakened one night by the hotel night porter who told me with pathetic excitement that the radio had just announced that Roosevelt had written a letter to Kalinin hinting at reestablishment of relations."

Within weeks, Maxim Litvinov, foreign commissar (minister) of the Soviet Union, was on the high seas bound for the United States. FDR, taking no chances with the State Department, decided to personally handle negotiations and had Litvinov brought to the White House for private discussions. Over several days the two men resolved the difficult issues of freedom of religion for Americans in the Soviet Union, which Russia did not wish to grant, and payment to Americans for their holdings in Russia seized by the Bolshevik government after the revolution and reached a gentleman's agreement on the size of the debt incurred by Russia prior to the Soviet takeover that had to be paid. Diplomatic relations between the two countries were resumed on November 16, 1933.

The following day at the cabinet meeting, Roosevelt proudly recounted how persuasive he had been with Litvinov, particularly on the subject of religion. After Litvinov said that they had all the freedom of religion in Russia they needed, and no one was punished for going to church, merely discouraged, he had replied as follows:

"You know, Max, your good old father and mother, pious Jewish people, always said their prayers. I know they must have taught you to say prayers . . ." By this time Max was as red as a beet and I said to him, "Now you may think you're an atheist . . . but I tell you, Max, when you come to die . . . you're going to be thinking about what your father and mother taught you . . ." Max blustered and puffed and said all kinds of things, laughed and was very embarrassed, but I had him. I was sure from the expression of his face and his actions that he knew what I meant and that he knew I was right.

Litvinov's reaction to the president's statement is unknown: whether it was agreement, amazement, or, as Frances Perkins hazarded, embarrassment. But the result was that the president got his way.

FDR sent as ambassador, as expected, William Bullitt and armed him with a long, detailed, unusual letter of advice, for if he was pleased that he had finally gotten America to recognize the potentially powerful nation, he was under no illusions about its dangerous strangeness:

Dear Bill: January 7, 1934

It is clear to me that the unusual difficulties presented by the problem of establishing an Embassy and Consulate in Moscow require unusual treatment. You will be more or less in the position of Commander Byrd—cut off from civilization and I think you should organize your expedition as if you were setting out on a ship which was to touch no port for a year.

FDR then went into a detailed list of what he would need: automobiles and the establishment of a commissary to supply all needs from food to office machines and supplies. He recommended bringing doctors (he suggested setting up a small operating room, as well as an isolation ward for contagious diseases) and finding tennis courts for recreation. But it was his advice on diplomatic conduct that is most illuminating:

In addition to the points enumerated above, it seems to me essential that all our diplomatic, consular, military and naval representation in the USSR should be forbidden to indulge in spying of any kind and should be instructed to cultivate the frankest and most direct relations with the members of the Soviet Government. You will, of course, warn all the members of the staff of both Embassy and Consulate in Russia that they will be spied upon constantly and that they should be on their guard against communicating at any time official secrets of any kind to anyone.

In the Soviet Union, the news was greeted with great joy; the newspapers acclaimed Roosevelt as a hero. Large photographs of the president appeared on the front pages of all the newspapers, columns and columns were devoted to the story, and the event was painted as a personal victory for the president, who was—the highest praise a Communist could bestow—referred to as a champion of the working class. "The laboring masses of the Soviet Union warmly greet this new victory for the cause of peace," enthused *Pravda*. "It is necessary to pay full tribute to the initiative taken by the President of the United States. The question of normal relations was placed in his agenda after his inauguration. Mr. Roosevelt found it necessary to overcome not a few prejudices in American bourgeois circles before he was able to bring this matter to a successful conclusion."

Izvestia cast the event in terms of a class war: "The United States, the greatest capitalist power in the world, has at last been 'compelled' to establish normal diplomatic relations." It was, the editorial continued, "the end of a long drawn out struggle which the progressive elements of the American bourgeoisie had been carrying on for the recognition of the U.S.S.R." Because nothing was published in the Soviet Union without the knowledge and approval of Stalin, the articles in both papers amounted to a salute from Stalin to the president of "the greatest capitalist power in the world."

"By all appearances a decided and courageous political leader," Stalin was quoted as saying a month after recognition. "He is a realist and knows facts as they are."

When Ambassador Bullitt reached Moscow in December, Stalin gave him a dinner in the Kremlin, something unheard of in Russian diplomatic history. In his toast to FDR at the dinner he gave notice that he had been following FDR's political fortunes and political enemies, particularly Hamilton Fish, saying, "To President Roosevelt, who in spite of the mute growls of the Fishes dared to recognize the Soviet Union." In 1934, Stalin said to Bullitt, "President Roosevelt is today, in spite of being the leader of a capitalist nation, one of the most popular men in the Soviet Union." Later in the year Stalin seemed to entertain the idea that FDR not only was admirable but might, in fact, have in mind socialist goals, saying to the English journalist H. G. Wells, "Undoubtedly Roosevelt stands out as one of the strongest figures among all the captains of the contemporary capitalist world." Not that he had any doubts, he told Wells, "about the personal abilities, talent and courage of President Roosevelt. But if the circumstances are unfavorable, the most talented captain cannot reach the goal."

On no other person except Lenin did Stalin ever heap such praise.

Part of the reason Stalin so happily welcomed the new relationship with the United States was that Hitler, who had come to power in 1933, was beginning his propaganda campaign against Slavs, Jews, and other non-European races. *Mein Kampf,* the führer's part-autobiographical, part-political tract, published in the mid-1920s, was permeated with violent anti-Slav, anti-Soviet venom. In it Hitler was quite explicit about his plans to colonize Slav lands with worthy German farmers. ("If we talk about new soil and territory in Europe today, we can think primarily only of Russia and its vassal border states . . . the German plow which needs only to be given land by the sword.")

Stalin was hoping that the United States would help the Soviets by selling them various things they would need in case of war, a necessity because Hitler had made no secret of his plans for Russia. In 1936, Germany laid down the keel of the *Bismarck,* a battleship eight hundred feet long, carrying eight fifteen-inch guns, manned by a crew of more than two thousand men, capable of attaining a speed of thirty knots, although heavily armored—the largest ship Germany had ever built. Stalin decided the Soviet Union needed a battleship too—an even larger one. Because the Soviet Union did not have the facilities to build such a huge ship, he set out to have it built in the United States. Stalin appointed as his chief negotiator Sam Carp and gave his company, Carp Export & Import Corporation, $200 million—a huge sum in those days—to draw on, with full authority to enter into contracts with shipbuilders. There was precedent, as Stalin, history buff, knew: during the Crimean War with England ninety years earlier a private U.S. firm had built a steamship for the Russian government. Stalin instructed Carp to ask for a super battleship with sixteen-inch guns—guns even more powerful than the *Bismarck*'s. Carp, an American citizen who lived in Connecticut, brother to Molotov's wife, Polina, worked diligently on the project, but almost immediately he ran into problems caused by Chief of Naval Operations William Leahy and Secretary of the Navy Claude A. Swanson, both of whom, strongly anti-Communist as was most of the navy brass, in concert blocked the project. When word that the navy was blocking the proposed battleship deal reached Secretary of State Hull, he laid the matter to the president. At a cabinet meeting on April 3, 1937, recorded Harold Ickes, secretary of the interior, "It was evident that the President saw no objection to this ship's being built on one of our yards, and neither did Hull. The President told Swanson to tell any shipbuilding company that it was a private concern and that this was a private contract and it could do as it pleased about the matter."

However, naval officers at various ranks, all of whom viewed the Soviet Union as a potential enemy, threatened companies that wished to sign on to the project with the loss of future contracts. Bethlehem Steel, which had been working on designs for the ship, privately admitted that the Soviet order "would merely lead to impossible controversies with the Navy Department." Carp persevered. In February 1938, the battleship was again brought to Roosevelt's attention. FDR "expressed the hope that a battleship in accordance with the plans could be constructed in this country." On April 8, Roosevelt said again that he "saw no objection to the project or the disclosure of the design to the Russians." Still, construction had not yet started.

The importance of this project to Stalin cannot be overestimated. On June 5, 1938, Ambassador Joseph E. Davies was accorded what the world believed was a signal honor when he made his last formal parting call on President Kalinin and Premier Molotov before leaving and taking on his next post, as ambassador to Belgium. Upon arrival in the Kremlin, Davies first paid his respects to Kalinin, who said he could understand Davies leaving, for "the life of a diplomat in Moscow was not altogether agreeable and had its limitations; for the reason that contacts between officials of the Soviet Union and the Diplomatic Corps did not generally obtain as they did in other countries." Then Davies had been taken down a long corridor to another section of the building and ushered into Molotov's office. Scarcely were he and Molotov seated when Stalin walked in.

The rest of the diplomatic corps and Davies himself thought Stalin met with him because he was highly pleased with him—he continued to believe this for the rest of his life—but the reason Stalin met with Davies was that he knew Davies was a conduit to Roosevelt and he wanted to push forward getting the battleship built.

Stalin began the meeting by telling Davies that he couldn't understand why the battleship project was not going forward, that the Soviet Union was prepared to pay cash, that this would provide employment to the unemployed in America. He made the leading comment (given that he knew Davies and the president were close friends and knew the lack of progress on the battleship was because of opposition from high-level government personnel) that "if the President of the United States wanted it done he felt sure that the army and navy technicians could not stop it, and that it could be lawfully done."

Davies faithfully transmitted Stalin's concerns to FDR. Three days later, June 8, FDR, saying there was no objection to the project, that he "hoped it would be carried out," ordered the navy to assist the architects, shipbuilders, and Soviet officers to facilitate the building of what had now grown to an order for several ships. Further, FDR ordered that to get around uncooperative naval personnel, an officer of flag rank be appointed to take full charge of the project. On June 17 the State Department "relayed the good news" to the Soviet ambassador, Alexander Troyanovsky. Glacial progress followed; although one ship's hull was completed, bureaucratic opposition continued; no ship was ever built. The Hitler-Stalin pact put an end to the enterprise. From this episode Stalin might have learned that Roosevelt was sympathetic to the Soviet plight and the danger that Hitler represented but that he didn't always get his way.

Stalin stayed interested in keeping in America's good graces and making a good impression. When he was called by Grover Whalen, the head of the 1939 World's Fair in New York, sometime in 1937 about funding a Russian pavilion, Stalin agreed to talk to him and, at the end of a half-hour telephone conversation, to pay $4 million to put up a large pavilion in a choice location. It was Whalen's first large-scale foreign contract. The resulting first-rate Russian pavilion included a life-size copy of the interior of the Mayakovskaya subway station. So entranced were the various visitors and officials that the designer of the station, Alexey Dushkin, was awarded the Grand Prize of the fair.

The menace of Hitler was constantly at the forefront of Stalin's and Molotov's minds in 1938. Stalin was strengthening Soviet defenses. In April he stepped up Soviet production of airplanes to four hundred a month, forty-eight hundred a year. From 1934 to 1937 the percentage of the total Soviet government revenue devoted to military purposes rose from 3.3 percent to 22 percent. A third five-year plan was published and implemented to continue adding to the industrial strength of the country.

NINETEEN THIRTY-EIGHT was the year Germany's armies began marching across Europe. Hitler announced the *Anschluss* with Austria and accomplished it with a bloodless invasion on March 12. In September, in the misbegotten hope that this would slake Hitler's thirst for territory, Prime Minister Neville Chamberlain of Britain, Prime Minister Édouard Daladier of France, and Prime Minister Benito Mussolini of Italy flew to Munich and signed an agreement ceding Germany the Sudetenland, the German-speaking part of Czechoslovakia.

In 1939, as it became obvious that Hitler and his Wehrmacht were ready to spring again, the question that occupied the international community was not so much if as where the next strike would be.

Most Americans still thought of Europe's problems as being as far away as the moon. Isolationists believed the oceans were impenetrable moats that protected America from harm. Roosevelt didn't. He had been influenced at an early age by Admiral Alfred Mahan's *Influence of Sea Power upon History* (according to his mother, he buried himself in it "until he had practically memorized the whole book") and found incomprehensible the isolationist idea that America could retreat from the world, safe behind the Atlantic and the Pacific Oceans. From Mahan he had learned that if a country did not defend and patrol its oceans, its shores could always be breached; a nation's commerce, its economic health, depended on freedom of the seas.

The president decided to discuss the growing danger to the country in his annual message to Congress on January 4, 1939. He pondered over the right words for days, remembered the speechwriter Sam Rosenman, intent as he was to alert people and get his message across without raising the hackles of pacifists and isolationists—the vast majority of citizens—who still believed America could stay untouched, no matter what happened in Europe, no matter how many countries Hitler and Mussolini overran.

He had begun to prepare America for war in various ways, which he carefully didn't mention. He explicitly couched his words in terms of defense of American institutions and stressed religion throughout. He referred to God and religion nine times. "Storms from abroad directly challenge three institutions indispensable to Americans, now as always," he said. "The first is religion. It is the source of the other two—democracy and international good faith . . . Religion, by teaching man his relationship to God, gives the individual a sense of his own dignity . . . Democracy, the practice of self-government, is a covenant among free men to respect the rights and liberties of other nations of men."

On the other hand, he wanted to warn Hitler that America would fight if provoked too far. Therefore, he ended by saying, "In our foreign relations we have learned from the past what not to do. From new wars we have learned what we must do. We have learned that effective timing of defense and the distant points from which attacks may be launched are completely different from what they were twenty years ago."

To the three writers working with him on the speech—Tom Corcoran, Ben Cohen, and Sam Rosenman—he said, so that they were absolutely clear on how he felt about Chamberlain and the Munich Agreement, "We can do business with him [Hitler] all right but in the process we would lose everything that America stands for."

As the threat of Hitler grew, the countries within marching distance of the Wehrmacht sought to make alliances, the Soviet Union among them. Poland, the only country, after Hitler annexed Czechoslovakia and Austria, still remaining between Germany and Russia, was torn between fear of newly militant Germany and fear of its ancient borderland foe: Russia. The enmity between Russia and Poland dated back centuries. In Red Square stands the famous statue that commemorates the two Russian heroes—the prince and the butcher—who threw the Poles out of the Kremlin in 1612. The sculpture is the only structure besides Lenin's tomb in that vast space, testimony to how long and deep the quarrel between the two countries ran.

Even so, Polish public opinion—although muted in a feudalist society still run by colonels and landed aristocrats—was strongly anti-German. The colonels in power, however, and particularly Poland's powerful foreign minister, Jósef Beck, who controlled foreign policy, were strongly pro-German. Beck came away saying, after a meeting with Hitler at Berchtesgaden, "If the Soviet Union is militarily feeble, what good is it to be tied to it; if the Soviet Union is strong they will never leave." Even in the face of Hitler's insistent and patently false claims of Polish atrocities against Germans as the rationale for threatening to grab Danzig, the Polish port on the Baltic, as well as taking control of the Polish Corridor, Beck clung to the belief that Hitler was not going to attack Poland. It was a fatal mistake. (One interesting explanation for Poland's otherwise inexplicable mésalliance has always been a suspicion that Beck was a German agent and that Hitler had talked him into a German alliance by dangling before him the prospect of Poland's claiming a piece of the Ukraine. This has the ring of truth, for his young son Andrzej, whom he sent out of harm's way to Loomis, an exclusive prep school in America, would find, after his father's death, among his prized possessions a photograph album consisting of his father posed with Nazi generals and various officials of the Nazi government elite.)

STALIN WANTED AN ALLIANCE with Chamberlain and Daladier because there was no other choice: there were no countries other than Britain and France to which he could turn to protect the Soviet Union from Hitler.

He made a speech broadcast over the radio to the nation and the world on March 10, 1939, on the occasion of the Eighteenth Party Congress. To the assembled Soviet delegates in the great hall built in 1935, equipped with thirteen hundred desks, one for each representative of each republic, he said,

> But war is inexorable. It cannot be hidden under any guise. For no "axis," "triangles" or "anti-Comintern pacts" can hide the fact that . . . Germany has seized Austria and the Sudeten region, that Germany and Italy together have seized Spain—and all this in defiance of the interests of the non-aggressive states.

They [Great Britain and France] let her have Austria, despite the undertaking to defend her independence; they let her have the Sudeten region; they abandoned Czechoslovakia to her fate.

He accused both countries of pointing up "the weakness of the Russian army," "the demoralization of the Russian air force."

Why, he asked, was this happening? It looked like a one-sided war. Were the nonaggressive states weak? "Of course not. Combined, the nonaggressive democratic states are unquestionably stronger . . . England and France have rejected the policy of collective security and have taken up a position of neutrality."

The point of the speech of interest to the international community was Stalin's statement that if England and France took collective action, they were stronger: the war, he was saying to them, *could* be won. And that made Russia available as an ally.

Five days later, March 15, Hitler seized the rest of Czechoslovakia.

When Stalin touched on the possibility of an alliance with the Allies in his March speech, it amounted to a clear call to Britain and France: It was for Foreign Minister Litvinov to negotiate that alliance.

Litvinov, skilled diplomat, anglicized by many years of living in London as the Soviet ambassador to Great Britain, married to an Englishwoman, was known to be sympathetic to Britain. He was also a friend of America's. He had negotiated recognition of the Soviet Union by the United States with Franklin Roosevelt. During his time as foreign minister the Soviet government had indicated it was prepared to fight for Czechoslovakia and maintained a wary distance from Germany. Under Litvinov, Russia had joined the League of Nations and followed a policy of collective security in 1934. At that time Litvinov had negotiated the Franco-Soviet Pact of Mutual Assistance: Stalin called it "an obstacle to the enemies of peace." In 1936, Stalin had predicted how German aggression would break out upon the world: "History shows that when any state intends to make war against another state . . . it begins to seek frontiers across which it can reach the frontiers of the state it wants to attack . . . I do not know precisely what frontiers Germany may adapt to her aims, but I think she will find people willing to 'lend' her a frontier."

He had been right on the mark.

Stalin made those statements before Munich. The question before the world in 1939 was, would Britain pull back from the principle of collective security? A week went by after Stalin's speech with no reaction from Britain. Taking the initiative on March 18 at Stalin's direction, Litvinov proposed that France, Britain, Poland, Russia, Romania, and Turkey join together at a conference to draw up a treaty to stop Hitler. Chamberlain reacted negatively. As he wrote to a friend, "I must confess to the most profound distrust of Russia. I have no belief whatever in her ability to maintain an effective offensive, even if she wanted to. And I distrust her motives." Chamberlain had never quite gotten over the notion implanted in his brain as a youth by his father, Joseph, that the world should be run by the Teutonic nations, by which was meant England, Germany, and America. Nevertheless, realizing that he had not achieved "peace in our time" at Munich in September 1938, on March 31, 1939, Chamberlain announced to an approving House of Commons that Britain and France would guarantee Poland in case Hitler attacked it: "would lend the Polish Government all support in their power."

But that was no help to Russia.

On April 14, Lord Halifax, the powerful, aristocratic British foreign minister and the ex-viceroy of India (Churchill called him the Holy Fox), gave Britain's answer to Litvinov's March 18 proposal. He told the Soviet ambassador to Great Britain, Ivan Maisky, that the British government would not extend to his country a guarantee of support if it was invaded, as it had to Poland. This, it was reported, "enraged" Stalin.

Nevertheless, Litvinov, in Moscow, tried for the next six weeks to bring Sir William Seeds, the British ambassador to the Soviet Union, who spoke also for the French ambassador, Paul-Émile Naggiar, to the point of discussing a military and diplomatic alliance. However, the ambassadors offered nothing—no alliance, no guarantees. Britain was telling Russia to go it alone.

On April 16, Stalin took a giant step: he had Litvinov formally propose to Seeds that Russia, France, and Great Britain make a pact that would bind their three countries to declare war on Germany if they or *any* nation between the Baltic and the Mediterranean was attacked: "to render all manner of assistance including military in case of aggression in Europe against any one of these powers." The agreement, Litvinov stipulated, should be cast in the form of two pacts: Great Britain and the

Soviet Union, and France and the Soviet Union; each should conclude accords for immediate military support in case of aggression, similar to the pact recently concluded between Great Britain and Poland.

THE PROBLEM WAS POLAND. No matter who allied with whom, everyone except the Polish foreign minister, Beck (his faith in Hitler was unshakable), agreed Hitler, who periodically erupted into diatribes about his intentions to control the Polish Corridor and Danzig, would start the war by invading Poland. William L. Shirer, war correspondent and author of *The Rise and Fall of the Third Reich,* spent the first week in April in Poland. He found Poland a conundrum, observing, "Militarily and politically they were in a disastrous position. Their Air Force was obsolete, their Army cumbersome, their strategic position— surrounded by the Germans on three sides—almost hopeless . . . [T]he strengthening of Germany's West Wall made an Anglo-French offensive against Germany in case Poland were attacked extremely difficult. And finally it became obvious that the headstrong Polish 'colonels' would never consent to receiving Russian help even if the Germans were at the gates of Warsaw."

And yet, he saw incredulously, they relied on Germany.

In point of fact, if the German army marched on Poland, there was nothing Britain could do to stop it—no matter what any treaty said. Halifax used as his excuse for putting off serious negotiations with the U.S.S.R. Jósef Beck's refusal to allow Russian soldiers to enter his country, even to drive back a German army. In fact it was obvious to all, according to Shirer, that Britain could have forced the Poles to agree to Russian action on Polish soil if it had wanted to.

On May 1, Lord Halifax visited the Soviet embassy in London; it was the first time a British foreign secretary had set foot in the embassy since the revolution. But it became apparent that Halifax's attitude had if anything hardened: he told Ambassador Maisky that his government was not ready to enter into a pact with Russia.

IN AMERICA, PRESIDENT ROOSEVELT and Secretary of State Cordell Hull were apprehensively watching the growing danger to peace

Hitler represented. The president, and Hull, too, had come to the conclusion that if Britain and France made a pact with the Soviet Union, it would deter Hitler. They, too, saw that the combined military might of the three nations not only matched but dwarfed that of Germany. They also saw the danger: the possibility that Stalin, if he could not make a deal with Britain, might make a deal with Hitler. It would make sense for him; it would buy the Soviet Union time to build up its defenses. Joseph E. Davies, ex-ambassador to the Soviet Union, a highly independent thinker whom Roosevelt relied upon, reporting on European alliances from his listening post in Brussels, where he was now U.S. ambassador, prophesied, "The deciding element in Hitler's determination as to whether it will be peace or war this summer in Europe will be whether Britain and France will make a definite agreement with the Soviet Union." He and other knowledgeable Americans watched, for that was all they could do.

Stalin was getting interesting information about FDR's mind-set from his ambassadors. Alexander Troyanovsky, the first Russian ambassador to the United States (from 1933 to 1938), small, stocky, reserved, and well regarded, had met with Roosevelt six times over the years he had been stationed in Washington. He was called back to the Soviet Union in the summer of 1938, lived for months fearing arrest, and was spared because he was a longtime friend of Stalin. There is an unsubstantiated story that in one of the few known instances where Stalin exhibited compassion, Stalin saw Troyanovsky's name on a list of those to be killed, drew a line through it, and wrote "Do not touch." Troyanovsky had reported that Roosevelt was sympathetic to the Soviet Union, but was "being intimidated and to a great degree fooled by the State Department apparatus which is cooking various memos in neutralist spirit and in general is working in favor of the aggressors." Constantin Oumansky, Troyanovsky's replacement, who was loathed by Stimson and Hull (Hull would write that Oumansky was "insulting in his manner and speech . . . overbearing . . . protested our acts as if they were heinous offenses"), nevertheless had his ear to the ground and reported the president "strongly hates the Nazis and the Japanese" and that Roosevelt chafed at the restrictions the Neutrality Act put on him. He noted as well "the activization of the reactionaries who at present are mostly manifest at the Dies [House Un-American Activities] Committee . . . an office of daily baiting of the progressive wing of Roosevelt administration."

Stalin learned another interesting fact about FDR. The NKVD reported that Neville Chamberlain would probably not even be negotiating with Russia at all if it were not for the pressure FDR was exerting on the prime minister. The information came from Donald Maclean, master Soviet spy. Maclean, who had been recruited to Communism while at Cambridge and would later defect to the Soviet Union, was then, as third secretary in the British embassy in Paris, privy to all the discussions taking place between the British, the French, and the Russians. And, according to Maclean, Roosevelt virtually forced the British government to begin discussions with the Soviets. "Donald Maclean reported that . . . Roosevelt urged Chamberlain to enter into negotiations with Britain's European allies, including the Soviet Union, to contain Hitler. Our intelligence sources reported that the British government reacted reluctantly to this American initiative and had to be forced by Roosevelt to start negotiations."

Lord Halifax, along with most of his class, had a deep-seated fear of Communism. After meeting Hitler, he had said of the führer, "By destroying Communism in his country, he had barred its road to Western Europe . . . Germany therefore could rightly be regarded as a bulwark of the West against communism." He and other world leaders feared Russia not only because Communism as a system of government was Western Europe's worst nightmare but because, in 1939, the Soviet Union, the embodiment of the Communist model, seemed to be such a vibrant, functioning economy. Indeed the argument could be made (and in many circles it was) that the Soviet Union was more of a success story than America, still fighting its way out of the Depression, or the democratic countries of Europe, which were still trying to recover from World War I. Therefore Halifax continued to drag his negotiating feet as much as he could get away with, seemingly bound to discourage serious consideration of Russian overtures, hoping by this tactic at least to delay war, even if he could not avoid it.

April saw the launching of Germany's new super battleship, the *Bismarck*.

On May 1, Litvinov stood on the reviewing stand next to Stalin as the Red troops and guns and armor passed by at the great annual May

Day parade in Red Square. Soviet newspapers marked him out as "guest of honor." Presumably, Stalin had not yet heard about Halifax's latest rebuff to Maisky. But certainly by the end of the day Stalin had been notified of what had occurred in London, for two days later he abruptly dumped Litvinov and made Molotov, already chairman of the Council of the People's Commissars, the new foreign commissar. Soviet newspapers reported the change on a back page. It was totally unexpected. The German chargé d'affaires in Moscow reported that "the sudden change has caused the greatest surprise here, as Litvinov was in the midst of negotiations with the British delegation . . . appears to be due to a spontaneous decision by Stalin."

In personal terms, the change finally gave ascendancy to Molotov in what had been a decades-long rivalry with Litvinov for Stalin's ear. In political terms, it meant trouble for England, for Molotov was less pro-British and more trusting of the Germans than Litvinov. He had written a remarkably revealing letter to Stalin in 1933 (undoubtedly followed by others as the years passed): "Litvinov along with his unscrupulous circle is inclined to slide down the road of 'opposition' to the Germans . . . I consider it necessary to stop him."

In contrast, early on Litvinov had singled out Hitler's intention "to cut a road for expansion to the East by fire and sword . . . and enslave the Soviet peoples." In putting Molotov in charge of Soviet foreign policy, Stalin opened the door to negotiations with Hitler. If Stalin couldn't get a treaty with the Allies, he would take his chances with Hitler, and it would be harder to deal with Hitler if Litvinov, who was Jewish, was in charge of the negotiations.

Molotov had always been Stalin's closest companion, the only person who "would talk to his chief as one comrade to another." For Stalin, dealing with this urgent matter of protecting his country from war, having Molotov on the front line meant that he would learn every nuance, every change, every possibility out there; he would be more than able to negotiate with the Germans.

Molotov continued the negotiating sessions with Naggiar and Seeds, but two days after Chamberlain as much as declared in Parliament that Britain would not enter into a treaty with Russia, Stalin told Molotov to meet with Count Friedrich von der Schulenburg, the German ambassador to the Soviet Union, and start a discussion of trade relations between their two countries.

Germany wanted to neutralize the Soviet Union at this moment in time because Joachim von Ribbentrop, the Reich foreign minister, eager for war, had convinced Hitler that rapprochement with Russia would give the Reich the immediate chance (after invading Poland) to strike a mortal blow at Great Britain. And after Great Britain was conquered, it would be time enough to finish off Russia.

Molotov was at first confrontational. He accused Schulenburg and his government of negotiating in bad faith. Molotov assured Schulenburg that "Stalin was following the conversations with great interest, he was being informed about all their details."

The German Foreign Office in Berlin wasn't at all sure it would be possible to "turn" the Soviets. "We are of the opinion here that the English-Russian combination certainly will not be easy to prevent . . . The possibility of success is considered here to be quite limited," it advised Schulenburg.

Shortly thereafter, on May 31, Stalin had Molotov make a speech on the radio, the medium of choice for a major foreign policy speech, because Stalin and Molotov assumed not just all Russia but all interested countries would be listening.

Molotov now announced on the radio that Britain had neither guaranteed military aid to Russia if it were attacked nor guaranteed aid to the border countries. "We stand for peace and against aggression," he declared, "but we must remember Stalin's admonition that we cannot be used to pull the chestnuts of others out of the fire." He clearly made the point that Russia wanted an effective pact of mutual assistance with England and France that laid out the extent and character of the aid the Soviet Union expected, as well as the aid to be rendered to the border countries that were guaranteed in the event of hostilities. Molotov included for his Russian audience (as well as British, French, and German listeners) a warning that the possibility of rapprochement with Germany shouldn't automatically be excluded. In 1938, Germany had wanted to open trade relations with the Soviet Union, he explained. Talks then were broken off, but, he continued, "The conversations may be renewed."

Of course, they already had been.

The use of the radio at this moment was indicative of a turning point. If Stalin had only wanted to warn France and England, Molotov could simply have met with the British and French ambassadors. What *was* necessary was for Molotov to go on the radio to prepare the Russian people for such an enormous change of policy.

Molotov mentioned only one world leader by name in the broadcast: Roosevelt—a clear signal that Stalin was aware of the president's efforts on his behalf. On April 14 the president had sent a message to Hitler in which he listed thirty-one countries he asked him not to attack for at least ten years. The main effect of the message had been negative, unfortunately, for Hitler held the message up to ridicule in a speech to the Reichstag that William Shirer described as "the most brilliant oration he ever gave." However, FDR's message had been met with appreciation in the Soviet Union. Now Molotov stated that the destruction by the German state of international treaties "was the answer of Germany to the proposal imbued with the spirit of peacefulness of the President of the United States, Roosevelt."

Within a short time Molotov was taking the lead in meetings with Schulenburg and had put political as well as economic issues between their countries on the table for discussion.

The next Soviet negotiating step took place in London and was a challenge to Halifax. Would he come to Moscow to negotiate seriously and iron out differences? asked Maisky.

Halifax replied, "It was really impossible to get away."

Anthony Eden, who had previously been foreign secretary, horrified by Halifax's rudeness, volunteered to go in place of Halifax; Chamberlain vetoed the idea. Maisky asked Halifax a second time to journey to Moscow; again he refused. It was impossible for him to leave London, he said, "for the present."

Given that Chamberlain had traveled to Munich to bargain with Hitler, the foreign secretary's repeated refusal to travel to Moscow was a slap in Stalin's face.

ROOSEVELT BADLY WANTED to get to Stalin, to add his voice to those who were telling him not to make a deal with Hitler. He found a messenger at hand. Ambassador Troyanovsky was being replaced, was coming to the White House for his farewell visit to the president on June 6, and would be debriefed in Moscow. FDR gave him a simple message. "Tell Stalin," he said, "that if his government joined up with Hitler, it was as certain as that the night followed the day that as soon as Hitler had conquered France, he would turn on Russia, and it would be the Soviets' turn next."

MEIN KAMPF HAD SOLD in the millions in Germany by the mid-1920s and had appeared in an English edition in 1933. British rulers had read Hitler's words that Russians and Jews were scum, words brought home in his continuing public pronouncements that Germany had a right to the Slavic farmland, particularly the Ukraine. The German master race needed lebensraum, he had ranted: "The Russian space is our India. Like the English, we shall rule this empire with a handful of men." Having digested these words, the British can possibly be forgiven for thinking, as Hitler grew ever more violent and threatening, that there was no need to rush to conclude a treaty with the Soviet Union because there was no danger of Russia and Germany making a treaty. Indeed, they might have thought that the *process* of negotiating a treaty with Russia, whose form of government they feared might take root in their country, would serve them as well as or perhaps better than the treaty itself, because the negotiations themselves might make Hitler pause—or even stop—before making his next aggressive move. It appeared to be outside their imaginations to consider that Hitler and Stalin might link up. Negotiations would buy them time, maybe enough time to deter Hitler till spring, because it was well-known that after the first week in September, heavy rains made Polish roads impassable, and afterward came winter, when there was snow and ice and it would be even harder to start a war.

The Soviet press was the tool that Stalin now employed to jumpstart discussions with Britain. He had *Pravda* hurl charges of insincerity at the Allies. "The British and French Governments Do Not Wish an Equal Treaty with the Soviet Union," the front-page headline read on June 29. Stalin did not entirely close the door to Britain and France, as a close reading of the article showed. Also reported was that the author's "point of view regarding British and French insincerity is not shared by 'his friends.'"

ON SEPTEMBER 15, 1938, the day Chamberlain first traveled to Munich to try to deal with Hitler, Roosevelt had written to a good friend that war was "inevitable . . . Perhaps when it comes the United States will be in a position to pick up the pieces of European civilization and help them to save what remains of the wreck."

Now, almost a year later, as he watched the Soviet Union drifting into Germany's orbit, Roosevelt began to prepare in earnest. On July 5, 1939, in preparation for the war he could see looming on the horizon, he quietly issued a military order. It created a new institution, the Executive Office of the President; reporting to it from that moment on would be the Joint Board of the Army and Navy (the chiefs of staff), which coordinated all strategic plans, the Aeronautical Board, and the Joint Army and Navy Munitions Board, which controlled all military procurement programs. Whereas before the chiefs of staff had reported to the secretary of war and the secretary of the navy, now all military planning—all questions of strategy, tactics, and operations—would come to him. He would hold all the reins in his hands.

As the warm days of July passed, the French, British, and American ambassadors in Berlin were wiring their governments that they found it increasingly apparent that the German general staff was preparing for war in August. By that time, they pointed out, the harvest would have been gathered, the fortifications would be ready, and the reservists whom they saw trickling into Berlin would be assembled in large numbers in military camps.

Ambassador Davies returned from Belgium on the *Queen Mary*, which docked in Manhattan on July 17. By 12:30 p.m. the next day he was at the White House having lunch with Roosevelt, briefing him on what Belgians with ties to German leaders had learned of Hitler's plans. As they discussed the war that they both were sure was coming, Davies advised the president that based on the knowledge he had gleaned from business and diplomatic sources, he believed Hitler and Ribbentrop expected to break Stalin away from England and France. He predicted that Hitler would make war on Poland before the party rally in Nuremberg in September.

Davies also told FDR that in Brussels they "were praying for the amendment of the Neutrality Act, in the belief that it might possibly deter Hitler and at least delay the war." Davies noted in his diary, "These statements gave him no surprise. It simply seemed to confirm his deep pessimism."

In fact, Davies's words galvanized the president. Armed with Davies's information that a change in the Neutrality Act might avert war, Roosevelt called a meeting later that same day of key senators to see if he could persuade them to amend the act immediately so that America could help by sending armaments abroad. He hoped Davies's additional evidence at this moment in time, with Stalin teetering between Germany and the Allies, with the Allies loath to commit to Stalin, would get the Senate moving. He held the meeting upstairs in his study. Present were Secretary of State Cordell Hull, Vice President John Nance Garner, and, crucially, the Republican senator William E. Borah, the ranking minority member of the Foreign Relations Committee, the key to the opposition, plus other senators. FDR opened the meeting by talking about the power and influence of Senator Gerald Nye, Republican of North Dakota, whose extreme isolationist views were blocking change. Borah interrupted. With a sweeping gesture he said, "There are others, Mr. President." FDR was so taken aback he asked Borah to repeat what he said, which Borah did, emphatically, repeating, with conviction, that "no war would occur at least in the near future . . . Germany isn't ready for it." Hull, deeply upset, predicted there would be war before the end of summer. He offered to let Borah see the cables he was getting and argued the case for repeal of the act. According to participants, he had tears in his eyes and was on the edge of losing self-control, so greatly was he outraged by Borah's brusque manner and his arrogance in thinking that he knew more about Germany than the State Department. The meeting went on until midnight, at which point Garner said, "Well Captain, we may as well face the facts. You haven't got the votes and that's all there is to it." The Senate was a hurdle Roosevelt could not, in the summer of 1939, overcome.

MOLOTOV HAD NOT GIVEN UP on negotiating with Naggiar and Seeds. He now convinced them that the Soviet Union wanted to enter into military discussions "immediately" in Moscow and that a military mission should be sent to Moscow forthwith to sign an agreement of mutual assistance. Halifax finally agreed to this.

The pressure on the British Foreign Office and most particularly on Halifax and the close group surrounding him, and their resistance to concluding a meaningful treaty with the Soviet Union, can be seen in a comment senior British diplomat William Strang made: "The history of the negotiations for [the triple alliance] is the story of how the British government were driven step by step, under the stress of Soviet argument, under pressure from Parliament and the press and public opinion polls, under advice from the Ambassador at Moscow, and under persuasion from the French, to move towards the Soviet position."

On July 31, Admiral Sir Reginald Drax and General Joseph Doumenc, the British and French negotiators, presumably armed with authority to conclude a military pact, and their staffs set off for Moscow. Their mode of travel was extraordinarily inefficient. The British navy was still the greatest in the world, but instead of putting the diplomats on a decent ship or, even more practically, on an airplane (Chamberlain and Daladier had flown to Munich), Halifax dispatched the group on the *City of Exeter,* a slow freighter. The *City of Exeter* took ten days to reach Leningrad.

The meetings between Schulenburg and Molotov continued as the *City of Exeter* proceeded east. Schulenburg, as an enticement to Stalin, now assured Molotov that Germany would "safeguard vital Soviet Baltic interests."

Molotov was doing a brilliant job holding off Schulenburg. Schulenburg was by no means sure that Stalin would go through with a treaty with Hitler. In fact, he informed the Wilhelmstrasse, he was extremely doubtful: "My over-all impression is that the Soviet Government is at present determined to sign with England and France if they fulfill all Soviet wishes."

Back in London, Chamberlain decided to stick to his plans and leave—on August 5—on a fishing trip to the trout streams of Scotland. The American ambassador in London reported, Chamberlain "hopes to be away a reasonable time."

ROOSEVELT WAS INFORMED by Cordell Hull of the status of discussions between the Soviet Union and England and France at the 2:00 cabinet meeting on Friday afternoon, August 4. FDR was aware that the *City of Exeter* was still on the high seas. Directly after the cabinet meeting, working with Undersecretary of State Sumner Welles, in a last-ditch effort to stop Stalin from making a treaty with Hitler, Roosevelt wrote a personal message to him. How to deliver the message was the tricky question. It was decided to send it, because the president vitally wanted Stalin to read it—but didn't want to get caught out having sent it—in a highly secret, roundabout way, but it took eleven days in that summer of endless negotiations before it reached Molotov and almost two weeks before Roosevelt heard of Stalin's reaction. On that Friday also, in Washington, the U.S. commercial agreement with the Soviet Union facilitating trade was renewed.

The *City of Exeter* arrived in Leningrad on August 10, and on August 12 Drax and Doumenc were ready to begin talks with their Russian opposite numbers. Because the treaty under discussion was military, and the Russians expected serious negotiations to be concluded, the Russian delegation was headed by the commissar of defense, Kliment Voroshilov. Voroshilov had with him as advisers the most senior Soviet military leaders, including General Boris Shaposhnikov, chief of the general staff of the Red Army; the commander in chief of the Red Air Force; and the commander in chief of the Red Navy. In contrast, the Allied negotiating team that faced them was a motley crew: General Joseph Doumenc was the commander of the First Military Region for France, and Admiral Sir Reginald Drax was the naval aide to King George VI. Accompanying Drax was Air Marshal Sir Charles Burnett, a pilot, who was not, according to the German ambassador to London, even a strategist.

The meeting was held in the Spiridonovka Palace, an imposing Gothic mansion from tsarist times that provided a backdrop of spacious rooms decorated with gold ceilings, brocaded walls, and exquisite Oriental rugs, which had been designated the official place to entertain foreign emissaries by the Ministry of External Relations. Because it was a warm day, the doors to the carefully tended pleasant garden were thrown open as the men sat talking and smoking around the table.

Drax arrived without written credentials giving him the authority to negotiate. (A crucial week passed before his papers arrived.) Russia had 120 infantry divisions ready to fight if there was war. Voroshilov asked how many British troops would be ready to fight. Five regular divisions and one mechanized division, Drax answered. Voroshilov was stunned. Russian intelligence had gotten British troop strength wrong; Britain was much weaker than they had believed. So was France. Voroshilov asked the key question, adding it was "the cardinal point to which all other points are subordinate": Would Poland agree to permit Soviet troops to enter the country to fight if the Germans invaded? British instructions to Drax were to duck the question, to answer that surely the Poles and the Romanians would invite the Red Army in. On August 17 Voroshilov proposed the talks adjourn until the question was answered. The delegations met again on August 21, but since the question remained unanswered, the talks were terminated for good.

With the clarity of hindsight it can be seen that the Allies were not negotiating in good faith. Before the conference had begun, Seeds had written, "I am not optimistic as to the success of military conversations . . . but to begin them now would give a healthy shock to the Axis Powers and a fillip to our friends, while they might be prolonged sufficiently to tide over the next dangerous months." Sir Charles Burnett, the pilot, after four days in Moscow wrote to London, "I understand it is the Government's policy to prolong negotiations as long as possible if we cannot get acceptance of a treaty."

As the *City of Exeter* had set off, the American chargé d'affaires in London had cabled Washington, "the military mission which has now left for Moscow has been told to make every effort to prolong discussions until October 1."

The British Foreign Office was not negotiating in good faith.

ROOSEVELT HAD JUST APPOINTED Laurence Steinhardt, previously ambassador to Sweden and Peru, U.S. ambassador to the Soviet Union. Steinhardt had arrived in Moscow and presented his credentials to Molotov on August 10, the day the *City of Exeter* reached Leningrad.

Great precautions were taken with Roosevelt's secret message to Stalin. In order not to raise the ire of American isolationists eager to find traces of FDR's meddling in European politics, it had been addressed to Steinhardt and signed not by FDR but by Sumner Welles. It was sent by the direct safe wire that the State Department relied on between Washington and the U.S. embassy in Paris. From Paris, because both telephone and telegraph wires throughout Europe were known to be routinely tapped, the embassy was instructed to follow the usual safe but maddeningly slow procedure of entrusting it to a courier. The second secretary of the embassy handed it to Steinhardt nine days later, the morning of August 14. It was planned that Steinhardt would personally give it to Molotov, who would, presumably, repeat its contents to Stalin. Steinhardt immediately requested an appointment with Molotov and personally presented the letter to him on August 15.

The letter begins,

My Dear Ambassador, The President has asked me to send you these urgent lines . . . Were the axis powers to gain a victory, the position of both the United States and of the Soviet Union would inevitably be immediately and materially affected thereby. In such event the position of the Soviet Union would be affected more rapidly than the position of the United States . . . The President could not help but feel that if a satisfactory agreement against aggression on the part of other European powers were reached, it would prove to have a decidedly stabilizing effect in the interest of world peace.

Roosevelt was asking Stalin to stay away from Hitler.

Molotov listened carefully to Steinhardt. Then he explained where his government stood. Steinhardt, with Molotov's assent, took notes.

Molotov told him that his government was interested not in "merely general declarations" but in "a determination of the action to be taken under specific conditions or circumstances—and that there shall be mutual obligation to counteract aggression . . . All the negotiations with Britain and France which have taken place thus far we value, in so far as they may lead to an agreement for mutual defensive assistance." Steinhardt asked his opinion as to the probable outcome of the negotiations. Molotov answered, "We have spent much time negotiating—this shows we expect the negotiations to succeed—but we are not to be blamed for the delay."

Molotov said that he well understood Roosevelt could not take any "immediate" part in European affairs "but that he knew that President Roosevelt held close to his heart a deep interest in and desire for the preservation of world peace and that for this reason his Government would attach the greatest interest and the utmost importance to the views just expressed."

The president's message was too little and too late to change anything. That very evening at 8:00 Molotov met with Schulenburg. Schulenburg cabled that he found Molotov "quite unusually compliant and candid . . . Significant is his quite clearly expressed wish to conclude a non-aggression pact with us." Molotov agreed Foreign Minister Ribbentrop should come to Moscow "to lay the foundations for a definite improvement in German-Russian relations" and conclude an economic agreement followed by a nonaggression pact with the Soviet Union.

When Ribbentrop read the cable, he was beside himself with excitement. He could hardly contain himself. He sent a telegram marked "URGENT" to Schulenburg telling him to call upon Molotov and inform him that the Reich foreign minister could fly to Moscow "any time after Friday, August 18."

On August 20, Schulenburg, as directed, presented to Stalin a cable on a sheet of paper with no letterhead, addressed to "Herr Stalin": it was from Hitler. It was altogether conciliatory and polite:

> The conclusion of a non-aggression pact with the Soviet Union means to me the establishment of a long-range German policy . . . I am convinced that the substance of the supplementary protocol desired by the Soviet Union can be cleared up in the shortest possible time if a responsible German statesman can come to Moscow and negotiate . . . The Reich Foreign Minister has full powers to draw up and sign the non-aggression pact as well as the protocol.
>
> I should be glad to receive your early answer. Adolf Hitler.

Stalin cabled back immediately, "I hope that the German-Soviet Nonaggression Pact will mark a decisive turn for the better in the political relations between our two countries," and stated that Joachim von Ribbentrop, foreign minister of the Reich, could arrive August 23.

Ribbentrop, thrilled as he was, now worried that this trip wouldn't come off—that Stalin might change his mind—sent a telegram to Schulenburg the following day: "Please do your best to see that the journey materializes."

Meanwhile, the German army was readying for war. A column a half mile long—made up of battle-ready soldiers, huge trucks carrying armaments including sixteen-foot guns, trucks on caterpillar treads— was seen heading for the German barracks in Gleiwitz, two miles from the Polish border. The British war minister, Leslie Hore-Belisha, observed by reporters in shorts on the beach in Cannes on August 20, after being handed a telegram, was further observed dressed and on a train heading for Paris within a half hour. In Scotland, Neville Chamberlain packed up his gear, left his cherished trout streams, and caught the night train to London.

Ribbentrop arrived in Moscow in Hitler's private plane, a well-appointed Condor, on Wednesday, August 23. With him were nine diplomats, including the German undersecretary of state, the chief of protocol, and the chief of the German Foreign Office's Eastern Department. Underlining the importance of the mission, Stalin greeted the delegation when it arrived at the Kremlin.

Meetings between the German and the Soviet officials were held throughout the afternoon and evening and on into the night. Ribbentrop telephoned Hitler at 1:00 a.m. to tell him that the pact had been signed. The news was immediately flashed over German national radio, and because it assured Russia's unconditional neutrality no matter what actions Germany undertook, *The New York Times* reported, it "created the greatest elation in all political circles." According to Steinhardt, Stalin personally conducted the negotiations with Ribbentrop, and when they were concluded, Ribbentrop drank a toast to Hitler and "the revival of the traditional German-Russian friendship." According to the diaries of several German officers who were present, Ribbentrop even went so far as to repeat the Berlin joke making the rounds that "Stalin will yet join the Anti-Comintern Pact."

Announcement of the pact appeared in *Pravda* and *Izvestia* later the same day. Although it was not part of the public document, in return for the promise of Soviet neutrality (article 2: "To refrain from supporting in any way any country at war with the other"), Hitler had reluctantly agreed that the Soviet Union could have the Baltic States and the part of Poland contiguous with the Soviet Union.

Stalin had regained lands the tsars had ruled.

When Hitler, at Berchtesgaden, was notified, he "stared into space for a moment, flushed deeply, than banged on the table so that the glasses rattled and exclaimed in a voice breaking with excitement, 'I have them! I have them!' 'Now, Europe is mine.'"

The next day, there being no reason to spend more time talking with the English and French representatives, Voroshilov, with two other members of the Politburo, Georgy Malenkov and Nikita Khrushchev, went duck hunting at Voroshilov's hunting preserve. (Khrushchev mistakenly remembered the day as a Sunday, but otherwise his recounting of events is eminently plausible.) The weather was perfect; they all had great success at bringing down ducks. Afterward the three men went to Stalin's dacha, where they sat around talking, drinking, and finally eating as the day ended and night fell and the ducks were plucked, dressed, and cooked for dinner. There was nothing Stalin enjoyed better than sitting around a dinner table for hours, talking but also listening to his inner circle far into the night, their conversation loosened by the constant flow of liquor and food. This day Stalin thought he had taken a huge step to safeguard—at least in the near future—his country from attack. He believed he had bought off Hitler with the promise of not joining forces against him. This day Stalin, remembered Khrushchev, was brimming with information about the draft of the Friendship and Nonaggression Treaty. Ribbentrop had brought it with him, and with some changes, Stalin informed them, it had just been signed in the Kremlin. The relaxation of the tensions that had consumed Stalin for almost a year—since Munich—was marked; he was expansive and happy. He "was in a very good mood and was joking a lot." He told the assemblage that "when the British and French representatives who were still in Moscow found out about the treaty the next day, they would immediately leave for home . . . [They] didn't really want to join forces with us anyway . . . Of course it's all a game to see who can fool whom. I know what Hitler's up to. He thinks he's outsmarted me, but actually it's I who have tricked him."

Stalin believed that he had bought time, that Hitler would dispose of Britain and France before he turned on Russia.

FDR, TOO, DECIDED to go on vacation. His home in Hyde Park, in the Hudson River valley, was scarcely cooler then Washington. He left the morning of August 12, bound for New York City to board the USS *Tuscaloosa* for a cruise in Canadian waters the same day the negotiations at Spiridonovka Palace got under way. He was planning to visit his house on Campobello Island, in New Brunswick, Canada, where he had spent so much time with his family. He had been felled by polio there in August 1921 and had not seen it since. Before polio he was a tall (six feet one), slender, handsome, stylishly dressed man, whom Woodrow Wilson described as "the handsomest young giant I have ever seen." After being crippled by the disease, he didn't look like the same person. Nor was he. "It was exactly as if all trivialities in life had been burned [out] in him. A steel had entered his soul," observed Sumner Welles. He had been taken off Campobello more dead than alive.

The USS *Tuscaloosa* was a very grand ship, fit for a president. It was a heavy cruiser of the New Orleans class, commissioned in 1934, sixty-one feet wide, almost six hundred feet long, manned by seven hundred sailors.

With him were his usual traveling companions, Pa Watson and Ross McIntire, plus the naval aide Daniel J. Callaghan. However, given the grave international situation, planning had turned the ship into a command center so that FDR would be able to deal with whatever political crisis occurred. For this purpose also on the *Tuscaloosa* were three secretaries to take dictation, help write a speech, or issue a press release, Dorothy Brady, Henry Kanee, and Bill Hassett; the White House telephone operator Louise Hachmeister, uniquely able to locate key people by telephone (no mean trick in those days); and Dewey Long, chief of the White House Transportation Office.

FDR was intent on fishing, relaxing, sitting in the sun, as well as visiting Campobello Island. Traveling northeast, anchoring first at Halifax Harbor, Nova Scotia, the cruiser arrived at Campobello Island at 1:00 p.m. on August 14. FDR quickly left the ship, presumably in one of its whaleboats, visited his house, which he must have found a distressful experience—to be at the site of where personal tragedy struck—and he was back on the *Tuscaloosa* three hours later. The *Tuscaloosa* steamed farther east, to Sydney Harbor on Cape Breton Island.

Watson, McIntire, Callaghan, and FDR fished off the back of the *Tuscaloosa* until they reached the Bay of Islands, Newfoundland, then, in the late afternoon, FDR and the others, lowered into whaleboats, fished for salmon in the Humber River for a few more hours. At 7:44 a.m. the next day the *Tuscaloosa* reached Petitpas Point, where FDR wanted to fish in another section of the Humber. The fishing must have been excellent, although there is no record of what was caught, because FDR and his friends fished for five hours before returning to the *Tuscaloosa*. They had planned to continue north through the Strait of Belle Isle to look at a large grounded iceberg, then circle Newfoundland, but heavy fog made that inadvisable. It was decided to start back to Halifax, Nova Scotia. Along the way the *Tuscaloosa* anchored off Bird Rock Island in the Gulf of St. Lawrence so the president and his companions could have a last chance to fish for salmon in the whaleboats, but they were back aboard and the *Tuscaloosa* was under way for Halifax at twenty knots an hour and a half later. Monday at 3:00 p.m.

they were anchored in Halifax Harbor. A courier from Washington, the U.S. postal inspector Leo DeWaard, came aboard with a special mail sack for the president. FDR was due back in Washington on Friday morning, August 25.

Monday evening German radio broke the news, interrupting a musical program, with the announcement that Germany and Russia had decided to sign a nonaggression pact. The next day, August 22, the tenth day of Roosevelt's cruise, the news made headlines in the German press.

Roosevelt and Hull and Davies had not only been discussing and trying to head off such an outcome for most of the summer; they had been looking toward the next step: dealing with it, which, they had decided, meant doing nothing to drive the Soviet Union even more tightly into Hitler's arms. *The New York Times* gave the best description of the administration's reaction because its reporter had been briefed by the State Department. According to the *Times,* the announcement of the nonaggression pact "caused little surprise in State Department circles. Chancellor Adolf Hitler's willingness to sell Russia war materials . . . had been taken as a tangible demonstration by Herr Hitler to Joseph Stalin that Germany no longer planned a direct assault on the U.S.S.R., and it was thought that Joseph Stalin desired, if possible, to play a passive part in Europe."

It reflected Roosevelt's singularly accurate, sympathetic view.

FDR queried Hull and Welles as to whether he should rush back to Washington. They advised no. Roosevelt ignored their advice and ordered the ship's captain to prepare for a 6:00 a.m. departure the next morning, August 22, heading the *Tuscaloosa* for Annapolis. That afternoon Harry Hopkins came aboard for a secret, unscheduled visit to give Roosevelt the latest news. Presumably, Hopkins had with him drafts of the messages that would go out over Roosevelt's name two days later to Adolf Hitler and President Ignacy Mościcki of Poland urging them to seek a peaceful solution.

Roosevelt's cable, issued at midnight to Hitler on August 23, emphasized world peace and asked him to agree to "refrain from any positive act of hostility for a reasonable and stipulated period" and to submit "these controversies to an impartial arbitration in which they can both have confidence." To President Mościcki of Poland, FDR suggested that "the controversy between the Government of Poland and the Government of the German Reich might be made the subject of direct discussion between the two governments," or it "might be conciliation through a disinterested third party."

To save time, the *Tuscaloosa,* heading south at top speed, proceeded to Sandy Hook, New Jersey, instead of Annapolis, anchoring there at 8:00 a.m. on Thursday, August 24. By early afternoon, well rested, FDR was back in the White House talking to Welles and Hull, working out how to deal with his worst nightmare: the alliance between Germany and the Soviet Union. The president's messages to the two leaders were released.

Mościcki cabled his polite but discouraging reply the next day. He thanked FDR for his "important and noble message." Direct negotiations between governments, he wrote, were "the most appropriate method of solving difficulties which may arise between states," but "the method of conciliation through a third party as disinterested and impartial as Your Excellency" was also "a just and equitable method in the solution of controversies."

FDR cabled Mościcki's response to Hitler immediately, noting that "the Polish government is willing, upon the basis set forth in my messages to agree to solve the controversy which has arisen . . . by direct negotiation or through the process of conciliation." "All the world prays that Germany, too, will accept." Hitler never replied. Within days of the pact's announcement, the French government had seen to it that all the paintings in the Louvre's Grande Galerie and exhibition rooms were packed up and moved to the Château de Chambord in the Loire valley. Only the sculptures, heavy and difficult to transport, remained. The British embassy advised its citizens in Poland to leave as soon as possible, "in view of the considerable danger of a rupture in German-Polish relations."

In England the news of the pact was received with stunned amazement. English newspapers didn't let the government entirely off the hook. The *Daily Herald,* for instance, commented on the "criminal hesitation on the part of the British and French governments in their relation with Russia," adding, "But it can provide no excuse for what is a bigger betrayal of peace and of European freedom even than Munich."

Lord Ismay, who would the next year become Churchill's chief of staff, admitted, "I had never expected that our belated and low-powered mission to Moscow would achieve anything," but, like many others, he was amazed at the speed of the negotiations between Hitler and Stalin. The treaty was struck, it seemed, overnight.

A treaty with Hitler was so bizarre for the Soviet Union, even to Politburo members, given that Hitler had said so many times that his master race would crush the Slavs and that Soviet leaders were the scum of humanity, that the pact was never mentioned at party meetings nor referred to in talks in public. "We couldn't admit outright that we had reached an agreement on peaceful coexistence with Hitler. Coexistence would have been possible with the Germans in general, but not with the Hitlerite fascists," explained Nikita Khrushchev. The hope they all expressed privately was that before he turned on them, Hitler would, because of the treaty, attack Britain and France.

Nine days after the treaty was signed, on September 1, the Wehrmacht invaded Poland. After eighteen days of fighting not a single Polish division was left: 450,000 troops had been taken prisoner; eight hundred airplanes had been destroyed or captured. On September 17, the Red Army entered eastern Poland: Poland ceased to exist.

The United States chose to see the Russian invasion, as Hull wrote in his *Memoirs,* as Stalin's way "to keep Hitler's legions from approaching too close to Russia . . . We [FDR and Hull] did not wish to place her on the same belligerent footing as Germany, since to do so might thrust her further into Hitler's arms . . . Hitler had not abandoned his ambition with regard to Russia."

Privately, FDR was furious. He referred to Communism in a message to Joseph Kennedy, U.S. ambassador to Great Britain, as "the Russian form of brutality" and passed on to him a joke: "Suppose you had two cows. The Socialist would take one and let you keep one. The Nazi would let you keep both cows but would take all the milk. The Communist would take both cows."

Within weeks Roosevelt had convened a special session of Congress to repeal the neutrality law, allowing countries (England and France) to buy military weapons. Immediately, the Wilhelmstrasse charged Roosevelt with being "unneutral." Hitler had a healthy respect for FDR, tinged with fear, according to William L. Shirer; within a year Hitler would regard FDR as the strongest enemy in the way of his path to world domination.

Roosevelt's moderate reaction to Stalin's pact with Hitler would bear fruit in the fall of 1940. Hitler wanted Stalin to send Molotov to Berlin to discuss future plans for world domination at the expense of Britain. Stalin, resisting Hitler's pressure, insisted that Molotov's visit to Berlin not take place until after November 5, the date Roosevelt would be reelected for his third term.

Stalin made a remarkable admission to the Turkish foreign minister a short while after signing the pact: "The English and French, especially the English, did not want an agreement with us, considering that they could manage without us. If we are guilty of anything it is of not having foreseen all this." Thirty-five years later Khrushchev would still defend the rationale for making the treaty: "If we hadn't made that move, the war should have started earlier, much to our disadvantage. As it was, we were given a respite."

It is interesting to note that Stalin received messages that summer of 1939 from Hitler and from Roosevelt, but he received no messages from either Chamberlain or Daladier.

Hans Frank, the German governor-general of occupied Poland, on October 31 announced, "The Poles do not need universities or secondary schools; the Polish lands are to be turned into an intellectual desert . . . The only educational opportunities that are to be made available are those that demonstrate to them their hopelessness or their ethnic fate." And indeed, the Germans kept their word: when the Red Army liberated Poland, it found no buildings usable as schools, no school equipment, no scientific material, no laboratories. What the Germans could not destroy they shipped back to the fatherland.

8

BARBAROSSA

H e felt it was coming, even if he wouldn't admit it. By early June, according to one observer, Stalin was physically such a wreck that his doctor ordered him to go to his dacha in Sochi for a rest. His complexion was yellow, his eyes red, his hands trembled.

For several years Stalin had lived with the knowledge that it was only a matter of time before Hitler turned on Russia: it was to buy time that he had made the treaty with Ribbentrop. Starting in January 1941, Soviet diplomats stationed at listening posts all over the world, plus the extensive Soviet intelligence network, sent in reports to the Kremlin that Hitler was planning to attack the Soviet Union in June. Stalin wouldn't believe them. He had made up his mind that Hitler would honor the treaty through the summer of 1941. His own generals tried to tell him that invasion was imminent, but because he rarely tolerated and even more rarely was swayed by the opinions of others, most of his circle adjusted their ideas to his. The many who disagreed with him were forced to keep their mouths shut. There were even some, such as Voroshilov, who believed he was right because he was the great, all-seeing Stalin. Voroshilov would say to those such as Vladimir Dekanozov, the Soviet ambassador to Germany, on the scene in Berlin, who was reporting the unmistakable signs that Germany was preparing for war, "How could you allow yourself to argue with Comrade Stalin! He knows more and can see further than all of us!"

In January 1941, Sam Woods, the U.S. commercial attaché in Berlin, acquired and sent to the State Department Hitler's December directive for Operation Barbarossa, passed to him by an anti-Nazi German in the dimness of a dark movie theater. Woods gave the outlines of the three-pronged military offensive Hitler was planning and reported that bales of rubles had been printed and that staffs stood ready to administer captured Russian territories. Sumner Welles gave the information to Ambassador Oumansky.

A few months later one of Ōshima Hiroshi's cables to his superiors in Tokyo gave the information given to him by Hermann Göring—the number of planes, the numbers and types of divisions that would be mobilized against the Soviet Union, and the time: early summer. (Signals Intelligence had run into a problem and couldn't read the messages for a short time because the Japanese had instituted a new keying system. The Signals Intelligence Service cryptographer who broke the code and pieced together this message admitted he "was too excited to sleep that night.")

Roosevelt, when informed, told Welles to warn Oumansky a second time, which Welles did in late March. "My government will be very grateful for your confidence. I will inform it immediately of our conversation," replied Oumansky.

British intelligence also read the signs of impending German aggression, leading Churchill as well to warn Stalin. Stalin reacted to Churchill's warning negatively: he didn't trust Churchill. After digesting Churchill's warning, the premier growled to Zhukov, "We're being threatened with the Germans, and the Germans with the Soviet Union. They're playing us off against each other." (Years later Molotov would say, "Could Churchill be trusted in this matter? He was interested in pushing us into a conflict with the Germans as quickly as possible, how could it be otherwise?")

The Chinese Communist leader, Chou En-lai, from Chungking, warned Stalin that a German invasion would take place on June 21.

In Tokyo under cover of being a German correspondent, Richard Sorge, who ran a network of agents and had befriended Eugen Ott, the German ambassador to Japan, reported to his Russian handlers on May 15 that the war would begin between June 20 and June 22. On May 19 he reported the very precise (and correct) information that there were nine German armies, 150 divisions, massing near the Russian border. Sorge, however, was suspected of being a double agent. The suspicion rested upon the fact that he had been named as probably untrustworthy by the Soviet officers accused of owing allegiance to Germany who had been executed during the purges in 1937. Nevertheless, because Stalin always insisted on seeing all information, Sorge's reports were passed on to him on June 9 by General Semyon Timoshenko and General Zhukov, along with other, similar reports. Stalin was scornful of the material and angrily dismissed it, saying, "There's this bastard who's set up factories and brothels in Japan and even deigned to report the date of the German attack as 22 June. Are you suggesting I believe him too?"

It is ironic that Stalin's paranoid fears of betrayal that had led him to kill so many generals during the purges now prevented him from using Sorge's information, so detailed and so correct. But "no amount of warning message—whether from London or Tokyo—could shift his *idée fixe*," Gromyko would later write.

It must be said that Hitler covered the military buildup brilliantly. A disinformation campaign had been put into operation by the intelligence arm of the German general staff, the crux of which was that Germany was going to finish off England before attacking the Soviet Union and further that all the overt actions that pointed to an invasion of the Soviet Union were intended to foster in the British a false sense of security so that they would not be ready for the onslaught until it was too late. So thorough was the disinformation campaign that Operation Barbarossa managed to take not just the Russian people but the German people "almost completely" by surprise. Even Count von der Schulenburg, the German ambassador to Moscow, was reportedly kept in the dark and, led to believe Hitler would not declare war, endeavored to convince Stalin of that fact.

This was in spite of the fact that the plans had been in the works for six months: on December 18, 1940, the Wehrmacht had been instructed "to be prepared to crush Soviet Russia in a quick campaign, even before the conclusion of the war against England."

On May 20, General Filipp Golikov, head of Soviet military intelligence, told Stalin that the Soviet spy known as Starshina, who worked in the headquarters of the Luftwaffe, was repeatedly warning him of German war preparations. Stalin directed that Starshina be reprimanded. Then, annoyed, he added, "Perhaps you can send your 'source' from the staff of the German air force to go fuck his mother. This is not a 'source' but a disinformer."

Having decided not to cross Stalin again, on May 31, 1941, Golikov reported to him that German preparations were directed against England: "The German command [is] continuing concurrently its movement of troops to Norway . . . having in view the execution of the main operation against the British Isles." ("I admit," he later told someone, "I distorted intelligence to please Stalin because I feared him.")

Some preparations were made. Timoshenko and Zhukov prevailed on Stalin to agree to call up 800,000 reservists at the end of April. On May 1 all roads leading out of Vladivostok were closed. On May 4, Stalin took over the title of prime minister from Molotov, thus concentrating power in his own hands. Extreme attention to keeping Hitler happy continued. On May 8 the Soviet Union withdrew recognition of the governments in exile of Norway and Belgium and recognized the puppet governments set up by the Nazis. On May 10, Ambassador Steinhardt reported, "There had been a great increase in the quantity of goods arriving in Vladivostok for rail shipment to Germany."

Barbarossa was one of the best-telegraphed punches in military history. Wrote the U.S. ambassador to Rome, William Phillips, in his diary the day of the invasion, "This morning's early broadcast brought the news which we have been expecting daily." Cables reaching the U.S. embassy in Moscow literally "burned with guesses" as to what day the invasion would occur. Four dates were repeated often enough that they stood out in his mind as the best bets: May 1, May 15, May 23, and June 15.

Because Stalin was turning a deaf ear to all reports, it followed that fellow Georgian Lavrenti Beria, head of the NKVD, always currying favor with Stalin, remained silent on the subject. When Ambassador Dekanozov, a friend of Beria's and also a Georgian, reported to him that Germany was preparing an attack, Beria cold-bloodedly suggested to Stalin that Dekanozov not only be recalled but be punished. Stalin rationalized as self-serving the many warnings received from sources in other countries.

Even as those warnings became more specific and the German border buildup more obvious, Stalin clung to his hope that Hitler would not attack. He went to great lengths *not* to provide Hitler with any excuse to commence hostilities. In May he granted Schulenburg's request that he allow groups of Germans to search for graves of soldiers who had perished in World War I on Russian soil. When he admitted this in a meeting with Timoshenko and Zhukov, both generals were stunned by the news because it was such a blatantly transparent excuse for the Germans to survey Russian troop positions. When Timoshenko told him there was "increasing infringement of Soviet air space," Stalin answered, "I am not sure that Hitler knows about those flights." Stalin then told them that Hitler had told the Soviet ambassador Dekanozov that troops had been transferred to the Soviet border as a ruse—to throw off London from knowing it was about to be invaded. He made sure that the Soviet products it had contracted to send to Germany continued to be sent in good time. The U.S.S.R. was shipping more than half of the Third Reich's phosphates, asbestos, and manganese and a third of its nickel and oil. The Japanese foreign minister, Yōsuke Matsuoka, visiting Moscow in April, reinforced Stalin's trust in Germany with a new spin. Matsuoka told him, "insisted," that he thought the Germans were intentionally circulating rumors of an attack as a way to make sure the Soviet Union continued to meet German supply requirements.

At the annual May Day parade, Stalin placed Ambassador Dekanozov next to him on Lenin's tomb as a public gesture of friendship toward Germany. On June 14, certainly at the command of Stalin and Molotov, *Pravda* published a Tass communiqué that could only have been printed as information directed at Hitler. The communiqué blamed England for spreading rumors that Germany and the Soviet Union were close to war and stated, "Rumors that Germany intends to break off relations with the USSR have no basis in fact. The recent movement of German troops, freed from operations in the Balkans, to eastern and northeastern Germany has other motives having nothing to do with Soviet-German relations. Rumors that the USSR is preparing for war with Germany are untrue and provocative. Attempts to portray the summer maneuvers of the Red Army as hostile to Germany are absurd."

"I am certain that Hitler will not risk creating a second front by attacking the Soviet Union. Hitler is not such an idiot and understands that the Soviet Union is not Poland, not France, not even England," Stalin said on June 15.

Even as Ambassador Ivan Maisky reported suspicious German activities from London, he, too, couldn't believe the invasion would happen. "Hitler is not ripe for committing suicide. And the attack against the USSR is virtually suicide," he wrote in his diary on June 18.

Not all of Stalin's circle, however, were taken in. Georgi Zhukov, tough, alert, in his mid-forties, the brilliant general who had defeated the Japanese in 1937, the son of a cobbler, as was Stalin, whom Stalin appointed chief of staff earlier in 1941, and Commissar of Defense Semyon Timoshenko, commander of the northwest front, both tried to persuade Stalin to mobilize the troops. So did Andrei Alexandrovich Zhdanov, senior member of the Politburo. Stalin explained his thinking to Zhukov one night at dinner at his dacha in Kuntsevo after Zhukov had asked that defenses be bolstered on the western frontier. Replied Stalin, "In secret, I will tell you that our ambassador had a serious conversation with Hitler personally and Hitler said to him, 'Please don't worry about the concentration of our forces in Poland. Our forces are retraining.'" Zhukov persevered, which only infuriated Stalin, who said, "Do you want a war because you don't have enough medals? If you're going to provoke the Germans on the frontier by moving troops there without our permission, then heads will roll." Stalin then had left the room, slamming the door behind him.

EVERYONE AT THE AMERICAN EMBASSY knew the attack was coming. Embassy staff had seen to it that a large supply of food and drink was stored in the embassy cellar. The day before the invasion every woman employed at the embassy was put on a plane to Sweden or Iran. The male staff members who remained waited for the inevitable.

Saturday, June 21, was the summer solstice, the longest day of the year, the start of summer. It had been a long, cold winter, the sun had suddenly broken out, the parks were thronged. It was a day for rest and relaxation in Russia. Sir Stafford Cripps, British ambassador to Moscow, had predicted Hitler would choose a Sunday: "It gives him a small advantage: on Sunday the level of alert of his opponents is lower than usual." The Sunday after the solstice meant a Sunday when the Russians would be even more off guard.

The evening of June 21 members of the Politburo were gathered in Stalin's apartment in the Kremlin discussing measures to take in the event that war with Germany became a reality. According to Anastas Mikoyan, Stalin was still in denial: he was aware it was June, that Napoleon had attacked in June, but June 1940 had passed, and May had just passed, and there had been no war; perhaps the rest of June 1941 would also pass peacefully. They had all been on alert for so long. General Dmitri Pavlov, commander of the Red Army on the western front, was at the theater (a short while later he would be tried by a summary court-martial and shot); Andrei Zhdanov was in Sochi. Stalin went back to his dacha in Kuntsevo for dinner. A little after 9:00 p.m. he received a call from General Zhukov, who had gone to general staff headquarters and was monitoring the situation, telling him that a deserter had just crept over the border from Poland, at great danger to himself, to tell Red Army headquarters that the German army was going to cross the river Bug with rafts, boats, and pontoons that very night. Stalin suggested that the deserter might have been sent by the Germans to provoke him into beginning hostilities, that German generals might be acting on their own to force Hitler's hand. Nevertheless, he ordered Timoshenko and Zhukov to the Kremlin, to which he returned. After they discussed the various options open to them, the following confusing, conflicting orders that clearly indicate Stalin's ambivalent state of mind were sent out to all troops:

FOR IMMEDIATE EXECUTION:

1. On June 22–23 1941, it is possible there will be a surprise attack by the Germans . . .
2. The task of our troops is to not respond to any provocative actions that might result in serious complications . . .
   a. During the night of June 22, 1941, secretly occupy firing positions in the fortified areas along the state frontier.
   b. Before dawn on June 22, 1941, disperse to reserve airfields all aviation, including troop aircraft, carefully camouflaging it.
   c. All units bring themselves to combat readiness. Troops are to be kept dispersed and camouflaged.
   d. Bring air defense to combat readiness without calling on additional staff. Prepare all measures for blackout of cities and installations.

3. Take no other measures without special permission.

Red Army units received this directive in the early morning hours of June 22. As if this were not enough, Stalin told Marshal Timoshenko,

"Will you please tell [General] Pavlov that Comrade Stalin has forbidden to open artillery fire against the Germans." Stalin had returned to Kuntsevo. At dawn Zhukov called Stalin to tell him the invasion had started. Again Stalin returned to the Kremlin; Zhukov and Timoshenko found him there "very pale . . . sitting at the table clutching a loaded unlit pipe in both hands . . . bewildered," saying, "A provocation of the German officers . . . Hitler surely does not know about it."

Beginning at 3:15 on the morning of June 22 three million German soldiers, plus another half a million Romanian, Finnish, Hungarian, Italian, and Croat troops, coordinating their attack from the Finnish border to the Black Sea, equipped with 700,000 field guns—some marching on foot, some riding in one of the 3,600 tanks or one of the 600,000 motor vehicles, some mounted on one of the 600,000 horses—spilled over the Soviet western border. Over their heads flew 500 bombers, 270 dive-bombers, and 480 fighters.

Because the Germans, using various pretexts, had been allowed to fly reconnaissance missions over the Russian border and had checked out the airfields, army bases, and command centers for the better part of a year, the Luftwaffe easily and quickly found its targets; the immediate devastation was huge: twelve hundred Soviet planes were lost the first day. The commander of the western front's air forces was so stunned he committed suicide. The commander of the Ninth Mixed Air Division fled. He was later found and shot.

Stalin still refused to believe, as he told his staff, that Hitler had sanctioned the invasion. It was not until Count Friedrich von der Schulenburg handed the German declaration of war to Molotov that Stalin was convinced. "They fell upon us, without making any claims, not demanding any negotiations, they made a vile attack like bandits," said Stalin, at last coming face-to-face with reality.

It was Molotov, not Stalin, who, at noon on June 22, spoke to the Russian people, concluding his speech with a vow: "Our cause is just. The enemy will be defeated. Victory will be ours!" It would be July 3 before Stalin, using virtually the same words, spoke to the people.

In three days the Wehrmacht advanced 150 miles. Within a week the Germans captured 400,000 soldiers, damaged more than four thousand planes beyond repair, and penetrated 300 miles into Russia, capturing Minsk. Another 200,000 soldiers were captured the second week.

After the first few days Stalin, finally facing the enormity of his mistake, seemingly stunned, silently acknowledging his profound failure to read the signals properly, left the Kremlin and retired to his dacha in Kuntsevo, apparently in the grip of a nervous breakdown. For days he wouldn't answer the telephone and made no calls. Reportedly, he began heavy bouts of drinking. On June 29 he burst out, to the assembled Molotov, Voroshilov, Zhdanov, and Beria, "Lenin left us a great inheritance and we, his heirs, have fucked it all up!"

The next day, when Molotov, Beria, and Voroshilov visited him, again he feared for a moment they might have come to arrest him. They hadn't. Then, realizing that at this, his most vulnerable moment, he was still in charge and his staff wanted him to stay in charge, he reassumed control.

STALIN EMERGED FROM HIS RETREAT with a new sense of purpose. He reached out for help. He came to the realization that if the Soviet Union were to survive, it would need allies. On July 3 he gave a speech reassuring the populace, speaking as their leader, but also speaking to Roosevelt and Churchill, laying out the groundwork for an alliance with the United States and Great Britain. He spoke, remembered Maisky, in a dull, colorless voice, "often stopping and breathing heavily," but his words were effective. He called the war by the name it would go down with in Russian history, the people's Great Patriotic War, and like Roosevelt he realized that the war would result in a new relationship between the Soviet Union and the rest of the world. The Russian struggle, he said, "will merge with the struggle of the peoples of Europe and America for their independence, for democratic liberties. It will be a united front of the peoples who stand for freedom and against enslavement."

Once back in control, Stalin reorganized all aspects of defense and assumed even more power. A war cabinet, called the State Defense Committee, or GKO, was formed. Its members initially were Molotov, Beria, the Politburo member Georgy Malenkov, and Voroshilov. Within a few weeks Stalin became chairman of the GKO, commissar of defense, and, on August 8, supreme commander in chief. His generals began calling him Supremo. Two days later, on August 10, the GKO ordered that new Siberian divisions be formed comprising Russian, Ukrainian, and Belorussian troops, to be ready for combat for the period September 15 to November 15.

Stalin had always been an obsessive worker, but now he worked eighteen-hour days and became overwhelmed sometimes with petty details, such as the placement of mines and the distribution of weapons, details best left to others.

One general, Dmitri Volkogonov, remembered that when he "lost" the whereabouts of a train for a short while, telling Stalin it was at one station when it was at another, Stalin said to him, " 'If you don't find it, general, you'll be going to the front as a private.' As he left, white as a sheet." Alexander Poskrebyshev, Stalin's personal watchdog and executive assistant, who was always either at Stalin's side or waiting outside his office ready for commands, said, "See you don't slip up. The boss is at the end of his tether," ominous because the efficient Poskrebyshev knew his boss. By his own admission Stalin had hired him because he was so ugly: "One day Stalin sent for me and said: 'Poskrebyshev, you have a frightful look about you. You'll terrify people.' And he engaged me." Some people thought he had a hangman's look, with his narrow shoulders and big head. Tubby, stocky, bent over, with a long, crooked nose, he had eyes that reminded the English interpreter A. H. Birse of a bird of prey. When he sat at a table only his head was visible. He had become indispensable.

There was great confusion in the first days of the war that had nothing to do with the German army: it was caused by inexperienced officers. In the 1937 purge 3 out of 5 marshals, 15 out of 16 army commanders, 60 out of 67 corps commanders, and 136 of 199 division commanders had been executed. Now generals were thrust into positions of authority who didn't have adequate training and background; they caused great damage. Four generals, including Pavlov, were tried on the charge that they were involved in an anti-Soviet conspiracy and the intended collapse of the command of the Western front. Stalin crossed out that charge and, in bold strokes, wrote, "None of this nonsense . . . showed cowardice, lacked authority and efficiency, permitted the breakdown of command." They did not deny their guilt but said they would make up for it in battle. They were not given the chance: they were found guilty and shot.

By mid-September Kiev had fallen, and another 453,000 Red soldiers had been taken prisoner.

In the beginning, because it was official German policy that the Slavic population should be severely reduced, many of the captured Red soldiers were herded into fenced open fields: some starved to death; some were shot. "We are only taking very few prisoners now," wrote one German soldier to his wife on June 27, 1941, "and you can imagine what that means." An official German report in December noted that between 25 and 70 percent of the Red Army prisoners died en route to prison camps. According to World War II historian and authority on Nazi Germany Gerhard Weinberg, the German military's own figures show that ten thousand prisoners of war were shot or killed by hunger and disease *every single day* for the first seven months of the war. To this figure, which amounts to two million, must be added the more than one million Soviet citizens who also died in this period.

Conditions for captured Red soldiers improved slightly as the Germans realized that if they fed and housed some prisoners at least minimally, the prisoners could then perform necessary labor. But because all Slavs were officially considered an inferior race, the soldiers treated them as such. The idea of abiding by the Geneva Convention for prisoners of war was never even considered.

ON THE EVENING of June 22, Roosevelt motored to Bethesda, Maryland, to have dinner at the home of the glamorous princess Märtha of Norway. The morning following the invasion he telephoned Acting Secretary of State Sumner Welles (Secretary of State Cordell Hull was ill) several times, then summoned him to his study. He had to hammer out a statement of American intentions.

Roosevelt knew that if Hitler emerged victorious from the Soviet Union, with the oil of the Caucasus, the grain of the Ukraine, and the manpower of Russia at his fingertips, with Hirohito and Mussolini as his allies, he would rule not just Western Europe but the world. Therefore the Soviet Union had to be helped. But there was strong opposition in America to aiding the Communist country. Some Americans were against aid to Russia because they believed the country was doomed and help a waste of American resources. Others were against aid to Russia because they thought Stalin was as dangerous as Hitler and wanted the two of them to fight it out and destroy each other. Still others were against aid because they thought America impregnable, protected as it was by its oceans. Senator Burton K. Wheeler, Democrat from Montana, the spokesman for the America First Committee, the most powerful isolationist group in the country, against any aid, had proclaimed in February that even giving FDR the power to run Lend-Lease would mean plowing under every fourth American boy.

The president had to assuage people's fears and swing public opinion to his side before he could even think of sending aid to the Soviet Union. He couldn't get too far ahead of the electorate. If he made *too* strong a speech, the isolationists would pounce. That had happened to him four years earlier, in 1937, when he had first tried to warn Americans about Hitler. He had spoken then of the spreading world lawlessness, of how important quarantines were to protect the health of a community against the spread of disease: he had been roundly and widely condemned as warmongering. He didn't mind drawing some isolationist rhetoric if that was the price of waking up other sections of the populace, but he had been too early, and the upshot had been that he hadn't accomplished anything. He later said to his speechwriter and friend Sam Rosenman, "It's a terrible thing to look over your shoulder when you are trying to lead—and find no one there." After passage of Lend-Lease in March he had curbed his warnings of war to such an extent that he worried his cabinet. He had in fact taken to his bed for ten days with some vague disease Dr. McIntire refused to describe, informing the press only that the president was too weak to transact business. FDR was incommunicado for a particular reason: he didn't want to be pushed into saying that America was ready to do something. "I am not willing to fire the first shot," he privately explained, canceling a speech he had been scheduled to give.

The month before Barbarossa a German sub had sunk the American ship *Robin Moor* in the South Atlantic. Weeks passed before the passengers and crew, floating in small lifeboats, were discovered and rescued by friendly vessels. Only then did the sinking become known. The incident gave Roosevelt the opportunity to make a tough anti-Nazi speech to Congress on June 20, two days before Hitler struck. Said FDR, using one of his favorite styles, sarcasm, "We must take the sinking of the Robin Moor as a warning to the United States not to resist the Nazi movement of world conquest. It is a warning that the United States may use the high seas of the world only with Nazi consent."

Roosevelt remained silent in the days following the German invasion. He had a problem: "I couldn't say we needed Russia on our side to win the war because Russia is not our kind of country and I couldn't be pictured as a communist sympathizer. But the reality of life is that as Great Britain needs the U.S., so we need Russia to help defeat a formidable foe." He let Welles talk for him—let him test the water. Welles gave a statement to *The New York Times* in which he carefully didn't say America would help the Soviet Union, but stated "Hitler and Hitler's armies are today the chief dangers to the Americas. . . . To the present German Government the very meaning of the word 'honor' is unknown."

Welles noted, significantly, Roosevelt's concern with religion—his awareness of the lack of it in Soviet society.

The year before, on September 16, 1940, Congress had passed the first peacetime draft in the country's history; however, the draftees had been inducted for only one year. Their time was almost up. The selective service extension was coming up before Congress a few weeks later in August, and it was very unpopular. There was a real chance that there were not enough votes for passage. The House majority leader John McCormack, counting forty-five Democrats against the bill and thirty-five undecided, worriedly told Stimson that he was losing control of his people, which made Roosevelt even more cautious. Aid to Russia was imperative, but if selective service didn't pass, America would have no army to speak of: no power. FDR couldn't afford to antagonize Congress. He needed public opinion on his side.

By mid-July the Soviet Union was in dire straits. It had lost 2 million soldiers, 3,500 tanks, and more than 6,000 planes. On July 17, Smolensk, on the road to Moscow, fell. Within a short time the Wehrmacht, advancing, captured another 300,000 Red Army soldiers and 3,000 tanks.

Four days after Holland was invaded, it surrendered; eighteen days after Belgium was invaded, it surrendered; five weeks after Norway was invaded, it surrendered. France took the longest: six weeks.

How long could Russia last?

WELLES'S STATEMENT ON JUNE 24 was printed almost in its entirety in *The New York Times*. He was quoted as saying that as between a communistic dictatorship and a Nazi dictatorship, there is no choice, as far as the people of this country are concerned. The United States maintains the principle of freedom of worship as undeniable, whereas that right has been denied their peoples by the Russian and German governments. "But Hitlerism and its threat of world conquest . . . is the main issue before the world. Hitler's armies are today the chief dangers of the Americas."

To give himself breathing space, test the strength of the opposition, FDR had Welles say the next step America might take was "hanging in the air"—possibly Lend-Lease would be extended, possibly not.

Senate opposition to the very idea of aid for Russia was immediate and vocal and reported in full. The Missouri senators were the worst. "It's a case of dog eat dog," proclaimed Senator Bennett Clark from Missouri. The other senator from Missouri, Harry Truman, felt the same way: "If we see that Germany is winning we ought to help Russia and if Russia is winning we ought to help Germany and that way let them kill as many as possible."

No Russian would ever forget Truman's statement.

On Tuesday, Roosevelt answered questions at a press conference at which he pledged that the United States would "give all possible aid to Soviet Russia." But he deliberately blunted the import of these words by telling reporters that "until this government obtained a list of what Russia needed . . . no moves could be made toward supplying her wants." He wouldn't be pressed. He joked, "Shoes and socks from Garfinkel's . . . Orders for planes and tanks took longer to fill. 'Is the defense of Russia the defense of the United States?' a reporter asked, whereupon, 'Mr. Roosevelt suggested that the reporter ask another type of question such as, How old is Ann?' "

Even though the Lend-Lease Act gave FDR the power to send munitions and armaments to the government of any country whose defense the president deemed vital to the defense of the United States, Roosevelt had to bring the country along with him. He knew that opposition to sending actual matériel to Russia would be fierce.

Proclaimed ex-president Hoover, "Now we find ourselves promising aid to Stalin and his militant conspiracy." The *Chicago Tribune* asked, "Why should we help an Asiatic butcher and his godless crew . . . We can resist the filthy disease." Even the liberal *New York Times* was not sure it was a good idea to help Russia: "Stalin is on our side today. Where will he be tomorrow?"

There were other, more practical objections, based on the belief that it was useless to send aid because Russia was doomed to defeat, a belief voiced by William Bullitt, America's first ambassador to the Soviet Union, who addressed the American Legion in midsummer: "I know no man in Washington who believes that the Soviet Army can defeat the German Army. The probability is that after severe losses Hitler will seize the vast resources of the Soviet Union and will then prepare an overwhelming force for the conquest of Great Britain, then of South America and the United States." Ambassador William Phillips, in Rome, thought the same. "It is clear that Germany is determined to get the control of the Ukraine and the oil from the Caucasus, and I suppose in due course she will succeed in doing so," he wrote in his diary. British intelligence predicted the Wehrmacht would reach Moscow "in three weeks or less."

FDR, therefore, continued to keep his plans as low-key and vague as he could. On June 30, Secretary of the Navy Frank Knox made a speech in which he said the time had come to use the navy to clear the Atlantic of the German menace. Reporters leaped on the secretary, wanting to know if Knox had checked the idea with Roosevelt. FDR held a press conference at his home in Hyde Park. Would he comment on Knox's speech? the reporters asked. He wouldn't. Lolling in a shirt open at the neck and seersucker trousers (an unusually casual outfit in those days), the president told reporters that he was "just sitting around and taking a swim each afternoon." He gave "no indication" of aggressive naval action. FDR's bête noire, Representative Hamilton Fish, congressman from FDR's home district, Hyde Park, was conducting a poll on the question of going to war. The reporters asked the president for his reaction. By way of reply, FDR told a story about President Coolidge, who after church one Sunday told his wife that the minister had preached about sin. "What did he say?" Mrs. Coolidge asked. "He was against it," Coolidge answered. Roosevelt continued, "That was very much like Mr. Fish's poll. Anybody obviously would vote only one way on the question, Are you against war? Of course, we are all against war."

Five days later Roosevelt ordered the first brigade of U.S. troops to Iceland, to protect the Western Hemisphere. On July 9 he sent identical letters to the secretary of war and the secretary of the navy requesting the preparation of "over-all production requirements required to defeat our potential enemies." He asked them to "explore the munitions and mechanical equipment of all types which would be required to exceed by an appropriate amount that available to our potential allies."

On July 11, FDR added a new entity to the government intelligence setup so that information would come directly to him instead of through the channels already in existence. He appointed William J. Donovan, a much-decorated hero of World War I, whom he had known at Columbia Law School and had wanted in his cabinet in 1939, to be "Coordinator of Information," head of a new intelligence service that he would create that would analyze and collate national security information and be accountable only to the president. Donovan's operation became the Office of Strategic Services (OSS), which operated behind enemy lines and reported directly to Roosevelt. FDR, however, who always liked to keep his sources competing for his ear, did not tell Donovan U.S. cryptographers had broken the enemy codes.

A Russian wish list of goods reached the president. On July 23 he directed his appointments secretary, General Pa Watson, to "get the thing through" within two days.

On July 25, responding to Japanese aggression in French Indochina, Roosevelt announced an embargo on oil for Japan, against the advice of General Marshall and Admiral Harold Stark, chief of naval operations.

As Roosevelt had originally set up Lend-Lease in March, it was to be run by a four-man advisory committee consisting of the secretaries of the Treasury, war, navy, and state, with Harry Hopkins in charge as the executive secretary. Hopkins pulled in his friend Edward R. Stettinius, who had reorganized U.S. Steel, to make it more efficient. Stettinius shrank the ninety days it was taking to process an order, each of which Roosevelt had to sign, to three days. There were bottlenecks throughout the system: army and navy officers, loath to help the hated Russians, dragged their feet. FDR was impatient with everyone. Among other people FDR telephoned was General Marshall, to tell him to find railroad experts to assist the Russians in keeping the Siberian railway out of Vladivostok open. On August 1, at a cabinet meeting, the president was visibly angry. Wrote Secretary of War Stimson, "The President made a big row in Cabinet this afternoon in regard to munitions for Russia. He pranced in [a very odd description of a paraplegic; Stimson must have been furious], saying that the Russian war had been going on for six weeks and the Russians had been wanting arms and had been promised arms for six weeks and they had been given a run-around here in Washington and nothing had been done for them." FDR went on that he was "sick and tired of hearing that the Russians are going to get this and they are going to get that . . . Whatever we are going to give them, it has to be over by the first of October, and the only answer I want to hear is that it is underway." FDR then proceeded to order that so many planes be immediately diverted from the United States to the Soviet Union that he also upset General Marshall. "Can the president survive the political attacks which will come if we undertake maneuvers this fall without planes?" Marshall mused out loud at a staff conference the next day.

Roosevelt, unmoved, then made sure that the Soviet government knew what he was doing. He had Sumner Welles write to Ambassador Oumansky that "the government of the United States has decided to give all economic assistance practicable . . . issuing unlimited licenses permitting the export to the Soviet Union of a wide variety of articles."

In an opinion poll taken on August 5, 38 percent of the U.S. population said they were in favor of Lend-Lease for the Soviet Union. That was probably higher than Roosevelt expected. FDR next, much to the dismay of Stimson, appointed a special administrator, Wayne Coy, who had worked with Hopkins on Works Progress Administration (WPA) programs in the Midwest and had a reputation as a superb organizer, to facilitate shipments to the Soviet Union and cut through the red tape. Much of the immediate problem had to do with making the British give up airplanes that had been allocated to them and that they were counting on receiving. But Stimson knew this was just the beginning of his problems: he was going to have trouble holding on to armaments for American soldiers.

Harry Hopkins, in London working out Lend-Lease problems with Churchill, wired FDR on July 25 that he thought it would be a good idea if he flew to Moscow: "Air transportation good and can reach there in twenty-four hours. I have a feeling that everything possible should be done to make certain the Russians maintain a permanent front even though they be defeated in this immediate battle. If Stalin could in any way be influenced at a critical time I think it would be worth doing by a direct communication from you through a personal envoy."

FDR wired him back two days later to go. Ivan Maisky, Soviet ambassador to London, undoubtedly wired ahead to Stalin his very positive assessment of Hopkins, "a man who had retained his loyalty to the democratic traditions of President Lincoln."

Hopkins's flight was horrendous. He went by PBY to Archangel in extremely bad weather. From there Soviet pilots took him in an American Douglas transport to Moscow. He was taken to meet with Stalin virtually immediately upon arrival:

> He welcomed me with a few swift Russian words. He shook my hand briefly, courteously. He smiled warmly. There was no waste of word, gesture, nor mannerism. It was like talking to a perfectly coordinated machine, an intelligent machine. Joseph Stalin knew what he wanted, knew what Russia wanted, and he assumed that you knew . . . He offered me one of his cigarettes and he took one of mine. He's a chain smoker, probably accounting for the harshness of his carefully controlled voice. He laughs often enough, but it's a short laugh, somewhat sardonic, perhaps. There is no small talk in him. His humor is keen, penetrating. He speaks no English, but as he shot rapid Russian at me he ignored the interpreter, looking me straight into my eyes as though I understood every word that he uttered.

The meeting lasted two hours. Hopkins made it clear that he came as a personal representative of FDR, who wished to aid the Soviet Union in its fight against Germany.

Stalin's first words were virtually a testament to how devastated he had been by Hitler's perfidy: "The Germans were a people who without a second's thought would sign a treaty today, break it tomorrow and sign a second one the following day. Nations must fulfill their treaty obligations, or international society could not exist."

His stated needs were enormous. He wanted twenty thousand anti-aircraft guns, a million rifles: "Give us anti-aircraft guns and the aluminum and we can fight for three or four years." He wanted, he told Hopkins, to have a conference at which all information could be exchanged regarding the capabilities and designs of Soviet and American tanks, guns, and planes. Hopkins quizzed him on specifics. Hopkins, impressed, told Sir Stafford Cripps, the British ambassador, that Stalin in every case but two gave him every figure and statistic that he asked for out of his head.

So eager was Stalin for U.S. aid that "he wanted me to tell the president that he would welcome the American troops on any part of the Russian front under the complete command of the American Army."

Hopkins said he told Stalin that he "doubted that our Government, in event of war, would want an American army in Russia but I would give his message to the President."

Photographs of Hopkins and stories about his offer of U.S. help covered the front pages of all Soviet newspapers the next day.

In a separate meeting with Molotov, Hopkins was alerted to the Soviet apprehension as regarded Japan. Molotov "stated that the one thing he thought would keep Japan from making an aggressive move would be for the President to find some appropriate means of giving Japan what Mr. Molotov described as a 'warning.'"

Stalin told Hopkins that the people in the conquered countries "and countless other millions in nations still unconquered could receive the kind of encouragement and moral strength they needed to resist Hitler from one source, and that was the United States. He stated that the world influence of the President and the Government of the United States was enormous . . . Finally he asked me to tell the President . . . the problem of supply by next spring would be a serious one and that he needed our help."

Hopkins met with Stalin twice—two long and satisfactory meetings, as he described them to FDR—and came away impressed with the morale of the people. "There is unbounded determination to win," he reported.

The U.S. press was not happy with Hopkins's trip. A typically sly comment was in *The Knoxville Journal:* "A man as susceptible to leaf-raking projects as Harry always was, is likely to give away more than we've got."

On August 2, FDR sternly gave Coy directions to push goods to Russia: "Nearly six weeks have elapsed since the Russian War began and we have done practically nothing to get any of the materials they asked for on their actual way to delivery . . . Get out the list [of materials] and please, with my full authority, use a heavy hand—act as a burr under the saddle and get things moving." He advised Coy that there were two categories of goods: first, material to be delivered in time to take part in battles in October; second, material that physically could not get there before October 1.

On August 12 the U.S. House of Representatives passed—by one vote—the extension of the Selective Service Act.

Roosevelt had arranged to meet with Winston Churchill at Argentia Harbor off Placentia Bay in Newfoundland, where the U.S. Navy had just placed into commission a new base. Part of the attraction for FDR was that it was a very hot summer and the cool northeastern coast made it the ideal time for a cruise in those waters, but he loved cruises in any weather. On August 3 he boarded the *Potomac* in New London, Connecticut, proceeded the next day to New Bedford, Massachusetts, where he fished and received visitors as onlookers and reporters watched. Then, under cover of darkness, the *Potomac* went around the southern end of Cuttyhunk Island and proceeded to Martha's Vineyard. There he secretly transferred to the heavy cruiser USS *Augusta,* waiting off Menemsha in the midst of seven U.S. warships, and the flotilla proceeded up the coast. He rendezvoused with Churchill on August 8. The original purpose of the trip had been so he could talk over the problem of the defeat of Germany with Churchill, but the meeting produced a statement of common principles that became famous as the Atlantic Charter.

Churchill's comments about FDR have been widely reprinted; the prime minister would probably have been hurt if he had known what FDR's first impression had been of him. "He is a tremendously vital person and in many ways is an English Mayor LaGuardia!" wrote Roosevelt, referring to the short, stout, and voluble mayor of New York City.

The two leaders declared that their countries sought no territorial aggrandizement, respected the right of all peoples to choose the form of government under which they lived, and hoped to establish a peace that would afford to all nations the means of dwelling in safety within their own boundaries.

Much scrutiny has been directed at FDR's refusal to have any mention in the Atlantic Charter of a postwar world security organization other than the vague "establishment of a wider and permanent system of general security." Its absence rested on the president's fear of arousing the opposition of America Firsters and other isolationist Americans. He thought mention would prematurely create "suspicion and opposition" to the creation of a world peace organization.

But more interesting is that Churchill was less than enthusiastic about the basic concept of the Atlantic Charter and went along only reluctantly. "There was some question about it being made applicable to the Pacific. Winston had not wanted that . . . FDR had pressed to make clear the meaning of the charter being of universal application," Mackenzie King confided to his diary after a private talk with the president.

In fact, the charter proclaimed the death knell for colonial empires. Europe, under the thumb of Hitler, and America, bent on helping Europe, heard only that countries should be safe within their own borders. But the charter was a call for nationalism that the third world heard. It would take years to make its way around the globe, but the fire had been lit among colonial peoples: India heard it first. Churchill only went along because he had to: Britain's life was at stake; only America could save it. And that meant Churchill did not dare cross FDR. "You'd have thought he was being carried up into the heavens to meet God," commented Harry Hopkins of Churchill, who was with him day and night on the *Prince of Wales* as the ship made its way from England to Argentia Harbor.

Churchill had subsequently gone before the House of Commons and explained that self-government did not apply to the British Empire: "We had in mind, primarily, the restoration of the sovereignty, self-government and national life of the States and nations of Europe under the Nazi yoke." FDR had deliberately pushed Churchill into a statement loosening England's colonial ties, according to his son Elliott, knowing he could not refuse. Elliott includes several pithy Roosevelt comments in his book *As He Saw It*. For example, while waiting for Churchill to arrive, FDR said, "I think I speak as America's president when I say that America won't help England in the war simply so that she will be able to continue to ride roughshod over colonial peoples."

Roosevelt was also aware that Churchill disliked, distrusted, and underestimated the Soviet Union. (Even the day after Hitler's attack on Russia, Churchill's secretary, John Colville, wrote in his diary, "The PM . . . castigating Communism and saying the Russians are barbarian. Finally he declared that not even the slenderest thread connected Communists to the very basest type of humanity.")

The night before Churchill's arrival FDR said to Elliott, "'I know already how much faith the P.M. has in Russia's ability to stay in the war.' He snapped his fingers to indicate zero." Hopkins had come away from his recent visit to Moscow believing the Russians would win: "He's able to convince me."

After meeting with Churchill, FDR quoted the prime minister as saying, "When Moscow falls . . . when Russian resistance ceases . . . war matériel to the Soviets was destined just to be war matériel captured by the Nazis."

Roosevelt, the consummate politician, managed to get his message from Argentia out to the world and charm Churchill at one and the same time. The Argentia statement, as Roosevelt had intended, not only provided a beacon of hope to those millions who Hitler now ruled but ignited the dreams of colonial peoples all over the world. In India, particularly, much to Churchill's chagrin, it aroused nationalist sentiments.

As for the prime minister, he cabled Clement Attlee, "I am sure I have established warm and deep personal relations with our friend."

FDR's opening gambit about his meeting with Churchill to the press when they caught up with him aboard the *Potomac* in Rockland Harbor, Maine, several days later was clever: it was a ten-minute description of the "remarkable religious service" held aboard the ship the previous Sunday.

THE RUSSIAN PEOPLE were particularly encouraged because the joint FDR-Churchill statement also declared that there was going to be a conference to cover Soviet supply needs.

Stalin, told there would be a conference in Moscow immediately to work out specific aid and schedules, a week later was still waiting to hear about specific arrangements. Impatiently, he informed Ambassadors Steinhardt and Cripps that Russia was ready for consultation "at the earliest possible moment."

German bombers were pounding Moscow, forcing Stalin, Molotov, and staff, including Poskrebyshev, to take refuge in the Kirov metro station. The metro system had been built hundreds of feet deep in 1934 in anticipation of just such a contingency.

As each day passed, the German army was moving farther into Russia. On August 20 the siege of Leningrad began. Hitler's viciousness was stunning. He issued the following directive to his army targeting Leningrad: "It is proposed to approach near to the city and to destroy it with the aid of an artillery barrage . . . No. 9— . . . the Hermitage . . . No. 192—Young Pioneer's Palace . . . No. 708—Institute for Mother and Child Care." The German navy had asked that the wharf and harbor be spared for its use. The request had been refused by the high command of the armed forces because "it is intended to surround the city and then raze it to the ground." Hitler intended to starve the 2.2 million people into submission; he declared, "Requests to be allowed to surrender will be rejected . . . We have no interest in preserving any part of the population of that large city."

THE PROSPECT OF THE CONFERENCE, noted Cripps after seeing Stalin on September 9, acted like a tonic on the premier: "Stalin seemed much more confident and less depressed than last time I saw him and I think that this may be because the conference is now going to actually happen very soon."

It must have taken an enormous effort on Stalin's part to create this impression on Cripps. On September 8, German troops' pummeling of Leningrad took such a great toll that Voroshilov, close to despair, was thinking of surrendering the city. The city was now entirely cut off. On September 11, Stalin sent General Zhukov to take over command from Voroshilov. Access to Leningrad was difficult and dangerous. Finnish troops were advancing from the north, and Nazi troops were advancing from the south, which meant that to gain access, Zhukov had to fly over either Lake Ladoga or the front line. Therefore Stalin, afraid Zhukov might be killed on his way, told him that the order appointing him as the new commander would only be issued "when you arrive in Leningrad."

Zhukov arrived safely and transformed the city's defense. (Later, Eisenhower would say of Zhukov, "In Europe the war has been won and to no man do the United Nations owe a greater debt than to Marshal Zhukov.") Voroshilov, fearing the surrender of the city would mean the Baltic fleet would fall into German hands, had given the order to scuttle it. Zhukov countermanded the order, transferred the fleet's guns so they could provide additional firepower to defend the city, and gave the inhabitants renewed hope. He also issued a statement that any soldier who abandoned his post without permission would be shot. On September 19, Germans shelled the city for eighteen hours.

ROOSEVELT WAS PUSHING his staffs to set production schedules that he could count on so that "substantial and comprehensive commitments" could be made to Stalin. Averell Harriman, leading the U.S. contingent that was going to Moscow, flew first to London to confer with the leader of the British group, Lord Beaverbrook, British minister of supply. Reacting to Russian news, Roosevelt pushed up Harriman's schedule so that he and Beaverbrook would reach Moscow closer to September 25 than October 1. Meanwhile, Ambassador Oumansky had informed FDR that Moscow (Stalin) was bitter about the credit situation, meaning that the Soviet Union didn't have the funds to cover the goods that Roosevelt was pushing at them.

By September 15, Harriman was in London linking up with Beaverbrook and encountered a vexing problem: Beaverbrook attempted to put Britain instead of America in control of the mission to Russia. Beaverbrook, told by Churchill, "Your function will be not only to aid in the forming of the plans to aid Russia, but to make sure we are not bled white in the process," declared to Harriman that *he* would decide how much of what the United States had previously agreed to supply to Britain his country would release to the Soviets. Harriman retorted that in that case there was no reason for him to go to Moscow. Beaverbrook backed down, which put an end to Churchill's scheme.

FDR was monitoring the situation. He personally cabled Harriman that he would be sending him last-minute "total number of tanks by design and month that can be exported from this country irrespective of source of funds. Important that your mission . . . determine on distribution of our exportable tanks. All that I have said about tanks applies equally to airplanes." He wrote to Stimson to supply him with the number of planes Harriman could offer Stalin each month beginning October 1 through July 1: "I want this figure irrespective of the source of funds . . . As a rule of thumb, particularly as it concerns the 4-engine heavy bomber, I suggest 50 percent of our output."

On September 26, Morgenthau advised Harriman by cable, "It was the president's desire to see that the Soviet Government would have the dollars it needed to meet current needs."

When Harriman and Beaverbrook arrived in Moscow on September 28, the city was already under attack. "We could see the flash of the Russian anti-aircraft guns at night," remembered Harriman. Roosevelt had provided Harriman with an upbeat letter from him to give to Stalin. The letter ended, "I want particularly to take this occasion to express my confidence that your armies will ultimately prevail over Hitler and to assure you of our great determination to be of every possible assistance."

Harriman and Beaverbook met with Stalin and Molotov in the Kremlin for three consecutive evenings, Stalin's preferred time for appointments. At the first meeting, which started at 7:00, a list of Russia's needs was submitted and discussed. Stalin stated that in the air Germany was 50 percent stronger than Russia and that the tank situation was much worse, Germany having three or four to Russia's one, and the tanks more important—"the tanks are the deciding factor . . . rather than the air." Six committees were set up to discuss specific needs: aviation, army, navy, transport, raw materials (including food) and equipment, and medical supplies. Harriman noted (without comment) that Stalin was particularly interested in receiving a large amount of barbed wire—four thousand tons a month. At the second meeting the following evening, Stalin declined the offer of field guns and mortars, stressing that they needed anti-aircraft guns and antitank guns in great numbers. He also wanted the United States to send a long list of raw materials, which Harriman thought were reasonable requests and which he would recommend. (He would later tell FDR, "The quantities requested are considered to be modest in view of the extent of the Russian effort and Russian losses.") As the discussions continued, Beaverbrook noted that Stalin must have received bad news about Wehrmacht advances: "He was very restless, walking about and smoking continuously, and appeared to both of us to be under an intense strain . . . [H]e spoke on the telephone three times, always dialing the number himself." He informed them early that he had to leave at nine. Quite possibly he had heard what would be announced the following day: that Hitler had decreed the beginning of a decisive offensive against Moscow.

At the third meeting the following evening, Stalin was more in control, and when Harriman gave answers to the seventy requests for needed items that had been submitted, Stalin said he had a new request, for trucks: they badly needed eight to ten thousand a month. The day before, Harriman had cabled FDR that "Stalin believes the Germans now have at least three times as many tanks as the Russians." Immediately, FDR had cabled him back authorization to triple the monthly rate tanks would be made available to Stalin. As Beaverbrook and Harriman went through the list with this new information, they could see

Stalin's "growing satisfaction." "You are pleased?" asked Beaverbrook. Stalin smiled and nodded. Litvinov, who had been translating, bounded out of his chair and cried out, "Now we shall win the war."

Harriman, too, was energized as they finished their agreement on the list of items to be shipped. He told his secretary that he had just accomplished the most important thing in his life. "He looked," the secretary noted, "like the cat that had swallowed the mouse."

The last evening there was a banquet in the great hall of the eighteenth-century Kremlin Palace built by Catherine the Great, the entrance to which was by a magnificent staircase. The room was lit by six prerevolutionary candelabra; the chairs, in all their imperial glory, were covered in gold leaf. Stalin presided, sitting between Harriman and Beaverbrook at a great table that stretched the length of the room. He wore a simple but well-cut dove-gray jacket. He shook hands with everyone, greeting most of them personally.

As Harriman noted,

> The quantity and quality of the food was impressive, but the more remarkable thing was the atmosphere . . . One of the greatest battles of history was raging not more than a hundred miles away. Through dinner and the evening one was impressed with their great assurance . . . There was an air of safety and confidence—of calm resolution and of unshakeable courage.

This feeling was reinforced when in the midst of dinner the air raid sirens suddenly went off. Then anti-aircraft guns went off in the courtyard, and as they paused, Stalin rose and proposed a toast: "Gentlemen, to the gunners."

In stark contrast to the dire straits of the country, the banquet was lavish. There were endless hors d'oeuvres, beginning with caviar, followed by various fish and cold suckling pig, followed by hot soup, salmon, chicken, duck, partridge, vegetables, mushrooms in sour cream, ice cream and cakes, and ending with assorted fresh fruits flown in from the Crimea.

In front of each man were a number of bottles containing pepper vodka, red and white wine, Russian brandy, and at dessert champagne.

Stalin drank out of a very small glass, about the size of a double pony of brandy. He drank his first toast in pepper vodka, drank only part, and poured the rest out into one of his larger glasses. He then filled the small glass with red wine, filling it frequently. He drank champagne out of the same glass. He put one of the other glasses in front of him over the champagne bottle "to keep in the bubbles." He ate caviar with a fork and ate plentifully. He appeared relaxed and kept looking around the room.

During the toasts Stalin would stand up, his glass on the table, and when he liked the sentiment of the toast, which was in most cases, he clapped his hands and then drank his toast. When he toasted FDR, he ended with the words "May God help him," which so surprised Harriman that he later had the words checked to make sure he had heard them correctly.

ROOSEVELT HELD A PRESS CONFERENCE that same day, at which he spoke about giving Russia "the greatest aid possible." He also pointed out that religion was permissible under the Soviet constitution.

Harriman would write of Stalin that he was "a man who knows the whole problem of Russia's military supplies, who hardly needs to check a fact . . . He is as quick in his mental qualities as he is slow in physical movement. And he hates Hitler—hates him with an unmeasured hatred." Because the aid promised was of such great psychological as well as military importance to the Russian people, Beaverbrook and Harriman sought to reassure the Soviet people that "it has now been decided to place at the disposal of the Soviet Government practically every requirement for which the Soviet military and civil authorities have asked." All of which was given great prominence in the Soviet press.

The Moscow protocol, as it would be called, would save Russia. The list of goods that Roosevelt committed to send to the Soviet Union was astounding. It included shipments every month of 400 planes, 500 tanks, 5,000 cars, 10,000 trucks, and huge quantities of antitank guns, anti-aircraft guns, diesel generators, field telephones, radios, motorcycles, wheat, flour, sugar, 200,000 pairs of boots, a million yards of woolen overcoat cloth, as well as 500,000 pairs of surgical gloves and 15,000 amputation saws. Shipments began virtually immediately. By the end of October ships carrying 100 bombers, 100 fighter planes, and 166 tanks—all with spare parts and ammunition—plus 5,500 trucks were on the high seas.

There was a problem. The American embassy and military staff, including Major Ivan Yeaton, U.S. military attaché, were largely hostile to Soviet survival. Most of them—career diplomats and military personnel alike—deeply mistrusted the Soviet leaders and tried to subvert FDR's all-out aid effort. This was known to General James H. Burns, whom FDR personally picked to go to Moscow to supervise aid to the stricken country. Burns, who had been watching the unproductive situation for some time and who approved only of Lieutenant Colonel Philip Faymonville, U.S. military attaché, sent a memo to Hopkins in August describing the negative attitudes of the American personnel stationed in Moscow: "With the exception of Faymonville there is little sympathy with the President's policy of maximum Lend-Lease aid to Russia in the spirit of the good neighbor and the sincere friend and based upon principle that helping Russia helps U.S. The organization in Russia lacks the teamwork, prestige, dignity, ability and respectability essential to the important work involved and is not a credit to America." He recommended to Hopkins that Faymonville immediately become head of Lend-Lease in Moscow.

Colonel Faymonville, a West Point graduate who had been in Moscow as U.S. military attaché on and off starting in 1934, was hated and ostracized by his American co-workers and superiors, whose fear of Communism was such that they believed that because he spoke Russian and was sympathetic to Russian culture, he was a traitor to his country. In 1939 the army sent Faymonville back to the United States and asked the FBI to try to turn up derogatory information on him, upon the expectation that he was a homosexual. The FBI, examining his life from schooltimes onward, discovered no evidence of what would at that time have been sexual deviation, indeed, found only respect and praise for his work. When Hopkins announced that Faymonville would not only be in charge of Lend-Lease in Moscow but be promoted to brigadier general, army brass, including General Marshall, were stunned and tried to block the move, arguing that Faymonville was oblivious to instructions. The effort failed. As Marshall admitted, "Hopkins had power in representing Russians. His power could always override mine because of his closeness to the president." Faymonville had other powerful friends—Joseph E. Davies, for one. Davies had written to FDR in 1939 that "both Molotov and Stalin expressed confidence in the judgment, capacity and fairness of our Military Attaché, Lieutenant Colonel Philip R. Faymonville."

The U.S. ambassador to the Soviet Union, Laurence Steinhardt, was scared and barely functioning. Three days after the invasion he packed up and shipped twenty-three cases and seven trunks out of the country so hurriedly that they went off without tags or labels of identification of any kind. At the end of August he sent his wife, Dulcie, and their fifteen-year-old daughter to Stockholm. He sent, without asking for permission, the first secretary of the embassy, Charles E. Dickerson Jr., together with other personnel, to Kazan on the Volga with a freight car full of possessions. He *thought* the Russians would hold out. "It is more probable than improbable that history will repeat itself," as he told the writer Erskine Caldwell, whom he saw in Moscow.

He did a number of things that Stalin heard about and didn't like. As the subject of contacts between their two nations came up in the conversations, it rapidly became clear to Beaverbrook and Harriman that Stalin disapproved of Steinhardt. Stalin complained to Beaverbrook that the ambassador accepted what others told him: "absurd" stories about the fall of Moscow. Stalin knew he had sent embassy staff to Kazan and that twice in the first six weeks of the war he had panicked, thinking there was no hope for Moscow. "Stalin's denunciation was severe," according to Beaverbrook.

Stalin asked Beaverbrook what he thought of Ambassador Oumansky. Beaverbrook diplomatically replied that Oumansky, in his "enthusiasm," went to too many people with requests, thereby irritating them. Oumansky was also very unpopular in Washington. Marshall didn't like him, and Stimson loathed him, noting in his diary, "He is nothing but a crook . . . Hoover and the FBI have a record on him which show that at one time he was in the pay of the German Government . . . He is a slick, clever little beast, very different from the two honest and straightforward Russian peasants who are with him."

Both men would be replaced.

As he spoke, Beaverbrook noticed that Stalin was drawing numberless pictures of wolves, filling in the background with red pencil.

Stalin was correct in complaining about Steinhardt, whose health was breaking down under the strain. Steinhardt evidently panicked periodically: he sent a cable to Washington on October 7 that he was returning to Washington, then changed his mind, and cabled Washington on October 13 that he was postponing his departure.

THE SIEGE OF MOSCOW, code-named Typhoon by the German general Fedor von Bock, in charge of the operation, began in September, with two million men assembled into three armies. In terms of the number of people involved as well as the stress it laid on the country, it was the greatest battle of the war. It would, according to the historian Rodric Braithwaite, author of *Moscow, 1941: A City and Its People at War,* claim 926,000 Soviet lives before it ended.

At first Wehrmacht progress was swift. On October 3, Adolf Hitler, speaking in Berlin, said the Red Army was already broken and would never rise again. By October 5 three German fronts were close to encircling the city. Zhukov, ordered by Stalin to return to Moscow, arrived on October 8. On that day 600,000 Muscovites were mobilized to mine the main bridges and tunnels, build barricades, create obstacles, dig trenches, and destroy all remaining industrial sites. In all, 498 companies and 210,000 workers were packed up, put on rails, and transported to the east. (Many had already been moved: by November more than 700 factories had been put on railway cars and taken to the Urals, more than 300 to Siberia, and more than 400 to areas behind the Volga.)

On October 9, Otto Dietrich, Hitler's spokesman, announced that Marshal Timoshenko's armies and Marshal Semyon Budenny's armies had been routed: "For all military purposes Soviet Russia is done with. The British dream of a two-front war is dead."

On October 10, Major Yeaton cabled Washington that the end of resistance was in sight. (Hopkins, who had spoken with Yeaton in Moscow in July, wrote to tell Secretary of War Henry Stimson to ignore this information: "I can not see how any Military Attaché could get any reasonable expression of opinion from commuters or the general public which would be worthwhile.") Nevertheless, Stimson was deeply worried. "The news is very bad from Russia," he wrote in his diary. "The Germans have been making big progress and it's Nip and Tuck whether they won't carry out their plan and finish the campaign before winter."

Major General Sir Hastings Ismay, Churchill's chief of staff, thought Moscow would fold within three weeks. *The New York Times* stated, "We are not yet compelled to abandon hope that the Russian armies may be saved, that a new front may be formed." The paper quoted

FDR's statement: "It is time for this country to stop playing into Hitler's hands and unshackle our own."

In England there was a growing clamor for immediate military action to save Russia. The popular call was for a cross-channel invasion by British troops, the reasoning being that Hitler had put all his men into the Soviet battle, leaving the entire coast from northern Norway to Spain only lightly guarded. It was the furthest thing from Churchill's mind. He was concentrating his troops for the battle in North Africa.

FDR HELD A PRESS CONFERENCE a few days later in which he announced that large amounts of supplies had been sent to Russia within the past few days. He further stated that all the munitions that were promised for October at the Moscow Conference, including tanks, airplanes, and trucks, would be sent to Russia before the end of the month, with most of these supplies leaving U.S. ports within two days' time. He also stated that the staffs had worked through the past weekend to rush supplies to the ports.

Richard Sorge had continued to send war information from Tokyo. His status had risen after his message giving the exact date of the German invasion: now considered credible, he was asked to find out whether Japan had plans to attack the Soviets in the Far East on the Manchurian border. On September 14 he cabled the information that Japan had decided not to strike the U.S.S.R. His later cables, the last one on October 4, continued to substantiate this information. Stalin decided he had no choice: he had to call in the bulk of the Far Eastern troops guarding the Manchurian border or lose Moscow. But the distance the army had to travel was huge—thousands of miles—it would take weeks for it to arrive. In the very possible event that the Japanese *might* pounce if they thought the border significantly unguarded, deployment of troops away from the border was hidden as much as possible from the Kwantung army. According to the Soviet historian Roy Medvedev, Stalin summoned General Joseph Apanasenko, commander in chief of the Far Eastern army, together with others of the Far Eastern staff, to the Kremlin, on October 12. Gennady Andreevich Borkov, the first secretary of the Khabarovsk regional committee of the All Union Communist Party, remembers receiving the urgent telephone call from Stalin asking him to fly to Moscow.

Stalin called me by top secret control operated communication line. . . . Throughout the years of my work in the Far East and elsewhere Stalin has never called me by phone. That is why I was greatly surprised when I heard his voice in the receiver . . . "Hitler is preparing an offensive to Moscow; we do not have enough troops to save the capital" . . . Finally, he repeated once again, "Fly immediately with the fastest military aircraft."

[Upon our arrival, Stalin] invited [us] to sit at a long table covered with green broadcloth. At first, he did not take a seat, but walked along the room in silence, [then] stopped in front of us and began, "Our forces in the western front are engaged in very difficult defensive combat, with a total crushing defeat in the Ukraine. Ukrainians in general behave badly, many surrender, the population welcomes the German forces."

A short pause. He took a few steps back and forth in the room. Stalin again stopped in front of us and continued, "Hitler has launched a large-scale attack of Moscow. I have to withdraw troops from the Far East. I am asking you to understand our situation."

I felt a chill in my back and cold sweat on my forehead . . . "The question is not only of the loss of Moscow but probably of the fate of the state . . ."

He spread his papers on the table, and pointing his finger to the details of the strength of our front, turning to Apanasenko began listing the numbers of the tank and motorized divisions, artillery regiments, and other major units, which Apanasenko was to send to Moscow immediately.

Borkov remembers that Stalin then asked Apanasenko how many antitank guns he had, and when Apanasenko gave the number, Stalin said, " 'Load these guns for dispatching too . . .' Apanasenko jumped off from the table and screamed . . . 'What are you doing . . . In case the Japanese attack, what would I defend the Far East with? . . . Demote me, shoot me, but I won't give the guns.' At this point Stalin said 'Calm down comrade. Why worry about these guns? Leave them to yourself.' "

Another of the generals present remembers Stalin saying, "You should do everything not to give Japan any grounds to join the war, to open what would become for us the second front. If you provoke a war in the Far East, we would try you by martial laws. Good-bye."

On October 14 the Germans broke through Russian lines at Mozhaisk, seventy-five miles west of Moscow, which meant Moscow was *almost* in their grasp.

The first 48 Curtiss P-40 planes were in Russia, assembled and ready for active service, on October 8. FDR cabled Stalin on October 13 that 166 tanks would leave the United States in two days, 200 planes in ten days, 5,500 trucks before the month was out. An indication of the chaos that prevailed in Moscow at this juncture is that this cable is missing from Russian files, and the next message FDR sent, on October 25, informing him that Russia had finally, definitely been included under Lend-Lease, was lost until spring.

Given the uncertainty and the nearness of German troops, on October 15 Stalin gave the order to evacuate the city. October 16 was a day of terror in Moscow. The Moscow police had been sent to the front. The city closed down: there were no buses, no trolleys; the metro stopped running. The streets were jammed with panicked people—families, possessions, baggage—all trying to move out of the city, amid a rain of soot swirling overhead as office workers set their files on fire.

All government officials, including Molotov, who was to go as deputy head of government, and all diplomats, were ordered to Kuibyshev, at the confluence of the Samara and Volga Rivers, six hundred miles away. The general staff was to go to another city on the Volga; the research institutes, educational institutions, and theaters were to go to yet other destinations. All important buildings in Moscow were wired with explosives; all important records went to Kuibyshev.

Stalin's library and personal papers were packed and sent to Kuibyshev; his railroad car and a DC-3 stood ready for his departure. The diplomats, told that Molotov and Stalin would join them, were ordered to board a special train for Kuibyshev. Together with other important Muscovites, the diplomats boarded the train shortly after midnight in a darkness lit only by flashes from nearby anti-aircraft guns; heavy sleet was falling. The trip took five days. Such was the chaos that the only food and water aboard were the supplies the passengers had with them. German soldiers came close to capturing the train—fought off by a Russian cavalry corps that counterattacked at the last moment. But the shelling had damaged the rail line, necessitating repairs and a very slow pace. On the train were also all members of the Bolshoi Theatre and the Bolshoi Ballet and some artists, including Aram Khachaturian and

Dmitri Shostakovich. All survived the trip by foraging when the train stopped at village stations and collective farms along the way.

The first Siberian troops, the Beloborodov division, arrived that same terrible day, immediately taking positions on the main roads to Moscow. They were followed by naval as well as army divisions. With their arrival Stalin changed his mind about leaving Moscow and ordered all the commissars—all except Molotov, who went to Kuibyshev—to stay with him.

General A. P. Beloborodov, commander of one of the Far Eastern divisions, wrote later in his memoirs of the rushed trip to get to Moscow in time: "The railmen gave us the green light. We spent no more than five–seven minutes at the key junctions. They would detach one engine, hitch another, filled with water and coal—and we would be again moving ahead! Exact schedule, strict control. As a result, all 36 troop trains with the division crossed the country from east to west at the speed of an express train. The last troop train departed from Vladivostok on 17 October."

On October 30, FDR cabled Stalin the news that he was helping the Soviet Union in the most direct and efficient way at his command:

> I have approved all of the items of military equipment and munitions and have directed that the utmost expedition be used to provide so far as possible the raw materials. I have ordered that the deliveries begin at once and be maintained in the greatest possible volume.
>
> In order to remove any financial obstacles I have also directed that arrangements be effected immediately whereby shipments up to the value of one billion dollars may be made under the Lend Lease act.
>
> I propose, subject to the approval of the Government of the USSR, that no interest be charged on the indebtedness incurred as a result of these shipments and that the payments on such indebtedness by the Government of the USSR begin only five years after conclusion of the war and completed over a period of ten years thereafter.

The cable, paraphrased because of concern over code safety, went to Steinhardt in Kuibyshev, who gave it to Vyshinsky, also in Kuibyshev, on November 2. Vyshinsky cabled the paraphrased version (essentially true in all respects to the original) to Stalin the next day. It took another day for Stalin to cable FDR back his appreciation and gratitude. His message closed, "With respect to your proposal . . . that personal direct contact should be immediately established between you and me . . . I share your desire with satisfaction and am prepared to do everything necessary to make this possible."

By that time Moscow was in such dire straits that Stalin wanted to feature the welcome news (with photographs) on the front pages of Soviet newspapers, but Steinhardt had to stop him. "[It] may be dangerous. Roosevelt has taken decision to grant the USSR a one billion dollar loan without the knowledge of Congress," he told Vyshinsky.

Steinhardt was on the verge of collapse. On November 3, he wrote to Hull of "the mental and physical strain . . . aggravated by the extraordinarily disagreeable conditions of life . . . war conditions . . . I broke a molar in half." He is sure, he writes, that Moscow's fall is a matter of time. Molotov has gone back to Moscow. "Until Moscow falls, which may not be for some time, it seems unlikely that they [Molotov and Stalin] will come to Kuibyshev." He writes further that he will stick it out if he cannot be relieved. Two days later he gets the answer to his plea: a soothing cable from Roosevelt telling him he will be replaced by "someone who is fully acquainted with detailed problems of American production and supply."

November 6 and 7 were solemn days of commemoration in the Soviet Union: in 1941 they marked the twenty-fourth anniversary of the Russian Revolution. The German army was a scant thirty miles from Moscow. On November 6, Stalin, for purposes of propaganda, decided to hold the traditional eve of anniversary party for political workers and deputies but to hold it out of sight, in the Mayakovskaya subway station, famous for its beautiful aluminum arches. A dais was set up for the Politburo at the end of the platform. On one track stood a train with open doors from which sandwiches and soft drinks were dispensed.

Stalin gave a rousing speech about Germany's miscalculation: "They seriously counted on creating a universal coalition against the USSR, on enlisting Great Britain and the USA in this coalition, after frightening the ruling circles of these countries with the spectre of revolution . . . Far from being isolated, the USSR acquired new allies in the shape of Great Britain, the United States and countries occupied by the Germans." Far from weakening, "the reverses of the Red Army only served still further to strengthen both the alliance of the workers and peasants." Stalin then went into the question of why they were suffering reverses. And here he pushed for a second front: "There are no armies of Great Britain or the United States of America on the European continent . . . The situation at present is such that our country is waging a war of liberation single-handed . . . But neither can there be any doubt that the appearance of a second front on the European continent—and it must unquestionably appear in the near future [loud applause] will materially ease the position of our Army." He also gave figures for Russians killed, 350,000, and missing, 378,000, since the start of the war that he knew were far, far from the truth.

The next day, against the advice of most of his staff, who thought it too dangerous (when he brought up the idea, Molotov and Beria thought they had misheard him, according to General Volkogonov), Stalin decided to hold the traditional parade and commemoration in Red Square—to celebrate as if Moscow were not under siege. He ordered a fighter "umbrella" over the city. If there was an air raid during the parade, Stalin said, the dead and wounded "must be quickly removed and the parade allowed to go on." He ordered that cameras be trained on the troops as they marched, undoubtedly to show the photographs of intact Red forces that would give the lie to the führer's assertions that the Red Army was finished. Luckily, it snowed, preventing German bombers from even attempting to disrupt the parade.

The event became a statement of Russian resistance and courage. With the members of the Politburo, Stalin stood on the mausoleum and watched as generals mounted on white horses, lines of Russian T-34 tanks, and columns of troops passed by. He spoke for thirty minutes, inspiring everyone with his self-assurance. His words were broadcast all over the Soviet Union. He started in a low-pitched voice, slow almost to the point of halting, as he often did.

Andrei Sakharov, then twenty years old, later famous for helping develop the Russian atomic bomb, related that even though he knew it was a carefully staged speech, it made a powerful impression on him as well as everyone else listening. A correspondent for the Overseas Press would never forget its impact. "The war is won," a Red Army colonel said to him as they stood at a railway station east of Moscow.

"How do you know?" asked the correspondent, Ralph Parker.

"By that face," the colonel answered, pointing at a middle-aged workman who had halted at the sound of Stalin's voice. "I saw his broad face slowly break into a smile. His rough hands went to his head and removed his cap. Then, quickly, he pressed it to his cheeks, down which tears had begun to stream."

All around him, Parker noticed, "people stood transfixed by their leader's voice and turned rapt faces towards Moscow whence it came."

Stalin started the speech with an unusual acknowledgment of the extraordinary contribution women were making to the war effort (farms were 90 percent operated by women, factories 60 percent):

> Men of the Red Army and Red Navy, working men and working women, collective farmers—men and women, workers in the intellectual professions, brothers and sisters in the rear who have temporarily fallen under the yoke of the German brigands, and our valiant men and women guerrillas who are destroying the rear of the German invaders . . .
>
> We have temporarily lost a number of regions, the enemy has appeared at the gates of Leningrad and Moscow. The enemy reckoned that after the very first blow our army would be dispersed, and our country would be forced to her knees. But the enemy gravely miscalculated.
>
> The enslaved peoples of Europe who have fallen under the yoke of the German invaders look to you as their liberator . . . The war you are waging is a war of liberation, a just war.

The soldiers marching in Red Square returned to their posts, picked up their positions, returned to the war.

By November 16, German troops had crossed the river Lama at the opening of the Moscow Canal. Klin, fifty-three miles northwest of Moscow, fell on November 24. On November 28 other German troops, proceeding south, were about twenty miles from the Kremlin. General Heinz Guderian was advancing from the south.

By the beginning of November, German soldiers could see the highest points of Moscow through their field glasses.

On November 23, Vyshinsky informed Ambassador Cripps the time had come for the British to send experts into the Caucasus to help arrange for the destruction of the oil wells. Then two things happened.

The temperature dropped to minus four degrees Fahrenheit, which didn't impede Red soldiers dressed for the cold but was disastrous for the lightly clad German troops who had been told they would triumph before winter set in. Then, a few days later, Soviet ski troops began attacking the German rear. On December 5, Zhukov, at the head of the Siberian divisions, went on the attack: the Soviet counteroffensive began. The German onslaught ground to a halt.

By December 6 the Germans had been pushed back from Klin, Yasnaya Polyana, 124 miles south of Moscow, and other key points. *Pravda* wrote on December 13, "The enemy has been wounded but not killed." By December 18, Stalin was discussing with Sir Stafford Cripps the serious deterioration of German morale in the armies on the front and his belief that there were no German reserves left.

DECEMBER 7 WAS a rare warm winter day in Washington. Neither Roosevelt, nor most members of his cabinet, nor the Joint Chiefs of Staff were ready for the Japanese attack on Pearl Harbor. There had been signs for weeks that the Japanese were going to hit *somewhere*. On the previous evening Roosevelt had been shown a map of Indochina with pencil marks showing Japanese ships approaching the Malay Peninsula, leading him and senior military officers to think the attack would be in that region. FDR heard the news of the attack from Frank Knox, secretary of the navy, who called him at 1:47 p.m. FDR called Hull and Stimson to tell them the news immediately. A bit later he called Davies, whose response was "Thank God!" These two succinct words were recorded by Maxim Litvinov, who had just arrived in Washington as the new ambassador from the Soviet Union, replacing the unpopular Constantine Oumansky, and with his wife was having lunch with Davies. Litvinov would later say that Roosevelt, as well as everyone in his close circle, was happy to be drawn into the war. Davies remembered saying to the president, "It was a terrible thing, but it was providential."

Litvinov, recorded Davies, was initially not happy at the idea of America's entering the war, because he was worried that it might impede the flow of American goods and weapons to the Soviet Union.

That evening FDR drew his cabinet together in the Oval Office. "He began," wrote Stimson, "with his fine sense of history, by telling us that this was the most serious meeting of the Cabinet that had taken place since 1861." Wrote Perkins after the meeting, "In spite of the horror that war had actually been brought to us, he had, nevertheless, a much calmer air. His terrible moral problem had been resolved by the event."

Weeks before, the famous journalist Edward R. Murrow and his wife, Janet, had been invited to the White House for dinner on December 7. They arrived to find, as a result of the Japanese attack, that Roosevelt was in constant meetings and could not stop for dinner and that they were expected to eat the light supper of scrambled eggs and pudding that Eleanor Roosevelt usually provided on Sunday evenings, which they did. Janet Murrow went home, and Murrow waited, hoping to see the president. Finally, near midnight, Murrow was rewarded; he saw Roosevelt come out of the Oval Office exhausted and angry, exclaiming, "Our planes were destroyed on the ground." Roosevelt had ordered beer and sandwiches. As they ate, he kept saying to Murrow, beating on the table, "On the ground, mind you, ON THE GROUND!"

America was readier than anyone knew. FDR had put the U.S. Navy on a shipbuilding spree. There were only 17 battleships in commission but 15 on order, of which 4 were scheduled to be completed by the end of 1942. The navy had 7 aircraft carriers and 11 on order, although completion would be in 1944. There were 18 heavy cruisers, 8 on order, of which 4 would be afloat in 1943. There were 19 light cruisers and 40 more on order, the first to come out of the yards before the end of the year. There were 172 destroyers on hand and 192 on order. There were 113 submarines on hand and 73 on order. One was almost finished, 27 scheduled to be finished in 1942, 24 in 1943, the rest later.

The Japanese attack on Pearl Harbor impelled Roosevelt to try to bring about war plans conferences as soon as possible involving China, the U.S.S.R., Britain, and America. Roosevelt's first message to Stalin after the Japanese attack must be read in this light. It is interesting in that it appeared to be as much for Chiang Kai-shek's eyes as for Stalin's. FDR wanted to have a conference, he told Stimson, with important members of the Allied governments in Washington toward the end of December, and to this goal he was sending similar cables to Chiang, Churchill, and Stalin.

Chiang declared war against Japan, Germany, and Italy on December 8. He then asked the Soviet ambassador to China, Alexander S. Panyushkin, to join him and declare war against Japan. There was reason for him to hope this would happen soon. As Chiang cabled his minister of foreign affairs in Washington, T. V. Soong, "The Chief Soviet Military Advisor expresses his personal opinion . . . that the Soviet declaration of war against Japan is verily a matter of time and procedure." Soong passed this information on to Welles. Litvinov met with Hull on December 11, four days after Pearl Harbor, and told him this was not going to happen. He "proceeded to say" to Hull "that he had received the final decision of his Government today and that it was not in a position to cooperate with us at present in the Japanese Far Eastern area; his Government is fighting on a huge scale against Germany and that to take part with us in the Far East would mean a prompt attack by Japan."

During this conversation Hull gave Litvinov the erroneous news, for the first but by no means the last time, that Japan was going to invade Russia, saying, "I now have information . . . to the effect that Japan, notwithstanding the terms of the Russo-Japanese neutrality agreement, is now under the strictest commitment to Germany to attack Russia and another country fighting against Germany." Litvinov, according to Hull, would not be drawn into commenting. Hull then vaguely threatened Litvinov, saying to him, "If Russia should refrain from cooperation with us in the East while we continue to aid her there will be a constant flow of criticism about why we are aiding Russia."

Roosevelt's message to Stalin is dated December 14:

First, I am suggesting to Generalissimo Chiang Kai-shek that he call a conference immediately in Chungking consisting of Chinese, Soviet, British, Dutch and American representatives. This group would meet not later than December seventeenth and report to their respective governments in the greatest confidence by Saturday, December twentieth. This would give us the preliminary picture of the joint problem from the angle of Chungking.

Second, I am asking the British to assemble a military-naval conference in Singapore . . .

Third, I should be very happy if you personally would talk with American, British and Chinese representatives in Moscow and let me have your suggestions as to the whole picture by Saturday, the twentieth.

Fourth, I am during this coming week covering the same ground with British missions here and will send you the general picture from this end.

Litvinov, in sending on the cable to Stalin, wrote an accompanying explanation:

> Roosevelt has just summoned me and presented to me a message for immediate transmission . . . The President opened the conversation by saying that Chiang Kai-shek would like to turn Chungking into the center of allied actions and that in his desire to satisfy him in a certain way Roosevelt is making the present proposal; however further [in the conversation] he said that he attached great significance to the conferences he proposed. It seems to me that Roosevelt would like to satisfy the public opinion to a certain degree in its demand of united allied actions and blaming him for not involving us earlier into conferences on Pacific matters . . . To my reservation that the conferences will probably discuss the problems of war with Japan . . . Roosevelt replied that he understood and that our representative in Chungking would, of course, be unable to officially take part in the conference . . . *It is possible that Roosevelt would like to involve us, however indirectly and verbally, into an anti-Japanese action and that all this has been the sole and only purpose of his proposals.* (Italics mine)

Although dated December 14, FDR's message was only transmitted the following afternoon at 4:20.

Stalin wrote back a polite but puzzled message, explaining that he had only received FDR's cable on December 16 and saying, "As there was no mention of the object of the suggested conferences in Chungking and Moscow, and there was only one day left before their opening, I thought I might be able, in conversation with Mr. Eden, who had just arrived in Moscow, to elucidate the question of the objects of the conferences . . . It transpired, however, that Mr. Eden has no information on this point, either."

FDR abandoned the conference idea; the cable to Churchill was never sent. Trying to involve Stalin in the battle against Japan ceased, for the moment. Churchill, in any case, was scheduled to visit the White House within the week.

Stalin had sent Chiang Kai-shek a friendly cable a few days earlier apologizing for Russia's nonparticipation in the war on Japan, explaining, "Russia today has the principal burden of the war against Germany . . . Under the circumstances the Soviet today ought not to divert its strength to the Far East . . . I beg you therefore not to insist that Soviet Russia at once declare war against Japan."

But then he had added, "Soviet Russia must fight Japan, for Japan will surely unconditionally break the Neutrality Pact. We are preparing to meet that situation, but it takes time to prepare."

The State Department received a copy of this cable on December 16. Welles, reading it, was so excited he immediately rang FDR and read it to him over the phone. In this offhand way, Stalin intimated to Roosevelt that, although not at present, at some point Russia could be expected to enter the war against Japan.

THE ENTRANCE OF AMERICA into the war had a salutary effect on Stalin, at least for a short time: his first reaction was that America would wipe both Germany and Japan into the dust in a matter of months. Even the fact that Archangel was becoming icebound could not curb his sudden optimism.

An evening meeting with Eden and Cripps ten days after Pearl Harbor found Stalin in high good humor. Not only was America in the war, but the Wehrmacht advance had ground to a halt. His thoughts went to protecting Russia in the future. He tried to push them into signing documents setting postwar boundaries; on view for the first time was his plan to protect Russia from further invasions. That meant there had to be a Poland strong enough to resist becoming the staging ground for yet another German invasion. But even though they couldn't agree and nothing was signed, they all—Maisky and Molotov were also present— finished up round the table with champagne, all sorts of cold dishes, and caviar. Stalin, according to Cripps, stuck with the caviar, "of which he eats large quantities . . . We had a long gossipy talk after the main conversation had finished and a good deal of laughter and chaffing." In the conversation Stalin "was most encouraging both as to his front and as to his estimate of the Japanese situation. *He thought they would not last much more than six months.*" (Italics mine)

9

ROOSEVELT, STALIN, AND
THE SECOND FRONT

The opening of the second front was the single most important move America could make to aid Russia and the single most contentious issue between Roosevelt and Stalin in the first years of the war. It was close to being an obsession with Stalin: the first thing he asked of Churchill and Roosevelt because, in the early months of the war, when the German army was poised on the outskirts of Moscow, he was desperate for a plan that would force Hitler to draw off his army from Russia.

U.S. military circles strongly backed the plan: a second front had been Eisenhower's idea from the start because driving straight into Germany was the single most efficient use of troops. In January 1942, as a lowly colonel in the War Plans Division of the general staff, Eisenhower had written a note to himself: "We've got to go to Europe and fight." Marshall agreed, and the planning began. Shortly thereafter Marshall promoted Eisenhower to brigadier general and made him head of the War Plans Division. By February 28, Eisenhower had finished the cross-channel invasion plan and submitted it to Marshall. It called for a buildup of forty-eight divisions to land in northern France between Calais and Le Havre, where the channel was narrowest, in the fall of 1943, to march into Germany. It would be protected by a force of fifty-eight hundred planes. It also called for a possible small-scale invasion of France later in 1942, code-named Sledgehammer, the establishment of a bridgehead in the fall of 1943, and exploitation of the bridgehead in the spring of 1943, when the full-scale invasion would take place. The express purpose was to "divert sizable portions" of the German army from Russia; the operations were to be "so conceived and so presented to the Russians that they will recognize the importance the support rendered." The plan was adopted because it made such sense.

Stimson, in his pivotal position as secretary of war, called it the surest road to the shaking up of Hitler's forces in Russia in 1942, the surest road to the führer's ultimate defeat. Stimson talked with Roosevelt endlessly over the ramifications and importance of the cross-channel invasion. It would save Russia "by making a powerful attack through Great Britain into France preceded by air," as Stimson wrote in his diary in early March. But it meant the buildup and housing of U.S. forces in England and the involvement of British soldiers and British aircraft in the invasion itself. It would only work if the British were solidly behind it: success rested on British cooperation.

On March 31, 1942, four months after Pearl Harbor, FDR decided the time had come to put the plan into action. He drafted a cable to Stalin inviting Molotov to Washington to discuss a matter "involving the utilization of our armed forces in a manner to relieve your critical western front. This objective carries great weight with me . . . Time is of the essence." But probably because he didn't yet have the British commitment, FDR didn't spell out that he was referring to the second front. More to the point, he didn't send the message. Instead, he held on to it. He drew together Secretaries Stimson and Knox, Generals Marshall and Arnold, Admiral King, and Harry Hopkins for another war plans conference. The results were gratifying: the men were unanimous in their conviction that a cross-channel invasion was the wisest course and that the British had to be an integral part of the invasion plan.

Reinvigorated by the strength and unanimity of his advisers, Roosevelt sent off a cable to the prime minister: "Your people and mine demand the establishment of a front to draw off pressure on the Russians, and these people are wise enough to see that the Russians are killing more Germans and destroying more equipment than you and I put together."

At the same time he decided to send General Marshall and Harry Hopkins to London to put the urgency of the invasion plans directly before Churchill, Eden, and the British general staff, who he knew were wavering. In contrast to their hesitant leaders, the British people favored a cross-channel invasion. At the end of March twenty thousand people demonstrated in Trafalgar Square for the opening of a second front. The headline in the *Sunday Express* read "Strike in Europe Now!"

Marshall and Hopkins arrived in London on April 8 and immediately plunged into discussions with Churchill and the British War Cabinet. The next day Hopkins cabled Roosevelt that he had had not one but two meetings with the prime minister and that his response had been "sympathetic. It seemed that the outlook was hopeful for agreement right down the line."

Another day passed. Another cable came from Hopkins: "The discussions with the Former Naval Person and the British Chiefs of Staff were progressing very satisfactorily." Encouraging, but far from a commitment. Nevertheless, the morning of April 11, Roosevelt released the cable to Stalin inviting Molotov to Washington. It was delivered to Maxim Litvinov at twelve noon, as we know because FDR, in a very unusual move, carefully wrote that information on its face.

Because FDR's cable did not spell out *exactly* what he had in mind, Stalin wanted more information. On April 14, Ambassador Litvinov visited the White House in search of it.

In London, at 10:00 p.m. that same day, Marshall and Hopkins met with Churchill and the British Defense Committee at 10 Downing Street for more discussion of the cross-channel invasion. The Americans felt as if they had finally worn the British down. Beaches between Le Havre and Boulogne were selected as possible landing points; April 1, 1943, was agreed upon as the earliest possible invasion date. The War Cabinet appeared solidly in favor of the invasion plans. Churchill wrote of the "momentous proposal" under consideration, "I had no hesitation in cordially accepting the plan . . . There was complete unanimity on the framework."

Hopkins cabled the news to FDR the next day: "At long meeting last night of Defense Council, Chiefs of Staff, Former Naval Person, Marshall and I, British Government agreed to our main proposal."

Marshall cabled *his* boss, Secretary of War Stimson, "The British Government now intended to proceed immediately and energetically with all necessary preparations for the major operation." Both Hopkins and Marshall were elated.

Mackenzie King, the prime minister of Canada, was visiting the White House at the time. Eleanor Roosevelt wrote of her husband, "He had no real confidantes." But King, in fact, *was* FDR's confidant. Roosevelt shared his thoughts with King, an old friend, and explained his reasons for various actions he had taken in a way that was, for him, uncharacteristically open. King, seven years older than Roosevelt, had been at Harvard working on his Ph.D. when Roosevelt was an undergraduate. FDR, oddly, had two sets of people he felt comfortable with: navy men and social workers. Virtually every member of his personal staff was a navy man. Hopkins, Perkins, and Eleanor Roosevelt herself all had backgrounds in social work, as did King, who had worked with Jane Addams at Hull House. FDR found in him an astute observer and a sympathetic ear. King was in Washington as a member of the Pacific War Council, which had met that afternoon. After dining with the members of the council, FDR asked King upstairs to his oval study so they could have a private talk. As he often did with people he brought to his study, Roosevelt, already seated on a large leather sofa, requested King to sit next to him for their after-dinner conversation. He then launched into a matter, as King wrote in his diary, "too secret" to bring up earlier. He had said to the Pacific War Council, earlier in the day, that he had sent Hopkins and Marshall to London to urge an offensive action that would help relieve the pressure on the Russians by creating another front.

Now, wrote King in his diary, "bringing his hand down on the part of the sofa that was between us, [he] said 'I have got word tonight that a favourable decision has been reached. The favourable decision being that agreement had been come to between the British and Americans to begin the offensive against the Germans very soon . . . [I]f Russia were to be defeated by the Germans, it would be better for the offensive to take place before the defeat occurred.'"

Observed King, FDR "seemed to be much relieved" that word of agreement had come to him that night. But, King also noted in his diary, FDR had an unrealistically high estimate of the number of British troops. *He* thought there were about one hundred divisions, whereas, King wrote, it was *his* best guess, based on recent information he had received, that there were far fewer—between sixteen and twenty.

Stalin answered Roosevelt five days later, on April 20: "Let me thank you for the message which I received in Moscow the other day. The Soviet government agrees that it is necessary to arrange a meeting between V. M. Molotov and yourself for an exchange of opinions on the organization of a second front in Europe in the immediate future . . . It goes without saying that Molotov will also stop in London."

A strong, independent Poland to stand between Germany and the Soviet Union was Stalin's number one postwar aim because he believed a future German invasion of Russia was inevitable. Since the fall of 1941, Stalin had been pressuring Churchill and Eden to sign a treaty recognizing Russia's boundaries as including the Baltic States, setting Poland's eastern boundary on the Curzon Line, and compensating the Poles by giving them German territory to the west. Earlier, in the dark days of December 1941, for two days running Stalin had tried to talk Sir Stafford Cripps, British ambassador to Russia, who was in Moscow, into a secret agreement recognizing Russia's boundaries as of 1941, which included the Baltic States and a new border with Finland. When Cripps told him it wasn't possible at that time for Britain to enter into any such agreement, Cripps thought he "eventually more or less gave up" on the idea, but he hadn't. In March, having succumbed to Stalin's demands, Churchill had felt driven to explain to Stalin he had written to Roosevelt "urging him to approve our signing agreement with you about the frontiers."

Roosevelt had refused. He thought it a terrible mistake—an abandonment of the Atlantic Charter, abandonment of the principle of self-determination, the glue holding together so many disparate, downtrodden nations. He knew Churchill was amenable to Russian demands, in fact, eager to please Stalin, and was also beginning to discuss deals and postwar settlements with governments in exile headquartered in London. The previous July, FDR had asked Churchill to make "an overall statement . . . making it clear that no post war peace commitments as to territories, populations or economics have been given." Churchill ignored the request. In addition to being an abandonment of principle, FDR believed it bad policy. President Wilson had been seriously handicapped at Versailles by commitments made to which he was not a party; FDR wanted to make sure he had a free hand.

Rather than pushing Churchill on the subject again, Roosevelt had resorted to diplomatic indirection. He had had Sumner Welles, the correct, elegant undersecretary of state, make a strong statement to Edward Wood, always referred to as Lord Halifax, the tall, gaunt, worldly, and even more elegant ex-viceroy of India, who was the British ambassador to America. Halifax, a good friend of the queen's who had once volunteered that he thought Göring "attractive" and Goebbels "likable," also, voicing another concept that Roosevelt looked upon with horror, had spoken of the need of having Germany constitute the balance of power against Russia after the war. Roosevelt told Welles what to say. Welles, who lived in a grand mansion off Dupont Circle and weekended at another grand neo-Georgian mansion of forty-nine rooms high on a hill over the Potomac in Maryland, was well equipped to face down the ambassador. He accordingly announced to Halifax in February that he was following specific instructions from the president to tell Halifax that FDR had read all his documents and "only one word had come into the President's mind and that was the word 'provincial.'" This stunning affront to the polished, aristocratic diplomat took a moment for Halifax to absorb. Welles, pausing to give Halifax time to recover, continued that Roosevelt had stated that a secret agreement guaranteeing the Soviet Union its 1941 frontiers "was not a matter that could be discussed at this time." Then Welles, driving the knife in still further, told him that FDR considered that the proposed nature of security which should rightly be accorded to the Soviet Union was something "he himself would discuss . . . directly with Stalin."

Churchill wanted to sign the boundary agreement because he never trusted Stalin; it was always in the back of the prime minister's mind that Stalin might turn on his allies—double-cross them—and again team up with Hitler. (Stalin had the same fear about Churchill—that he would negotiate with Hitler.) Churchill's acquiescence in Stalin's demands to set boundaries, then, must be seen as a bribe that he thought necessary to keep him on the right side.

FDR, on the other hand, found the idea of Stalin's linking up with Hitler, given the extremely vicious conduct of the German army in the Soviet Union and the extraordinary statements Hitler had made for years about his plans for the Slav race, a very remote eventuality. And, FDR believed, Stalin had reason to rely upon *him*. He was, after all, the American president who had had the sense to recognize Soviet Russia, which Lenin had sought from the first day he was in power, and he had done it in spite of all the problems doing it entailed. Tangible evidence of Stalin's attitude toward FDR was that the Soviet press, controlled by Stalin, was historically complimentary to Roosevelt. Just that January 30, FDR's sixtieth birthday, *Izvestia* had published a highly flattering article about him, containing the genuinely nice things Stalin had said about him in his interview with H. G. Wells in 1934. Stalin had cited the president's outstanding personal qualities of initiative, courage, and determination. Stalin had called him the preeminent leader of the capitalist world.

To explain his moves to Churchill regarding Stalin, Roosevelt wrote the prime minister an artful note shortly before he sent Hopkins and Marshall to London: "I know you will not mind my being brutally frank when I tell you that I think I can personally handle Stalin better than either your Foreign Office or my State Department. Stalin hates the guts of all your top people. He thinks he likes me better, and I hope he will continue to do so."

FDR was sure Stalin would continue to rely on America, and on him personally, to pull Russia through. Furthermore, the idea that Stalin would capitulate was nonsense. The German army was in possession of millions of acres of Russia; the German air force and navy were sinking Allied ships loaded with critical supplies of armaments, food, and clothing; German soldiers were killing Russians in sickening numbers. Stalin couldn't surrender: Hitler was in the process of erasing Soviet culture, destroying the nation. German soldiers were famously herding millions of captured Red soldiers into open fields and letting them die from exposure and starvation. As they conquered towns and villages, German soldiers were deliberately defacing and destroying national treasures. Stalin must certainly have sensed how deliberate the destruction was.

Stalin had made a deal with Hitler once. Roosevelt was sure he wouldn't make that mistake again.

On the other hand, as Roosevelt also knew, Stalin had good cause not to rely on Churchill. FDR didn't believe setting a bad precedent, of caving in to Stalin's demands, would improve Stalin's respect for the prime minister. As he told Secretary of the Treasury Henry Morgenthau in March, "Every promise the English have made to the Russians, they have fallen down on . . . The only reason we stand so well with the Russians is that up to date we have kept our promises."

There was, of course, more to it than that. Churchill was an inveterate, eloquent anti-Bolshevik; he was on record as saying vile things not only about the Soviet Union but about Stalin personally. "Civilization is being completely extinguished over gigantic areas while Bolsheviks hop and caper like troops of ferocious baboons amid the ruins of cities and the corpses of their victims" was one of his choice remarks. He had also been quoted, in a double slur, as describing the Soviet leaders as "a rabble from the gutters and ghettos of Eastern Europe." He described Stalin as "a callous, a crafty and an ill-informed giant." The prime minister no longer vented his anti-Bolshevik remarks in public, but he hadn't changed his opinion. His first remark to his secretary, John Colville, after learning that Hitler had invaded Russia, was "If Hitler invaded Hell I would make at least a favourable reference to the Devil in the House of Commons."

Stalin had sent Molotov to London before Washington to work out such a boundary treaty, expecting that Roosevelt would be forced to recognize such a treaty as a fait accompli. Therefore, two days after he cabled Roosevelt, Stalin cabled Churchill that Molotov would stop in London prior to arriving in Washington. Notified of Molotov's travel plans, FDR and Hull worked out a course of action to block the Russian foreign minister from signing such a treaty. Roosevelt suggested a compromise to the British Foreign Office: the Lithuanians, Latvians, Estonians, and Finns who did not want to be Russian would have the right to leave their countries with their properties. When Molotov arrived in London, Anthony Eden presented the idea to him. Molotov rejected it.

Roosevelt and Hull then cabled John Winant, the American ambassador in London, an impressive-looking man with a Lincolnesque face, who had been head of the International Labour Organization and as such was well-known in the Soviet Union, that if a boundary treaty was signed, "we might have to issue a separate statement clearly stating that we did not subscribe to its principle and clauses . . . [T]here was no other course we could logically pursue." Winant relayed this information to Molotov at a meeting at the Russian embassy on the evening of May 24. Molotov "listened attentively and said that the President's views on this matter warranted serious attention."

The result was Molotov left London with an unsigned treaty of alliance between the Soviet Union and Britain: it contained no mention of boundaries.

Molotov arrived in Washington on Friday, May 29. His flight from London was delayed for a day and a half in Iceland by bad weather. Once over America, his Russian pilots, either unaware of the need for identifying their plane or not realizing the importance of so doing, even though they were flying a Russian bomber, made no radio contact until they were very close to the capital. As Reilly, the head of the president's security, later wrote, the unidentified plane "had us in a swivet as it was tracked southward toward Washington . . . The Russians weren't telling anybody anything even over Philadelphia."

By the time Molotov was on the ground in Washington at the air force's Bolling Field, the plane's identity had been established, and Hull and Litvinov were at the airport waiting to greet him. He was immediately taken by limousine to the White House and at 4:00 p.m. ushered into Roosevelt's study, where the president, Hopkins, Litvinov, and Hull were waiting for him. Tea was served. Molotov would later note to Stalin that this was the only conversation with Roosevelt at which Hull was present.

Molotov was a very uneasy traveler and off balance at the tea because he had not been given a chance to change clothes or freshen up. "Straight from the aerodrome," he complained to Stalin, "I was driven by car to meet Roosevelt," thus arriving at the White House "somewhat disheveled and unwashed." The White House butler Alonzo Fields would write that Molotov's "eyes would dart around with the glint of a fox waiting to spring on his prey." Having Litvinov present at his first meeting with FDR was another reason for Molotov's uneasiness: they didn't get along. Hopkins felt the tension between the two men. Litvinov "obviously doesn't like the idea of Molotov being the big shot," Hopkins noted, which in turn made Molotov uncomfortable. Molotov appeared unused to traveling outside the Soviet Union. A large chunk of black bread, a roll of sausage, and a pistol were in his bag, according to the valet whose duty it was to unpack it.

FDR didn't know what to expect of Molotov, as he later told Daisy Suckley. He thought it might be rough going, having heard "he is *not* very pleasant, and *never smiles*."

As the first meeting with Molotov got under way, the president was disturbed by the stilted nature of the conversations caused by the wait as each statement was translated, compounded by the interpreters, who occasionally stopped to discuss shades of meaning with each other. Observed Hopkins, "It was pretty difficult to break the ice, although that did not seem to be due to any lack of cordiality and pleasantness on the part of Mr. Molotov." It was rare that Roosevelt dealt with interpreters: his French and German were excellent, and one of the reasons he had gotten along so well with Ambassador Litvinov was that Litvinov spoke English. But also the initially stiff, correct Molotov was a far cry from the roly-poly, voluble Litvinov.

The Russian interpreter was Vladimir Pavlov, whom Molotov had brought with him and who would become a familiar presence to Americans. Pavlov was only twenty-seven, but he was a gifted linguist who had been on Molotov's staff for three years. He would be Stalin's interpreter in Moscow and at the Tehran and Yalta Conferences. The American interpreter was Samuel H. Cross, head of the Russian Language Department at Harvard. Cross would never again be used, because several weeks after Molotov left, Cross, having drunk too much at a dinner, had proceeded to entertain a Cambridge assemblage with a report of the conversations.

Roosevelt called Daisy the next day and told her Molotov was a "visiting fireman [who] comes from Shangri-La and speaks nothing but Mongolian."

As they drank tea, Molotov, testing the waters as to FDR's commitment to the war in Europe over the war against Japan, threw out the comment that Hitler was the chief enemy. Roosevelt agreed and mentioned the "repeated" statements he had made that America would remain on the defensive in the Pacific until Hitler was beaten. "It had been difficult to put this view across, but it was now accepted," he explained.

The president inquired about Nazi treatment of Soviet prisoners of war, raising the concept that the Soviet Union and Germany might adhere to the Geneva Convention. But, as Hopkins wrote, "you don't have to know very much about Russia, or for that matter Germany, to know there isn't a snowball's chance in hell for either Russia or Germany to permit the International Red Cross really to inspect their prison camps." Molotov said that it would be a mistake from a propaganda view, that Russian prisoners were getting a very bad deal; twenty-six prisoners recently escaped from Norwegian prison camps came back telling of starvation and beatings on the part of Germans. (In fact, the death rate over the course of the entire war for Red Army soldiers taken prisoner was more than 50 percent; for the first months of the war it was considerably higher.)

After a brief rest and a walk with Maxim Litvinov, who, it had been decided, would be excluded from the conversations to follow (as Hull would be), Molotov, Hopkins, the president, and the interpreters reassembled in the study at 7:40 for cocktails, mixed by the president, dinner, and conversation that lasted late into the evening.

Roosevelt began, while serving cocktails, to expound on his favorite subject: his ideas about a postwar organization to preserve the peace. He explained to Molotov that there would be an enforcement agency consisting of four policemen—the United States, the Soviet Union, Britain, and China—who would be the only countries permitted arms. Other nations might join the first four after experience proved they could be trusted. The organization would have inspection privileges, and "if any nation menaced the peace, it could be blockaded and then if still recalcitrant bombed." He said that his thoughts were preliminary and that he wanted Stalin's input.

Molotov replied that it would be "a bitter blow" to Poland and Turkey, not to mention France, if they were not at the outset permitted to have an army. Wouldn't they balk at being defenseless?

Roosevelt went no further with the discussion of nations' disarming. In fact one reason he was so specific about who would have arms and who would not was that the plan would also curtail Soviet armaments. His plan for the postwar limitation of arms included limiting the arms of the four policemen. "If you cannot beat the devil, join him," he said to Mackenzie King, apropos of Stalin, six months after Molotov's visit. "Russia was going to be very powerful. The thing to do was to get plans definitely made for disarmament."

Molotov stated that he wanted to verify that Roosevelt knew no negotiations over frontiers had taken place in London. Roosevelt said yes, he knew, and "he was glad the frontier problem had not been mentioned . . . The present was not the moment."

He seemed to take it as a natural outcome that Stalin and Churchill had both bent to his will.

Once they were seated for dinner, Molotov began to ably set forth his arguments for a second front. He presented the case that it was in the best interests of the Allies to draw off Hitler's forces while Russia was still strong, for if they could draw off forty German divisions, the Red Army could strike a decisive blow and shorten the war. He showed how all their countries would benefit.

Roosevelt said it was a matter not of manpower and matériel but of transportation—of landing craft.

Molotov asked about the state of public opinion toward his country in America. Roosevelt replied that the mass of the population was "more friendly" than Congress.

After dinner Roosevelt moved the party to his upstairs study and, as usual with the principal guest, asked Molotov to sit next to him on the couch. Roosevelt would have been chagrined—or perhaps he would have laughed—if he had read Molotov's characterization to Stalin of their after-dinner talk sitting on the couch: Molotov appeared not to have enjoyed it. "After dinner there was a rather long, but quite barren talk," he cabled Stalin. And, he noted, the president had tried to make him agree that he was a better host than Churchill: "Roosevelt asked me whether Churchill had received me like this, hinting at the unaffected and candid style of his reception. I replied that I was very pleased with Roosevelt's hospitality, as well as with Churchill's, who had sat with me two evenings till nearly two in the morning."

As they talked, Roosevelt assured Molotov that he was pushing his generals to get ready for the main cross-channel invasion that would take place in 1943. Saying his generals were not in favor, he spoke also of sacrificing men and landing six to ten divisions in France in 1942: "It is necessary to make sacrifices to help the USSR in 1942. It is possible that we shall have to live through another Dunkirk and lose 100,000–120,000 men."

Molotov replied that the landing of six to ten divisions was not enough. He spoke of the severe battles that the Red Army expected to fight during the summer.

Roosevelt then returned to his ideas for the postwar world, saying he wanted to start the process of disarmament after the war in such a way that peace could be established for at least twenty-five years.

The postwar world was also on Stalin's mind, of course, as evidenced by his express push for a treaty with Britain that would settle Russia's postwar boundaries. Stalin would now find out through Molotov that FDR's mind was set on initial plans for an organization of nations that could ensure a lasting peace. And it sounded as if he wanted Stalin not just to go along with his vision of a peaceful postwar world but to help him plan it. Roosevelt was essentially offering him a postwar partnership: *almost* saying, "Look here. I want you to help me run the world."

Each evening Molotov sent Stalin a report on the day's conversations. For this purpose he had brought with him a small staff of secretaries from Moscow. He cabled these thoughts of Roosevelt to Stalin. Stalin cabled him back to agree with the president:

> Roosevelt's considerations about peace protection after the war are absolutely sound. There is no doubt that it would be impossible to maintain peace in future without creating a united military force by Britain, the USA and the USSR, capable of preventing aggression. It would be good to include China here. As for Poland, Turkey and other States, I think we can well do without them, because the military power of three or four States is quite enough. Tell Roosevelt that you have communicated with Moscow, thought this matter over and come to the conclusion that Roosevelt is absolutely right and that his position will be fully supported by the Soviet Government.
>
> [STALIN]

Molotov's room was across the hall from Hopkins's. Although it was almost midnight when the meeting in Roosevelt's study broke up, Hopkins paid Molotov a visit. He wanted to make sure Molotov gave the best possible presentation the next day in his conferences with the president, General Marshall, and Admiral King on the necessity of opening a second front. He urged Molotov to paint the blackest possible scenario of the Soviet position because the military men "do not see an acute need to open the second front . . . Draw a gloomy picture of the Soviet position to make the American generals understand the gravity of the situation." He wanted Molotov to dispel any notion among the Joint Chiefs that the Soviet Union could hold out if there was no second front in the offing to draw off Hitler's hordes. Hopkins also suggested to Molotov that it would be "very useful" if he met with the president half an hour before the conference began to tell *him* about the seriousness of the situation his country faced. (This latter piece of information must also have placed in the back of Molotov's mind the idea that the president was not as fired up as he should be by the plan.)

The Soviet situation *was* in fact deteriorating. There were 217 enemy divisions and twenty brigades on the Soviet-German front. Kharkov and Kerch had fallen. Sevastopol, which had been under siege for seven months, was about to fall: it would surrender July 7. The Wehrmacht had the Soviet Second Shock Army on the northwestern front in a noose. Stalingrad was under siege. (In August, Hitler, sure Stalingrad was about to fall, convened a meeting to deal with military problems in the city after its capture, "which it was assumed would take place in a week.")

Leningrad was in the eighth month of its agony. On the Crimean front 278,000 Russian soldiers had been killed, wounded, or taken prisoner. In all, the total loss of Soviet soldiers in the eleven months they had been fighting exceeded 2 million. Molotov would not have to exaggerate, just paint the picture as it was.

The next morning, Saturday, Molotov, who had asked to meet Eleanor Roosevelt, was taken to her sitting room. They talked, with Pavlov translating, "about social reforms in his country and mine," wrote Eleanor Roosevelt. (She noticed that he often began talking before the translation was finished.)

Next, taking Hopkins's advice, Molotov met alone with the president. At eleven, Hopkins, General Marshall, and Admiral King arrived, and the discussion of the second front began in earnest. Molotov, taking his cue from Hopkins, spoke at length about the crucial importance of quick intervention on the part of Britain and America, warning that if the Red Army was *not* able to hold out, "Hitler's strength would be correspondingly greater, since he would have at his disposal not only more troops, but also the foodstuffs and raw materials of the Ukraine and the oil wells of the Caucasus." He emphasized that if Great Britain and America mounted a second front and drew off forty German divisions, "the war would be decided in 1942." If in 1943, the war would be even tougher to win than 1942.

He requested a straight answer as to the U.S. position on the second front.

"Could we say to Mr. Stalin that we are preparing a second front?" asked Roosevelt of General Marshall.

"Yes," replied the general.

Roosevelt then authorized Molotov to tell Stalin, "We expect the formation of a second front this year."

Once that crucial statement was made, FDR expounded on postwar matters, specifically on his ideas of an international trusteeship council to administer the former colonial possessions that would be taken away from weak nations. He indicated he wanted Stalin's input. He also gave

Molotov the bad news that to build up the forces for the second front in Britain, it would be necessary to cut back on Lend-Lease; Stalin would have to agree to reduce previously agreed-upon tonnage: "Ships could not be in two places at once."

A luncheon for Molotov followed the meeting. Present, among others, reflecting Roosevelt's continual strategy of keeping Congress in the foreign policy loop and on his side, were Senator Tom Connally, head of the Senate Foreign Relations Committee, and Representative Sol Bloom, head of the House Committee on Foreign Affairs.

At one point Roosevelt asked Molotov what he had thought of Hitler, because he had talked with him more recently than anyone else.

Molotov's visit to Berlin to meet with Hitler in mid-November 1940 had caused a sensation, but it was known to Roosevelt and Hull that Molotov had stood his ground and refused to fall in with Hitler's plans to dismember the British Empire. It was also known that Hitler and Ribbentrop had exerted all the pressure they could to make Molotov's visit take place earlier—just before the presidential election rather than after—because they thought the specter of Molotov and Hitler in conference *might* scare Americans and bring about Roosevelt's defeat. Stalin, understanding this, had held off Molotov's visit.

Molotov now replied that "obviously Hitler had been trying to create a good impression upon him. But he thought he had never met two more disagreeable people to deal with than Hitler and Ribbentrop." Roosevelt replied with the odd piece of knowledge that Ribbentrop had been in the champagne business. Molotov said that "he had no doubt Ribbentrop was better in that line than in diplomacy."

After lunch FDR and Molotov repaired to the president's study, where FDR greeted the officers and crew of Molotov's bomber and his clerical staff. He gave Molotov a large picture of himself in a splendid frame, on which he had inscribed, in violet ink, "To my friend Viachslav Molotov from Franklin Roosevelt, May 30, 1942." He also handed him a list of the eight million tons of Lend-Lease material to be produced for the Soviet Union while telling him that only four million tons could be shipped because of the demands inherent in the buildup of men and armaments in Britain for the cross-channel invasion.

On Sunday afternoon, May 31, after Roosevelt met with Marshall, King, and Hopkins, Hopkins drafted a cable from Roosevelt to Churchill. The key sentence: "I am, therefore, more anxious than ever that Bolero [the building up of the invasion forces and supplies in Britain] shall begin in August and continue as long as the weather permits."

Stalin cabled Molotov to "try to get the following from the President" on the question of supplies from America:

1. Organization of one convoy of ships monthly from American ports directly to Archangelsk [Archangel], escorted by US Navy.
2. Monthly supply of 50 B-25 bombers by air through Africa to be delivered to us in Basra or Teheran.
3. Monthly supply of 150 Boston-3 bombers for us delivered to the ports of the Persian Gulf to be assembled there.
4. Monthly supply of 3,000 trucks for us delivered to the ports of the Persian Gulf to be assembled there.

Molotov delivered this document (minus Stalin's name) to Roosevelt on Monday morning. At this meeting Roosevelt took the opportunity to return once more to the subject of the postwar world. He told Molotov to "tell Mr. Stalin" that he had a new thought: "Instead of requiring interest on wartime advances, all the United Nations should work out a plan covering a long-term repayment of capital only." This could only have been a great relief to Stalin.

FDR followed this up by telling Molotov that although he had already developed his ideas about disarming Germany and Japan, and discussed the role of the four nations as the guarantors of eventual peace, he had omitted one point: what to do with the many islands and colonial possessions all over the world "which ought, for their own safety, to be taken away from weak nations . . . Mr. Stalin might profitably consider the establishment of some form of international trusteeship over these islands and possessions."

Molotov replied that Stalin was in full accord with the president's ideas. Roosevelt then discussed the abandonment of the mandate system, where small islands had been given to various nations, including Japan and Germany. But he mentioned the British and the French, who "ought not to have them either." Over a long period, FDR said, these islands should be put under an international committee of three to five members. From there FDR went into a discussion of colonial possessions, particularly Indochina (Vietnam), Siam (Thailand), the Malay

States, and the Dutch East Indies. Such possessions would have to be readied for self-government, he said, for "a palpable surge toward independence was there . . . and the white nations thus could not hope to hold these areas as colonies in the long run." Molotov "expressed his conviction that the President's proposals could be effectively worked out." Illustrating the complexity of his personality, FDR then warned Molotov that he would have to terminate the conversation soon because he had invited the Duke and Duchess of Windsor to lunch at 12:00. The duke at that time was governor-general of the Bahamas: he had been shunted off to the Bahamas in 1941 to keep him far away from the European Fascist leaders who had been courting him. The duke was a classic illustration of a colonial white ruler who was, in spite of everything, very popular in some American circles. It is intriguing that Roosevelt announced this odd social engagement to Molotov. Like many Americans, in spite of his philosophical convictions, Roosevelt liked to socialize with royals.

Before he left, Roosevelt summed up second front plans and went over the revised list of armaments and equipment that the Soviet Union could expect, now cut in half by the needs of building up armaments and soldiers to Britain for the second front. For the second time he said, "We expected to set up a second front in 1942," adding, as an incentive, "Every ship we could shift to the English run meant that the second front was so much the closer to being realized."

There was some discussion about the news release that would be jointly announced in Washington and Moscow after Molotov had safely returned; the key sentence read, "In the course of the conversations full understanding was reached with regard to the urgent task of creating a second front in Europe in 1942." General Marshall told Hopkins that he felt that the sentence was too strong and urged that there be no reference to its taking place in 1942. "I called this particularly to the president's attention," Hopkins recounted, "but he, nevertheless, wished to have it included."

Stalin was eagerly waiting to hear what Molotov was accomplishing in Washington in his conversations with Roosevelt and his military staff. Cautious, meticulous, Molotov was transmitting what he thought was most relevant, but Stalin wasn't satisfied with the level of detail Molotov was supplying. He sent Molotov a blistering cable on June 3:

1. The Instance [Stalin] is dissatisfied with the terseness and reticence of all your communications. You convey to us from your talks with Roosevelt and Churchill only what you yourself consider important and omit all the rest. Meanwhile, the Instance would like to know everything, what you consider important and what you consider unimportant.
2. This refers to the draft of the communiqué as well. You have not informed us whose draft it is . . . We are having to guess because of your reticence.
3. We consider it expedient to have two draft communiqués— one on the negotiations in Britain, and another on the talks in the USA.
4. We further consider it absolutely necessary that both communiqués should mention, among other things, the subject of creating the second front in Europe and that full understanding has been reached in this matter.

On June 4, Molotov cabled Stalin the text of the communiqué he had worked out with Roosevelt the previous day:

In the course of the conversations, full understanding was reached with regard to the urgent task of creating a second front in Europe in 1942. In addition, measures for increasing and speeding up the supply of planes, tanks and other kinds of war materials from the United States to the Soviet Union were discussed. Further discussed were the fundamental problems of cooperation of the Soviet Union and the United States in safeguarding peace and security to the freedom-loving peoples after the war. Both sides state with satisfaction the unity of their views on all these questions.

Stalin's next cables indicate that he was happier with Molotov's reportage and, more important, believed that American troops would be on Russian soil within the year. Stalin cabled to Molotov:

We shall have to accept Roosevelt's proposal to reduce our request for tonnage and confine ourselves to deliveries mostly of arms and industrial equipment . . . In all probability this [reduction] is needed by the USA and Britain to release tonnage for bringing troops to Western Europe in order to create a second front.

Stalin's cable to Litvinov after Molotov left shows, in addition, that he was fully aware that the British were lukewarm at best on the enterprise:

> You must inform Roosevelt of the Soviet Government's agreement to reduce our requests for tonnage . . . and state in addition that the Soviet Government is doing this to ease the US shipment of troops to Western Europe in order to create a second front there in 1942, in compliance with what is stated in your communiqué agreed between Molotov and Roosevelt. In our opinion this might hasten British consent to the organization of the second front this year.

Roosevelt's reaction to Molotov's visit was measured. He wrote to Churchill that it was "a real success. We have got on a personal footing of candor . . . He warmed up far more than I expected." He told Daisy that although he had been warned that he would find Molotov "frozen," "[I] got him to smile & be quite human." However, thinking about Molotov six months later, he described him to Mackenzie King as an imperialist, definitely a pejorative characterization, given Roosevelt's mind-set.

Hopkins thought the visit a success. Shortly after Molotov left Washington, he wrote to Ambassador John Winant what can be taken as not just his view but FDR's: "I am sure that we at least bridged one more gap between ourselves and Russia . . . [I]t must be done if there is ever to be any real peace in the world. We simply cannot organize the world between the British and ourselves without bringing the Russians in as equal partners. I would surely include the Chinese. The days of the policy of the 'white man's burden' are over. Vast masses of people simply are not going to tolerate it and for the life of me I can't see why they should."

MOLOTOV RETURNED TO MOSCOW by way of London. While he was there, the treaty of alliance between the Soviet Union and Great

Britain was finally signed—with no mention of borders. Churchill, warningly, put into Molotov's hand an aide-mémoire regarding a second front in 1942: "Britain could 'give no promise, but provided it appears sound and sensible' the landing on the Continent planned for August or September would take place." The aide-mémoire concluded that Britain was putting maximum effort into an invasion in 1943.

In the Soviet Union coverage of Molotov's trip and the agreements he secured with Britain and America was, by Russian standards, "spectacular." Editorialized *Pravda*, "At countless meetings throughout the country the workers, *kolkhozniki*, intellectuals, soldiers, officers and political workers of the Red Army are expressing the greatest conviction that the strengthening of these bonds [between the Big Three] will hasten final victory . . . 1942 must become the year of the enemy's final rout. Our Soviet people have reacted with great satisfaction to the complete understanding concerning the urgent tasks for the creation of a Second Front in 1942."

Shortly afterward there was a meeting of the Supreme Soviet, the first since the start of the war. The twelve hundred deputies, many in native dress, convened in the hall of the Supreme Soviet. Each delegate sat behind a desk equipped with a loudspeaker. All members of the State Defense Committee—everyone of importance in the government— were present. Molotov spoke about the agreement with Great Britain, which "in the enemy camp . . . has caused confusion and angry hissing," and about the agreement on the second front, which "can be seen from the identical Anglo-Soviet and American-Soviet communiqués . . . Both communiqués declare that in the negotiations 'complete understanding was reached with regard to the urgent tasks of creating a second front in Europe in 1942.'"

Other statesmen spoke after Molotov. Zhdanov, a friend of Stalin's and a member of the Politburo who represented Leningrad, talked of "the urgent tasks for the creation of a Second Front in Europe in 1942 . . . Hitler and his bloody clique will be crushed in 1942."

The proceedings were broadcast all over the Soviet Union on the government-controlled radio station.

The next day's coverage by *Pravda* included lines written by the celebrated Soviet writer Ilya Ehrenburg: "Already the small children of France, looking across the misty sea, are whispering: 'There's a ship over there.' And the name of the ship is the Second Front."

Pravda described how all over the Soviet Union workers were being informed about Russia's powerful new allies.

During his talks with Roosevelt, Molotov had said a few times that a second front was a *political* rather than a military matter. Once he had gone so far as to state, "Though the problem of the second front was both military and political, it was *predominantly* political," adding, "If you postpone your decision you will have eventually to bear the brunt of the war."

However, directly upon his return to Moscow he wrote FDR a very straightforward letter in which he expressed "the great satisfaction I feel in having reached a full understanding concerning the urgent tasks connected with the creation of a second front in Europe in 1942 for speeding up the rout of Hitlerite Germany and concerning cooperation of our countries in the postwar period in the interests of all freedom-loving peoples."

Much later Molotov would say that in fact he never believed the second front was going to come off: "I remained calm and realized this was a completely impossible operation for them. But our demand was politically necessary . . . I don't doubt that Stalin too believed they would not carry it out."

Stalin knew by this time from many sources that Roosevelt was committed to the second front but Churchill was not. Roosevelt had said as much to Molotov; Maisky had explicitly informed Stalin that the president was for "the speediest possible opening of a second front but that Churchill was stubbornly resisting." Throughout the summer of 1942, plans seemed to go ahead to house and handle the incoming numbers of troops in England. The idea that the Soviet Union had allies was certainly a psychological help to the hard-pressed Russians, and it was apparent to everyone that the German expectation of a second front meant Hitler had to hold off sending more soldiers into Russia.

In fact, the prime minister and his staff had decided in April that the plan was not feasible: they just hadn't told their allies. Some Britons in positions of power were uneasy about their lack of candor. Major General Hastings Ismay, head of the British Office of the Minister of Defense, was among those who thought it a great mistake to have, in a sense, hoodwinked Marshall and Hopkins: "Our American friends went happily homewards under the mistaken impression that we had committed ourselves to both Roundup and Sledgehammer . . . When we had to tell them, after the most thorough study of Sledgehammer, that we were absolutely opposed to it, they felt that we had broken faith with them . . . I think we should have come clean, much cleaner than we did, and said, 'We are frankly horrified because of what we have been through in our lifetime.'"

FDR'S OVERRIDING DESIRE in 1942 was to get American boys into the fight against Hitler. He finally settled on an invasion of French North Africa, code-named Torch. Torch had one great attraction for the president. It put American troops in the war against Hitler in 1942. It was a political need he felt he had to fulfill—to the American people and to Stalin. "If Sledgehammer is finally and definitely out of the picture, I want you to consider the world situation as it exists at that time, and determine upon another place for U.S. Troops to fight in 1942," he had written to Hopkins and Marshall.

Roosevelt kept pushing.

He sent Hopkins, Marshall, and King back to London in July for another try at second front invasion plans. When they reported that the British were still opposed, he wrote to them,

Hopkins, Marshall and King,

Your two messages of July 22 do not wholly take me by surprise and I agree that mere acquiescence in the part of our friends is not sufficient.

I therefore repeat the directive that some other offensive be worked out for American forces in 1942.

People in and out of government, watching as he mulled over a decision, often criticized Roosevelt for being indecisive. A better description is that he saw all sides of a policy and took his time—sometimes an inordinately long time—thinking things over. He now proceeded to overrule the advice of the Joint Chiefs of Staff and his secretary of war: American soldiers would fight Germany in 1942, if not in France, then in North Africa. He also overruled Admiral King and others, who, wanting to defeat Japan and let the Soviet Union fight on alone, called for more troops and armaments in the Pacific in a bid to make U.S. forces concentrate on the war with Japan.

Secretary of War Henry Stimson, initially against a North African invasion, finally gave in and backed Torch, realizing that Roosevelt had a point: it *was* important from a morale point of view that U.S. troops get into the fight against Hitler. But in his diary he vented his anger and worry at the venue chosen: "It may not ripen into immediate disaster . . . It will be a lodgement more or less like that of the British at Gallipoli."

The decision on Torch was made in July. On August 13 orders were cut for Eisenhower to launch the expedition in conjunction with the preparations for the advance westward of the British Eighth Army, then reorganizing on the El Alamein line.

Eisenhower was furious. He called the day the decision was made "the blackest day in history." He thought it a waste of time to invade the rim of a continent with no strategic merit, and dangerous besides. Marshall, too, thought it foolhardy. Arguing that it would be "far safer," Marshall proposed that if the British would not go ahead with the cross-channel invasion, "we make a real drive in the Pacific," an argument that, Stimson wrote, "the president flatly vetoed." Even later FDR's decision rankled Marshall, who would write, "We failed to see that the leader in a democracy has to keep the people entertained. That may sound like the wrong word, but it conveys the thought."

The British had won: the second front was postponed. The invasion of French North Africa was of course a joint U.S.-British operation. Roosevelt, however, prevailed on a small point: wanting America to see its boys battling German troops, he ordered that only American soldiers were to take part in the first wave that went ashore; American soldiers had to hit the beaches first. He offered up an excellent rationale for Churchill: "The French will offer less resistance to us than they will to the British . . . I feel very strongly that the initial attacks must be made by an exclusively American ground force."

A total of sixty-five thousand soldiers, roughly half American and half British, took part in the operation. Roosevelt was right about the American public: the first American unit to make contact with the German army was wildly applauded, celebrated for years.

Stimson thought the operation only succeeded because Roosevelt was lucky. In *On Active Service in Peace and War,* the book he co-wrote with McGeorge Bundy, the following appears: "Stimson always considered Torch the luckiest Allied operation of the war, but he was prepared to admit that those who had advocated the operation could not be expected to see it in that light; the President had won his bet."

What Roosevelt knew was that Americans were vocally fretting that their boys had not yet seen action against Hitler's army. There was a congressional election coming up on November 3. Ever the politician, he knew it would win votes for the administration if the populace saw U.S. soldiers storming ashore in French North Africa. The electorate, which scarcely more than a year earlier had been against the war, was now gung ho for American soldiers to fight to help Russia in the battle against the monster Hitler. "Please," he said to General Marshall, "make it before election day." But it was not until Sunday, November 8, that U.S. forces hit the beaches. As a result, Democrats had to deal with a whopping setback in Congress: Republicans gained ten seats in the Senate, forty-seven in the House.

Stalin was genuinely disappointed at the non-start of the second front and gave free rein to his emotions. On October 3 he chose to vent his spleen on the thirty-two-year-old Moscow Associated Press correspondent Henry Cassidy, who had submitted questions to him: "The aid of the Allies to the Soviet Union has so far been little effective. In order to amplify and improve this aid only one thing is required: that the Allies fulfill their obligations completely and on time." Stalin's statements made headlines around the world. "Stalin Says Aid from Allies So Far Is 'Little Effective'; STALIN SAYS ALLIES HAVE AIDED LITTLE," ran the headline in *The New York Times* two days later.

Within a month, however, he had been notified of Torch and immediately realized that it was going to help Russia's plight. In his big speech of the year, on November 7, the anniversary of the revolution, he was not only statesmanlike but appreciative of collaborating with Britain and the United States. "In their hunt for oil and for Moscow, the German strategists have got into difficulties," he said amid cheers. "Their summer plans have failed . . . The Anglo-Soviet-American coalition has all the possibilities for victory, and they will win."

He was asked if there would be a second front. "Yes, there will be one," he answered, "sooner or later, because it is no less essential for our Allies than us."

The embassy chargé d'affaires Loy Henderson, not usually inclined to notice signs of Russian cooperation or acknowledgment of America, reported from Moscow that the speech "represents another step forward in the direction of closer cooperation between the Soviet Union and its allies. I believe and already have received indications that Soviet officials are interpreting the speech as a directive for the display of greater friendliness toward the United States and Britain."

That was definitely what Stalin had in mind. He wanted his allies and his enemies to know for sure just how pleased he was. A few days later he replied at length to another set of questions from the Associated Press correspondent Cassidy:

Dear Mr. Cassidy,

I am answering your questions which reached me on November 12.

    1. What is the Soviet view of the Allied campaign in Africa?

    Answer: The Soviet view of this campaign is that it represents an outstanding fact of major importance demonstrating the growing might of the armed forces of the Allies and opening the prospect of disintegration of the Italo-German coalition in the nearest future.

    The campaign refutes once more the skeptics who affirm that the Anglo-American leaders are not capable of organizing a serious war campaign. There can be no doubt that no one but first-rate organizers could carry out such serious war operations as the successful landings in North Africa across the ocean. . . .

10

POSTWAR PLANNING

FDR had been devastated when the League of Nations had gone down to defeat in the Senate in 1919. He had strongly felt the first prerequisite of a peaceful world was the creation of an organization in which all the nations of the world were members. As the vice presidential candidate in 1920, running with James M. Cox, three-time governor of Ohio, he made more than eight hundred speeches, always pressing the issue of the League of Nations. It was "the dominant issue of the campaign" and "a practical necessity." He had watched with increasing frustration as President Wilson had become ever more ineffectual and America fell back into isolation. His conviction that world peace depended upon nations' working together never wavered. He would later characterize it as "the first great agency for the maintenance of peace," but gradually, as he studied league provisions, he realized that much of it had to be reworked. In 1923 he submitted a world plan to Edward Bok, editor of the *Ladies' Home Journal,* who had set up a competition for an American peace award. FDR called the organization he envisioned the Society of Nations. It was to be run by an executive committee whose permanent members would be America, Britain, France, Italy, and Japan, and there would be an international court of justice. It never received any notice, because Eleanor Roosevelt became one of the judges, and he had to withdraw his entry.

As the world began to fall apart in 1939, FDR's thoughts returned to the importance of creating a world government. He gave to Hull and the State Department the job of creating the blueprint for such an international organization.

FDR put Undersecretary of State Sumner Welles in charge of the project. Under FDR's guidance, Welles put together a small, eclectic group of State Department people and outsiders with special knowledge in international affairs to begin to outline a postwar organization. "The President," according to Welles, "warmly endorsed the need for starting such preparations without delay." For some months this group met every Saturday in Welles's State Department office together with another State Department officer, Leo Pasvolsky, chief of the Division of Special Research and special assistant to the secretary of state. Welles reported "frequently" to the president on the group's progress, at which times the president helped "skope" the organizational outline.

By the time FDR created the Map Room in 1942, he had settled in his mind four basic questions concerning the postwar world: first, that he was going to control its structure; second, that it would involve the creation of an organization to which every nation would belong; third, that within the organization, four powerful allied nations would run herd on the rest of the world; fourth, that these powerful nations would include not just Britain, Russia, and America, so deeply involved in the war, but, breaking with his generation of white supremacists, China. Having settled on the broad outlines of his ultimate world plan, he went about protecting it to make sure it did not become a subject of conversation or of speculation, either of which would attract attention and enemies. He devised an interesting and simple solution to limiting the possibility that unknown eyes would find out what he was up to: he made the Map Room, where the cables to and from the three world leaders originated, the most secret, the most closely guarded room in the White House. It was off-limits to his cabinet, the chiefs of staff, and senators, unless specifically invited. The contents of the Map Room, the functions of the Map Room, everything about the Map Room, reflected this. Permission to enter was hard to come by. Guarded at all times by a uniformed White House police officer, the Map Room was located on the ground floor of the White House, directly across the corridor from the family elevator, and next to the doctor's office. On the inside of the entrance door was a captioned cartoon of three monkeys. Under each printed caption was a penciled caption, which Roosevelt was responsible for. According to a Map Room officer, Roosevelt had dictated the comments to Henry Stimson one evening. The caption for the first monkey, "sees everything," whose eyes were wide open, had underneath it, written in pencil, "something." The caption for the second monkey, "hears everything," with a hand to his ear, had underneath it the penciled comment "a little." The caption for the third monkey, "tells nothing," with a hand over his mouth, had underneath it, in pencil, "less."

But that was just the tip of the iceberg. FDR wanted to make sure that no member of the U.S. military no matter how senior—knew what his relationship was with Churchill, Stalin, and Chiang Kai-shek: knew what he was planning with them. Given that all cables to and from these world leaders were coded in the Map Room, they still had to be carried by either the army or the navy. So that neither service head had a full record of U.S. foreign policy, he devised a novel solution: every cable he sent to one of the three had to be transmitted through Navy Department communications and coding facilities, and every cable they sent to him had to be transmitted through War Department circuits. This meant that routinely the secretary of war, Stimson, and the secretary of the navy, Knox, saw only half the messages and Hull saw none. Presumably, Hull saw those messages Roosevelt or his close staff—Hopkins and Admiral Leahy, who became chief of staff to the president following his return from Vichy France in late spring 1942—thought he *should* see.

The file cabinets were unique in that they contained the *only* complete file of these messages in existence.

Maps and charts covered the four walls of the room. Clear plastic, overlaid with grease-penciled comments, updated constantly as couriers from the War and Navy Departments came in with the latest battle news, marked the position of Allied and enemy troops. Colored pins, in different sizes and shapes depending on the type of ship, marked the position of ships on the ocean charts: blue for American, orange for Japanese, red for British, gray for Italian, and black for German. So that it was possible to view this information up close, all desks, chairs, tables, and file cabinets were grouped in the center of the room. A small round table that could double as a dining table, where Roosevelt occasionally entertained guests, was in the center as well.

Unrestricted entry to the Map Room was limited to Hopkins and Leahy. Knox, refused entry one day, went complaining to FDR, who kidded him about his lack of control over navy personnel but did not put him on the entry list. Code officers, three army watch officers and three navy watch officers, were on duty around the clock. When Roosevelt traveled, all communications to and from him were routed through the

Map Room. Roosevelt's obsession with secrecy was intended to address the problem of possible opposition to his policies: no knowledge—no opposition. No one in government, knowing only one side of the correspondence, could gainsay his grand world plans. His soothing explanation of this odd arrangement to the Map Room staff was that "the army and the navy would be reluctant to entrust the Map Room with their most secret information if 'politicians' were allowed to nose around." It made the staff feel particularly important.

Typically, in the afternoon, Roosevelt would be wheeled to the Map Room to see the latest war developments and messages. Then, although no one realized with what regularity Roosevelt needed treatments of any sort, most afternoons he would go next door and sit in the dentist's chair he had had installed in the doctor's office and have his sinuses treated and his legs massaged.

In 1943, FDR chose *The Saturday Evening Post,* the nation's most popular magazine, to familiarize the world with his postwar vision. Four Norman Rockwell paintings, each illustrating one of FDR's Four Freedoms, had appeared on the cover in consecutive issues of the magazine and had been wildly popular, spiking circulation well up in the millions. Soon thereafter Roosevelt decided *The Saturday Evening Post* would be the perfect vehicle to introduce and publicize the United Nations. He gave an interview to Forrest Davis, the world-famous journalist who had covered the Scopes "Monkey" trial as a friend of Clarence Darrow's and had been the foremost reporter on the kidnapping of the Lindberghs' child. Davis's article "Roosevelt's World Blueprint" appeared on April 10, 1943.

Davis described FDR's ideas of how the yet-to-be-formed United Nations would control a future rogue state, for example, Germany. Step one, if the country did not cease preparing for war, there would be a quarantine sealing borders accessible by rail, air, river, canal, and highway and blocking all communication by radiogram, telephone, telegraph, and post. With the halting of importation of food, news, and raw materials and the cessation of clearing of foreign contracts, paralysis would grip the country. Exchanges would close; the country would shut down. Step two, if preparations still did not cease, the UN would announce that the country's strategic centers would be "bombed to destruction."

Roosevelt was publicizing his get-tough concept in his effort to show his practical side. As Davis explained it, "He is concentrating on power; dealing with problems of power politics in contrast to what the pundits describe as welfare politics." He also, Davis wrote, "deeply feels that mankind should not be subjected to a second disaster of the magnitude of Versailles in one generation."

Davis also wrote that FDR did not fear the rise of Communism, but this was put very delicately, so as not to raise hackles: "He inclines to believe the revolutionary currents of 1917 may be spent in this war, and the future—as in the post-Napoleonic era—devoted for many years to reconstruction and social as well as international peace."

And finally, Davis reported the joker in the deck: "As matters stand, the shape of the postwar world depends more on Stalin than on Roosevelt or the British leaders. It is not too much to say that he can have the kind of world he desires."

It is quite possible that Roosevelt gave the interview just to send this message to Stalin.

For all his get-tough concept, Roosevelt's plan for a world organization policed by Great Britain, Russia, America, and China, linked as it was in his mind with a world at peace, meant to him that the United States would have to keep only a minimal army after the war was over. This influenced his plans for the design of the Pentagon, the huge military headquarters in the planning stage in 1941. FDR, who had an architect's eye and in fact had designed a number of buildings, including two cottages on his estate in Hyde Park, the post office in Rhinebeck, New York, and the naval hospital in Bethesda, Maryland, one Friday sprang on his cabinet the idea that the Pentagon would be a cubic block of a building with either no windows or very few, lit by artificial light, and ventilated "artificially," as Stimson described it with alarm. ("I should absolutely refuse to live in a building of that type," he confided to his diary.)

FDR's reasoning behind this radical notion was his vision that following victory and the creation of the United Nations peacekeeping force, America's armed forces would radically shrink to such a point that the Joint Chiefs and their support staff would rattle around in the huge new building: the windowless, well-ventilated Pentagon would then become the repository for all armed forces personnel records. What is remarkable is that this was FDR's idea in 1941. He expected opposition: "The War Department will doubtless object to giving up the Pentagon building but it is much too large for them, if we get a decent peace." He stuck with the idea. "After the war is ended all the personnel records of the Armed Forces should be placed in the Pentagon building," he told his budget director, Harold Smith, just before the Yalta Conference.

FDR's vision for the inclusion of China was founded on solid personal logic. With an eye to the future, he believed that a co-equal Asian presence in the United Nations was necessary not only to make it fully representative of the world but to ensure its very survival. Therefore, he insisted on China's inclusion as a policeman, even though it was at present fighting a Japanese invasion and riven by a civil war. His view, unique in his generation of leaders, was that the white race should not rule the world and was *not* innately superior to other races. Because he viewed China as a temporarily sidelined nation fully as competent as any white nation, he could see it as a balance to Russia in terms of geography and population: the two countries shared the longest border in the world. The Soviet Union was a country of 165 million people in Roosevelt's time; America was a country of only 130 million: China dwarfed them both.

FDR had asked Welles to deliver the message to Lord Halifax that his attitude was "provincial" because Halifax, and Churchill as well, were thinking only of Europe when they envisioned Germany balancing Russia. Roosevelt was thinking about a postwar world where China as well as America could act as a check on Russia's power; he just wasn't talking about it. He eventually revealed this to Mackenzie King, the wise, discreet prime minister of Canada, who bared secrets only to his diary. One night in 1942 after dinner at the White House, FDR took King upstairs to his study and unburdened himself: "The President said he would like to discuss tonight the question of disarmament and bringing Stalin into the picture. He said that was very necessary." Then, King wrote, FDR "asked me if I remember the saying of Senator Watson. 'If you cannot beat the devil, join him.' He said Russia was going to be very powerful. The thing to do now was to get plans definitely made for disarmament." Later in the evening, King wrote in his diary, FDR repeated Watson's "If you cannot beat him, join him" and then went on to say, "It was clear that the U.S., Britain, China could not defeat Russia. The thing to do was to get them all working on the same lines. He then came to what he said was confidential and added: *for God's sake, don't give me away.*"

FDR's idea was that not only would the four policemen keep the peace but, working together, each policeman would by force of circumstances be monitored by the other three. The situation of necessarily working in harness, so to speak, would be a check on Russia, and the inclusion of China would help keep Russia from going rogue.

The doctrine of unconditional surrender was another aspect of Roosevelt's world vision. It, too, solved a number of problems. Most important, unconditional surrender took care of a peace conference: there needn't be one. That was a great plus for FDR, always haunted by Versailles. There would be no negotiated peace: without a peace conference he could stay in control; terms could be decided upon on an ad hoc basis as each Axis country surrendered.

It was a popular idea in Washington. In late May 1942, an influential State Department subcommittee, chaired by Norman Davis, friend to both Hull and Roosevelt, recommended to the president, "On the assumption that the victory of the United Nations will be conclusive, unconditional surrender rather than an armistice should be sought from enemy states except perhaps Italy."

At the end of December the Joint Chiefs of Staff fell into line, recommending to the president that it be applied to *all* Axis powers: "It has been recommended by representatives of the Joint Chiefs of Staff that no armistice be granted Germany, Japan, Italy and the satellites until they offered the 'unconditional surrender' of their armed forces." Early in January, FDR told the Joint Chiefs that unconditional surrender would from then on be a basic Allied policy. Having embraced it, Roosevelt refused to explain, define, or otherwise soften the policy. As he advised Hull in a memo, definitions would be useless, for "whatever words we might agree on would probably have to be modified or changed the first time some nation wanted to surrender." Learning from Mackenzie King early in December 1942 that Churchill expected a peace conference, FDR put his hands to his face, shook his head a bit, "then said . . . that he did not know that there would be any peace conference. As far as he was concerned there would be total surrender." He added, "There might be a series of small conferences dealing with different aspects at different times to avoid anything in the nature of a Versailles conference."

Unconditional surrender also dovetailed with FDR's intent of making sure that after *this* war, as opposed to World War I, the German people would know that their army had been defeated, that no German could say, as the German soldier Herbert Richter, quoted in *The Nazis: A Warning from History* by Laurence Rees, had said, "We didn't feel beaten at all. The frontline troops didn't feel themselves beaten, and we were wondering why the armistice was happening so quickly and why we had to vacate all our positions in such a hurry because we were still standing on enemy territory."

Roosevelt announced the policy of unconditional surrender at a news conference with Churchill at Casablanca on January 24, 1943. The announcement, according to Churchill, took him by surprise, although he had already agreed to it in substance. It was thought at the time that Roosevelt wanted to reassure Stalin, so pressed by the Wehrmacht, that America and Britain were going to pursue the war to the bitter end. Unconditional surrender was popular in the United States. Eighty-one percent favored it in a poll: most people in America thought Germany might start another war.

Roosevelt always cited his hero, General Ulysses S. Grant, as the inspiration for this policy—this plan to be magnanimous but to force the enemy to surrender without terms. Grant's words to the Confederate commander general Simon Buckner after the capture of Fort Donelson on February 16, 1862, had been "No terms except unconditional and immediate surrender can be accepted," and Grant had stuck to that policy during the war, making sure it applied to Lee. Roosevelt could never resist embellishing a story in the interest of making it better, and he became quite enthusiastic as time went on about Grant. This is how he explained Grant's policy of unconditional surrender to Hull: "The story of Lee's surrender to Grant is the best illustration. Lee wanted to talk about all kinds of conditions. Grant said that Lee must put his confidence in his (Grant's) fairness. Then Lee surrendered. Immediately Lee brought up the question of Confederate officers' horses, which belonged to them personally in most cases, and Grant settled that item by telling Lee that they should take their horses home as they would be needed in the Spring plowing."

Needing to address the fears of many that he sought a vindictive peace, Roosevelt had taken to the radio on February 12 to explain more fully what he had in mind: "To these panicky attempts to escape the consequences of their crimes we say—all the United Nations say—that the only terms on which we shall deal with an Axis government or any

Axis factions are the terms proclaimed at Casablanca: 'Unconditional Surrender.' In our uncompromising policy we mean no harm to the common people of the Axis nations. But we do mean to impose punishment and retribution in full upon their guilty, barbaric leaders."

In March 1943, at a lunch meeting in his study with Eden, Hull, and Hopkins, FDR reiterated the policy. According to Hopkins's notes, "He wanted no negotiated armistice after the collapse; that we should insist on total surrender with no commitments to the enemy as to what we would or would not do after this action."

As the war progressed, Roosevelt was pressured by Hull and others to soften his stance: the argument was made that the draconian nature of the statement impelled the satellite nations to go on fighting. Stalin, speaking through Molotov, was of that opinion and asked Ambassador Harriman for a precise definition of unconditional surrender, on the premise that the lack of explanation played on people's fears and kept the satellite countries from surrendering. Roosevelt refused to define the term. When Hull tried to push him, he wrote back in a letter on January 17, 1944:

> Frankly, I do not like the idea of conversations to define the term "unconditional surrender." Russia, Britain and the United States have agreed not to make any peace without consultation with each other. I think each case should stand on its own merits in that way.
>
> The German people can have dinned into their ears what I said in my Christmas Eve speech—in effect, that we have no thought of destroying the German people . . . on condition of course, that they get rid of their present philosophy of conquest . . . Whatever words we might agree on would probably have to be modified or changed the first time some nation wanted to surrender.

Stalin understood FDR's decision, volunteering, diplomatically, to Ambassador Harriman, on June 10, 1944, that "so far as the German surrender was concerned, there was no disagreement."

Roosevelt agreed in June 1944 to ameliorate the policy as it applied to the satellite countries. As Molotov and Stalin downplayed the propaganda aspects of unconditional surrender to hasten capitulation by the satellite countries, FDR agreed that the term "unconditional surrender" could be omitted from propaganda information relating to the satellite countries. Generally speaking, a satellite country had to break with Germany and fight alongside the Allied armies, including the Red Army, pay an indemnity to the U.S.S.R. for the damages it had inflicted, and repatriate Soviet and Allied prisoners of war.

There were those who thought that Roosevelt's unconditional surrender policy prolonged the war because it caused such fear among the Germans, and possibly it did. Roosevelt was aware that it might. He thought it a principle to uphold because it would deter future wars.

"There had been a good deal of complaint among some of the nice, high-minded people about unconditional surrender, that if we changed the term 'unconditional surrender,' Germany might surrender more quickly . . . that it is too tough and too rough," he said to a reporter in Honolulu in 1944.

"Unconditional surrender still stands?" asked the reporter.

"Yes. Practically all Germans deny the fact they surrendered in the last war, but this time they are going to know it," Roosevelt answered.

STALIN, MEANWHILE, had a different approach to the postwar world. Thinking less loftily than FDR, he was concerned only with Russia's place in the world. It was his basic belief that although the countries of Europe might eventually go Communist because it was a superior economic system, and that the capitalist system would founder, it was going to take a long time—twenty or thirty years. Therefore, there had to be peace while the process took place. Propaganda would be the only tool to hasten this (inevitable) process: force was not part of his equation. As he said to the newspaper publisher Roy Howard, "We Marxists believe that revolution will occur in other countries as well. But it will only come when it is considered possible or necessary by the revolutionaries in those countries. Export of revolution is nonsense. Each country, if it so desires, will make its own revolution, and if no such desire exists, no revolution will occur." (Germany, for instance, he believed entirely unsuited for Communism: Stalin was on record as saying Communism was "no more fit for Germany than a saddle for a cow.")

Stalin firmly believed he could turn the Soviet Union into a society superior to the West. According to Marx and Engels, in capitalist societies bankers and industrialists got rid of competitors, discouraged technological innovation, and were therefore inefficient. Socialism was more efficient and would do better. His belief was founded on the fact that he had eliminated unemployment in the Soviet Union, provided food, shelter, education, and health care where there had been minimal or none before. He had presided over the top-to-bottom reorganization of Soviet society. His five-year plans had produced remarkable results, although at great cost, little comprehended at the time. The execution of these plans required great courage and utter ruthlessness, according to Joseph E. Davies. Stalin had turned the Soviet Union, a backward society, into an industrial state that had to be reckoned with. Collectivizing the farms—involving the murder and deportation of millions of agricultural workers, the virtual extinction of the kulaks—in the end worked to change Russia forever. In 1928 the Soviet Union had produced 4.3 million tons of steel; by 1938 that figure had risen to more than 18 million tons. The production of trucks went from 700 per year to 182,000. In the space of ten years Soviet Russia, an agricultural society, had become an industrial society.

So Stalin had reason to believe that his economic model was in fact as good as Marx and Engels had posited.

But the war had destroyed his country. It had to be rebuilt. For that to take place, Stalin needed a long peace. That meant he needed partners.

The history of Russia is a history of invasions. In the earlier years of the century, as civil war raged across the land, Stalin had taken part in battles against German, English, and Polish invaders. Germany was now striking at Russia for the second time in twenty years.

Stalin had been twenty-six in 1905, when Russia had been so humiliated by the Battle of Tsushima in the Sea of Japan, the largest sea battle in history. Japan had been menacing Russia ever since.

Stalin was a student of history, obsessed with the history of Russia. This was reflected in his huge library—more than twenty thousand books—mostly concerned with history and political theory, all bearing marks of his attention. His notes and underlinings of key passages indicate his reverence for Marx and Lenin. His volumes on the Napoleonic Wars, Vipper's history of Greece, von Moltke's *Franco-German War of 1870–71,* and other histories of the previous wars between Germany and England and Russia, as well as works on the Russian tsars, were all heavily annotated.

Stalin's aim: to make Russia secure from invasion, something it had not been for generations.

Talking with Harriman and Beaverbrook in October 1941, with German artillery fire so close it lit up the Moscow sky, Stalin proposed what he had sought two years earlier: a permanent military alliance with Britain that would extend into a postwar treaty. Plus, he wanted to talk about postwar boundaries. When Beaverbrook brushed him off with the comment that it would be enough to win the war, it undoubtedly brought back to him memories of his failed 1939 attempt at a treaty with Britain that would stop Hitler, particularly because Halifax was still in Churchill's government. Stalin wanted to have the results of his talks with Harriman and Beaverbrook recorded: he asked for a written agreement, something neither Beaverbrook nor Harriman expected or were prepared for. Harriman reported that he felt "embarrassed" and began speaking about the Atlantic Charter as constituting a program for peace. At the time, the exchange proved at least one thing was sure: Stalin believed Hitler would be beaten.

What was *not* absorbed, then or later, was the depth of Stalin's desire that Britain and America and Russia remain friends in the post-war world. He wanted to make sure that the Soviet Union would not be unceremoniously abandoned after the war was over. It was the Russians, in January 1942 in London, who proposed the founding of what would be called UNRRA, the United Nations Relief and Rehabilitation Administration. That is to say, it was Stalin, for nothing happened on this scale unless he had agreed to it. The Soviets' idea—as they were reeling back from the Wehrmacht—was to found an internationally controlled, manned, and operated relief organization for those countries "which experienced especially severe suffering from Hitler's aggression." The Russian proposal included the provisions that all countries should be "on the basis of equality," that there should be a secretariat of four or five—Britain, the Soviet Union, and two or three other delegates who would run the organization: all decisions had to be by unanimous vote. By 1943, Roosevelt's concept of the four policemen as the powerful overall authority in the postwar world had been accepted by Russia as the proper governing group, and organization of the UNRRA was taking place in Washington in meetings between representatives of the four: Maxim Litvinov for the Soviet Union; Lord Halifax for Britain; the Chinese ambassador Wei Tao-ming for China; and Dean Acheson, whose office adjoined Hull's office in the southwest corner of Old State.

Acheson, back for his second stint in the Roosevelt administration, was assistant secretary of state. That the germ of the concept for UNRRA was Russian has been largely forgotten.

The UNRRA four met for the first time on January 11, 1943, to begin hammering out administrative and policy matters. The narrow Soviet interpretation of the countries that would be aided—only those suffering from Hitler's aggression—was broadened to comply with the concept of the Atlantic Charter. The main battle, though, according to Acheson, was over the Soviet position that all decisions by UNRRA had to be unanimous. Litvinov battled hard, and when he left, the issue was still undecided and would stay so until September, when majority rule was finally inked in. This was one of the early Soviet capitulations to U.S. policy. "On the whole, the three of us did rather better with the USSR in our negotiation than many of our successors have done since, not due, I hasten to add, to our skill but to the Soviet desire for relief assistance," wrote a pleased Acheson. Under pressure from their colleagues, Halifax and Acheson agreed that although the director general would be an American, there would be a Russian and a Chinese deputy director general.

UNRRA would begin work under the stewardship of Herbert Lehman, ex-governor of New York, as Roosevelt announced just before he left for the Tehran Conference. By mid-May most of the large and small issues had been settled, and a draft agreement on the establishment of UNRRA acceptable to each of the four nations had been drawn up.

Stalin in other ways was accommodating to Roosevelt's wishes. There was his about-face on religion. He now condoned churchgoing and reinstated the church metropolitans, a huge change for the Russian people. At Christmas in 1943, when for the first time in years the churches were open for Christmas prayers, Moscow's fifty churches were jammed. At the Bogoyavlensky Cathedral, where Patriarch Sergei celebrated the Christmas service, worshippers were packed in so tightly that many found it difficult to raise their arms to make the sign of the cross. When Kathleen Harriman went to the Old Believers Church in Moscow the following Easter, she found the same situation. It was so packed, she wrote her sister, "I couldn't get my hands up from my sides." Where previously the premier had been inaccessible, he was now seeing a stream of Roosevelt's people: Ambassador Joseph E. Davies,

Cordell Hull, Wendell Willkie, Ambassador Hurley, Ambassador Harriman. He answered questions posed by Western journalists. He received Winston Churchill when he came to Moscow.

Stalin, in fact, guided by his aim to set the future of Russia, had become by Russian standards amazingly open to his new allies. He, like Roosevelt, was thinking way ahead. In late spring of 1943 he recalled the Soviet Union's diplomats with the most intimate knowledge of their allies, America and Britain, back to Moscow to help him plan for the postwar world. Litvinov would leave at the end of May. Maisky was notified in mid-August that he had been appointed deputy people's commissar for foreign affairs. As chairman of a special government commission on reparations, he was recalled to work out what the Soviet Union would ask of Germany when the war was over. News of the recalls set rumors swirling in all three capitals to the effect that the sudden change was an expression of Stalin's displeasure with his allies (the press and other diplomats in Moscow immediately attributed the recall to a deterioration in relations of the Big Three; even Gromyko was reporting that there was speculation the recall augured "a certain sharp turn" in Soviet foreign policy). To counteract these damaging rumors, Stalin took the unusual step of assuring FDR none of the rumors were true, that the change had been made for a reassuring reason. "Stalin," Ambassador William Standley reported to FDR, "stated to me personally his desire to have near him for instant consultation these individuals who were thoroughly conversant with the situation in London and Washington." Standley reported that Molotov as well told him that the recall of the diplomats was necessitated by the need of their advice, because there was a dearth of knowledge in the Soviet headquarters.

The change of ambassadors made a difference. Molotov was less worldly and more cynical about Russia's new allies than Stalin. Litvinov, who had been foreign commissar in 1930, was historically strongly anti-Hitler. Under him, the Soviet Union had made a treaty with France in 1934 and joined the League of Nations. It had taken Molotov until 1939 to undermine Litvinov and replace him as foreign commissar, and it had happened only because Stalin had decided to change Soviet foreign policy and throw in his lot with Hitler. Stalin was aware of their differing worldviews. It was not until FDR offered openhanded aid to the Soviet Union in the form of Lend-Lease, after Barbarossa in 1941, that

Litvinov regained professional status and became the new ambassador to America.

Molotov, in his role of foreign commissar, generally limited Stalin's access to information from ambassadors because he wanted Stalin to turn to him for information. He made it particularly difficult for Litvinov, who was more pro–United States and much more comfortable with Americans and who enjoyed good relations with Joseph E. Davies and Dean Acheson, among others, whom he saw socially. (Litvinov was having breakfast with Joseph E. Davies on December 7, having just arrived in the United States, when FDR called to tell Davies that the Japanese had bombed Pearl Harbor. Litvinov had arrived that morning to take up his duties as ambassador to the United States.)

In May 1943, about to return to Russia, Litvinov paid a farewell call on Sumner Welles, asking him not to make any record of their conversation (Welles ignored the request and made detailed notes, which follow). In light of the fact that Stalin was bringing him home to help him plan for the future, it is interesting to read Litvinov's half-truths, lies, and jealous ravings because they provide a window into this diplomat's mind. Certainly he, like anyone else in his position, would inevitably have been unhappy at the idea of giving up Washington, D.C., the center of power and the good life, for war-torn Moscow. He and Acheson had become friends, their wives, Ivy Low Litvinov, an Englishwoman, and Acheson's wife, Alice Stanley Acheson, were painting companions. Indeed, the two couples were together at so many dinners where Acheson was seated next to Ivy Litvinov that she often asked him to use his long legs to find her dinner shoes, which she had the habit of kicking off under the table.

Litvinov, in his farewell visit to Welles, told him "his successor as Foreign Commissar [Molotov] had removed from the Foreign Commissariat every important official who had any experience with the outside world and any personal knowledge of the United States or of the Western democracies." He had decided to go home, he explained, to see if he could persuade Stalin to listen to him. His recommendations were never followed now, he said, and he doubted that Stalin even saw them: "He was completely bereft of any information as to the policy and plans of his own Government . . . even been forbidden by his Government to appear in public or to make any public speeches." Litvinov said that when he got to Moscow, he was going to explain to Stalin the role pub-lic opinion played in a democracy: he wanted to impress on him that public opinion was a determining factor in the creation of government policy in America.

(At Tehran, Stalin learned from Roosevelt's own lips how crucial public opinion was, as they talked about the future of Poland and the Baltic States.)

Litvinov told Welles that he believed that the peace of the world depended "very largely upon understanding and cooperation between the Soviet Union and the United States . . . Without the achievement of this, he did not believe that any international organization was con-ceivable or that the peace of the world could possibly be maintained."

Litvinov now showed his understanding of his own country's psyche and gave Welles some welcome news. In reply to Welles's statement that "all nation members of the United Nations organization must be privi-leged to afford their peoples the right of free speech, of free assembly, of freedom of worship and of freedom of information," Litvinov said that "he believed his Government would be wholly in accord with the establishment of some general principle of this character."

The new ambassador appointed to the United States was Andrei Gromyko. He was able, was young (thirty-three), spoke excellent En-glish, and was suited for the position. Gromyko was called behind his back "Old Stone Face" because he put on such an impenetrable mask, but, according to Acheson, he had a dry, sardonic sense of humor "when he chose to turn it on."

Litvinov understood Western foreign policy in a way that Molotov and Stalin did not. Molotov and Stalin believed—Gromyko described it as the party line—that the French and the British had just been pre-tending to negotiate with the Soviet Union that fateful summer of 1939 and that their real aim had been to push Hitler into war against the U.S.S.R. Litvinov, on the other hand, did not believe they had had such a nefarious plan, and he was open about his views, making him suspect in the eyes of Molotov and Stalin. Molotov's belief in Britain's untrust-worthiness underlay his policies and his advice to Stalin.

Litvinov might have been expecting the worst upon his return to Russia, but he soon found out that his position was secure. The fact that Gromyko reported to Stalin that when he saw FDR in July, FDR asked him "how Litvinov was," and Gromyko responded by saying that "Litvinov was well," undoubtedly helped.

His thoughts on foreign policy, written after his arrival in Moscow, dated June 2, were noted as read by Stalin and Molotov and bear heavy underlining by Molotov. As such, they are interesting to read.

"I came to the conclusion that he [FDR] was entirely convinced in the need of opening the second front as soon as possible . . . However, he was, probably, gradually being deviated from this conviction by his military advisers and particularly by Churchill," Litvinov had written.

Litvinov in the same memo also laid out a course of action for the Soviet Union. "If we wish to eliminate existing misunderstandings and to prepare conditions for mutual cooperation, then the following measures and arrangements suggest themselves":

1. To create a body for permanent military-political contact with the president and the War Department in Washington.
2. To initiate discussion of postwar problems in the press and public debate.
3. To place our ambassador in a position where he can speak frequently in front of the American public . . .
4. To discuss, with London and Washington simultaneously, the emerging political problems.

A month after Litvinov's recall Maisky received a call from Molotov notifying him that he too was to move to Moscow: He was being appointed deputy people's commissar of foreign affairs.

Stalin was careful where Roosevelt was concerned. The decision, taken at the Trident Conference in Washington by Roosevelt and Churchill at roughly the same time, to again postpone the second front had resulted in Stalin's sending an angry message of protest to Roosevelt. But the message, received by FDR on June 11, wasn't as angry as it could have been: Stalin edited and toned down the message. "Now, without any consultation or advice, you and Mr. Churchill made the decision, postponing the British-American invasion of Western Europe." Stalin took out "without any consultation" and added the date, so that the message read "Now, in May 1943 you and Mr. Churchill made the decision, postponing the British-American invasion of Western Europe."

In August, Stalin again edited the text of a message to Roosevelt, once again toning down the rhetoric. The message had started out "Since the opening of the second front this year has again been post-poned by the British and American governments, our army has to strain its forces to the limit." Stalin deleted the sentence so that the message starts out on a very different footing: "Only now, having come back from the front, I can answer your message of July 16th." The message goes on to explain the powerful German summer offensive and states, "I have at the present time to put aside other questions and my other duties" to direct the action at the front. Stalin then suggests that he, too, thinks they need to iron out major issues, writing, "I consider that a meeting of the responsible representatives of the two countries would positively be expedient."

These various events—the recall of first Vyshinsky, then Maisky, the toning down of the messages to FDR, including excision of a remark about the lack of a second front, the heavy editing in Stalin's hand, and his suggestion that "responsible representatives" should meet, which was taken to mean the foreign ministers of the three countries—show Stalin's new sensitivity to his allies, and particularly to Roosevelt. He had evidently read Litvinov's memo. It had dawned on Stalin that he was being taken seriously not just by the president of the United States but by the prime minister of Great Britain, who had been snubbing him for years.

He wanted to serve on commissions with them, as became appar-ent. Stalin wrote to FDR that the three countries should establish a military-political commission "with the purpose of considering the questions concerning the negotiations with the different Governments disassociating themselves from Germany."

Stalin had always admired, even had a sneaking love of, America. The famous German writer Emil Ludwig had picked up on that when he was interviewing him in 1931:

LUDWIG: I notice that in the Soviet Union everything Ameri-
    can is held in very high esteem, I might even speak of a worship
    of everything American.
STALIN: You exaggerate. We have no especially high esteem for
    everything American, but we do respect the efficiency that the
    Americans display in everything in industry, in technology, in

literature and in life. We never forget that the U.S.A. is a capitalist country. But among the Americans there are many people who are mentally and physically healthy who are healthy in their whole approach to work, to the job on hand. That efficiency, that simplicity, strikes a responsive chord in our hearts. Despite the fact that America is a highly developed capitalist country, the habits prevailing in its industry, the practices existing in productive processes, have an element of democracy about them, which cannot be said of the old European capitalist countries, where the haughty spirit of the feudal aristocracy is still alive.

When Ludwig had asked him for positive feedback on Germany (this was before Hitler came to power), Stalin appeared to be at a loss to think of anything in Germany he admired and replied, "It gave the world such men as Marx and Engels. It suffices to state the fact as such."

With the gift of hindsight we can see that Stalin by the summer of 1943 has seen the future and Russia's place in it as a world power. He is readying his country for the world stage. He institutes serious changes: he is literally dressing those Russians whom the world sees—the soldiers and the diplomats—allowing religion to take its rightful place in the social fabric of the country (although grudgingly), setting up military academies to train the next generation of Red Army officers, and, seeing the value of having a powerful friend, writing to Roosevelt that indeed they should work together on various commissions.

Litvinov was given the title of chairman of the Foreign Ministry's Special Commission on Post-war Order and Preparation of Peace Treaties and given a competent staff; Maisky became chairman of a special government commission in charge of the reparations program, which would deal with Germany; and Andrei Gromyko became de facto head of the Soviet team at Dumbarton Oaks working out the articles and basic formation of the United Nations.

Litvinov had under him on the commission Solomon A. Lozovsky, assistant people's commissar for foreign affairs, and Dmitry Manuilsky, as well as three foreign policy experts, one of whom, Eugene Tarle, was a famous historian.

At the same time Churchill was also thinking of the future and Britain's place in it. Churchill, famously, was worried about the Balkans and about preserving the empire. It was at this point that Harriman, in London coordinating Lend-Lease, told Churchill that Roosevelt had decided to have an exclusive meeting with Stalin. Churchill was strongly negative; he feared that he would lose his special relationship with FDR. Harriman now spent hours trying to convince him that an effort by FDR to talk Stalin out of his shell, broaden his views, and make him more cooperative would be better for all of them.

Churchill thought, in any case, as he admitted to Harriman, as they continued their conversations over the weekend of June 26–27 at his country estate, Chequers, that Stalin's "unrelenting pressure for a second front in 1943 springs from his designs on the Balkans. What better way to keep the Western Allies from landing in the Balkans than to tie them down in a long and costly battle for Western Europe?" He feared this meeting without him, even to the point of saying, "I do not underrate the use that enemy propaganda would make of a meeting between the heads of Soviet Russia and the United States . . . [M]any would be bewildered and alarmed thereby."

It was Stalin, actually, who put his foot down about meeting with Roosevelt alone. He must have sensed that it would arouse Churchill's fears and would gain him nothing. He refused a meeting à deux.

II

PROBLEMS AND SOLUTIONS

For as many years as Stalin had tried to fend off a German invasion, he had tried to fend off one by Japan, Russia's other dangerous enemy, which had defeated it in 1905. In the spring of 1941, a bare two months before Operation Barbarossa, he had succeeded in negotiating a brilliant coup. Hitler was on the move, Belgrade had just surrendered, and the Japanese foreign minister, Yōsuke Matsuoka, was in Moscow. Japan was preparing for war with the United States, and wanting to make sure Stalin did not pounce on Manchuria, Matsuoka sought a treaty with the Soviet Union. Foreign Ministers Matsuoka and Molotov finalized the details and put their signatures on the Japanese-Soviet Nonaggression Pact on April 13. The signing of the pact had been such an enormous relief to Stalin that his self-control vanished: he was seen drunk. Following the signing, he and Matsuoka drank throughout the night and into the morning. At 6:00 a.m. the two were seen at the Yaroslavsky station staggering arm in arm toward Matsuoka's train. "We'll organize Europe and Asia," the happily drunk Stalin was heard to say, as he put Matsuoka into the train. He remained on the platform until the train pulled away.

At Tehran in November 1943, Stalin had said to FDR, who welcomed the statement, "Once Germany was finally defeated, it would then be possible to send the necessary reinforcements to Siberia and then we shall be able by our common front to beat Japan." Stalin had first transmitted this thought to Roosevelt via Averell Harriman, who although not yet ambassador, was in Moscow in August 1942. Stalin told Averell Harriman to tell FDR that Japan's defeat was essential: "Eventually she [Russia] would come in . . . Japan was the historic enemy of Russia and her eventual defeat was essential to Russia's interests." With this background, the U.S. military was ready with battle plans for a joint U.S.-U.S.S.R. war with Japan: it was just waiting for the right moment to present them to Stalin. It had come at Tehran; FDR gave the premier the Joint Chiefs of Staff document outlining planned U.S. operations against Japan, which was predicated on a joint U.S.-U.S.S.R. attack: "With a view of shortening the war, it is our opinion that the bombing of Japan from your Maritime Provinces, immediately following the beginning of hostilities between the USSR and Japan, will be of the utmost importance, as it will enable us to destroy Japanese military and industrial centers." The United States planned a force of from one hundred to one thousand four-engine bombers, the number to depend on the facilities Russia could make available in the Maritime Province. Stalin had scanned the document and agreed to coordinate the offensives of the two countries, but there was no further discussion: it was just, basically, a thought for the future.

Molotov brought the matter up with Harriman the month after the Tehran Conference, as Harriman was settling into life in Moscow as the new ambassador. The way he did it indicated just how worried he and Stalin were that the Japanese would get wind of the plan.

Harriman had tried hard to avoid the posting to Moscow. Roosevelt had asked him to take over as ambassador from Steinhardt in 1941, but Harriman had refused, pleading that he would be more useful to Roosevelt as a roving ambassador. "I had just seen what a hopelessly restricted life the foreign diplomats led in Moscow, the way they were fenced in," he admitted. But Admiral Standley, the ambassador chosen, had not worked out, and when Roosevelt asked Harriman again, Harriman reluctantly said yes.

On December 26, Harriman had his first big news to give to Roosevelt. Molotov, he notified FDR, nervously ("reading from a paper which he preferred not to give me in writing") told him "that the Soviet Government was ready to begin cooperation in regard to the Pacific war.

"I replied that I knew you would be glad to learn that the Soviet government was ready to begin cooperation in regard to the Pacific war . . . Molotov interrupted me to say that Stalin had made this quite clear."

Molotov's nervousness stemmed from fear that Japan would find out: its powerful Kwantung army was as always deployed on the Manchurian border, presumably ready to attack. It could cause great mischief, if provoked, by sabotaging the Trans-Siberian Railway, Russia's link with the Maritime Province, which at its eastern end ran within a few miles of the Manchurian border.

In February 1944, Stalin met with Harriman a number of times to define what he meant by Soviet participation. At their first meeting he told Harriman "categorically" that the Soviet Union would provide facilities in the Far East for three hundred U.S. heavy bombers. When Harriman told him General Arnold contemplated there might be as many as a thousand bombers, Stalin replied, "Then we must build new fields. We will see what is possible."

Stalin continued, "When German resistance in the West begins to weaken, divisions will be sent to the Far East . . . As soon as these forces are transferred, the Soviet government will cease to fear Japanese provocation and may even provoke the Japanese itself. It is too weak to do so now." He said that the GKO had started reequipping the Soviet air force: four infantry corps of twenty to twenty-two divisions would be transferred to the Far East.

Stalin also volunteered that a Soviet officer had recently been approached by the chief of the Japanese general staff seeking an audience with him, saying, by way of explanation, that the Germans meant nothing to the Japanese. Stalin related that he had refused to see the man, adding, "Let them go to the Devil." He also wanted FDR to know that he had been told that the Japanese were reported to be evacuating plants and machinery to Manchuria and Japan, building a new inner defense line that would run around the islands, and that, if pressed, they would not defend their outer perimeter and Indonesia.

Shortly after D-day FDR asked Harriman to query Stalin again as to his specific plans for entering the war. When Harriman saw Stalin on June 10 he told him the president "was anxious to know how soon Stalin would be ready to initiate secret talks on the use of American air forces on Soviet bases in the East and also coordination of naval plans." Stalin said he expected Russia to play a more active role in the war and saw "one of joint cooperation in waging war on land and sea as well as in the air," that he had already discussed the matter of Soviet bases with the commander in chief of the Red Far Eastern Air Force, that there were twelve suitable airfields for four-engine bombers in the area between Vladivostok and Sovetskaya Gavan, and that the United States could expect to receive the use of six or seven of them for their bombers. Stalin emphasized, as was usual when the subject was Japan, the need for utmost secrecy, explaining that the Japanese were not interfering with Russian shipping in the Pacific, with the result that supplies, including fuel, were being accumulated in Vladivostok "legally." Stalin asked about the possibility of receiving several hundred four-engine planes. "The president," said Harriman, "would like nothing better than to have *combined* American-Soviet air operations against the Japanese." Roosevelt hoped, Harriman continued, that discussions between U.S. and Soviet military as to preparations would start immediately. "No time should be lost and the sooner the discussions started the better it would be," said Stalin. Stalin also inquired about FDR's health. Harriman reported that he replied that the president always had sinus trouble in the winter months, but "as to the present status of the president's health I said that he was very well and in full strength and vigor."

In August, FDR wrote to Stalin urging joint cooperation in the Pacific "when you are ready to act . . . There is nothing we could do now that would be of more assistance in preparing to bring the Pacific war to a speedy conclusion." Stalin replied, "I have received your message on the Pacific Ocean matters. I understand the significance you attach to these matters . . . I am confident at the same time that you are well aware to what an extent our forces are strained in order to secure success for the unfolding struggle in Europe. All this allows us to hope that the time is not far off when we shall attain a solution of our urgent task and will be able to take up other questions."

In September, Stalin, evidently having expected to hear more specifics from FDR about the Pacific war, was worried, Harriman reported, as to whether or not the United States was going to *allow* Soviet participation. "Stalin inquired," Harriman cabled, "whether we wished to bring Japan to her knees without Russian assistance or whether you still wished as you suggested in Tehran Russian participation . . . what were the plans for the defeat of Japan, and particularly what part the Allies desired to assign to Russia." He "appeared anxious to know specifically what role we would want Russia to play. He gave every indication of being ready and willing to cooperate *but did not want to be an uninvited participant.*"

On October 15 and 16, 1944, meetings were held at the Kremlin at which the U.S. military, the Russian military, and the British discussed the first moves against Japan. Present was the young, able general Aleksei Antonov, chief of Soviet operations; General Shevchenko, chief of staff of Soviet Far Eastern forces; General Deane, head of the U.S. military mission in Moscow; Harriman; and the British generals Brooke and Ismay, who were there for information and support. (Churchill was also in Moscow, there to bring Stalin up to date on Allied decisions. It was at this time that he and Stalin concurred on their percentages deal in Romania, Bulgaria, and Greece.) Stalin stated to the assembled military chiefs, "Sufficient supplies could be accumulated in three months to maintain the Soviet forces [in the Far East] for a period of one and a half to two months. This would be sufficient to deal a mortal blow against Japan."

For a moment his mind suddenly wandered to a humiliating moment in Russia's past. It became obvious that what was driving him was history: "There was no similarity between 1904 and 1944," he said abruptly. "Russia was alone in 1904, and the Japanese were free to move where they wished. Russia was no longer alone." No one had mentioned the 1904 war between Russia and Japan, which had ended so badly for Russia. He had been twenty-six at the time, and it obviously had made a great impression on him. The war had ended in the disastrous Battle of Tsushima in the Sea of Japan in May 1905. In that struggle, which must rate as the most decisive and humiliating battle in the history of naval warfare, the Japanese navy, in the space of a few hours, sank, captured, or put out of commission all of Russia's warships—twelve battleships, seven cruisers, five minelayers, and three transports—while losing only three small torpedo boats. Russia had been forced to sign the humiliating Treaty of Portsmouth, which gave Japan the southern half of Sakhalin Island and granted it control of the rail system Russia had built in Manchuria, as well as Port Arthur and Dairen, the warm-water ports on the Liaodong Peninsula.

Stalin quickly returned to the subject at hand. He said again Russian operations against Japan could commence "three months or several months" after the defeat of Germany, adding that he thought it would be a short war and therefore a three-month supply for sixty divisions would be sufficient.

At a meeting the next day Stalin said that when he and Roosevelt next met, he believed the two of them would be able to come to a joint agreement on the war with Japan and that until then the question should be studied from a military and political point of view. The group then settled down to work. General Deane presented an outline of America's general strategy. America had bombers—the biggest, the most lethal bombers in the world, he said: it needed airfields in the Maritime Province to service these bombers so they could wreak the greatest damage on Japan.

The Soviet Union had the largest army in the world, and Stalin, basically, was volunteering it. He now described what his army would need in the way of food, armaments, and logistical support. He presented his needs in terms of a two-month war, the food and fuel and vehicles necessary, he calculated, for the force of 1.5 million men he would supply: three thousand tanks, seventy-five thousand motor vehicles, and five thousand planes—all deliveries to be completed by June 30, 1945.

He commented that in the initial stages of the war it would be necessary to bomb Japan from the Vladivostok and Primorye area. It would be more feasible, however, "to bomb northern Japan from Komsomolsk and Sakhalin." Pursuit planes would be used primarily to protect the Trans-Siberian Railway. The Japanese would of course attack the railroad by air during the first stages of the war, but when the Russian invasion proceeded southward there would be less need to protect the railroad.

Stalin then launched into a detailed discussion of Soviet strategy, beginning with "his" weakness in the event of a premature Japanese attack (Molotov's great worry), and then outlined the general plans for a strong land offensive to encircle and knock out the Japanese forces in Manchuria. He spoke without notes and without hesitation.

He asked General Deane what the chiefs of staff thought Soviet objectives should be. Deane gave them as follows:

1. To secure the Trans-Siberian Railroad and the Vladivostok and Komsomolsk area.
2. To establish a United States–Soviet Strategic Air Force.
3. The Soviet land operations to destroy the Japanese forces in Manchuria.
4. Concurrently, to secure the route across the Pacific in order to safeguard supplies and to open up the port of Vladivostok.

In response to a question from Stalin, Deane said only Soviet land operations in Manchuria were contemplated.

Stalin replied, "We cannot be limited to the Manchurian region. We shall strike direct blows from different directions in Manchuria. But to have real results we must develop outflanking movements—blows to Kalgan and Peking . . . The problem that faces us is to prevent the Japanese from withdrawing from China into Manchuria . . . Regarding the other objectives set forth by General Deane—I have no objection." It was evident Stalin feared Japanese troops would be moved from China to the Manchurian border if Peking was not attacked, a parallel thought to the American fear that Japanese troops would be moved from the Manchurian border to Japan proper if the Red Army did not engage them.

In response to a question from Deane, Stalin indicated on a map that there would be outflanking movements through Ulan Bator and Kalgan, following "the old Mongol route."

"What about the Kurile Islands?" Harriman asked. "Would it be of interest for U.S. forces to occupy the northern Kurile Islands in order to secure the supply route?" The marshal replied that would be of great interest, that all the sea positions should be strengthened and then the North Korean ports should be occupied by Soviet land and sea forces. The Japanese, he continued, would probably make their first attack on Vladivostok and Petropavlovsk to secure the airfields there.

Harriman said U.S. plans were being prepared for naval action and seizure of the northern third of the Kurile Islands. Because these islands, now Japanese, had belonged to Russia in the nineteenth century, the idea that they would be wrested from Japan, and therefore would again become Russia's possession, was welcome news for Stalin.

General Deane announced that American battle plans contemplated the invasion of Japan in the closing months of 1945, and then he asked a crucial question: Did the Russians place higher priority on the buildup for the ground forces or on strategic bombing? Stalin replied, "Both at the same time . . . The Americans would cut off the Japanese garrisons on the southern islands and the Russians would cut off the land forces in China." Stalin once again stressed the need for secrecy to prevent the Japanese from embarking on "premature adventures."

Harriman inquired about the delivery of bombers. Stalin said fields and facilities would be ready in about two weeks and he wished to receive ten to twenty bombers as a first installment.

On a map Stalin outlined the planned Red Army offensive that would start in the Lake Baikal area and sweep through Outer and Inner Mongolia to Kalgan, Peking, and Tientsin, thus keeping separate the Japanese forces in China and Manchuria. Obviously pleased at the way the discussion was proceeding, Stalin said it was a "grand undertaking . . . We must break the Japanese spine."

It was agreed that General Deane and General Antonov would talk with their naval opposite numbers.

On December 14, Harriman had another long meeting with Stalin. They covered general information on shipping and delivery of U.S. goods to the Far East and the upcoming meeting—wherever it would take place—Stalin was to have with Roosevelt and Churchill. Harriman told Stalin that American plans included preparations for supplying Petropavlovsk, which would become a very important base for navy and air force operations, and that information would have to be exchanged between their opposite numbers. (Harriman reported to FDR of the meeting that Stalin "was in general well pleased with what has so far been promised. I assured him that both you and the Joint Chiefs of Staff were anxious to do everything possible both as to supply and shipping. I stressed the need for detailed planning . . . He gave me his assurance that he would authorize the General Staff promptly to begin discussions.")

At Tehran, Roosevelt had mentioned only that the warm-water port of Dairen, now known as Dalian, could possibly be returned to Russia, knowing this was not all Stalin would ask for in return for Soviet participation in the war. Now the price had to be settled. Harriman was requested to meet with Stalin and find out what it was, to say FDR "was anxious to know what were the political questions indicated by him which should be clarified in connection with the entry of the USSR into the war against Japan." Harriman put the question to him in his office. Stalin walked into the next room, returned with a map in his hands, and said that Lower Sakhalin and the Kurile Islands should be returned to Russia and that Russia would like to lease the ports of Dairen and Port Arthur. In addition, said Stalin, he "again" wished to lease the Chinese Eastern Railway lines in Manchuria from Dairen to Harbin, northwest to Manzhouli, and east to Vladivostok. Stalin, gratifyingly, reported Harriman, "specifically reaffirmed his intention not to interfere with the sovereignty of China in Manchuria," adding that he was interested in maintaining the independence of Outer Mongolia. Stalin was asking

General Georgi Zhukov, the savior of Leningrad, 1945

Stalingrad was totally destroyed. Solitary walls and chimneys mark where houses once stood.

Churchill arriving aboard the USS *Augusta* for the Atlantic Conference, August 1941.
FDR put on his braces, which he rarely did aboard a ship, so as to be standing as he
greeted the prime minister.

The USS *Arizona*, Pearl Harbor, 1941

Secretary of State Cordell Hull and Ambassador Maxim Litvinov greet Foreign Minister Molotov as he arrives in Washington, May 1942.

U.S. A-20 attack bombers being readied for shipment

for the territories Russia had ceded to Japan by treaty in 1905, plus the Kurile Islands, which Russia had owned at an earlier time.

Previously, in discussions about future bomber strikes, Antonov and Stalin had cautioned that U.S. planes could not in any case arrive on airfields in the Maritime Province and Kamchatka until ten days before war commenced. Suddenly, on December 17, General Antonov announced, "After careful calculation we have determined that the Soviet forces will need all the air and naval bases in the Maritime Province and that therefore American air and naval forces will be unable to operate from there." Harriman seemed to take this change of plans as a personal affront, as another instance of Stalin's arbitrariness, telling FDR about it in a cable on December 29: "It is fair to say that almost all our requests generally are turned down out of hand without explanation. In no sense can I report that our military mission is being treated as that of an ally . . . [T]hey are persistent, overbearing." However, at the same time, continued Harriman, Antonov informed him that the United States could use and commence surveying Kamchatka. No explanation was forthcoming—normal Soviet behavior—but FDR's knowledge of geography was encyclopedic. (Once during the war he had stunned Deputy Prime Minister Walter Nash of New Zealand during a conference: Nash had suggested American forces occupy a small Pacific island near New Zealand. FDR said, "No, not that island; an island nearby called Mangareva would be better." Nash had never heard of the island. "Oh, it's in the Tuamotu Archipelago, in the postal zone of Tahiti," FDR informed him. "I know the place because I am a stamp collector.")

The president would have realized, as Harriman did not, that the Maritime Province was *too* close to Japan for Soviet comfort, forming, in fact, the eastern Manchurian border; it would be hard to keep U.S. activity there a secret: the abrupt change was likely because of the Soviets' mortal fear that the Japanese, discovering the American presence, would attack before the Red troops were armed and ready. General Curtis LeMay was using the Marianas as his base for the B-29s that were bombing Tokyo to smithereens, so although Kamchatka was a good deal closer to Japan, airfields there were not crucial.

Harriman's complaints were followed by his admitting, "My personal relations with Marshal Stalin, Mr. Molotov and other members of the Foreign Office are pleasant."

FDR BACKTRACKED ON TWO COMMITMENTS he had made
to the Soviet Union, both sensitive issues with the Russians, who were
always suspicious even in the best of circumstances, given their distrust
of all foreigners. Both incidents reveal American paranoia to have been
on a par with Russia's, although better hidden.

In November 1943, FDR and the War Department had authorized
Brigadier General Donovan, legendary head of the OSS, to set up an
OSS intelligence mission in Moscow in return for a matching Soviet
intelligence liaison mission in Washington. Such a setup would ease
problems that were arising during joint operations between the two
countries. Britain had such a mission exchange with Russia in place:
four NKVD officers were stationed in London; British Special Operations Executive personnel were stationed in Moscow. Such an action
did not mean that any seriously compromising material was exchanged.

Donovan met first with Molotov, who, favorably impressed with
OSS intelligence operations, sent him on, accompanied by General
Deane, to the Commissariat of Internal Affairs, the NKVD headquarters. There the two men met with Lieutenant General Pavel Fitin, chief
of the External Intelligence Service. Fitin was blond, blue-eyed, thirty-
six, with a pleasing smile, according to Deane, while Major General
Alexander Ossipov, head of the section dealing with subversive activities in enemy countries, looked to be a suitable companion for Boris
Karloff. Donovan charmed the Russians, volunteered descriptions of
suitcase radios, plastic explosives, and other special spy equipment the
OSS had developed, and described how the OSS introduced agents
into enemy territory. Donovan also discussed the types of training U.S.
agents received. Fitin liked the idea of the intelligence exchange, according to General Deane, citing how desirable it would be if the United
States could be informed if Soviet agents were preparing to sabotage an
important German industrial establishment or railroad, and the reverse.
But Fitin then darkly asked Donovan if he had come to the Soviet Union
"solely for the purpose of offering cooperation or whether he had some
other intentions." "I could not help but snicker at this further evidence
of Soviet suspicion," wrote Deane (unaware that his own country was
even more suspicious). Donovan neutrally replied to Fitin that he had
no other intentions.

Their relationship changed entirely upon agreement to the exchange of personnel. Previously, when Deane had business with Fitin, he first had to phone Fitin's assistant, who would take his time before passing on Deane's message to Fitin. The awkward and time-consuming process took hours or sometimes days before Deane finally succeeded in speaking to Fitin. But after the meeting Fitin gave him the telephone numbers for himself and for Ossipov. "It was my first telephone number in Russia and I felt that I had achieved a tremendous victory," Deane later wrote. For the first time Fitin and Ossipov accepted an invitation to dine at the American embassy. By January 5 the four had agreed on the size and composition of the personnel exchange: Colonel John Haskell and a small team would come to Moscow to represent Donovan; Colonel A. G. Grauer together with his assistants would represent Fitin and Ossipov in Washington.

The spy chiefs had finished most of the details of the exchange, as Donovan explained to Harriman:

> I have arranged with Government agencies here engaged in intelligence and subversive activities as follows:
> 1. The Soviets will establish a liaison with OSS in Washington and I have agreed to set up a unit here reporting to the Ambassador and the Military Mission, and agreed to designate Col. John Haskell Chief Representative.
> 2. There is agreement on exchange of intelligence material.
> 3. Also regarding reciprocal examination and exchange of special devices and equipment.
> 4. Joint operations in such theatres as may be agreed.

Donovan was aware there were U.S. worries, particularly among the Joint Chiefs of Staff, about whether or not the action would expose America to Soviet spies. He went about quelling their suspicions. In March he sent a clear, persuasive memo to Admiral Leahy, always privately wary of Soviet intentions, whom he knew to be lukewarm about the idea:

> The Attorney General in his talk with me suggested that the impression might be created in this country that this was an invitation to the OGPU to come to America. As I answered your question, however, that already happened when Amtorg established its

offices here. [There were twenty-five hundred Soviets working at Amtorg in New York and an equal number in Washington.] . . . It does seem an invalid argument to say that the addition of four or five other representatives on an open basis to work with OSS on matters concerning our joint operation against the common enemy would provide any greater facilities for undercover activities . . . For the first time, we have an opportunity to find out just how our strongest ally carries out important agencies in its war effort . . . It is as essential to know how your allies conduct their subversive work as to know how your enemy does it.

In mid-March, Harriman received a bombshell: FDR called off the project. A cable came from the president that gave evidence of careful thought (FDR's handwritten changes in italics) telling him the exchange had to be canceled and ordering him to inform Molotov. FDR couched it in personal terms in an attempt to take the sting out of it, aware that Stalin had been told numerous times of the anti-Soviet sentiment in the United States:

> The question presented has been carefully examined here and has been found to be impracticable *at this time.*
>
> Please inform ~~Stalin~~ *the Marshal* when you have an opportunity that for purely domestic political reasons *which he will understand* it is not appropriate *just now* to exchange these missions. *The timing is not good.*

Harriman tried to change FDR's mind in a long cable:

> The Soviet acceptance of the idea was perhaps welcomed by us all the more because it was the first tangible evidence of the spirit of cooperation which was voiced at the conferences in Moscow and Tehran.
>
> We were received cordially by Molotov . . . We were informed that after consideration the Soviets accepted Donovan's proposal for an exchange of missions . . . The Soviet Mission, consisting of Colonel Grauer and about six assistants plus the usual wives are ready to leave for Washington . . .
>
> For the last two and a half years we have unsuccessfully

attempted to penetrate sources of Soviet information and to arrive at some basis of exchange and mutual confidence. We have now, for the first time, penetrated one intelligence branch . . . But if we now close the door on this branch of the Soviet Government, I cannot too strongly express my conviction that our relations with the Soviet Government will be adversely affected in other directions.

J. Edgar Hoover, head of the FBI, had gotten wind of the project and as always, seeing *all* Russians as dangerous spies, threatened FDR, warning him that if he didn't cancel the exchange, there would be "an unfavorable public reaction" if it became public knowledge. With Hoover strongly against the idea, and his implied threat that it would become public knowledge in an election year, the idea was dead. (Hoover saw Communists everywhere; he would a few years later warn Truman that his secretary of state, Dean Acheson, was the head of a Communist cell.) FDR responded to Harriman's plea by cabling him, "The domestic political situation was the predominant factor in my decisions," and noting that it "may" be helpful if Harriman reemphasized to Stalin that the exchange of missions "had to be deferred because of timing."

J. Edgar Hoover also compromised another project. At Tehran, FDR had asked Stalin to facilitate improvement of radio communications between their two capitals by allowing the establishment of a U.S. radio station in Moscow and a Russian radio station in Washington. Because of atmospheric and other problems, cables to and from Moscow and Washington were taking days instead of hours to reach their destinations. Britain had already set up reciprocal radio stations with the U.S.S.R. in their respective capitals. General Deane, working with the Red Army staff, had gone to work in the months after Tehran, spending December and January setting up the U.S. radio station in Moscow. Then, in March, the War Department suddenly informed him that under U.S. law no foreign government could be given the privilege of operating a radio station in the United States. This was such a great setback in terms of efficiency as well as personal relations that Harriman thereupon suggested to Roosevelt that he use his wartime powers and get around the provision by extending the privilege for the duration of the war only. He pointed out how important better communications were for the furtherance of Allied plans (the air force was about to send in a thousand men to operate U.S. bombers for a shuttle-bombing operation at three Soviet airfields). But in any form the idea drew the ire of J. Edgar Hoover, historically paranoid about and on the lookout for Communist conspiracies. The FBI chief declared it "a highly dangerous and most undesirable procedure." On March 15, FDR wired Harriman to drop it, with the excuse that the military staff had (after all the months of pushing for better communications) suddenly found out that communications were quite all right the way they were: "The Joint Chiefs of Staff are of the opinion that the establishment of a Soviet radio station in Washington and an American station in Moscow is at the present time unnecessary. Therefore please take no further action toward the establishment of a Soviet radio station in Washington."

Because more efficient, reliable communications between the two countries were so necessary and so lacking, Deane suggested to the Russians that a relay through Algiers would at least improve the situation. But Molotov and Stalin were annoyed: if a Soviet radio station in Washington was not possible under American law, said Molotov, "the Soviet Government is unwilling to consider any other alternative."

Deane went to work on Molotov, pushing the idea of a hookup through Algiers as a viable alternative that would improve communications; both knew something had to be done. The Red Army staff, aware that relaying through Algiers would at least be an improvement, was also working to change Molotov's—essentially Stalin's—mind.

Would U.S. paranoia prevent even this setup? Harriman wrote questioning FDR about it; FDR wrote him back, this time determined to get results: "With reference to radio communications between the USSR and the United States . . . I understand that this matter is still under negotiation." He added to it in his own hand "*and is proceeding toward a satisfactory conclusion.*"

Harriman later learned that indeed J. Edgar Hoover had objected, as had Chief of Staff Admiral Leahy, both using the argument that if it became known the president had sanctioned a Soviet radio station in Washington, his enemies and the right-wing press would tag him as a Communist. In fact, the specter of adverse publicity was a threat disguised as advice: if FDR went ahead, Hoover *could* make it known to the broad band of isolationists, America Firsters, and those many Americans afraid of Communism that FDR had permitted the installation of a Soviet radio transmitter in Washington, and he *might,* as a result, lose the next election.

STALIN SEEMED ABLE and motivated to brush aside questions about Roosevelt's basic reliability just as Roosevelt brushed aside questions about him. Now, after these two incidents, the exchange of secret agents and setting up radio stations in each other's capitals, where FDR had changed his mind and backed away, Stalin said of him, "The president is my friend, we will always understand each other." This remark, which was repeated to FDR in July, perhaps prompted FDR's remark about Stalin to the assembled delegates of the Dumbarton Oaks Conference at a reception at the White House the following month: "At Tehran the Marshal and I got to know each other. We got on beautifully. We cracked the ice, if there ever was any ice; and since then there has been no ice."

By the spring of 1944, the Red Army had liberated more than three-quarters of occupied Soviet territory. Stalin's May Day speech underlined the importance of the alliance: "We must follow hot on the heels of the wounded German beast and finish it off in its own lair . . . [W]e must deliver from German bondage our brothers the Poles, the Czechoslovaks and other peoples of Western Europe . . . It can be accomplished only by the joint efforts of the Soviet Union, Great Britain and the United States of America, by joint blows, delivered in the East by our troops and in the West by the troops of our Allies."

Stalin made a widely quoted comment about Roosevelt to Milovan Djilas on the eve of D-day—that he wouldn't slip a kopeck out of your pocket, whereas Churchill would. The comment is usually misinterpreted, because it is in the middle of a long diatribe about Churchill, and, usually when quoted, stands alone and out of context. Stalin had been speaking about Great Britain and said, "They [the English] find nothing sweeter than to trick their allies. During the First World War they constantly tricked the Russians and the French. And Churchill? Churchill is the kind who, if you don't watch him, will slip a kopeck out of your pocket. Yes, a kopeck out of your pocket! By God, a kopeck out of your pocket! And Roosevelt? Roosevelt is not like that. He dips in his hands only for bigger coins. But Churchill? Churchill—even for a kopeck." He continued on about English duplicity.

The Normandy invasion took place on June 6. On that day 160,000 men hit the Normandy beaches, within weeks to be joined by a million more men, transported there by the largest armada ever assembled.

The next day Stalin cabled FDR that the Red Army would perform as promised: "The summer offensive of the Soviet troops . . . will begin in the middle of June . . . The general offensive will develop in phases by successive throwing in of armies into the offensive operations . . . I pledge to give you timely information about the progress of the offensive operations." At roughly the same time, Stalin said to Harriman, "We are going down a good road."

There was no public word out of Stalin for a week as U.S. and British forces battled German fortifications up and down the French coast. Finally, on June 13, Stalin gave his allies unqualified public praise in *Pravda:* "After seven days' fighting in Northern France one may say without hesitation that the forcing of the Channel along a wide front and the mass-landings of the Allies in Northern France have completely succeeded. This is unquestionably a brilliant success for our Allies. One must admit that the history of wars does not know of an undertaking comparable to it for breadth of conception, grandeur of scale, and mastery of execution."

On June 21, Stalin gave FDR more details abut the major Russian offensive that would pin down German divisions, promising, "Not later than in a weeks time will begin the second turn of the summer offensive of the Soviet troops. In this offensive will participate 130 divisions, including armored tank divisions . . . I hope that our offensive will render substantial support to the operations of the Allied troops in France and Italy."

A few days later, when the U.S. embassy showed the first motion pictures of the invasion, two Soviet marshals plus some two hundred high-ranking officers showed up. "The interest was intense." On July 4, Molotov went to lunch at the American embassy—the first time he was ever known to dine at a foreign embassy.

FROM FDR'S POINT OF VIEW, one of the most important messages he sent Stalin was the one that had gone out on February 23, 1944, on the subject of postwar international monetary collaboration and the "possible" convocation of a United Nations monetary conference. International monetary instability had been a major factor behind the two world wars and the Depression.

U.S. plans for the Bank for Reconstruction and Development and the United Nations Stabilization Fund had been in the works since the week after Pearl Harbor, when Secretary of the Treasury Morgenthau had requested Harry Dexter White to be the architect and create plans for international monetary instruments. White, special assistant to Morgenthau, who would become the driving force behind the agreement, worked for the next year more or less in constant contact with his British counterpart, John Maynard Keynes, adviser to the British Treasury, who was also working on a blueprint for postwar economic cooperative organizations, but necessarily from the point of view of protecting the British Empire. Those involved—Morgenthau, White, and Keynes— wanted to start publicizing their work and enlisting the support of foreign governments in the spring of 1943. Roosevelt, always sensitive to tipping his hand before he had to and giving enemies (in this case isolationists) time to marshal their arguments, stopped Morgenthau, telling him it was "too early . . . We haven't begun to win the war."

After leaks regarding the project—stemming from the many conversations and memos that had been sent out to the governments involved—made further secrecy impossible, White's draft was sent out to the finance ministers of the Allied governments, including the Soviet Union, in late April. The idea by that time had been widely discussed and acclaimed. *Fortune* magazine did a major article endorsing the need for postwar international monetary cooperation between countries. Gromyko assured Morgenthau that the Soviet Union was "keenly interested" in the proposals being developed for both the fund and the bank. In December, White gave two copies of the "final" preliminary draft agreement relating to the bank to the Soviet embassy secretary, Vladimir Bazykin, noting to him that this draft was also being sent to Britain, China, and Canada, also noting that FDR's most difficult problem would be getting the measure through the Senate. In January 1944, the first Russian monetary technicians, as they were called (the International Monetary Fund required technical knowledge), finally arrived in Washington.

FDR's message to Stalin asking him to take part in the meeting to hammer out postwar international economic collaboration went out a month later. Stalin answered, in the affirmative, three weeks later: "I consider as quite expedient the establishment at the present time of a United Nations apparatus for the working of these questions."

Stalin had an excellent grasp of economic theory. "What is the main task of planning?" Stalin had asked at a meeting of Russian economists early in 1941. The meeting had been called to update official Soviet economic texts. At this meeting Stalin had commented on the latest Soviet textbooks explaining Communist economic theory. Minutes of the meeting show Stalin's analysis of the drafts of two books that government economists had submitted to him to critique. Mainly, his comments were that those in charge of the books should concentrate on saying everything clearly, simply, without exaggeration. He gave them an example, "The planned economy is not our wish; it is unavoidable or else everything will collapse. We destroyed such bourgeois barometers as the market and trade, which help the bourgeoisie to correct disproportions," changing it to "The planned economy is as unavoidable for us as the consumption of bread . . . The main task of planning is to ensure the independence of the socialist economy. This is absolutely the most important task."

In the midst of this conversation with economists (a lecture not expected to see the light of day outside the Soviet Union), which showed Stalin deeply involved in analyzing and rephrasing passages, he had, the minutes show, suddenly veered off the subject into mentioning FDR in a favorable light: "I had Wells [the British author H. G. Wells] into this office and he told me that he didn't want the workers in power and didn't want the capitalists in power. He wants the engineers to rule. He said that he is for Roosevelt whom he knows well and speaks of as an honest man committed to the men of the working class. They are disseminating the ideas of the reconciliation of classes with the petit-bourgeoisie." Then Stalin had returned to the task at hand, urging the economists to write more simply and to clarify the relationship of socialism and capitalism, reminding them, "There is no need to forget that we emerged from capitalism."

A world where Russia would be safe to continue rebuilding itself, which seemed likely if Roosevelt were at the helm—a period of world economic stability—was certainly to Stalin's liking. He took steps to signal his wish to be part of the planning. Not only did he agree to take part in the conference, but he invited the quintessential proponent of capitalism, Eric Johnston, president of the U.S. Chamber of Commerce, to visit Soviet Russia. Johnston was approvingly quoted in *Pravda* in February as saying that American businessmen wished to sell and export goods and services and "not ideologies and political concepts." Nor did Stalin stop with Johnston. In roughly the same time period, *The Foundations of Marxism,* a major Russian economic journal, published an article officially lowering the tone of opprobrium to capitalism, thereby opening the way to making competition between socialist and capitalist economies ideologically acceptable.

The plan that White drew up had sections that neither the British nor the Russians were happy with, but Roosevelt, with his fine sense of timing, felt that the monetary conference *must* convene that summer and that the differences would be ironed out by the conferees when they met. Morgenthau needed both Britain and Russia to sign on to the joint statement if the conference was going to be effective and a new world economic order created. At first Stalin was lukewarm. After reading the preliminary documents, he thought the questions intrusive. He wanted a provision for unilateral Russian definition of the gold value of the ruble and objected to White's requirements for Soviet gold payments into the International Monetary Fund. It looked as if the Soviet Union would not sign on to the joint statement. Morgenthau worriedly appealed to Gromyko in Washington and Harriman in Moscow to press Stalin to agree to it, falsely (taking what he later described as "an awful chance") advising Harriman to tell Stalin that the British had already signed on to the draft, thereby taking an unusual step that probably saved the future of the conference. Stalin agreed. Molotov requested Harriman to come to his office at 11:30 p.m., at which time he read to him the following: "The government of the USSR has not yet succeeded in studying fully the basic conditions in question. However, if it is necessary to the government of the United States to have the voice of the USSR to secure due effect in the external world, the Soviet government agrees to give instructions to its experts to associate themselves with the project of Mr. Morgenthau."

Morgenthau was naturally gratified, as he reported to FDR: "Yesterday I called up both Harriman in Moscow and Gromyko here to put all the pressure I could on them to get the Russians to come along . . . I thought you would be most pleased that the Soviet government decided to go along with us 'to secure due effect on the rest of the world.' In other words, they want to be associated with us in the eyes of the world." As Morgenthau said to Harry Dexter White, "England and Russia have to make up their minds on two vital things for them . . . 1. Is Russia going to play ball with the rest of the world on external matters, which she has never done before and, 2. Is England going to play with the United Nations or is she going to play with the Dominions? Now, both of these countries have to make up their minds, and . . . I am not going to take anything less than a yes or no from them." Presumably, both countries gave in, realizing that what Secretary of the Treasury Henry Morgenthau was aiming at was not simply U.S. hegemony but helping all countries get back on their feet after the war and develop and grow through trade and investment.

On April 21 the "Joint Statement by Experts for the Establishment of an International Monetary Fund" was finally ready. Morgenthau informed FDR he would send out invitations on May 1, commence informal drafting on May 10, and convene the first session at the end of May. "Well done. You are hereby authorized to go ahead," replied FDR.

The Mount Washington Hotel, a sprawling 350-bedroom white stuccoed Western version of a Spanish Renaissance castle located in Bretton Woods, New Hampshire, cool, accessible, famous, was chosen as the venue. FDR approved the draft of the invitation, the list of American delegates presented, and the title, "The United Nations Monetary and Financial Conference." "That's good," he remarked. "Here's where you get a medal, Henry."

Roosevelt convened the conference; forty-four nations sent delegations.

The hotel, closed for three years, less than ready, was described by one of the participants as a mixture of luxury, chaos, and inefficiency. Participants found that the windows in their rooms didn't always open or close and the taps ran irregularly. However, the days were warm, the evenings were cool, the food was good, and a sprawling veranda running the length of the hotel encouraged mingling and conversation. The American delegation included Henry Morgenthau, the chair; Harry Dexter White; the president of the First National Bank of Chicago; Dean Acheson from the State Department; the chairman of the Federal Reserve; a Vassar economics professor; and, to make sure Congress would be supportive of the outcome, two congressmen and two senators.

From the outset it was apparent that although it didn't "show" in the negotiations, which were difficult because so many countries were involved and so much was at stake for each one of them, it was the consensus of most members of the American delegation that even though the country was devastated and its loss of life astounding, "Russia doesn't need the Fund . . . It has a complete system of state trading— state industry."

"But the Fund needed Russia," White said. Senator Charles Tobey, a member of the delegation, agreed. "World cooperation must have Russia," he said.

The Soviet delegation consisted of M. S. Stepanov, the deputy people's commissar of foreign trade and the head of the delegation; the deputy commissar of finance; the head of the Monetary Division of the Commissariat of Finance; a doctor of economics; and the head of the Monetary Division of the Commissariat for Foreign Trade.

In spite of their numerous objections, in the off-hours the Soviet delegates were quite friendly. Twice there were volleyball games between the American delegates and the Russian delegates, both of which the Russians won. The Russians also socialized at the late-night Bretton Woods Hotel nightclub, where everyone, well lubricated, would congregate and sing each other's songs.

The members of the Soviet delegation objected to the quota allotted their country in the International Monetary Fund, on the basis that its trade with America was going to greatly increase after the war. They expected a quota equivalent to 10 percent of the fund, which would give them 10 percent of the votes, but they were now told they would have $800 million, which was less than a tenth. Said Stepanov, "The proposed formula was based upon past economic data such as foreign trade and that since it was hoped that the foreign trade of all countries would be increased, particularly that of the Soviet Union and the United States, the calculations for the quotas should be based on future prospects rather than past statistics." Stepanov then came to the crux of his argument: the Soviet quota should equal the British.

He also pointed out that Soviets were of the opinion that countries occupied or devastated by the Germans should receive a reduction in their gold contribution to the international fund.

The American delegation proposed to Stepanov a quota of $1.2 billion on condition there were no more concessions.

Stepanov replied that he had only asked for a reduction of 25 percent in initial gold contribution and couldn't "decide . . . without the consent of Moscow." He held that the Russians would have "especially heavy" reconstruction expenses and therefore couldn't go with Morgenthau's wish for a subscription of $1.2 billion. He could only agree to a Russian contribution to the bank of $900 million. Not having the authority to change his figure, he cabled Moscow for direction.

Russia's position caused worldwide concern. "Still awaiting a reply from Moscow on the amount of gold it is willing to pay into the proposed $8,500,000,000 international monetary fund, the United Nations Monetary and Financial Conference remained stalled," reported *The New York Times* on July 14. More days went by.

Meanwhile, Eric Johnston was in Moscow being given the VIP treatment by Stalin. He was allowed to visit parts of the Soviet Union that had not been seen by an American since 1926 and given a long "conversation" with the premier. The timing of his visit, from the standpoint of demonstrating to the countries of the world that Russia expected to become a responsible member of the postwar world, was absolutely perfect. *The New York Times,* under the headline "Chamber Head Says Stalin Appears Intent on Building Nation and Its Trade," quoted Johnston as saying there was "a feeling of definite need for a long period of peace . . . induced by the necessity to rebuild Russia after the terrible destruction of the war." Praise from Johnston, the president of the Chamber of Commerce, the organization representing the greatest concentration of capital wealth in the world—what could top that?

Still, at Bretton Woods, all waited for the answer to the question of Russia's contribution into the fund. Finally, word was gotten through to the Kremlin that their indecision was causing a definite crisis: Harriman, in Moscow, was instructed to meet with the commissar of finance and tell him that unless Russia responded immediately, Morgenthau was going to announce the final, definitive report without Soviet participation. Evidently, Stalin was scoping out the issue. Within three hours of Harriman's meeting with the finance commissar, Molotov was cabling the details to Stepanov. There was an hour to go before the final plenary session; it was seven in the evening in New Hampshire: Stepanov called Morgenthau to tell him "the answer is that he is happy to agree to your proposition . . . to increase our quota . . . to one billion two hundred million dollars."

It was a huge step, as well as another instance of Stalin's bending to FDR's will. With the inclusion of the Soviet Union, the conference succeeded in getting every one of the forty-four nations to agree to set up an international monetary fund to stabilize postwar currencies, stimulate world trade, and prevent economic rivalries that might endanger world peace. Stepanov was quoted in newspaper accounts as saying his country "was very anxious to cooperate with the rest of the United Nations in post-war matters and felt there was special need for some stabilized monetary system after the war."

The next day Morgenthau exultantly wrote to FDR that Molotov's agreement to lift the quota showed the Russian "desire to collaborate fully with the United States. Dean Acheson has just said that this was almost unbelievable . . . a matter of great political significance." Keynes, in a sense, went further. The Russians, Keynes wrote to a friend, "*want* to thaw and collaborate."

THE DAY BEFORE the conference ended, Colonel Claus von Stauffenberg came close to assassinating Adolf Hitler during a conference at Hitler's Rastenburg headquarters. Stauffenberg had placed a briefcase containing a bomb, timed to detonate ten minutes later, under the conference table where Hitler was working and exited the building. The bomb went off, killing four of the staff, but Hitler escaped with scorched clothes and burns on his arm and leg. Stauffenberg was apprehended and shot; his co-conspirators were rounded up and hanged. General Donovan, head of the OSS, knew of Stauffenberg's conspiratorial group because they had come to him for OSS assistance. If the assassination was successful, it was to have been followed by an uprising of the German underground, according to Donovan. However, the group had made plain to the OSS chief that they were strongly anti-Soviet and believed a peace dictated without Russia would be best for Germany. Donovan had gone to FDR to ask if the OSS could help the conspirators. FDR told the OSS chief, "If we start assassinating chiefs of State, God knows where it all would end. If the Germans dispose of Hitler, that is their prerogative, but the OSS must have nothing whatsoever to do with it." The president also told him, "The United States would never act without previous consultation with the USSR."

ANOTHER CHANGE STALIN MADE, in line with FDR's way of thinking, also happened in July. In a public relations move hailed at home and abroad, Stalin created the Council for Religious Affairs to act as liaison between the government and all religions except the Russian Orthodox Church, which had already been rehabilitated. This was the final step in the process of rehabilitating religion in Russia. Catholic churches were permitted to repair their buildings, buy printing presses, and generally function. Theological schools, closed since 1917, were permitted to reopen. The prestigious Moscow Theological Institute, housed in a four-hundred-year-old monastery, was the first to take advantage of the new law, but Gregorian Armenians were about to open a seminary near Yerevan, and the council was reported to be considering allowing Muslims in the Uzbek republic to open a school for mullahs. In Moscow the council was given a big beige-painted stone building for its headquarters, the gateway of which was identified by a gold-lettered black plaque with its name on it. It didn't mean any change in Stalin's thinking—a Communist who expected to rise had to be an atheist—but as a step to make the people newly grateful to him as supreme leader and to impress the world with his humanitarian rebirth, it made a great deal of sense.

No comment by Roosevelt has been discovered on this final loosening of the strictures against religion nor on Stalin's earlier relaxation of antireligious practices. Presumably, FDR just uttered a sigh of relief.

As the summer progressed, final arrangements were made for the Dumbarton Oaks Conference, where FDR's four policemen—America, Britain, Russia, and China—would meet to discuss how to form a world security organization. Dumbarton Oaks, which dated from the early nineteenth century and had once been the home of U.S. senator and vice president John C. Calhoun, had been transformed by Robert Woods Bliss, a career diplomat, into an exquisite Georgetown brick mansion. It was set in the midst of an unusual sixteen-acre garden designed by Beatrix Farrand that included pebble walks, lily ponds spanned by bridges, and stunning flower gardens. The interior, equally tasteful, contained a Renaissance music room where, on August 21, delegates from America, Britain, and Russia assembled. They sat around a U-shaped conference table covered with blotter pads and pencils as they decided upon the broad outlines of the postwar peacekeeping organization. The Russian ambassador, Andrei Gromyko, aided by a complement of Soviet experts on international law, headed the Soviet delegation; Alexander Cadogan, permanent undersecretary for foreign affairs, headed the British delegation; Undersecretary of State Edward R. Stettinius led the American delegation. Much to their chagrin, because of the ever-present Russian fears of provoking the Japanese, the Chinese delegation could not be seated until the Russian delegation had departed.

Gromyko, traveling with the Russian delegation, survived a grueling five-day plane trip that took him across Siberia and the Soviet Far East to Alaska, then across Canada and down into the United States. The group was delayed by hurricane-force winds, stranded in the tiny Siberian settlement of Uelkal in Chukotka on the edge of the Bering Sea. When they finally arrived at National Airport, they found, waiting to greet them there, Stettinius and the American delegation and Cadogan and the members of the British delegation. Having survived the trip, Gromyko was extremely sanguine regarding the conference. In fact, by Russian standards, ecstatic. Just that it was taking place made him optimistic. As he wrote to Stalin, "There are all grounds to believe that the USA will be interested in maintenance of peace . . . It is only in this light that we can interpret the readiness of the USA to take an active part in the international peace and security organization." As he wrote later, "Our approach was clear. We were determined to create such an organization and we were determined that it should be effective."

Because Roosevelt's basic concept of the four policemen as the most powerful international force to keep unruly nations in line had been discussed with Molotov and Stalin when Molotov visited Washington in June 1942, agreed to at the Moscow Conference in October 1943, and again discussed at length with Stalin at Tehran, the Russians found no surprises: the concept was now very familiar to everyone concerned, indeed was considered essential by both the British and the Russians.

The final document presented at Dumbarton Oaks was the result of five years of fine-tuning by FDR and the State Department. The four policemen were now the four permanent members of the eleven-member Security Council. The permanent members, acting together, constituted the UN Military Staff Committee that was in charge of all UN military enforcement actions. There was the General Assembly, to which all nations belonged, the International Court of Justice, the Economic and Social Council, the Secretariat, and various subagencies.

After some discussion initiated by Gromyko, France was agreed to as the fifth permanent member. As Stephen Schlesinger, author of *Act of Creation: The Founding of the United Nations,* noted, Roosevelt was advocating a six-member permanent Security Council—the sixth member to be Brazil, the largest country in South America, which was pushing its cause. Stettinius, aided by Leo Pasvolsky, director of State's Committee on Postwar Problems, successfully persuaded the president to drop the idea.

Stalin instructed Gromyko to fight for an absolute veto in the Security Council. Gromyko recalled it as an anxious time for him: "The work was exceptionally intense." It had been agreed among the three powers that a veto was necessary to block any military action against one of its members, even if that member was the aggressor. But Gromyko was instructed to demand that the veto be absolute: any world problem that one of the members did not want to discuss could be suppressed. This was unacceptable to both Britain and the United States, because it would mean any nation could control the agenda—in effect be the censor. The Soviet position, according to Gromyko, was based on the fear that the capitalist nations might gang up on the Soviet Union—the single socialist member of the council—and he wouldn't budge.

Not being able to resolve this impasse, that unanimity with the right of veto had to be a principle of the Security Council, Hull and Stettinius decided to invite Gromyko to have breakfast with FDR, to see if the president could change his mind. Such a thing—such an intimacy as breakfasting with the president—was viewed as indicating the extraordinary level of friendship extended by FDR. Stettinius asked Gromyko if he would be willing to discuss the matter with FDR over breakfast: of course he said yes. The meeting was held the next morning, September 8, with Stettinius present.

FDR immediately put things on a personal footing. He handled the meeting in such a way that he not only explained the U.S. position to Gromyko but gave Gromyko the feeling that he was "on the inside"—being present as he gave instructions to his undersecretary of state. He began by telling Gromyko some of his plans for his upcoming meeting in Quebec with Churchill, his hopes of another conference of the three chiefs of state as soon as possible, and his delight with the way things were going on both the Russian and the Allied fronts. He then read a wire from General Pat Hurley in China, which said that Molotov had told him that the Soviets were not interested in the Chinese Communists, that they were not really Communists anyway. Roosevelt commented that he himself thought they were agrarians.

FDR, often in a loquacious mood, took a leisurely while to get to a point. This trait served to disarm many people, but it made Stettinius restless. "The president finally came around to Dumbarton Oaks," he wrote. Gromyko, in the interest of security, had previously, in discussion with Cadogan and Stettinius, objected to the Economic and Social Council because his government was afraid the proposed peace organization might dissipate its energies on extraneous issues. He had also advocated the establishment of a permanent, always-ready international air force that could deal immediately with infractions. Now he said that if the United States objected to these positions, his country would drop them. But Gromyko "indicated pretty clearly" that though he could yield on these points, the one really difficult point was the voting question.

Roosevelt then got down to work to change Gromyko's mind on the voting question, persuasively rolling out arguments. First he cast the problem in personal terms: "Traditionally in this country, husbands and wives when in trouble never have the opportunity to vote on their own case, although they always have an opportunity to state their case." Then he threw in a bit of American history, stressing the American concept of fair play originating with the founding fathers. Then he pointed out how the Soviet proposal would give him problems in the Senate and finally wound up by saying that he thought "the issue of quick and immediate force" in the Senate could be met. Nothing worked. Gromyko explained to the president that "we did not have room to retreat from our position, just as our troops at Stalingrad knew that they could not retreat further east than the Volga." But he accepted FDR's remarks gracefully, according to Stettinius, and there was a discussion of "the way he could explain our position clearly to his people at home."

Would Gromyko consider it helpful if a message went out to Stalin? asked Stettinius, who could now be seen to be ready for just such an eventuality. In his hand he held a cable from FDR to Stalin outlining the difficulty of the voting question, stressing the traditional concept that in America parties to a dispute never vote on their own case, that an international organization that violated this concept would not be supported, and that smaller nations would feel the same way. Stettinius read it out.

FDR said he liked the message but wanted it redrafted to include his husband-and-wife simile "and be sent to Miss Tully [his secretary] for transmission."

Then, as was his style, to keep participants from getting bogged down in details, and as much for Gromyko's benefit as for Stettinius's, FDR became peremptory: the whole matter should be wrapped up by the end of the following week, he said. "I want at that time the document signed and a report from you that great success was achieved. This is an order to you."

As he finished, according to Stettinius, "Gromyko squirmed in his chair as I did in mine."

In spite of their basic disagreement, Gromyko still felt FDR's goodwill, felt that the president was looking for a way of removing difficulties to come to an agreement. He even thought that Roosevelt might give in on the veto, because he had agreed that all Security Council proceedings, other than "matters of procedure," must be agreed upon unanimously. But matters of procedure included the agenda, which meant any country could bring up any subject. This was not quite clear to anyone. Ten days later Gromyko said to Stettinius, "The Russian position on voting in the Council will never be departed from."

Even long afterward, Gromyko remembered how FDR had managed to project a feeling of respect and friendship, writing, "As the president was clearly concerned to find a means of reconciliation, I felt hopeful that the search for agreement would succeed."

The breakfast had an impact on Gromyko. The Soviets' thinking, as a result of their experience of invasions by Poles and Germans, was narrowly concentrated on preventing future invasions, thus they focused exclusively on the creation of what Gromyko was calling, tellingly, an international organization not of peace but of safety. Having given no thought to social and economic issues, the Russians at first thought them distractions. But significantly, later in the day of the breakfast, Gromyko agreed to the Economic and Social Council, and as a quid pro quo Stettinius and Cadogan agreed to reinstate the expulsion proposal Gromyko had been pressing for.

Deciding on details was hard work: by midnight even the name of the organization had come under serious scrutiny. In his book *Memories,* published in 1989, Gromyko uses "cosy," a very odd word to describe stately Dumbarton Oaks. ("The three delegations met in a cosy house in Dumbarton Oaks.") As applied to this large, elegant mansion, it is a singularly inappropriate word. It is a distinctly emotional recollection linked to his time with Stettinius, Cadogan, and Roosevelt. Evidently, Gromyko, while working out the details of the plan that would keep the world at peace and punish aggressors, felt for the first time that he was part of a close-knit team and was comfortable with the knowledge, as he wrote, that "the participants all must reach agreement."

There was still one major time bomb, however, at Dumbarton Oaks, which neither the president nor Gromyko wanted to even touch upon, and that was Stalin's demand, relayed by Gromyko the first day of the conversations, August 21, and which he agreed not to bring up again, that all sixteen Soviet republics, which had been granted sovereignty just the year before, be members of the General Assembly. Stettinius had told the president about it immediately. Roosevelt had responded, "My God," and instructed Stettinius to tell Gromyko privately that he could never agree to it. FDR wrote to Stalin in the same vein, telling him that to raise this question at the conversations would imperil everything. His solution was to offer Stalin a carrot, the question could be raised later, after the organization was formed: "The Assembly would then have full authority to act." Stalin, who also did not want to imperil what he considered Roosevelt's project, wrote back agreeing to postpone the issue: "I hope to have an opportunity to explain to you the political importance of the question brought up by the Soviet delegation at Dumbarton Oaks."

FDR planned to talk Stalin out of the sixteen votes when they met, but Stettinius was so afraid that knowledge of the Soviet demand would derail further discussion on the composition and details of the world organization he omitted it from the regular minutes circulated to the delegates; it appeared only in a second set of minutes that he locked in his safe.

Following the breakfast Stalin wrote a thoughtful cable to FDR:

I also hope that these important discussions may end successfully. This may be of serious significance for the further strengthening of cooperation of our countries and for the whole cause of future peace and security . . . The initial American proposal that there should be established a special procedure of voting in case of a dispute in which one or several members of the council are directly involved, seems to me correct . . . Among these powers there is no room for mutual suspicion . . . I hope that you will understand the seriousness of the considerations expressed here and that we shall find a harmonious solution of this question as well.

Preparing Soviet citizens for what was to come with peace, Soviet newspapers gave the Dumbarton Oaks conversations extensive coverage, printing important sections of the draft agreement, emphasizing "almost exclusively" the necessity for concord and unanimity among the great powers responsible for the enforcement of peace. The Soviet press also reflected a new awareness of Russia's role in the world. Subjects such as the postwar administration of colonies and the future status of the Kiel Canal were featured. Soviet citizens were being groomed for the future, for when their country would take its rightful place at the peace table.

At the same time, Stalin and by extension the Russian public, uneasy with the thought that possibly FDR might not be reelected in November, continued steadfastly to identify with Roosevelt and urge his reelection. As Stalin said to Harriman, "The president *would* be reelected. Dewey was no match for him and no American of sound mind would wish to change the head of the government in the middle of a war. There was no comparison between Dewey and the President. Dewey was an ignorant man—the president was a first class politician on a world scale. The president was *sure* to be reelected."

Just to make sure that their several differences of opinion did not scuttle plans for a world organization before they met—which would not be until after Roosevelt's State of the Union address in January— Roosevelt told Harriman to advise Stalin that even if he continued his objection to the voting procedure, he "did not wish a 'no' but wanted the matter kept open for further discussion."

In spite of the disagreement over the veto Stalin was unusually happy at the prospects for peace that the new world organization promised. In his annual eve of anniversary speech of the great socialist revolution on November 6 he made this clear:

What means are available to prevent fresh aggression on the part of Germany, and if war breaks out nevertheless, to strangle it at the very outset . . . Apart from the complete disarming of aggressor nations there is only one means of achieving this: to set up a special organization consisting of representatives of the peaceful nations, for the protection of peace and for ensuring security; to place at the disposal of the leading body of this organization the minimum of armed forces necessary to prevent aggression, and to make it the duty of this organization to utilize these armed forces without delay . . . This must not be a replica of the League of Nations of sad memory, which possessed neither the powers nor the means with which to prevent aggression. It will be a new, special, fully-empowered international organization, which will have at its disposal all that is necessary for protecting peace and preventing fresh aggression.

Further, he stated that comity among nations was key:

Can we count on the activities of this international organization being sufficiently effective? They will be effective if the Great Powers who have borne the brunt of the burden of the war against Hitler Germany continue to act in a spirit of unanimity and harmony. They will not be effective if this essential condition is violated.

As Christmas approached, Roosevelt asked Stalin to meet with an officer from Eisenhower's staff to coordinate the efforts of the Red Army on the eastern front and the Allied armies on the western front, promising to maintain "complete secrecy." Eisenhower's armies were fighting the Battle of the Bulge, as it was called, Hitler's last counterattack, which was causing the bulge in the Allied line, while at the same time the Red Army had crossed the Vistula and was making giant strides toward Berlin. Stalin wired back immediately, "Naturally, I agree with your proposal as well as I agree to meet the officer from General Eisenhower and to arrange an exchange of information with him."

FDR HAD DECIDED to see the New Year in with champagne from Stalin. It was just a small gathering of friends and family, including children and grandchildren, upstairs in FDR's study at the White House. There was "much anticipation" as the first bottle of champagne from the case, which came, the accompanying note explained, from Stalin's home republic of Georgia, was poured into everyone's glass.

The shock was that everyone hated it, agreeing it was "too sweet," "awful," "quite undrinkable." But midnight had arrived—there was nothing else—so they all raised their glasses. Then everyone, including the president, toasted "Uncle Joe."

12

THE NEW WEAPON:
THE ATOMIC BOMB

In the 1930s fission was *the* hot topic among physicists all over Europe. Western scientific journals were publishing hundreds of articles on fission. And then, suddenly, Russian scientists noticed that the Western journals were publishing no articles on fission. Then they noticed in the early 1940s that an enormous number of English and American physicists and engineers had inexplicably vanished from their teaching assignments, their committees, their departments, their institutes—vanished as if into a black hole—causing puzzled Soviet intelligence to label the obviously serious but unknown project Enormoz. As if this weren't enough, the final tip-off to Russian scientists that Western governments were working on nuclear fusion and hiding their work was the reception given an article the brilliant twenty-two-year-old Soviet nuclear physicist Georgii Flerov co-wrote with another Soviet physicist, titled "Spontaneous Fission of Uranium," that was published in the *Journal of Physics:* it evoked no response—not one letter, not one comment. The cutoff date, the Russian nuclear physicists realized, was June 1940: after that, mention of fission ceased in all Western scientific journals. Ironically, Western scientists had instituted the giant secrecy policy to discourage development of the bomb in Germany—the specter of Hitler armed with such a weapon was unimaginable—without realizing that the result was like waving a red flag to the world. Quickly, the NKVD chief Beria's spies were assigned to find out where the nuclear scientists were and what they were doing, and quickly Russian nuclear scientists were informed that the United States was building an atomic bomb. Soviet nuclear scientists, too, were working in the exciting new field of nuclear fusion, even though Americans did not realize it. The Russian nuclear scientist Igor Vasilievich Kurchatov, as head of a research team, was putting the finishing touches on a cyclotron in 1939. In November 1940, he presented a paper on the possibility of nuclear chain reactions at a conference on nuclear physics in Moscow. By June 1941, Kurchatov's cyclotron was ready to start operation. The day Hitler invaded the Soviet Union was the day it was supposed to start up. With their country facing possible extinction, they could not continue, the cyclotron was closed down, and physicists went to work on projects of more immediate need for their country.

Flerov, very junior in the Russian scientific hierarchy, single-handedly tried to persuade the Russian scientific community to restart nuclear research in spite of the war. He wrote letters to senior Soviet nuclear scientists stating the case to restart nuclear research. After being profoundly rebuffed, he finally wrote directly to Stalin, warning him that other countries were working on developing a nuclear bomb, and strongly recommended that work resume in the Soviet Union: "This letter is the last, and after it I will lay down my arms and wait until the problem is solved in Germany, Britain, or the USA. The results will be so huge that there will be no time to decide who was guilty of the fact that we abandoned this work here in the Union."

Flerov wrote this letter in April 1942. The next month Stalin called a meeting of top Soviet scientists seeking their advice: Abram Fedorovich Ioffe, founder of the Leningrad Institute of Physics and Technology; Vitaliy Grigorievich Khlopin, chairman of the Soviet uranium commission; Peter Kapitza, a protégé of the New Zealand scientist Ernest Rutherford, who would be awarded the Nobel Prize in 1978; and Vladimir Vernadski, founder of the State Radium Institute of Leningrad. Writes Richard Rhodes, author of *Dark Sun: The Making of the Hydrogen Bomb,* the scientists unanimously confirmed the importance to Russia of developing a bomb. After some hesitation, Stalin said, "We should do it." But implementation would have to wait. The war in the spring of 1942 was going very badly. The nation was in the iron grip of the Wehrmacht. Stalingrad was close to being lost; Leningrad was under siege, its citizens dying of starvation. It simply wasn't possible.

The Nobel Prize winner Enrico Fermi, an Italian-born naturalized American citizen, set off the first nuclear chain reaction ever in Chicago on December 2, 1942. The information took about eight weeks to reach Soviet intelligence and was instantly made known to Stalin. Virtually the first moment the tide of war changed in favor of the Soviet Union—on February 11, following the surrender of General Friedrich Paulus at Stalingrad—Stalin ordered the creation of a committee to develop atomic energy for military weapons. Kurchatov was appointed director on the "uranium project," as it became known, in 1943. There was initially opposition among some of the older scientists to Kurchatov's appointment (he was just forty). But he was a year older than J. Robert Oppenheimer, head of the Manhattan Project the Russians spied upon and so admired, whom Enrico Fermi and Niels Bohr had both worked under.

All concerned knew they were far behind their Western colleagues, so Lavrenti Beria ratcheted up spying activities on U.S. and British developments. Kurchatov and his team, eager to learn of the latest developments in chain reaction, "often visited" Beria in his office on the third floor of the Lubyanka to read the information he had gathered. On the basis of Beria's information, by March 1943, Kurchatov learned the location of the seven most important nuclear research centers in America and had identified the twenty-six scientists who were key. By July, Soviet spies had purloined and delivered 286 classified publications on nuclear research to Beria. Kurchatov began designing a small graphite–natural uranium reactor, although he couldn't proceed very far because of a lack of graphite and uranium.

In October 1943, Russia tried to recruit the brilliant Danish nuclear physicist Niels Bohr, then in London, to work for them. Bohr was the ex-director of the Institute of Theoretical Physics in Copenhagen, the recipient of the Nobel Prize in Physics in 1922 for his work on the structure of atoms. Learning that the Germans were about to round up all Jews in Denmark, British agents had stuffed him in the belly of their unarmed Mosquito bomber, until then the British diplomatic pouch, and flew him out of Stockholm. Shortly after his arrival in London, the Soviet embassy gave him a letter from the top Soviet physicist, Peter Kapitza, who wrote "to let you know that you will be welcome to the Soviet Union where everything will be done to give you and your family a shelter and where we now have all the necessary conditions for carrying on scientific work." Aside from notifying U.S. and British authorities of its existence, Bohr ignored the letter.

In February 1944, Beria appointed Pavel Sudoplatov, legendary Soviet spymaster, the director of a new, autonomous NKVD agency, Department S, charged with improving the gathering, utilization, and dissemination of atomic intelligence. From then on money was no object: all the members of Department S—as well as all atomic energy personnel—were given access to special food, top medical care, nice apartments, dachas, and special scrip with which to shop at special stores.

But nuclear research in the Soviet Union was on a very small scale. Kurchatov's staff in January 1944 numbered only sixty-five at his main laboratory. The supply of uranium was woefully short: their first big cache of uranium would be the 750 pounds Soviet physicists seized from German scientific laboratories in Vienna in the spring of 1945.

IN THE UNITED STATES, Roosevelt was alerted to the importance of developing an atomic bomb by a letter from Albert Einstein: the year was 1939. The letter—the writing and the attribution—was primarily the work of Leo Szilárd, a Hungarian nuclear physicist with whom Einstein had worked in Germany who was determined to wake FDR to the importance of America's developing an atomic bomb. Szilárd composed the letter aided by another Hungarian, Eugene Wigner, then a professor at Princeton, during that crucial summer—the summer of 1939—when Stalin was teetering between Britain and Germany. The letter described the real danger that Hitler might acquire an atomic bomb through the work of German scientists, the leaders in the field of nuclear research. To make sure Roosevelt read the letter, Szilárd asked Einstein, as the most famous scientist in the world, to sign it. At the beginning of August, Szilárd, the final typed version in his pocket, never having learned how to drive, had his friend Edward Teller, a Hungarian nuclear physicist with a car, drive him out to Peconic, Long Island, where Einstein was living, to secure his signature. Einstein, according to Teller, read the letter with great care. As he signed it he said it would be the first time that nuclear energy would be used directly instead of indirectly through the processes in the sun. Szilárd enlisted the aid of Alexander Sachs, a friend of FDR's and an economist, to present it to the president. Because of the international situation, it took Sachs until October 11, the day FDR wrote to Kalinin to show restraint in Russian dealings with Finland, to get an appointment. On that fateful day, to emphasize the danger, Sachs read the letter to him. The letter reads, in part,

> Some recent work by E. Fermi and L. Szilárd, which has been communicated to me in a manuscript, leads me to expect that the element of uranium may be turned into a new and important source of energy in the immediate future.
>
> . . . It may become possible to set up a nuclear chain reaction in a large mass of uranium by which vast amounts of power and large quantities of new radium-like elements would be generated. Now it appears almost certain that this could be achieved in the immediate future.
>
> This new phenomena would also lead to the construction of bombs.

Sachs recalled that he added his own fear: "A large nuclear chain reaction . . . could be achieved in the immediate future . . . [A] single bomb of this type [then thought too heavy for a plane to carry], carried by boat and exploded in port, might very well destroy the whole port together with some of the surrounding territory." Roosevelt replied, "Alex, what you are after is to see that the Nazis don't blow us up." Sachs wanted to make sure Roosevelt was sufficiently aware that steps had to be taken immediately, so he went back to see him the next morning. FDR greeted him with the question "What bright idea have you got now?" Sachs then, according to his later (1950) recollection, told him a story of how Robert Fulton had advised Napoleon to build a fleet of steamships to transport his troops onto English soil and that Napoleon had scoffed at the idea. There was a silence, according to Sachs, after which FDR asked a servant to bring in a bottle of rare Napoleon brandy and, when he returned, to uncork it and pour each of them a glass. As they clicked their glasses, FDR told Sachs he would take action immediately. He gave Einstein's letter to Edwin "Pa" Watson, his military aide, with what amounted to an order: "This requires action." Ten days later, Saturday, October 21, Leo Szilárd, Eugene Wigner, who would later be awarded a Nobel Prize for his work on the project, and Edward Teller, brilliant nuclear physicist working in America, all Hungarian-born physicists who had fled beyond Hitler's reach, were meeting with army and navy brass to fill them in and jump-start the project. Shortly thereafter—further galvanizing Roosevelt—Szilárd, Einstein, and Sachs informed him that unless he did something more immediately, Szilárd was going to publish "in detail" how to set up a chain reaction in uranium. Roosevelt thereupon approved "a systematic mobilization of scientists in America for war." American development of the bomb had begun.

Learning that progress in nuclear fission research was also proceeding in Britain, Roosevelt wrote Churchill that they should work with each other, "in order that any extended efforts may be coordinated or even jointly conducted." He instructed Vannevar Bush, a brilliant engineer turned inventor who wore many hats—he was an MIT professor, president of the Carnegie Institution, and director of the U.S. Office of Scientific Research and Development—to draft a letter "to open up discussions of the matter [with the British] at the top."

In October 1941, the committee in charge of the project was designated Section-1. The bomb project thereafter, ironically (same designation in Russia), came to be known as S-1, which was how Stimson, as secretary of war in overall charge, always referred to it. On the committee were Vannevar Bush; James Conant, forty-eight, president of Harvard and a chemist; Stimson; and General Marshall.

In September 1942, Brigadier General Leslie R. Groves, U.S. Army deputy chief of construction (he had just finished supervising building the Pentagon), was made executive head of development of the enterprise. By this time Roosevelt realized its importance. He informed Bush in March 1942 the program should be "pushed not only in regard to development, but also with due regard to time. This is very much of the essence." In December 1942, Oppenheimer was appointed director.

The Manhattan Project, staffed by an amalgam of foreign and American scientists, engineers, and mathematicians, under the umbrella of Bush and Stimson, *was* huge and was nursed along by FDR from the outset as a military weapon that America clearly must have. At its peak it employed 120,000 people and built and ran thirty-seven installations, at a cost of more than $2 billion. The work continued to rely heavily on the brilliance and expertise of émigré scientists, mostly Jewish, whom Hitler had caused to emigrate: Hans Bethe, Edward Teller, Enrico Fermi, James Franck, Eugene Wigner, and Szilárd. No one yet thought of the Soviet Union as a possible nuclear threat: it was the specter of Nazi development of a nuclear device that preoccupied them all—the nightmare of Hitler armed with a nuclear bomb.

The great difference between the American and the Russian effort was money and manpower: America had lots of both. The Russian effort did not and virtually limped along, while America progressed by leaps and bounds.

FROM THE EARLIEST DAYS, knowing it was a problem he had to solve, FDR mulled over when and whether to inform the Soviet Union about the bomb and the potential dangers of doing so. He talked it over with a number of people: Henry Stimson, Mackenzie King, Vannevar Bush, Felix Frankfurter, Niels Bohr, and Churchill.

Niels Bohr, brilliant, dignified, white-haired, pipe smoking, professorial, had left England to live in the United States, where he became an adviser on the Manhattan Project. Bohr believed that to avert a disastrous arms race and the possibility of atomic annihilation, knowledge of the bomb *had* to be shared. Felix Frankfurter, a Supreme Court justice, a former Harvard Law School professor (Oliver Wendell Holmes and Louis Brandeis both allowed him to choose their law clerks), and a good friend of the president's, met Bohr one day at a tea at the Danish embassy in Washington. After talking to him, Frankfurter became sure of the rightness of Bohr's conviction. Frankfurter was uniquely close to FDR; he alone (except for Churchill) was exempt from calling FDR Mr. President: he called him Frank. When he talked, Roosevelt listened. Frankfurter and FDR discussed the bomb during a long lunch in the president's office on March 13, 1944. The specter that the bomb might become either the greatest boon or the greatest disaster to humankind weighed heavily on both their minds. Frankfurter told FDR about Bohr. Frankfurter later wrote, "I was with the President for about an hour and a half and practically all of it was consumed by this subject. He told me that the whole thing 'worried him to death,' and he was eager for all the help he could have in dealing with the problem."

FDR, on the basis of what Frankfurter told him, without seeing Bohr, immediately decided Bohr should go to London and see Churchill. Specifically, he authorized Frankfurter to "tell our friends in London that the President was most eager to explore the proper safeguards in relation to X." Further, he asked Frankfurter to arrange a meeting between him and Bohr. Much has been made of the oddity of FDR's packing Bohr off to see Churchill without first talking to him himself. But this was the period when FDR was in terrible physical shape. He had a cough he couldn't get rid of, severe headaches, trouble sleeping, clogged sinuses, and various "aches & pains," according to a worried Daisy Suckley. To his press secretary, Bill Hassett, he said he felt "like hell." His daughter, Anna, had finally cornered his doctor, Ross McIntire, and insisted that her father get a complete checkup at Bethesda Naval Hospital. On March 27 he was seen and given tests by Lieutenant Commander Howard G. Bruenn, chief of cardiology at the hospital. Bruenn found that he was close to collapse: suffering cardiac failure of the left ventricle, hypertension, acute bronchitis, and an enlarged heart. He put him on a low-calorie diet to make him lose weight and cut his smoking down to ten cigarettes a day from twenty (FDR wrote to Hopkins, "Luckily they still taste rotten") and his drinking down to one and a half cocktails at cocktail time. He also put him on digitalis, had him sleep in a hospital bed that raised his head and torso to make breathing easier, and visited the president every morning to take his blood pressure and monitor his condition. More to the point as far as Bohr was concerned, Bruenn had also severely cut down on Roosevelt's appointment schedule—both his work and his social life. Shortly, on the severely reduced activity schedule, so comprehensive that the president even took dinner in bed, Roosevelt began to recover. Within ten days, according to Bruenn, FDR's lungs cleared up of fluid, his heart was a more normal size, his coughing stopped. At the beginning of April he went down to Hobcaw Barony, Bernard Baruch's twenty-three-thousand-acre estate in South Carolina, for several weeks for a complete vacation. When he first arrived, he could barely make an early dinner before retiring to bed, but almost immediately he began to perk up and had friends and family down to visit (including his wife, Daisy Suckley, and Lucy Rutherfurd), and by the time he came back, he was recovered.

Soon after, Bohr was in London as FDR directed, to meet with Churchill; with him was his son Aage, also a nuclear physicist. Their meeting with the prime minister, held at 10 Downing Street, was a disaster. "It was terrible. He scolded us like two schoolboys," according to Aage. Not content with being rude to the Bohrs, Churchill reproached his friend and scientific adviser Lord Cherwell for arranging the meeting with Bohr. "I did not like the man when you showed him to me, with his hair all over his head." In fact, as Churchill proceeded to make absolutely clear, he was adamant that "Tube Alloys," the British code name for nuclear fission, remain secret from the Soviet Union: the bomb would serve to protect Britain forever. He would be happy if Stalin *never* had the bomb.

Bohr sent FDR a long memo in July 1944. He told him of Kapitza's request upon learning that he had fled to London that he come to Russia to do scientific research, thus alerting FDR that Russia was working on nuclear fusion. Bohr's memo also pointed out that when Germany was defeated, it would "release immense resources for a full scale effort within the Soviet Union," giving added weight to his plea that collaborating would forestall "a fateful competition."

Roosevelt discussed the memo with Frankfurter. On August 26 he met with Bohr and his son in the White House for an hour and a half. Aage reported,

> Roosevelt agreed that an approach to the Soviet Union . . . must be tried . . . In his opinion Stalin was enough of a realist to understand the revolutionary importance of this scientific and technical advance . . . He mentioned that he had heard how the negotiations with Churchill in London had gone, but added that the latter had often reacted in this way in the first instance. However, Roosevelt said, he and Churchill always managed to reach agreement, and he thought that Churchill would eventually come around to sharing his point of view in this matter. He would discuss the problems with Churchill at their forthcoming meeting and hoped to see my father soon afterwards.

Bohr was merely the most forceful scientist who advocated sharing knowledge with Russia as the best, most prudent course. From the first, there had been discussions between the scientists and the military involved in the Manhattan Project about the need for (the nuclear scientists' position) or the danger of (the military's position) informing and sharing information with Russia. An important ingredient in any decision was an estimate of how long a lead time America would have. If the bomb could be kept an inviolate secret for quite a number of years, the thinking among the military (excepting General Marshall) was that there was no need to tell Russia. But if it could not be, and the scientists were agreed that it could not be, the matter of an arms race had to be faced. And secrecy in any case was a two-edged sword. It could turn a friend into an enemy: If nuclear parity was simply a matter of a few years, was secrecy—and the anger and distrust it would inevitably cause—a wise course? Of all those in on development of the bomb, Churchill held the most extreme view: he felt so strongly he once wrote, "Even six months will make a difference should it come to a show-down with Russia." Virtually all nuclear scientists, believing the secret would last a much shorter time than did the generals, advocated sharing knowledge. General Groves, quintessential engineer who always had, according to someone who worked with him, absolute confidence in his own decisions, would go on record as saying that only America was competent to build an atomic bomb; it would take anyone else ten years.

As the matter was being considered, the Russians did something so startling it should have pushed all kinds of buttons in American military minds, but it didn't: the Soviet Purchasing Commission, under Lend-Lease, at the request of Kurchatov, asked for eight tons of uranium oxide and eight tons of uranium salts. General Groves, absolutely sure Americans could build anything faster and better than anyone else on earth and that America had somehow pulled the wool over Soviet eyes as far as atomic research was concerned, decided to allow the request, according to Michael Gordin, author of *Red Cloud at Dawn,* on the grounds that the Russians didn't know America was working on the bomb and to deny the request would tip them off. He granted them one thousand pounds of uranium salts and two thousand pounds of unenriched uranium metal. This didn't pull the wool over Russian eyes any more than not mentioning nuclear fusion in scientific journals had in 1940. In September 1944, FDR changed his mind about who should know about the bomb. He was in an indecisive frame of mind that fall in Quebec: he also changed his thinking on the treatment of Germany and the timing of the planned peace conference with Churchill and Stalin. All three decisions—sharing knowledge, dismantling Germany, the upcoming peace conference—were undone.

The president and Churchill were meeting in Quebec at the Citadel, the fortress residence of the governor-general of Canada, as Dumbarton Oaks was winding down. Henry Morgenthau had journeyed there to present his plan for "converting Germany into a country primarily agricultural and pastoral in character." Majdanek, the grisly German extermination camp in Lublin, Poland, with its warehouses stocked with roomsful of the gold fillings, toys, shoes, dresses, suits, and coats of the murdered that would be shipped to Germany, had been discovered six weeks earlier: revulsion of anything German was high. On September 15, FDR put his initials on Morgenthau's "pastoral Germany" document stripping Germany of all industry. (So did Churchill, who was initially against the idea but had been "converted" to its possibilities.) However, when the plan was made public, and the idea torn to pieces, FDR promptly changed his mind and retreated from it, pretending he hadn't really ever been for the idea. (He later baldly stated to Stimson he had been misunderstood, which made Stimson furious, because he knew this wasn't true. Stimson wrote about it in his diary: "He spoke of this paper as something that had been put over on him in Quebec and which he had never fathered. I had a copy of it in my pocket, fished it out, and showed his initials at the bottom of it. Then he said he had made a great mistake and has admitted that with great frankness since.")

FDR's second change of mind also took place in Quebec. It had to do with the timing of the upcoming peace conference, which Stalin was also going to attend. Roosevelt threw out the idea to meet not in February, as they had been discussing, but very soon, on October 30—six weeks away. This was more in the nature of a trial balloon than a full-blown decision, but still, it is a mark of FDR's mental state and was caused by his worry that he wouldn't be reelected in November. He divulged this worry to Prime Minister Mackenzie King, telling him, "We cannot get our people to register, cannot get the vote out," that soldiers were barred from voting in several states that were favorable to him. His plan, therefore, as he told Churchill, Eden, and King, was to have the international peace conference begin at the end of October— seven days before the presidential election. He dropped this idea on them, presumably, to see if they thought that a preelection conference would enhance his profile with voters. All three said no, it was a terrible idea. FDR attempted to defend it, saying that the idea was "to show that no time was being lost." But their arguments—that it would confuse the American public, that his opponents would find flaws in the proposal, that it would be much more effective for people to vote for him to carry out his peace plans at a future conference—all carried the day. He dropped the idea.

At the conclusion of the conference, FDR and his party, including Admiral Leahy and Dr. Bruenn, who now saw the president daily to monitor his health, boarded FDR's railroad car, Ferdinand Magellan, at 6:00 p.m. on September 16, arriving at Hyde Park the next morning at 9:00. Churchill arrived, also by train, with his secretary, Marian Holmes, on the morning of September 18.

Virtually the entire U.S. military establishment dreaded Churchill's U.S. visits because he generally interfered with their plans and had been such an eloquent critic of the cross-channel invasion. The Joint Chiefs and Stimson would always remember that Churchill had been able, in 1942, to argue FDR out of mounting a cross-channel invasion in 1943. Stimson, particularly, was wary in the extreme of the prime minister, although he carefully vented his annoyance only to his diary. Polite in public, he fumed in private: after Churchill had gone to work on FDR in the spring of 1943 to further delay the cross-channel invasion, he had caustically written, "Churchill arrived last night with a huge military party evidently equipped for war on us, determined to get his own way." They—Stimson and the Joint Chiefs of Staff—had been finally able to hold off Churchill on that matter, but now, at Hyde Park on September 18, 1944, FDR changed his mind for the third time in the space of a week, and Churchill temporarily prevailed in the matter of the bomb. (Hopkins was also at Hyde Park but, according to his biographer Robert Sherwood, was "completely out of touch" with atomic developments.)

FDR and Churchill spent the day together the day Churchill arrived, and both put their initials on an extraordinary memo stating that the atomic bomb should be a secret between the two of them. This aide-mémoire reads like pure Churchill and is unlike anything Roosevelt ever agreed to before or later about the bomb: "The suggestion that the world should be informed regarding Tube Alloys [code name for the bomb] with the view to an international agreement regarding its control and use, is not accepted. The matter should continue to be regarded as of the utmost secrecy; but when a bomb is finally available, it might perhaps, after mature consideration, be used against the Japanese, who should be warned that this bombardment will be repeated until they surrender."

Churchill even succeeded in persuading FDR (at least for that moment) that Bohr was a dangerous Communist sympathizer, for the aide-mémoire concludes, twisting Bohr's warning that the Russians had tried to recruit him to work on *their* nuclear project to mean the exact opposite, "Enquiries should be made regarding the activities of Professor Bohr and steps taken to ensure that he is responsible for no leakage of information, particularly to the Russians."

FDR packed Churchill off with a spanking display of presidential power, riding with him to the Poughkeepsie railroad station, their car surrounded by other cars full of bodyguards and G-men who leaped on the running boards. It made, according to Churchill's secretary, "a terrific show." The prime minister, immensely pleased with what he had accomplished, finished off the day with a triumphal cable to the Australian prime minister: "This Conference has been a blaze of friendship and unity." The next day he sailed on the *Queen Mary,* bound for England.

History will never know what happened—never know how or why Churchill prevailed. The likeliest explanation is that FDR, with no one around to urge caution before signing, figuring that he would marshal his arguments later and reverse himself, decided to go along with Churchill, as he had for a breathtaking moment gone along with Morgenthau about making Germany a pastoral nation. After all, an aide-mémoire did not commit him to anything he could not undo. And as Roosevelt was heard to say after one of his last meetings with Churchill, "Yes, I *am* tired! So would you be if you had spent the last five years pushing Winston uphill in a wheelbarrow."

FDR was immediately uneasy about signing the aide-mémoire. Four days later, back at the White House, he spent a long afternoon meeting with Vannevar Bush and Lord Cherwell, worriedly discussing the future of the bomb and atomic energy, knowing that both men thought the policy of secrecy was wrong. He even entertained second thoughts about its use under *any* circumstances against Japan, posing "the question of whether this means should actually be used against the Japanese or whether it should be used only as a threat with full-scale experimentation in this country." FDR must have sounded rather equivocal on the subject, or perhaps he asked for first-class ammunition to dismantle opposition to sharing control of the bomb with other nations, for Bush, with the aid of James Conant, twelve days later produced a document that completely repudiated the path set out in the aide-mémoire. In a document obviously written to counteract it, Bush and Conant, putting their heads together and their knowledge on the line, wrote and co-signed a clear refutation of the stupidity of such a course of action and sent it to Stimson, who, as secretary of war, was their immediate boss and overall head of the Manhattan Project. They were precise. The subject: "Concerning Future International Handling of Subject of Atomic Bombs."

After describing and analyzing the state of U.S. atomic power and its military potentialities in points 1 and 2 the memo gets to

> Point 3. <u>Present Advantage of United States and Great Britain Temporary.</u>
>
> . . . It would be possible for any nation with good technical and scientific resources to reach our present position in three or four years. Therefore it would be the height of folly for the United States and Great Britain to assume that they will always continue to be superior in this new weapon . . .
>
> Point 4. <u>Impossibility of maintaining complete secrecy after the war is over.</u>
>
> It has been necessary to bring a vast number of technical men into the project. Information in regard to various aspects of it is therefore widespread. Furthermore all the basic facts were known to physicists before the development began. Some outside the project have undoubtedly guessed a great deal of what is going on . . . In view of this situation it is our strong recommendation that plans be laid for complete disclosure of the history of the development and all but the manufacturing and military details on the bombs as soon as the first bomb has been demonstrated . . .
>
> Point 5. <u>Dangers of partial secrecy and international armament race.</u>
>
> . . . It would be extremely dangerous for the United States and Great Britain to attempt to carry on in complete secrecy further developments of the military applications of this art. If this were done Russia would undoubtedly proceed in secret along the same lines.

Point 6 outlined how the international exchange of information should be handled.

Bush and Conant totally refuted the idea of secrecy, in fact argued that it would be the most dangerous path America could take: they proposed the free interchange of information under the auspices of the international organization that was in the process of formation.

Stimson was naturally impressed by their knowledge and advice: he now had in his hands a document written to him by the heads of the Manhattan Project telling him that secrecy wouldn't work. On December 30 at a preluncheon meeting he and General Groves met with FDR to bring the president up to date on the progress of the bomb. Groves informed FDR that the first bomb, expected to produce the equivalent of a ten-thousand-ton TNT explosion, "should be ready about 1 August 1945." That meant certain issues were coming to a head: decisions had to be made. The next day, Sunday, Stimson was FDR's only appointment; he met with the president in a "wrap-up-of-the-year" hour-long conference in the Oval Office at noon. Stimson wrote in his diary that after bringing FDR up to speed on Eisenhower's progress in the Battle of the Bulge, he gave him his views on the future of S-1 and Russia. He writes that he told him that Russia should be told, but not just yet, and that FDR thought it a good idea:

> I told him of my thoughts as to the future of S-1 in connection with Russia; that I knew they were spying on our work but that they had not yet gotten any real knowledge of it and that, while I was troubled about the possible effect of keeping from them even now that work, I believed that it was essential not to take them into our confidence until we were sure to get a real quid pro quo from our frankness. I said I had no illusions as to the possibility of keeping permanently such a secret but that I did not think it was yet time to share it with Russia. *He said he thought he agreed with me.* (Italics mine)

Stimson's statement made a great deal of sense. Relations between the United States and Russia had survived a number of bumps in 1944, as Harriman was reporting. Stimson was suggesting a road to a destination. As the months went by, Stimson became surer and surer that Russia had to be included in an international atomic knowledge framework. At the same time, neither he nor FDR was thinking of a simple giveaway of the information: they expected to make Stalin work for it;

pressure should be brought on Stalin to conform to alliance standards. That was the meaning of "a real quid pro quo."

By this time FDR must have realized that Churchill was pretty much alone even among his own people in his view that information on the bomb should be kept from the Russians. The British ambassador to the United States, Lord Halifax, who had, prewar, harbored strong anti-Russian sentiments, now thought the information should be shared with them. So did Chancellor of the Exchequer Sir John Anderson, the scientist in Churchill's cabinet in charge of the atomic project. Anderson proposed notifying the Russians when the first test was expected, writing in a March 1944 memo that there was "much to be said for communicating with the Russians in the near future the bare fact that we expect, by a given date, to have this devastating weapon; and for inviting them to collaborate with us in preparing a scheme for international control." Lord Cherwell, a physicist and another of Churchill's scientific advisers, was also in favor of telling the Russians about the bomb. It seemed to most reasonable men to be the most reasonable thing to do.

FDR drew Stettinius into discussions about the bomb soon after appointing him secretary of state. As was often the case, the conversation took place in FDR's ship-lined study. Although FDR had kept Hull in the dark about the bomb, he told Stettinius almost immediately, saying that "the time had been reached for the State Department to come into the atomic picture." Stettinius immediately became very much involved, monitoring Soviet espionage activity in the United States, which, he quickly learned, was considerable, so he as well as Stimson knew "the Russians certainly had an indication of what was taking place."

Roosevelt had made up his mind so completely by Yalta about wishing to share information about the bomb with Russia that during the conference he went to work on Churchill to convince him it was a timely idea. Not only had his top advisers convinced him that sharing the information was the wisest course, but he knew beyond the shadow of a doubt that Stalin not only knew about the Manhattan Project but was pushing Soviet intelligence to find out more: Stettinius had told him on the second day of the conference that the nuclear race had already begun, that the Soviet Union had 125 spies on the job, that he should therefore be prepared to discuss it with Stalin—because he "might ask us about it." (Stettinius had actually been working with

General Marshall to hammer out what FDR should say to Stalin about the bomb.) In addition, Stettinius told FDR, there was a new threat: there was a French scientist in Montreal working on the bomb who was known to be sympathetic to the Soviet Union; he might leak crucial information to Russian agents.

As a result, shortly thereafter, FDR shocked Churchill—his way of preparing him for the inevitable—by casually announcing that he thought it was time to bring Stalin in on the secret, "on the grounds that de Gaulle, if he heard of it, would certainly double-cross us with Russia." Naturally, Churchill was furious.

Right after the conference Vannevar Bush again told Stimson he wanted to share nuclear information with the Soviet Union. Stimson as a result told Harvey Bundy, his assistant on atomic matters (also, like Stimson, a member of Yale's Skull and Bones), "Bush is so delighted at the news which came this morning of the agreement at Yalta that he is anxious to be very chivalrous to the Russians on this subject." Stimson agreed with Bush that it was a good idea, only suggesting to wait a bit so it could be used as a bargaining chip, specifically "to hold off conferences on the subject until we have some more tangible 'fruits of repentance' from the Russians as a quid pro quo for such a communication to them." It was not a question of whether or not Stalin should be told, in other words; it was a question of employing the information in a fruitful way.

Bush had another idea on the subject and came in to talk it over with Stimson two days later. He proposed a general pooling among nations of *all* scientific research and an interchange of everything susceptible to military use—the purpose being to prevent nations from developing secret plans for secret weapons during peacetime. Stimson thought it was a good idea in terms of Russia but again advised waiting; first, work had to be done: "It would be inadvisable to put it into full force yet until we had gotten all we could in Russia in the way of liberalization in exchange for S-1."

The matter of the bomb weighed heavily on the secretary of war both in terms of administrative duties and as a moral problem, because he was the person directly responsible for the entire undertaking. By March, Stimson received the information that there was definite progress on the bomb; it was coming along on schedule. By then Germany was heading for defeat, Russian and Allied armies were pressing into

Germany's heartland, and administration estimates were that victory would be declared by summer. Where in Japan the bomb should be dropped, whether or not to give the Japanese notice, what to do about the Russians, became subjects that needed to be solved very soon. It was a huge burden for Stimson.

On Monday, March 5, Stimson talked it over with Bundy again: "We are up against some very big decisions. The time is approaching when we can no longer avoid them . . . [I]t is by far the most searching and important thing that I have had to do since I have been here in the office of Secretary of War because it touches matters which are deeper even than the principles of present government." How to handle Russia and the bomb were still on his mind at the end of that same day. As General Marshall was preparing to leave for home (their offices were connected; there was a door in between), Stimson wrote in his diary, he "gave him a little talking to on the subject. He is one of the very few men who know about it and I wanted to get him thinking on this postwar set of problems."

Prime Minister Mackenzie King, FDR's old Harvard friend, was visiting the White House on March 9. Arriving in the late afternoon, he had been directed to FDR's oval study, where he found Eleanor having tea. When FDR was wheeled in, King went up to the president and kissed him on the cheek. ("He turned it toward me for the purpose.") King had not seen FDR since September, in Quebec, and his initial reaction was that he "looked much older," his face was "very much thinner," but he was told this was because he had intentionally lost weight. As the visit wore on, his concern for FDR's health was tempered by the president's staying power. After a late, informal dinner with Eleanor and Anna Boettiger in the small family dining room, Roosevelt asked King to return with him to his oval study. They talked for hours, King in a chair he pulled up opposite FDR, sitting on the well-worn leather sofa. "We talked steadily from 8:30 until 20 past 11 when I looked at the clock. I thought it was about 10. The president said he was not tired; he was enjoying the talk," King wrote in his diary. King was privy to nuclear fusion matters because Canada was an important uranium source. Midway through the conversation King brought up the bomb. "When I asked about certain weapons that might be used," King wrote in his diary later that night, "he said he thought that would be in shape by August; that the main difficulty was knowing just how to have the material used over the country itself." King wrote he then asked another question on the subject, to which Roosevelt replied that "he thought the Russians had been experimenting and knew something about what was being done. *He thought the time had come to tell them how far the developments had gone. Churchill was opposed to doing this. Churchill is considering the possible commercial use later.* I said it seemed to me that if the Russians discovered later that some things had been held back from them, it would be unfortunate." (Italics mine)

Six days later, on March 15, just a month before he died, was the last time FDR spoke of advising Stalin of the existence of the bomb. He and Stimson had a long lunch in the small, cheerful, south-facing Sun Room on the third floor of the White House. FDR unloaded on Stimson his worry that in fact the bomb project itself was going to fail. FDR told Stimson that he was having last-minute jitters over rumors that he had been "sold a lemon" (the massive outlays on developing the bomb)—the bomb might not work! Stimson reassured him (it was, he knew, a common opinion among those not fully informed), noting that Nobel Prize scientists (four) "and practically every physicist of standing" were involved in the project. It wouldn't fail. Then, according to Stimson, who was spending more and more time on matters relating to the bomb ("It is approaching its ripening time and matters are getting very interesting and serious"),

> I went over with him the two schools of thought that exist in respect to the future control after the war of this project in case it is successful, one of them being the secret close-in attempted control of the project by those who control it now, and the other being the international control based upon freedom both of science and of access. I told him that those things must be settled before the first projectile is used and that he must be ready with a statement to come out to the people on it just as soon as that is done. *He agreed to that.* (Italics mine)

On March 24, FDR saw the speechwriter Robert Sherwood in his office: he needed input on his two upcoming speeches, one he was to give on Jefferson's birthday, April 13, the other opening the San Francisco Conference a short while later. He asked Sherwood to find him a Jefferson quotation on the subject of science to include in the Jefferson

Day speech. Obviously, the atomic bomb was very much on his mind. A week later FDR went down to Warm Springs. Two weeks later he was dead. There is little doubt which road Roosevelt would have taken if he had lived. International control based on freedom of access was practically a Roosevelt hallmark: a strong international organization was his goal in life. His plan for the postwar limitation of arms from the start had been based on parity among the four policemen. Holding a club over Stalin's head, which was what withholding information on the bomb amounted to, would have been just the action he was trying to avoid. It would put Russia in an inferior position, which was Churchill's aim, not his. *He* wanted to keep Stalin within reach, keep him within the community of nations, not drive him out. The most influential men in the British cabinet, and the most influential men in America involved in the bomb, all advocated sharing control with the Soviet Union as the only way to avoid an arms race. Many historians assert that because FDR had not yet told Stalin about the bomb, he had decided against it. However, FDR probably thought the time to tell Stalin would be after a bomb had been successfully detonated, which, he had been informed, was months away. In April FDR was concentrating on getting what he considered the greatest project of his lifetime, the United Nations, up and running. His mind was centered on San Francisco: he had to get there, make a speech, and launch the world government. After that he would deal with Stalin and the bomb. The time was not yet ripe.

13

YALTA

From the moment the date and place of the final conference with Stalin was set, FDR looked as if a great load had been lifted off his shoulders, according to his friend and speechwriter Sam Rosenman. He seemed to gain strength and began to look forward to the trip with an enthusiasm and exuberance he hadn't shown in years. The reason was obvious to those who knew him well: he expected the outcome to be the fruition of his dream, the birth of an organization that would have the power to keep nations within their own borders. If he could pull it off, he would go down in history as the chief and only architect of the first world government. Probably he did not think of it in such grandiose terms: it was not his style. He was into results: for him it would mean he had created an instrument that would end world wars. It would also mean that he had succeeded where Wilson had failed.

The conference meeting place was Stalin's choice, Yalta, in the Crimea. The Crimea, so far from America, so far for FDR to travel, was chosen because Stalin wouldn't travel farther than the Soviet coast of the Black Sea, and without Stalin there would be no United Nations, no successful framework on which to build the postwar world. Churchill would have gone virtually anywhere, although he was very grumpy about Yalta, saying to Harry Hopkins, "If we had spent ten years on research we could not have found a worse place."

On the other hand, Harriman reported to FDR that two naval officers had reported to him that the town of Yalta was "extremely neat and clean by Russian standards. The climate in winter is reasonably favorable, with average temperature of 39 degrees Fahrenheit in January and February." Harriman had also reported to FDR, on December 15, that Stalin's report about his doctors seemed honest and that he had hoped they would meet shortly after FDR's inauguration. Nevertheless, on December 19, FDR, having no knowledge of the gigantic preparations that had been going on since November to make Yalta habitable, told Harriman to again suggest to Stalin that they meet in the Mediterranean, possibly at Taormina. It was also true that as he was not only head of state but commander in chief of Soviet forces, Stalin had to be close to and in constant contact with his staff, which was possible in the Crimea, a part of Russia. So Yalta, nine hundred miles from Moscow, fifty-seven hundred miles from Washington, it was.

FDR was a master manipulator of people. He instinctively knew how to keep Stalin and Churchill working together. His approach to both men is best illustrated in a subtly brilliant comment he once made to Churchill that at one and the same time laid out his plan of approach to the Russian, notified the prime minister that patience was required, and left him in charge. He put it as follows: "We are all in agreement . . . as to the necessity of having the U.S.S.R. as a fully accepted and equal member of an association of the great powers formed for the purpose of preventing international war. It should be possible to accomplish this by adjusting our differences through compromise by all the parties concerned *and this ought to tide things over for a few years until the child learns to toddle.*" Roosevelt was brilliant at sizing up people. He could intuit other people's views of reality and appeal to them. He could lay out a path that made sense from where other people stood; in the process of understanding, he could lead them forward to accept his goals as theirs.

He was setting out for a peace conference with one leader who exerted control over the black and Asian populations of the world and another leader who threatened to exert control over populations along its vast western borders. He had served notice on Churchill of his intentions as regards the British Empire: he had forced Churchill to allow India to sign the first United Nations document of January 1, 1942, thereby giving India de facto dominion status. Later that summer, in the Atlantic Charter, he had gone a long way to encouraging independence—firing up the hopes—of Gambia, Indochina, Singapore, Egypt, Burma, Kenya, South Africa, and Malaya: key holdings of Britain and France. But his power was limited, as far as Churchill went, to the power to persuade. Without breaking the ties of friendship, he managed to use it to the utmost to put Churchill on notice that he wanted Britain to begin to free its colonies. However, as the war wound down, the job at hand was to prevent Stalin's takeover of Poland. The world was watching not England but the Soviet Union. FDR had to protect the rights of one of the most grievously mistreated nations in the world—Poland. If there was to be a peaceful future, if there was to be an international security organization powerful enough to stop authoritarian regimes from invading other countries, he had to make Stalin see that that meant he had to behave. The fact that the Poles were continually quarreling among themselves (as they had been at least since the time of Catherine the Great) made pressuring Stalin to allow them to choose their own new leaders all the more difficult.

ROOSEVELT WAS UNDER no delusions about either leader. With these two men he was going to create what he hoped was going to be a brave new world, at the center of which would be a powerful peace organization: the United Nations. He knew—it was common knowledge even then—that Stalin was guilty of "the indiscriminate killings of thousands of innocent victims." He had said as much to the American Youth Conference at the White House in February 1940. And in the midst of the war, possible evidence surfaced about his murder of a group of Polish officers when they had been Russian prisoners of war and the subsequent efforts to cover up the crime. FDR paid the story no attention. He knew Churchill was seriously flawed as well. History has dealt harshly with Stalin but has been kind to Churchill: one reason is that the prime minister was a brilliant writer, and it is his version of history that has come down to us and blinded us to his amoral actions. He was almost as much of a trial to FDR as Stalin. Four months earlier, the previous October, Churchill, meeting with Stalin in the Kremlin, had cynically proposed that he and Stalin specify to each other which Balkan country they wanted to control. Churchill had written his percentages on a piece of paper, ceding Stalin 90 percent control in Romania, Britain 90 percent in Greece, and splitting Yugoslavia. Stalin had shoved the paper back to Churchill without comment, suggesting Churchill keep it. Such a bargain was anathema to the president, intent on the creation of a peace organization obviating such deals.

Roosevelt was strongly against colonialism and the consequences of powerful nations' controlling weaker nations; he also knew that Churchill was a racist and believed in colonial empires. FDR was dedicated to the philosophy that one nation should not control another. In the first year of his presidency he had repudiated America's right to intervene in the affairs of South American countries and within a short time recommended self-government for Puerto Rico, pushed Congress to pass an act giving independence to the Philippines after a ten-year period of transition, relinquished the right of the United States to control Panamanian territory and unilaterally the canal, relinquished the right of the United States to intervene in Cuban affairs, and ordered the last U.S. marines to leave Haiti.

He did this because he believed that colonialism was not only morally wrong—in that colonial peoples were always initially overwhelmed, usually slaughtered, and *always* exploited—but also structurally damaging to world peace. (He knew firsthand of the true nature of British colonialism from his Delano grandfather and his Delano great-uncle, seafaring trading partners, who were in Hong Kong in 1841 and saw and were appalled by British brutality. "I truly wish John Bull could meet with one hearty repulse and great slaughter from the Chinese," his great-uncle had written in his diary, preserved as a Delano family treasure.) Not only was it morally indefensible, but FDR's view was that because colonial empires were a mark of power, as well as a reservoir of manpower for a nation's armed forces, the pursuit of empires led to war. Because Britain was the greatest colonial power in the world, not even friendship could break down FDR's reserve toward its leader, even if he was, at the same time, the prime minister's friend.

FDR had begun his battle to make Churchill loosen Britain's hold on its jewel in the crown—India—during Churchill's first visit to the White House. He encountered fierce resistance. According to Churchill, "I reacted so strongly and at such length that he never raised it verbally again." FDR didn't give up: he changed tactics. His friendship with Churchill was a given, they were linked by history, by heritage, by race, but Churchill was a racist. Roosevelt was acutely aware of it and tried to intervene. Churchill's racist view was the reason he had initially been against China as the fourth policeman. Observed the prime minister's doctor, "To the President, China means four hundred million people who are going to count in the world of tomorrow, but Winston thinks only of the color of their skin." After the Atlantic Conference, Churchill had gone before the House of Commons to explain that what he and the president had agreed on—the right of nations to self-determination—had no effect on British policy in India or other parts of the empire. His credo was "Why be apologetic about Anglo-Saxon superiority, that we were superior, that we had the common heritage which had been worked out over the centuries in England and had been perfected by our constitution."

In *The Hinge of Fate*, his history of the war, Churchill wrote, "No great portion of the world population was so effectively protected from the horrors of the World War as were the peoples of Hindustan [India]." Nothing could be further from the truth. British rule over India was every bit as brutal as Stalin's rule over Russia. He had Britain declare India at war with Japan without bothering to consult Indian leaders. In November 1941, Churchill instituted a scorched-earth policy in Bengal that came to be known as the Denial Policy. Soldiers were ordered to seize all the rice they could find: they stripped silos and storehouses, took seed crops. The rationale was that the policy would deny food to the Japanese, who threatened to invade the country. Soldiers also impounded all industrial and pleasure transport—all boats, including Bengali fishermen's boats, all bicycles, including those used by the population to get to work. Their store of rice gone, denied transport to search for food, Bengalis began starving to death in ever-increasing numbers. The starvation policy served to swell the ranks of the British Indian Army: Indian men enlisted in great numbers as a sure way to get fed. Those stationed in India served without weapons, for Churchill was fearful they would be turned on the English.

Roosevelt had attempted to intervene, using as his excuse that American equipment and soldiers bound for the Burma Road and China, transported by rail across India to Assam near the Burmese border, were in constant danger of Japanese attack and that Indians should be given rights and treated as prospective equals so that they would be incentivized to repel any Japanese incursions. He sent Colonel Louis Johnson, former assistant secretary of war, to New Delhi early in 1942 as his personal representative. Johnson's mission: to try to persuade the viceroy to give Indians *some* power over their lives and a hope of dominion status after the war, thereby motivating them to make their peace with the British. At the same time as he sent Johnson to India, FDR wrote to Churchill suggesting that as a solution he follow the arc of British-American history, which he proceeded to outline: that he set up "what might be called a temporary government, headed by a small representative group, covering different castes, occupations, religions and geographies—this group to be recognized as a temporary Dominion Government." FDR told Hopkins, who was in London coordinating U.S.-British military plans, to discuss his ideas with Churchill, which Hopkins did. That discussion, however, according to Hopkins, which had taken place over a weekend at Chequers, had been a disaster. Upon hearing about Johnson's mission, Churchill had gone wild with rage. Hopkins later described the scene to Stimson. "When he found that the President had sent his fantastic mission of Louis Johnson to India . . . the string of cuss words lasted for two hours in the middle of the night, it was vivid."

Churchill, who had fought in India as a young cavalry subaltern, afterward spoke of Indians as "among the most miserable and brutal creatures of the earth . . . pernicious vermin." The viceroy ruled with an iron hand: there was press censorship, arrest without warrant, detention without trial, and limited Indian access to higher education, industry, and civil service.

On October 16, 1942, a cyclone and tidal wave hit Bengal, ruining fields, houses, and the ability of the people to go on with their lives. In the face of this disaster, rice denial continued as British policy; indeed rice was shipped from Bengal to Ceylon. As a result, 13 percent of the population of Bengal died of starvation. Because Indians were not permitted to travel abroad and had no access to international telephone or telegraph, and their leaders were in jail, there was no way for Bengalis to make their plight known to the world.

After the tidal wave, FDR replaced Johnson with William Phillips, State's most competent diplomat, head of the OSS in London, as his personal representative. He directed Phillips to push his philosophy "favoring freedom for all dependant peoples at the earliest possible date." By the time of Phillips's arrival, late in 1942, Indians in great number, led by Mahatma Gandhi and Jawaharlal Nehru, completely outraged by British high-handedness, had rebelled, and the viceroy had retaliated by killing ten thousand Indians and putting ninety thousand in jail. Twenty-five thousand members of the Congress Party, including Nehru and Gandhi, who were being held incommunicado, remained in jail. Phillips's request to interview them was denied. Told Gandhi, whom he despised, was fasting, Churchill commented, "We had no objection to his fasting to death if he wanted to . . . He is a thoroughly evil force, hostile to us in every fiber."

He also said, "It is alarming and nauseating to see Mr. Gandhi, a seditious Middle Temple lawyer, now posing as a fakir of a type well known in the East, striding half naked up the steps of the Vice Regal palace to parley on equal terms with the representative of the King-Emperor."

Churchill claimed that the fighting was caused by bad blood between the Hindus and the Muslims, which was not true. In fact, as it had done in the past, British policy was to foster enmity between the two groups. "I am not at all attracted by the prospect of one united India, which will show us the door," he admitted.

A month later, on November 11, 1942, Churchill made his famous comment: "I have not become the King's First Minister in order to preside over the liquidation of the British Empire." The next day, according to Leo Amery, minister for India, Churchill "went off the deep end in a state of frantic passion on the whole subject of the humiliation of being kicked out of India by the beastliest people in the world next to the Germans . . . [Churchill] knows as much of the Indian problem as George III did of the American colonies." It wasn't from a lack of ships or food stocks or information that food was withheld: it was because Churchill wouldn't allow it. Over the winter the situation only got worse. The governor of Bengal informed British authorities, "Bengal is rapidly approaching starvation." Even the viceroy, insulated from reality in his very grand palace, which boasted a huge circular throne room and a banquet hall that seated 140 guests routinely served by lines of footmen dressed in crimson and gold, finally became concerned. (After a visit, the Prince of Wales had remarked to the viceroy, "This is the way royalty should really live.") Alarmed, in late October 1943, the viceroy cabled the prime minister, "Bengal famine is one of the greatest disasters that has befallen any people under British rule and is dangerous to our reputation here." Churchill ignored the cable. Phillips minced no words in his report to FDR: "Many of the rural areas in Bengal are foodless, with the villagers wandering into the cities to die there of starvation. Deaths from starvation on the streets of Calcutta are reported to have become so numerous that prominent European members of the community have addressed open letters to the municipal authorities requesting that more adequate means be found for the removal of the bodies."

Word of the growing disaster began seeping out to the British public. The archbishop of Canterbury called for daily prayers for the starving Indians. The House of Commons unanimously voted to send food. Churchill was unyielding; he fought the House measure to a standstill, retorting he "did not care what the House thought." Amery asked the British War Cabinet to send in food. Churchill dominated the cabinet: the offer was refused. Mackenzie King and Roosevelt offered to send in food. Their offer was refused. Wrote Hull in his *Memoirs,* putting the best face on it while still managing to tell the truth, "We made efforts to secure from the all too inadequate rice stocks in the Western Hemisphere an allocation of rice for India. The British representatives on the Combined Food Board in Washington insisted, however, that the responsibility for Indian food requirements be left to Britain, and we perforce had to agree." Nor did the passage of time soften Churchill's views. In July 1944, Viceroy Archibald Wavell reported, "Winston sent me a peevish telegram to ask why Gandhi hadn't died yet." In the fall of 1944 in Quebec, Churchill baldly maintained to FDR and Mackenzie King that the starvation "has been due to the hoarding of food by the people themselves for speculative purposes." Six weeks later Churchill began an address to the War Cabinet, according to the minister for India, with "a preliminary flourish on Indians breeding like rabbits and being paid a million a day by us for doing nothing about the war."

Responding to a comment on India at dinner a few weeks after Yalta, John Colville, Churchill's private secretary, recorded in his diary, "The PM said the Hindus were a foul race protected by their mere pullulation from the doom that is their due and he wished Bert Harris [Sir Arthur Harris, marshal of the air force] could send some of his surplus bombers to destroy them." Modern estimates are that at least 1 million and perhaps as many as 3 million died.

In his travels to Casablanca and Tehran, FDR had visited Gambia, French Morocco, Egypt, and Malta, holding private talks with nationalist leaders wherever he could. Firsthand knowledge of the conditions in these countries reinforced his desire to press for the end of colonial empires. "The Big Four—ourselves, Britain, China, the Soviet Union—will be responsible for the peace of the world . . . These powers will have to assume the task of bringing education, raising the standards of living, improving the health conditions—of all the backward, depressed colonial areas of the world. And when these areas have had the chance to reach maturity, they must have the opportunity extended them of independence . . . If this isn't done, we might as well agree that we're in for another war."

Gambia, a British protectorate on the coast of Africa, particularly bothered FDR: "It's the most horrible thing I have ever seen in my life . . . The natives are five thousand years back of us . . . The British have been there for two hundred years—for every dollar that the British have put into Gambia, they have taken out ten."

Phillips returned to the United States in April 1943 at FDR's request, to brief him personally on conditions in India. "I said that all India was looking to him for help and that my continued presence in India would put him in a false position unless there was a change in the British attitude. He agreed," Phillips wrote in his diary.

AGAINST THIS BACKDROP of colonial violence, the same month Phillips debriefed him, FDR learned—although the evidence given him was ambiguous—of Stalin's great crime, Katyn.

As German soldiers retreated in the spring of 1943, the government of Nazi Germany broadcast the electrifying news that its troops had discovered the mass graves of ten thousand Polish officers in the Katyn Forest near Smolensk, Russia, all of whom had been shot in the back of the head. They charged the deed had been done by the Russians in 1940. This was indeed the case. The killings had been carried out because the NKVD and Stalin believed that the officers, the cream of the Polish army, who were indeed anti-Soviet, were potentially dangerous to the Soviet Union because, blinded by their hatred of Russia, in 1939 they had sought to ally themselves with Hitler. The Polish government in exile in London had repeatedly queried the Kremlin as to what had become of these officers, previously held as prisoners by the Soviet Union, particularly because letters from the soldiers to their families had ceased after March 1940. Faced with Polish charges that Premier Władysław Sikorski had been stonewalled by Stalin in December 1941 when he had asked him as to the fate of the officers, plus the demand by the Polish government for an investigation by the International Red Cross that the Kremlin would be unable to control, Stalin severed relations with the Polish government. Sikorski withdrew his request for an investigation. Stalin was so determined to evade all guilt he put himself way out on a limb in the letter FDR received from him on April 21:

> The recent conduct of the Polish Government towards the Soviet Union is regarded by the Soviet Government as absolutely abnormal and contrary to all rules and standards governing relations between allied countries.
>
> The campaign of calumny against the Soviet Union, initiated by the German fascists regarding the Polish officers they themselves slaughtered in the Smolensk area, on German-occupied territory, was immediately taken up by the Sikorski government and inflated in every possible way by the official Polish press. The Sikorski government, far from taking a stand against the vile fascist slander of the Soviet Union, did not even see fit to ask the Soviet government for information or explanations.
>
> The Hitlerite authorities, after perpetrating an atrocious crime against the Polish officers, are now engaged upon an investigation farce for the staging of which they have enlisted the help of certain pro-fascist Polish elements picked up by them in occupied Poland, where everything is under Hitler's heel and where honest Poles dare not lift their voices in public.

FDR gave him the benefit of the doubt. As a result, he was solely concerned with the political repercussions of the Soviet Union's breaking off relations with the Polish government:

> I can well understand your problem but I hope in present situation you can find means to label your action as a suspension of conversation with the Polish Government in exile rather than a complete severance of diplomatic relations.
>
> It is my view that Sikorski has not acted in any way with Hitler gang, but rather that he made a ~~stupid~~ mistake in taking the matter up with the International Red Cross. Also I am inclined to think that Churchill will find ways and means of getting the Polish Government in London to act with more common sense in the future.

The Russian government had mounted an amazing disinformation campaign to disguise its deed. It dug up thousands of bodies, planted false evidence on the corpses, and then invited a group of U.S. and British journalists, including Kathleen Harriman, Averell Harriman's daughter, who lived and worked with her father at Spaso House, to inspect the site. The group was sent down in a special train that Kathleen described as "sumptuous." The cover-up effort was gruesomely meticulous. Kathleen's description follows. Once at the site,

> we began a tour of each and every one of the graves. We must have seen a good many thousand corpses, or parts of corpses, all in varying stages of decomposition but smelling about as bad. Some of the corpses had been dug up by the Germans in the spring of '43 after they'd first launched their version of the story . . . The most convincing bit of evidence was that every Pole had been shot thru the back of the head with a single bullet. Some of the bodies had their hands tied behind their back, all of which is typically German . . . The Germans say that the Russians killed the Poles back in '40, whereas the Russians say the Poles weren't killed until the fall of '41 . . . Though the Germans had ripped open the Poles' pockets, they'd missed up on some written documents. While I was watching, they found one letter dated the summer of '41, which is damned good evidence.

An apparently convinced Averell Harriman cabled his conclusions to FDR:

> The evidence that made the greatest impression to substantiate the Russian case was 1. That the preponderance of soldiers so far exhumed are enlisted men rather than officers as claimed by the Germans. 2. The methodical method of the killing, each man having been executed by one shot in the base of the skull. 3. That the papers exhibited were dated from November 1940 to June 1941. 4. The description by witnesses of the unsuccessful attempt to evacuate the Poles when the Germans broke through to Smolensk and of Poles working on the roads in the area for the Russians and the Germans during 1941.

THE RUSSIANS USED TO call Yalta the Cowes of the Crimea, after the ultra-fashionable and beautiful English seaport town on the Isle of Wight off the south coast of England that had been the playground and meeting place of the tsars and Queen Victoria. Situated on a peninsula on the north coast of the Black Sea, offering a sheltered harbor, Yalta was set in a dramatic coastline of towering, snow-covered granite peaks that dropped down to green hills, beaches, and the sea. After the revolution the villas and palaces built by the tsars and grand dukes were converted to sanitoriums and rest homes: the remaining vineyards, magnificent cedars, and lovely green sloping countryside had kept Yalta beautiful. Now the harbor, the fields, the roads, were in various stages of destruction and ruin. The Germans had looted and damaged as much as they could before their hasty retreat. Most of the buildings were heavily damaged by shell fire; the few stores still standing were boarded up.

To ready Yalta for the conference was a task of heroic proportions. Before the war a town inhabited by 2,250 people, Yalta had only 234 residents and nineteen undamaged houses—the rest were roofless shells—by the time the German army retreated in 1944. The Livadia Palace, where the conference would take place, and the Yusupov Palace that Stalin chose for his residence were both still standing only because the Germans had not had time to blow them up, but windows were shattered, walls smashed, floors ruined, plumbing and heating destroyed, and furniture nonexistent. Beria and the NKVD were given the task of supervising the herculean project of rebuilding the roads to and within Yalta and rebuilding, repairing, and furnishing the residences. As with all projects in Stalin's era, it was energetically and successfully carried out. An army of workmen was sent in to repair the damage and make the buildings habitable. Another army of workmen repaired the roads. According to one foreman, the workday began at five in the morning and went until midnight, after which briefings were held, totals accounted for the day, and tasks set for the following day. Crews worked for two weeks at full tilt, then, exhausted, were given time off to recover, before returning for another all-out two-week stint. Linen, china, and flatware collected from various public and private sources came from Moscow. Fifteen hundred trainloads of material arrived for the Livadia Palace alone. Kitchens, laundries, bathrooms, and telephone systems, plus two autonomous electric installations at each palace, were installed.

When it was noticed some key item was missing, work details commandeered it from those remaining houses within driving distance. Moscow hotels were stripped of their staffs, furniture, plates, china, kitchen utensils, and bedding.

According Roosevelt his status of primus inter pares, Stalin saw to it that he was housed in the Livadia Palace, the fifty-room Renaissance-style edifice built by the last tsar, Nicholas, which was the conference venue. Nicholas, with the self-indulgence that marked his reign, had put thirteen hundred workers to work on his summer palace in April 1910, and Livadia was finished in September 1911. The palace had been designed with the very latest in modern conveniences: central heating, electricity, and an elevator, and because the royal family enjoyed seawater, seawater was pumped into the royal bathrooms. The grounds were extensive and beautiful, containing miles of allées lined with cypress, cedar, yew, and bay trees that stretched up the side of the mountain and down to the sea and beach. The tsar and tsarina and their four daughters and hemophiliac son vacationed only four times in the magnificent palace before Nicholas was forced to abdicate and a short while later executed, along with his entire family. It was said that fearing assassination for years, he had slept in a different bedroom at Livadia each night he was in residence; sometimes, FDR later told reporters, he would even change bedrooms during the middle of the night. According to Lord Moran, Churchill's doctor, Stalin said, with a grin, that the only place where one could be certain of finding the tsar was in the bathroom first thing in the morning.

Roosevelt's inauguration for his fourth term was Saturday, January 20. It took place on the South Portico of the White House, rather than at the Capitol, and was watched by a relatively small group of two thousand people gathered on the South Lawn: because of wartime security measures it had to be kept small, without parades or flyovers. FDR told Harriman he planned to leave for Yalta at the earliest practicable date after it. Molotov, worried that Yalta wouldn't be ready, having been given a start date of February 10 for the conference, asked him not to rush it. When the first Americans arrived at the Livadia Palace, Romanian prisoners of war were still at work planting shrubs and repairing the roads, and inside, doorknobs and the last plumbing fixtures were being put into place.

Great care was taken to make sure not only that Roosevelt would be comfortable but that his special needs would be met. To make sure that the president could be wheeled, and stay in his wheelchair no matter in which of the three palaces a meeting or a dinner was held, wherever there were stairs, ramps were installed. (Replacing stairs with ramps was a usual courtesy extended for presidential visits: ramps had been built at the Citadel in Quebec for FDR's visits there.) Some measure of the magnitude of the undertaking that went into making FDR comfortable may be taken from the fact that besides the listed army, navy, and diplomatic staffs necessary for the conference, FDR would be bringing and need housing for another thirty people: eight servants, sixteen Secret Service men, and six White House staff.

The Livadia Palace, called the White Palace because its exterior was white granite, was now camouflaged brown and pink, according to Admiral C. E. Olsen, in charge of seeing to American needs. Roosevelt was given a suite of rooms on the ground floor, the rooms Nicholas and his son, Alexei, had used. They consisted of a bedroom, a study, a dining room, and, a most rare prized possession at Livadia, a bathroom that was built from scratch. No expense was spared. His bedroom, with three floor-to-ceiling windows facing the sea, was paneled in yellow satin, his study was paneled in red velvet. His dining room, with chestnut walls and an intricate walnut ceiling, originally the tsar's billiard room, designed in the English sixteenth-century style with windows facing the courtyard, had miraculously survived as originally constructed; above the fireplace was a cartouche of Nicholas, and a painting of a winter scene hung behind FDR's chair. When the suite was finished and the Russians learned that FDR had wanted his rooms painted the blue of the sea, they repainted his bathroom blue. Then, worried about the particular shade—whether or not they had got it right—they repainted it three times. For the same reason—worry over the color scheme (Kathleen Harriman wrote home, "The Soviets just couldn't make up their minds which oriental colors looked best")—the Oriental rugs for the suite were changed four times, which meant moving out the furniture each time.

Hopkins's room was next to FDR's. Because he was so ill, he rarely left it except to attend plenary sessions. In spite of his ill health FDR was relying on him for advice again. (Losing his battle to send Hopkins to the sick bay aboard the USS *Catoctin,* Dr. McIntire tried to restrict him to his bedroom. He basically subsisted, according to Stettinius, on coffee, cigarettes, an amazingly small amount of food, paregoric, and sheer fortitude. Lord Moran, Churchill's doctor, wrote of Hopkins that he looked much worse than the president, "Physically he is only half in this world. He looked ghastly.") Anna Boettiger and Kathleen Harriman also shared a room near the president. Kathleen finally met FDR, who, she wrote to her sister, is "absolutely charming, easy to talk to, with a lovely sense of humor. He's in fine form." (Kathleen Harriman would provide a classic example of the inaccuracy of memory. After FDR died and people assumed that he was already terribly sick at Yalta, she had a new thought. "I was horrified at the way he looked," she would say in 1987.) Edward R. Stettinius, whom FDR had appointed secretary of state in December to replace Hull, who had resigned because of ill health, was also one of the lucky ones on the ground floor in a two-bedroom suite overlooking the sea. Everyone else—there were forty-three members in the delegation—was on the second floor. General Marshall was given the tsar's bedroom upstairs. Admiral King was housed next door in the empress's bedroom. The rest of the military staff had to share quarters: six major generals shared one room, twelve brigadier generals and ten colonels another. The bathroom situation was dire: as many as thirty men shared one bathroom. Water buckets and pitchers were placed in these rooms. State Department personnel were also squeezed into rooms.

By this time Roosevelt had made his peace and gained influence with State Department personnel. In Stettinius he had a man who would do his bidding, did not have the tender ego of Cordell Hull, and was a good administrator. For that reason Stettinius was at Yalta, whereas Hull had been frozen out of Tehran; Charles Bohlen had become liaison between FDR and the State Department as well as interpreter. Brought along for their expertise, were H. Freeman Matthews, director of European affairs, and Alger Hiss, deputy director in the Office of Special Political Affairs, who had been administrative head at Dumbarton Oaks and would be later convicted of perjury on the charge of spying for Russia.

Roosevelt, with his sense of history and his architectural bent, must have appreciated the fine palace where he spent so much time. But being housed in the last palace built by a foolish monarch who, if he had been alive, would have been only fourteen years his senior must have reinforced his intention to set the world on a course that would avoid the excesses, lawlessness, and carnage of the past.

To ensure two-way high-speed radio communications between Yalta and Washington, the U.S. Signal Corps set up communications from the Livadia Palace to the USS *Catoctin*, anchored in Sevastopol, by stringing landlines over the fifty miles. To ensure that FDR knew the latest war news, a map room was set up for him in the palace.

The moment any American opened a door leading outside, three NKVD men dressed in long dark blue overcoats and shabby black caps appeared out of nowhere. Security troops were also very much in evidence, all magnificent physical specimens in gray and blue uniforms.

The Yusupov Palace, where Stalin chose to live, in Koreis on a hill above the sea, was between the Livadia Palace and the Vorontsov Palace, about a twenty-minute drive each way. It was situated right under a steep, snowcapped mountain and was on a smaller scale than the other two. It had a unique history. Stalin, dedicated revolutionary that he was, must have felt a sense of achievement and pleasure to be staying there, for it had belonged to Prince Felix Yusupov, in the earlier years of the twentieth century not only one of the richest men in Russia but one who could have served as the poster boy of the decadent prerevolutionary ruling class that ran Russia into the ground. Ironically, both Stalin and Yusupov had lived in St. Petersburg at the same time, although leading wildly different lives. Stalin, then an escaped revolutionary, was furtively putting out the first issues of *Pravda* while hiding from the Okhrana, while Yusupov, nine years younger, a daring, stunningly beautiful bon vivant cross-dresser, was habituating St. Petersburg clubs and restaurants exquisitely dressed in his mother's clothes and jewels, causing such a sensation that photographs of him so attired regularly appeared in the local magazines. However, it was as the murderer of Gregory Rasputin, the faith healer who held such power over Nicholas and Alexandra, that Yusupov earned undying fame. Yusupov had lured Rasputin to his palace in St. Petersburg, served him tea, Madeira wine, and cakes, all of which he had laced with cyanide. However, he had evidently not administered a lethal enough dose, for Rasputin failed to drop dead. Yusupov thereupon whipped out a pistol, shot him, wrapped the body in heavy linen, shoved it into a car, drove to Petrovski Island, and dropped it off a bridge into the Moika River. Exiled for the deed by the tsar, Yusupov, taking money and possessions with him, went to live in Paris, thereby making him one of the lucky members of the Russian nobility who was out of the country before the revolutionary violence exploded.

German soldiers had bivouacked in the Yusupov Palace, leaving it in ruins. Reconstruction crews paneled the walls in oak, resurfaced the floors, brought in furniture, and rebuilt the kitchens. The most interesting change, however, was that Stalin used only a side door while he was in residence instead of the grander front door, and he had the large room he chose to live in close by that entrance divided into two rooms, one of which he used as his bedroom, the other as his office. The furnishings brought in for him, preserved by the state, were standard Soviet issue—austerely bland: a utilitarian bed with a plain honey-colored wooden headboard and matching wardrobe and simple desk and bookcase. Whether he did not feel comfortable in the large rooms, whether it was an ostentatious reminder to his staff of the excesses of prerevolutionary Russia that Bolshevism had remedied, whether he felt safer in small rooms, can only be a matter of conjecture. He was certainly seriously concerned with his personal safety: Beria's bedroom was next door but one. Molotov's bedroom and office, in contrast to Stalin's, were in their original configuration. Molotov had a piano installed in his office and unlike Stalin enjoyed the luxury of a balcony overlooking the sea. So that Stalin could see newsreels from the front and stay current with the progress of the war, the billiard room in the basement was turned into a movie theater, with a huge screen at one end, a wall with openings for a projector at the other, so that Stalin could see the latest films of the war. The only room in the villa on the grand scale of the other palaces was the dining room, a good fifty feet long and more than twenty-five feet high, dominated by a huge half-moon window, the glass of which had been shattered and replaced for the conference. This is where Stalin hosted his dinner. The household staff that prepared meals, all the china, glass, and silver used, came from the Metropol and National hotels in Moscow.

Churchill was installed in the Vorontsov Palace, properly grand, with part-Scottish, part-Moorish flourishes, designed by an English architect, which the Germans had not had time to trash. It boasted towering turrets, Gothic windows, magnificent spaces, sweeping views of the sea on one side and the stark granite peak of Mount St. Peter's on the other; six huge fierce white marble lions guarded the wide flight of stone steps leading down to terraces and the sea. There were intricate oak ceilings and paneled walls in many rooms and a blue drawing room where Rachmaninoff and Chaliapin had performed. Churchill's large bedroom on the ground floor featured floor-to-ceiling windows facing the sea. As at the Livadia Palace, bathrooms were scarce: there were two sinks with cold taps only and two baths in the entire palace. The Vorontsov Palace was the farthest from the Livadia Palace, about a half-hour drive along a road that was well paved but had many hairpin turns.

Because the NKVD had been in charge of renovations as well as staffing, the palaces were thoroughly bugged, as were the cars the Soviets provided. Stalin saw summaries of conversations; unlike at Tehran, however, he no longer asked for verbatim extracts of the conversations. Quite possibly this was because the material Beria was supplying was so boring: all U.S. personnel had been warned that everything they said would be overheard by the Russians, that every room was bugged, and presumably the English participants had been also.

The level of care, effort to please, and pervasiveness of surveillance are illustrated by one incident. Churchill's daughter Sarah Oliver, a WAAF section officer, remarked to someone one day that lemon juice improved the taste of caviar. Shortly thereafter a lemon tree, covered with lemons, appeared in the garden near the dining room at the Vorontsov Palace.

The smartly dressed staff that saw to the daily needs of all the participants was in sharp contrast with the cleaning crews that operated at night when everyone was in bed. Then shabby porters polished the floors by skating about in their bare feet on top of rag mops, while women swept up with bundles of twigs.

A line of warships—Russian and American—stood off the coast. Prior to the conference Beria had the NKVD make security sweeps of the area; they found and arrested, according to him, hundreds of spies and confiscated thousands of guns, including more than seven hundred machine guns. During the conference four NKVD regiments remained on guard.

BY THE END OF JANUARY everyone watching the three leaders knew that *something* was up: Hopkins had left Rome for no one knew where; the president was nowhere to be seen on his birthday, January 30; Churchill and Eden had both disappeared. The NKVD, learning through espionage organs they monitored that the Germans were trying to pinpoint the exact location where the three leaders would meet, ordered that eight Soviet air divisions of the Black Sea Fleet be on constant patrol around the Crimea while they were there.

The afternoon of the day he left for Yalta, FDR's personal preparations for the trip included having John Mays, the dignified, courteous black man who had doubled as the official White House greeter and barber since the time of President Taft, cut his hair. While this was taking place, he was having a last-minute discussion with James Byrnes, director of mobilization and reconversion, about Yalta matters. FDR asked Byrnes to go to Yalta to provide expertise on trade as well as economic data "certain to come up." He had told Morgenthau that there would be no "finance people" at Yalta as an excuse not to talk about a long-term loan to Russia: the fact that he asked Byrnes along meant that he was reconsidering.

At 10:00 p.m. on January 22, FDR was driven to the siding under the Bureau of Engraving, where his private railroad car, the armor-plated Ferdinand Magellan, with three-inch bulletproof windows, waited. By 11:00 p.m. he was in bed. This siding was the usual place for FDR to board, both because it was private and because the siding floor was level with the floor of the car, so FDR could be wheeled directly from the auto to the railroad car. The Magellan consisted of the president's suite: bedroom, bathroom with shower, plus three more bedrooms, a dining room, a kitchen, and a lounge. (Although there were adequate toilet facilities in every car, FDR's shower was the only one on the train.) A communications car containing a diesel-powered radio that kept FDR in touch with the Map Room using special codes, four sleeping cars, a dining car, and a lounge car for the other passengers made up the rest of the train. Accompanying FDR, besides Byrnes, were his daughter, Anna; Admiral Leahy; Ross McIntire; Admiral Wilson Brown; General Pa Watson; Dr. Bruenn; Edward J. Flynn, consummate Democratic politician and former head of the Democratic Party; and his press secretary, Steve Early. (Flynn was a last-minute addition; FDR planned that his attendance at Yalta would give Flynn added prestige in everyone's eyes and that after the conference he would visit Moscow and the pope and work on improving relations between the Roman Catholic Church and Russia.) The Filipino mess crew from Shangri-La, the presidential retreat in Maryland, who would prepare all the president's meals at Yalta, were in one of the sleeping cars. Hopkins and Stettinius were waiting at Malta. As FDR slept in his bedroom, the train, which had right-of-way over all other trains (all of which had to keep clear of the Magellan by at least twenty minutes—taking to a siding if necessary), continued on at the smooth-riding maximum speed of forty miles an hour. The usual precautions were in play: army guards watching over the train as it headed south were particularly visible as the train passed trestles, culverts, switches, and crossings; where highways closely paralleled the tracks, motorized units patrolled. The Magellan arrived on schedule before dawn at Newport News, Virginia. Waiting in the harbor was the USS *Quincy*, the fast new heavy cruiser that had fired the first gun at the Normandy landings and would weigh anchor, with the president's party on board, before the sun came up.

FDR had confided to Daisy that he was worried the conference would be tiring ("thinks it will be very wearing, and feels that he will have to be so much on the alert, in his conversations with Uncle Joe and W.S.C.") but that he was looking forward to the ship's voyage itself. When he went aboard, he told her, "he would get into the elevator, go up to his cabin on the upper deck, have breakfast, then go forward on the deck and get the sea air and spray." And that was what occurred: "We came on board & had breakfast, and by the time we were through we were out in the stream & heading out, wrote FDR."

At dusk that first day FDR sat on deck with Anna watching the Virginia coastline slip by. He pointed out, secure in the knowledge that Anna was discreet, complicit as she was in keeping from Eleanor his many meetings with Lucy Rutherfurd, whom he had promised Eleanor years before never to see again, the spot where Lucy's family used to live. "That's where they had their plantation," he remarked.

Ten days of salt air during the day, almost smooth seas, a morning nap ("take another nap after breakfast") and an afternoon nap (Anna would report that the president "slept and slept"), communal lunches and dinners served in his cabin, followed by a movie, and resting ten hours at night (as he told Stettinius) was just what Roosevelt thrived on. There were no nasty surprises: twice ships in the convoy thought they had picked up sound contacts from enemy submarines, but both turned out to be false alarms. He was, according to William Rigdon, "a merry guest" at his birthday party on January 30, when five rival groups

FDR, notes in hand, announcing the policy of unconditional surrender to the press and to Churchill, Casablanca, January 24, 1943

Churchill and his military staff: Field Marshal Sir Alan Brooke on Churchill's right, General Hastings Ismay directly behind the prime minister.

Churchill, Averell Harriman, Stalin, and Molotov, August 1942

Stalin usually smoked a pipe, although occasionally he switched
to cigarettes.

James Conant, Vannevar Bush, and Brigadier General Leslie R. Groves at Hanford, Washington, one of the Manhattan Project sites, 1943

Igor Kurchatov, right, director of the Soviet Union's nuclear program, and Andrei Sakharov

U.S. ambassador to Britain John Winant, FDR, Secretary of State Edward R. Stettinius, and Harry Hopkins aboard the USS *Quincy* at Malta

Stettinius and Molotov at Saki airfield, waiting for FDR's plane to make an appearance, February 3, 1945

FDR meeting privately with Stalin before the first plenary session February 4, 1945. Their interpreters, Vladimir Pavlov and Charles Bohlen, are on the right.

FDR meeting privately with Churchill during a break in the first plenary session.

FDR waiting for the first plenary session to begin. Whenever possible, he was the first into any meeting: he would be wheeled in and seated in a normal chair, his wheelchair would be spirited away before other participants appeared.

First plenary session under way

Stettinius, FDR, and Stalin during a break in the conference

The Big Three posing for the cameras

The closing lunch, February 11; note Churchill spooning caviar, always served in abundance.

aboard the *Quincy* baked and presented to him five birthday cakes. Rigdon reported that "he worked with his usual deft touch on a big batch of mail . . . ate about as usual, was not disturbed at all by the first few days of rough seas . . . talked and laughed and told stories, was lively at the pre-dinner cocktail parties."

Byrnes had a slightly different story about the president from Rigdon's, however. FDR had a cold, according to Byrnes, who was disturbed by his appearance, and stayed in his cabin a great deal, but by the time they reached Malta, the cold was gone, and altogether FDR had improved "greatly." He attended the field meet the crew put on on the fantail of the ship: sailors competing in three-legged races and at a tug-of-war. In the evening after dinner he watched every movie shown: *Our Hearts Were Young and Gay, Here Come the Waves, The Princess and the Pirate, Laura, To Have and Have Not*. Even though Byrnes was aboard because FDR had told him he needed him to supply postwar U.S. production numbers, he engaged him in little or no talk about his upcoming role. Their conversations were about the great organization that was coming into existence that would, Roosevelt believed, be his crowning achievement. Byrnes concluded, after spending eleven days on the *Quincy,* "Our chief objective for the conference was to secure agreement on the Dumbarton Oaks proposals for the creation of an international peace organization." FDR did not seem concerned about how any other issue would be handled.

As the *Quincy* sailed slowly into Malta harbor at 9:30 a.m. on February 2, Bohlen, watching, described the sun glistening on the waves, a cloudless sky, flags on British warships as well as on the walls of the city snapping in the light breeze, salutes from the British men-of-war, and the rolling cheers of spectators crowding the quay as they saw Roosevelt sitting on deck, his black cape wrapped around his shoulders.

Churchill awaited. He came aboard for a long-anticipated lunch upon FDR's arrival, bringing his daughter Sarah Oliver and Anthony Eden. For a change he was in civilian clothes, not his regular naval uniform. Both he and FDR were in high spirits, according to others, and indulged in much joking and talking about the Atlantic Charter, which they remembered they had never signed, and about China and Madame Chiang. However, there was a momentary break when the prime minister referred to China as "the great American Illusion"; the president was curt, according to Stettinius. As he had attempted before the Tehran Conference, Churchill sought to engage FDR in conversations that would lead to their presenting a united front to Stalin: FDR wouldn't play along.

"Pleasant but no business whatsoever done," recalled Anthony Eden of the lunch. The "business" Eden had in mind was the Yalta agenda: FDR refused to discuss it. Unfazed, Eden and Churchill arranged to be invited for dinner aboard the *Quincy* that evening, "specifically for this purpose."

The dinner was no more successful than the luncheon, from Churchill and Eden's point of view. Sarah Oliver and Anna Boettiger were present, and undoubtedly as FDR planned, it was a purely social evening. (Harry Hopkins had been invited but was too sick to attend.) "Impossible even to get near business," Eden reported, later complaining, "We were going into a decisive conference and had so far neither agreed what we would discuss nor how to handle matters with a Bear who would certainly know his own mind." In fact it was exactly this British desire for partnership that Roosevelt was bent on avoiding: the game was his to play alone. He wasn't intending to share power. Contrary to Eden's claim, Stettinius had met with him the previous day and reviewed those conference matters FDR *wanted* his British allies to know about. Wrote Sarah Oliver, "My father and all the British party felt a withdrawing of the former easy understanding," conveniently forgetting that the same thing had happened at Tehran.

The *Quincy* dinner went on much too late. It wasn't until 10:15 that Churchill, Eden, and Sarah Oliver left the ship. FDR had hoped to be airborne by 10:00, but it was 11:00 p.m. before he and his party drove to Luqa, the RAF airfield on Malta, and boarded the *Sacred Cow*.

Although FDR was not the first president to fly (that milestone belonged to his cousin Theodore), he was the first to fly while in office; the *Sacred Cow* was the first presidential airplane, and this was the president's first use of it. A remodeled Douglas C-54, in its commercial version known as a DC-4, it had a cabin for FDR fitted out with a full-length couch that made up into a bed, an armchair, a desk, and a uniquely large picture window to satisfy the president's unfailing interest in viewing the lands he was flying over. Maps that pulled down were set into the wall. In line with his passion for all things marine, a painting of a clipper ship hung on the wall above the couch/bed. Forward of FDR's cabin were two compartments, each with double seats.

Behind the passenger cabin was an elevator that could lift FDR, in his wheelchair, into and out of the plane, which eliminated the telltale and therefore dangerous thirty-foot ramp that had previously marked out any plane transporting FDR. FDR had not been enthusiastic about the prospect of a specially built presidential airplane: he didn't much like flying, because air travel seemed to aggravate his sinus condition, and he was concerned at the cost, so in contrast to his railroad car, appropriately named Ferdinand Magellan, he let others find a name for the plane. As a consequence, when he learned that the ground crews who guarded it and the fliers who tested it were all referring to the aircraft as *a* sacred cow, FDR let the name stand: *Sacred Cow* became the official name.

The flight to Saki, the nearest airfield to Yalta in reasonable condition (it had a solitary metal strip runway), on the west coast of the Crimean Peninsula ninety miles from Yalta, took almost seven hours.

The Secret Service head, Mike Reilly, in Yalta preparing for the presidential visit, had been alerted that trigger-happy Russian anti-aircraft gunners, mistaking English and American planes for German, had been shooting at and occasionally hitting Allied aircraft. In fact, Russian gunners had just accidentally shot down a British transport plane near Saki on February 1, killing ten passengers, six of them from the British Foreign Office. Because the route of the *Sacred Cow* would put it directly over several of the Soviet batteries, the U.S. Air Force decreed that a U.S. soldier who could identify his plane had to be placed in command of every Russian anti-aircraft battery on or near the route FDR would fly. When Reilly presented this requirement to General Artikov, Artikov refused to sanction it, prompting Reilly to say, "No Roosevelt then." Artikov, forced to take it up with Stalin, came back a day later, "obviously amazed," remembered Reilly, volunteering, "Stalin says 'absolutely.'" As a result, at every Russian anti-aircraft station along the Malta-Saki flight path, as the *Sacred Cow* and the other planes, flying without lights and with radios silent, roared overhead, a U.S. sergeant stared up into the sky: there were no more incidents.

Escorted by five Lockheed Lightnings, the *Sacred Cow* came in just after noon at the Saki airfield. The field was outlined by Russian guards standing every twenty feet, tommy guns visible. It had been swept clear of every snowflake. Churchill's plane arrived shortly after, at which point Roosevelt was lowered by the plane's elevator to the ground and wheeled into a nearby open jeep provided by the Russians, and the two met. Waiting on the field to greet FDR were Molotov, Deputy Foreign Minister Vyshinsky, General Antonov, Ambassador Gromyko, Ambassador F. T. Gusev, Stettinius, and Harriman. The president reviewed the guard of honor and listened to the "spectacular" brass band waiting to greet him. As Cadogan recorded, not too admiringly, in his diary, smoking a ten-inch cigar, "the PM walked by the side of the President, as in her old age an Indian attendant accompanied Queen Victoria's phaeton." There were three refreshment tents on the field dispensing everything from glasses of hot tea with lemon and lump sugar to brandy, champagne, dishes of caviar, smoked salmon, fresh butter, cheese, soft- and hard-boiled eggs: the repast was extensive and lavish and served on china plates and in crystal goblets. Refusing any food, FDR was lifted into a waiting Packard, also supplied by the Russians, and when the ceremonies and the music finished, his motor caravan started out for Yalta. With him in his car were his daughter, Anna, and Mike Reilly. There was two inches of snow on the ground; it was sloppy underfoot. A few sections of the road were paved, but most of it was pretty rough and muddy. The ninety-mile trip took six hours: a Sherman tank would have found it tough going, according to Dr. McIntire, following in another car. The cars were well guarded as they proceeded slowly along the uneven road. Red Army soldiers, many of them young women, all armed with Springfield rifles (old but still deadly sniper rifles supplied by Lend-Lease), formed an unbroken line for the entire passage, springing to attention as the cars came into view. The caravan passed the ruins of war: burned-out tanks, gutted houses, damaged rail equipment. Sarah Oliver, in her father's car, described it as "a countryside as bleak as the soul in despair."

STALIN TRAVELED TO THE CRIMEA by rail ensconced in his private railroad carriage, the green bulletproof saloon car that contained his bedroom with a big, comfortable double bed, desk, chairs, and mirror, a bathroom with shower, a conference room with expandable table that twelve could sit around with curtains that could be drawn for privacy, and a kitchen. The route of the train was through Tula, Orel, and Kursk, where great battles had been fought and where the devastation was unremitting. Shelling had destroyed the landscape: of whole towns and villages, only remnants remained; sketchily built log cabins now took the place of train stations. The train stopped as rarely as possible, if at all, because homeless refugees jammed every station. After three days the train reached Simferopol, the nearest station to Yalta, where Stalin transferred to a car, probably another armored Packard the train carried in one of its cargo carriages, and he too was driven down to Yalta. Unlike at Tehran, where he had brought only Voroshilov, whom he rarely consulted, Stalin had with him a full complement of advisers: as FDR had hoped, Stalin was learning the ropes of diplomacy. With Stalin on the train were his secretary, Poskrebyshev; General Nikolai Vlasik, in charge of Stalin's personal security detail; Molotov; Admiral Nikolay Kuznetsov, commissar of the navy; General Antonov, of the Red Army; Vyshinsky, Molotov's deputy for foreign affairs; Marshal of Aviation Sergei Khudyakov; and Maisky. (Andrei Gromyko would come from Washington; F. T. Gusev, ambassador to Great Britain, would come from London.)

NKVD preparation for the conference was thorough. According to Pavel Sudoplatov, in charge of special tasks for the NKVD (the man in charge of planning Trotsky's murder in Mexico), Molotov gathered together the top personnel of all the intelligence services at the end of December and asked them for information: their opinions of German strength to continue the war, their opinions on possible areas of future peace settlements with America and Britain. They told him what must have been good news: neither the British nor the American delegation had a coherent postwar policy toward Eastern European countries; "the Americans were ready for a compromise . . . that a flexible position on our part would ensure a fair division of influence in postwar Europe." Military intelligence personnel, according to Sudoplatov, believed "the political turn of events . . . was easy to predict." Presence of the Red Army in the liberated areas would mean the de facto provisional governments would come under their control, even if there was democratic voting.

FOLLOWING PRACTICES THAT HAD BEEN HONED by the Russians for years, developed to cope with their endemic suspicion and fear of foreigners, Sudoplatov was ordered to analyze every American participant known to be coming to Yalta as to personality and attitude and to provide a psychological portrait of each of them. (Alger Hiss, according to Sudoplatov, was identified as "highly sympathetic to the interests of the Soviet Union and a strong supporter of postwar collaboration between American and Soviet institutions" but was *not* described as an agent.)

IN LINE WITH FDR'S PRACTICE of acquainting Stalin with his thinking on issues ahead of time, which he had first instituted when Molotov was visiting Washington in 1942, he had told Harriman to bring up with both Molotov and Ambassador Maisky in advance the subjects he wanted to discuss at Yalta. Molotov's diary of January 20 shows that while downplaying the thought that there was an agenda ("The president, of course, does not mean to suggest any agenda"), Harriman, in fact, presented exactly that to Molotov. The agenda included "all the matters dealing with treating Germany, including partition of Germany and others . . . all the matters left open after the Dumbarton Oaks conference. Next, the president wants to talk about Poland. He also wants to discuss the political and military aspects of the war in the Pacific, as well as in Europe," according to Molotov's diary.

What questions would Marshal Stalin like to raise? Harriman asked. Replied Molotov, "The Soviet government has not developed any agenda and would not suggest one . . . Marshal Stalin will be ready to discuss any questions the President may want to arise." As at Tehran, Stalin passed. Indicating that the subject of postwar trade and loans would probably be on the table, Harriman also noted that James Byrnes, head of industrial mobilization, would be in the president's party.

Harriman met with Maisky later that same day. Maisky was very knowledgeable of FDR's concerns; their conversation was fruitful. Maisky made careful notes. "The president is primarily interested in two questions: a) the future international security organization . . . At present the political atmosphere in the USA is rather favorable . . . for strengthening America's participation in the future international agency. We should seize the moment. Later isolationism can again take hold and create unnecessary difficulties. b) Postwar fate of Germany . . . It comes down to two issues: the problem of Germany's partitioning, the problem of reparations from Germany." Here FDR authorized, according to Harriman, a huge carrot: "Once Germany was out of the war, loans for the Soviet Union would be discussed." He asked them, according to Maisky, "to detail the wish list of the Soviet side . . . as well as to outline their own measures so that with the war's end *the American industry could come down to delivering on the Soviet orders immediately.*" (Italics mine)

Stalin had been counting on and working on a loan at least since November 1943. At that time Harriman had pointed out at a meeting with Anastas Mikoyan, commissar for foreign trade, that the granting of a long-term loan to the Soviet Union enabling it to buy American manufactured goods would be in the self-interest of the United States as a means of assuring full employment during the period of transition from wartime to peacetime economy. A few days later, after further discussion, Harriman had written to Washington to make sure it understood "that this question of reconstruction is considered by the Soviet Government as, next to war, the most important political as well as economic problem that confronts them." Immediately after Tehran, Molotov pursued the idea. At the end of October 1944, Gromyko had suggested to U.S. Lend-Lease officials a loan of $6 billion for a period of thirty years, the money to be used to purchase American manufactured goods—railcars, engines, rails, gas pipes, and the like. On January 3, 1945, Molotov formally requested of Harriman a $6 billion loan in postwar credits over thirty years at an interest rate of 2.5 percent. Harriman favored the loan and transmitted details to Washington. However, at that time the just-appointed secretary of state, Edward Stettinius, had decided that granting such a large credit to the Soviet Union would deprive the United States of its "bargaining" position. He was particularly obdurate, taking this narrow view in response, according to Morgenthau, to the recent Soviet action of taking 170,000 Germans from Romania to Russia for forced labor. At a late morning meeting with FDR on January 10 in the Oval Office, Stettinius had out-argued Morgenthau and persuaded FDR not to raise the issue at Yalta. According to Morgenthau, Stettinius accomplished this by refusing to show FDR Harriman's cable saying how important the large credit was to Molotov and Stalin, describing the scene as follows: "He wanted to read it . . . The president finally said, 'Well, after all, we are not having any finance people with us and I will just tell them we can't do anything until we get back to Washington . . . I think it's very important that we hold this back and don't give them any promises of finance until we get what we want.'" Harriman, in Moscow briefing Maisky, far away from the argument taking place in the Oval Office, gave Maisky the mistaken *impression* that the loan was going to be discussed.

Harriman's briefing to Maisky included the questionable information that FDR did not see any future in battling the Soviet Union over control of Poland: "At this particular late stage the President does not see any point for discussion—e.g. situation in Poland is *fait accompli.*" Maisky would also have reported, from his conversation with Harriman, that "the problem of colonies is not yet highly urgent."

Stalin also received input from Andrei Gromyko, whom he wanted present at Yalta. Gromyko advised the premier that "the United States government will be forced to recognize the Polish provisionary government." On the issue of voting in the Security Council, Gromyko advised standing pat: "Americans and the British will have to make concessions on this issue." On the other hand, Gromyko also advised Molotov that before he left Washington, he had been talking with Stettinius and Leo Pasvolsky, who raised with him the issue of smaller nations' appealing the actions of great powers in the Security Council, and, he concluded, "Discussion of issues without voting and passing decision might be O.K. with us . . . since in this case a possibility that the Council passes decisions against us would be ruled out."

The views of F. T. Gusev, Russian ambassador to Britain, who would also be at Yalta, as to what matters should be discussed at the conference were solicited. Presumably, because he was wrong about Russian entry into the war against Japan ("the Americans and the British are probably no longer interested in our entering the war against Japan") and Stalin didn't suffer fools, his role was minor.

Litvinov, absent from the conference, undoubtedly blocked from attending Yalta by Molotov, made perhaps the most accurate assessment of American positions. In January he had predicted, "The USA is not interested in the fate of the Baltic [republics] or Western Ukraine and Belorussia. Under the press of the known circles, Roosevelt will, probably, make 'ideological' reservations. He may, for instance, suggest a plebiscite in the Baltic [republics] without attaching any significance to his proposal. Finally, he will put up with the inevitable and recognize the borders we desire."

Stalin's key advisers, then, reported that FDR would be amenable to Soviet positions on Poland's government and borders, that he looked favorably on the long-term loan, and that the American stand on the veto in the Security Council was not as dangerous as previously thought.

Roosevelt, Churchill, and Harriman brought their daughters; Hopkins's son Robert was also present. Anna Boettiger, whom FDR had not permitted to attend the Tehran Conference, was especially thrilled to be at Yalta. Her mother had wanted to go, but Anna, who had become so important to her father as organizer, with Daisy Suckley, of his leisure time, prevailed. She didn't feel in the least guilty for being chosen: "If Mother went, I couldn't go . . . Harriman and Churchill were bringing their daughters, and there would be no wives." Sarah Churchill Oliver, who had been at Tehran, whom her father found helpful and good company, was his aide-de-camp. Kathleen, who lived with her father at Spaso House and worked with him, quite naturally accompanied Harriman to Yalta. Missing was Stalin's daughter, Svetlana, eighteen, who spoke excellent English. She and her father were barely on speaking terms. He had sent her first serious boyfriend, a Jewish journalist, to Siberia and had reluctantly permitted her marriage to Grigory Morozov, fellow classmate at Moscow University, who was also Jewish, whom he also disapproved of. Svetlana was in any case five months pregnant. (Stalin also had two sons; the elder, Yakov, by his first wife, had been taken prisoner by the Germans. An offer to Stalin was made through Count Bernadotte to swap Yakov for Field Marshal Paulus, but Stalin had regretfully refused: "I had to refuse . . . What would they have said of me, our millions of Party fathers . . . ? No, I had no right." Yakov was subsequently killed. Although it was never conclusively proved, the most common account of Yakov's death was that he hurled himself against the outer prison fence, forcing his guards to shoot him. Stalin's second son, Vasily, entered the war at twenty as a captain and at twenty-four had been promoted to lieutenant general. Young, spoiled, not up to the responsibility, unfit to command, he became an alcoholic.)

IT WAS AGAINST THIS BACKDROP that Roosevelt worked to further his ideas for a peaceful future world at Yalta, worked to fashion a world organization strong enough to keep a nation from spilling out of its borders into another nation's territory—worked to end war. He had two partners: both ready to oppress foreign nations to save their own, neither willing to admit it. There was, of course, a world of difference between Churchill and Stalin. If you were within Churchill's magic circle—if you were white—you were safe. No one was safe with Stalin. Except, possibly, Molotov and FDR.

British disagreements with Roosevelt, of course, were more like disagreements among members of a family. British mistrust of Stalin ran much deeper. As Churchill said of Stalin, in a statement that at the same time reveals his antagonism bordering on hatred, "Trying to maintain good relations with a communist is like wooing a crocodile. You do not know whether to tickle it under the chin or to beat it over the head."

Eden and Churchill were aware that with Roosevelt in control of the form the postwar world would take, they had a problem: his bedrock disapproval of the principle of white supremacy, upon which rested the British Empire and Britain's right to rule its colonies. But they looked beyond the president's philosophical mind-set and believed he saw economic gain as a side benefit. FDR, Eden believed, "did not confine his dislike of colonialism to the British Empire alone, but it was a principle with him, not the less cherished for its possible advantages." FDR "hoped that former colonial territories, once free of their masters, would become politically and economically dependent upon the United States." Neither Eden nor Churchill understood FDR's idea that independence, not dependence, was the best economic solution to the world's problems. Nor did they understand that he believed the pursuit and maintenance of colonial empires was a root cause of World War II (as did Stalin). Roosevelt saw the future as a world of independent nations, always excepting the British and Soviet subject nations, kept in check by a world security organization—a UN force—policing the world. Neither Eden nor Churchill understood this. Stalin did; Molotov probably did not.

Yalta must be seen against this backdrop of Churchill's deep mistrust of Stalin, as well as Stalin's deep mistrust of Churchill, their joint (measured) confidence in Roosevelt's sense of history and fair play, and Roosevelt's view that he could handle both men and make them get along. Roosevelt, with his keen insight, formulated the idea that he could act as moderator between the two leaders before he had even met Stalin. He saw himself as the leader, the forger of the future alliance of nations when the war was over. As he explained to Mackenzie King a year after Pearl Harbor, "I doubt if Winston and Stalin together could have their minds meet over some of these postwar questions. I could perhaps act as a medium between them, in helping to bring them together. It seems to me that when there are two great powers that come near each other but never quite combine, there is always a bit of a barrier in between them. I could perhaps help to get views reconciled."

It was indeed a common thought of those watching the three leaders at Yalta that Roosevelt was the intermediary between the other two, and it is visually enforced: in photographs FDR is always between them.

Roosevelt's optimistic view of himself as moderator/peacemaker gives a good clue to his conduct at Yalta and shows that he saw no roadblocks between Stalin and Churchill that he could not bridge. He was looking forward to the conference with the firm expectation that he would be the moderator.

The conference went on for eight days. Sun and overcast seemed to alternate each day. The temperature stayed at a steady fifty degrees. Each afternoon the three heads of state met in a long plenary session, usually lasting four hours, seated around the round table in the grand ballroom of the Livadia Palace. The following morning the foreign ministers and military chiefs met to settle the questions that the plenary session had left unresolved. There were dinners given by each leader. FDR and Churchill both met privately with Stalin; they did not themselves meet except at lunch.

As at Tehran, Roosevelt was not only the chair of the conference but in control in every way. His first act upon arrival at the Livadia Palace was to direct Harriman to call on Molotov at the Yusupov Palace to work out conference plans with Stalin. Harriman transmitted to Molotov Roosevelt's request that Stalin meet with him at the Livadia Palace the following afternoon to discuss the military question, after which the plenary session would begin at 4:00 and be attended by the military staffs and the foreign secretaries as well as themselves. FDR also directed Harriman to tell Molotov that he wanted to give the first dinner—small, unofficial—following the first plenary session. After conferring with Stalin, Molotov told Harriman that Stalin, whose days always started late, preferred that the plenary session start at 5:00 rather than 4:00; he would therefore call on FDR at 4:00; he accepted the dinner invitation.

It must be noted that Churchill and his staff were informed rather than consulted on conference plans, which must have been an aggravation to them.

The next morning FDR met with his military chiefs on the sun-porch overlooking the sea. It was a beautiful clear day; the water was calm as a millpond. At 10:30, Stettinius, Harriman, Matthews, Hiss, and Bohlen joined them, and there was general discussion of U.S. positions. At 4:00 p.m. FDR and Bohlen waited in Roosevelt's red velvet study at the palace. Stalin and Molotov, accompanied by their interpreter, Pavlov, arrived promptly in a large black Packard limousine. The two leaders met, observed Bohlen, as two old friends, grasping each other's hands, both smiling.

The military situation, which Harriman and Molotov had agreed should be the first thing their leaders discussed, was, FDR and Stalin both now acknowledged, considerably improved since their last meeting. Stalin informed FDR that the Soviet armies were moving very successfully onto the line of the Oder River. FDR replied that he had made a number of bets on board the *Quincy* coming over as to whether the Russians would get to Berlin before the Americans got to Manila.

Stalin said he was certain the Americans would get to Manila first. (They did, entering it the next day.)

Roosevelt then said he had been "very much struck by the extent of German destruction in the Crimea and therefore he was more blood-thirsty in regard to the Germans than he had been a year ago." In line with the profile he wished to present to Stalin of being no closer to Churchill than he was to Stalin, FDR picked up on his remark that Churchill had taken such exception to at Tehran, saying that "he hoped that Marshal Stalin would again propose a toast to the execution of 50,000 officers of the German army."

Stalin replied that everyone was more bloodthirsty, that the destruction in the Crimea was nothing compared with that which had occurred in the Ukraine; the Germans were savages and seemed to have a sadistic hatred for the creative work of human beings.

Roosevelt informed Stalin that Eisenhower was planning an offensive for February 8 and another on the twelfth but that the main blow would take place in March. He asked that General Eisenhower and his staff be permitted to communicate directly with the Soviet staff through General Deane in Moscow, as the armies were getting close enough to have contact between them, rather than going through the chiefs of staff in London and Washington as they had been doing. (General Marshall, citing British reluctance for the change, which he had to overrule, had asked FDR to discuss this with Stalin.) Stalin agreed, promising to work out the details.

As the conversation turned to France's role, FDR, knowing from Tehran that Stalin shared his negative view of de Gaulle, spoke of his conversation with de Gaulle in Casablanca two years earlier, when de Gaulle had compared himself with Joan of Arc as the spiritual leader of France and Clemenceau as the political leader.

Stalin replied that "in actual fact the French contribution at the present time to military operations on the Western Front was very small and that in 1940 they had not fought at all."

FDR then said he would now tell the marshal something indiscreet, because he would not wish to say it in front of Prime Minister Churchill, namely that the British for two years had had the idea of artificially building up France into a strong power that would have 200,000 troops on its eastern border to hold the line for the period required to assemble a strong British army. He said the British were a peculiar people and wished to have their cake and eat it too.

They then discussed the German zones that each of them would occupy. FDR said he would have preferred the northwest zone but the British seemed to think that the Americans should restore order in France and then return political control to the British. Stalin asked whether FDR thought France should have a zone. FDR attached great importance to giving France a zone of occupation, and Stettinius had made this known to Eden at Malta, but aware of Stalin's strong negative view of all things French, he now said that "it was not a bad idea," then added that "it was only out of kindness."

Both Stalin and Molotov then spoke up vigorously and said that would be the only reason to give France a zone.

As it was almost five, Roosevelt suggested they proceed to the grand ballroom to begin the first plenary session, which they did.

14

ORGANIZING THE WORLD

The entrance to the grand ballroom, the White Hall, more than forty yards long, was through handsome white Corinthian columns, past a huge white marble statue of Penelope. Seven tall French doors looking out on a courtyard ran the length of the room on the left, facing seven tall arched windows on the right looking out on the mountains. The ornate ceiling was punctuated by 280 well-concealed recessed lights that would discreetly turn on as the late afternoon meetings extended into the evening. At the far end of the ballroom, near a huge white marble fireplace, was the large round table around which the conference participants would sit. The table, covered by a beige cloth, was surrounded by banks of wooden chairs; in the inner bank were three armchairs reserved for the leaders. In front of each chair was a box of cigarettes and cigars. A brisk log fire crackled in the great fireplace.

Both FDR and Churchill were seated at the table by the time Stalin, followed by his advisers, walked into the room. Churchill rose to greet him; Stalin went to FDR to shake his hand.

Roosevelt always sat with his back to the fireplace. His advisers, who sat in the outer ring, were General Marshall, Admiral King, General Deane, General Laurence Kuter, U.S. Army Air Forces (in place of General Hap Arnold, recovering from a heart attack), and General McFarland in place of General MacArthur. Stalin's delegation consisted of Admiral Kuznetsov, General Antonov, Air Marshal Khudyakov, and Vyshinsky. At this first meeting Hopkins was absent, too ill to attend, but he was present at all subsequent sessions.

The president always wore a business suit, either gray or blue, with a handkerchief peeking out from his breast pocket. Stalin and Churchill wore military uniforms, Churchill sometimes the uniform of a colonel, according to Stettinius, while Stalin wore a plain light khaki uniform that buttoned up high around his neck, with a star with a red ribbon on his left breast.

There was, obviously, no head to a round table, but if there had been, FDR would have sat there. Wherever he was, whether with U.S. personnel or with foreigners, with heads of state such as Churchill, whether in Washington, Quebec, Casablanca, or Tehran, FDR always presided over every group, everywhere, every time. Nor was it just governments that accorded him, as the American president, so much respect: ordinary people adored him. In the far reaches of the world he was larger than life. Carlo Levi, in those years a best-selling author, tells how, on entering a hovel—in a miserable village in godforsaken Calabria—in 1945, he saw on the wall a crucifix, a picture of the family's absent son, and a picture of Roosevelt. His dominance was a fact FDR was conscious of and took for granted. On the evening he arrived at Yalta, as he was having dinner with his daughter, Anna, the Harrimans, Leahy, and Stettinius, FDR was particularly aware of his position: the only chief of state at the conference. Stettinius generously attributed the fact that he was smiling to his "rich sense of humor," but the realization, as he observed that because he was the senior officer present, "people were going to come to see him," obviously made FDR happy. It *might* have crossed his mind, for a fleeting moment . . . master of the world?

As the White Hall became silent and conversation at the round table ceased, with everyone seated, Stalin now, as host, spoke, to request that FDR preside. FDR stated that he was very happy to open such a historic meeting in such a lovely spot; he thanked Stalin for the effort expended in making it comfortable in the midst of war. He proposed that the talks be conducted in an informal manner in which each would speak his mind frankly and freely. Lest anyone in the room think him naive, ingenuous, or simply mouthing platitudes, he added that he had discovered through experience that the best way to conduct business expeditiously was through frank and free speaking. (He would undoubtedly have agreed with Emily Dickinson's poem, however: "Tell all the truth but tell it slant.")

Then, demonstrating his steady, optimistic frame of mind, in a comment primarily directed at Stalin, he said, "We understand each other much better now than we had in the past, and month by month our understanding grows." (While this might have been true for himself and Stalin, it was at the same time a directive for Churchill, who, he hoped, was absorbing his words.) He then called for military assessments from each country; "military questions, particularly those on the most important front of all, the Eastern Front, should be the subject of discussion," and in this casual way the conversation began, with Russia as the center of attention. He requested of Stalin that he have a staff officer give a detailed report.

Roosevelt had asked Stalin in late December to meet with an officer from Eisenhower's staff to coordinate the efforts of the Red Army on the eastern front and the Allied armies on the western front. At that time Eisenhower's armies were fighting the Battle of the Bulge, Hitler's last offensive action of the war, while at the same time the Red Army had crossed the Vistula and was advancing toward Berlin. Stalin had wired back immediately, "Naturally, I agree with your proposal as well as I agree to meet the officer from General Eisenhower and to arrange an exchange of information with him." The result had been that Air Marshal Arthur Tedder, Eisenhower's deputy, and other officials from SHAEF, Supreme Headquarters Allied Expeditionary Force, flew to Moscow and met with Stalin in his office in the Kremlin on January 15. Tedder had explained to the premier how the Germans were being pushed back to their frontier and shown him the various positions on maps. Stalin explained that only the lack of clear weather was holding his armies back from starting their offensive in aid of the Allied armies but that they would now advance in spite of the weather. "We have no treaty but we are comrades," he told Tedder. "It is proper and also sound, selfish policy that we should help each other in times of difficulty. It would be foolish for me to stand aside and let the Germans annihilate you; they would only turn back on me when you were disposed of. Similarly, it is to your interest to do everything possible to keep the Germans from annihilating me."

Stalin had been pleased with the exchange of information and with Tedder's explanation of impending operations. As the conference wound up, he told Tedder, "That is what I like. A clear, businesslike statement, without diplomatic reservations." To FDR, Stalin had written, "Mutual information is sufficiently complete. The exhaustive answers have been given on the matters in question by both sides. I should say that Marshal Tedder makes the most favorable impression."

Building on this first genuine interchange of military information, the Russians came to Yalta prepared to match the session with Tedder in openness. Now, at Stalin's bidding, General Antonov, deputy chief of the Soviet general staff, reading from a document, outlined the various Soviet military positions and the results of the Red Army offensive. He explained to the assemblage that Soviet forces had begun their January offensive earlier than planned—in heavy fog, in spite of extremely low visibility—in order to take pressure off the Allied soldiers who were pinned down and suffering casualties in the Ardennes, that in eighteen days of advance Soviet troops on the eastern front moved forward with an average speed of fifteen to eighteen miles a day, and that they were now, in some areas, on the Oder River.

When President Roosevelt inquired as to whether German railroad gauges had to be altered to accommodate Russian rolling stock, Stalin picked up from Antonov: "The greater part of the German railroad lines would remain of their customary gauge."

Following Antonov's presentation, General Marshall summarized the situation on the western front. The Germans had been repulsed in the Ardennes ("the German bulge in the Ardennes had now been eliminated"), the Allies were on the offensive in the southern sector of the line north of Switzerland, and Field Marshal Montgomery, commanding the British Twenty-First Army Group and the U.S. Ninth Army, was driving toward Düsseldorf. Plans were being finalized to cross the Rhine, but not until March 1 because of ice conditions and the strength of the current.

The conversation continued with General Marshall supplying information about the western front, Churchill asking for Russian help in the submarine war by taking out Danzig, where the submarines were built, and Stalin making longer and longer explanatory statements—detailed analyses of Russian tactics and troop movements and of German losses. He described how special Soviet artillery "break-through" divisions carrying from three hundred to four hundred guns operated. It became increasingly obvious that Stalin was indeed the knowledgeable, hands-on head of Russia's military forces.

There was a jarring note. "What were the wishes of the Allies in regard to the Red Army?" Stalin asked, expansively. Churchill answered. He "wished to express the gratitude of England and he was sure of America for the massive power and success of the Soviet offensive." The answer annoyed Stalin. He didn't want gratitude for doing the right thing, he testily replied. "The Soviet Union was not bound by any agreement at Tehran to conduct a winter offensive," he said, "and despite what some people had thought no demand or request had been received." He mentioned this, he continued, "only to emphasize the spirit of the Soviet leaders . . . who acted on what they conceived to be their moral duty to their Allies."

In spite of this interchange, Sir Alexander Cadogan, British under-secretary of foreign affairs, said of the day's discussions, "I have never known the Russians so easy and accommodating. In particular Joe has been extremely good. He *is* a great man, and showed up very impressively . . . He's obviously got a very good sense of humour—and a rather quick temper."

As he had at Tehran, Churchill at times spoke as if he and FDR were a team. Now he mentioned "the complete confidence which the president and he felt in the Marshal." Roosevelt, as at Tehran, did not return the compliment. If anything, this transparent habit of Churchill's undoubtedly grated on Russian ears. That the Russians felt the difference between the two leaders was commented on by Gromyko, who was decidedly struck by Roosevelt's friendliness and Churchill's antagonism. Gromyko would recall, "While Roosevelt reacted to Stalin's remarks calmly, even with understanding, Churchill did so with barely concealed irritation. The British prime minister tried not to show his feelings, but his cigars gave him away. He smoked far more of them when he was tense or excited. The number of his cigar stubs was in direct proportion to the stresses of the meeting. Everyone noticed it, and mocking remarks were made about it behind his back."

The reverse was also true: Stalin's antagonism toward Churchill was likewise apparent. "Stalin had a liking for Roosevelt," observed Gromyko, "which could not be said about his attitude towards the British Prime Minister." Gromyko saw it as political as well as personal: "The difference in attitude had to do with the politics."

Roosevelt's dinner followed this first plenary session. His Filipino mess staff from Shangri-La, the president's wartime retreat on Catoctin Mountain, who also had only arrived the day before, managed to turn out and serve, with minimal help from the maître d' and staff of the Hotel Metropol in Moscow, the group sent down to take care of Roosevelt's needs, a dinner that included some American dishes such as chicken salad, southern fried chicken, and beef and macaroni, and some Russian fare: consommé, sturgeon, caviar, and hot vegetables. (So important was FDR's diet to his health that Harriman had notified Molotov that the president would eat food brought in from the USS *Catoctin* that would be cooked by his own staff.) Five kinds of wine plus vodka and Russian champagne provided the fodder for the usual numerous toasts. The dinner was in what had been Nicholas's chestnut-paneled billiard room; on one wall hung a Russian winter scene, on another a portrait of the tsar. The Americans: Stettinius, Harriman, Byrnes, and Bohlen; the British: Eden, Archibald Clark Kerr, and Birse; and the Russians: Molotov, Vyshinsky, Gromyko, and Pavlov were present. For a change, possibly because his hands shook more than usual, FDR did not make the cocktails, as he usually did. (All his life FDR had episodes of heightened tremor. In late 1942, Mackenzie King had noted in his diary that when the president poured him some tea in his office, "his hand was very shaky." As he got older, people would attach more significance to his tremor.)

The mood among the diners was indeed convivial. Molotov and Stettinius drank toasts to each other. When Molotov said he hoped that Stettinius would soon visit Moscow, FDR "immediately interjected, 'Ah-ha, he wants him to go to Moscow. Do you think Ed will behave in Moscow as Molotov did in New York?'" Roosevelt was a great teaser, according to Stettinius, and was suggesting that the Secret Service men assigned to show Molotov the sights in 1942 had taken him around theaters and shops and to nightclubs as well. Stalin happily replied, "He could come to Moscow incognito." Stalin, who was, Stettinius noted, smoking Lucky Strikes, asked FDR whether he had actually sent a cable asking for five hundred bottles of Russian champagne but then said—postwar credits for Russia obviously very much on his mind—he "would give it to the president on a long-term credit of thirty years." The ice was broken, but FDR decisively switched the subject, replying, "There is one thing I want to tell you. The prime minister and I have been cabling back and forth for two years now, and we have a term of endearment by which we call you, and that is 'Uncle Joe.'" Stalin asked what it meant. FDR repeated that it was a term of endearment, "as though he were a member of the family." Stalin appeared to be offended, although FDR had called him Uncle Joe to his face the last day at Tehran. At this point Molotov stepped in to say no one should be deceived: "He is just pulling your leg. We have known this for two years. All Russia knows that you call him 'Uncle Joe.'"

As the dinner drew to a close, Stalin, in a reference to the difference of opinion about the veto in the Security Council, put forth the idea that the three great powers who had liberated the small powers from German domination should have the unanimous right to preserve the peace of the world. "It was ridiculous to believe," he said, "that Albania would have an equal voice with the three Great Powers . . . He would never agree to having any action of any of the Great Powers submitted to the judgment of the small powers."

FDR genially agreed that the three great powers "represented at this table" should write the peace. After a bit of discussion, Churchill made a toast to the proletarian masses of the world, then gave a graceful quotation: "The eagle should permit the small birds to sing and care not wherefore they sang."

At some point Vyshinsky turned to Bohlen and said that Americans "should learn to obey their leaders and not question what they were told to do." Bohlen retorted he "would like to see him go to the United States and tell that to the American people." Vyshinsky grinned and replied he would be glad to go.

Stettinius noted, as the toasts went on, that Stalin was being careful to stay sober, drinking down half the vodka in his glass at each toast, then refilling it with water when he thought no one was looking. (Vyshinsky was noted doing the same thing.) The atmosphere was so friendly that FDR called for more champagne to be served, and when Stalin suggested at 10:00 that it was time to leave, that he had to return to his military duties, FDR said no. Stalin thereupon said he would stay until 10:30, but he actually stayed until after 11:00.

MONDAY, FEBRUARY 5

The days were consumed with meetings. The three foreign ministers met each day at noon at each palace in succession (unlike their bosses, who always deferred to FDR and let him run their meetings, Eden, Molotov, and Stettinius took turns presiding, and the venue changed to the presiding minister's residence). They conferred through lengthy lunches about the various matters that had been discussed at the previous day's plenary session. Each afternoon Stettinius, Eden, and Molotov would meet and brief their heads of state. The generals and admirals also met each day to coordinate war plans.

The second plenary session began at 4:00 p.m. FDR opened the session by stating that the subject matter under discussion would be the political aspects of the future treatment of Germany. The first question to be discussed, he said, was the zones of occupation, which had been agreed upon by the three of them, leaving the question of whether France should or should not have a zone of occupation and, if so, if it should sit on the Allied Control Commission. He handed a map of the zones to Stalin.

Stalin stated that he wanted a number of issues settled as to the future of Germany: All had been in favor of dismemberment at Tehran, were they still? Would each set up a separate government? "If Hitler surrendered unconditionally would we deal with his government?" In addition, he brought up the question of reparations.

FDR replied that the treatment of Germany, as he understood it, would grow out of the zones of occupation. Stalin replied that he wished to find out whether or not it was the joint intention to dismember Germany: "If Germany is to be partitioned, then in what parts . . . At Tehran FDR suggested partition into five parts . . . The prime minister in Moscow talked of partition in two parts . . . Hadn't the time come for decision?"

Churchill answered, saying that in principle the British government agreed to dismemberment, but the actual method was much too complicated a matter to settle in four or five days. If he were asked how Germany should be divided, he would not be in a position to answer, "and for this reason he couldn't commit himself to any definite plan for the dismemberment of Germany." Eliminating Prussia from Germany "would remove the arch evil—the German war potential would be greatly diminished . . . We are agreed that Germany should lose certain territories conquered by the Red Army which would form part of the Polish settlement," but there was the question of the Rhine, the industrial areas of the Ruhr; all required careful study. But now, he concluded, "all that was required was a final agreement on zones of occupation and the question of a zone for France."

Stalin replied that the surrender wasn't clear to him: "Suppose, for example, a German group declared they had overthrown Hitler and accepted unconditional surrender. Would the three governments deal with the group?"

Churchill said in that case Britain would present the terms of surrender. It would not negotiate with Hitler or Himmler. The three allies would consult together before dealing with any group and then immediately submit the terms of unconditional surrender. Would it not be wise to add a clause then, saying that Germany would be dismembered, without going into details? asked Stalin. He didn't think dismemberment an additional question. But Churchill thought it unnecessary to discuss with the Germans, "only among themselves . . . there was not sufficient time . . . it was a problem that required careful study." But Stalin wanted the matter clarified.

As the two bickered, FDR stepped in to change the tenor of the dialogue. They were both talking about the same thing, he said soothingly: Stalin meant that they should agree on the *principle* of dismemberment, which he personally favored, as he had stated at Tehran. Then he digressed—one of his favorite methods of tamping down personality clashes, giving everyone time to settle back while he talked. Dismemberment would reverse a historic trend, he reminisced: forty years earlier, when he was in Germany, German communities dealt with their provincial government—for instance, if in Bavaria, one dealt with the Bavarian government, and if in Hesse-Darmstadt you dealt with that government; only recently had everything become centralized. Winding up, he said that he still thought the division of Germany into five or seven states was a good idea.

Or fewer, interrupted Churchill, with which FDR agreed.

The prime minister went on to say that he didn't think there was any need to inform Germans of policy: they must surrender and then await their decision. FDR, saying public discussion of the problem of dismemberment would be a great mistake, suggested the matter be referred to the foreign ministers, with a request that they submit a recommendation as to how to handle the issue and report back to them in twenty-four hours. But Stalin had more to say before the matter was dropped; he wanted dismemberment clearly laid out: Germany was threatened with internal collapse because of the lack of bread and coal. Such rapid developments made it imperative that the three governments not fall behind events but be ready to deal with the question when the German collapse occurred. He said he fully understood the prime minister's difficulties. He felt the president's suggestions might be acceptable and summarized them as follows: (1) agree in principle that Germany should be dismembered; (2) refer the matter to the foreign ministers; (3) add to the surrender terms a clause stating that Germany would be dismembered without giving any details.

FDR said he shared Marshal Stalin's idea of the advisability of informing the German people at the time of surrender of what was in store for them. Churchill, again disagreeing, stated his view that it would make the Germans fight harder. FDR and Stalin said there was no question of making the decision public. At this point the conversation stopped as all three agreed to turn the matter over to the foreign ministers and let them determine how to include a reference to the intention to dismember Germany into article 12 of the terms of surrender.

Roosevelt then turned their attention to the issue of adding a French zone of occupation to their own three zones. Churchill assured Stalin that if there *were* a French zone, it would come out of the British and American zones and it would not affect the proposed Russian zone: all he sought at Yalta was that the Soviet government would agree that the British and American governments should have the right to work out with the French the latter's zone of occupation. Stalin probed as to whether or not granting a zone to France would not serve as a precedent for other countries. Churchill's answer and explanation for the request was that Britain needed help: the occupation might be a lengthy one. Britain was not sure it could bear the burden alone; France could be of real assistance. But, he added, tripartite control of Germany might then change to four-nation control.

But a fourth power in the control machinery for Germany might bring up complications, said Stalin. He suggested instead that the British get help from France or Holland or Belgium, *without* any right to participate in the three-power decisions. At this point Churchill revealed what lay behind his stand: he said Britain needed France to play a very important role; as the largest naval power, France could be of great help in the administration of Germany; Great Britain did not wish to bear the whole weight of an attack by Germany in the future; it was essential that France be relied upon to assist in the long-term control of Germany. Also, he added, Britain needed France because it was problematical how long U.S. forces would remain in Europe.

As they discussed the addition of France, Stalin smiled, saying that "this was an extremely exclusive club, restricted to a membership of nations with five million soldiers. Churchill quickly corrected him and said three million."

Stalin interrupted to ask FDR to express an opinion as to how long U.S. troops would be staying in Germany. Not much more than two years, the president replied: "I can get the people and Congress to cooperate fully for peace but not to keep an army in Europe for a long time. Two years would be the limit." (There was already a groundswell of public opinion demanding the return home of U.S. forces when the war was over; it was a continuing concern of General Marshall's.) Churchill continued: France should have a large army; it was Britain's only ally and would help Britain share the burden. France should come in; he wanted to see its might grow to help keep Germany down.

FDR agreed with Churchill: France should have a zone, but he thought it a mistake to bring in any other nation.

If France were included in the control machinery, it would be difficult to refuse other nations, said Stalin, repeating that he wished to see France a strong power. But, he continued, that could not destroy the truth—which was that France had contributed little to the war and had opened the gate to the enemy. He therefore thought the control machinery should be run by those who have stood firmly against Germany and have made the greatest sacrifices in bringing victory.

Churchill agreed that France had not been much help in the war, but, he said, it still remained Germany's nearest neighbor: in the future it would stand guard on the left hand of Germany. Eden said the French had pressed them to be on the Allied Control Commission. Stalin admitted they had raised the question in Moscow.

FDR pulled the discussion to a close, saying he favored the French request for a zone. But he agreed with Stalin that they should be excluded from the control machinery, otherwise other countries—such as the Dutch, suffering because the Germans had destroyed the dikes and inundated Dutch farmland with saltwater and at least five years must pass before the flooded lands would be suitable for cultivation—might claim a voice in the Allied Control Commission.

Said Stalin, Britain should speak for France on the Allied Control Commission: French participation would serve as a precedent for others. He had the last word, noting that there was agreement that France should have a zone but not be on the Allied Control Commission and that the three foreign ministers should study the problem and report back.

Stalin then said he wanted to discuss the question of reparations. Earlier that day, at the foreign ministers' luncheon at the Yusupov Palace in Koreis, as Molotov and Stettinius had discussed reparations from Germany, Molotov had taken the opportunity to express the hope Russia would receive long-term credits from America. He expected this to be relayed to FDR. As Molotov had been told in January, FDR had authority from Congress to extend credits only during the life of the Lend-Lease Act: Congress would have to pass a new act for long-term (postwar) credits. Discussions and planning should begin; Stettinius told Molotov at the lunch that he was ready to discuss the matter "either here or later in Moscow or Washington."

FDR was well briefed on the subject of reparations. At Stettinius's request, the head of the OSS, William Donovan, had prepared an estimate of Soviet war damages for the purposes of discussion. The OSS finding was that Russia had lost approximately $16 billion of fixed capital in 1937 prices—25 percent of its capital—not counting manufacturing inventories and personal property, which the OSS fixed at $4 billion. (In the western part of Russia alone seventeen hundred cities and towns had been destroyed.)

Roosevelt opened the discussion by saying that besides themselves there was the question of the desires and needs of the small powers, the question of manpower, and the question of what Russia wanted. He said America did not want reparations in the form of labor, "and he was sure Great Britain held the same view."

Stalin replied, "We have a plan for reparations in kind but we are not ready to talk about manpower." At this point Hopkins, possibly getting restless, wrote a note he slid over to FDR, referring to Russia's manpower needs: "Why not take all Gestapo-Nazi storm troopers and other Nazi criminals?" FDR ignored it.

Stalin instructed Maisky to present Russia's plan.

Maisky, attractive and forceful, spoke perfect English. He had been the Russian ambassador to Britain and in London had become friends with George Bernard Shaw and H. G. Wells before being called back to Moscow to work out the program of Russia's reparations demands. Maisky explained that the Soviet Union envisioned reparations being in two forms: transfer of (German) factories, plants, machinery, machine tools, and rolling stock abroad, which should terminate two years after the war, and yearly payments in kind for a period of ten years; the most important industries to be nationalized under Allied supervision for a period of ten years. To safeguard the future security of Europe, he continued, it would be necessary to reduce German heavy industry by 80 percent: Germany's economic needs could be met with 20 percent of its heavy industry. All German enterprises that could be utilized for war purposes should be subject to representatives of the three powers. Priorities among countries should be established, based on their proportional contribution and their losses. As to Russian losses, he said, the figures were so astronomical that reparations could not cover them. He closed with the exact amount Russia wanted: not less than $10 billion of total reparations in kind over a ten-year period.

Churchill made a long speech objecting: he didn't like the idea of reparations, particularly expressed in dollars. He discussed how difficult it had been in the last war to extract *anything* from Germany. While admitting that Russian losses were much greater than those of any other country, he touched on how Britain had suffered, how the British government had disposed of the bulk of its assets abroad. He said no victorious country was so burdened in an economic sense as Great Britain, and he very much doubted that large reparations from Germany would benefit the British Isles. He was haunted by the specter of a starving Germany: "If you wished a horse to pull a wagon, you would at least have to give it fodder."

Stalin "observed that was right, but care should be taken to see that the horse did not turn around and kick you."

Roosevelt interrupted to calm them both down. After the last war the United States had lost a great deal of money; it had lent more than $10 billion to Germany. This time it would not repeat its past mistakes. Germany should live but not have a higher standard of living than the U.S.S.R. He was in favor of extracting the maximum in reparations from Germany but not to the extent that its people would starve. He would help the Soviet Union retain the reparations in kind it needed, as well as German manpower to reconstruct devastated regions: he envisioned a Germany that would be self-sustaining but not starving.

Maisky threw out some figures: "What is ten billion dollars? It is 10% of the United States budget this year. It is six months war expenditure of Great Britain. It is one and one quarter times the United States peacetime budget and two and one quarter times the British each year." The prime minister's doubts are unfounded, he said. Germany will be able to live a decent life, and we must not forget that it will have no burden of military expenditures.

Churchill, ignoring the reparations figures, agreed on setting up a reparations commission but said it should be kept secret. Stalin agreed: it should be kept secret.

Stalin brought up France: it could not expect to get reparations, he stated; it only had eight divisions in the war, whereas Yugoslavia had twelve and the Lublin government thirteen.

The three leaders agreed that the main directives to a committee on reparations would be decided and clarified by the foreign ministers at their next meeting but that there would be a reparations commission that would sit in Moscow. The session ended at 7:45 p.m. The three leaders retired to their quarters for the evening.

FDR had a relaxed dinner in his quarters with Marshall, King, Stettinius, Leahy, McIntire, Byrnes, Brown, Steve Early, Kathleen and Averell Harriman, and his daughter, Anna, and then retired. "It was," according to Stettinius, "purely a family dinner at the end of a hard day."

Stalin worked on a different time frame, arising late in the day and working through the night into the early hours of the morning. His staff by necessity adjusted their lives to his. As head of his country's armed forces, he spent a great deal of time with his generals, particularly General Antonov, to formulate war plans, learn the latest battle news, and view recent film footage brought in from the various fronts. Stalin made it a point to talk with the members of his delegation most evenings to check their assessment of the day's conversations and held at least one cocktail party for his staff at which he greeted each of the more than fifty people by name, asked and answered questions, and was remembered by Gromyko as listening attentively to the replies. Gromyko recounted one such query he got from Stalin, probably because he thought he had made an impression on his leader. "What are the main social elements that Roosevelt can count on for support inside his country?" Stalin asked him. Gromyko remembered summing up his thoughts and answering, "His domestic policies may encroach to some extent on the interests of large monopolies, and right-wing extremists sometimes make the absurd accusation that he is sympathetic to socialism, but it's only a propaganda ploy by people who don't want the USA to have good relations with the USSR. At the moment, Roosevelt as president has no rival. He feels secure." Gromyko felt that his words had an impact on Stalin because he spoke knowledgeably as the ambassador to America; he felt he had added to Stalin's esteem of and reliance on the president.

Once, when FDR felt poorly and took to his bed, Stalin went to visit him, taking along Molotov and Gromyko. "We sat with him," recalled Gromyko, "for maybe twenty minutes, while he and Stalin exchanged polite remarks about health, the weather, and the beauties of the Crimea." After they left, Stalin asked, rhetorically, "Why did nature have to punish him so? Is he any worse than other people?"

TUESDAY, FEBRUARY 6

Breaking the pattern he had set at Tehran of not socializing with the prime minister (having, he must have felt, set his relationship with Stalin on a firm footing), FDR invited Churchill, together with Sir Alexander Cadogan, to have lunch with him in his dining room at the Livadia Palace, joining Byrnes, Hopkins, and Harriman. FDR amiably kept the conversation off politics. "Quite agreeable and amusing," recorded Cadogan of the lunch, "but not awfully useful."

Meanwhile, the foreign ministers, meeting at the Livadia Palace, had lunch in the palace sunroom, with its big bay window looking out over the sea below.

During the day Stalin telephoned Marshal Zhukov, according to Marshal Vasili Chuikov, author of *The End of the Third Reich,* who heard both sides of their telephone conversation because he happened to be sitting close to Zhukov at the moment it took place. "Where are you, what are you doing?" Stalin asked Zhukov. Zhukov replied, "I am at Kolpakchi's headquarters, and all the Army Commanders of the Front are here too. We are planning the Berlin operation." Realizing that that meant they were only some forty miles from Berlin, Stalin replied, "You are wasting your time. We must consolidate on the Oder and then turn all possible forces north, to Pomerania to join with Rokossovsky and smash the enemy's 'Vistula' group." By this conversation Stalin delayed Russia's entry into Berlin: he must have made the decision because he thought the specter of the huge Red Army sweeping into Berlin would look frighteningly aggressive to FDR and particularly to Churchill, always suspicious of him.

At 4:00 p.m. the third plenary session began. Seated with FDR were Bohlen, Stettinius, Hopkins, Byrnes, Leahy, and Harriman. Stalin's group was down to six: Molotov and Maisky, Gusev, Gromyko, Pavlov, and Vyshinsky. Stalin was smoking Russian cigarettes. Churchill was seated between Eden and his interpreter, Major Birse.

FDR asked if the foreign ministers, who met each day at lunch, had anything to report. Stettinius, chair for the day, replied that he could report "full agreement" to the insertion of the word "dismemberment" after the word "demilitarization" in the German surrender terms but that Molotov had an additional phrase he wanted to put in. Molotov's suggestion at the meeting had been the addition of the sentence "In order to secure peace and security of Europe, they will take measures for the dismemberment of Germany." He now replied (obviously having taken it up with Stalin) that he was withdrawing his proposed words.

Stettinius reported that the foreign ministers needed more time to deal with the subjects of France, the Allied Control Commission, and reparations.

Churchill, speaking of the French zone and reflecting the view of each of them that German aggression was going to remain a threat, said that the knowledge that U.S. troops would be going home in two years made France more important: "Great Britain alone would not be strong enough to guard the western approaches to the Channel."

Roosevelt saw an opportunity to point up the importance of the United Nations. He said that when he had spoken of the troops, he had spoken "on the basis of present conditions." With the formation of the international organization the American public "might change their attitude in regard to the question of maintaining troops in Europe." He then launched into a discussion of the plans for the international organization agreed to at Dumbarton Oaks. He said he was not as optimistic "as to believe in eternal peace, but he did believe fifty years of peace were feasible and possible." He asked Stettinius to explain the U.S. position on voting in the Security Council, which was still a bone of contention. Stettinius outlined the voting proposal FDR had sent to Stalin and Churchill in December. ("Procedural matters" meant what subjects could be brought up for discussion.)

1. Each member of the Security Council should have one vote.
2. Decisions of the Security Council on procedural matters should be made by an affirmative vote of seven members.
3. Decisions of the Security Council on all other matters should be made by an affirmative vote of seven members including the concurring votes of the permanent members; provided that, in decisions under Chapter VIII, Section A, and under a second sentence of paragraph 1 of Chapter VIII, Section C, a party to a dispute should abstain from voting.

Stettinius pointed out that the proposal called for unqualified unanimity of the permanent members on all major decisions relating to the preservation of peace, including all economic and military enforcement measures: at the same time any member state would have the right to present its case, thus protecting the crucial freedom of discussion for all parties. He closed with the statement "It is our earnest hope that our two great Allies will find it possible to accept the President's proposals."

Stalin had said the first evening that he would never agree to having *any* action of any of the great powers submitted to the judgment of the small powers. As FDR knew from Gromyko's reaction at their breakfast meeting in September, this was a very touchy subject to the Russians. Stalin had also written to him on the subject in late December; he wouldn't agree to *any* restriction on the use of a nation's veto: "I have, to my regret, to inform you that with the proposed by you wording of this point I see no possibility of agreeing." Now Stalin merely asked if there was anything new in the statement—any change from the voting proposal FDR had sent to Stalin and Churchill in December. When Stettinius said there had been a minor drafting change, Molotov said that he needed time ("wished to study" the change) and would be ready to discuss it the next day.

Churchill had also been having a problem with the veto and the voting procedure. At FDR's dinner the first night, after Stettinius had heard Eden trying to explain it to the prime minister, Stettinius explained it to Churchill at length. Eden had later admitted to Stettinius it was the first time the prime minister realized what the question was all about.

Churchill, since then firmly in the president's camp, now stated that he found the president's new proposals on voting entirely satisfactory: if reservation were not made for free statement of their grievances by small countries, the matter would look as though the three great powers were trying to rule the world. He launched into a long statement of how a matter such as China's demand that Britain return Hong Kong would be handled: China could raise the question, but in the last analysis Great Britain would be protected by the veto under paragraph 3.

Stalin probed. Would Egypt be a member of the assembly? Suppose Egypt raised the question of the return of the Suez Canal?

Churchill didn't like the question. He replied that he hoped the marshal would let him finish his illustration about Hong Kong. He continued that under paragraph 3, Great Britain would have the right by its veto to stop all action by the Security Council. Britain didn't have to return Hong Kong; however, China should have the right to speak, and so should Egypt, if it had a complaint about the Suez Canal. He then, however, expanded into America's position, saying that the same considerations would apply if Argentina raised a complaint against the United States.

After this non sequitur FDR stepped in to remind them of what they had said at Tehran regarding their supreme responsibility to make a peace that would command goodwill from the overwhelming masses of the peoples of the world.

Stalin wasn't ready to agree on the voting procedure: he announced he wanted to have the document to study, giving the excuse that hearing it orally, he found it impossible to catch all of the implications. But then, by his questions, it was obvious that he was not comfortable with the assurances that the veto power of the permanent members of the council would sufficiently protect the Soviet Union. He now said he didn't believe any nation would be satisfied with simply expressing its opinion. The Dumbarton Oaks proposals already gave the right of discussion in the assembly: China would want more than to express an opinion on Hong Kong; China would want a decision, and the same was true of Egypt.

Stalin's annoyance at Churchill now surfaced: he digressed. "What powers had Mr. Churchill in mind when he spoke of a desire to rule the world . . . He was sure Great Britain had no such desire, nor did the United States and that left only the U.S.S.R. . . . It looks as though two Great Powers have already accepted a document which would avoid any such accusation but that the third has not yet signified its assent." He then, echoing FDR's choice of words, said that ten years from now none of them might be present and there was, therefore, an obligation to create for future generations an organization that would secure peace for at least fifty years. The main thing was to prevent quarrels in the future between the three great powers: a covenant must be worked out that would prevent conflicts between the three great powers.

Stalin again said he had less than perfect understanding of the voting issue. Stettinius would later write that it wasn't that Stalin was uninformed on the subject, that in fact he had given rather careful study to the question and hadn't yet made up his mind. Now Stalin brought up the League of Nations in 1939, when, at the instigation of England and France, which had mobilized world opinion against the Soviet Union, it had been expelled from the organization.

FDR, realizing that nothing would be gained by continuing on the subject, stepped in to close the discussion. The last word was his: there was no means of preventing discussions in the assembly; full and friendly discussions in the council would serve to demonstrate the confidence the great powers had in each other.

There was then a short break. When they reconvened, FDR rather tentatively suggested they move on to Poland, as they had agreed to do the previous day, and so began the most contentious discussion on the Yalta agenda: the future of Poland.

Stalin had broken off relations with the Polish government in exile in London as a result of that government's call for investigation of the Katyn massacre. The Soviet Union now recognized the new de facto government, the so-called Lublin or Warsaw government, also called the Polish Committee of National Liberation, that had taken over the administration of Poland. The United States and Britain continued to recognize the government in exile in London.

FDR plunged in, beginning the discussion with two ideas, both of which Stalin disagreed with. Said FDR, as the eastern frontier there was tentative agreement on the Curzon Line, to which the American people were in general favorably inclined, as he had so stated at Tehran, but he raised the suggestion that Stalin now bend the line and give Lvov and the oil lands southwest of Lvov to Poland. He softened the request, saying he wasn't making a definite statement, but he hoped Marshal Stalin would make the gesture. Before Stalin had a chance to reply, FDR went on to the second idea, saying that opinion in the United States was against recognition of the Lublin government on the ground that it represented a small portion of the Polish people: people want a government of national unity and, he added, a Poland that will be thoroughly friendly to the Soviet Union for years to come. Stalin said that Poland should maintain friendly relations not only with the Soviet Union but with the other Allies.

Roosevelt said solving the Polish question would be a great help to everyone; he didn't know any members of either government, but he had met Stanisław Mikołajczyk (head of the Polish Peasant Party, formerly head of the London government in exile), who impressed him as a sincere and honest man.

Churchill spoke next, saying the Curzon Line was not a decision of force but one of right. Having delivered this conciliatory idea, however, he threw out a challenge to Stalin: he wanted to see the Poles have a home where they could organize their lives as they wished, saying it was the earnest desire of the British government that Poland be mistress in its own house and captain of its soul. It must not be forgotten, he said, that Great Britain had gone to war to protect Poland, had no material interest in Poland, but the question of its future was one of honor.

At this warning to Stalin to keep his hands off the Polish people, Stalin suggested a ten-minute intermission: he must have wanted to collect his thoughts.

When they resumed, Stalin was obviously angry. He rose from his chair and, remaining standing, spoke in a quietly controlled voice as he marshaled his arguments:

> Mr. Churchill had said that for Great Britain the Polish question was one of honor . . . but for the Russians it was a question both of honor and security. It was one of honor because Russia had many past grievances against Poland and desired to see them eliminated. It was a question of strategic security . . . because throughout history Poland had been the corridor for attack on Russia . . .

During the past thirty years Germany twice has passed through this corridor . . . Poland was weak. Russia wants a strong, independent and democratic Poland. It is not only a question of honor for Russia but one of life and death.

Still standing, Stalin then addressed the border issue:

It is necessary to remind you that not Russians but Curzon and Clemenceau fixed this line . . . The line was established against their will. Lenin had opposed giving Bialystok Province to the Poles but the Curzon Line gives it to Poland. We have already retreated from Lenin's position . . . Should we then be less Russian than Curzon and Clemenceau? We could not then return to Moscow and face the people . . . I would prefer to have the war go on although it will cost us blood in order to compensate for Poland from Germany.

Stalin continued, pointing out that there had been a good chance for fusion between the various parties in the fall and that in the meeting between Mikołajczyk, Stanisław Grabski, and the Lublin Poles, various points of agreement were reached.

Roosevelt and Churchill remained silent.

The fact was many members of the Polish government in exile, holdovers from the pre-1939 government that had been pro-German, openly talked of the next war against Russia. Harriman, who, even though he had become increasingly annoyed at Russian stubbornness, had explained the problem to FDR in late March 1944: "They are terrified of Germany coming back and are unwilling to have a Polish government that might follow a Beck policy of alliance again with Germany." There was no doubt the émigré group, the Polish government in exile, which both Britain and the United States had recognized, was pro-German. Anthony Eden also saw the émigré government as untrustworthy: "Privately they say that Russia will be so weakened and Germany crushed that Poland will emerge as the most powerful state in that part of the world." As the Poles continued squabbling among themselves, it was almost inevitable that as the Red Army liberated Poland, it would put into power Poles who would do its bidding.

Stalin had first written to FDR about Poland the previous February. Then he had carefully edited a cable, pointing out (the edit is in his handwriting) that the principal role of the Polish government in exile "is played by hostile to the Soviet Union pro-fascist imperialist elements," citing the historically anti-Russian general Kazimierz Sosnkowski, commander in chief of the Polish armed forces in the West, as the prime example. Stalin had had the idea that Polish Americans might serve as political ballast in a new Polish government and requested that two Poles living in America, Father Stanislaus Orlemanski, a Catholic pastor, and Oskar Lange, a professor of economics at the University of Chicago, both of whom considered the Polish government in exile insufficiently democratic, be granted passports so they could come to Moscow. He met with both men because he hoped patriotic American Poles such as Lange would take part in the government, Lange to become director of foreign affairs. Both he and Molotov thought that a Polish government containing Americans would ensure a government friendly to the Soviet Union. Stalin told Lange, in his desire that Lange become a Polish citizen, "Cooperation and understanding between the Soviet Union, the United States, and Great Britain was not a matter of expediency but was being established on firm and permanent lines."

There were *some* reasonable men in the émigré government in London, Stalin had acknowledged. The premier, Stanisław Mikołajczyk, head of the Polish Peasant Party, was one. The best, most reasonable man in the government, he was not anti-Soviet, but he did not control the other members of the government. FDR had met with him at the White House, after which he had advised Stalin to meet him, writing, "He [Mikołajczyk] is fully cognizant that the whole future of Poland depends upon the establishment of genuinely good relations with the Soviet Union." After reading a special GRU tape of the FDR-Mikołajczyk meeting that clearly showed the president supporting Stalin's position vis-à-vis the Poles (quite possibly leaked by the State Department), Stalin also met with Mikołajczyk. The GRU report read,

> During the visit of the Polish prime minister to Washington, Roosevelt insisted on the removal from the Polish government of the anti-Soviet elements of Sosnkowski's group, as well as on agreeing by the Poles to the border along the Curzon Line. He also insisted that the [Polish] government enter into working contact with the Polish patriots in Moscow and the Polish divisions in the eastern

front . . . Mikołajczyk agreed to act in the spirit of Roosevelt's suggestion, however, only in case of complete support by the Polish
émigré circles in London.

Reassured again of FDR's support, Stalin had written FDR shortly
after D-day that he hoped for a strong, independent, and democratic
Poland, with a government of Polish statesmen from England, America,
the U.S.S.R., "and especially democratic statesmen in Poland itself and
also . . . the Curzon Line as the new border between the USSR and
Poland." But in the meantime, as the Red Army beat back the Germans
and entered Poland, the Russian government set up the Polish Committee of National Liberation to administer the government.

As had been the case in 1939, Poland continued to be tragically
ill-served by its principal statesmen. Mikołajczyk and his government
argued about which of two Polish constitutions should be recognized:
the constitution of 1921 or the severely authoritarian one adopted in
1935. They argued over boundaries; there was talk of a Polish civil war.
In August, Stalin wrote to FDR that possibly the Polish groups were
beginning to work together; the Polish Committee of National Liberation offered Mikołajczyk the post of premier and four portfolios out
of eighteen: "Both the Polish National Committee and Mikolajczyk
expressed the wish to work together . . . One may consider this as the
first stage in relations between the Polish Committee and Mikolajczyk
and his colleagues. We shall hope that the business will go better in the
future." It didn't. It was in every way a difficult situation. The Warsaw uprising made things worse. When the Red Army reached the east
bank of the Vistula in late July 1944, instead of aiding the woefully
outnumbered and ill-equipped Warsaw patriots who had risen up to
fight the Nazis and were desperately trying to free their capital by themselves, the Red Army ground to a halt. As became known only later, the
Germans threw four new armored divisions into the battle. Marshal
Konstantin Rokossovsky, commander of the First Belorussian Front,
himself a Pole born in Warsaw, told Stalin the army had no choice but
to fall back. Looking for information, Alexander Werth, the unusual
BBC journalist who remained in Russia throughout the war, found and
interviewed Rokossovsky a few days later. "Wasn't the Warsaw rising
justified?" he asked. "No, it was a bad mistake . . . [T]he rising would

have made sense only if we were on the point of entering Warsaw," answered Rokossovsky.

As a result of Rokossovsky's decision, while the world watched in horror, the German army proceeded to kill or wound nearly 250,000 Poles and level what was left of Warsaw. Churchill tried, enlisting FDR's tepid support, to have Allied planes drop supplies into the beleaguered city. In September, after agreeing to some aid for Warsaw, Stalin characterized the situation to the effect that it was like some dirty face helping to disgrace a fair face. Harriman, among others, was upset with Stalin at the time, thinking it a callous, calculated act, but he later realized things were not as they seemed, some twenty years later admitting as much to Arthur Schlesinger. He then said, of the uprising, it "was the London Poles thinking they could put it over on the Russians by seizing Warsaw." Mikołajczyk, who could not persuade his cabinet to agree to Stalin's borders, was replaced by a minister who "made the situation even worse and created a precipice between Poland and the émigré government," Stalin advised FDR.

Now, at Yalta, Stalin charged, the London government was sending agents into Poland to harass the Red Army as it moved through Poland, had killed 212 military men, attacked supply bases, and set up radio stations in violation of regulations. "We will support the government which gives us peace in the rear."

Roosevelt decided to give Churchill the last word before they broke up. The British and Soviet governments have different sources of information, said Churchill. He could not feel that the Lublin government represented more than one-third of the people, nor would it be maintained in power if the people were free to express their opinion. "The British government could not agree to recognizing the Lublin government of Poland," he concluded.

FDR had begun the session, and Churchill had ended it, by telling Stalin that they would not recognize the Lublin government, but Stalin had made a powerful presentation.

It was 8:00 p.m. when the session adjourned. Each leader retired to his residence for the evening. Roosevelt had a quiet dinner with his daughter, Anna, Byrnes, Leahy, Harriman, Harriman's daughter Kathleen, Early, and Ed Flynn. Hopkins remained in his bedroom. Later FDR met with Bohlen to discuss a final draft of a message to Stalin about Poland that he wanted Stalin to read before the next day's plenary session. FDR had sent Hopkins and Stettinius to Paris, Rome, Naples, and London in late January to take the temperature of Europe, to make sure there were no surprises in store at Yalta, and to keep Churchill on message. In London, Hopkins had soothed Churchill's ruffled feathers over a variety of issues where FDR had overruled him. The United States and Britain were at loggerheads over Italy. Churchill wanted King Victor Emmanuel on the throne; Roosevelt didn't, writing to the prime minister, "The old gentleman, I am told, only clicks before lunch." They also differed on Count Carlo Sforza as Italy's foreign secretary. FDR's anticolonial stance also worried Churchill. And, the crowning blow, FDR had refused Churchill's request to spend more than one day at Malta.

While Hopkins calmed Churchill, Bohlen had met at the Polish embassy with Mikołajczyk, who proposed as a solution an interim governmental committee consisting of prominent Poles who had remained in Poland and prominent Poles who had fled. FDR liked the idea and set Stettinius, Bohlen, and Hopkins to refine the proposal so he could present it to Stalin as a finished idea. In their evening meeting Bohlen showed FDR the final draft:

> My dear Marshal Stalin: I want to tell you in all frankness what is on my mind . . . I am greatly disturbed that the three great powers do not have a meeting of minds about the political setup in Poland. It seems to me that it puts all of us in a bad light . . . to have you recognizing one government while we and the British are recognizing another . . . I am sure this state of affairs should not continue and that if it does it can only lead our people to think there is a breach between us, which is not the case. I am determined that there shall be no breach between ourselves and the Soviet Union. Surely there is a way to reconcile our differences.
>
> You must believe me when I tell you that our people at home look with a critical eye on what they consider a disagreement between us at this vital stage of the war. They, in effect, say that if we cannot get a meeting of minds now when our armies are converging on the common enemy, how can we get an understanding on even more vital things in the future . . .
>
> . . . We cannot recognize the Lublin government as now com-

posed . . . I suggest we invite here to Yalta at once Mr. Bierut and Mr. Osóbka-Morawski from the Lublin government and also two or three from the following list of Poles, which according to our information would be desirable as representative of the other elements of the Polish people in the development of a new temporary government which all three of us could recognize and support: Bishop Sapieha of Cracow, Vincente Witos, Mr. [Zygmunt] Zurowski, Professor [Franciszek] Buyak, and Professor [Stanisław] Kutzeba.

If to those were added Polish leaders from abroad such as Mr. Mikolajczyk, Mr. Grabski and Mr. Romer, the United States Government, and I feel sure the British Government as well, would then be prepared to examine with you conditions under which they would dissociate themselves from the London government and transfer their recognition to the new provisional government . . .

It goes without saying that any interim government which could be formed as a result of our conference with the Poles here would be pledged to the holding of free elections in Poland at the earliest possible date. I know this is completely consistent with your desire to see a new free and democratic Poland emerge from the welter of this war.

The letter was dispatched to Stalin.

WEDNESDAY, FEBRUARY 7

In the morning FDR worked over the latest White House mail, brought by a courier the previous evening. At noon he conferred with Hopkins, Harriman, Byrnes, and Bohlen in his study. He then lunched with his daughter, Ed Flynn, and Pa Watson.

Stettinius, Eden, and Molotov met at the Yusupov Palace. The army of landscape workers had done an incredible job bringing back the formal gardens to their original state. Stettinius remarked on their beauty, on the statues and pools. Then he and Eden and Molotov worked over the various issues they had been given by the plenary session.

FDR opened the plenary session a few minutes after 4:00 p.m., stating that in regard to the Polish question he did not attach any importance to the continuity or legality of any Polish government, because "there hasn't really been any Polish government since 1939. It is entirely in the province of the three of us," he said, "to help set up a government—something to last until the Polish people can choose." He then turned the meeting over to Molotov to give the summary of matters he, Eden, and Stettinius had worked on earlier at the Yusupov Palace.

Molotov stated that they had agreed that France would have a German zone of occupation, that he and Stettinius wanted the European Advisory Commission to decide whether France should participate in the Allied Control Commission, but that Eden disagreed, wanting France placed on the Allied Control Commission right away. Next, Molotov reported that it had been decided that a reparations commission consisting of a representative from each of the three allies be formed, that it work out a detailed plan, and that it be located in Moscow.

The conversation then returned to the previous day's discussion of the ramifications of giving France a zone in Germany. Churchill gave a long speech. He was "unconvinced" that the French could be given a zone without becoming a member of the Allied Control Commission; such a situation "would cause endless trouble. If we were strict in our zones, they might be lenient in theirs, and vice versa." French participation wouldn't mean they could attend a conference such as Yalta, he continued. Churchill forcefully said that the matter of whether the French should be part of the Allied Control Commission should be settled before the conference ended. FDR, trying to avoid conflict, spoke of postponing the decision for two or three weeks instead of two or three days, but Churchill pointed out that once they separated, a decision would be more difficult.

Stalin backed FDR. The three governments had been able to settle a good many things by correspondence, he said. FDR then said he agreed with Stalin that France should not join the foreign ministers.

Then the president suggested they talk further about Poland. Stalin stated that he had received FDR's message suggesting that they invite two representatives from the Lublin government and two representatives from other Polish groups to Yalta and work out with them the holding of free elections in Poland. He said he had tried to reach the Lublin Poles by telephone and was not successful. As for the others, Witos and Sapieha, he doubted they could be located in time to come to Yalta. Because, he continued, Molotov was working on some proposals that appeared to approach the president's suggestions, but they had not yet been typed out, he suggested that Molotov give the Soviet view on Dumbarton Oaks, knowing full well that what Molotov was going to report would make FDR very happy.

Molotov thereupon announced that subsequent to Stettinius's explanations of the president's proposals, and Churchill's remarks, the Soviet government now felt that these proposals fully guaranteed the unity of the great powers in the matter of preservation of peace. They were entirely acceptable: there was full agreement on the subject. They accepted the veto in the Security Council.

The convoluted announcement that Stalin had agreed to the veto meant the moment had finally come to call for the convening of a conference to set up the United Nations.

However, following this extremely welcome news, Molotov continued with the unwelcome news that the Soviet Union wanted the admission of the Ukraine, White Russia, and Lithuania as members of the General Assembly.

Without giving FDR a chance to speak about the issue of the veto, Molotov continued his argument regarding extra votes for the Soviet Union, launching into a discussion of the dominions of the British Commonwealth that had gradually and patiently achieved their places as entities in international affairs. It was only right, therefore, that three, or at least two, of these Soviet republics find a worthy place among the members of the assembly. He repeated that he fully agreed with the president's proposals and withdrew any objections or amendments but would request that at least two of the Soviet republics be given a chance to become equal members of the world organization.

FDR wrote a note that he passed to Stettinius: "This is not good."

FDR thereupon made the longest speech he had made at the conference. Stalin had just given him an unexpected gift, a great gift, he said, in agreeing to accept that a veto in the Security Council could not be invoked as regards the agenda. As he thought through his response, he touched on the various ramifications of such an action. He started by saying that acceptance of the voting formula was a great step forward. The next step was summoning a conference to set up the United Nations, possibly at the end of March, or possibly within the next four weeks. Then, comparing the different governmental structures of Britain, America, and Russia, he said that Molotov's suggestion should be studied, particularly in the light of the possibility that if the larger nations were given more than one vote, it might prejudice the thesis of one vote for each member. He touched on Brazil, larger than America but smaller in population, Honduras and Haiti, small in area but large in population. He then brought up other countries associated with the United Nations that had broken relations with Germany but were not at war. The important thing, he felt, was to proceed with plans for a conference and at the conference consider the question of nations not members of the United Nations. The foreign ministers should work it out.

However, Churchill now proceeded to undermine the president, exhibiting his antagonism to a world government to preserve peace, in a statement that also exposed his basic racism: Great Britain, he said, could not agree to any organization that would reduce the status of the dominions or exclude them from participation. His heart went out to mighty Russia, and he could understand its point of view, as it was represented by one voice in comparison with the British organization, which had a smaller population, if only white people were considered. But, he said, he could not exceed his authority, and as he had just heard this proposal, he would like to discuss it with the foreign secretary and possibly communicate it to London.

Roosevelt, momentarily at a loss for words, said his recommendations were somewhat different: he had merely meant that the foreign ministers should study the proposal, as well as the time and place, and decide who should be invited.

Churchill attacked again. He was against holding a meeting so soon, he said: he foresaw difficulties in a March meeting; the battle would be at its height; he doubted whether representatives would be able to give it full thought. He was as negative as he diplomatically could be. (Eden would later write that Churchill had spoken up against the proposed conference at the foreign ministers' meeting earlier in the day.)

FDR calmly replied that he had only in mind an organizational meeting; the world organization itself would probably not come into being for from three to six months after the conference.

Churchill again argued against the idea, on the grounds that some nations would still be under the German yoke, represented by governments in exile; other countries were starving and in misery, such as Holland; other countries had not suffered at all in the war. How could such a gathering really undertake the immense task of the future organization of the world?

Because Churchill's opposition was so strong and so unexpected, while he talked, Hopkins scrawled a hasty, ungrammatical note to FDR saying, "All of the below refers to Churchill's opposition to early calling of conference of United Nations. There is something behind this talk that we do not know of its basis. Perhaps we better to wait till later tonight what is on his mind." FDR scrawled back, "All this is rot! local politics." Hopkins then wrote, "I am quite sure now he is thinking about the next election in Britain."

FDR thereupon, in his low-key way, keeping control, contented himself with repeating his proposal having to do with the basic formation of the United Nations Conference: the foreign ministers should consider the Soviet proposal regarding membership, the date and place of the conference, and what nations should be invited.

Churchill, saying he must emphasize that it was not a technical matter but a matter of great decision, agreed reluctantly.

Stalin, who for a change had been on the sidelines because the debate was between FDR and Churchill, now supported FDR, remarking that the foreign ministers would *not* make decisions but merely report back on the conference.

It was time for a short intermission for light refreshments—which probably all three needed.

When they reconvened, Churchill proposed that the foreign ministers consider the question of Iran. Roosevelt made a short speech about Iran and what he had seen there during the Tehran Conference and then, having said his piece, gave the floor to Molotov for his proposals on the Polish question.

Molotov then read the Soviet position:

1. The Curzon Line should be the eastern frontier with a digression in some regions of five to eight kilometers in favor of Poland.
2. The western frontier should extend from Stettin and farther to the south along the river Oder and then the river Neisse.
3. Some democratic leaders from Polish émigré circles should be added to the Polish Provisional Government.

4. The enlarged Polish Provisional Government should be recognized by the Allies.
5. The Polish Provisional Government should call the population of Poland to the polls for organization by general voting.
6. Molotov, Harriman, and Clark Kerr were entrusted with the
   discussion of the question of enlarging the Polish Provisional
   Government and submitting their proposals to the consideration of the three governments.

Molotov then said that they had been unable to reach the Poles in
Poland by telephone: time would not permit summoning them to the
Crimea as the president wished.

Roosevelt said he felt progress had been made but that he didn't
like the word "émigré" in the proposal, on the grounds that you could
find enough Poles in Poland for the purpose. He repeated that he didn't
know any of the London Poles except Mikołajczyk: he asked for an
opportunity to study Molotov's proposals with Stettinius. Stalin agreed.

As Churchill began to speak, FDR scribbled to Stettinius, "Now
we are in for 1/2 hour of it." Building on FDR's objection to "émigré,"
Churchill said he shared the president's dislike of the word, but for him
it meant a person driven out of a country—he didn't like to use it. He
then evinced worry over moving Polish frontiers too far to the west,
saying that it would be a pity to stuff the Polish goose so full of German
food that it got indigestion. Stalin remarked, wryly, that most Germans
had already run away. Churchill then announced that he had another
comment: a reference in Molotov's proposal should be made to other
democratic leaders from within Poland itself. Stalin agreed, and the
words "and from inside Poland" were added to the end of paragraph 3.
The meeting adjourned.

FDR dined at 8:30 at Livadia with his daughter, Anna, Harriman,
Kathleen Harriman, Byrnes, Leahy, and Stettinius. Later, privately, he
explained to Stettinius that he believed Stalin felt a vote for the Ukraine
in the General Assembly was essential because his position in the
Ukraine was difficult and insecure. He also explained his own reasoning: the most important things were to maintain unity, defeat Germany,
"and then get them all around a table to work out a world organization." He closed by reminding Stettinius that the real power was in
the Security Council and each country in that body had only one vote.

After all, what practical difference would it make to the success or failure of the assembly for the Soviet Union to have two additional seats?

Much later, when FDR had retired, Stettinius, mulling over where the April 25 conference should be, turned over in his mind Chicago, Cincinnati, Hot Springs, and Miami. But when he presented his ideas to FDR the next day, "none of these places quite clicked in Roosevelt's mind . . . He asked me to study the matter further, come up with a better suggestion, saying, . . . 'We haven't hit it yet.'"

THURSDAY, FEBRUARY 8

FDR had a late morning meeting with Harriman, Bohlen, Hopkins, and Byrnes and lunched alone with Anna in his study. Later in the afternoon he was scheduled to meet privately with Stalin.

The matter of the Soviet Union having three votes in the General Assembly now took an unexpected turn. Stettinius was in FDR's study in the afternoon, briefing him on what had taken place at the foreign ministers' meeting earlier in the day. He had found himself, he told FDR, odd man out in opposing the idea, because Eden, wanting seats for the dominions and India, had backed Molotov's position of seating the Ukraine and White Russia. FDR said, "Somehow or other we would now have to accept the proposal." Stettinius, not entirely agreeing, was in the process of telling FDR that he had not backed down, the matter was not yet settled, when, at 3:45, Stalin walked in. "We have had good agreement at the Foreign Minister's meeting," the secretary of state had just finished saying to FDR, as Stalin arrived. Stalin immediately inquired whether there had been agreement on the extra seats question. Then, according to Stettinius, FDR "waved his hand and told Stalin that agreement had been reached on *everything*." Stalin asked, "Even on the extra votes?" Before Stettinius could answer, FDR said yes. Stettinius blamed himself for the confusion: *he* had not been quick enough on his feet. But his hands were tied; the deed was done. He left.

THE PURPOSE OF THE MEETING with Stalin was to discuss Soviet entry into the war against Japan. Present were Harriman, who had worked with Stalin on the various details since the previous October, Bohlen, Molotov, and Pavlov.

Roosevelt opened the meeting by saying that with the fall of Manila, the time had come to establish new air bases and begin intensively bombing Japan, thereby possibly avoiding the actual invasion of the Japanese islands, thus saving American lives.

Before the meeting, the Joint Chiefs had sent a memo under FDR's name asking Stalin two questions: "Is it essential that a supply line be kept open across the Pacific to Eastern Siberia? Will U.S. bases be permitted to operate from Komsomolsk-Nikolaevsk or some other suitable area in the Maritime Province?"

Stalin now replied that he had no objection to bases at Komsomolsk and Nikolaevsk, but Kamchatka would have to be left to a later stage in view of the presence there of a Japanese consul. FDR then handed two more memos to Stalin, one having to do with American use of airfields in the vicinity of Budapest, the other a request for U.S. experts to view bombing damage in enemy territory now held by the Red Army. Stalin said he would give the necessary orders.

The intrusion of U.S. personnel in Red Army vicinities was one of the least desirable requests from the Soviet point of view: it automatically raised Russian hackles. Stalin could not refuse FDR's request, but he could, and did, immediately ask for a quid pro quo: "Mr. Stettinius had told Mr. Molotov there was a possibility that the United States would have surplus shipping property after the war which might be sold to the Soviet Union."

FDR replied that a change of legislation would be necessary but that he hoped surplus shipping could be transferred on credit without any interest. He then added a sweetener: the ships could be transferred for a fixed sum on credit that would include the cost of the ship less depreciation; in twenty years the entire credit would be extinguished. FDR said, further, that he hoped the Soviet Union would interest itself in a large way in the shipping game.

Stalin, not surprisingly, thought the idea was a very good one, that it would ease the task of the Soviet Union in the future, and volunteered the thought that Lend-Lease was a remarkable invention, that in former wars some allies had subsidized others but this had offended the allies receiving the subsidies. Lend-Lease, however, produced no such resentment, and he called it an extraordinary contribution.

FDR, pleased, answered that he had dreamed up the idea while cruising on the *Potomac:* he had thought and thought of a way to help the Allies and at the same time avoid the difficulties inherent in loans and had finally hit upon the scheme.

With FDR in such a generous mood, Stalin took the occasion to name his price: the political conditions under which the U.S.S.R. would enter the war against Japan.

All Americans, not just the U.S. military, were horrified by the bloody viciousness and fanaticism of the Japanese they had witnessed during the winter. When U.S. forces invaded Tarawa in the Gilbert Islands, they were attacked by 2,563 Japanese soldiers who all, except for eight taken prisoner, fought to the death. It was the same story with the Japanese soldiers defending the Marshalls and Kwajalein: Japanese soldiers were choosing to fight to the death rather than surrender; their death rate was averaging more than 98 percent, which meant huge U.S. fatalities. But it was when U.S. troops landed on Saipan, the largest island in the Marianas, where there were twenty thousand Japanese civilians, that America learned that Japanese civilians were as fanatic as their soldiers. U.S. troops could only watch as mothers, gripping their children's hands, fathers throwing their children before them, leaped off the cliffs into the sea rather than surrender. The intense battle over Saipan, particularly, made Americans dread the upcoming U.S. invasion of the home islands, knowing Japan would fight to the last man, in the process killing as many Americans as they could, which meant U.S. casualty rates were going to be huge. General MacArthur estimated that a million Americans would die in just the first phase, the invasion of Kyushu, the southernmost island, planned for November 1. D-day would be a picnic compared with the invasion of Japan. The desire for Russian help became intense for the obvious reason that if the Red Army entered the war, fewer American soldiers would die. The Joint Chiefs of Staff, as well as Marshall and Leahy individually, therefore, for the better part of a year, had been strongly advising Roosevelt that Soviet entry into the war against Japan was an absolute necessity. The memos kept coming across his desk. "We should make every effort to get Russia into the Japanese war before we go into Japan, otherwise we will take the impact of the Jap divisions and reap the losses, while the Russians in due time advance into an area free of major resistance," advised MacArthur. "I will not consider going into any part of the Japanese islands unless the Japanese armies in Manchuria are contained by the Russians." Two weeks before Yalta, an official memo came from the Joint Chiefs: "The Chiefs of Staff suggest that Marshal Stalin be asked that necessary administrative steps be taken to make collaboration between the U.S. and U.S.S.R. work more efficiently and rapidly and that he also be asked to state what inefficiencies and delays his own people have experienced in working with the U.S." Five days later the Joint Chiefs underlined the urgency to FDR with another memo: they were "working towards the U.S.S.R. entry into the war against Japan . . . Russia's entry at as early a date as possible consistent with her ability to engage in offensive operations is necessary to provide maximum assistance to our Pacific operations."

Another memo specified exactly what FDR should tell Stalin at Yalta:

a.   We desire Russian entry at the earliest possible date consistent with her ability to engage in offensive operations.
b.   We consider that the mission of Russian Far Eastern Forces
should be to conduct an all-out offensive against Manchuria
to force the commitment of Japanese forces and resources
in North China and Manchuria that might otherwise be
employed in the defense of Japan.

Japan was Russia's historic enemy. Stalin had introduced William Bullitt, America's first ambassador to the Soviet Union, to Marshal Alexander Egorov, Soviet chief of staff, in 1934 as "the man who will lead our Army victoriously against Japan when Japan attacks." The only time Stalin was ever seen drunk was when, ecstatically relieved, he was packing off the Japanese foreign minister at the train station after negotiating the Japanese-Soviet Nonaggression Pact of April 13, 1941.

Gaining back what Russia had lost to the Japanese in the Treaty of Portsmouth was now his goal. He knew that earlier in the year Roosevelt had publicly announced to the Pacific War Council, the gathering of ambassadors and heads of state of nations fighting Japan in the Pacific, exactly what he was going to give Russia:

Japan should be stripped of their island possessions . . . that Russia, having no ice-free port in Siberia, is desirous of getting one and that Marshal Stalin looks with favor on making Dairen a free port for all the world, with the idea that Siberian exports and imports could be sent through the port of Dairen and carried to Siberian territory over the Manchurian railroad in bond. He agrees that the Manchurian Railway should become the property of the Chinese government. He wishes all of Sakhalin to be returned to Russia and to have the Kurile Islands turned over to Russia in order that they may control the straits to Siberia.

The Kuriles were the connecting chain of forty-seven islands extending from Hokkaido, Japan, in the south, to the Russian peninsula of Kamchatka, in the north. Russia had ceded the Kuriles to Japan in 1875; the islands controlled passage into the Sea of Okhotsk and Russia's eastern shoreline.

Complementary motives governed the conversation between the two leaders: the U.S. desire to assure Russian entry into the Japanese war to save American lives; the Soviet Union's desire to regain the territory Japan had taken away from it in 1905, plus the Kurile Islands, and, equally important, to be party to the destruction of Japan's dreams of empire. Japan's acquiescence in this rearrangement of its possessions was considered irrelevant by both parties: Roosevelt, alone, had the power to draw boundaries because it was necessary to the U.S. war effort to bring the Soviet Union into the war; the Senate would not see it in the same light as drawing Poland's boundaries after the Red Army had liberated Poland.

U.S. war plans called for an American invasion of Japan in November. That meant, given the logistics involved, Roosevelt and Stalin had to come to an agreement immediately. In fact, Roosevelt and Stalin had been working on the assumption that Russia would enter the war since Tehran; for months massive amounts of U.S. Lend-Lease material had been secretly moving across Siberia to arm the Soviet forces that would face the Kwantung army.

The question for Roosevelt was, would Stalin settle for the return of what Russia had lost to Japan in the Treaty of Portsmouth, or would he seriously push for the Kurile Islands, which were without a doubt choice real estate? The U.S. Navy was eyeing them, intrigued with the idea of establishing a base in the islands, possibly under the aegis of the United Nations, although it is not clear whether FDR had been apprised of this.

Roosevelt had told the Pacific War Council that Stalin wished to have all of Sakhalin and the Kurile Islands, but he hadn't said he agreed that Stalin should have them. But on the other hand, why should Japan? The massacre at Palawan six weeks earlier was fresh in American minds: in that appalling incident the Japanese had marched 150 American POWs—soldiers—into a trench on the Philippine island, poured gasoline into it, and incinerated the men: one had escaped to tell the tale.

Soviet spies had obtained and Stalin had read a State Department memo recommending that neither the southern part of Sakhalin nor the southern part of the Kurile Islands be ceded to Russia. The memo must have raised the level of Stalin's concern: he had no idea if it had influenced FDR, or if, indeed, FDR had even seen it. Stalin knew what he wanted; he had no assurance he would get it. Probably FDR was not sure himself.

Why *should* Russia enter the war? It had to be offered a valuable carrot. Stalin knew beyond a doubt that America was stronger than Japan and that it was now simply a matter of time and planning before U.S. forces invaded the Japanese home islands. It wasn't a matter of necessity that made getting Russia into the war so important to U.S. war planners and to FDR: it was a matter of lessening the number of Americans who would die in the process. The atomic bomb was not yet ready and therefore could not be counted upon. The matter came down to enlisting Russian fighting forces to spare American lives.

There were several reasons for Stalin to enter the war: for territorial gain and for the prospect of future aid, reparations, and peaceful relations with America. Both men had need of each other.

Now, as they talked, was Stalin's moment of truth. He said he and Ambassador Harriman had already conversed about the political conditions under which he would agree to enter the war. Roosevelt, of course, knew every word they had spoken at their meeting in the Kremlin on December 14. He had, in fact, ordered Harriman to meet with Stalin to find out what, exactly, *was* his price, and it had been relayed to him. As Stalin and Harriman had talked, Stalin had gone into the next room, brought out a map, and said to Harriman, "The Kurile Islands and Lower Sakhalin should be returned to Russia." Then Stalin had drawn a line around the southern part of the Liaodong Peninsula, including Port Arthur and Dairen, and told Harriman, "The Russians wished again to lease these ports and the surrounding area . . . wished to lease the

Chinese-Eastern Railway [in Manchuria] . . . he specifically reaffirmed his intention not to interfere with the sovereignty of China in Manchuria." It was with relief that FDR had learned that Stalin had no designs on Mongolia, that he wanted Mongolia to remain "an independent entity." FDR had had seven weeks to think about it.

Roosevelt held no brief for Japan. Why should he? On balance, as the aggressor, Japan deserved to lose land, as did Germany. Without preamble, FDR gave Stalin his answer, saying he had received a report of this conversation: there would be no difficulty whatsoever with the southern half of Sakhalin and the Kurile Islands going to Russia; in regard to a warm-water port in the Far East, they had discussed that point at Tehran, and he had then suggested that the Soviet Union be given the use of a warm-water port at possibly Dairen. He went on to say that either Russia could outright lease Dairen from the Chinese, or Dairen could be a free port under some form of international commission. He added that he preferred the latter method because of Hong Kong: he hoped the British would give back the sovereignty of Hong Kong to China and that it would become an internationalized free port. He said he knew Churchill would have strong objections to this suggestion.

Stalin, not rising to the bait, brought up the Manchurian railways; he wanted the rail lines the tsars had had. FDR replied that there were two ways of achieving that: to lease them, or to create a commission composed of one Chinese and one Russian.

Stalin wanted every *i* dotted, every *t* crossed. "It is clear that if these conditions are not met it would be difficult to explain to the Soviet people why Russia was entering the war against Japan. They understood clearly the war against Germany, which had threatened the very existence of the Soviet Union. But they would not understand why Russia would enter a war against a country with which they had no trouble." Roosevelt replied that he had not yet spoken about this to Chiang Kai-shek because anything said to the Chinese was known to the whole world in twenty-four hours. Stalin replied that it wasn't necessary to speak with the Chinese yet. Then, changing the subject, he said, "It would be well to leave here with these conditions set forth in writing agreed to by the three powers." FDR agreed. Stalin suggested that it wouldn't be time to speak to the Chinese until twenty-five Soviet divisions could be freed from Europe and moved to the Far East. He ended with the comment that in regard to the question of a warm-water port, the Russians would not be difficult, and he would not object to an internationalized free port.

In the space of a few minutes the two had come to an understanding.

Roosevelt thereupon moved the conversation to the subject of Korea. He "had in mind" that Soviet, American, and Chinese representatives should form a trusteeship and based on the Philippines, which it had taken about fifty years to prepare for self-government, that the Korean trusteeship might be for a period of twenty to thirty years. Stalin replied that the shorter the period, the better. FDR, in his continuing campaign to distance himself from British policy, then slyly brought up what he called a delicate matter: he did not feel it was necessary to invite the British to participate in the Korean trusteeship, "but he felt they might resent this." Stalin replied, in another light moment, that they would most certainly be offended. "In fact," he said, "the Prime Minister might kill us." The British should be invited.

FDR then brought up Indochina. He also had in mind a trusteeship for it, although he knew again that the British did not approve, as it might affect Burma, part of the British Empire. FDR described the Indochinese as "people of small stature, like the Javanese and Burmese . . . not warlike." He then repeated a thought he had voiced many times over many years: "France had done nothing to improve the natives since she had the colony."

FDR next touched on de Gaulle, whom both disliked. He told Stalin that de Gaulle had asked him for ships to transport French troops to Indochina. "Where was De Gaulle going to get the troops?" Stalin asked. De Gaulle said he was going to find the troops when he could find the ships, replied FDR, and then added in another light moment, "up to the present I have been unable to find the ships."

FDR then spoke of China: "For some time we had been trying to keep China alive." Stalin dryly replied that in his opinion China would remain alive. He did say, however, that there needed to be some new leaders around Chiang Kai-shek, that although there were some good people in the Kuomintang, he did not understand why they were not brought forward. FDR informed Stalin of steps he had taken: General Albert Wedemeyer and General Patrick Hurley, America's new ambassador, were "making progress in bringing the Communists in the north together with the Chungking government." He virtually agreed with Stalin about the lack of leadership: "The fault lay more with the

Kuomintang and the Chungking Government than with the so-called Communists." Stalin replied that he didn't understand why they didn't get together and present a united front against the Japanese. "Chiang Kai-shek should assume more leadership." Stalin was not that fond of either Chinese side, being no fonder of Mao Tse-tung than of Chiang. He occasionally called Chinese Communists "margarine Communists," according to Harriman's secretary, Robert Meiklejohn.

The conversation stopped. They had already run a bit over their time. From start to finish the meeting, each word of which was necessarily repeated by the interpreters, only took a little over half an hour. In that brief time the two leaders pretty well settled the Far East. Neither Molotov nor Harriman spoke a word, according to Bohlen's minutes.

When Admiral King, chief of naval operations, was informed that the Russians would definitely enter the fight against Japan, he was immeasurably relieved, commenting, "We've just saved two million Americans."

15

SETTLING ISSUES

At the foreign ministers' meeting at Vorontsov Palace that morning, at which Eden, the day's chair, presided, Stettinius had succeeded in convincing Eden and Molotov that FDR's desire that the conference on the world organization take place almost immediately—not later than the latter part of April—in America was sound and should be adopted.

The fifth plenary meeting began slightly late, at 4:15. FDR, delighted at the outcome of the foreign ministers' meeting, opened by congratulating the foreign ministers and asking Eden to give a report. Eden announced to the assemblage that following the wishes of the president, they had settled on Wednesday, April 25, as the date to convene the United Nations Conference, the meeting to take place in America. They had found membership a thorny issue: they recommended that only those nations that had signed the UN Declaration by the end of the Yalta Conference be invited, that when the conference convened, the members would then decide the list of original members; at that time the delegates of the U.K. and the United States would support the proposal to admit to original membership the two Soviet Socialist Republics.

Stalin raised a possible problem: ten states at the conference that would be original members had no diplomatic relationship with the Soviet Union. He found it somewhat strange for the Soviet Union to work with states that had no desire to have diplomatic relations with it to build a world security organization. What could be done?

FDR replied that most of these states wanted to have relations with the Soviet Union "but had just not gotten around to doing anything about it." There were a few, however, he admitted, where the influence of the Catholic Church was "very strong." (The Catholic Church was a thorn in FDR's side; official Catholic opposition to any Communist state was a threat that might turn the Catholic vote in America's eastern cities against FDR and his policies. FDR pointed out to Stalin that the Soviet Union had sat down with these states at Bretton Woods and UNRRA conferences. But Stalin protested that the new organization was different: at this conference they were to consider the vital question of the establishment of world security.

FDR then explained about the South American countries: Sumner Welles had told six of them that breaking diplomatic relations with the Axis was sufficient. Frankly, FDR said, it was a mistake on Welles's part in not advising them to declare war instead of merely breaking off diplomatic relations. He had sent letters to the presidents of the six countries urging them to declare war: Ecuador had just done so.

Stalin next brought up Argentina. "I am not for the Argentines," he said. "I do not like them; but I do desire there should be no logical contradiction; the nations which declared war would feel not quite at ease with those nations that have not declared war, who were trying to speculate on who would win and who generally were not straight in their behavior."

FDR replied that it was his idea to invite only those associated nations that have declared war. Stalin asked by what date. FDR replied, right away. Put a time limit on them.

"Say, the first of March."

"All right, the first of March."

There was then some discussion about countries such as Turkey and Egypt. Would they be acceptable if they declared war by March 1? The answer was yes.

FDR said that the matter of the Ukraine and White Russia should be presented to the conference and that all three had agreed to support it. Stalin worried that somehow membership for the Ukraine and White Russia would be blocked. He requested that the two republics sign the UN Declaration. Molotov asked if the two Soviet republics could become members of the assembly if they too signed by March 1.

Churchill supported the idea, mentioning "the martyrdom and suffer-
ings of the Ukraine and White Russia." FDR explained that it was a
technical question: they had been discussing new countries to add to
the list, but this was about giving a great power three votes instead
of one; it was a matter that should be put before the conference: all
three had agreed to support them. Stalin asked again if the Ukraine and
White Russia could sign the UN Declaration. FDR said a third time
that that would not overcome the difficulty. Stalin then said he would
withdraw his proposal.

During the morning FDR, who with his staff had worked over
Molotov's proposals regarding Poland, had sent a reworked proposal
to Eden and Molotov incorporating new elements. His proposals were
now close to those of Molotov, according to Roosevelt: he wanted
Molotov's comments.

FDR's proposal in essence was as follows:

1. There was no objection to point one, that the eastern boundary of Poland should be the Curzon Line with modifica-
   tions in favor of Poland in some areas of from five to eight
   kilometers.
2. No objection to the western frontier extending from Stettin up to the line of the Oder, but "there would appear to be
   little justification to the extension of the western boundary of
   Poland up to the Western Neisse River."
3. Concerning the future government of Poland it was proposed
   that Molotov, Harriman, and Clark Kerr be authorized to
   invite to Moscow Mr. Bierut, Mr. Osóbka-Morawski, Bishop
   Sapieha, Mr. Vincente Witos, Mr. Mikołajczyk, and Mr.
   Grabski to form a government along the following lines.
4. Three of the above, representing the Presidential Office of the
   Polish Republic, will undertake the formation of a government consisting of representative leaders from the present
   Polish Provisional Government in Warsaw, from other democratic elements inside Poland, and from Polish democratic
   leaders from abroad.
5. This interim government will pledge itself to the holding of
   free elections as soon as conditions permit for a constituent
   assembly to establish a new Polish constitution.

6. When a government is formed, the three governments will
    then proceed to accord it recognition as the Polish Provisional
    Government.

Molotov started with the last point: Would it mean that the London government would then disappear? Churchill answered yes. Stalin wanted to know what would happen then to the property and resources of the London government. Churchill assured him that withdrawal of recognition would take care of that. FDR agreed: the property would go to the new government.

A short recess was then declared, during which tea and coffee and light refreshments were served.

Molotov was the questioner upon resumption of the session. The proposals they made the day before had been based on certain realities, he said. The Soviet government had felt it would be useful to have discussions on the basis of enlarging the government, given that the Lublin, or Warsaw, government "stands at the head of the Polish people and enjoys great prestige and popularity . . . We might have some success if we start from the basis that the present government should be enlarged . . . The people who now compose the Polish Provisional Government have been closely connected with the great events of the liberation of Poland, but Messrs. Mikolajczyk, Grabski and Witos have not been." His observations, he said, applied not only to the question of a new government but also to the proposed presidential committee. Additional difficulty might result from the creation of a presidential committee because there already existed a national council, which of course could be enlarged.

In regard to the question of frontiers, Molotov was glad to note complete agreement on the eastern boundary, but on the western boundary there was no unanimity. The provisional government stood for the western frontier as outlined in the Soviet proposals.

Molotov did not exclude the possibility that some Poles from abroad could be involved, but he was not a bit sure about Mikołajczyk. The president had proposed five names; it would be a good idea to invite the three members of the provisional government (Bolesław Bierut, Edward Osóbka-Morawski, and General Michał Rola-Żymierski) and two from the president's list.

FDR asked whether Molotov meant that the presidential committee should be avoided.

Molotov answered that it would be better to avoid the presidential committee and enlarge the National Council and the provisional government. He and Harriman and Clark Kerr could discuss the question of how to enlarge the National Council and the provisional government with three representatives from the Polish Provisional Government and two persons from the president's list.

Churchill spoke eloquently. He noted that they were now at the crucial point of this great conference: "We would be found wanting by the world should we separate recognizing different Polish governments . . . If the British Government brushed aside the London government and went over to the Lublin government there would be an angry outcry in Great Britain . . . We had no special feeling for the Polish government in London, which in my opinion had been foolish at every stage . . . If they were to give up the London government it must be evident that a new start had been made on both sides from equal terms."

FDR said all were agreed on the necessity of free elections and that the only problem was how Poland was to be governed in the interval. Having phrased it this way, he was putting Stalin on notice that he expected the government they were wrestling over would be of short duration.

Stalin answered that he could assure the conference that the people running the government were popular. "The three leaders . . . had not fled from Poland but stayed on in Warsaw and had come from the underground . . . What puzzles the Polish people is that a great event—the liberation of their country by the Red Army has occurred . . . For many years the Poles had hated the Russians and with reason, since three times the Tsarist government had participated in the partitioning of Poland . . . The liberation of Poland had changed the attitude and old resentments had disappeared . . . The driving out of the Germans by the Red Army had been received by the Poles in the light of a great national holiday." Then, addressing himself to Churchill's concern, Stalin continued, "We have different information—the best method, therefore, would be to summon the Poles from different camps and to learn from them. Why could we not deal with an enlarged Polish government? It would be better to deal with the reconstruction of the Provisional Government rather than to attempt to set up a new one."

FDR asked how long it would be before elections could be held in Poland. Stalin replied it might be possible in a month provided no catastrophes occurred on the front and the Germans began to beat them. With that bit of welcome news, FDR ended the discussion, proposing that the matter be referred to the foreign ministers for study, and this was agreed to. The meeting adjourned at 7:40.

FDR had fifty minutes to rest and change before it was time to leave for the Yusupov Palace in Koreis, where Stalin was giving a dinner in his honor. Going with him were Stettinius, Leahy, Byrnes, Harriman, Flynn, Anna Boettiger, Kathleen Harriman, and Bohlen. When the party arrived at the Yusupov Palace, they found, to their surprise, among the guests, the British and Russian chiefs of staff. In spite of the absence (because of some failure of communication) of the American military, the evening was in many ways the high point of the conference.

The good camaraderie among them started almost immediately, remembered Stettinius: "As we were having vodka and caviar before going into dinner Molotov edged up to me and asked, 'We have agreed upon the date, where is the [UN] conference to be held?'" Stettinius had been working with FDR on finding a suitable place for the conference somewhere in America. Many cities had been considered and rejected for one reason or another. Stettinius had awakened the previous night at about 3:00 a.m. with the clear picture in his mind that San Francisco should be the venue: he had checked it out with FDR in the afternoon, but FDR had merely said, "It sounds most interesting." Now, remembered Stettinius,

> I crossed the room and leaned down to Mr. Roosevelt who was still in his little portable wheel chair, and said, "Molotov is pressing me for a decision as to a place for the conference. Are you ready to say San Francisco?" The president said, "Go ahead, Ed, San Francisco it is." I went back to Molotov and told him that Mr. Roosevelt had just approved the selection of San Francisco. Molotov beckoned to Eden and we stood in front of an open fire in the presence of Roosevelt, Churchill, and Stalin, and drank vodka in the Crimea to the success of the San Francisco conference to open April the 25th, just eleven weeks later.

Two huge tropical plants framed the entrance to the dining room, which was dominated by a great half-moon window set high in the wall. The dinner itself was epic. "Great quantities of food, thirty-eight standing toasts, and mosquitoes under the table," wrote Admiral Leahy ruefully in his diary. The dinner, which started at 9:00 p.m., consisted of twenty sumptuous courses, during which there were (according to another count) forty-five toasts.

Stalin was in an unusually happy, expansive mood. He was as host seated in the middle of the fifty-foot-long dinner table, with FDR on his right and Churchill on his left. Opposite were Molotov, Eden, and Stettinius.

Stalin led off with a toast to Churchill, toasting him as the bravest governmental figure in the world, who had carried on the fight when England stood alone: he knew of few examples in history where the courage of one man had been so important. He then toasted FDR, saying of him, even though his country was not directly imperiled, he had been the chief forger of the instruments that had led to the mobilization of the world against Hitler. FDR in his toast took the opportunity to reiterate his goal of a world at peace. He spoke of the atmosphere at the dinner as that of a family, that each of them was working in his own way for the interests of his people, that their objectives were to give every man, woman, and child on earth the possibility of security and well-being.

Harriman said afterward he'd never seen Stalin in such great form. "The Bear was at his most friendly," agreed Sarah Churchill. Kathleen Harriman, too, thought he really *was* terrific: "He enjoyed himself, was a splendid host and his speeches meant something more than the usual banalities." He even, at times, according to Kathleen, "just sat back and smiled like a benign old man, something I'd never thought possible." Furthermore, he kept leaping to his feet to talk, once calling himself a "garrulous old man." He teased Ambassador Gusev, mimicking his dour look, then wound up about him, "He is a gloomy old man, but sometimes gloomy men are more reliable than likeable ones."

"He toasted Churchill as the great leader who'd taken command when England was without fighting allies," recalled Kathleen. "His tribute to the President was harder to explain. Stalin talked about America miles from the war and her leader who prepared her for that war. He talked about allies in war and allies in peace and that allies deceived each other only if they thought they could get away with it. Deceiving was impossible among equals."

During the dinner FDR noticed Beria, who as the person in charge of security at the conference had not been present before at an event. "Who's that in the pince-nez opposite Ambassador Gromyko?" he asked Stalin.

"Ah, that one. That's our Himmler . . . That's Beria," replied Stalin loud enough so that, FDR noticed uncomfortably, Beria could hear him.

Stettinius remembered that during the dinner FDR suddenly had a coughing fit "and couldn't speak . . . It lasted a long time. Something due to nerves." Perhaps it happened following this comment by Stalin. At some point Stalin toasted the hardworking interpreters, "who worked while we were enjoying ourselves." Bohlen answered his toast with the rephrasing of a line from *The Communist Manifesto:* "Interpreters of the world, unite; you have nothing to lose but your bosses." Stalin absorbed the words, then laughed, got up from the table, went and clinked glasses with Bohlen, and congratulated him on his "wit."

A mark of Stalin's unusually benign mental outlook was his behavior toward FDR: he left his seat "quite regularly," one onlooker noticed, to pat the president on the back.

Stalin even waxed philosophical: "History has recorded many meetings of statesmen following a war. When the guns fall silent, the war seems to have made these leaders wise, and they tell each other they want to live in peace. But then, after a little while, despite all their mutual assurances, another war breaks out. Why is this? It is because some of them change their attitudes after they have achieved peace. We must try to see that doesn't happen to us in the future."

Roosevelt replied, "I agree with you entirely. The nations can only be grateful for your words. All they want is peace."

"We felt we were at the focus of history and that justice was standing by, scales in hand," recalled Gromyko.

Byrnes made a toast "to the people of our respective countries—the workers on farms and in factories—who did not wear the uniform but whose contribution made possible our victories." Stalin liked the toast so much he rose, went over to him, and, wrote Byrnes, "clinked his glass with mine in approval of the sentiment. The truth is, he is a very likeable person."

The dinner continued until 1:00 a.m. according to one account, until 2:00 a.m. according to another. It had been a long, ultimately fruitful day. After it Stalin undoubtedly met with his marshals to learn what was happening with the Red Army and issue new orders. FDR went home to bed.

FRIDAY, FEBRUARY 9

FDR began the day meeting with Stettinius to talk about Poland, instructing him to drop the idea of a presidential committee and present a compromise statement to the plenary session.

At 11:00 a.m., he and the American chiefs of staff together with Churchill and the British chiefs of staff met to hear the final report of the Joint Chiefs on the various theaters of war. Churchill expressed the opinion that Russia should join them in calling on Japan to surrender unconditionally: this might lead it to ask what mitigation could be extended if it accepted the ultimatum. FDR said he doubted whether this would have much effect on the Japanese, who still seemed to think they might get a satisfactory compromise and therefore "would be unlikely to wake up to the true state of affairs until all of their islands had felt the full weight of air attack." FDR and Churchill and Marshall agreed on the advantages of the Combined Chiefs of Staff, which had simplified the solution to the many problems until now, and agreed their military staffs should continue to collaborate.

Gromyko conferred with Stalin during the morning. FDR's staff had written up the Far East agreement the president and Stalin had worked out the previous afternoon: Stalin wanted Gromyko's translation. Gromyko produced it and gave it to Stalin. It had a marked effect on the premier, according to Gromyko: "Stalin was so pleased by Roosevelt's letter. Several times he walked across the room with it, as if he didn't want to let go of it, and he was still holding it when I left it."

FDR had invited Churchill to lunch, which was served, as usual, by the Filipino staff in FDR's dining room. The president, again desiring it to be a purely social lunch, this time invited all three daughters— Sarah Oliver, Anna Boettiger, and Kathleen Harriman—to dine with them, plus Leahy and Byrnes. There was casual conversation initiated by Byrnes who teasingly suggested giving Puerto Rico, Hawaii, and Alaska votes in the General Assembly.

The foreign ministers' meeting began at noon, also at Livadia. Stettinius, the presiding officer, opened the meeting by saying that after consideration he agreed with Molotov's position of the day before that the creation of a presidential commission should be dropped. Following through on FDR's directive to find common ground, he continued that the British "Provisional Government," the American "Government of National Unity," and the Soviet "Polish Provisional Government" agree that the new government should be composed of members of the present Polish Provisional Government, augmented with members of other democratic elements inside Poland and some Polish leaders from abroad.

Eden questioned the popularity of the Lublin government among the Polish people and defended the reputation and the presence of Mikołajczyk as reassuring to the British people. He touched on the 150,000 Poles fighting with the British army.

Molotov replied that the Russians wanted to hold general elections as soon as practical, and that would do away with all the difficulties. Stalin had said the provisional period would be perhaps one month, the prime minister had mentioned two. However, right now the question was the rear of the Red Army; there were obstacles in the rear. An impossible situation might arise, which was why he had suggested reorganization be on the basis of the present Lublin government with the democratic elements from within and without the country added. As far as Mikołajczyk, the Poles themselves must decide.

Eden said if the Lublin government controlled the elections, they would not be free; Stettinius stated he supported Eden's views in full. Molotov then, after reading the translation of the American proposal, said he had to consult Stalin. Eden and Molotov continued to argue about a Lublin government as opposed to a more fully representative government.

Stettinius suggested that unless the foreign ministers could get away from the words "existing Polish government," no agreement could be reached. Because they were deadlocked on the issue and further argument appeared fruitless, Stettinius suggested that they report to the plenary session just that state of affairs: that they had not reached an agreement.

They then discussed the principles governing reparations. Maisky suggested that the Moscow Commission accept the total of $20 million as a basis for its studies. Eden retorted that the prime minister was strongly against stating a figure.

Stettinius suggested that while not mentioning a sum, they could merely state that 50 percent of the total sum would go to the Soviet Union: Molotov did not object.

THE AMERICAN AND SOVIET chiefs of staff were also meeting at Livadia. They had one topic: coordinating the upcoming Russian and American invasion of the Japanese home islands. They set to it, in contrast with the foreign ministers' meeting, with a singleness of purpose.

General Antonov explained that he had only minor changes to make in the plans that he had worked out with Harriman and Deane in October in Moscow. He went over a list of Soviet needs, plans, and answers to American questions:

a. The main change he had to report was that some units that were supposed to be already moving to the Far East were still in the center of the line on the Russian front and so were behind schedule.

b. Specific supply routes—sea and air—needed to be worked out for food and petroleum after the outbreak of hostilities.

c. The U.S. Air Force could begin operating in the Komsomolsk-Nikolaevsk area without delay.

d. U.S. assistance for the defense of Kamchatka was desired: it was a great distance from the bulk of Soviet military strength.

e. Pre-hostility preparations, including construction and storage of U.S. stockpiles in eastern Siberia, were being prepared for U.S. air units.

f. A survey party from Fairbanks to Kamchatka, being so visible to the Japanese, had to wait until the last moment.

g. The Soviets will take southern Sakhalin unassisted by the U.S. forces. It would be one of their first operations. They would open the Strait of La Pérouse.

h. General Antonov assured General Marshall that combined planning between the two armies "will proceed vigorously."

i. The U.S. request for additional weather stations had been approved.

In reply to a question from General Marshall, General Antonov stated that the Soviets were already shipping supplies, fuel, and such: upon completion of hostilities in Germany the shipments would accelerate. Marshall then asked how many divisions per week could be moved from the German to the Japanese front. Antonov replied that a three-month period was required. As they adjourned, they all expressed pleasure "at the free, frank, clear, and definite interchange of information between the Russian and the American military staffs."

The sixth plenary meeting convened at 4:00 p.m.

FDR opened the meeting by asking Stettinius to report on the foreign ministers' meeting. Stettinius stated that the American idea of creating a Polish presidential committee had been dropped, that Molotov was presenting certain new American considerations to Marshal Stalin, and that the three foreign ministers thus far had not reached agreement on the matter.

Molotov stated that they were eager to come to an agreement; he suggested that the first sentence of Stettinius's proposal be changed. It had read:

> The present Polish Provisional Government be reorganized into a fully representative government based on all democratic forces in Poland and including democratic leaders from Poland abroad, to be termed the Provisional Government of National Unity.

Molotov suggested:

> The present Provisional Government of Poland should be reorganized on a wider democratic basis with the inclusion of democratic leaders from Poland itself and from those living abroad, and in this connection this government would be called the National Provisional Government of Poland.

He also suggested that the sentences dealing with the three ambassadors observing and reporting on the elections be eliminated on the grounds that it would be offensive to the Polish people.

Churchill cautioned FDR not to hurry the decision on Poland, that hurried decisions were a great mistake.

FDR then proposed that Stettinius finish his report and they then adjourn for half an hour in order to study Molotov's changes. Stettinius proceeded to summarize the discussion on reparations. Then he wound up with a matter he said had so far been overlooked: at Dumbarton Oaks it had been decided that the five governments with permanent seats on the Security Council should consult with each other as to the establishment of trusteeships and dependent areas. Hearing the words "trusteeships" and "dependent areas," Churchill suddenly interrupted and, in a tantrum that was so amazing that James Byrnes, who took shorthand, included it in his book *Speaking Frankly,* said, "I absolutely disagree. I will not have one scrap of British territory flung into that area. After we have done our best to fight in this war and have done no crime to anyone I will have no suggestion that the British Empire be put into the dock and examined by everybody to see whether it is up to their standard."

He closed, according to Hopkins, with words to the effect that he would never consent under any circumstances to the United Nations' thrusting interfering fingers into the very life of the British Empire, and he kept muttering, "Never. Never. Never."

Churchill's outburst so amused Stalin that he rose from his chair, walked up and down beaming, and, at intervals, broke into applause. FDR tried to stop the prime minister. "I want Mr. Stettinius to finish the sentence he was reading," he said. Churchill began to calm down after Stettinius said that the subject was in reference not to the British Empire but to the Japanese mandated islands in the Pacific. But, still not entirely calm, he suddenly demanded of Stalin how *he* would feel if the suggestion was made that the Crimea should be internationalized for use as a summer resort. Stalin smugly replied he would be glad to give the Crimea as a meeting place for the three powers.

A brief adjournment was called, during which coffee and tea and light refreshments, as usual, were served.

When the meeting resumed, FDR applied himself to the task of finding common ground on which they could all come together. He said,

> I find that it is now largely a question of etymology. We are nearer than we have ever been before. I believe there is a chance of real agreement to settle this question of the period before the Poles can hold their elections. I suggest that the words [of Molotov's

amendment] be changed to The Polish Provisional Government now functioning in Poland. Mr. Molotov proposes the elimination of the last sentence. I suggest that some gesture be made to show that there will be an honest election . . . A little more work by the three foreign ministers tonight . . . might settle the question.

The genius of FDR, who knew that they both relied on him, was that his words forced them to see things *his* way: by saying they were close to agreement, he made them see the areas of agreement rather than the areas of disagreement.

There followed a long conversation between Churchill and Stalin. Churchill said he knew there were bitter feelings among the Poles and fierce language had been used by Osóbka-Morawski in regard to the London government and that he understood the Lublin government had declared its intention to try as traitors the members of the Polish Home Army. He said these reports caused great anxiety and perplexity, and he wanted observers at the elections. Stalin said there were some very good people among the Poles, that they fight among themselves. He said something that would resonate much later: "Mikolajczyk is a representative of the Peasant Party. The Peasant Party is not Fascist and will take part in the elections. Those candidates will be allowed to stand."

FDR said he wanted to add a word: the elections were the crux of the matter; it was true, as Marshal Stalin said, that the Poles were quarrelsome; he wanted assurance for the six million Poles in America that the elections would be freely held.

At the beginning of the meeting the Declaration on Liberated Europe, originally drafted by the State Department and revised by Stettinius and FDR, approved by the foreign ministers at their morning meeting, had been distributed to the participants. It was a stirring document, invoking the Atlantic Charter—the right of all peoples to choose the form of government under which they will live.

Stalin now said that he had one small change to propose, which was an added sentence: "Support will be given to the political leaders in those countries who have taken an active part in the struggle against the German invaders."

FDR pointed out that the foregoing conversation was the first use of the declaration, in that it included the phrase "to create democratic

institutions of their own choice." And further, that the next paragraph
(3) contained the following statement: "to form interim governmental authorities broadly representative of all democratic elements in the
population and pledged to the earliest possible establishment through
free elections of governments responsive to the will of the people."

Stalin replied, "We accept paragraph three."

FDR now uttered his famous simile: "I want this election in Poland
to be the first one beyond question. It should be like Caesar's wife. I did
not know her but she was pure." Stalin immediately quipped, "They
said that about her but in fact she had her sins." Roosevelt did not rise
to the bait, instead answering, "I don't want the Poles to be able to question the Polish elections. The matter is not only one of principle but of
practical politics."

FDR proposed that they leave the final wording to the foreign ministers. But before they did, Stalin suggested another compromise in the
wording: delete the word "present" from "present Provisional Government," and say "the Polish government which acts in Poland."

Churchill, still smarting from the mention of trusteeships, agreed to
the declaration "as long as it was clearly understood that the reference
to the Atlantic Charter did not apply to the British Empire." By way
of explanation he said he had once been on record as interpreting the
Atlantic Charter (mistakenly) as affecting the British Empire and had
sent a copy of this interpretation to Wendell Willkie. Retorted FDR, to
laughter, "Was that what killed him?"

Molotov had the last word on Poland, with the suggestion that the
following phrase be added: "and there will be secured a wide measure of
support to the men in those countries who have taken active part in the
struggle against German occupation."

Churchill now suggested preparing lists of war criminals and discussing the holding of trials. FDR replied that he was not ready for this
question. After a few minutes, FDR called for adjournment.

FDR, CHURCHILL, AND STALIN retired to their respective quarters. FDR had a working dinner with General John E. Hull, the army's
top planner for the war in the Far East; General Kuter, who would command the Pacific Air Forces; Leahy; and Vice Admiral C. M. Cooke.

After dinner he worked on the White House mail that had arrived by courier during the plenary session. It would go out first thing the next morning.

The three foreign ministers, charged by FDR with resolving the unresolved issue of Poland, met at the Yusupov Palace at 10:30 p.m., Molotov presiding. Eden announced that his government would not approve Molotov's formula (as they now referred to the proposed statement), and Molotov objected to Eden's proposed formula. There was even argument as to whether they were discussing the American formula with amendments added or the prime minister's words: it was a lengthy but, Bohlen wrote, amicable discussion.

The following text was finally agreed on:

A new situation has been created by the complete liberation of Poland by the Red Army. This calls for the establishment of a provisional Polish government more broadly based than was possible before the recent liberation of western Poland. The provisional government now functioning in Poland should be reorganized on a broader democratic basis with the inclusion of democratic leaders from Poland itself and from those living abroad. This new government will then be called the Polish Provisional Government of National Unity. Mr. Molotov, Mr. Harriman, and Sir Archibald Clark Kerr, are authorized to consult in the first instance in Moscow with members of the present provisional government and with other democratic leaders from within Poland and from abroad with a view to the reorganization of the present government along the above lines. This Polish Provisional Government of National Unity would be pledged to the holding of free and unfettered elections as soon as practicable on the basis of universal suffrage and secret ballot. In these elections all democratic and anti-Nazi parties would have the right to take part and to put forth candidates.

When a Polish Provisional Government of National Unity has been properly formed in conformity with the above, the three governments will then accord it recognition.

However, in spite of Bohlen's writing for the record that it was an amicable discussion, it was not. Stettinius had proposed the addition of a further sentence: "The ambassadors of the three powers in Warsaw, following such recognition, would be charged with the responsibility of observing and reporting to their respective governments on the carrying out of the pledge in regard to free and unfettered elections." Molotov absolutely refused to include any variation of these words.

There was disagreement on another issue. Stettinius and Eden refused to accept Stalin's proposed addition of the following sentence to the draft Declaration on Liberated Europe: "Support will be given to the political leaders in those countries who have taken an active part in the struggle against the German invaders."

Both of these matters were referred to the next plenary session.

SATURDAY, FEBRUARY 10

In spite of all the disparate loose ends, FDR had a sense that it was time to wind up the conference. At their morning meeting, saying that he had already been away too long, had pressing problems back in Washington, and had made plans to see Ibn Saud, Haile Selassie, and King Farouk, FDR told Stettinius he had to leave the next day: he would tell Stalin and Churchill later in the day. Stettinius was not surprised.

FDR had already decided in early January that the conference should not extend past five or six days. As he had done at Tehran, he got his way not by announcing that it was time for the conference to end but by saying he was going to leave. A few days earlier he had warned Stettinius that he planned to leave possibly on February 9 or 10, certainly by February 11. As they spoke, Stettinius told FDR about the battle the previous evening with Molotov to insert words giving Harriman and Clark Kerr the right to observe the Polish election process. FDR replied, "If we agree to withdraw this sentence, it must clearly be understood that we fully expect our ambassador to observe and report on the elections. If the statement of this fact irritates the Russians, we can drop the statement, but they must understand our firm determination that the ambassadors will observe and report on the elections in any case."

Stettinius met with Eden and Molotov as usual at noon. It was Eden's turn to preside, therefore the meeting was at the Vorontsov Palace.

Stettinius stated that FDR was ready to withdraw the offending sentence "on the understanding that the president would be free to make any statement he felt necessary on Poland relative to his receiving information from his ambassador on the question." Eden stated that he did not wish to indicate that he approved of the withdrawal. Stettinius agreed and in his acknowledgment indicated that he thought FDR was wrong; he, too, "of course, preferred the document as it existed . . . The president was so anxious to reach agreement that he was willing to make this concession."

Molotov then announced he had several new amendments: "as soon as practicable" should be changed to "as soon as possible," certainly a minor change, but his next amendment was major. He wanted the end of the last paragraph changed to read, "The Governments of the United States of America and Great Britain will establish diplomatic relations with the Polish Government as has been done by the Soviet Union." Stettinius said he could not agree with the latter change, which would have put the Soviet Union in charge of *any* future Polish government. Eden also objected, stating the obvious: that it was most necessary that the three allies move together in recognizing the new government. Molotov then brought up again the issue of Poles' raising difficulties in the rear of the Red Army. As was the usual case, the matter was dropped, with the thought that it could be revisited later.

The Declaration on Liberated Europe was the next subject of discussion. Stettinius said he had discussed the Soviet amendment stating that "strong support will be given to those people in these countries who took an active part in the struggle against German occupation" with FDR, and the president would not accept it. Molotov then suggested a few minor word changes that Eden and Stettinius agreed to, following which Molotov agreed to drop his amendment regarding U.S. and British acceptance of the new Polish government following Russia's lead. The issue of reparations was next. Eden stated the case against taking too much from Germany: Britain did not want to finance and feed Germany at a later date as a result of reparations. Whether reparation payments should be for five or seven or ten years was discussed and again amounts.

FDR had lunch at Livadia with Anna, Kathleen Harriman, Leahy, Admiral Brown, and Byrnes, who was leaving immediately after lunch. Meanwhile, following the foreign ministers' conference, at 2:00 Harriman went to the Yusupov Palace, where he met with Molotov to work out the final terms for Russia's entry into the war in the Far East. Molotov handed him a paper outlining Stalin's demands, as he and FDR had discussed two days earlier:

1. *Status quo* in the Outer Mongolia should be preserved.
2. The former rights of Russia violated by the treacherous attack of Japan in 1904 should be restored viz:
   a) the southern part of Sakhalin as well as all the islands adjacent to this part of Sakhalin should be returned to the Soviet Union,
   b) possession of Port Arthur and Dairen on lease should be restored.
   c) the rights possessed by Russia before the Russo-Japanese war to the operation of the Chinese-Eastern Railroad and the South-Manchurian railroad providing an outlet to Dairen should be restored on the understanding that China should continue to possess full sovereignty in Manchuria;
3. The Kurile Islands should be handed over to the Soviet Union. The Heads of the three Great powers have agreed that these claims of the Soviet Union should be unquestionably satisfied after Japan has been defeated. For its part the Soviet Union expresses its willingness to conclude with the National Government of China a pact of friendship and alliance between the USSR and China in order to render assistance to China with its armed forces for the purpose of liberating China from the Japanese yoke.

FDR wanted the following changes made, Harriman informed Molotov: Port Arthur and Dairen should be free ports, and paragraph 2c should cover the alternative of the railways being operated by a Chinese-Soviet commission. In addition, Harriman said, FDR wanted the concurrence of "the Generalissimo," Chiang Kai-shek. The changes were (additions italicized):

   b) ~~possession~~ *lease of the port areas of* Port Arthur and Dairen ~~on lease~~ should be restored, *or these areas should become free ports under international control.*

c) Add the following after the word "Manchuria," at
the end of the paragraph "*or these railroads should be
placed under the operational control of a Chinese-Soviet
Commission.*"

Add final paragraph:

*It is understood that the agreement concerning the ports and
railways referred to above requires the concurrence of Generalissimo Chiang Kai-Shek.*

After checking the revised document, FDR told Harriman to resub-
mit it to Stalin, which Harriman did. The two leaders met at 4:30 in
FDR's study. At that time Stalin told FDR he was willing to have Dairen a free port, but that Port Arthur was to be a Russian naval base,
and therefore required a lease. FDR agreed to the change. Then Stalin conceded that it would be more appropriate for the Manchurian
Railroad to be operated by a Chinese-Soviet commission, agreed that
the generalissimo should be notified and his concurrence sought, and
stated he wished FDR (not himself) to seek this out from the generalissimo. FDR said he would send an army officer from Washington to Chungking carrying a letter of instruction to the American
ambassador to ensure secrecy, which was the main, indeed overriding
concern.

The final draft was drawn up to be read and signed the next day by
FDR, Stalin, and Churchill.

THE SEVENTH PLENARY SESSION in the grand ballroom was
scheduled to start a bit later than usual, at 4:50, on account of this
meeting. It actually started even later, because Stalin met briefly with
Churchill who urged him to accept the foreign ministers' compromise
wording on Polish elections. Roosevelt was as usual already seated at his
place at the great round table, with his back to the log fire burning in
the fireplace, when the two entered the room. Each, singly, went up to
FDR and apologized for being late.

FDR opened the meeting by asking Eden to give a report on the
progress achieved at the foreign ministers' meeting. Eden then read the
final version of the statement on Poland they had agreed upon. It basically reflected Western, rather than Eastern, terms: there had never been

a free, unfettered election on the basis of a secret ballot in the history of Eastern Europe.

> A new situation has been created by the complete liberation of Poland by the Red Army. This calls for the establishment of a Polish Provisional Government which can be more broadly based than was possible before the recent liberation of Western Poland. The Provisional Government which is now functioning in Poland should therefore be reorganized on a broader democratic basis with the inclusion of democratic leaders from Poland itself and from Poles abroad. This new Government will then be called the Polish Provisional Government of National Unity.
>
> Mr. Molotov, Mr. Harriman, and Sir A. Clark Kerr, are authorized to consult in the first instance in Moscow with members of the present Provisional Government and with other democratic leaders from within Poland and from abroad with a view to the reorganization of the present Government along the above lines. This Polish Provisional Government of National Unity shall be pledged to the holding of free and unfettered elections as soon as possible on the basis of universal suffrage and secret ballot. In these elections all democratic and anti-Nazi parties would have the right to take part and to put forth candidates.
>
> When a Polish Provisional Government of National Unity has been properly formed in conformity with the above, the Government of the USSR, which now maintains diplomatic relations with the present Provisional Government of Poland, and the Government of the United Kingdom and the Government of the U.S.A. will establish diplomatic relations with the new Polish Provisional Government of National Unity, and will exchange ambassadors by whose reports the respective Governments will be kept informed about the situation in Poland.

The hours of wrangling had produced a document that all could live with. For FDR and Churchill, there was the promise of free, unfettered elections and the reorganization of the Soviet-controlled government on a "broader and more democratic base"; for Stalin, there was the elimination of the official presence of Harriman and Clark Kerr when the voting would actually take place. In all ways it was an amazing document for Stalin to sign, reflecting, as it did, none of his values, only those of a truly democratic philosophy of government. Observed Churchill's doctor, Lord Moran, privy to all that transpired at Yalta, "One cannot help noticing Stalin's deference to the President's opinions . . . This frame of mind does not come naturally to Stalin. It must cost him great effort. What is behind it all?"

As they continued talking, Churchill observed that there was no mention of Polish boundaries in the document. FDR explained that he was reluctant to have a public declaration on this subject for a very good reason: he had no right to make an agreement on boundaries; that must be done by the Senate.

Molotov suggested they could say that the Curzon Line was generally representative of the opinion of all present and say nothing about the western frontier. But Churchill disagreed, saying they must say that Poland is to get compensation in the west; also that they must discuss it with the Polish government before the line was drawn. Molotov liked this, replying, "Very good."

The next subject Eden brought up was a minor matter, having to do with the Declaration on Liberated Europe: the exact wording of the penultimate paragraph. It was finally resolved as follows: ". . . shall consult together on the measures to discharge the joint responsibilities set forth in this declaration." Eden then asked for approval of the foreign ministers' proposal on France hammered out the previous evening: "In issuing this declaration the three powers express hope that the Provisional Government of France will associate itself with them."

At this point FDR entered the conversation. Stettinius, Freeman Matthews, who had been counselor at the American embassy at Vichy, Harriman, and Hopkins had all been championing Churchill's view to FDR that if France had a zone in Germany, it *had* to be on the Allied Control Commission. The unanimity of his advisers finally succeeded in convincing the president and finally overcame his antagonism to de Gaulle, whom he neither liked nor trusted. Now FDR abruptly said, "I have rather changed my opinion. I was opposed to France sitting in on the Commission of Three, the Control machinery. The more I think of it the more I think the prime minister's contention that a country which has an area to control cannot do so without sitting in on the Control Commission. I think it would be easier if France is on that Control Commission to get De Gaulle to agree to this Declaration and other things. I would like Stalin to think about it."

In fact, at the time FDR had changed *his* mind, he had notified Stalin, who had said that "since this was the president's considered decision he would go along with it."

Now Stalin said, simply, "I agree."

There was then a short discussion of the Yugoslav government that was in formation in which FDR did not take part.

The next big subject was reparations. Churchill had the first word, stating that his government had instructed him not to mention figures; FDR went along with his idea not to mention money. Stalin stated he wanted only a monetary expression of what goods cost, not money: monetary sums mentioned were only expressions of the value of reparations in kind. Roosevelt worried that people at home would *think* of reparations in terms of dollars and cents. Churchill replied that he didn't understand what was to be published. FDR answered that nothing was to be published.

These words do not do credit to the emotions exposed nor give the details of the arguments generated during what reads like a reasonable disagreement. Disagreement was intense, particularly between Churchill and Stalin, and the written record as given in *Foreign Relations of the United States* is incomplete. Recounted Hopkins, "Stalin rose and gripped the back of his chair with such force that his brown hands went white at the knuckles. He spat out his words as if they burnt his mouth. Great stretches of his country had been laid waste, he said, and the peasants put to the sword. Reparations should be paid to the countries that had suffered most. While he was speaking no one moved." Stettinius also noticed Stalin's unusual emotional state: "Stalin . . . spoke with great emotion, and even passion, in sharp contrast to his previous manner. On several occasions he arose, stepped behind his chair, and spoke from that position, gesturing to emphasize his point. The terrible German destruction in Russia obviously had moved him deeply. Although he did not orate or even raise his voice, he spoke with intensity." He wanted it spelled out not only that in principle Germany would pay reparations but that when the Reparations Commission met in Moscow it would take into consideration the U.S.-U.S.S.R. figure setting reparations at $20 billion, with the Soviet Union receiving fifty percent.

Churchill, objecting, read out a telegram from the British War Cabinet stating it was inadmissible to include any figure without further investigation, and the figure of $20 billion was too great.

During the discussion Hopkins advised FDR to support Stalin, passing him the following note: "The Russians have given in so much at this conference that I don't think we should let them down. Let the British disagree if they want to." FDR then suggested the matter be left to the Reparations Committee in Moscow.

In the face of Churchill's opposition and Roosevelt's refusal to be pinned down as to whether a figure should be mentioned, Stalin proposed the following formula: (1) that the heads of the Governments had agreed that Germany must pay compensation for the damages caused to the Allied nations as a result of the war, and (2) that the Moscow Commission be instructed to consider the amount of reparations.

Churchill agreed, and asked whether FDR did.

"The answer is simple," he replied. "Judge Roosevelt approves and the document is accepted."

As the conversation on reparations finally wound down, Stalin leaned over toward Gromyko and asked him for his opinion of FDR: "What should I make of Roosevelt? Does he really disagree with Churchill, or is it just a ploy?" Gromyko's answer shows how an intelligent person remained in Stalin's good graces: by showing an understanding of possibilities and nuances and at the same time exhibiting the proper skeptical attitude toward capitalist leaders. He replied, "There are differences between them, but one must be aware that he is correct in his behavior towards the British Prime Minister. Even so, that same correctness would never stop him bringing unofficial pressure on Churchill. If he [FDR] hasn't done this, I hardly think it accidental."

Gromyko definitely had a point: when FDR felt strongly about something his view prevailed. Would FDR press the point and agree to the $10 billion figure? Whose side was he on?

As the meeting broke at 6:00 p.m. for a fifteen-minute rest and tea break, Stalin pushed back his chair, and Gromyko heard him mutter, "It's possible the USA and Britain have already agreed on this with each other."

Stettinius noticed that the president's hand shook as he drank his tea.

Gromyko, *wanting* everything to go well between Roosevelt and Stalin, sought out Hopkins, who he knew was also in favor of rapprochement between Roosevelt and Stalin, and confided to him Stalin's skepticism about Roosevelt's commitment. Hopkins thereupon wrote a note to FDR: "The Marshal thinks you did not back up Ed [Stettinius] relative to Reparations—and that you sided with the British—and he is disturbed about it. Perhaps you could tell him privately later."

When they reconvened, FDR announced that he wanted to revisit the discussion about Poland's frontiers. During the earlier discussion Hopkins had sent FDR a note of warning: "Mr. President: You get into trouble about your legal powers and what senate will say." To help solve the problem, FDR had asked Stettinius to confer with his staff for a possible solution; while they were conferring, according to Stettinius, FDR "suddenly looked up at us and said, 'I've got it' . . . Instead of the first three words, 'The three powers,' he would like to substitute, 'The three Heads of Government consider.' In the second sentence he proposed eliminating the words 'three powers,' and in the last sentence, the word 'feel' instead of 'agree' should be used." That turned the statement from a governmental commitment to an expression of views that FDR could safely sign:

> The three Heads of Government consider that the Eastern frontier of Poland should follow the Curzon Line with digressions from it in some regions of five to eight kilometers in favour of Poland. It is recognized that Poland must receive substantial accessions of territory in the North and West. They feel that the opinion of the new Polish Provisional Government of National Unity should be sought in due course on the extent of these accessions and that the final delimitation of the Western frontier of Poland should thereafter await the Peace Conference.

Stalin now suggested an addition to the text to indicate that Poland should receive the return of her ancient frontiers in East Prussia and on the Oder. FDR at this point laughed and asked how long ago these lands had been Polish. Molotov replied very long ago but they had in fact been Polish. FDR said, "This might lead the British to ask for the return of the United States to Great Britain," and said to Churchill, "Perhaps you would want us back?" Stalin replied, "The ocean prevented this." After a few more exchanges, FDR announced that he had to leave the next day at 3:00 p.m.

There remained the question of hammering out the final communiqué: he suggested that if they met at eleven the next day, it could be finished by lunch. Both Stalin and Churchill objected: they thought that wouldn't be enough time, but FDR was obdurate. Stalin said he felt it was impossible to complete the work in view of the dinner Churchill was planning and suggested the dinner might be canceled: this was not seriously considered. The meeting adjourned. The foreign ministers were given the task of agreeing on the wording of the final draft communiqué the Big Three would sign. It was 8:00 p.m.

A half hour or so after the adjournment, FDR and Stalin were on their way to Vorontsov: Churchill was giving the final dinner. It was a very small, select guest list: Roosevelt, Stettinius, and Bohlen; Churchill, Eden, and Birse; Stalin, Molotov, and Pavlov.

The presidential party was the first to arrive at Vorontsov. They were greeted by a regimental guard lined up on the steps of the palace. They entered the palace, which looked more like a castle, to find themselves in a grand vestibule measuring some forty feet wide, the walls of which were lined with large portraits of famous Russian generals in full dress uniforms. Walking through that, they were ushered into a small, beautifully furnished reception room. Cocktails, according to Stettinius, were not served until Stalin and Molotov arrived. A short while after the Russians entered, all moved into the ornate, Moorish-style dining room. The dinner was elaborate and had many courses. Menus were at each place, listing the following: caviar, pies, salmon, sturgeon in aspic, game, sausage, suckling pig with horseradish sauce, and vol-au-vent of game for the first course; game bouillon and cream of chicken for the second course; white fish with champagne sauce and baked kefal for the third course; shashlik of mutton, wild goat from the steppes, and mutton pilaf for the fourth course; roast turkey, roast quail, roast partridge, and green peas for the fifth course; ice cream, fruits, petits fours, roasted almonds, and, finally, coffee finished the dinner.

There were many toasts, but there was also business done. FDR found time to reassure Stalin on the reparations issue, as Hopkins had suggested. Stalin told Churchill that he was unhappy with the way the reparations issue had been settled; Churchill finally backed down. The three, talking together, agreed to state in the protocol the concrete dollar amount that Stalin so desired to have mentioned: that Russia and America would take as a basis of discussion the figure of reparations as $20 billion, half to go to Russia, and that mention would be made in the communiqué that Germany would pay for the damage it had caused the Allied nations.

They toasted each other. Churchill proposed a toast to Stalin's health, remarking that he hoped the Marshal had a warmer feeling for the British than he had had in the past, that the great victories of the Red Army had made the Marshal more mellow and friendly, the fires of war having wiped out old animosities.

Roosevelt reminisced about an incident involving the Ku Klux Klan, the American organization that he described as hating Catholics and Jews. He had been the guest of the president of the chamber of commerce when he visited a small southern town, he recounted, and had asked the president whether the Italian sitting on one side of him and the Jew on the other were members of the Ku Klux Klan. The president told him they were considered all right because everyone knew them, thus illustrating how difficult it was to have any prejudices—racial, religious, or otherwise—if you really knew people. Stalin observed that "this was very true."

FDR then proposed a toast both prescient and thoughtful to the prime minister that illustrated how sensitive he was to information and how capable of reacting to it. He must have felt in his bones that Churchill would be voted out of office when the war ended. He now said Churchill had been in and out of government "and it was difficult to say whether he had been of more service to his country within or outside the government . . . He personally felt that Mr. Churchill had been perhaps of even greater service when he was not in the government, since he had forced people to think." (He would tell Mackenzie King in March that he intended to see if he could help Churchill get reelected.)

Stalin, showing an ignorance of American politics, asked FDR whether a Labor Party existed in America. FDR replied that it did not, although labor was "extremely powerful."

FDR mentioned that he was meeting the three Near Eastern kings, including Ibn Saud, at which point Stalin brought up what he called the

Jewish problem, which, he said, was a very difficult one: they had tried to establish a Jewish homeland in Birobidzhan, but after a few years they had scattered. FDR answered that he was a Zionist. Stalin said he was one in principle but he recognized the difficulty. This brought Stalin in mind of his treaty with Hitler: he stated that if it had not been for Munich and the Polish-German treaty of 1934, he would never have made the treaty with the Germans in 1939.

When Stalin said to FDR that he didn't think they could complete the work of the conference by three o'clock the next day, FDR replied that if necessary he would wait over until Monday; Stalin expressed gratification.

Conference staff worked through the night to get the various agreements into final form for the Big Three to sign the next day: the final plenary session was set for noon.

SUNDAY, FEBRUARY 11

While both Churchill and Stalin felt FDR should stay longer, in fact when they convened at noon for the final plenary session, they found there was little to do except make small changes in the documents: one of Churchill's changes had to do with substituting a word for the word "joint," which to him meant British lamb on Sunday. An interesting change, initiated by Stalin, was to request that the final communiqué not say that it had been the president who had put forth the proposal on the voting procedure: he was not against its being made public that the U.S. proposal had been adopted; he just didn't think the reference to the president belonged in the communiqué; his change was adopted.

There were, however, some final fireworks. Churchill and Eden were shown for the first time the Far East agreement Stalin and FDR had worked out: it caused an immediate row. Presented with the document as a fait accompli, both were furious. Eden advised Churchill not to sign the agreement. As they argued and FDR remained out of the argument, which meant he was not going to insist on Churchill's signature, both Englishmen became even more furious. Worse, according to Eden, was that the argument was "in front of Stalin and Roosevelt," Eden being against Churchill's putting his signature to the document, Churchill maintaining he *must*. (Neither FDR nor Stalin ever commented upon

this.) Eden and Churchill decided to call in for advice Alexander Cadogan, ex-British ambassador to China. Cadogan, agreeing that Churchill
should not sign the document, backed Eden. Churchill would not be
dissuaded; he and the British general staff were deep into plans to recap-
ture Malay, Singapore, and Burma. Noting that their authority in the
Far East would suffer if they were not signatories, and therefore not parties to any later discussions, he signed. Eden's view of Roosevelt changed:
where before he had admired Roosevelt fairly unreservedly (except for
what Eden considered the president's unnatural bias against colonialism), he now thought FDR devious. He would write in his memoirs,
"For those who attributed Roosevelt's decisions to illness, it must be
remembered that though the work of the Conference was strenuous
enough to keep a man even of Churchill's energy occupied, Roosevelt
found time to negotiate in secret, and without informing his British col-
league or his Chinese ally, an agreement with Stalin to cover the Far East.
This document was, in my judgment, a discreditable by-product of the
Conference." Churchill did his best to hide the disagreement from the
world, later calling it an American affair that was not Britain's to shape.

FDR had written a letter the day before formally asking Stalin to
support him if he felt it necessary, to win the support of Congress and
the American people, for the United States to have two more votes in
the General Assembly. Stalin now handed FDR a letter saying that he
was prepared to officially support the president's proposal. FDR took
measures to keep the matter secret for the time being; in fact, according
to Hopkins, he was "extremely anxious" that no aspect be discussed,
even privately.

When it came to the matter of actually putting their signatures on
documents, the Big Three at first couldn't agree on who should sign
first. FDR said Stalin should sign first because he was such a wonderful
host, but Stalin objected on the grounds that if his was the first signature, everyone would say he led: he insisted he be in last place. Churchill
then pointed out, "If you take the alphabet I'll be first. If you take age
I also come first." In the end, the report of the conference and the
protocol on German reparations, the main trilateral documents, bore
the signature of Churchill first, Roosevelt second, and Stalin third. The
agreement regarding the entry of the Soviet Union into the war against
Japan, however, was signed in a different order: it was the sole agreement signed first by Stalin, then by Roosevelt, and lastly by Churchill.

Much was left out of the documents that were made public. There was no mention of the extra votes for the Soviet Union, the word "dismemberment" was left out for fear it would increase German resistance, and the voting procedure in the Security Council and the matter of territorial trusteeships were not mentioned, because they first had to be cleared with France and China, which were going to be the other two permanent members of the Security Council.

The final lunch, with FDR as host in his dining room at Livadia, followed. With FDR were Leahy, Stettinius, Hopkins, Harriman, and Bohlen. Churchill's group consisted of Eden, Clark Kerr, Cadogan, and Birse. With Stalin were only Molotov and Pavlov. Stettinius asked Molotov if he could have the painting of a winter scene that was hanging on the wall behind FDR as a memento of their collaboration. Molotov gave it to him. Stettinius's thank-you letter, sent from Cairo, read, "It will occupy a place of honor at my farm in Virginia which I hope you will be able to visit sometime soon."

The lunch went on until 3:45, after which FDR left by car for Sevastopol to view the terrible destruction there that Stalin had told him about: the Germans had left not one house standing. According to the *New York Times* reporter Harrison Salisbury, it looked like a city of the dead. (According to the mayor, "If a room has three walls and a ceiling we count it in good shape.") After a brief tour FDR would spend the night on the USS *Catoctin*. An added bonus for this plan was that the drive would take him by Balaclava, where he could see the site of the Charge of the Light Brigade, the famous field that lay between two ridges a quarter mile apart. The following morning the president left for Saki, where the *Sacred Cow* awaited to fly him to Egypt. There he would board the USS *Quincy*, anchored in the Great Bitter Lake, in the Suez Canal, have one day of rest, and then meet the three kings, Ibn Saud, Farouk, and Haile Selassie, who were coming aboard the *Quincy*, one after the other: he particularly wanted to learn about Palestine. Then he would sail for home. (Admiral Leahy, witness to the Churchill-FDR wars over the wisdom of mounting a second front, wrote in his diary that when Churchill learned FDR was meeting with the three kings, the prime minister hastily arranged to do the same thing, "undoubtedly with the purpose of neutralizing any accomplishment the President may have made during his talks with the three kings.")

16

POST-YALTA PROBLEMS

The report on the conference was released on February 12. Congratulatory cables flooded in from friends and enemies alike. Said the Republican ex-president Herbert Hoover, "It will offer a great hope to the world"; William L. Shirer called it "a landmark in human history." Even Arthur Vandenberg, Michigan's isolationist Republican senator, was moved to state that the conference "reaffirms basic principles of justice and undertakes for the first time to complement them by direct action." The American press was generally wildly enthusiastic. *Time* magazine wrote, "All doubts about the Big Three's ability to cooperate in peace as well as in war seem now to have been swept away." *The Christian Science Monitor* editorialized, "The Crimea Conference stands out from previous conferences because of its mood of decision . . . The meeting at Yalta was plainly dominated by a desire, willingness and determination to reach solid decisions." The *New York Herald Tribune* also hailed it as a positive accomplishment: "The conference has produced another great proof of Allied unity, strength and power of decision." *The Washington Post* joined in the praise: "The President is to be congratulated on his part in this all-encompassing agreement."

Meanwhile, FDR was returning home on the *Quincy,* arriving back in Newport News, Virginia, the last day of February. The sixteen-day ocean voyage was designed to give FDR time to rest and recover from the conference, but Harry Hopkins, again extremely ill, had to leave the *Quincy* to check into a hospital. And FDR's loyal friend, military aide, and appointment secretary, General Edwin "Pa" Watson, who had suffered a stroke, was in a coma aboard the ship. FDR had company to distract him: his daughter, Anna, and Leahy were aboard, as well as his doctor, Ross McIntire, and his naval aide, Admiral Brown, but to liven things up and get some work done, FDR, always media conscious, summoned the speechwriter Sam Rosenman, on a mission in London, to travel with him and work on the speech he would give to Congress, plus his three favorite White House correspondents, Merriman Smith, Douglas Cornell, and Robert G. Nixon. The four came aboard at Algiers on February 18.

Although the *Quincy* was heavily guarded by two cruisers, seven destroyers, and a canopy of warplanes, when it passed through the Strait of Gibraltar, a group of P-38s and a blimp were added, and the ship was preceded by a minesweeper: two Allied ships had been sunk the previous day in the area, possibly by enemy submarines. The minesweeper picked up a sonar signal, dropped a depth charge, but saw no evidence of a kill. Two days later Watson died. Observed Rosenman, "It was plain to all of us how deeply affected he was." FDR spent the days resting and reading, sitting on deck when the sun shone, lunching in his cabin with Leahy, Rosenman, and Anna. Cocktail time was the usual, with FDR mixing the cocktails, as he so enjoyed doing, the drinks usually accompanied with liberal amounts of the caviar FDR had received from Stalin. In the evenings, on a screen set up in Admiral Leahy's cabin, there were movies. FDR watched every evening except the last, when he and Rosenman worked on his speech. As the *Quincy* crossed the Atlantic, the precaution of zigzagging during the day and running darkened at night continued.

On February 23, FDR held a press conference for the three correspondents. His first thoughts were of the United Nations.

Q: Do you conscientiously believe that the Conference can be the foundation of world peace for more than the generation of the men who are building that peace?

THE PRESIDENT: I can answer that question if you can tell me who your descendants will be in the year 2057.

Q: Can we look forward?

THE PRESIDENT: We can look as far ahead as humanity believes in this sort of thing. The United Nations will evolve into the best method ever devised for stopping war, and it will also be the beginning of something else to go with it.

His balanced view of his two allies was very much in evidence: Indochina, now Vietnam, was on his mind, as was Hong Kong, which he had discussed with Stalin. What seemed to bother him, however, was Churchill's imperial mind-set: he decided it was time to give it another shaking. What Churchill thought when he read FDR's comments has never been recorded: perhaps the prime minister's aides succeeded in keeping them from him. FDR was devastating on the subject of Churchill. In talking with the journalists about the Pacific, he said Indochina had been worrying him for two years: it wasn't ready for independence—it should not be given back to the French—it should be under a trusteeship until it was ready, although the British wouldn't like that because Burma might be next. "It might bust up their empire," FDR said.

He answered the questions the three threw at him.

Q: . . . All [that] territory out there, he [Churchill] wants them all back just the way they were?
THE PRESIDENT: Yes, he is mid-Victorian on all things like that.
Q: This idea of Churchill's seems inconsistent with the policy of self-determination?
THE PRESIDENT: Yes, that is true.
Q: He seems to undercut the Atlantic Charter. He made a statement the other day that it was not a rule, just a guide.
THE PRESIDENT: The Atlantic Charter is a beautiful idea. When it was drawn up, the situation was that England was about to lose the war. They needed hope.

It was not until a few days before the *Quincy* reached Hampton Roads, Virginia, that FDR began serious work on the speech with Rosenman. "None too soon," according to an impatient Rosenman, barely satisfied with a completed third draft before they docked. (In all there would be six drafts.)

A healthier Harry Hopkins was waiting for FDR the day he got back and present at both lunch and dinner. FDR spoke to a packed joint session of Congress on March 1. For the first time ever he spoke from his wheelchair, asking the audience for forgiveness with such a sure touch that no one gave it a second thought, particularly because he spoke for an hour with energy, wit, and incisiveness. The speech was generally well received, even by discerning journalists such as Arthur Krock of *The New York Times,* who wrote, "He made it so promptly and in such good temper he visibly and favorably impressed the auditors at the joint session. This was evident in their faces, in the volume and placement of their applause."

The speech was a careful description of what had gone on at the conference, and in his statement of the failed diplomacy the United Nations would replace, it specifically repudiated Churchill's "percentages agreement" with Stalin:

> The Crimea Conference was a successful effort by the three leading Nations to find a common ground for peace. It ought to spell the end of the system of unilateral action, the exclusive alliances, the spheres of influence, the balances of power, and all the other expedients that have been tried for centuries—and have always failed. We propose to substitute for all these, a universal organization in which all peace-loving Nations will finally have a chance to join.

FDR himself was happily relieved at what they had accomplished at Yalta. He told Daisy that "the conference turned out better than he dared hope for."

In Russia comments bordered on euphoria, and because the press was virtually an extension of Stalin, it reflected Stalin's sense of accomplishment, his feeling that the Soviet Union had accomplished its goals. The description of FDR's speech took up two-thirds of the foreign news pages of Russian morning newspapers the day following the speech. *Pravda* editorialized that the alliance of the Big Three has "not only its historical yesterday and its victorious today, but its great tomorrow as well . . . It saw each decision by President Roosevelt, Prime Minister Churchill and Premier Stalin contributing to a speedier victory and a more stable peace." *Izvestia* described the conference as "the biggest political event of current times—an event that will enter in history as a new example of coordinated solutions of complicated questions in the interest of peace and democracy" and informed its readers of the "deep and firm impression that the three leaders left this time better friends than ever before. Not the slightest sign of friction developed at any time during the meeting."

Soviet factory workers held "spontaneous" meetings, spurred on by radio announcements of the conference—impromptu speakers making such comments as "We'll be in Berlin soon . . . The hour of retribution has arrived." Reference to the UN organization to maintain peace and security very evidently touched a nerve throughout the Soviet Union: many Russians, remembering their prewar pariah status, believed this powerful new organization, of which their country would be a founding member, would protect them from German aggression.

Stalin told General Zhukov that he was "very pleased" with what had transpired at Yalta; "Roosevelt had been most friendly," he said. Molotov spread the word to Soviet ambassadors that the Soviet Union was happy with the Yalta decisions. "The general atmosphere at the conference was very friendly. We consider the conference as a positive development on the whole and specifically on Poland, Yugoslavia, and reparations," he told them in case they were in doubt.

There seemed to be general agreement that the measures hammered out at the conference were such that all three leaders could live with them. On voting in the Security Council, where the power of the United Nations would rest, in the face of FDR's insistence, Stalin had dropped the power to control the agenda. Poland had been a compromise for all. In dealing with Poland, FDR had his hands tied because the Red Army was in command of Poland, but he had drawn Stalin into public promises of an amazing nature. Stalin had signed a document that stated that the Polish government would *not* be the one imposed by the Red Army but would instead be reorganized on a broader democratic basis, that it would include democratic leaders from Poland itself and from Poles abroad, and, astoundingly, that it would oversee the holding of "free and unfettered elections as soon as possible on the basis of universal suffrage and secret ballot."

As Churchill told the War Cabinet later in February, "If the terms of the communiqué agreed with Premier Stalin were carried out in good faith, all would be well. If, on the other hand, effective reality were not given to those undertakings, our engagement would be altered."

Stalin had even signed the Declaration on Liberated Europe, which specified as a Big Three aim the democratization of *all* of Europe:

(c) to form interim governmental authorities broadly representative of all democratic elements in the population and pledged to the earliest possible establishment through free elections of governments responsive to the will of the people; and (d) to facilitate where necessary the holding of such elections.

One major reason Stalin went along with Roosevelt on these stirring words, as the historian Geoffrey Roberts has pointed out, is that he expected that Communists were going to win leadership roles in free and open elections in the newly liberated countries: he thought the populace would embrace not just the Red Army, which had freed them, but a Soviet-dominated government. And some of the actions of the Lublin government in Poland, such as long-overdue land reform, were well received. In addition, the Moscow press announced shortly after Yalta that Russia would assist in the reconstruction of Warsaw: it would provide technical assistance and pay 50 percent of the cost.

Stalin had no idea how unpopular the strong-arm manner of Russian governance was. He thought, in fact, that with care, the Communist parties in the Slavic countries were going to grow in strength. As he said in April to Georgi Dimitrov, head of the Bulgarian Communist Party, "There should be no rush to hold elections . . . Issues have to be found on which the peasants could be won over to the Communist Party."

So why *not* stay allied with FDR? America was the most powerful country in the world.

Another reason given for Stalin's agreement with the Yalta documents, clearly antithetical to Soviet-style government, is a widely cited statement Molotov made that in effect implies Stalin never intended to honor the words he had signed on to. "Do not worry," Molotov asserts Stalin told him, "work it out. We can deal with it in our own way later. The point is the correlation of forces." This is quite clear, but these sentences were followed by another thought, added by Molotov, that is also obvious—and usually these next sentences are left out: "It was to our benefit to stay allied with America. It was important." In other words, both Stalin and Molotov, in their own way, were admitting that alliance with America was crucial for them: devastated by Germany, Russia needed American help, needed America's hand to help it rebuild. In February 1945, they expected that help would be forthcoming. Also, being pragmatists, Stalin and Molotov definitely didn't want to antagonize the most powerful country in the world.

Stalin made a speech on February 23 celebrating the Red Army on its twenty-seventh anniversary and marking how close it was to victory:

> The Red Army completely liberated Poland and a large part of Czechoslovakia, occupied Budapest and knocked out of the war Germany's last ally in Europe, Hungary, captured the major part of East Prussia and German Silesia, and hewed a road for itself to Brandenburg and Pomerania, the approaches to Berlin.
>
> The Hitlerites boasted that no enemy soldier had set foot on German soil for over a hundred years and that the German army had fought and would fight only on foreign soil. An end has now been put to this German boastfulness.

ARRANGEMENTS AMONG THE BRITISH, the American, and the Russian staffs had been in the discussion stage for months before Yalta regarding treatment of released prisoners of war of their three countries. At Yalta, although there had been no discussion at the Big Three level, measures had been finalized and documents signed specifying how each country would handle released prisoners of war:

> Each ally will provide food, clothing, medical attention and other needs . . . until transport is available for repatriation. In caring for British subjects and American citizens the Soviet government will be assisted by British and American officers. Soviet officers will assist British and American authorities in their task of caring for Soviet citizens liberated by the British and American forces, during such time as they are on the continent of Europe or in the United Kingdom, awaiting transport . . .
>
> We are pledged to give every assistance consistent with operational requirements to help to ensure that all these prisoners of war and civilians are speedily repatriated.

However, an American soldier and a Russian soldier were looked upon and treated differently by their respective countries. An American soldier was an individual with family ties, a member of a community, a voter, a *citizen*. A Soviet soldier was a cog in a machine, an expendable individual who served the state. This led to serious differences in the way each government treated its soldiers. Beyond this was the incontrovertible fact that the Russian nation was desperately poor and Russians were used to primitive conditions brought on by the war while Americans were used to the niceties of life. Hundreds of thousands—indeed literally millions—of Russians, made homeless by the war, were on the move, crowding roads and trains, overwhelming transportation facilities, taking shelter anywhere they could. As Russian prisoners of war came stumbling out of German prison camps, in most cases the Russian government expected them to make their own way to wherever they were going. As American prisoners of war, many of them injured aviators, stumbled out of the camps, the American government sought to provide them with immediate medical aid, new clothes, American food, clean beds, and transportation to speed their journey home: it was hard for the Russians to understand this. The idea, expressed at Yalta, that "we are pledged to give every assistance" simply had a different meaning to the Russians. They ordinarily transported POWs and sometimes their own troops in boxcars with no heat or sanitary arrangements. Harriman seemed to think it "unbelievable" that in at least one Russian camp, the freed Americans were mixed in with civilians; food, consisting of barley soup, bread, potatoes, tea, and coffee, was served only twice a day; and there were no delousing facilities. (He was conveniently forgetting that bedbugs and other vermin were a fact of life in Russia: that just before FDR had arrived at the Livadia Palace, the American staff, who thought they had scoured every inch of the palace, at the last minute had to spray it liberally with DDT.) Deane wanted to send in medical and other support staff to care for the freed soldiers: Molotov balked, fearing that Americans were using caring for their prisoners merely as a pretext to send in spies to report on Polish conditions. Also, as Molotov told Harriman, his people should be dealing with the Polish Provisional Government. General Deane had made careful, indeed elaborate plans to succor the released prisoners: a U.S. ship waited offshore with food, medical supplies, and clothes; small contact teams were ready and waiting to enter the POW camps. One team consisting of an American doctor and an officer chosen by Deane *were* permitted to go to Lublin with a load of supplies to care for the prisoners; however, they were not permitted to travel, and, most upsetting to Deane, no further personnel were permitted to enter. Instead, the Russians urged all American POWs to make their way to Odessa in the Ukraine: from there they would be flown out to Moscow.

Roosevelt and Stalin exchanged messages on the subject. FDR's first message, basically written by Stimson along the lines requested by General Deane and sent March 3, mentioned "the difficulties which are being encountered in collecting, supplying and evacuating American ex-prisoners of war and American aircraft crews who are stranded east of the Russian lines." FDR dictated the closing sentence to Stimson to put the message on a personal level: "In view of your disapproval of the plan we submitted what do you suggest in place of it?"

Stalin answered promptly that he had consulted "our local representatives . . . On the territory of Poland and in other places liberated by the Red Army, there are no groups of American prisoners of war, as all of them, except the single sick persons who are in the hospitals, have been sent to the gathering point in Odessa, where 1,200 American prisoners of war have already arrived and the arrival of the rest is expected in the nearest future."

General Deane was sure there were still stray Americans in Poland and wanted permission to look for them: permission was denied. He appealed up the chain of command, and Deane was sufficiently powerful and sufficiently angry to engage FDR in his cause.

Another message went out over FDR's signature containing some very strong words:

> With reference to the question of evacuation of American prisoners from Poland I have been informed that the arrangement for General Deane with a Soviet Army officer . . . has been cancelled . . . I have information that I consider positive and reliable that there are a very considerable number of sick and injured Americans in hospitals in Poland and also numbers of liberated U.S. prisoners in good health who are awaiting entrainment . . . to transit camps in Odessa . . . I cannot understand your reluctance to permit American officers means to assist their own people.

FDR's criticism didn't make Stalin change policy, but it did sting him into an explanation. Stalin replied, making corrections in his own hand (Stalin's handwritten changes shown in italics), in a message that went out on March 22. The exceptional care he took with this message might have been grounded in another event. On March 20, American fighter planes attacked clearly marked Soviet planes over territory held by Soviet troops in Germany. Although, according to the U.S. military mission report, the Soviet pilots tried to avoid an air battle, U.S. fighters pursued and shot down six Soviet planes, killed two Soviet pilots, and seriously wounded a third. This was the second instance of an attack by American fighters on Soviet planes over territory occupied by Soviet troops. Stalin chose not to bring the matter up with FDR:

> In regard to the information which you have about a seemingly great number of sick and wounded Americans who are in Poland, and also those who are waiting for departure for Odessa or who did not get in touch with Soviet authorities, I must say that that information is not exact. In reality, on the territory of Poland by March 16 there were only 17 sick Americans, except a number of Americans who are on the way to Odessa. *Today I have received a report that very soon they (17 persons) will be taken to Odessa by planes . . .*
>
> . . . The matter concerns the interests of the Soviet armies at the front and Soviet commanders, who do not want to have extra officers with them, having no relation to military operations but at the same time requiring care for their accommodation, for the organization of meetings and all kinds of connections for them, *for their guard from possible diversions on the part of German agents who have not yet been caught . . .*
>
> Our commanders pay with their lives for the state of matters at the front and in the immediate rear . . .
>
> In addition to this I have to say that former American prisoners of war liberated by the Red Army are in Soviet prisoner-of-war camps in good conditions, at any rate in better conditions than former Soviet prisoners of war in American camps where they have been partially placed together with German prisoners of war . . .

In a rare moment of reflection, Harriman had admitted to Washington on March 10 that if it hadn't been for Russian soldiers, many Allied POWs wouldn't even have been rescued: "The war prisoners say that as the Red Army advanced the Hitlerites took energetic steps to evacuate the camps where the Americans, English and Frenchmen were concentrated to the interior of Germany. Only the quick movement of the Soviet troops westward made possible the freeing of the war prisoners from captivity."

The condition of the Soviet camps where American soldiers were being held—"sleeping on the floor, utterly no sanitary and washing facilities," the lack of doctors—drove Harriman, from Moscow, to suggest retaliation to FDR in the form of limiting the movements of Russian contact agents in France caring for released Soviet citizens. FDR refused, answering that it didn't appear "appropriate" for him to even send Stalin another letter on the subject.

Eventually, all the American and British POWs in Poland were found or made their own way to Odessa. Most reported helpful, grateful Russians; the worst stories were tales of stolen watches. From Odessa all the soldiers were flown out and repatriated. In a short time the matter had resolved itself.

POW tales of all sorts reached Washington. Henry Stimson records the more balanced Washington view of the Polish prisoner-of-war situation, writing in his diary of

> two boys he had talked with, a [U.S.] captain and a lieutenant, loud in their praise of the basic kindness of Russian troops. They had seen a great many on this long trek which they had made on foot and had been treated with uniform kindness. They described the Russians as rough and the fare which the Russians were able to give them as very poor fare compared with the rations we are accustomed to . . . They found that the Russians uniformly had a very high opinion of the United States as the one country they wished to get along with.

FDR regarded these clashes with a different eye than did his staff on the front line. He refused to view them as anything other than minor, momentary disputes, and, by so doing, rendered them as such. When Mackenzie King came to visit the White House on March 9 for several days, FDR described the Crimea Conference and never mentioned the POW exchange of messages. He told King as they had tea the first afternoon that Stalin "had a good deal of humor, that he . . . liked him, found him very direct." FDR was consistently upbeat: he didn't think "there was anything to fear particularly from Stalin in the future—he had a big program himself to deal with." After dinner with Eleanor and their daughter, Anna, FDR took King upstairs to his oval study, where the prime minister settled into a chair opposite FDR, who sat as usual on his leather couch. There FDR filled him in in more detail. He spoke of Churchill doing 80 percent of the talking at Yalta and again stressed Stalin's sense of humor. Once, when Churchill was making a long speech, said FDR, "Stalin put up his hand to the side of his face . . . and winked one of his eyes as much as to say: there he is talking again."

He told King that he felt "before the end of April, as far as Europe was concerned, it should be over . . . Once Europe was over, Japan would collapse very soon thereafter . . . possibly three months." (For FDR to give such a short time frame for Japan's collapse meant he knew the bomb was almost ready.) He also volunteered that quite possibly the war in Europe would be over before the San Francisco Conference was finished. The conversation between them went on until 11:45: King actually suggested breaking it off earlier, worried he was tiring FDR, but the president wouldn't hear of it.

So upbeat was FDR that he confided to the Canadian prime minister his plans to make a triumphal European tour. He had been invited by the king and queen of England to visit in May, after Germany surrendered, but that seemed too soon he said, he expected it would be June. (By which time Churchill's wife, on a Red Cross tour of Russia, would be back in England, Churchill had assured him.)

FDR's plans were precise and elegant, he told King: "to go from the ship to Buckingham Palace and stay there, and then to drive with the King through the streets of London, and at the weekend, spend time with Churchill at Chequers. Also giving an address before the Houses of Parliament and get the freedom of the city of London . . . He would also like to pay a visit to Queen Wilhelmina in Holland, stay at the Hague. From there, he would perhaps pay a visit to Paris but would not say anything about that till the moment came."

King concluded, "He and Churchill have worked out plans quite clearly contemplating that the war will be over before June . . . A sort of triumphal close to the war itself."

FDR also confided to King that Stalin was waiting until he could bring all his divisions up to the front near Manchuria and would then break off relations with Japan.

But following the prisoner-of-war exchange of messages, which worked out to the satisfaction of both countries, there occurred another, larger problem. It came about through the resurgence of the Russians' fears that their allies might make a separate peace with Germany. According to Stimson, it was precipitated by Churchill. Stimson laid it to what he characterized as the prime minister's "erraticness."

The Russians were always on the watch for signs of treachery, and occasionally their concern was justified. In April of the previous year *Pravda* ran a story from "reliable Greek and Yugoslav sources" that Ribbentrop had met with two British officials in a seacoast town in the Pyrenees "to find out the conditions of a separate peace with the Germans. It is understood that the meeting did not remain without results," the article stated darkly.

On March 9, Alexander Kirk, ex-ambassador to Egypt, now political adviser to Field Marshal Harold Alexander, notified Stettinius that the SS general Karl Wolff, Germany's highest-ranking officer in Italy, had arrived in Lugano, Switzerland, near the Italian border, with a small staff to negotiate the "definite surrender" of the German army in Italy. Kirk's cable from Caserta stated that the information had been preceded by ten days of indefinite rumors and reports and appeared to be reliable.

Alexander explained to the Combined Chiefs of Staff that Wolff stated that the German commander Albert Kesselring had been contacted but was not yet won over to the plan and that he—Wolff—was planning to convince him it was the only way to avoid further German bloodshed in a cause that was hopeless. Further, it was so secret that Heinrich Himmler, head of the SS and Wolff's boss, was unaware of the plan. As evidence of his good faith, Wolff had been pressed to release and produce the leader of the Italian underground resistance movement, which he had done. Alexander further informed headquarters that he intended to send General Lyman Lemnitzer, U.S. deputy chief of staff, and General Terence Airey, British chief of intelligence, to Bern.

On March 12, Alexander informed Molotov of the possible negotiations in much the same language as his cable to the Combined Chiefs of Staff. He told him that his representatives were preparing to go to Switzerland "in order to handle the situation," that if the German rep-

FDR addressing Congress March 1, 1945, upon his return from Yalta. Although it was the first speech he ever gave sitting down, it was well received.

FDR and his cabinet, 1945. The table was curved to give FDR a clear view of all participants.

General Dwight D. Eisenhower and Marshall, Allied headquarters, Algeria, June 1943

Eisenhower viewing his first death camp, Ohrdruf, just liberated by the 4th Armored Division. Dead bodies were strewn in piles everywhere; the stench was appalling; Eisenhower was stunned.

FDR at work at his cottage in Warm Springs, Georgia, a few days before he died

The last photograph of FDR, taken by Nicholas Robbins on April 11, 1945, the day before FDR died

The train bringing FDR's body from Warm Springs to Washington, D.C.

Churchill, Truman, and Stalin at Potsdam, July 1945

Henry L. Stimson, Stettinius, and James Forrestal, secretary of the navy, 1945

Eisenhower bids good-bye to Stimson

Stimson receives the Distinguished Service Medal from Truman just prior to his last Cabinet meeting

Secretary of Commerce Henry Wallace arriving at the White House the day after the bomb was dropped on Nagasaki

Truman with members of his cabinet. From left to right: Secretary of State James F. Byrnes, the president, Secretary of the Treasury Fred M. Vinsom, and Attorney General Tom Clark.

resentatives seemed genuine, they must fulfill certain expectations: they must have written evidence that they have Kesselring's authorization; they will meet with the OSS at night at either the American or the British legation; Lemnitzer and Airey will be present.

Molotov informed Harriman that the Soviet government did not object to negotiations in Bern, but it wanted General V. N. Dragun, chief of the Soviet Mission on War Prisoners in France, General Ivan Susloparov, chief of the military mission in France, plus another unnamed officer to take part in the conversations.

General Deane thought the presence of *any* Russians a terrible idea, as he wrote to General Marshall: "The success of the mission might be jeopardized." Harriman felt the same: such a mission "has no justification . . . It is not a capitulation of a Government as in the case of Bulgaria or Rumania." So did Clark Kerr: "It is not intended that any terms of surrender should be discussed at Berne."

As FDR would find out from Henry Stimson on the eleventh, Molotov assumed that Soviet representation would be accepted at this meeting mainly because Churchill had raised his expectations. Stimson wrote about the matter in his diary two days running: As a result of Churchill's interference, the British chiefs of staff, instead of notifying the Soviet Union about these preliminary Bern discussions, had asked for their agreement. Stimson saw FDR on the eleventh. The next day the secretary of war wrote,

> Apparently Churchill . . . overruled the arrangement of the two staffs, namely that we should notify the Russians but not ask their assent. He has instructed the British staff to defer final action until we get the Russians' assent. This I think is a grave mistake. It adds delay to a movement which must be conducted rapidly.

On the thirteenth, as Russian anger escalated, Stimson wrote of the prime minister,

> Somehow or other the English papers fell into the hands of Churchill and he overruled his staff and sent a note inviting the Russians to come and did this after our people had sent off their letter which simply notified the Russians.

FDR was bothered enough by the contretemps to give Mackenzie King, who was visiting him at the White House, an earful. King wrote in *his* diary on March 13,

> The President was agreeable to having this [the Bern meeting] done in a way which would see that the Army surrendered and were properly treated and that Kesselring might himself have his men saved. If this were done, he believed it would help to speedily end the war. He had cabled Churchill about it, but Churchill, without communicating back with him, had communicated with Russia to ask if Russia was agreeable. Russia took the position that she wanted three Generals present. The President said Russia really had nothing to do with the Italian campaign. He was afraid Winston had acted too suddenly and they had made the situation very difficult.

Two days later FDR had General Donovan in for a meeting, presumably because he was head of the OSS and could give the president an update on what was actually happening in Bern.

In the discussion related to what the British and Americans involved considered the outrageous behavior of Molotov and Stalin, no one—not FDR, not Stimson, not Harriman, not Alexander—took into account the Russians' basic fear of a double cross: the fear their Western allies might either be selling them out or, as a result of the proposed surrender of German troops in Italy, allow Hitler to concentrate his remaining forces against the Red Army on the eastern front. It is understandable, in view of their concentration on saving American lives, but it did not endear them to the Soviets in charge.

Certainly Molotov's anger was palpable. Molotov had always been less certain of Russia's new allies than Stalin. A worried Molotov had cautioned Stalin in 1944, "Germany will try to make peace with Churchill and Roosevelt." "Right," Stalin had answered, "but Roosevelt and Churchill won't agree." Now Stalin wasn't so sure. Now, suddenly, he too was furious. Probably it was the combination of the Polish situation and the Bern talks that made Stalin do something he knew would seriously affect his relationship with FDR: under pressure from Molotov the marshal announced that Gromyko, not Molotov, would represent the Soviet Union at the San Francisco Conference. FDR was devastated. He wrote two messages to Stalin, both dated March 24:

> Recalling the friendly and fruitful cooperation at Yalta between Mr. Molotov, Mr. Eden, and Mr. Stettinius, I know the Secretary of State has been looking forward to continuing the joint work . . . for the eventual realization of our mutual goal, the establishment of an effective international organization to insure a secure and peaceful world. Without the presence of Mr. Molotov the Conference will be deprived of a very great asset . . . I am afraid that Mr. Molotov's absence will be construed all over the world as a lack of comparable interest on the part of the Soviet Government in the great objectives of the Conference.

FDR's second message to Stalin dealt with the surrender negotiations (the words in italics were added in FDR's hand):

> The facts are as follows: . . . unconfirmed information was received in Switzerland that some German officers were considering the possibility of arranging for the surrender of German troops in Italy . . . When this information reached Washington, Field Marshal Alexander was authorized to send officers . . . to Switzerland to ascertain the accuracy of the report, and if it appeared to be of sufficient promise to arrange . . . for a conference at his headquarters in Italy to discuss the surrender. *Soviet representatives would, of course, be present if such a meeting could be arranged* . . . Soviet officers to be present at Field Marshal Alexander's meeting with German officers when and if such a meeting is finally arranged *in Berne* to discuss details of a surrender *at Caserta* . . . *It is in the same category as would be the sending of a flag of truce to your general at Koenigsberg or Danzig.*

Stalin's reply three days later dealt only with Molotov's absence from the San Francisco Conference. "I and Mr. Molotov regret it extremely but the convening . . . of a sessions of the Supreme Soviet of the USSR where the presence of Mr. Molotov is absolutely necessary, is excluding the possibility of his participation . . ." (It wouldn't be until Roosevelt died and Stalin ordered him to go to San Francisco that Harriman would discover that it was Molotov who elected not to go to San Francisco: he didn't want to miss the meeting of the Supreme Soviet.)

It wasn't until March 29 that Stalin dealt with the issues FDR had raised.

> The Soviet Government could not have given a different answer . . . I agree to negotiations with the enemy on such matter only in the case when . . . there will be excluded a possibility for the Germans to maneuver and to use these negotiations for shifting of their troops to other sections of the front and, first of all, to the Soviet front . . . I cannot understand why representatives of the Soviet Command were refused participation in these negotiations and in what way could they cause inconvenience . . . For your information I have to tell you that the Germans have already made use of the negotiations with the Allied Command and during this period succeeded in shifting three divisions from Northern Italy to Soviet front.
>
> The task of coordinated operations . . . announced at the Crimea Conference is to bind the troops of the enemy to the place of their location and not to give the enemy any possibility to maneuver and shift troops . . . This is being violated . . .
>
> As a military man you write me you will understand that it is necessary to act quickly . . . It is regretted that an analogy does not suit this case. German troops at Koenigsberg and Danzig are surrounded. If they surrender they will do it in order to avoid annihilation . . . The German troops in Northern Italy are not surrounded and they do not face annihilation.

FDR in turn was furious. The cable as much as accused the Anglo-American military command, as Stalin called it, of colluding with the enemy. Harriman was asked to ascertain whether this was Stalin's thinking or the thinking of someone else in the Politburo. Harriman answered that the words and reasoning were Stalin's.

FDR called in as advisers Stettinius, Sumner Welles, Assistant Secretary of State Archibald MacLeish, and Bohlen to discuss the situation and draft a reply. Wrote Bohlen of their meeting with FDR in the White House, "It was one of the few times that I saw him angry. He was seated at his desk at the White House, his eyes flashing, his face flushed, outraged that he should be accused of dealing with the Germans behind Stalin's back." FDR's strong cable in reply to Stalin touched on troop movements:

> There is no question of negotiating with the Germans in any way which would permit them to transfer elsewhere forces from the Italian front . . . We intend to do everything within the capacity of our available resources to prevent any withdrawal of the German forces now in Italy . . .
>
> . . . Your information about the time of the movements of German troops from Italy is in error. Our best information is that three German divisions have left Italy since the first of the year, two of which have gone to the Eastern front. The last division of the three started moving about February 25, more than two weeks before anybody heard of any possibility of a surrender.

Another message went out from FDR to Stalin that same day on the subject of Poland, but Stalin, furious at FDR's cables about the Bern negotiations and the fact that the Soviet Union had been excluded, chose to ignore it and blast back his anger at FDR.

There is no doubt he was terribly upset. There was no way for anyone outside Stalin's immediate circle to know it, but his cable was not only handwritten by him but heavily self-edited. It also showed that those around him, probably Molotov, were exacerbating his fears of betrayal. There was no doubt the Bern conversations had hit all the wrong buttons:

> *I have received your message on the question of negotiations in Bern. You are absolutely right that in connection with the affair . . . "has developed an atmosphere of fear and distrust deserving regrets."*
>
> *You insist there have been no negotiations yet.*
>
> *It may be assumed that you have not been fully informed. As regards my military colleagues, they, on the basis of data which they have on hand, do not have any doubts that the negotiations have taken place and that they have ended in agreement with the Germans . . .*
>
> *I think my colleagues are close to truth . . .*
>
> *I understand that there are certain advantages for the Anglo-*

*American troops as a result of these separate negotiations in Bern or in
some other place since the Anglo-American troops get the possibility to
advance into the heart of Germany almost without any resistance on
the part of the Germans, but why was it necessary to conceal this from
the Russians and why your Allies—the Russians, were not notified?*

*As a result of this at the present moment the Germans on the West-
ern front in fact have ceased the war against England and the United
States. At the same time the Germans continue the war with Russia,
the Ally of England and the United States.*

It was not necessary to know that Stalin had written this message
in his own hand to detect the depth of his conviction that he was being
double-crossed—it was obvious. So obvious that FDR responded to it
with a deeply personal message of his own:

I have received with astonishment your message . . . containing
an allegation that arrangements which were made between Field
Marshals Alexander and Kesselring at Bern "permitted Anglo-
American troops to advance to the East" . . .

I have told you that,

1) No negotiations were held at Bern;
2) That the meeting had no political implications whatever;
3) That in any surrender of the enemy army in Italy there
   could be no violation of our agreed principle of unconditional surrender;
4) That Soviet officers would be welcomed at any meeting
   that might be arranged to discuss surrender.

I must continue to assume that you have the same high confidence in my truthfulness and reliability that I have always had in
yours.

I have also a full appreciation of the effect your gallant army
had had in making possible a crossing of the Rhine by the forces
under General Eisenhower . . .

I have complete confidence in General Eisenhower and know
that he would certainly inform me before entering into any agreement with the Germans . . .

I am certain that there were no negotiations in Bern at any

time, and I feel that your information to that effect must have come from German sources which have made persistent efforts to create dissension between us in order to escape in some measure for responsibility for their war crimes. If that was Wolff's purpose in Bern your message proves that he has had some success.

With a confidence in your belief in my personal reliability and in my determination to bring about together with you an unconditional surrender of the Nazis, it is astonishing that a belief seems to have reached the Soviet Government that I have entered in an agreement with the enemy without first obtaining your full agreement.

Finally I would say this, it would be one of the great tragedies of history if at the very moment of victory now within our grasp, such distrust, such lack of faith should prejudice the entire undertaking after the colossal losses of life, matériel and treasure involved.

Frankly I cannot avoid a feeling of bitter resentment toward your informers, whoever they are, for such vile misrepresentation of my actions or those of my trusted subordinates.

No one could speak truth to Stalin and have it penetrate—except Roosevelt, as is shown by what happened next. As foreign minister, Molotov met with Naotake Satō, Japanese ambassador to the Soviet Union from time to time. It was Satō's job to keep track of Soviet intentions to honor the neutrality pact between their two countries, particularly sensitive as U.S. forces pushed them back toward their home islands. Molotov had been extremely careful to give no hint of a change in the Soviets' attitude toward Japan, no hint that they were deeply involved in war plans against Japan with the United States. Satō had reported home, as late as after a February 22, 1945, meeting with Molotov, "Molotov as usual was amiable and smiling and I was conscious of the warmth of his personality throughout the interview."

Now, on the afternoon of the day Stalin received FDR's message, all that changed. Molotov called Satō into the Kremlin at 3:00 p.m. and declared that the Soviet Union wished to denounce its nonaggression pact. The reason given: "Japan, an ally of Germany, is helping the latter in her war against the USSR. Japan is fighting against the United States and Britain, which are allies of the Soviet Union." The news was suddenly blared out on loudspeakers on Moscow's cold, sleet-filled streets and all over the nation by radio.

In Japan, the cabinet fell. In America and England there was jubilation: doubts and worries about Stalin had begun to surface, particularly after it had been revealed that at Yalta Roosevelt had agreed to give the Soviet Union three votes in the proposed General Assembly; now there was a collective sigh of relief.

FDR by this time was in Warm Springs. He had boarded his railroad car, the Ferdinand Magellan, at 4:00 p.m. on the twenty-ninth, a few hours after the meeting with Stettinius, Bohlen, and MacLeish. Earlier in the day he had made it a point to talk to every member of his cabinet, according to Secretary of Labor Frances Perkins, and had checked up on last-minute matters and given his opinion or his approval of their actions. Admiral Leahy walked with FDR as he got into his car and left the White House for the Bureau of Engraving, where the Magellan waited. "He was cheerful, as usual," Leahy recalled, "and as he came to the door and got in his car, I remarked, 'Mr. President, it's very nice that you are leaving for a vacation. It is nice for us, too, because when you are away we have much more leisure than when you are here.' Roosevelt laughed and replied, 'That's all right Bill, Have a good time while I'm gone because when I come back I'm going to unload a lot of stuff on you.'"

Traveling with him were Daisy Suckley and Laura Delano, known as Polly, his eccentric, entertaining, purple-haired, flamboyant (especially in contrast to Daisy) cousin who also lived in Rhinebeck. He was looking forward to days of rest, relaxation, and bathing in the Warm Springs pool filled with the restorative water that came from the mineral springs. His home there, the Little White House, which he had built in 1932, was a one-story white cottage of simple frame construction; Daisy, in her bedroom in the cottage, could hear (and report to Dr. Bruenn) every coughing spell he had during the night. Others of his group were in cottages close by. The healing waters were an attraction, certainly for the president, but also he was away from Eleanor, which meant he could have Lucy Rutherfurd come and visit and be totally relaxed about it.

Molotov's announcement to Satō must have been a great relief for the president. At least *one* gamble was paying off. However, even though he had reset Stalin's fears about their relationship, Stalin did not give up on two points, as he wrote in his next message to FDR: "We Russians believe that in the present situation at the fronts when the enemy is confronted by the inevitability of capitulation, at any meeting with the Germans on the question of capitulation by representatives of one of the Allies, arrangements have to be made for the participation in this meeting of representatives of the other Ally." And Stalin was still bothered by the great disparity between the resistance the German army was putting up between the eastern front and the western front: "They continue to fight savagely with the Russians for some unknown junction Zemlianitsa in Czechoslovakia which they need as much as a dead man needs poultices, but surrender without any resistance such important towns in Central Germany as Osnabruk, Mannheim, Kassel." He also complained that some of the military information supplied his generals by Marshall "did not correspond to the actual course of events on the Eastern front in March" (while at the same time asking that Marshall continue to supply available data about the enemy).

And yet Stalin must have known that all Germans were in dread of the Red Army and were desperate to avoid surrendering to them. Hitler had deliberately instilled fear of Russians into the German people. In a message from Hitler read over the radio on February 24, he talked of the Jewish-Bolshevik plague and warned that if the Red Army triumphed, "the old men and children will be murdered, women and girls will be degraded as barracks whores. The remainder will march to Siberia."

But it didn't take Hitler to raise the awareness of German soldiers of what the Red Army had in store for them and their famous capital city. They knew that Red soldiers were looking forward to exacting revenge for the horrors they themselves had inflicted on Russians; they knew they had treated captured Russians—be they civilian or military—like scum. Red soldiers and civilians, having witnessed German atrocities— prisoners penned in open fields left to die, villages gutted, civilians torched and shot, cultural icons desecrated—were naturally filled with hatred for everything German.

Stalin made only token efforts to restrain his soldiers. He knew what he was about to unleash, as he told Milovan Djilas:

You have, of course, read Dostoevsky? Do you see what a complicated thing is man's soul, man's psyche? Well then, imagine a man who has fought from Stalingrad to Belgrade—over thousands of kilometers of his own devastated land, across the dead bodies of his comrades and dearest ones! How can such a man react normally? And what is so awful in his having fun with a woman, after such horrors? You have imagined the Red Army to be ideal. It is not ideal, nor can it be, even if it did not contain a certain percentage of criminals—we opened up our penitentiaries and stuck every-body in the army.

Soldiers of the Red Second Guards Tank Army, queried after the war wound down, supplied the information that 20 percent of them had relatives sent as slave labor to Germany and 90 percent had a relative killed or injured by German soldiers; they came from 2,430 villages the Germans had burned to the ground. The Germans, knowing the Red soldiers wanted revenge, dreaded the approaching Red Army, resisted them tooth and nail, and tried to lay down their arms to an American or British general. "The Germans had concentrated their forces against us as they prepared to surrender to the Americans and the British," Stalin later told Khrushchev.

STALIN HAD SUMMONED his military commanders to Moscow on March 25 to finalize plans for taking Berlin. A force of 2.5 million men, 41,000 guns, 6,250 tanks, and 7,500 planes had been assembled. An event happened that pleased Stalin enormously. On the evening of March 31, General Deane and his British counterpart, Admiral Ernest Archer, together with Harriman and Clark Kerr, met with him in his office at the Kremlin to deliver a cable to him from General Eisenhower. In it Eisenhower informed Stalin that he intended to bypass Berlin and concentrate on encircling and isolating the industrial Ruhr—to strike first in the center and subsequently to effect a linkup with the Red Army in the Regensburg-Linz area with a view to neutralizing the redoubt, Hitler's last line of defense. Eisenhower asked Stalin to cable back his intentions and let him know whether their plans meshed. Stalin, very pleased, answered that he agreed on all points: that Eisenhower's plan of dividing German forces by uniting the Soviet and Allied armies fell in with the Soviet plan, that the principal Soviet blow would be about the second half of May, that enemy forces on the eastern front were being gradually increased by divisions from northern Italy and Norway. He also included a sentence that probably amused Eisenhower: "Berlin has lost its former strategic significance. Therefore the Soviet High Command is considering the assigning of second rank forces on the Berlin salient." This was such a bald lie that Eisenhower probably didn't believe it. But Eisenhower was intent on avoiding Berlin: General Omar Bradley had given him an estimate that taking Berlin would cost 100,000 American lives (the Berlin siege would cost the Russians 361,367 casualties). Why should he waste American lives when he knew Stalin was eager to get there first? Eisenhower had made no secret around SHAEF headquarters of his aversion to taking Berlin: Berlin is "no longer a particularly important objective . . . I regard it as militarily unsound at this stage . . . to make Berlin a major objective, particularly in view of the fact that it is only 35 miles from the Russians . . . The function of our forces must be to crush the German armies rather than to dissipate our own strength in the occupation of empty and ruined cities." It didn't make sense to Eisenhower to sacrifice American lives when the city was going to be a four-power island in the middle of the Soviet zone. This view fitted in perfectly with Roosevelt's inclination, which was to let the Russians teach Germany its final lesson ("The German people as a whole must have it driven home to them that the whole nation has been engaged in a lawless conspiracy against the decencies of modern civilization," he had said to Stimson the previous summer), and with that of Marshall, who was very protective of American troops. Marshall was on record as saying, "Personally, and aside from all logistical, tactical or strategic implications I would be loath to hazard American lives for purely political purposes."

Stalin not only didn't put his second-string commanders in charge of the assault on Berlin; he initiated a competition for Berlin between General Rokossovsky and General Zhukov.

Stalin was ever after grateful to Eisenhower. Nikita Khrushchev recalled, "In conversations with his inner circle Stalin always stressed Eisenhower's decency, generosity, and chivalry in his dealings with his allies. Stalin said that if it hadn't been for Eisenhower, we wouldn't have succeeded in capturing Berlin . . . Berlin would have been occupied by the Americans . . . in which case . . . the question of Germany might have been decided quite differently."

Eisenhower had notified none of the people he should have before sending his cable to Stalin: not the Combined Chiefs of Staff, not his own deputy, Air Marshal Tedder. This unusual procedure, which essentially kept the prime minister out of the loop, was FDR's way of stopping Churchill from interfering with the decision: it is pure Roosevelt. Allowing the Red Army to take Berlin had added attractions for FDR besides saving American lives. He had never gotten over the mistake the Allies had made after World War I of not making the Germans experience defeat: German soldiers returning home in 1918 had been greeted by cheering crowds; Berlin never saw a foreign soldier. The entrance of the Red Army into Berlin now—a ragtag, vengeful, undisciplined force—would ram home to Germans the folly of their ways. FDR thought the Russians deserved their revenge; it was their due.

When the prime minister learned of Eisenhower's plan—which was immediately—he attempted to change it. He cabled a long, detailed message to FDR the next day that was all a buildup to the same subject— Berlin: "The fall of Berlin will be the supreme signal of defeat to the German people . . . The taking of Berlin by the Russians may lead them into a mood which will raise grave and formidable difficulties . . . [W]e should march as far east into Germany as possible and should Berlin be in our grasp we should certainly take it." He accused FDR of changing plans they had agreed upon, a valid charge FDR never addressed. FDR's answer—a long, soothing, evasive, detailed discussion of Allied military plans—was mainly drafted by Marshall, but FDR told Daisy that it was he, knowing what the plans were, who "sent an explanation to W.S.C. backing up Eisenhower."

Three days after FDR died, Eisenhower ordered the U.S. Army to halt at the Elbe. "Where in the hell did you get this?" asked General William Simpson. "From Ike," answered General Bradley.

17

ROOSEVELT DIES

In mid-March, FDR was according himself the luxury of still being undecided as to whether to attend the opening or the closing of the San Francisco Conference, admitting as much to reporters in a press conference on March 13. But as to his belief in the rightness of his policies—that was something entirely different—he was steadfast: working with the Soviet Union was imperative. Having Russia one of the four policemen remained to his thinking the way to keep some modicum of control over the marshal. Driving FDR was not the idealistic idea that he and Stalin, America and the Soviet Union, were going to be friends, but his realistic assessment, as he had explained it to Mackenzie King, that "Russia was going to be very powerful. The thing to do was to get plans definitely made for disarmament." What other mechanism besides the yet-to-be-created Security Council could conceptually level the playing field? It stood to reason to FDR that he had to have the most dangerous force in the world—Stalin—inside the tent, which meant dealing firmly and fairly with Stalin while avoiding a split.

He had articulated this idea very clearly in the exceedingly short but pointed inaugural address he had delivered, standing on the south porch of the White House on a bitterly cold morning (hatless, capeless) just before leaving for the Yalta Conference. It contained a section clearly directed not only at Stalin but at Allied decision makers watching how he handled Stalin and at Soviet decision makers wondering if he was on the level: "We have learned the simple truth, as Emerson said, that 'The only way to have a friend is to be one.' We can gain no lasting peace if we approach it with suspicion and mistrust or with fear. We can gain it only if we proceed with the understanding, the confidence, and the courage which flow from conviction." Every action Roosevelt took in the few months left to him flowed from this idea. Churchill must have listened to the speech (and to most of the ideas FDR expressed in 1945) with a sinking heart.

FDR was above all practical, but his practicality wasn't visible to his contemporaries. His insistence on unconditional surrender, another of his initially startling ideas, was not a philosophical approach to ending hostilities but a practical and effective way to avoid negotiating a peace. A negotiated peace was much to be avoided because it meant at best conferring with his allies in advance and at worst a peace conference: in either case he wouldn't be in absolute control. By insisting on unconditional surrender, FDR could deal with each nation—in turn—as circumstances dictated and make decisions on an ad hoc basis. The president had dressed the idea up in a charming story he loved to tell: how magnanimous General Grant had been, telling General Lee after he had surrendered, "Let the horses go back to the fields, get back to the art of peace." But there was nothing magnanimous about the idea: unconditional surrender was the path to power.

His obsession, his absolute dedication to the formation of the United Nations, as well, was a practical approach to solving a problem— preventing an arms buildup—that he believed would be the most effective way to keep peace among nations. A peace organization would be the most efficient method of arms control, and arms control was the key to world peace. In the muscular United Nations FDR envisioned, the four nations (five, with France), necessarily making decisions together, were going to constitute the military force that would act as policemen to the world. And as the nations worked together, they would be watching each other, checking on each other as well as on the rest of the world. FDR's insistence on the inclusion of China as the fourth policeman, even though it was paralyzed by internal and external strife, was as well on practical grounds. Asians were important in terms of future demographics, he knew, because of their enormous population, but there was another asset: China would be a check on Russia. China and Russia shared the world's longest border; they would be watching each other.

Now, in March, with the San Francisco Conference almost upon him, FDR was looking forward to the time when the UN was up and running and its power could be tested, according to King's diary; "he would welcome some outbreak between a couple of countries, with a view of testing out the machinery of use of forces. Let them see how it works before making too many treaties as to military undertakings."

Conscious as he was that he was head of the most powerful nation in the world, why was he giving Stalin so much rope? He felt he had to. FDR had stipulated to Stalin what he considered necessary regarding Poland during the Yalta Conference: "I don't want the Poles to be able to question the Polish elections. The matter is not only one of principle but of practical politics." He expected Stalin to live up to this. He didn't really expect a free, American-style election: Poland's history, like Russia's, was one of despotic rule, and it was not going to change overnight, but he did expect Stalin to give the Polish people some measure of autonomy by including various disparate groups in the government. And appearances counted.

He undoubtedly realized that Stalin was motivated by fear of a resurgent Germany, because Stalin had expressed the thought so often. Whether or not he realized the depth of that fear is a question that cannot be answered. At the end of March, Stalin voiced this fear to a visiting Czech delegation:

> We are the new Slavophile-Leninists, Slavophile-Bolsheviks, communists who stand for the unity and alliance of the Slavic peoples. We consider that irrespective of political and social differences, irrespective of social and ethnic differences, all Slavs must ally with one another against the common enemy—the Germans . . . Many think the Germans will never be able to threaten us again. This is not so . . . It is impossible to get rid of the Germans, they will remain . . . We will be merciless towards the Germans but our allies will treat them with kid gloves. Thus we Slavs must be prepared for the Germans to rise again against us.

On FDR's last day in Washington, at the meeting where Bohlen had seen him angrier than he had ever seen him before, the assembled group in the Oval Office of Stettinius, MacLeish, Bohlen, Leahy, and assistant State Department secretaries had worked with him on a second message to Stalin concerning Poland. Molotov was behind the rejection of Clark Kerr and Harriman's suggestions of Poles for the interim commission to come to Moscow. The message that went out over FDR's signature, co-signed by Churchill, pointed out that this was wrong: "The Warsaw government cannot under the [Yalta] agreement claim the right to select or reject what Poles are to be brought to Moscow by the Commission for consultation. Can we not agree that it is up to the Commission to select the Polish leaders to come to Moscow[?] . . . It is obvious to me that if the right of the Commission to select these Poles is limited or shared with the Warsaw Government the very foundation on which our agreement rests would be destroyed."

It has been overlooked by historians that besides abrogating the treaty with Japan, Stalin made another concession after receiving FDR's emotional cable of August 4: he changed his mind about the composition of the Polish government. It didn't seem that way from the opening sentences of the message—"Matters on the Polish question have really reached a dead end"—but then he went into a detailed, reasonable discussion. Stalin quoted Molotov as quoting to him a variety of Clark Kerr and Harriman's statements: "No member of the Provisional Government will be included in the composition of the Polish government of national unity . . . Each member of the Moscow commission [must] be given the right to invite an unlimited number of people from Poland and from London." These were misstatements, undoubtedly supplied by Molotov.

But having supplied these quotations to buttress his case—at much greater length and with more specificity—Stalin then backtracked. It is quite possible that this message was a collaborative effort with Molotov. It is also quite possible that he now realized that what Roosevelt and Churchill were asking of him was not to give up power in Poland but to observe the rules they had set up at Yalta. Stalin wrote that the reconstruction of the Polish Provisional Government "means not its liquidation but just its reconstruction by way of broadening it," that the provisional government had to be recognized "as the greatest force in Poland as compared to those singletons who will be called from London and from Poland," and that Polish leaders who really strove to establish friendly relations between Poland and Russia would be the ones chosen. He suggested a similar setup to that established in Yugoslavia: "As regards the numerical correlation of old and new ministers . . . there could be established approximately a similar correlation which was realized in respect to the Government in Yugoslavia." (The ratio in Yugoslavia was twenty-one Tito appointees, six from other groups.) He closed with a definite peace offering: "I think that, taking into consideration the above-stated remarks, a harmonious decision on the Polish question can be reached in a short time."

Stalin then made a very specific, significant concession, by way of a message to Churchill, his biggest critic, which he made sure the president saw—instructing Gromyko to deliver both of his messages to FDR simultaneously. It was major: "If you deem it necessary I shall try to induce the Provisional Polish Government to withdraw its objections to inviting Mikolajczyk, provided he publicly endorses the decisions of the Crimea Conference." Because Molotov had put himself in charge of choosing the delegates to the Polish Provisional Government, and was on record with Harriman and Clark Kerr as strongly protesting Mikołajczyk's inclusion, this was indeed a serious concession: it meant Stalin was offering to overrule Molotov.

At the same time as FDR was knocking heads with Stalin, he was having a problem keeping Churchill in line. Churchill was pushing him to take a tougher, confrontational stand on Poland. FDR restrained him in cable after cable. "I very much hope, therefore, that you will not send any message to Uncle Joe at this juncture—especially as I feel that certain parts of your proposed text might produce a reaction quite contrary to your intent," he cabled Churchill on March 11. The next day, another prod, writing to the prime minister, "The Yalta agreements, if they are followed, should correct most of the abuses alleged in your 909." Three days later, another strong statement—basically a lecture—that Churchill should adhere to FDR's point of view: "I cannot agree that we are confronted with a breakdown of the Yalta agreement . . . I cannot urge upon you too strongly the vital importance of agreeing without further delay on instructions to our Ambassadors . . . I . . . continue to feel that our approach would be better calculated to achieve the desired result." Next, a reminder: "You will recall that the agreement on Poland was a compromise between the Soviet position that the Lublin Government should merely be 'enlarged' and our contention that we should start with a clean slate . . . The wording of the resulting agreement reflects this compromise . . . If we attempt to evade the fact that we placed somewhat more emphasis on the Lublin Poles than on the other two groups . . . I feel we will expose ourselves to the charge that we are attempting to go back on the Crimean decision."

He was also reminding Churchill that Stalin had to be brought in on policy decisions, writing to the prime minister on March 22, responding to a cable Churchill wanted to send the German high command regarding German treatment of prisoners, "If Marshal Stalin agrees, I will go forward with you." And again, discussing Greece, in April, FDR warned Churchill against setting up a bilateral commission: "This would look as though we, for our part, were disregarding the Yalta decision for tripartite action in liberated areas and might easily be interpreted as indicating that we consider the Yalta decisions no longer valid."

Marshall and Stimson believed he was following the right path, indeed had no choice, as is evident in a passage Stimson wrote in his diary at the beginning of April:

> We simply cannot allow a rift to come between the two nations without endangering the entire peace of the world . . . Marshall told me that he had anticipated these troubles and thought they would be pretty bad and irritating but thought that we must put up with them. I told Stettinius that in retrospect Russia had been very good to us on the large issues. She had kept her word and carried out her engagements. We must remember that she has not learned the amenities of diplomatic intercourse and we must expect bad language from her.

The next day, April 3, Stimson went further in articulating FDR's policy of accommodation in the face of problems. He didn't have to name names; he was thinking of Harriman and Deane—in Russia and on the firing line—dealing with Molotov virtually every day; he and Marshall saw things as FDR did:

> There has been growing quite a strain of irritating feeling between our government and the Russians and it seems to me that it is a time to use all the restraint I can on these other people who have been apparently getting a little more irritated. I have myself been in the various crises enough to feel the importance of firm dealing with the Russians, but, as Marshall agrees, what we want is to state our facts with perfectly cold-blooded firmness and not show any temper.

A good part of the problem regarding Harriman and Deane was that they had been in Moscow too long. The life of a foreign diplomat in Moscow was enough to try anyone's soul. Followed everywhere, unable to freely mix with Muscovites, always fighting mountains of government red tape, waiting weeks and months for decisions that were always delayed because of the pervasive Russian fear of making a decision without authorization, they were emotionally exhausted. And life at Spaso House itself was hard. The house was gloomy because some of the windows had been boarded up, and the food was inadequate, even with infusions of packages from America, as was the heating system: the most popular room in the house belonged to Robert Meiklejohn, Harriman's secretary, who had rigged up a kerosene stove, the warmth of which attracted everyone, including Clark Kerr and Harriman. The final irritation was Christmas packages that took until April to reach them. Nothing, really, had changed in Moscow since FDR had advised Bullitt in 1933, "You will be more or less in the position of Commander Byrd—cut off from civilization and I think you should organize your expedition as if you were setting out on a ship which was to touch no port for a year."

If FDR presented a confident face to Churchill, nevertheless he had qualms. Very uncharacteristically, he unburdened himself to Chester Bowles, the brainy former advertising man who served in his administration in various capacities and who would become special assistant to the first secretary-general of the United Nations, Trygve Lie:

> We've taken a great risk here, an enormous risk, and it involves Russian intentions. The Russians have got enormous problems, they're flat on their back, their whole country has been devastated, and if they have any sense they're going to pull in their horns for twenty years and be people you can live with. I don't think they've changed their concepts basically about communism but I do think that the practical problems of their suffering that they've gone through and their physical devastation is going to make them adjust to the world somewhat differently. And we should encourage them in every way we conceivably can. At the same time we ought to keep our guard up to make sure that they don't switch gears, but I don't see why they would.

Then, according to Bowles, he went on to say,

> "However certain things are beginning to worry me" and he told
> me the story of a Polish camp in Poland where a lot of American
> prisoners were held and they agreed at Yalta that America was to
> fly in doctors and nurses. The Russians had taken over the area and
> had held them up, and he was firing off cables to our Embassy in
> Moscow. There were two or three other things . . . He said, "I'm
> worried. I still think Stalin will be out of his mind if he doesn't
> cooperate, but maybe he's not going to; in which case we're going
> to have to take a different view."

"Worried" though he was, this statement shows that FDR was not
being taken in by Stalin, as so many of his critics have claimed over the
years. To the contrary, it shows him pursuing a policy of accommodation because he expected it to work out. The POW situation had been
a momentary blip, had been resolved and receded into the background,
as he had hoped.

FDR sent a cable carefully admonishing Churchill, also worked out
on his last day in Washington, March 29:

> I have likewise been watching with anxiety and concern the
> developments of Soviet attitude since the Crimea Conference. I
> am acutely aware of the dangers inherent in the present course of
> events.

On April 5, in Warm Springs, FDR held a press conference. Sergio
Osmeña, president of the Philippines, with whom he had been discussing the date for the granting of independence for the country, was
visiting him. FDR told the reporters from the press pool he was giving
them a story he wanted them to release on the day he returned to Washington, which, he said, would be in another week or ten days.

They asked him about the extra votes Russia was going to get in
the General Assembly. FDR gave them a fulsome, charming anecdote,
whether true or not no one knows:

> Stalin said to me—and this is the essence of it—"You know there
> are two parts of Russia that have been completely devastated. Every

building is gone, every farm house, and there are millions of people living in these territories—and it is very important from the point of view of humanity—and we thought, as a gesture, they ought to be given something as a result of this coming victory. They have had very little civilization. One is the Ukraine, and the other is White Russia. We all felt—not any of us coming from there in the government—we think it would be fitting to give them a vote in the Assembly. In these two sections, millions have been killed, and we think it would be very heartening—would help to build them up—if we could get them a vote in the Assembly."

He asked me what I thought.

I said to Stalin, "Are you going to make that request of the Assembly?"

He said, "I think we should."

I said, "I think it would be all right—I don't know how the Assembly will vote."

He said, "Would you favor it?"

I said, "Yes, largely on sentimental grounds. If I were on the delegation—which I am not—I would probably vote 'yes.'"

That has not come out in any paper.

He said, "That would be the Soviet Union, plus White Russia, plus the Ukraine."

Then I said, "By the way, if the Conference in San Francisco should give you three votes in the Assembly—if you get three votes—I do not know what would happen if I don't put in a plea for three votes in the States." And I said, "I would make the plea for three votes and insist on it."

It is not really of any great importance. It is an investigatory body only. I told Stettinius to forget it. I am not awfully keen for three votes in the Assembly. It is the little fellow who needs the vote in the Assembly. This business about the number of votes in the Assembly does not make a great deal of difference.

Then FDR was asked, "They don't decide anything, do they?" And he replied, "No."

The next evening, April 6, FDR had the idea of a stamp commemorating the UN that would say simply, "April 25, 1945, Towards United Nations." The postmaster general, Frank Walker, was located, and it was quickly arranged that following the president's approval of the design, such a stamp would be issued on April 25, the day the San Francisco Conference convened.

Warm Springs had been good for FDR. He seemed to be gaining strength. Whereas at the end of March, in Washington, Dr. Bruenn had noted he was working too hard and looked "very badly (grey)," after a week in Warm Springs, Bruenn observed a "decided improvement." Daisy, too, thought FDR was mending. He mentioned to her that he was looking forward to retiring the following year, "after he gets the peace organization well started." In her diary for April 8 she wrote, "He is very slowly improving each day. It shows in different ways. He sits a little straighter in his chair, his voice is a little clearer and stronger, his face is less drawn and he is *happier.*" The next day Lucy Rutherfurd and her friend Elizabeth Shoumatoff, who was going to paint a portrait of FDR, arrived. Daisy wrote that evening, "F. looks splendidly."

Roosevelt had a major speech to give for Jefferson's birthday, April 13, that would be carried by all the major radio networks. On the morning of April 11 he worked on the final draft with Dorothy Brady, one of his secretaries. He used the Jefferson quote Sherwood had supplied as the opening salvo in an argument to share knowledge of the atomic bomb with Russia.

"Thomas Jefferson, himself a distinguished scientist, once spoke of 'the brotherly spirit of science, which unites into one family all its votaries of whatever grade and however widely dispersed throughout the different quarters of the globe.'"

FDR segued from that to say, "Today, science has brought all the different quarters of the globe so close together that it is impossible to isolate them one from another.

"Today we are faced with the preeminent fact that, if civilization is to survive, we must cultivate the science of human relationships—the ability of all peoples, of all kinds, to live together and work together at peace."

Besides working on his speech that morning, FDR dealt with the cables, memos, letters, and legislative bills that had to be dispatched every day. He looked over and okayed three important messages, one to Stalin and two to Churchill, that came from the Map Room for his approval: they were in perfect tune with his policies. It is notable that all three cables had to do with keeping Churchill, Stalin, and himself on the same page. They also show FDR's method of control: he was declaring to both leaders that the misunderstandings over Bern were "minor," and by so categorizing them, he made them minor.

To Stalin he wrote,

> Thank you for your frank explanation of the Soviet point of view of the Bern incident which now appears to have faded into the past without having accomplished any useful purpose.
>
> There must not, in any event, be mutual mistrust and minor misunderstandings of this character should not arise in the future. I feel sure that when our armies make contact in Germany and join in a fully coordinated offensive the Nazi Armies will disintegrate.

The message went, as all such messages did, back to the Map Room, for transmission by cable to Harriman at the U.S. embassy in Moscow: upon receipt Harriman was expected to notify Molotov and present it at the Kremlin.

FDR's first message to the prime minister had to do with a cable to the German government Churchill wanted him to co-sign to allow the Red Cross to feed the starving civilian population in German-occupied Holland. "You may send it as a joint message provided it is approved by Stalin," wrote FDR.

FDR's second message to Churchill shows beyond a doubt that he had not changed his mind about how to deal with Stalin; it is, in fact, an affirmation of that policy:

> I would minimize the general Soviet problem as much as possible because these problems, in one form or another, seem to arise every day and most of them straighten out as is the case of the Bern meeting.
>
> We must be firm, however, and our course thus far is correct.

After finishing off all the matters that needed his attention, FDR broke for lunch with his women: Daisy, Laura Delano, Lucy Rutherfurd, Lucy's friend Elizabeth Shoumatoff, and his secretary Dorothy Brady. In the afternoon he went out on the porch with Dorothy Brady and put the finishing touches on the Jefferson Day speech. He told his secretary Grace Tully that he would start work the next morning on his speech to the United Nations.

It was a lovely day, "wonderful warm air," according to Daisy, so later in the afternoon she and Lucy and Fala and FDR went out for a two-hour drive.

Morgenthau was expected for dinner. When he arrived at 7:00, he found FDR sitting in front of the card table, his legs up on a wicker stool, alcohol, ice, and glasses in front of him, mixing cocktails. "I was terribly shocked when I saw him," Morgenthau recalled, "and I found that he had aged terrifically and looked very haggard. His hands shook so that he started to knock the glasses over, and I had to hold each glass as he poured out the cocktail." He took two cocktails and then seemed to feel a little bit better. He talked about San Francisco. " 'I am going there on my train and at three o'clock in the afternoon I will appear on the stage in my wheelchair, and I will make a speech.' Then he grimaced," according to Morgenthau, "clapped his hands, and said 'And then they will applaud me and I will leave.' "

Meanwhile, Harriman, in Moscow, fed up with Molotov and Stalin after all the wrangling he and Clark Kerr had been having with them over the Polish government, and thinking FDR's message minimizing conflict was wrong, instead of presenting it to Molotov, held on to it. He now cabled FDR "respectfully" suggesting that he delay giving Stalin the cable so that the president and the prime minister could take the same line to Stalin, and—even *more* significantly—Harriman suggested to the president that the word "minor" be deleted from the cable because, Harriman wrote, "I must confess that the misunderstanding appeared to me to be of a major character." Roosevelt didn't care what it looked like to Harriman, he cared about getting along with Stalin, and he didn't want any blowups: he wasn't going to let a rift happen. Leahy, in Washington, knew this—knew that FDR didn't agree with Harriman—and the morning of the twelfth sent from the Map Room, for Roosevelt's approval, the following cable for him to send to Harriman: "I have replied to Churchill's 940 by quoting my message to Stalin. Churchill is therefore fully informed and there is no necessity of your delaying delivery of my message to Stalin. Your second question. I do not wish to delete the word 'minor' as it is my desire to consider the Berne misunderstanding a minor incident."

FDR woke up the next morning with a slight headache and a stiff neck. Dr. Bruenn rubbed his neck. He spent the morning hours, as usual, in front of the stone fireplace, sitting, as he so often did, in his leather armchair drawn up to the card table, now covered with the White House mail—reading, okaying, signing the various documents put in front of him by Hassett. Because the pouch came unusually late, he knew there would not be time to start on his San Francisco speech before lunch. He spoke with Dewey Long, in charge of White House travel arrangements. His plan was to be in Washington on April 19 and leave at noon the next day for San Francisco. Now FDR told Long that he wanted the train to follow the direct rather than the scenic route to San Francisco.

Leahy's suggested message to Harriman that would bear FDR's signature if he approved went out from the Map Room to Warm Springs at 10:50 a.m. At 1:06 the Map Room received Roosevelt's one-word cable: "Approved." Nine minutes after that, at 1:15, the president said, looking at Daisy and putting his left hand up to the back of his head, "I have a terrific pain in the back of my head." He lurched forward, lost consciousness. He never regained it. At 3:30 p.m., he died.

His magnificent plans—of personally presiding over the San Francisco Conference, of then going on a triumphal European tour, of getting off the ship and being driven through London amid cheering crowds to Buckingham Palace to be the guest of the king and queen of England, of possibly being the first secretary-general of the United Nations ("the moderator," as he thought of it) following his presidency—vanished. People all over the world felt the sudden loss of his leadership. Tommy Corcoran, an early member of his administration, voiced many people's dreams of FDR's postpresidential future when he wrote, "I thought that once the war was over, he would resign the Presidency in order to head up . . . the United Nations, and chair the world."

Although it is often thought the cause of FDR's death was high blood pressure and a weak heart, these were contributing factors but were *not* the immediate cause of his death, according to Dr. Bruenn, who characterized the stroke as "a bolt out of the blue." Bruenn diagnosed the event as a subarachnoid hemorrhage caused by a cerebral aneurysm. Such an aneurysm could have been present for years. It could have burst anytime: FDR could have died years before.

THERE WAS AN EMBASSY farewell party in progress at Spaso House for the departing foreign service officer John Melby on April 12 when, well past 1:00 a.m., the officer on duty called Ambassador Harriman to tell him he had just heard on a late-night radio broadcast that the president had died. The party was beginning to wind down as Harriman went back into the party room to make the announcement, and as he finished, the music stopped and everyone left.

Because Stalin was a night owl who routinely worked until the early hours of the morning and all his associates in the Kremlin kept the same hours, when Harriman telephoned Molotov to tell him the news, Mikhail Potrubach, Molotov's aide, still on duty, answered the phone. Harriman told him he would like to see Stalin and Molotov "in the afternoon, earlier if possible," then, five minutes later, he called again to request a meeting with Molotov that same night. According to Potrubach, "The ambassador was obviously not quite himself." After relaying this request to Molotov, Potrubach called back to say that Molotov would come to Spaso House "immediately, if this is convenient for him."

When the usually reserved, coldly proper Molotov arrived at Spaso House, remembered Harriman, "he seemed deeply moved and disturbed . . . stayed for some time talking about the part President Roosevelt had played in the war and in the plans for peace, of the respect Marshal Stalin and all the Russian people had had for him and how much Marshal Stalin had valued his visit to Yalta . . . I have never heard Molotov talk so earnestly." An appointment with Stalin was arranged for Harriman the next evening in the Kremlin.

When Harriman walked into Stalin's office at 8:00 the next evening, Molotov, as usual, was present. Stalin was never known for any display of emotion, no one ever remarked on or saw him greeting anyone with anything but a perfunctory handshake, but now he stood, and, as he greeted Harriman, he grasped his hand and held on to it. The tall, lean Harriman and the short, thickset Stalin remained standing until Stalin released Harriman's hand and they sat down. The marshal, according to Harriman, was "deeply shaken and more disturbed than I had ever seen him."

Stalin proceeded to ask questions about the circumstances surrounding Roosevelt's death. He wanted to make sure he wasn't poisoned. Then he said he did not believe "there would be any change in American policy under Truman," undoubtedly hoping that his statement would elicit a response, either positive or negative. Harriman responded reassuringly and explained the overriding reason FDR had chosen Truman: "The President knew that he would need Senate approval of his peace plans . . . This was one of the main reasons he had chosen Senator Truman as his running mate." He then briefed Stalin on the uncertainties and changes that Truman's sudden accession to the presidency would naturally create, after which Stalin exclaimed, "President Roosevelt has died but his cause must live on. We shall support President Truman with all our forces and all our will."

Their talk turned to the San Francisco Conference, and Harriman mentioned Roosevelt's disappointment that Molotov was not going to be present, the president's worry that the absence of the Soviet foreign minister would be taken as suggesting a rift between Russia and the other powers, whose foreign ministers would be there, or even that Russia did not consider the United Nations of paramount importance. Stalin replied that he wanted to give immediate assurance to the American people to indicate his desire to continue on a cooperative basis with his country, whereupon Harriman suggested if that was the case, he send Molotov to San Francisco. Further, that on the way Molotov should stop in Washington to meet Truman. Stalin asked a few questions: Was Harriman expressing his personal views? Were they the views of the new president and the secretary of state? After Harriman assured him the views were his but his government would confirm them, "Marshal Stalin then stated categorically Mr. Molotov's trip to the United States, although difficult at the time, would be arranged." Molotov had not entered the conversation proper, but while they were talking, remembered Harriman, "Mr. Molotov kept muttering, 'Time, time, time.'" Harriman was observing the impediment to Molotov's presence at San Francisco: it was Molotov himself. In front of the American ambassador Molotov was showing his reluctance to obey orders. He was the one who had decided against going to San Francisco: Stalin had apparently acquiesced. Now Stalin had taken matters into his own hands, and Molotov would have to go whether he wanted to or not. As they parted, Stalin reassuringly said to Harriman, "Our policy regarding Japan as agreed to at the Crimea Conference remains unchanged."

Stalin ordered the Soviet nation into mourning. All government agencies in Moscow were ordered to display mourning flags on their buildings. It was an unheard-of occurrence, that the bourgeois leader of a capitalist country should be so honored. Kathleen Harriman wrote to her friend Pamela Churchill, "Jesus it was a shock. Red flags with black borders hung from all houses today throughout Moscow—something I'd never guessed would happen." Virtually the entire Soviet nation, people at every level of society, reacted as if they had lost a real friend. It was "suggested" by the all-powerful Council of People's Commissars that all government agencies hang flags of mourning from their buildings, which of course they did. Not just flags flew black borders, but the front pages of all Soviet newspapers announcing the president's death were bordered in black as well: his death dominated the news for days. The front page of *Izvestia* on April 13 featured Stalin's condolence letter to Eleanor Roosevelt, in which he called the president "the great organizer of the struggle of freedom-loving nations against the common enemy and . . . the leader in the cause of ensuring security world over." Soviet archives show that Molotov and Stalin actually collaborated on this letter and that the words about "the great organizer" are in Stalin's handwriting and replaced Molotov's wordier "the friend and comrade-in-arms in the struggle against our common enemy." *Izvestia* also, tellingly, in view of the Marxist emphasis on class struggle and the fact that Stalin looked through the paper before it was published, described Roosevelt not as a capitalist but as an ally of workers: FDR "pursued the 'New Deal,' which aimed at restricting monopolies and at improving the social conditions of broad masses of people . . . the leader of the great democracy across the ocean." The article dwelled on Roosevelt's "progressive thinking, his irreconcilability in the face of fascist aggression and desire to ensure security in the future."

Stalin's letter to President Truman, in which he wrote of Roosevelt's historic role as "the greatest politician on an international scale and a spokesman for peace and security after the war," was also prominently displayed. *Pravda* had a long article headlined "The Spokesman for Peace and Security," which ended, "Let this friendship tempered in the time of war, flourish, as a really grand monument to President Roosevelt, who passed away untimely." As well *Pravda* devoted space to all the details of the funeral in the capital and even printed excerpts from the Jefferson Day speech Roosevelt was scheduled to give the day after he died, including his plea for the end of wars: "The work, my friends, is peace. More than an end of this war—an end to all wars. Yes, an end, forever, to this impractical, unrealistic settlement of the differences between governments by mass killing of peoples."

Harry Hopkins sent a cable to Stalin, the first sentence of which was a warning that FDR's death was going to mean trouble for the Soviet Union: "I want you to know that I feel that Russia has lost her greatest friend in America. The President was deeply impressed by your determination and confidence that the Nazi tyrants of the world will be driven from power forever." Stalin tacitly acknowledged the warning in his reply: "I agree completely with you . . . I personally feel deep sorrow in the loss of a trusted friend—a man of great spirit."

The Communist Party and the NKVD, following the government policy of checking and analyzing public opinion of important events, found Russians alarmed by the question of what Roosevelt's successor's attitude toward them would be, because he had become such a super-star in their world, but also because they were aware of the continuing undercurrent of anti-Russian sentiment in America "The news of the death of the U.S. President Franklin Roosevelt was met in Moscow with a feeling of sincere condolence and deep regret for the untimely death . . . Simultaneously, a feeling of alarm is expressed . . . if Roosevelt's successor, Truman, continues Roosevelt's policy in the most important issues of war, peace, and postwar security, as well as toward the Soviet Union."

Peace and security: that was what Roosevelt stood for in the mind of the Russian people and, it became clear when Hopkins came to Moscow in late May, in Stalin's mind as well.

There was a simple funeral service at the embassy two days later. It drew the top brass of all branches of the Soviet armed forces, Molotov and all the members of his commissariat, all the senior foreign diplomats in Moscow, every member of the U.S. embassy staff, and every U.S. soldier and visiting journalist in Moscow.

Later that same day Harriman went to the Kremlin to talk to Stalin. Several weeks earlier, against all orders, an American air crew at Poltava had put an anti-Communist Pole in an American uniform, stashed him in their plane, and smuggled him out of the air base. Stalin now, to Harriman, angrily accused the entire U.S. Air Force of conspiring with the anti-Communist Polish underground. That meant, Harriman angrily retorted, Stalin was "impugning the loyalty of General Marshall." Stalin's reply was interesting for its bluntness as well as for its implied apology: "I would trust General Marshall with my life. This wasn't he but a junior officer." Harriman took the unusual moment after this statement to say that FDR thought the principal issue clouding U.S.-Soviet relations was Poland and that when Molotov was in America he should therefore try to find common ground on the subject with Stettinius and Eden. The result was surprising. Molotov, who was as usual present, "grumbled . . . But Stalin assured Harriman that Molotov would go under instructions to find common ground . . . 'The sooner the better,' he said, overruling his unhappy foreign commissar."

18

HOPKINS TURNS BACK
THE CLOCK

For FDR, haunted by the memory of how the Senate had trashed President Wilson, always conscious of the crucial power of the Senate to make or break foreign policy, Truman had a great attraction: he was an honest, hardworking, popular senator. To have him, as vice president, pushing the United Nations would greatly improve the chances of Senate approval of the world peace organization and the final peace terms.

But although FDR knew Truman was a hard worker and honest, he never took the time to educate him, bring him into his inner circle—in fact had barely communicated with his new vice president. His attention was still focused on winding down the war, the unconditional surrender of Germany, and supervising the creation of the new organization that was going to take place at San Francisco—all of which was almost upon him. Educating the new VP would come later in the summer. "FDR's one really great wish is to get this international organization for peace started," confided Daisy Suckley to her diary on March 31. "Nothing else counts, next to that." Truman never even entered the Map Room while FDR was president: his first visit was after FDR died.

Molotov's stopover in Washington began well enough but from the Soviet point of view ended in disaster. When the foreign minister arrived, Truman paid a brief call on him at Blair House, the official residence for important foreign visitors, where Molotov was staying, and they exchanged short, polite amenities. The next day Molotov met with

Truman in the Oval Office at 5:30. Present were the two interpreters, Bohlen and Pavlov, the two ambassadors, Harriman and Gromyko, and Leahy.

Truman had carefully, in a short time, brought himself up to speed on foreign policy. He studied the Yalta transcripts and documents; he spoke with his foreign policy experts. In preparation for Molotov's visit he had called together Stettinius, Stimson, Marshall, Secretary of the Navy James Forrestal, Harriman, and Deane to brief him on their views and the line they thought he should take with the foreign commissar. Stettinius, while not advocating any change in relations with Russia, told Truman that the situation in Poland was grave, that he had heard the Russians were preparing to insist the Lublin government be recognized and represent Poland at San Francisco. Stimson, worried there might be a change of FDR's policy in view of Soviet intransigence, advised Truman "to be very careful and see whether we couldn't get ironed out on the situation without getting into a head on collision." (He also knew that the notion of a free, unfettered election in Poland was pie-in-the-sky, writing in his diary that night, "I know very well from my experience with other nations that there are no nations except the U.S. and the U.K. which have a real idea of what an independent free ballot is.") Marshall supported Stimson's "let's keep getting along" approach, but the others—Forrestal, Deane, Harriman, and Leahy— were of a different mind-set: backing a get-tough stance. Leahy, who, in fact, was tutoring Truman on how cavalierly Stalin was violating his Yalta pledges, noted that there was definitely a consensus of opinion— four (Forrestal, Deane, Harriman, and Leahy) to two (Marshall and Stettinius)—that Truman should take "a strong American attitude" toward Molotov.

There are different versions of the interchange that took place when the president and Molotov met in the White House. There is agreement that Molotov led off by inquiring about the still-secret agreements reached at Yalta regarding the Far East: Was Truman prepared to honor them? Truman assured Molotov the commitments would be honored. They then discussed Poland.

According to Bohlen, as Molotov started talking about those Poles who were working against the Red Army (which was a fact), Truman "firmly and briskly" said he wished Molotov to inform Stalin of his concern over the Soviet failure to live up to the agreement made at Yalta.

At this point, "Molotov turned a little ashy and attempted to steer the discussion back to the Far East," but Truman closed off the conversation, saying, "That will be all, Mr. Molotov. I would appreciate it if you would transmit my views to Marshal Stalin," and dismissed him.

Truman remembered the conversation differently. He remembered Molotov as saying, "I have never been talked to like that in my life," to which *he* had replied, "Carry out your agreements and you won't get talked to like that." However, Truman's naval aide Admiral Robert Dennison, although never commenting on this particular interchange, obliquely did just that when he recalled various instances of misremembering to the historian Wilson Miscamble, author of *From Roosevelt to Truman*. Dennison told Miscamble that after "a perfectly normal and amiable conversation with a caller . . . after the caller left he would say to me, in effect, 'I certainly set him straight,' or 'I let him have it,' . . . the president's remarks having no conceivable relation to the conversation I had just heard." And neither Bohlen nor Gromyko corroborated Truman's version of what he said, although both agreed on his abruptness. Gromyko wrote of the conversation, "Quite unexpectedly—still in the middle of our talk—Truman suddenly half rose and gave a sign to indicate that the conversation was over." Gromyko would also note, "Almost at once serious strains developed in Soviet-US relations."

Harriman maintains that he was shocked at Truman's bluntness: "I was a little taken aback, frankly, when the president attacked Molotov so vigorously." Not because he thought Molotov's sensibilities had been offended, for "he could be rough and tough," but "I did regret that Truman went at it so hard because his behavior gave Molotov an excuse to tell Stalin that the Roosevelt policy was being abandoned." Leahy, on the other hand, thought Truman had reacted well, writing that Truman's attitude toward Molotov "was more than pleasing to me."

Roosevelt had been the glue holding together the alliance. Without him, without his iron hand in the velvet glove, it was rapidly fraying.

Harriman's change of heart actually began before FDR's death. He not only tried to change FDR's last message to Stalin, disapproving of its conciliatory tone, but wrote the president a cable that at the last moment he decided not to send. Frank Costigliola, author of *Roosevelt's Lost Alliances*, found it in Harriman's files at the Library of Congress. In it Harriman made the implausible charge (to FDR!) that FDR's policies had "been influenced from a sense of fear" and went on to detail the "almost daily . . . outrageous . . . insults" to which he was being subjected. He had enough sense not to send the cable, for if one thing was clear, it was that Roosevelt never feared Stalin and would not take kindly to an ambassador who posited such a thought. The unsent cable remained in Harriman's files. The sentiment that underlay it, that Russia and America were no longer allies, would be unleashed by U.S. and British statesmen before FDR was cold in his grave.

In March, FDR had chosen his friend Dr. Isador Lubin, a brilliant, bald, bespectacled economist and statistician, to be the U.S. representative on the Reparations Commission in Moscow with the rank of ambassador. Lubin, holding a similar get-tough view on Germany as FDR, had taken the job on the understanding that Germany would be carefully administered and be allowed only light industries except for coal. He had planned to leave for Moscow on April 15 with his staff of ten: holding the rank of ambassador, he would be staying with Harriman at Spaso House. FDR, in line with his mind-set of giving the Germans lessons to drive home to them the error of their ways, thought Lubin particularly fitted for the post: "It is a very nice thing to have the man in charge of reparations over in Germany be a Russian Jew." But Truman had other thoughts and other priorities. On April 28 he replaced Lubin with *his* good friend Ed Pauley, treasurer of the Democratic National Committee: Pauley, who to his credit was a skilled negotiator, would have the rank of ambassador; Lubin would go as Pauley's assistant, with the rank of minister.

THE RUSSIAN PEOPLE, and most of those in the government, about to wreak vengeance on Germany and be released from the horror Hitler had visited upon them, had only positive thoughts about America. Three weeks after Roosevelt's death, on May 9, the news that Germany had surrendered was announced to the general public in the Soviet Union (a day later than in America and Britain). As it was announced by loudspeakers, which on every corner in Moscow also blared out "The Star-Spangled Banner" along with "The Internationale," crowds of Russians started walking toward the American embassy on Mokhovaya Street. The embassy, easily identified by the prominent American flag it flew, was on a square three or four city blocks wide that backed onto the west wall of the Kremlin; above the wall could be seen the Byzantine domes of the Kremlin buildings. As the day went on, the crowd continued to grow until it filled the square; Muscovites stood there waving, cheering, pressing against the sides of the building, pushing past the police. Because Harriman was still in Washington, George Kennan, as U.S. chargé d'affaires, was in charge of the embassy. Watching from inside, he decided, in view of the nonstop enthusiasm, to put a Soviet flag up next to the Stars and Stripes. As new roars of enthusiasm came from the crowd, the ordinarily cool, collected Kennan decided a short speech of appreciation had to be made and, accompanied by a sergeant in uniform, climbed outside the building onto a ledge formed by the top of a column slightly above the crowd. He shouted out, in Russian, "Congratulations on the day of victory. All honor to the Soviet allies." This resulted in new roars of approval. The crowd pressed closer under the pedestal, then hoisted up a Soviet soldier until he was level with Kennan and the sergeant. The soldier proceeded to kiss and embrace the sergeant and then "relentlessly" pull the sergeant down into the crowd. Watching him bob "helplessly" over the sea of hands, almost disappearing from view before finally escaping, Kennan successfully retreated back into the building. The crowd stayed on until well into the evening, resisting the continuous attempts of the Soviet police to make them move. Nowhere else in Moscow was there such a grand demonstration of joy.

On May 11, Germany having surrendered, Truman, prompted by the law that made Lend-Lease a wartime program, abruptly, without thought of consequences—that countries were counting on receiving agreed-upon goods necessitated by the war against Germany—ordered that Lend-Lease be shut down immediately, with the exception of matériel destined for the Soviet Union for use in the war against Japan. Truman did not think to give notice to prepare countries for the action. The loading of ships carrying Lend-Lease supplies to all countries including Russia stopped, partially loaded ships were unloaded, ships mid-ocean were turned toward home. Nor had Truman consulted with the State Department. When Stettinius found out, he called the order an "untimely and incredible step." Stalin and Molotov were stunned and formally protested, inasmuch as the shipments had been mutually agreed upon between officials of both countries. Molotov cautioned Gromyko, "Do not barge in with pitiful requests. If the U.S. wants to cut off deliveries, it will be all the worse for them." Truman, realizing he had made a mistake as it applied to the always ready-to-take-umbrage Soviet Union, rescinded the order immediately: ships in port were reloaded, and ships at sea were told to continue on their way. But he had damaged the American-Soviet relationship: Stalin took it as an anti-Soviet move, knowing it would never have happened if FDR were alive. He took it as Truman's warning to Russia to behave.

The next anti-Soviet move was Churchill's. On May 12, exactly one month after FDR's death, Churchill sent a cable to the president using for the first time the phrase "iron curtain." He wrote, "An iron curtain is drawn down upon their front. We do not know what is going on behind. There seems little doubt that the whole region east of the line Lübeck-Trieste-Corfu will soon be completely in their hands." In fact, Churchill had been anxiously sure for two years that Stalin was going to double-cross his allies. He had confided to Anthony Eden, in early January 1944, a month after reluctantly agreeing to a second front, "Of course once we get on to the Continent with a large commitment, they [the Russians] will have the means of blackmail, which they have not at present, by refusing to advance beyond a certain point, or even tipping the wink to the Germans that they can move more troops into the West." He had gone further, which partially explains his continual insistence to FDR on upholding Poland at the expense of the Soviet Union: "Every effort must be made to reach complete understanding with the United States, and Poland is an extremely good hook." Churchill thought Soviet insistence on running things in Eastern Europe the prelude to a Russian military move on Western Europe. This is made clear by his order to General Montgomery, the supreme British military officer in Germany, immediately after the German surrender. The prime minister, according to Montgomery, at a meeting on May 14, " 'got steamed up about the Russians' and told him not to destroy the weapons of the one million German soldiers who had surrendered to him in case 'we might have to fight the Russians with German help.' " Three weeks later Churchill expressed the same thought in another cable to Truman—asserting that Western Europe was in danger: any U.S. troop withdrawal from Germany will mean "bringing Soviet power into the heart of Western Europe."

Truman, to his credit, was as wary of Churchill as of Stalin. His first opinion of his two allies after becoming president, he would later tell Dean Acheson, was that *both* were grasping, rogue leaders not to be trusted. Churchill was out for what he could get for his country, Truman wrote to Acheson: "Britain only wanted to control the Eastern Mediterranean, keep India, oil in Persia, the Suez Canal and whatever else was floating loose." Stalin was worse, in his eyes, bent on becoming another Hitler: "Russia had no program except to take over the free part of Europe, kill as many Germans as possible and fool the Western Alliance." The difference in the two, Truman seemed to have concluded, was not their methods but their prey. (Others in positions of influence besides FDR had been wary of Churchill since the start of the war. It was a commonly held belief among Washington insiders that Churchill was more concerned over preserving Britain's position in Europe than in preserving peace. Leahy would write, "This was consistent with our staff estimate of Churchill's attitude throughout the war.") Still, even if Truman faulted the aims of both, in the spring and summer of 1945, his problem was with Russia, and Churchill's advice seemed to make sense.

Stalin, meanwhile, was carefully keeping his word to Churchill on Greece. When he and the prime minister had made their famous percentages agreement in Moscow in 1944, Greece was declared 90 percent British predominance. When there was a Communist outbreak in Athens in 1944, Stalin decreed that no assistance be given. In January, shortly before Yalta, he again refused to help the Communists: "I advised not starting this fighting in Greece . . . They've taken on more than they can handle. We cannot send our troops into Greece . . . The Greeks have acted foolishly." He would continue to keep his hands off Greece for the remainder of the year.

THE SAN FRANCISCO CONFERENCE convened thirteen days after FDR died. FDR had pushed for the early date to make sure that when the Allied nations gathered together to draft the charter for the world security organization, they were still working together in wartime harness. Even so, there were many arguments: ratification was a near thing. It took fifty-one days of debate, negotiation, and drafting, at times exceedingly rancorous, always complicated because there were delegates from forty-six countries who each had issues, concerns, and egos, before the charter was finished. Of Truman's opening speech, which he gave over the radio from Washington, Anne O'Hare McCormick, a *New York Times* journalist, framed the worrisome thought in many heads when she damned it with faint praise: "President Truman's was not the magic voice of Franklin Roosevelt, but it was the voice of a man bent on the same end." Would it be enough?

The U.S. delegates, headed by Stettinius, president of the conference, aided by Anthony Eden, had carried the day on the issue of membership: the Ukraine and White Russia would become members of the United Nations, as FDR had promised Stalin and Molotov at Yalta, but to accomplish this, Stettinius had had to enlist the votes of the ministers of the nineteen South American countries with whom he had just signed a treaty fostering hemispheric cooperation. The Latin countries had exacted a price for their support: they would vote in favor of the Soviet republics on condition that Argentina, a virtual ally of Hitler's throughout the war until it switched sides and declared war on Germany on March 27, immediately become a member. Inasmuch as the decision had been made at Yalta that only countries that had declared war by March 1 were eligible for immediate membership, this was a violation of the Yalta accords. Molotov saw in the seating of Argentina, because it *was* a violation of the Yalta accords, a chance to push for acceptance of the Polish Provisional Government, which, not yet approved as the Polish government, also would be a violation of the Yalta accords. He coerced Jan Masaryk, foreign minister of Czechoslovakia, into making a motion to seat the provisional Lublin government. After Masaryk had finished his speech in favor of seating the provisional government, Stettinius rose to make a strong argument against it, invoking Yalta: "I remind the Conference that we have just honored our Yalta engagements in behalf of Russia. I also remind the conference that there are other Yalta obligations . . . One of them calls for a new and representative Polish Provisional Government. Until that happens, the Conference cannot, in good conscience, recognize the Lublin government. It would be a sordid exhibition of bad faith." Stettinius carried the day: Masaryk's motion was resoundingly defeated.

Molotov called a press conference: five hundred journalists showed up, filling the ballroom of the St. Francis Hotel. Molotov told the assemblage if Argentina, with its checkered past of siding with the enemy, became a member, Poland should be reconsidered. He said, with truth, Poland "had suffered so much in this war and had been the first country to be invaded whereas Argentina had, in effect, helped the enemy." Although Molotov lost his cause (the U.S. stand was overwhelmingly favored), he evoked worldwide sympathy, both because Argentina was so universally abhorred even in Latin America and because, as he pointed out, if the case against Poland was that it was not an independent state, then India and the Philippines, controlled by Britain and the United States, should not be admitted either. The U.S. media—newsmagazines and newspapers—joined in the condemnation of the seating of Argentina. Even the conservative journalist Arthur Krock, writing in *The New York Times,* worried the United States had gone too far: "It would not be an unreasonable view on the part of Mr. Molotov that the United States is the leader of an irresistible conference bloc of more than twenty of the forty-eight members . . . There is a general feeling that every effort must be made from now until the charter has been completed to deal sympathetically with future Russian proposals lest the Moscow authorities decide that something resembling a steam-roller of a national convention is being used against them." Cordell Hull voiced his concern: he thought Stettinius had caved in to pressure from the South American bloc. But Stettinius felt he had had no choice: he owed it to the South American republics to seat Argentina; the damage to good relations with the Soviet Union could be contained.

As Masaryk revealed to Bohlen, when they met later in the evening in the bar of the Fairmont Hotel, he had made the motion to invite the Lublin government only because Molotov had sent him a note "out of the blue" saying that "Czechoslovakia must vote for the Soviet proposition in regard to Poland, or else forfeit the friendship of the Soviet government."

Of the many issues fought out between the forty-eight countries before the charter was finally approved, the most difficult and the most crucial was the veto in the Security Council that had supposedly been hammered out at Yalta: it was the centerpiece, the rock, upon which the organization was founded, and with its acceptance by Stalin and Churchill at Yalta, FDR had carried the day. The agreement had been that procedural matters could not be vetoed: although a nation could veto any *action,* any *matter* could be brought up for discussion in the Security Council. Because there were so many issues regarding the United Nations Charter that had to be resolved by all the nations, the final discussion on the veto was taken up only after weeks had passed. Before it was, Molotov, Eden, Harriman, and Bohlen had left (Stettinius as head of the conference had to stay to the bitter end) on the assumption that all the serious issues had been settled. Before their exodus, in a moment of great harmony on May 4, four days after Hitler had committed suicide, two days after the Russians had captured Berlin, Molotov, Eden, and Stettinius cabled Harry Hopkins, "At a dinner last night we three drank a special toast to you in sincere recognition of the outstanding part you personally have played in bringing our three countries together in the common cause. We regret that you are not with us at this moment of victory."

At earlier meetings on the veto the smaller nations had strongly voiced their concerns over the voting power of the five permanent members of the Security Council. Inasmuch as each one of the smaller countries had a vote in creating the charter, and as a bloc they could outvote the Big Three, their needs had to be addressed. It was not until May 26 that the permanent members of the proposed Security Council met in Stettinius's penthouse suite at the Fairmont Hotel to work out a reasonable, calming response to small-country fears that they would be bullied by the permanent members of the Security Council. Although it had been agreed at Yalta that the veto did not extend to setting the agenda—to so-called procedural matters in the Security Council—during the meeting Gromyko took the floor to announce the present Soviet view on the veto. In so doing, he threw a bombshell, saying that the Soviet Union's position now was that a nation should have the power to decide whether a matter *was* procedural: this would mean a nation could exercise its veto over what was brought up for discussion. Stettinius, stunned, pressed him to change his mind, but he wouldn't—he couldn't—he was following instructions given to him, it would be learned, by Molotov. The strong negative reaction made Gromyko cable Molotov: days went by as he waited to hear whether Molotov would back down. (Waiting for word from Moscow was something all the delegates had gotten used to, although none too happily.) Finally, on June 1, Gromyko announced that he had received his instructions: it was Molotov's view that the U.S. position—that no veto should be allowed on what he now called the first step of the chain of events leading to enforcement measures—was not right; that such a first step might ultimately lead to war. Because bringing a matter up for discussion was therefore a political issue, explained Gromyko, completely misinterpreting what had been agreed to at Yalta, bringing a matter up for discussion was subject to the veto, even if the nation exercising the veto was not involved.

Stettinius was stunned; so were all the Americans present. Their view was that if the Soviet view prevailed, the United Nations would be deformed at birth. Stettinius advised Gromyko, "If the Soviet Union insisted on this view the United States would not join the world organization." The following day, after a phone conversation with Truman in which he discussed the contretemps, Stettinius reinforced his warning to Gromyko: "It would be utterly impossible for us to join an organization holding veto power over discussion." Gromyko's response was that the United States was misinterpreting the Yalta accord.

Stettinius, entertaining the thought that perhaps Molotov was not sufficiently informing Stalin of the stands he was taking, decided to appeal directly to Stalin. He sent a cable to Moscow. Meanwhile, Bohlen and Harriman, as they were flying east to Washington, talked about sending Harry Hopkins to Moscow to see if, by meeting with Stalin, he could iron out the increasingly contentious issues between their two nations. Upon landing, they went straight to Hopkins's house in Georgetown. They found him in bed, looking "too ill even to get out of bed and walk across 'N' Street," but nevertheless told him what they had in mind. At the thought Hopkins, thrilled at the idea, suddenly became energized: he was ready to leave. Truman, too, had been thinking about sending Hopkins to Moscow. He had consulted James Byrnes, whom he would name secretary of state in early July, who was against it, and Cordell Hull, who was for it. He talked with Hopkins—these were difficult days for Hopkins, eager to go and not sure Truman would allow it—but Truman finally agreed that Hopkins could make the trip.

Accompanied by his wife, Louise, along to look after his health, Bohlen, and Harriman, Hopkins left Washington on May 23, flew to Paris, and arrived in Moscow on May 25.

On that day, possibly in response to the growing anti-Russian point of view among Americans (the army newspaper *Stars and Stripes* would shortly run an article that "volunteer troublemakers" in America who talk of possible war with Russia are "playing directly into the hands of warmongers"), Eisenhower assessed the U.S.-U.S.S.R. relationship in talking to his aide Captain Harry Butcher. Because as supreme commander Eisenhower had more experience working with the Russians than any other American, because Stalin respected him, and because later, when the situation changed, he would never refer to it, Eisenhower's sympathetic point of view has been lost to history:

> Ike said he felt that the American and British relationship with Russia was about at the same stage of arms-length dealing that marked the early contacts between the Americans and the British when we first got into the war. As we dealt with each other, we learned the British ways and they learned ours . . . Now the Russians, who have had relatively little contact, even during the war, with the Americans and the British, do not understand us, nor do we them. The more contact we have with the Russians, the more they will understand us and the greater will be the cooperation. The Russians are blunt and forthright in their dealings, and any evasiveness arouses their suspicions. It should be possible to work with Russia if we follow the same pattern of friendly cooperation that has resulted in the great record of Allied unity demonstrated first by AFHQ and subsequently by SHAEF.

Hopkins was given an appointment to see Stalin the evening following his arrival. The attention and time Stalin proceeded to give to Hopkins, a minister without portfolio, speaks to the extraordinary importance Stalin gave to his relations with the United States, his deep uneasiness as to their present state, and his desire to make the relationship endure. But there is only one explanation for the probing frankness of the dialogue itself: it was as if he *were* talking to the dead president, as if Hopkins were FDR's proxy. Stalin and Hopkins talked to each other at six meetings: the first meeting went on for ninety minutes, twice as long as any private conversation Stalin had had with FDR. During it Stalin indicated that he had a number of worrisome questions he wanted Hopkins to answer. For the head of the second most powerful nation in the world to accord such access to an out-of-office American should have been a signal to Truman of how vulnerable Stalin was at that moment and how much he counted on having a good relationship with America. So should the fact that as the meetings progressed, Stalin made concession after concession; Truman, new to the game: either did not realize the significance of what was happening, or he was deeply anti-Soviet.

The next evening, at the second meeting, Stalin said there was an impression that the American attitude towards the Soviet Union had perceptibly cooled. He gave five examples of actions that indicated that the Americans' attitude toward them had changed—that now the U.S. government was saying that the Russians were no longer needed. The first action was the Allied violation of the Yalta accord at the San Francisco Conference dealing with the immediate admission of Argentina to membership in the world organization: Argentina had not declared war by March 1, the date he and Roosevelt had set at Yalta. Why could Argentina not have been asked to wait three months? The second was the pressure now being exerted by the United States to add France to the Reparations Commission, when at Yalta it had been decided that only the three powers would sit on the commission. Why equate France with—place it on the same footing as—the Soviet Union? It looked like an attempt to humiliate the Russians. The third point was the attitude of the U.S. government on the Polish question. He said "anyone with commonsense" could see that at Yalta they had agreed to reconstruct the existing government: this meant that the present government was to form the basis for the new. The fourth point was the manner in which Lend-Lease had been curtailed. "If the refusal to continue Lend-Lease was designed as pressure on the Russians in order to soften them up," he said, "then it was a fundamental mistake." The fifth point had to do with the German fleet: in this Stalin digressed to compliment General Eisenhower, calling him "an honest man," who had made 135,000 German troops in Czechoslovakia surrender to the Soviet command instead of to the American army as they had tried to do. This was prelude to the question of why no part of the German fleet, which had caused so much damage at Leningrad, had been turned over to the Russians, even though the fleet had surrendered. He said he had written to both Truman and Churchill suggesting that at least one-third of the fleet be surrendered to the Soviet Union, had heard nothing except rumors the request might be turned down, and "if this turned out to be true it would be very unpleasant." This, he said, completed the list of his concerns.

Hopkins replied that he would first address the last point: the German fleet. He was able to state, he said, that America had no desire for any portion of it: it was being retained only for examination of possible new inventions and technical improvements. He then said the U.S. portion would probably be sunk, a statement that Stalin did not challenge, probably because Hopkins said he was sure the fleet would be divided three ways—among the United States, the Soviet Union, and Britain. Next Hopkins spoke of Lend-Lease, reminding Stalin—he thought it had been clear to the Soviet Union—that after the war with Germany there had to be changes in the legislation. He explained that the government agency that had authorized the Lend-Lease stoppage had countermanded the order within twenty-four hours.

At the end of Hopkins's explanation regarding the Lend-Lease stoppage, it appeared he had completely mollified Stalin: the premier said he hoped Hopkins would consider how it had looked from the Russians' side. Hopkins's last comment on the subject echoed a Roosevelt theme: "It would be a great tragedy if the greatest achievement in cooperation which the Soviet Union and the United States had worked out together on the basis of Lend-Lease were to end on an unsatisfactory note."

The next subject Hopkins addressed was the Reparations Commission: because France had a zone in Germany and was on the Allied Control Commission, it seemed reasonable to put France on the Reparations Commission, he said. Stalin objected on the grounds that Poland and Yugoslavia had suffered more. Hopkins suggested of the American position, "We would probably not insist in an unyielding manner."

Next Hopkins brought up the Argentine question and asked Harriman, who had been at San Francisco, to explain what had happened there. Harriman proceeded to blame the immediate seating of Argentina on Molotov: "If Mr. Molotov had not introduced the question of an invitation to the present Polish Government we might have been successful in persuading the Latin American countries to postpone the question of Argentina." Molotov mildly protested. Stalin closed the subject, in what amounted to a rebuke to Molotov, by saying, "In any event what had been done could not be put right and the Argentine question remained in the past."

Hopkins then said he wanted to bring up Poland and then unequivocally explained to Stalin just how important it was that he fall into line on the issue. Stalin did not interrupt him as Hopkins went into a very long explanation. Hopkins said he wished to state the U.S. position as clearly and as forcibly as he knew how: the question of Poland per se was not so important as the fact that it had become a symbol of America's ability to work out problems with the Soviet Union; the United States would accept any government that was desired by the Polish people and at the same time friendly to the Soviet Union; this was a problem that should be worked out jointly between the United States, the Soviet Union, and Great Britain, and the Polish people should be given the right to free elections, and Poland should be genuinely independent. But, Hopkins continued, the preliminary steps toward the reestablishment of Poland appeared to have been taken unilaterally by the Soviet Union together with the present Warsaw government and that *in fact the United States was completely excluded.* Hopkins said he hoped that the marshal would put his mind to the task of thinking up what diplomatic methods could be used to settle this question, keeping in mind the feeling of the American people; he himself was prepared to say not how it could be done but that *it must be done.* He was appealing to the marshal to help find a way to the solution of the Polish problem. In this he was echoing what FDR had written to Stalin in February 1944: "It is my earnest hope that while this problem remains unsolved neither party shall by hasty word or unilateral act transform this special question into one adversely affecting the larger issues of future international collaboration. While public opinion is forming in support of the principle of international collaboration, it is especially incumbent upon us to avoid any action which might appear to counteract the achievement of our long-range objectives."

Stalin asked Hopkins to take into consideration that in the course of twenty-five years the Germans had twice invaded Russia via Poland, which he said was a horrible thing to endure. He said Germany had been able to do this because Poland had been regarded as a part of the cordon sanitaire around the Soviet Union and that the previous European policy had been that the Polish government must be hostile to Russia; Poland, he said, had served as the corridor for the German attacks on Russia. It was in Russia's vital interest that Poland should be both strong and friendly. There was no intention to interfere in Poland's internal affairs, he continued. The Polish people did not desire collective farms or other aspects of the Soviet system. In this, he said, the Polish leaders were right because the Soviet system was not exportable: it must develop from within. Then Stalin said he wanted to comment on U.S. interests in the world: not only this war but the previous war had shown that without U.S. intervention Germany could not have been defeated; he therefore fully recognized the right of America as a world power to participate in the Polish question. He said Russia had acted unilaterally because it had been compelled to: the logic of the war demanded that the Soviet rear be assured, and the Lublin government had been of great assistance. (This was true, although Churchill continued to deny it. According to Meiklejohn's diary entry for June 8, Red Cross officials in Poland distributing aid were reporting that "a good part of the Polish underground army that fought the Germans is still underground fighting the Soviets.") Stalin told Hopkins that it was contrary to public policy to set up Soviet administration on foreign soil and pointed out that Soviet action in Poland had been more successful than British action in Greece. He said there were eighteen or twenty ministries in the present Polish government and four or five of these portfolios could be given to representatives from the British and U.S. lists. (Molotov whispered to Stalin, who then said he meant four, not five, posts.) He said if this was acceptable, "we could then proceed to consider what persons should be selected." He added that Mikołajczyk was acceptable, that it might be wise to ask some of the Warsaw leaders: if they could settle the composition of the new government. No differences remained, Stalin continued, because all agreed on free and unfettered elections. Having said all this and more, Stalin then said that there were three other questions to be settled: (1) policy in regard to the occupation of Germany, (2) Japan, (3) meeting of the three heads of government. On the latter subject he said, in reply to a question from Hopkins, that he was waiting to hear whether the president and the prime minister would meet in Berlin; he was prepared to meet them anytime. As regards Germany, he was prepared to name General Zhukov the next day. They agreed to meet the following evening, May 28, at 6:00 p.m.

The two meetings had reassured Stalin and Molotov to the point that before the scheduled 6:00 meeting, Molotov and Anastas Mikoyan, commissar of foreign trade, met with Harriman to give him their Lend-Lease requests for the second half of 1945.

The third meeting was even more reassuring than the first two. Stalin told Hopkins the Soviet army would be in position on the Manchurian border by August 8 (three months to the day after VE-day—as he had promised FDR). He said he would back Chiang Kai-shek "because no one else was strong enough . . . no Communist leader was strong enough to unify China." He said he had no territorial claims against

China, mentioning specifically Manchuria, and assured Hopkins that everywhere in China his troops would be fighting the Japanese, they would respect Chinese sovereignty. He "went out of his way" to say not Russia, only America, had the resources to aid China after the war. He further said Korea should be governed by a trusteeship under America, China, Britain, and the Soviet Union. Then, expecting that the invasion of Japan would be a joint Soviet-Allied operation, and assuming that Russia would share in the occupation of Japan, as in the occupation of Germany, Stalin said he envisioned an agreement with Britain and America as to occupation zones. In line with his concern to settle such matters, Stalin told Hopkins that there should be a peace conference, that planning for one should get under way: ironic in that now it was he, with FDR dead, who wanted to settle things.

On their fourth afternoon in Moscow, Hopkins and his wife went sightseeing and visited the world-famous Russian ballet school. When Hopkins met Stalin that evening at 6:00 and told him about their visit, Stalin admitted he had never seen the school. Hopkins said he was like the traditional New Yorker, who says, "I've lived here all my life but I've never yet seen the Statue of Liberty."

As they talked, Hopkins went into more detail about American expectations for Poland: there should be freedom of speech, the right of assembly, the right to worship at any church; all political parties except the Fascist Party should be allowed; all citizens should have the right of public trial, the right of habeas corpus.

Stalin replied that the principles of democracy were well-known and there was no objection on the part of the Soviet government, but the specific freedoms mentioned by Hopkins could only be applied in full in peacetime, and even then with limitations: nor could they apply without reservations to Fascist parties trying to overthrow the government. Hopkins reverted to the Yalta Conference, saying how pleased FDR had been after it was over, thinking the Polish matter "virtually settled." But, and here Hopkins stated a position FDR would never have taken, "he must say that rightly or wrongly there was a strong feeling among the American people that the Soviet Union wished to dominate Poland." (FDR actually expected Russia to dominate Poland; he just wanted Stalin to respect Polish rights.) And again Hopkins said they should be able—all three great powers—to settle the matter. This gave Stalin an opening: he blamed Britain, noting that "if one of them secretly did not wish to see it settled then the difficulties were real." But the meeting ended with an agreement that they would next discuss possible Polish candidates to be asked to come to Moscow to form the Polish government. At Hopkins's next meeting with Stalin on May 31, the fifth one, it was obvious that progress had been made: they exchanged the names of possible candidates; Molotov was no longer blocking Allied choices. Following the meeting Stalin had arranged a private dinner for the Hopkinses, to which he invited twenty of the most important men in the Politburo, with their wives, plus Harriman and his daughter Kathleen, General Deane, and other important Americans in Moscow. After dinner there was dancing. The long meeting, followed by the long dinner, with, as usual, many toasts, was a huge strain on Hopkins. It would show when, following dinner, Hopkins danced one dance with Ivan Maisky's wife, after which they sat down. Maisky then saw that Hopkins couldn't get his breath back, that there were drops of perspiration on his forehead. He felt his hand and found it limp and cold. Maisky recounted that he became anxious, and the anxiety showed: Hopkins looked at him and said, "You know, I've got a leave of absence from death."

But his recuperative powers and his will were also on display, and after the other guests had departed and he had regained his breath, speaking privately with Stalin, evidently having waited for the salubrious effects of the lavish dinner, dancing, and many toasts to kick in and make Stalin more accommodating, Hopkins asked about the sixteen London Poles who had traveled to Moscow and been charged with high treason and imprisoned, which Molotov had first informed Stettinius of in San Francisco and which Western newspapers had been enthusiastically tracking ever since. Hopkins said he hoped they would be released. He warned Stalin, aware that Stalin wanted to settle the many war's-end problems and territorial concerns that peace demanded, that if Polish matters were *not* resolved, they would probably take up most of the time at the Berlin meeting in July. Hopkins also mentioned another factor Stalin should keep in mind: "the many minority groups in America who were not sympathetic to the Soviet Union." He said relations between their two countries were threatened by these problems. Stalin said all sixteen men were guilty of matters that had not been made public, that Churchill had misled the United States in regard to the facts and had made the American government believe that the statement of the Polish London government was accurate when just the opposite was true. Stalin continued that he did not intend to have the British manage the affairs of Poland, that the British were conniving with the London Poles. He then made a concession, saying that the men had to be tried but that they would be treated leniently—that the only charge against the sixteen would be for illicit possession of radio sending sets.

Hopkins, his work done, made plans to leave Moscow. Meanwhile, the drama—the deadlock—over the veto in the Security Council in San Francisco was intensifying, as news headlines made clear. The first days of June, reported James Reston in *The New York Times,* the "Big Five" conferees, despite meeting four times in forty-eight hours, had been able to resolve nothing. The signing of the charter creating the United Nations was itself in doubt. Hopkins delayed his departure.

The small and medium-size nations, by their numbers holding the majority voting power, were beginning to fall in line with the American position, but still Gromyko, bound by his orders from Moscow, held out. "Many Nations Hit Soviet Veto Stand," headlined *The New York Times* on June 4. Stettinius, in desperation, with Truman's approval, cabled a request to Harriman to accompany Hopkins to ask Stalin "whether he realizes fully what the instructions sent to Gromyko mean and what effect the Soviet proposal would have upon the character of the world organization we are all trying to work out. Please tell him in no uncertain words that this country could not possibly join an organization based on so unreasonable an interpretation of the provision of the great powers in the Security Council . . . We will have to take the necessary steps to wind up the Conference here if we have nothing favorable from you in this regard."

The request for another meeting between Hopkins and Stalin was granted.

During this meeting Hopkins proceeded to persuade Stalin that Russia's very public stand restricting the agenda was casting Russia in a bad light and in addition was simply wrong. He described the formula agreed on at Yalta as one that safeguarded the freedom of discussion and the right of any member to bring before the council any situation for discussion. Molotov then made a short speech in which he said the Soviet position (his) was based squarely on the Crimea decision. There followed a private conversation between Stalin and Molotov during which, according to Hopkins's notes, even though it was in Russian,

Hopkins could see that Stalin "had not understood the issues involved, and had not had them explained to him." After Stalin and Molotov finished their conversation, Stalin said he had no objection to a simple majority being applied in discussions relating to pacific settlement. He then proceeded to overrule Molotov, saying he was prepared to accept the American position on the point at issue at San Francisco in regard to voting procedure. He was very clear. This was a major concession because controlling the agenda is not a neutral, procedural matter. It is indeed substantive.

Harriman, present as always, immediately ordered the change of policy cabled to Stettinius, who received it the same day, Soviet time being half a day ahead of U.S. time. As he bade good-bye to Stalin, Hopkins told him he was planning to leave for Berlin and looked forward to seeing the present state of Berlin and possibly the pleasant spectacle of finding Hitler's body. Stalin replied, in a comment that showed his already deeply suspicious nature that would in a few years blossom into full-blown paranoia, that he was "sure Hitler was still alive."

Hopkins and his wife left the next morning; in an unusual show of respect, Molotov accompanied them to the plane.

Upon receipt of the cable informing him of Stalin's change of policy on the veto, Stettinius invited Gromyko to his penthouse at the Fairmont. As Stettinius recalled the circumstances, he said to the Soviet ambassador, "I feel I owe it to you in all friendliness to tell you immediately of this word." As he told him of Stalin's change of mind, "Ambassador Gromyko's expression was rather strained and he had a ruddy complexion." The next morning, June 7, Gromyko heard from his own sources. Stettinius asked Gromyko to come to the Fairmont at 1:15, at which time he told him he planned that the forthcoming announcement would *not* indicate a victory of the United States over the Soviet Union. Gromyko, gratified, suggested they stress the importance of the unanimity of the five permanent members of the council. A meeting of the Big Five was scheduled for 3:00 p.m., at which time Stettinius announced that Gromyko had a statement to make. Gromyko then announced the new Soviet position. Immediately following the meeting Stettinius held a press conference to announce the news that no one member "can alone prevent" discussion, which was met with resounding applause from the assembled news and wire service reporters. When he told them they could leave "if they so desire," they bolted so fast "I could not help but laugh," recalled Stettinius. (The next day the news of the changed Soviet position was headlines round the world.) As Stephen Schlesinger has written, the conference was back on track.

Following the press conference, at 5:23 p.m., Stettinius telephoned Truman. "Well, it's all done," he told the president, "and it had the most electrifying effect you can possibly imagine . . . I went into the Steering Committee, which is the Chairmen of fifty delegations. I made my statement and got a terrific ovation. I went immediately from it into a press conference five minutes later. The press was as enthusiastic and warm as the Steering Committee itself . . . It really has electrified the whole situation here." Replied Truman, "It gives me a mighty good feeling too." Stettinius continued, "When they asked me how it happened, I said we worked this out in a spirit of good faith and mutual give and take and came out with an agreement agreeable to everybody. I think we are over the hump."

In the meantime, there was a discussion as to where the future headquarters of the United Nations should be located. The Soviet Union voted for the United States, because, according to Gromyko, "Moscow wanted to make sure the Americans did not lose their interest in international affairs. We were afraid the United States would revert to isolationism."

There would be one more roadblock put up by Gromyko at San Francisco, the issue of what might be discussed in the General Assembly: the wording, according to Gromyko, had been changed and enlarged since Dumbarton Oaks. "Russians Demand Curb on Assembly or They Won't Sign," ran the headline in *The New York Times* on June 18. After two days of arguing, Gromyko was given new orders. Stalin had again retracted his, or more probably Molotov's, objections, fallen into line, and agreed to the new language the others wanted: as in the Security Council, members had the right to bring up a new subject. Stettinius expressed "his personal and official delight at the splendid conciliatory attitude of the Ambassador and his government."

In June, then, because of Hopkins, Stalin was back on board as a functioning member of the alliance, had named Marshal Zhukov to the Allied Control Commission for Germany as the Russian representative (Eisenhower was the American representative), allowing the Control Commission to begin its work, had overruled Molotov's position that the agenda could be vetoed in the Security Council, and had agreed to changed language on the veto in the General Assembly, which literally allowed the United Nations to be born. Dr. T. V. Soong, the Chinese foreign minister, in San Francisco, was gratified at the way Hopkins's conversations with Stalin were going even before Stalin's about-face on the veto. "Mr. Hopkins had made good headway in his conversation with Stalin," he said to Stettinius on June 5, when Stettinius told him that Stalin wanted Soong to come to Moscow for conversations not later than July 1. For the time being, it looked as if Roosevelt's ground-work in creating the United Nations, which forced nations to work together, and in the process of working together influence and shape world events, was going to carry the day after all.

This seemed particularly possible because there were other Soviet changes: at the end of June it was announced that Patriarch Alexius was going to visit the United States to meet with members of the Rus-sian Orthodox Church. Molotov relaxed his continuing objections to the various Western-leaning Poles, and as a result the Poles themselves were grinding out a compromise government consisting of men associ-ated with the Peasant Party, the Socialist Party, and the Workers' Party. Invitations went out to a list of Poles that even Molotov agreed upon. On June 27 membership in the new Polish government was announced. Fourteen of the twenty-one posts went to members of the provisional government; Mikołajczyk was made deputy prime minister. The next day the new government took office. On July 5, Churchill and Tru-man recognized the new, reorganized Polish Provisional Government of National Unity. Poles themselves were pleased; even Polish intellectuals thought the makeup a fair compromise between the various factions. There was no way to know if and when the Yalta stipulation of free and unfettered elections would take place (the new government would not set a date), and it was only because of U.S. vigilance that the new gov-ernment did not succeed in dropping the word "Provisional" from its title, but harmony finally ruled, at least on paper. (The *New York Times* reporter Harrison Salisbury asked Mikołajczyk what he thought of Sta-lin. Mikołajczyk answered, "Stalin knows Poland well. We get along well in our conversation. I think he is the kind of man I can do business with.")

In essence, Stalin had taken control of the Soviet Union's foreign policy, taken it out of the hands of his foreign minister, and put it back into line with the Yalta decisions. The question is why. The only answer that makes sense is that he felt the Soviet Union needed the alliance, needed America. The contrasts between the United States and the Soviet Union in the summer of 1945 were huge. From a practical rather than an ideological perspective it wasn't that hard a decision: America was untouched by the war. By war's end it was supplying half of the world's manufacturing capacity, generating more than half of the world's electricity, and holding two-thirds of the world's gold stocks, and half of all the monetary reserves. It had suffered 405,000 casualties by war's end, .003 percent out of a population of 130 million. In contrast, the Germans killed 16 percent of the Russian population, 27 million Russians—out of a population of 165 million—so many that an exact number can never be ascertained. The Germans burned seventy thousand Russian villages and hamlets to the ground and destroyed 100,000 farms: twenty-five million Russians were homeless, wandering the roads and rail lines. They destroyed thirty-two thousand factories and sixty-five thousand railroad tracks. The war left Russia on its knees: Stalin needed America to rebuild Russia; he needed the thirty-year long-term loan, which is why it was uppermost in his mind when he laughed about FDR's champagne tastes at their first Yalta dinner. He thought it would be looked on favorably by Americans, not simply out of Christian charity, but because, given his understanding of economics and what he had been told by prominent American businessmen, after the war was over and America's factories would no longer be turning out armaments, capitalist America was going to need new markets for the new products its workers would produce.

Besides economic aid, he needed America's might to help keep Germany down in the future. The specter of German power was ever present even in the country's moment of defeat; the prowess of the German soldier and Germany's industrial efficiency were legendary: fewer than seven million German soldiers had wreaked all the damage. Russia needed the Grand Alliance. As Stalin had said, "The foundation for the alliance of the USSR, Great Britain and the USA lies not in chance and passing considerations but in vitally important and long-term interests." *Izvestia* reflected this: Russia would be great *because* it was allied with America and Britain. The government newspaper, by its nature an extension of Stalin's thinking, predicted, at the end of June, that the Big Three powers "will become the soul of the new organization and will be able to bring peace to the peoples of the world . . . One may say with confidence that the final text of the charter greatly outdistances all previous projects for establishing an international organization."

Truman assumed the presidency determined to honor his predecessor's policies, but he was still the same midwesterner who, in 1941, when Hitler invaded the Soviet Union, had said, "If we see that Germany is winning we ought to help Russia and if Russia is winning we ought to help Germany and that way let them kill as many as possible although I don't want to see Hitler victorious under any circumstance. Neither of them think anything of their pledged word." The statement had appeared in *The New York Times.* Do nations ever get along when their leaders loathe and mistrust each other? Four years later Truman's diary entry as he was meeting with Stalin at Potsdam and contemplating dropping the first atomic bomb again put Stalin on a par with Hitler: "It is certainly a good thing for the world that Hitler's crowd or Stalin's did not discover this atomic bomb." Stalin, in turn, had scant regard for Truman. "Stalin had no respect for Truman. He considered Truman worthless," recalled Nikita Khrushchev.

When Truman and Stalin met at Potsdam, they were almost confrontational. At the end of May, Stimson had assembled a group of scientists and government officials working on the bomb to find out their views on whether sharing information about atomic fusion with the Soviet Union was a good idea or not. The sentiment—virtually unanimous—was that the information should be shared to prevent an arms race. Present at the meeting had been Undersecretary of the Navy Ralph Bard, Assistant Secretary of State William Clayton, James Byrnes, Drs. Vannevar Bush, James Conant, J. Robert Oppenheimer, Enrico Fermi, Ernest O. Lawrence, Arthur Compton, and Marshall, Leslie Groves, and Harvey Bundy, whom Stimson used on various projects.

> The only suggestion which Committee had been able to give as to future control of the situation was that each country should promise to make public all work that was being done on this subject and that an international committee of control should be constituted with full power of inspection of all countries to see whether this promise was being carried out. I said I recognized that this was imperfect and might not be assented to by Russia, but that in that case we were far enough ahead of the game to be able to accumulate enough material to serve as insurance against being caught helpless.

Marshall, in fact, went on record as saying it would be a good move to invite Soviet scientists to witness the test at Alamogordo. (Only Groves, so sure of American exceptionalism and the superiority of American engineering know-how, thought it would be many years before the Soviets had the bomb.) On June 6, Stimson met with Truman to advise him what his gathering of informed scientists and government officials believed should happen, which he himself strongly agreed with. At the same time he restated his advice that disclosure should be coupled with changes in Soviet behavior, cautioning Truman that "no disclosure of the work should be made until all promises of control were made and established." Stimson and Truman then went over quid pro quos that might be put into place before taking the Russians into partnership. Truman, wrote Stimson, "said he had been thinking of that and mentioned the same things that I was thinking of, namely the settlement of the Polish, Rumanian, Yugoslavian, and Manchurian Problems."

At the beginning of July, Stimson and Truman, with Potsdam looming, again worked on the ticklish question of what Truman would say to Stalin about American progress on the bomb. According to Stimson's diary, they settled on the following dialogue, which was very similar to the approach that he and Roosevelt had settled on in March:

> We were busy with this thing and working like the dickens and we knew he was busy with this thing and working like the dickens, and that we were pretty nearly ready and we intended to use it against the enemy, Japan; that if it was satisfactory we proposed to then talk it over with Stalin afterwards, with the purpose of having it make the world peaceful and safe rather than to destroy civilization. If he pressed for details and facts, Truman was simply to tell him that we were not yet prepared to give them.

Then the bomb was detonated: the explosion, at Alamogordo, New Mexico—the mushroom cloud that rose, "a cosmic phenomenon like an eclipse"—changed the world forever. Seven days *after* Alamogordo, Truman met Stalin at Potsdam and told him that America had the bomb. But instead of the statesmanlike approach he and Stimson, based on the advice of the scientists and executives, had discussed so carefully, Truman merely bragged. No mention of collaboration, of making the world peaceful and safe, no mention of offering to share information in return for the settlement of the Polish, Romanian, Yugoslavian, and Manchurian problems.

The meeting took place at the Cecilienhof Palace, the sprawling faux-Tudor mansion built by the Hohenzollern family at Potsdam on the outskirts of Berlin. Stalin had arrived there a day late, explaining that "his doctor had insisted he come by train, not by air." Reportedly, he had had a slight heart attack. But it was not a last-minute decision. To guard the 1,195-mile route, Beria had stationed six men per half mile in Russian territory, ten men per half mile along Polish tracks, and ten men per half mile in German territory, plus eight armored trains that patrolled, plus seven NKVD regiments and nine hundred bodyguards, plus fourteen planes that circled overhead.

At a break in the conference the evening of July 24, Truman walked over to Stalin and carefully told him that the United States had developed a new weapon, "a new bomb far more destructive than any other known bomb, and that we planned to use it very soon unless Japan surrendered." Stalin listened impassively as Vladimir Pavlov translated, and he politely replied that he was glad to hear of it, that he hoped America would make "good use of it against the Japanese." He asked no questions. No one saw a flicker of emotion. Those Americans present— Stimson, Byrnes, now secretary of state, and Truman himself—all closely watching Stalin to see how he would take the news noticed his apparent lack of reaction. Pavlov would report "no muscle moved in his face." The Americans thought maybe he hadn't realized the importance of the information. Churchill thought the same: "I was sure that he had no idea of the significance of what he was being told."

Stalin was a good actor, and perhaps a better poker player: his reaction to Truman's statement had in fact been profound. Before he left Potsdam, hoping to speed up Russian progress on the bomb, he placed jurisdiction over the development of a Soviet bomb in Beria's hands, on the assumption that the dreaded head of NKVD would force a quicker pace of development. Beria set to work immediately, "making notes on a sheet of paper . . . organizing the future commission and selecting its members." Upon his return to Moscow, Stalin met with Igor Kurchatov, Russia's top nuclear physicist, to whom he said, "Ask for anything you need. There will be no refusals."

A few days after Truman informed Stalin about the bomb, Lieutenant George Elsey, his young, discreet naval aide, a graduate of

Princeton with a master's in history from Harvard, delivered a message from Stimson to Truman informing him that Stimson was preparing a statement for the president to release immediately after the first bomb was dropped, which could be any day. Truman thought about it for a moment, flipped the message over, and wrote on the back, "O.K. to release but not before August 2," the date the conference was ending. As he handed it to Elsey, Truman spoke revealingly, indicating just how differently he felt about Stalin than had FDR: "I want to be out of here before the news is out. I don't want to have to answer any questions from Stalin."

The bomb altered Stalin's view of FDR: "Roosevelt clearly felt no need to put us in the picture. He could have done it at Yalta. He could have told me that the atomic bomb was going through its experimental stages. We were supposed to be allies." Stalin was correct in this assessment of FDR. Stettinius had told the president on the second day of the Yalta Conference that the nuclear race had already begun: that the Soviet Union had 125 spies on the job, that he should therefore be prepared to discuss it with Stalin—because Stalin "might ask us about it." However, basic planning for the United Nations and the details of Russia's commitment to invade Manchuria were the topics that had to be settled. FDR had got as far at Yalta as mentioning to Churchill that he wanted to let Stalin in on the secret, but he had not yet brought Churchill round to accepting it. Sharing the atom was a complicated subject: discussion about it could wait.

Stalin had no knowledge of any of this, but even if he could point to FDR's silence on the subject, he also knew that FDR *might* have planned to tell him after the first successful nuclear detonation, and death had robbed him of the chance.

On August 6, when he learned that Little Boy, the first atomic bomb, had been dropped on Hiroshima, Stalin became ill, according to his daughter. He said to aides, the bomb "has shaken the whole world . . . The balance has been destroyed."

The Red Army facing the Kwantung army was the culmination of ten months of coordinated planning, during which America had been arming, transporting, and feeding the Red troops who now stood on the Manchurian border, ready to invade. On August 8, on schedule, the Soviet Union declared war on Japan. When Truman was told, he was annoyed. "They're jumping the gun, aren't they, Admiral?" he asked

Leahy. Leahy concurred. On August 9 at 1:00 a.m., one million Soviet troops crossed the border into eastern Manchuria: Stalin had made good on his promise. But later that same day the second atomic bomb, Fat Man, annihilated Nagasaki. To everyone in the Soviet Union the second bomb was a stunning blow. The timing made it look to them like a deliberate effort to rob the Soviets' entry into the war of any significance, to trivialize their military might by overmatching it—in short, as a warning to behave. The Red Army was powerful, but no match for the most powerful weapon in the world.

On August 10, Japan surrendered.

Dropping the second bomb had an unintended effect: the sheer horror at the damage it caused transfixed America, with the result that Americans hardly noticed the Red Army invasion. Most Americans then and now never realized the significance of Russia's entry into the war, never appreciated the fact that Russia had moved a million men across Siberia, were never aware that Russia had been expected to bear the brunt of the casualties if and when there was an invasion of Japan, never realized that there even was a Russian invasion. The Imperial Army had always dreaded fighting a two-front war, and now it faced one: the Soviet invasion had just as much to do with the Japanese surrender as the atomic bombs.

Molotov said, "The bombs dropped on Japan were not aimed at Japan but rather at the Soviet Union." The nuclear physicist Yuli Khariton voiced a common Russian reaction when he wrote that the two bombs had been dropped "as atomic blackmail against the USSR, as a threat to unleash a new, even more terrible and devastating war."

On September 2, VJ-day, Stalin went on the air in the Soviet Union to announce the end of the war: "Utterly defeated on the seas, on land and surrounded on all sides by the armed forces of the United Nations, Japan acknowledged her defeat and laid down arms." In closing, in a last nod to FDR's memory, he made mention of the four policemen: "Glory to the armed forces of the Soviet Union, the United States of America, China and Great Britain which have won over Japan."

Truman went on the air that same day to announce the end of the war to Americans. Buried halfway through his speech was mention of "gallant Allies in this war." He never named them.

EPILOGUE

The psychological and visual impact of the destruction caused by the atomic bombs was such as to virtually erase from American minds Russia's million-man invasion of Manchuria and its effect on Japan. Even Secretary of War Stimson was so mesmerized by the power of the bombs that he wrote in his diary, "On August 6 one B-29 dropped a single atomic bomb on Hiroshima. Three days later a second bomb was dropped on Nagasaki and the war was over."

The bomb caused great anxiety among the Russian people. But it did something more: it created for the first time a feeling of mistrust of America, the only nation Russians had previously and unreservedly considered their friend.

The anxiety and unease most likely would have been dissipated if, as many people in Britain and America advocated, the United States had included Russia in its plans for controlling and developing atomic energy and the bomb. And there *was* a moment, in late September 1945, when influential minds in Washington came close to advocating doing exactly that. It occurred at a cabinet meeting called September 21 by President Truman expressly to discuss the idea.

Secretary of War Henry Stimson was the prime mover behind the plan. Shortly after the bombs were dropped, Stimson had retreated to his cabin in the Adirondacks and, aided by his assistant secretary of war, John McCloy, hammered out a course of action—a proposal—he thought the United States should follow to avert an arms race that might endanger the world.

He sent it off to Truman on September 11 with a covering letter:

I believe that the change in attitude toward the individual in Russia will come slowly and gradually and I am satisfied that we should not delay our approach to Russia in the matter of the atomic bomb until that process has been completed. Furthermore, I believe that this long process of change in Russia is more likely to be expedited by the closer relationship in the matter of the atomic bomb which I suggest and the trust and confidence that I believe would be inspired by the method of approach which I have outlined . . . [U]nless the Soviets are voluntarily invited into the partnership upon a basis of co-operation and trust, we are going to maintain the Anglo-Saxon bloc over against the Soviet in the possession of this weapon.

In response Truman scheduled a cabinet meeting for September 21, 1945, with one topic only on the agenda: the atomic bomb and the peacetime development of atomic energy.

September 21 was a momentous day for Stimson: his last day as secretary of war, his seventy-eighth birthday. That morning he had his last official talk with General Marshall, his last lunch at the General Officers' Mess, and a last conference with President Truman, during which the president awarded him the Distinguished Service Medal. Finally, at 2:00 p.m., the cabinet met. Both Truman's appointments secretary Matthew J. Connelly and Secretary of the Navy James Forrestal took notes. Connelly in addition listed who agreed and who disagreed with Stimson's position.

Truman opened the meeting by calling for Stimson to express his views. Stimson laid out the case that the way to achieve a lasting peace was for the United States to share control of the atomic bomb with the Soviet Union: "I consider the problem with our satisfactory relations with Russia as not merely connected with but as virtually dominated by the problem of the atomic bomb . . . Having this weapon rather ostentatiously on our hip, their suspicions and their distrust of our purposes and motives will increase . . . We might also consider including in the arrangement a covenant with the U.K. and the Soviets providing for the exchange of benefits of future developments whereby atomic energy may be applied on a mutually satisfactory basis for commercial or humanitarian purposes."

Stimson told the group, "We do not have a secret to give away—the secret will give itself away. The problem is how to treat the secret with respect to the safety of the world." He explained that the technological information necessary to make the bomb was another thing entirely from the scientific knowledge shared by all atomic scientists. (Stimson had no intention of giving the Russians the secret ordnance procedures having to do with production of atomic bombs as weapons of war, the incoming secretary of war, Robert Patterson, noted.)

Out of the eighteen men present, including Vannevar Bush, director of the Office of Scientific Research and Development, there to present the views of the Manhattan Project scientists, thirteen, by Connelly's count, supported Stimson's idea that steps should be taken to share knowledge with Russia, although three thought implementation should wait. Four thought it a bad idea.

Bush informed the cabinet that in five years the Russians could get to the place "we are now in . . . We have no corner on knowledge or efforts of physicists." He therefore favored "giving Russia everything we have as regards the principles of atomic energy." Dean Acheson, undersecretary of state, attending in place of James Byrnes, the secretary, who was in London, offered the view that there was no alternative to sharing information: "The advantage of being ahead in such a race is nothing compared with not having a race"; he could not "conceive of a world in which we were hoarders of military secrets from our Allies, particularly this great ally." Secretary of the Treasury Fred M. Vinson disagreed, commenting, "If we give this information away, we should give information with respect to all war gadgets in order to be consistent . . . Unless other countries give us everything, this would be dangerous . . . If we give away the atomic bomb secret, we might as well forget the idea of compulsory military training, an adequate Army, Navy, and Air Force." Attorney General Tom C. Clark, a Texan, agreed with Vinson: "We should continue to carry a big stick."

At this point Truman, possibly shocked by the vehemence of the attacks on the idea, possibly shocked by the misinterpretation of what was being discussed, pointed out to the assemblage, "We are only thinking of an interchange of scientific knowledge—not contemplating giving away industrial knowledge." Postmaster General Robert E. Hannegan, a Missouri politician and the chairman of the Democratic National Committee, stated that he respected Stimson's judgment. An encouraged president then ventured that "relationships are improving between Russia, Great Britain and ourselves. In order to achieve a lasting peace, we must maintain mutual trust." Secretary of the Navy James Forrestal put forth the statement that there were two viewpoints to be considered, one with respect to military usage and one to civilian usage. He further said, "Trust had to be more than a one-way street." (In a memo he presented to the president at the meeting that showed his bias, he stated, "The Russians, like the Japanese, are essentially oriental in their thinking, and until we have a longer record or experience with them on the validity of engagements . . . it seems doubtful that we should endeavor to buy their understanding and sympathy. We tried that once with Hitler.") Secretary of Agriculture Clinton Anderson spoke next. He stated he was "inclined to agree with Vinson . . . We should hang on to secret of the bomb." Abe Fortas, undersecretary of the interior, a southerner whom Truman relied on who would later be appointed to the Supreme Court, made one of the more thoughtful comments: "If we protect the secret of the bomb we will hinder industrial application of atomic energy . . . It should be kept in mind that when the principles of atomic energy are used industrially, the secret of the atomic bomb will not keep long." Secretary of Commerce Henry Wallace followed, supporting Stimson, and asked the question "as to whether we should follow the line of bitterness or the broad line of peace . . . Science cannot be restrained." (Forrestal, showing his antipathy to Wallace, noted in his diary that Wallace was "completely, everlastingly and wholeheartedly in favor of giving it to the Russians.) The incoming secretary of war, Robert Patterson, supported Stimson. Secretary of Labor Lewis Schwellenbach, who had replaced Frances Perkins, supported Stimson; so did General Philip Fleming, head of the Federal Works Agency. Paul V. McNutt, head of the War Manpower Commission, also supported Stimson, commenting that he agreed with the principle of keeping your powder dry "but in this case it looked to him as if we couldn't keep our powder dry because of Bush's statement that our atomic power knowledge must necessarily eventually be equaled by the Russians." John B. Blandford, administrator of the National Housing Agency, supported giving the information to the Russians without even trying to get a quid pro quo. Three men—Julius A. Krug, chairman of the War Production Board; John Snyder, head of the Office of War Mobilization and Reconversion; and the Tennessee senator Kenneth McKellar, president pro tem of the Senate—also agreed with Stimson but advocated a cooling-off period of six months before the decision was implemented.

The consensus of the men must be seen in the light of Bush's comment that the secret could not be contained; therefore the issue was not one of security or of necessity but whether to treat Russia as an enemy or as a friend. Given the clear way Bush presented the issue, Truman understood what was at stake: the future friendship or the future enmity of the Soviet Union.

There is little if any doubt which course FDR would have followed. He would have shared control and knowledge of atomic energy with the Soviet Union, turning disclosure into a demonstration of friendship, gambling that such a course would reduce Soviet fears and insecurity and keep the Soviet Union a functioning nation within the international community. FDR had talked with Mackenzie King along those lines in March just weeks before he died. "He thought the time had come to tell them how far the developments had gone," wrote King in his diary on March 9, 1945, after his late-night post-dinner conversation with the president in his study.

TWO THINGS HAPPENED the day following the September 21 cabinet meeting: the ordinarily accurate *New York Times* presented an account of the meeting that bore little if any resemblance to what had taken place, and General Groves, in a widely reported speech that influenced a great many people, because as the engineer in charge of the Manhattan Project he was such an authority figure, said he thought the bomb should remain an American secret.

The bizarre page-one *New York Times* article was headlined "Plea to Give Soviet Atom Secret Stirs Debate in Cabinet: No Decision Made on Wallace Plan to Share Bomb Data as Peace Insurance." The *New York Times* Washington reporter Felix Belair Jr. had been duped. Someone, probably James Forrestal, had fed him a false account of what had gone on at the meeting. The long article repeatedly referred to the plan as the Wallace plan; Stimson was mentioned once, erroneously, as having said that the question should be "put up to a world body to be established at some future date," which was not what he believed at all. The article stated that the army and the navy "are prepared to resist the proposal to the hilt." Support for the idea, the *Times* account reemphasized several times, was from "Wallace adherents."

The effort to discredit the plan was incredibly effective—so effective it was doomed. Instead of a proposal from Stimson—a widely respected Republican who had served not just as FDR's secretary of war but as secretary of war under William Howard Taft and as secretary of state under Herbert Hoover—who had authorized the use of the atomic bombs and chosen the target cities, it became the idea of Henry Wallace, former vice president, a divisive figure who had barely been confirmed as commerce secretary, whom FDR had dropped as his running mate the previous year. *Time*, the most popular newsmagazine in America that routinely took and condensed material from newspapers, ran an article on the cabinet meeting the following week that echoed the *New York Times* account: "At a U.S. Cabinet meeting Henry Wallace and others cited scientific opinion that the secret could not be kept, argued that the bomb be made available to the United Nations Organization." *Life* magazine did a laudatory two-page spread on Stimson's retirement a short while later: there was a photograph of Stimson at the airport following the cabinet meeting walking through two lines of generals, including General Marshall, to the plane that would take him home; there was no mention of Stimson's last, momentous proposal to share information on the bomb with Russia. Retired to his beloved farm, Highhold, on Long Island, Stimson was soon sidelined by a heart condition.

WITHIN THREE YEARS, Forrestal, by then secretary of defense, would routinely refer to B-29s as "atomic carriers" to be stationed in Britain for use against Russia and advise Truman, "The only balance that we have against the overwhelming manpower of the Russians . . . is the threat of the immediate retaliation with the atomic bomb." In his diary less than a year before Russia exploded its first atomic bomb, Forrestal approvingly quoted the ambassador to Russia Walter Bedell Smith's assessment: "The Russians cannot possibly have the industrial competence to produce the atomic bomb now." The deception—whether by Forrestal or one of the other three documented opponents of Stimson's plan—was so effective that when *The Forrestal Diaries,* edited by Walter Millis, was published in 1951, Millis, evidently unaware that Truman's appointments secretary, Matthew J. Connelly, took notes and summarized discussions of all cabinet meetings, wrote of the September 21 meeting, "The underlying attitude of nearly all seemed closely in accord with Forrestal's contribution."

That such a gross misrepresentation of the issue discussed at the cabinet meeting could have prevailed is in itself an indication of the temper of the country: Americans were strongly against sharing information with Russia. Fifty-five out of sixty-one congressmen polled were opposed to the idea, as was 85 percent of the American public, according to a National Opinion Research Center poll. Preventing the Cold War was probably never an option after FDR's death. Perhaps the cabinet meeting can best be seen as a last, doomed effort to save an alliance America no longer thought wise.

WHEN BYRNES RETURNED to Washington a fortnight after the cabinet meeting, he stated he "felt himself in closest agreement with General Groves" and thought bringing Russia into partnership on atomic matters a mistake. "We must first see whether we can work out a decent peace," he explained. He decided a better plan was for the United Nations to set up a body to deal with atomic energy, ignoring, perhaps deliberately, that Stalin would consider such an action a slap in the face. In private, he stated "undue emphasis was being given to the views of the scientists on this subject." Truman, who had initially appeared to be on the fence, undoubtedly sensitive to the growing anti-Russian mood of the country, after a few weeks fell in with Byrnes's plan and decided not sharing was the safest, easiest route for America to take. At an impromptu press conference at a fishing retreat on Reelfoot Lake in Tennessee on October 8, he stated that the United States would not give away its engineering "know how" that produced the atomic bomb to any nation; others would just have to catch up with us. "Our possession of the atomic bomb and Russia's lack of it was not a factor in relations between the two countries," he said. He then, according to the news report, put a nail into future comity between the two nations with the comment that language difficulties precluded his meeting again with Stalin as he had at Potsdam, where "it was very difficult to translate into Russian the precise meaning of what he said in English and he always had to speak through an interpreter."

Anti-Russian feeling had always existed, even within FDR's closest wartime circle—even among key staff members, including Admiral Wilson Brown and Admiral Leahy—although in the interests of their careers and FDR's extraordinary personality, they, like many others, had kept their opinions well hidden when he was alive. In the Map Room, feeling secure, the always present Lieutenant Elsey many times heard both men speak critically of FDR. "Both were concerned at his 'globaloney,' the derisive term applied to the views of idealists preaching a 'One World' philosophy . . . They fretted aloud and often," Elsey remembered. After FDR's death anti-Russian sentiments, no longer in abeyance, took firm hold throughout the nation. On a day-to-day foreign policy level under Truman, men such as George Kennan, whose "Long Telegram" became the basis for America's postwar diplomacy of containment, and Joseph C. Grew, undersecretary of state, both of whom believed accommodation with the Soviet Union was neither possible nor desirable, both of whom had been against resumption of diplomatic relations with the Soviet Union in 1933, together with Averell Harriman, were the voices being listened to in day-to-day dealings with Russia. Kennan was so extreme he was against U.S. membership in the United Nations because Russia was a member. This was made crystal clear in a letter Charles Bohlen received from Kennan in February 1945 at Yalta in which Kennan negated Roosevelt's entire foreign policy. "I fail to see why we must associate ourselves with this political program, so hostile to the interests of the Atlantic community as a whole, so dangerous to everything which we need to see preserved in Europe," Kennan wrote to Bohlen, suggesting that "plans for the United Nations be buried as quickly as possible, because the only practical effect of creating an international organization would be to commit the United States to defend a swollen and unhealthy Russian sphere of power."

FDR was a pragmatist, a political problem solver. From the start he had assumed Soviet domination of Eastern Europe, assumed that Stalin's drive to achieve such domination was based on protecting Russia's borders. He would, if Stalin had insisted, have even acquiesced in the postwar Soviet domination of Finland. He had admitted as much in 1943 to Francis Cardinal Spellman, New York's archbishop, prior to Tehran. Poland, the Baltic States, Finland, he wrote, "better give them gracefully . . . What can we do about it?" He hoped, FDR had continued, that in ten or twenty years "European influence would bring the Russians to become less barbarian." FDR never admitted as much in public, and when he met Stalin at Yalta, the president had proceeded to set limits to Soviet domination of satellite countries that Stalin had signed on to and that he signed on to again in Moscow in June when pressed by Hopkins. FDR was looking to the future—gambling that Stalin, who had lived through two German invasions, was building his own cordon sanitaire of nations to forever protect Russia from future invading armies and had no military designs on Western Europe.

Finally understanding after discussions with Hopkins U.S. concerns with appearances and the necessity of measuring up to international expectations, Stalin had agreed in June to bring Polish dissidents such as Mikołajczyk into positions of authority in the government.

In spite of the shock of the bomb, a world where Russia would be safe to continue rebuilding itself—which meant a period of economic stability, which meant a friendly America—was certainly Stalin's postwar goal. Because of his faith in FDR, Stalin was crucially among the founders of the World Bank and the International Monetary Fund designed by FDR to foster world trade and economic stability, without being entirely in favor, because it was so important to FDR. It had come down to a question of trust.

Stalin's expectation that America would help Russia rebuild and grant Russia a significant loan even though FDR was dead had a solid basis: loan negotiations had been going on for the better part of two years. Harriman had discussed postwar American aid with Anastas Mikoyan, the commissar for foreign trade, several times in 1943. Molotov had presented the first formal Soviet request for a $6 billion postwar credit to Harriman in January 1945. Henry Morgenthau advocated increasing that amount to $10 billion. Eric Johnston, president of the U.S. Chamber of Commerce, who had visited Moscow in 1944, had assured Stalin that capitalist America was going to need markets to absorb the industrial capacity it had developed during the war and therefore a loan enabling Russia to buy American goods was in the interests of America as well as Russia. After their two-and-a-half-hour meeting Johnston noted that Stalin had an excellent grasp of American economic conditions, telling the *New York Times* reporter Harrison Salisbury, "He knows American production figures better than most of our own business men do. I know because knowing those figures is my business." Johnston, quintessential symbol of American capitalism, much impressed by the Russian leader, had told Stalin that he would do "everything he could to promote extension of credits by the United States to Russia for the purchase of American machinery for reconstruction and assured the Marshal that American business desired the development of the fullest trade and commerce with the Soviet Union in both directions." Stalin's economic policies were based on the economic theories of Dr. Eugene Varga, the brilliant Hungarian economist who had approved of the Bretton Woods plan and whom Stalin relied on and often consulted; Varga's analysis of the general crisis of capitalism, of capitalist stagnation, was a bedrock Communist belief and as such unquestioningly accepted by Stalin. With the knowledge that FDR's friend Secretary of the Treasury Morgenthau, as well as the State Department, was discussing the question of a postwar Russian loan, that it was generally accepted as a beneficial move to both countries, that FDR had always been on his side from the time he had tried to get a ship built in America in 1936 and had been so generous with Lend-Lease in the intervening years, Stalin must have been as certain as he was of anything that a loan would be granted.

Loan negotiations had stalled because FDR had notified administration officials in January 1945 to hold off further discussions until he met with Stalin, according to the historian Thomas Paterson. However, although it was on Stalin's mind—he mentioned a possible U.S. loan the first evening at Yalta (joking that if FDR wanted five hundred bottles of champagne he "would give it to the president on a long-term credit of thirty years")—FDR never brought up the subject during the conference. Nor did Stalin or Molotov. One can only speculate that FDR thought the timing wrong—that it was too early—and was waiting until the two nations joined forces in the invasion of Japan, while Stalin and Molotov were waiting for FDR to take the initiative.

Shortly after August 9, Stalin learned that the Export-Import Bank, which at that time had limited funds, was preparing to consider granting a $1 billion credit to Russia. Soviet officials applied for this smaller amount, offering 2.375 percent interest: the bank turned them down, on the grounds that the interest rate was too low, although shortly thereafter the United States offered the British a $3.75 billion loan at an interest rate of 2 percent. On September 17, Senator Claude Pepper of Florida, an advocate of aid for the Soviet Union, and the members of the House Special Committee on Post-war Economic Policy and Planning traveled to Moscow to see Soviet economic conditions. Meeting with Stalin, the participants discussed the original $6 billion loan. Trying to whet their appetite, Stalin reminded the legislators, "There are possibilities for the trade between the United States and Russia to increase." He told them Russia faced many years of building to repair the war damage and raise living standards and, in line with classic Marxist thinking on the dangers of overproduction in a capitalist society, pointed out, "Our internal market is bottomless and we can swallow God knows how much." Aware that many Americans feared and mistrusted the Soviet Union, during a special forty-five-minute interview with Pepper, he assured the senator that he wanted U.S. financial help to build up the living standard of the Russian people and not for the purpose of further development of military power. "It would be suicide for Russia to use any loan funds for military purposes," he said. The group got the impression from Stalin that he felt negotiations were "going along nicely for a six billion dollar credit."

The Russians waited. Absolutely nothing happened: there was no action on the loan, no action on credits. Asked about it, Truman denied the Russians had even applied for credits. The State Department then issued a statement that it wasn't America's fault: it had invited the Soviets to negotiate credits, and the Soviet Union had not responded. In March 1946, the State Department announced that the previous August the original Russian loan application had been lost during a transfer of the documents from the Foreign Economic Administration, which oversaw the Export-Import Bank, to the State Department: the papers had just been found. According to Arthur Schlesinger Jr., "This was impossible for the Russians to believe . . . It only strengthened Soviet suspicions of American purposes."

Russian suspicions of foul play turned out to be correct. Secretary of State James Byrnes later admitted he took pains to see that credits would not be granted by burying the pertinent folder: "I had it placed in the forgotten file, as I felt sure that Fred Vinson, the new Secretary of the Treasury, would not press it."

Stalin's still optimistic outlook on an Anglo-Russian alliance lasted into 1946 and can be seen in his answers to the questions put to him by Alexander Werth, the Russian-speaking BBC and *Sunday Times* journalist who had remained in Moscow throughout the war and wrote a powerful book about what it had been like, *Russia at War, 1941–1945*.

WERTH: Do you believe in a real danger of a "new war" concerning which there is so much irresponsible talk throughout

the world today? What steps should be taken to prevent war if
such a danger exists?

STALIN: I do not believe in a real danger of a "new war."

Those who are now clamoring about a "new war" are chiefly
military-political scouts and their few followers from among the
civilian ranks. They need this clamor if only: (a) to scare certain
naive politicians from among their counter-agents with the
spectre of war, and thus help their own Governments to wring
as many concessions as possible from such counter-agents; (b)
to obstruct for some time the reduction of war budgets in their
own countries; (c) to put a brake on the demobilization of
troops, and thus prevent a rapid growth of unemployment in
their own countries.

One must strictly differentiate between the hue and cry
about a "new war" which is now taking place, and a real danger
of a "new war" which does not exist at present.

WERTH: Do you believe that Great Britain and the United
States of America are consciously placing the Soviet Union in a
state of "capitalist encirclement"?

STALIN: I do not think that the ruling circles of Great Britain
and of the United States of America could create a "capitalist encirclement" of the Soviet Union even if they so desired,
which, however, I do not assert.

WERTH: Do you believe in the possibility of friendly and lasting co-operation between the Soviet Union and the Western
democracies despite the existence of ideological differences, and
in the "friendly competition" between the two systems to which
Mr. Wallace referred?

STALIN: I believe in it absolutely.

General Eisenhower, on his way to England aboard the ocean liner
Queen Mary, said at a news conference that he agreed with Premier Stalin's statement that no country wants war.

WHAT FDR HAD SO ASSIDUOUSLY worked to prevent—allowing
British and American diplomats, as the war wound down, to create
the appearance of an Anglo-Saxon coalition against the Slav nation—

became a reality after his death. Britain received a postwar loan, which it desperately needed; the Soviet Union, which needed it more, did not. Truman, swayed by his advisers, rejected sharing control over the atomic bomb with Stalin. So in the end, a fearful Stalin, the most paranoid of world leaders, was faced with an America that had refused to give up its weapons superiority and refused to grant his country aid. FDR had famously said in his first inaugural address, "The only thing we have to fear is fear itself." After he died, it slowly became apparent that fear again stalked the land. A different fear: fear of Russia.

On April 12, 1946, *Pravda* observed the anniversary of Roosevelt's death with a laudatory article about him. "The Soviet people saw in Mr. Roosevelt a friend of the Soviet Union," the newspaper stated. The article described FDR as "an enemy of isolationism as well as an opponent of those non-isolationists who considered and still consider today that the United States policy must consist of power politics with the aim of establishing the domination of American interests throughout the world."

Anthony Eden said at roughly the same time, "Had Roosevelt lived and retained his health he would never have permitted the present situation to develop. His death, therefore, was a calamity of immeasurable proportions."

Stimson had written, "Whether Russia gets control of the necessary secrets of production in a minimum of say four years or a maximum of twenty years is not nearly as important to the world and civilization as to make sure that when they do get it they are willing and co-operative partners among the peace-loving nations of the world."

On August 29, 1949, in Kazakhstan, less than four years after the fateful cabinet meeting in which Stimson advocated sharing control of atomic energy with Russia, the Soviet Union succeeded in exploding an atomic bomb. It was code-named First Lightning. The arms race was on.

Years later Stalin would say, displaying his still abiding affection for the fallen leader as well as his bedrock belief in the intrinsic superiority of the Communist system over the capitalist system, "Roosevelt was a great statesman, a clever, educated, far-sighted and liberal leader who prolonged the life of capitalism."

ACKNOWLEDGMENTS

I want to thank the MacDowell Colony. It was during my stay at the Colony that I conceptualized the chapters of this book.

The first person I must acknowledge is Svetlana Chervonnaya. She has been my patient adviser, translator, and font of information on all things Russian. Svetlana has supplied me with many documents from various Russian sources, as well as taking me into the Russian State Archive of Social and Political History (RGASPI) in Moscow to view Stalin's messages to Roosevelt.

I want to thank my very helpful readers. First, Professor Marilyn B. Young for her many observations, sound advice, and generous donation of that most precious commodity, time, and Professor Frank Costigliola for his interest, perspective, and archival knowledge of the period. I am also indebted to Stephen Schlesinger, William Levit, John Connor, and Pat Beard for their astute comments and continued interest in the manuscript, to Denie and Frank Weil for their helpful suggestions, and to General James Abrahamson. My thanks also to Susan Connor, who translated for me the original drafts of Stalin's messages to FDR that are in RGASPI and to Anthony Zannino, also a very helpful translator.

I am so grateful to Victoria Wilson, my amazingly intuitive editor, for her suggestions for changes and additions that have added greatly to the manuscript. I also want to thank her assistant, Audrey Silverman, who so ably kept the manuscript on track at Knopf, and Lydia Buechler, meticulous copy chief. I am deeply indebted to the late Arthur Schlesinger Jr. for setting me on the path that led to this book. I must thank Carl Pforzheimer for acquainting me with the Frederick Lewis Allen and Wertheim rooms at the New York Public Library at Forty-Second Street, where so much of the book was written, and Jay Barksdale for making my life there so pleasant.

I owe special thanks to Bob Clark, deputy director and chief archivist at the Franklin D. Roosevelt Presidential Library, for his help and guidance, as well as to the knowledgeable and always resourceful archivists Virginia Lewick, Matthew Hanson, Mark Renovitch, and Alycia Vivona. I also want to thank Richard Peuser at NARA for his assistance, as well as Randy Sowell at the Harry S. Truman Presidential Library, Amanda Pike at the Seeley Mudd Manuscript Library at Princeton, and Marcia Loveman, at the Lake Wales Library in Lake Wales, Florida, who facilitated my continuing search for documents from other libraries. I must mention as well the excellent assistance I was given by the staff of the Manuscript Division of the Library of Congress, and the staff of the Albert and Shirley Small Special Collections at the University of Virginia.

I was fortunate to receive historic Roosevelt family information from Diana Delano, background UN and UNRRA information from Dan Plesch, and information on John Maynard Keynes from Robert Skidelsky. And I want to thank Sergey Yurchenko, director of Livadia Palace, for the wonderful private tour he gave me.

I also want to thank Sally Mack for housing me while I did research in Boston at the Houghton Library, Andrea and Tim Corcoran while I was in Washington working at the Library of Congress, Ann Morse and Linda and Robert Butler for taking care of me in Hyde Park, New York, while I worked at the FDR Library, and Felicia Rogan for housing me in Charlottesville while I did research at the University of Virginia.

I must also thank Luis Lagera, from Bartow, Florida, who put all my scattered notes and documents into chronological order; and my agent, Fredrica Friedman.

NOTES

ABBREVIATIONS

APP: American Presidency Project, by Gerhard Peters and John T. Woolley, online

AVP RF: Archive of the Foreign Policy of the Russian Federation

CC: Closest Companion, ed. Geoffrey C. Ward

FDRL: Franklin D. Roosevelt Library

FRUS: U.S. State Department, *Foreign Relations of the United States*

LOC: Library of Congress

MDMS: My Dear Mr. Stalin, ed. Susan Butler

NARA: National Archives and Records Administration

NYT: New York Times

RGASPI: Russian State Archive of Social and Political History

1: CROSSING THE ATLANTIC IN WARTIME

5　It had been specially fitted: Rigdon, *White House Sailor,* 60.

5　"We are trying": Reilly, *Reilly of the White House,* 136.

7　"the easiest person": Strong, *The Soviets Expected It,* 47.

7　"as absolute as": Sherwood, *Roosevelt and Hopkins,* 138.

7　"I bank on": McIntire, *White House Physician,* 170.

8　"The United States": Freidel, *Rendezvous with Destiny,* 31.

8　"The tragedy of Wilson":Sherwood, *Roosevelt and Hopkins,* 227.

9　"with absorbed": Wehle, *Hidden Threads of History,* 134.

9　The Russians were behind: Acheson, *Present at the Creation,* 69.

10　"not a stripe": King Diary, Dec. 5, 1942.

10　"Winston, I have it": *CC,* 385.

11　"Chiang's troops": Elliott Roosevelt, *As He Saw It,* 142.

11　"immediately after the end of the war": Stalin to FDR, Oct. 30, 1943, in *MDMS,* 180.

12　"outstanding organizer": Montefiore, *Stalin,* 439.

12　By the fall of 1943: Harriman and Abel, *Special Envoy,* 253.

12　"I suggest that we": FDR to Stalin, May 5, 1943, in *MDMS,* 129.

13　"Should this proposal be": Stalin to FDR, Aug. 8, 1943, in *MDMS,* 151; fond 558, op. 11, files 366, note 22, Stalin Papers.

13 "the exact date of": Stalin to FDR, Sept. 8, 1943, in *MDMS*, 162.

13 "I cannot assume the delays": FDR to Stalin, Oct. 21, 1943, in ibid., 178.

13 "The whole world": FDR to Stalin, Nov. 8, 1943, in ibid., 182.

14 "We should have no": Isaacson and Thomas, *Wise Men*, 154; Kennan, *Memoirs, 1925–1950*, 57.

14 "You should go": Dallek, *Franklin D. Roosevelt and American Foreign Policy*, 532.

14 "Communicating through the State": Robert Skidelsky, on C-SPAN, May 29, 2006.

14 Nor did it help: Talk with Harry Hopkins, June 5, 1945, Robert Meiklejohn Diary. "He told how, early in the New Deal administration he had been sent on a trip to Europe, ostensibly to study housing but actually to check up on the Foreign Service."

14 "gross procrastination": Morgenthau, personal report to the president, Jan. 15, 1944, Morgenthau Diaries, book 694, FDRL.

14 "reach a large measure": Rosenman, *Working with Roosevelt*, 402.

15 "Deplorably untidy": Ismay, *Memoirs*, 214.

15 "an animated piece": *New Yorker*, Aug. 7, 1943.

16 "it was absolutely": Eleanor Roosevelt, *This I Remember*, 257.

16 "would advise me": Gromyko, *Memories*, 54.

16 "the only member": Doenecke and Stoler, *Debating Franklin D. Roosevelt's Foreign Policies*, 11.

16 "Remember how Wilson": Perkins, *The Roosevelt I Knew*, 340.

17 "made up the rules": Loy Henderson, Columbia Oral History Project, Columbia University.

17 "I learned": Hull, *Memoirs*, 2:1110.

17 "in his element": Wehle, *Hidden Threads of History*, 223.

17 "Please try": Hull, *Memoirs*, 2:1111.

18 "If I understood you correctly": Stalin to FDR, Oct. 6, 1943, in *MDMS*, 171.

18 "The Soviet Government welcomes": William Phillips Diary, based on the account of Cavendish Cannon, of the State Department, Nov. 12, 1943, Phillips Papers.

19 "The OM [old man] sat": Goodwin, *No Ordinary Time*, 471.

19 as *The New Yorker* described: E. J. Kahn, *New Yorker*, May 3, 1952.

21 "The destroyer in the escort": Dictated by Roosevelt, June 1, 1944, FDR Papers.

21 "while the President": Sherwood, *Roosevelt and Hopkins*, 978.

22 "Take me to the starboard": Rigdon, *White House Sailor*, 64.

22 "All goes well": *F.D.R.: His Personal Letters*, 4:1469.

22 "This will be": FDR, note in longhand, FDR Papers.

22 "There would definitely be": *FRUS, Conferences at Cairo and Tehran, 1943,* 254–55.

23 "We took up first": Stimson Diary, Nov. 9, 1943.

23 "this command should be": *FRUS, Conferences at Cairo and Tehran, 1943,* 204.

2: TRAVELING TO TEHRAN

25 As the three: Summersby, *Past Forgetting,* 173.

26 "Man's desire": Reilly, *Reilly of the White House,* 170.

26 "a horrible scene": Ward, *Before the Trumpet,* 118.

28 "aside from the declaration": Sherwood, *Roosevelt and Hopkins,* 771.

28 "it would be": Kimball, *Churchill and Roosevelt,* vol. 2, 597.

28 "It was unfortunate": Dec. 15, 1943, U.K. National Archives.

28 "that's what will": Elliott Roosevelt, *As He Saw It,* 165.

28 "lengthy, complicated": Dallek, *Franklin D. Roosevelt and American Foreign Policy,* 426.

29 "The American chiefs of staff": Ismay, *Memoirs,* 334.

29 "wanted the right": Pogue, *Ordeal and Hope,* 330.

30 "there was no time left": Ismay, *Memoirs,* 337.

30 "Winston said he": Moran, *Churchill at War,* 159.

30 "to continue the offensive": Major General Sir John Kennedy Diary, in Pogue, *Organizer of Victory,* 300–301.

31 "The Conference goes": Tully, *F.D.R.: My Boss,* 270.

31 "remain for two": FDR to Stalin, Nov. 22, 1943, in *MDMS,* 186.

32 "If I suggest": Sherwood, *Roosevelt and Hopkins,* 969.

34 "We have made": *FRUS, Conferences at Cairo and Tehran, 1943,* 397.

34 "a ramshackle house": Ismay, *Memoirs,* 337.

35 "The Russian Government talk as always": *FRUS, Conferences at Cairo and Tehran, 1943,* 439.

37 "I always agree": Salisbury, *Russia on the Way,* 256.

38 "We had a very unenlightening talk as always": Gorodetsky, *Stafford Cripps in Moscow,* 150.

38 "he had lived": Rachel Polonsky, *Molotov's Magic Lantern,* 64.

38 "It was easier": Svetlana Chervonnaya, e-mail to author, Aug. 9, 2010.

38 "The Kulaks are": Axell, *Marshal Zhukov,* 34.

39 "The Collective Farm policy": Winston S. Churchill, *Hinge of Fate,* 498.

39 "a good fellow": Dimitrov, *Diary,* 145.

40 "sending Comrade Voroshilov": Volkogonov, *Stalin,* 455.

40 "somewhat plump": Bohlen, *Witness to History,* 355.

40 "little and fat": Kathleen Harriman, Harriman and Abel, *Special Envoy,* 416.

41 "generals don't often": S. M. Shtemenko, *The General Staff in the War*

Years (Moscow: Voenizdat, 1989), http://militera.lib.ru/memo/russian/shtemenko/index.html; *Komsomolskaya Pravda,* May 7, 2007; *Lipetsk News,* April 11, 2007.

42 "he had clung": Volkogonov, *Stalin,* 498.

3: TEHRAN

44 "had not come": Harriman, memo of conversations at Tehran, Nov. 27, 1943, Harriman Papers.

45 "The Boss": Reilly, *Reilly of the White House,* 178–79.

46 "You will, of course": Bullitt, *For the President,* 75.

47 "Plainly it is": Moran, *Churchill at War,* 162.

47 "Everywhere you went": Reilly, *Reilly of the White House,* 179.

47 "all of them": Elliott Roosevelt, *As He Saw It,* 171.

48 "a small thing to do": Costigliola, *Roosevelt's Lost Alliances,* 196.

48 "I have a hunch": King Diary, May 21, 1943.

49 "I did not suggest": Kimball, *Churchill and Roosevelt,* 2:283.

49 "My Dear Mr. Stalin": FDR to Stalin, May 5, 1943, in *MDMS,* 129.

50 "Let's all get a drink": Werth, *Russia at War,* 617.

50 "I agree with you": Stalin to FDR, May 26, 1943, in *MDMS,* 134.

51 "in addition to": FDR to Stalin, June 16, 1943, in ibid., 141.

51 "You write to me": Stalin to FDR, June 24, 1943, in ibid., 144–45.

51 "act of treachery": FDR to Stalin, June 22, 1943, in ibid., 144.

51 he took the trouble: Stalin Papers, fond 558, op. 11, file 365.

51 "I thank you": Stalin to FDR, June 26, 1943, in *MDMS,* 147–48.

52 "The battles are": Stalin to FDR, Aug. 8, 1943, in *MDMS,* 150–51.

53 "Unfortunately, not one": Stalin to FDR, Oct. 19, 1945, in ibid., 174.

53 "I would gladly": FDR to Stalin, Oct. 21, 1945, in ibid., 178–79.

54 "as far as Basra": Hull, *Memoirs,* 2:1303.

54 "You are now": Excerpts from the Press Conference, Oct. 29, 1943, APP, http://www.presidency.ucsb.edu.

54 "Things are 'in a mess' ": *CC,* 250.

55 "There always was": Lash, *Love, Eleanor,* 399.

55 "His Scottish soul": *Roosevelt and Frankfurter,* 737.

56 "He is preparing": *CC,* 250.

56 "I still hope": *F.D.R.: His Personal Letters,* 3:1462.

56 "The possibility of traveling": Stalin to FDR, Nov. 5, 1943, in *MDMS,* 180–81.

56 "We won't get": Welles, *Where Are We Heading?,* 29–30.

57 "cannot be away": *CC,* 253.

57 "It was quite possible": King Diary, Dec. 5, 1942.

57 "a little worried": *CC,* 252.

58 "I have worked out": FDR to Stalin, Nov. 8, 1943, in *MDMS,* 181–82.

58 "is assigning high": *Sovetsko-amerikanskie otnosheniia, 1939–1945.*

58 "The fighting in Southern Europe": Werth, *Russia at War,* 687.

59 "Here Ivan the Terrible": Zubok and Pleshakov, *Inside the Kremlin's Cold War,* 16.

59 "The 'father of the people'": Bullock, *Hitler and Stalin,* 633.

59 "Membership in the Comintern": Dallin and Firsov, eds., *Dimitrov and Stalin,* 227.

59 "When we created": Ibid., 238.

60 "We ought to rush": Ibid., 253.

60 "that when he was ambassador": Werth, *Russia at War,* 617.

60 "It exposes the lie": Stalin, "The Dissolution of the Communist International," https://www.marxists.org/reference/archive/stalin/works/1943/05/28.htm.

60 "We have good": Birse, *Memoirs of an Interpreter,* 209.

61 "Fine uniforms": Werth, *Russia at War,* 676.

62 "his religious faith was the strongest": Arthur M. Schlesinger, Jr., *Coming of the New Deal,* 586.

62 "Freedom to worship God as their": *FRUS, 1941, General, The Soviet Union,* 1: 767.

62 "I believe there is": *F.D.R.: His Personal Letters,* Sept. 3, 1941, 4:1204.

63 "If Moscow could get": *FRUS, 1941, General, The Soviet Union,* 1:832.

63 "so that he might": Dallek, *Franklin D. Roosevelt and American Foreign Policy,* 297.

63 "The President wanted": Harriman, *America and Russia in a Changing World,* 16.

63 "the Soviets were": Sherwood, *Roosevelt and Hopkins,* 391.

64 "The old body snatcher": Perkins, *Roosevelt I Knew,* 146.

64 "Public opinion of the Soviet Union": Harriman Papers.

64 "Freedom for any religion": Harriman and Abel, *Special Envoy,* 103.

64 "I believe Litvinov": Hull, *Memoirs,* 2:1120.

65 In November 1942: *FRUS, 1942,* 3:142.

65 The following day: Volkogonov, *Stalin,* 470.

67 "parts the sky": Montefiore, *Stalin,* 461.

67 "Only a mere": Kahan, *Wolf of the Kremlin,* 214–15.

4: FIRST IMPRESSIONS

68 "Well, you know": Stimson Diary, May 1, 1942.

68 "get a little": Hull, *Memoirs,* 1:205.

68 "a solo performance": Stimson Diary, May 1, 1942.

68 "I had much to tell him": Phillips Diary, April 29, 1943.

69 "Conversation was his golf": Gunther, *Roosevelt in Retrospect,* 60.

69 "With a most engaging": Reilly, *Reilly of the White House,* 179.

70 "I caught him looking": *CC,* 299.

70 "He could make a casual": Jackson, *That Man,* 111.

70 "I never": Ickes, *First Thousand Days,* 127.

70 "about five feet six": Sherwood, *Roosevelt and Hopkins,* 344.

71 "I was struck": Deane, *Strange Alliance,* 24.

71 "Any American": Hull, *Memoirs,* 2:1311.

71 "sinister in appearance": Leahy Diary, Nov. 30, 1943.

71 "The foundation of Stalin's power": Montefiore, *Stalin,* 48.

72 On his desk was: Berezhkov, *History in the Making,* 211.

72 after his dinner guests: Montefiore, *Stalin,* 116.

72 "I had never met": Rosenman, *Working with Roosevelt,* 22.

73 "instinct for the basic": Schlesinger, *Coming of the New Deal,* 551.

73 "dominated his": Montefiore, *Stalin,* 49.

73 "the frank clear gaze": Schlesinger, *Coming of the New Deal,* 575–76.

73 "You know, Orson": Meacham, *Franklin and Winston,* 27.

73 "That was the Garbo": Gunther, *Roosevelt in Retrospect,* 62.

73 "My journey": Harriman and Abel, *Special Envoy,* 218.

77 "a striking example": Bohlen, *Witness to History,* 141.

77 "Marshal Stalin replied": *FRUS, Conferences at Cairo and Tehran, 1943,* 482–86.

81 Churchill had instructed: Ibid.

81 "make it clear": Foreign Office to Moscow, outward telegram, Oct. 26, 1943, U.K. National Archives.

83 "that the staffs work": *FRUS, Conferences at Cairo and Tehran, 1943,* 496.

84 "He seemed so dispirited": Moran, *Churchill at War,* 164.

84 "a poor and not": Alldritt, *Greatest of Friends,* 169.

84 "The Anglo-American plans": CAB/65/40/15, Minute 2, Dec. 15, 1943, U.K. National Archives.

85 "I think he felt": Dictated by FDR, June 1, 1944, FDR Papers.

85 "Tell the President": *CC,* 299.

86 "a direct threat": *FRUS, Conferences at Cairo and Tehran, 1943,* 508–9.

87 "The very Reich itself": Ibid., 510–14.

88 "Well, I'm glad": McIntire, *White House Physician,* 173.

88 "Winston burst out": Reilly, *Reilly of the White House,* 180–81.

89 "plainly put out": Moran, *Churchill at War,* 165.

5: A MEETING OF MINDS

91 "how happy he": *FRUS, Conferences at Cairo and Tehran, 1943,* 529.

91 "Mr. President," he said: Leahy, *I Was There,* 209.

92 "Mr. Churchill did not like": *FRUS, Conferences at Cairo and Tehran, 1943,* 530.

92 "This organization": Ibid.

92 "A European state would": Ibid., 531.

92 "doubted if the United States Congress": Ibid.

93 "that England and the Soviet Union": Ibid.

93 "it might be possible": Ibid., 531–32.

93 Stalin had written: *NYT,* Sept. 17, 1948.

94 "I hate the Germans": Roberts, *Stalin's Wars,* 12.

94 "we must have": *FRUS, Conferences at Cairo and Tehran, 1943,* 532.

94 "We have got to": Blum, *Years of War,* 342.

94 the first requisite of the peace: Gunther, *Roosevelt in Retrospect,* 116.

95 "I really feel": Jean Edward Smith, *FDR,* 587.

95 "After all China was a nation": *FRUS, Conferences at Cairo and Tehran, 1943,* 532.

95 "a strong and effective": Ibid., 532–33. Blum, *Years of War.* Bohlen's minutes are ambiguous as to when Stalin made the comment about the ease of converting factories, but Roosevelt's comment makes it clear that Stalin made this statement when Roosevelt was still in the room.

96 Stalin had demonstrated that he: *FRUS, Conferences at Cairo and Tehran, 1943,* 533.

96 "most certainly he would": Elliott Roosevelt, *As He Saw It,* 180.

96 "coincided with that": Deane, *Strange Alliance,* 42.

97 Churchill, stout and round shouldered: Montefiore, *Stalin,* 468.

97 tears in his eyes: Alldritt, *Greatest of Friends,* 173.

98 "with this preface": Moran, *Churchill at War,* 167.

98 "for about ten minutes": Winston S. Churchill, *Closing the Ring,* 368.

99 "I rapidly grew": Alldritt, *Greatest of Friends,* 169.

99 "If we are all": *FRUS, Conferences at Cairo and Tehran, 1943,* 546.

99 "no interest in any": Ibid., 546–48.

100 "Without that feeling": Moran, *Churchill at War,* 149.

100 "Mr. Churchill became": Alldritt, *Greatest of Friends,* 171.

100 "he was really": Bohlen, *Witness to History,* 146.

101 "all that was necessary to be solved": *FRUS, Conferences at Cairo and Tehran, 1943,* 550.

102 Roosevelt again tried: Ibid., 550–52.

102 "If the conditions": Ibid., 552.

102 As Elliott later remembered: Elliott Roosevelt, *As He Saw It,* 184–86.

103 "But a weak one": Ibid., 186.

104 "lost no opportunity": *FRUS, Conferences at Cairo and Tehran, 1943,* 553.

104 "What are we": Gunther, *Roosevelt in Retrospect,* 18.

105 "I propose a salute": Elliott Roosevelt, *As He Saw It,* 188.

105 "quasi-jocular fashion": Bohlen, *Witness to History,* 147.

105 "The conflict": Evans, *Third Reich at War,* 175.

106 "In a hundred years": Ibid., 171.

106 In December 1941: Ibid., 186. Evans's description of the soldiers' plight is well documented and horrifying.

106 "If I had my way": Hull, *Memoirs*, 2:1289.

106 "When the president": Harriman and Abel, *Special Envoy*, 178.

107 "Any such attitude": Elliott Roosevelt, *As He Saw It*, 188.

107 "The British Parliament": Winston S. Churchill, *Closing the Ring*, 374.

107 "As usual," Roosevelt said: Elliott Roosevelt, *As He Saw It*, 188.

107 Secretary of the Treasury: Stimson and Bundy, *On Active Service*, 584.

107 Churchill, usually known: This description is an amalgam of Montefiore, *Stalin*, 470, 554; Harriman and Abel, *Special Envoy*, 274; and Winston S. Churchill, *Closing the Ring*, 373–74.

108 "Russian, American, and British soldiers": Elliott Roosevelt, *As He Saw It*, 190.

108 "I had not been there": Winston S. Churchill, *Closing the Ring*, 373–74.

109 "When the time comes, we will": *FRUS, Conferences at Cairo and Tehran, 1943*, 555.

109 "What you said was": Elliott Roosevelt, *As He Saw It*, 191.

110 "He was," remembered Elliott: *Look*, Sept. 1946.

110 Yet there is evidence: *FRUS, Conferences at Cairo and Tehran, 1943*, 564.

111 "his great satisfaction": Ibid., 565.

111 "When would the Commander": Ibid.

113 "cookie pushers": Sherwood, *Roosevelt and Hopkins*, 774.

113 "there had been a question": Bohlen, *Witness to History*, 128.

115 "Iran is definitely": Stettinius, *Roosevelt and the Russians*, 180; Hull, *Memoirs*, 2:1507–8.

116 "This is a fine": Montefiore, *Stalin*, 30; Gray, *Stalin: Man of History*, 386.

116 "a frightening figure": Sarah Churchill, *Thread in the Tapestry*, 65.

117 "Stalin became gloomy": Berezhkov, *History in the Making*, 288.

117 "I want to tell you": *FRUS, Conferences at Cairo and Tehran, 1943*, 469.

6: CEMENTING THE ALLIANCE

119 "if we had everything": Rigdon, *White House Sailor*, 81–82.

120 "May I come in?": *Politicheskii zhurnal* [Political journal], April 5, 2004.

121 "Why is it, Mr. President": Manchester, *American Caesar*, 154.

121 "what we were doing": Perkins, *Roosevelt I Knew*, 84–85.

122 "was entirely convinced": Fond 06, op. 5, p. 28, file 327 ("Political and informational letters received from the Embassy of the USSR in the USA from Comrades Litvinov and Gromyko, May 22–June 29, 1943"), AVP RF. Read by Molotov, who marked it up with pencil.

122 "the classic British foreign policy of walling": Costigliola, *Roosevelt's Lost Alliances*, 192.

123 "absolutely impossible": *FRUS, Conferences at Cairo and Tehran, 1943*, 587.

123 "this dreadful rape": FDR to Lincoln MacVeagh, Dec. 1, 1939, in *F.D.R.: His Personal Letters*, 4:965.

123 "so better give": Doenecke and Stoler, *Debating Franklin D. Roosevelt's Foreign Policies*, 73.

123 "If the cession": Winston S. Churchill, *Closing the Ring*, 399.

124 "I am sick and tired": Frank Costigliola, "Broken Circle: The Isolation of Franklin D. Roosevelt in World War II," *Diplomatic History* 32, no. 5 (Nov. 2008): 705.

125 "downright rudeness": O'Sullivan, *Sumner Welles, Postwar Planning, and the Quest for a New World Order*, 183.

125 "All those Baltic republics": Costigliola, "Broken Circle," 705.

125 "world opinion would want": *FRUS, Conferences at Cairo and Tehran, 1943*, 595.

126 "The USA does not have": "Political and informational letters received from the Embassy of the USSR in the USA from Comrades Litvinov and Gromyko, May 22–June 29, 1943," fond 06, op. 5, p. 28, AVP RF.

126 "it would be helpful": *FRUS, Conferences at Cairo and Tehran, 1943*, 595.

126 "Churchill instantly reacted": King Diary, Dec. 5, 1942.

127 "felt that it was": *FRUS, Conferences at Cairo and Tehran, 1943*, 595.

127 "it was just an idea": Ibid.

127 Roosevelt described how he edged: Jackson, *That Man*, 135–36.

127 "after thinking over": *FRUS, Conferences at Cairo and Tehran, 1943*, 596.

128 "in the common cause": Ibid., 597.

128 "around the end of January": Ibid.

129 "at the expense of Germany": Ibid., 598.

129 "the evil core of German": Ibid., 600.

130 "must have the strength": Ibid., 603.

130 "whether Marshal Stalin": Ibid.

130 "Although I have tried": Churchill to Eden, personal minute, Jan. 4, 1944, U.K. Archives.

130 "Comrade Stalin declared": Roberts, *Stalin's Wars*, 188.

131 "For God's sake": Bohlen, *Witness to History*, 143.

132 "The conferences have": FDR Diary, December 1, 1943, FDR Papers.

133 "It seemed to me": Berezhkov, *History in the Making*, 303.

134 "The conference, I consider": FDR to Stalin December 3, 1943, in *MDMS*.

134 "I agree with you": Ibid., 194.

134 "probably going to": Stimson Diary, December 3, 1943.

135 "must be full": Stimson Diary, April 15, 1945.

135 "told me the President": Sherwood, *Roosevelt and Hopkins,* 803.

136 "I welcome the appointment": Stalin to FDR, December 10, 1943, in *MDMS,* 194; the original in fond 558, op. 11, file 367, note 55, Stalin Papers.

136 the cornerstone accomplishment: Elliott Roosevelt, *As He Saw It,* 213.

136 "The trip was almost": December 15, 1943, *CC,* 261.

136 "I have thus": Stimson and Bundy, *On Active Service,* 443.

137 "I thank the Lord": Stimson Diary, December 3, 1943.

139 "The road": *Tass,* Dec. 8, 1943.

139 "Stalin's signature": *Tass,* Dec. 12, 1943.

139 "The new association": "Embassy Interpretive Report on Developments in Soviet Policy Based on the Soviet Press for the Period December, 1943," Dec. 14, 1943, Harriman Papers.

141 The cable went on: Boyd, *Hitler's Japanese Confidant,* 111.

141 "I am distressed": Winston S. Churchill, *Closing the Ring,* 422.

142 "I do not remember": Rosenman, *Working with Roosevelt,* 411.

143 "It is the first time": Goodwin, *No Ordinary Time,* 480.

146 "A man hewn": Hassett, *Off the Record with FDR,* 226.

146 "You know," he said: Perkins, *Roosevelt I Knew,* 382.

147 "in reality": *FRUS, 1944, Europe,* 801.

147 "He began by emphasizing": Gromyko, *Memories,* 108.

148 "It is high time": Harriman and Abel, *Special Envoy,* 295.

148 However, calm was restored: Harriman to FDR and Hull, paraphrase of embassy telegram, Feb. 7, 1944.

148 "I like you but": FDR and Hull, telegram, February 7, 1944, Harriman Papers.

148 "The Commanders feel they": Kimball, *Churchill and Roosevelt,* 2:653.

148 "In Teheran U.J. was given": Ibid., 662.

7: STALIN SEARCHES FOR AN ALLY

149 Stalin, his faithful shadow: By a document signed by Lenin on January 22, 1918, Stalin was one of two people who could enter Lenin's office unannounced. Radzinsky, *Stalin,* 127.

149 "On the problem of our relationships": Fond 130 (Sovnarkom), op. 3, file 177, pp. 147, 151–53, GARF (State Archive of the Russian Federation).

150 "the principal force in the world": Williams, *American-Russian Relations,* 184.

150 "America knows where we stand": *NYT,* Dec. 1, 1930.

150 "The major issue is": Fond 06, Office of V. M. Molotov, AVP RF.

151 "He said not": Farnsworth, *William C. Bullitt and the Soviet Union,* 91.

151 "I go along": *F.D.R.: His Personal Letters,* 3:162–63.

151 "I think the menace": Jean Edward Smith, *FDR,* 342.

151 "Well, of course, you know": Blum, *Years of Crisis,* 55.

152 "awakened one night": Thayer, *Bears in the Caviar,* 47.

153 "You know, Max": Dallek, *Franklin D. Roosevelt and American Foreign Policy,* 81.

153 "Dear Bill": Bullitt, *For the President,* 73–75.

154 "The laboring masses": *NYT,* Nov. 19, 1933.

154 "The United States": *FRUS, Soviet Union, 1933,* 44.

154 "By all appearances": *NYT,* Dec. 28, 1933.

154 "To President Roosevelt": Bullitt, *For the President,* 67.

155 "President Roosevelt is today": Henderson, *Question of Trust,* 265.

155 "Undoubtedly Roosevelt stands out": H. G. Wells, *Modern Monthly,* Dec. 1934.

155 "If we talk about": Hitler, *Mein Kampf,* 950–53.

155 There was precedent: Foreman, *World on Fire,* 38.

156 "It was evident": Malcolm Muir Jr., "American Warship Construction for Stalin's Navy Prior to World War II: A Study in Paralysis of Policy," *Diplomatic History* 5, no. 4 (Oct. 1981): 340.

156 "would merely lead": Ibid., 343.

156 "expressed the hope": Ibid., 346.

156 "saw no objection": Ibid., 347.

156 "the life of a diplomat": Davies, *Mission to Moscow,* 341.

157 "if the President": Ibid., 346.

157 "relayed the good": Muir, "American Warship Construction for Stalin's Navy," 350.

158 "until he had practically": Sara Roosevelt, *My Boy Franklin,* 15.

159 "Storms from abroad": Franklin Roosevelt, "Annual Message to Congress," Jan. 4, 1939, APP.

159 "We can do business": Rosenman, *Working with Roosevelt,* 182.

160 "If the Soviet Union": Neumann, *After Victory,* 28.

161 "an obstacle to the enemies": Stalin, interview by Roy Howard, chairman of the board of Scripps Howard Newspapers, March 1, 1936, online at Marxists Internet Archive, http://www.marxists.org.

161 "History shows": *NYT,* March 8, 1936.

162 "I must confess": Chamberlain, private letter, March 26, 1939, in Shirer, *Rise and Fall of the Third Reich,* 460.

162 "would lend the Polish": Ibid., 465.

162 "to render all": *FRUS, 1939, General,* 1:235.

163 "Militarily and politically": Shirer, *Rise and Fall of the Third Reich,* 469.

164 "The deciding element in Hitler's": Davies, April 18, 1939, in *Mission to Moscow,* 442.

164 "Do not touch": Montefiore, *Stalin*, 233.

164 "being intimidated": Troyanovsky to Litvinov, April 13, 1938, fond 05-18-147, AVP RF.

164 "insulting in his manner": Hull, *Memoirs*, 1:743.

164 "strongly hates": K. A. Oumansky to Litvinov, Dec. 8, 1938, *Soviet-American Relations, 1934–1939*, 102.

165 "Donald Maclean reported that": Sudoplatov, *Special Tasks*, 97.

165 "By destroying Communism": Wright, *Iron Curtain*, 346.

166 "the sudden change": German chargé d'affaires to the German Foreign Office, telegram, May 4, 1939, Nazi-Soviet Relations.

166 "Litvinov along with": Molotov to Stalin, Oct. 2, 1933, fond 558, op. 11, file 769, p. 134, Stalin Papers.

166 "to cut a road": Bullock, *Hitler and Stalin*, 521.

166 "would talk to his chief": Montefiore, *Stalin*, 314.

167 "Stalin was following": Aug. 17, 1939, Nazi-Soviet Relations.

167 "We are of the opinion": May 27, 1939, Nazi-Soviet Relations.

168 "the most brilliant": Kennedy, *Freedom from Fear*, 423.

168 "was the answer": *FRUS, Soviet Union, 1933–1939*, 764.

168 "Tell Stalin," he said: Davies, *Mission to Moscow*, 450.

169 "The Russian space": Mukerjee, *Churchill's Secret War*, 34.

169 after the first week: Shirer, *Berlin Diary*, 186.

169 "point of view regarding": *FRUS, 1939, General*, 1:279.

170 "Perhaps when": F.D.R. to William Phillips, *Letters*, 4:810.

170 On July 5, 1939: Greenfield, *American Strategy in World War II*, 52. Greenfield cites R. Elberton Smith, *Army and Economic Mobilization*, in *United States Army in World War II*, 413–15.

170 "were praying": Davies, *Mission to Moscow*, 450.

171 "There are others": Hull, *Memoirs*, 1:651; Sherwood, *Roosevelt and Hopkins*, 133; Dallek, *Franklin D. Roosevelt and American Foreign Policy*, 192.

171 "Well Captain": Kennedy, *Freedom from Fear*, 423.

171–2 The history of the negotiations": Roberts, *Molotov*, 22–23.

172 "safeguard vital Soviet Baltic interests": Schulenburg to the German Foreign Office, telegram, Moscow, August 4, 1939, Nazi-Soviet Relations.

172 "hopes to be away": the chargé to the secretary of state, July 20, 1939, *FRUS, 1939, General*, 288.

173 "British instructions to Drax": Shirer, *Rise and Fall of the Third Reich*, 534.

174 "I am not optimistic": Ibid., 504.

174 "I understand it is": Ibid.

175 "My Dear Ambassador": Ibid., 293.

175 Molotov told him that: Steinhardt to Welles, Welles Papers, FDRL.

175 "quite unusually compliant": Aug. 16, 1939, Nazi-Soviet Relations.

175 "to lay the foundations": Aug. 14, 1939, Nazi-Soviet Relations.

176 telegram marked "URGENT": Ribbentrop to Schulenburg, Aug. 16, 1939, Nazi-Soviet Relations.

176 "Please do your best": Ribbentrop to Schulenburg, Aug. 21, 1939, Nazi-Soviet Relations.

176 The British war minister: *NYT,* Aug. 21, 1939.

177 "created the greatest": *NYT,* Aug. 24, 1939.

177 "Stalin will yet": Bullock, *Hitler and Stalin,* 619.

177 "To refrain from": *FRUS, 1939, General,* 1:342.

177 "stared into space": according to Albert Speer in Bullock, *Hitler and Stalin,* 617.

177 "Now, Europe is mine": Overy, *Russia's War,* 49.

177 went duck hunting: Khrushchev, *Khrushchev Remembers,* 128.

178 "was in a very good mood": Ibid.

178 "the handsomest young giant": Gunther, *Roosevelt in Retrospect,* 204.

178 "It was exactly": Welles, *Where Are We Heading?,* 123.

180 "caused little surprise": *NYT,* Aug. 22, 1939.

181 The British embassy advised: Ibid.

181 "I had never expected": Ismay, *Memoirs,* 97.

182 "we couldn't admit": Khrushchev, *Khrushchev Remembers,* 129.

182 "to keep Hitler's": Hull, *Memoirs,* 1:685.

182 "the Russian form of brutality": FDR to Kennedy, Oct. 10, 1939, in *F.D.R.: His Personal Letters,* 4:948.

183 "The English and French": Roberts, *Stalin's Wars,* 46.

183 "if we hadn't": Khrushchev, *Khrushchev Remembers,* 129.

183 "The Poles do not need": Evans, *Third Reich at War,* 34.

8: BARBAROSSA

184 "How could you allow": Montefiore, *Stalin,* 352.

184 Sam Woods: Lash, *Roosevelt and Churchill,* 354.

185 Hiroshi's cables to his superiors: Boyd, *Hitler's Japanese Confidant,* 21.

185 "My government will be": O'Sullivan, *Sumner Welles, Postwar Planning, and the Quest for a New World Order,* 185.

185 "Could Churchill be trusted": Chuev, *Molotov Remembers,* 28.

186 "There's this bastard": Montefiore, *Stalin,* 353.

186 "no amount of warning": Gromyko, *Memories,* 48.

186 "almost completely": Evans, *Third Reich at War,* 189.

186 "to be prepared": Gorodetsky, *Grand Delusion,* 85.

186 "Perhaps you can send": Roberts, *Stalin's Wars,* 67.

187 "I admit," he later told: Murphy, *What Stalin Knew,* 249.

187 "There had been a great": Letter from Steinhardt, May 10, 1941, Steinhardt Papers.

187 "This morning's early broadcast": Phillips Diary, June 22, 1941.

187 "burned with guesses": Thayer, *Bears in the Caviar,* 207.

188 "increasing infringement": Gorodetsky, *Grand Delusion,* 224.

188 Matsuoka told him: Bennett, *Franklin D. Roosevelt and the Search for Victory,* 20.

188 "Rumors that Germany": Murphy, *What Stalin Knew,* 187.

188 "I am certain": Braithwaite, *Moscow, 1941,* 54–55.

188 "Hitler is not ripe": Gorodetsky, *Stafford Cripps in Moscow;* Maisky Diary, June 18, 1941.

189 "In secret, I will tell you": Montefiore, *Stalin,* 342.

189 "Do you want": Lukacs, *Churchill,* 80.

189 "It gives him": Gorodetsky, *Stafford Cripps in Moscow,* 112.

190 A little after 9:00 p.m.: Chuev, *Molotov Remembers,* 28.

190 "FOR IMMEDIATE EXECUTION": Murphy, *What Stalin Knew,* 214–15.

191 "Will you please tell": Werth, *Russia at War,* 159.

191 "very pale . . . sitting": Gorodetsky, *Grand Delusion,* 311.

191 Beginning at 3:15: Evans, *Third Reich at War,* 178.

191 "They fell upon us": *Dimitrov and Stalin,* 189.

192 "often stopping and breathing": Maisky article in *New World Moscow,* Dec. 1964.

192 "will merge with the struggle": Radio address, July 3, 1941, Foreign Languages Publishing House, Moscow, 1946, prepared for the Internet by David J. Romagnolo, http://www.marx2mao.com/Stalin/GPW46 .html#s7.

192 reorganized all aspects of defense: Roberts, *Stalin's Wars,* 95–96.

193 "One day Stalin sent": Beria, *My Father,* 350n.

194 "We are only taking": Evans, *Third Reich at War,* 182.

194 According to World War II historian: Gerhard Weinberg, "The 2011 George C. Marshall Lecture," *Journal of Military History* 75, no. 3 (July 2011).

195 plowing under every: FDR obituary, *NYT,* April 13, 1945.

195 "It's a terrible thing": Rosenman, *Working with Roosevelt,* 167.

195 "I am not willing": Ickes, *Lowering Clouds,* 523.

195 "We must take": FDR, "Message to Congress on the Sinking of the *Robin Moor,*" June 20, 1941.

195 "I couldn't say we": James Roosevelt, *My Parents,* 161.

196 "Hitler and Hitler's armies": *NYT,* June 24, 1941.

197 "If we see": Ibid.

197 "give all possible": *NYT,* June 25, 1941.

197 "Now we find": Dunn, *Caught Between Roosevelt and Stalin,* 127.

197 "Stalin is on": *NYT,* Aug. 6, 1941.

198 "I know no man": Lash, *Roosevelt and Churchill,* 444.

198 "It is clear that Germany": Phillips Diary, June 22, 1941.

198 British intelligence predicted the Wehrmacht: Bradley Smith, *Sharing Secrets with Stalin,* 21.

198 Lolling in a shirt: *NYT,* July 2, 1941.

198 On July 9 he sent identical: R. Elberton Smith, *Army and Economic Mobilization,* 135.

199 "get the thing through": Lash, *Roosevelt and Churchill,* 364.

199 "The President made a big row": Stimson Diary, Aug. 1, 1941.

200 "Can the president survive": Pogue, *Ordeal and Hope,* 73.

200 "the government of the United States": U.S. Department of State Bulletin, Aug. 9, 1941.

200 "Air transportation good": Adams, *Harry Hopkins,* 234.

200 "a man who had retained": Maisky, *Memoirs of a Soviet Ambassador,* 178.

201 "He welcomed me": Adams, *Harry Hopkins,* 237–38.

201 "The Germans were a people": *FRUS, 1941,* 1:803.

201 "he wanted me to tell": Ibid., 813.

202 "and countless other millions": Ibid.

202 "There is unbounded": Hopkins to FDR, message, Aug. 1, 1941, Hopkins Papers.

202 "A man as susceptible": *Knoxville Journal,* Aug. 2, 1941.

202 "Nearly six weeks": FDR to Coy, memo, Aug. 2, 1941, LOC.

203 "He is a tremendously": *CC,* 141.

203 "establishment of a wider": Divine, *Second Chance,* 43.

203 "There was some question": King Diary, Dec. 5, 1942.

204 "You'd have thought": Dallek, *Franklin D. Roosevelt and American Foreign Policy,* 282.

204 "We had in mind": Stettinius, *Roosevelt and the Russians,* 245.

204 "I think I speak": Elliott Roosevelt, *As He Saw It,* 25.

204 "The PM . . . castigating": Gorodetsky, *Stafford Cripps in Moscow,* 115.

204 " 'I know already how' ": Adams, *Harry Hopkins,* 243.

204 "He's able to convince me": Elliott Roosevelt, *As He Saw It,* 22.

204 "When Moscow falls": Ibid., 30–34.

205 "I am sure I": Churchill to Attlee, Aug. 12, 1941, Imperial War Museum, London.

205 "at the earliest": *NYT,* Aug. 20, 1941.

205 "It is proposed": Axell, *Marshal Zhukov,* 91.

205 The German navy had asked: Kuby, *Russians and Berlin,* 35.

206 "Requests to be allowed": Hitler directive, Sept. 29, 1941, quoted in Radzinsky, *Stalin,* 489.

206 "Stalin seemed much more": Cripps Diary, Sept. 9, 1941, in Gorodetsky, *Stafford Cripps in Moscow,* 163.

206 "when you arrive": Axell, *Marshal Zhukov,* 179.

206 "In Europe the war has been won": Flagel, *History Buff's Guide to World War II,* 202.

207 Moscow (Stalin) is bitter: Oumansky to FDR, Sept. 11, 1941, FDRL.

207 "Your function will be": Churchill to Beaverbrook in Dallek, *Roosevelt and American Foreign Policy,* 295.

207 "total number of tanks": FDR to Harriman, cable, Sept. 18, 1941, Harriman Papers.

207 "I want this figure": FDR to Stimson, Sept. 18, 1941, Harriman Papers.

207 "It was the president's": Harriman Papers.

207 "We could see the flash": Harriman and Abel, *Special Envoy,* 84.

207 "I want particularly": FDR to Stalin, Sept. 29, 1941, in *MDMS,* 44.

208 "The quantities requested": Harriman to FDR, Oct. 29, 1941, Harriman Papers.

208 "He was very restless": Beaverbrook notes, Harriman Papers.

209 "growing satisfaction": Harriman to FDR, third meeting with Stalin, Harriman Papers.

209 "He looked": Abramson, *Spanning the Century,* 293.

209 "The quantity and quality": Harriman Papers.

210 "it has now been decided": Harriman and Beaverbrook, joint press release, Moscow, Oct., 1, 1941, Harriman Papers.

211 "With the exception of Faymonville": Burns to Hopkins, memo, Aug. 16, 1941, Hopkins Papers.

211 "Hopkins had power": Pogue, *Ordeal and Hope,* 75.

211 "both Molotov and Stalin": Davies to FDR, Jan. 18, 1939, FDR Papers.

212 "It is more probable": Interview with Erskine Caldwell, probably late August 1941, Steinhardt Papers.

212 "Stalin's denunciation": Beaverbrook's notes on meeting, Sept. 30, 1941, Harriman Papers.

212 "He is nothing but a crook": Stimson Diary, Aug. 5, 1941.

213 by November more than: Axell, *Marshal Zhukov,* 85.

213 "For all military": *NYT,* Oct. 10, 1941.

213 "The news is very bad": Stimson Diary, Oct. 10, 1941.

214 FDR held a press conference: Hopkins memo, Oct. 13, 1941, Hopkins Papers.

215 "Stalin called me": G. A. Borkov, *Zadolgo do saliutov* [Long before the Fireworks] (Poltava, 1994), 67–71. Other generals and party officials remember the meeting as taking place a few days later. All, including General Joseph Apanasenko and N. M. Pegov, first secretary of the Maritime Committee, agree the meeting was in the time period October 12 to October 15.

215 "You should do everything": N. M. Pegov, *Blizkoe-dalekoe* [The nearby and the far-out] (Moscow: Politizdat, 1982), 110–13, http://stalinism.ru/Elektronnaya-biblioteka/Vstrechi-so-Stalinyim/Page-9.html.

216 "October 16 was a day": Sakharov, *Memoirs,* 42.

217 "The railmen gave us": Medvedev, *Josef Stalin and Josef Apanesenko. The Far Eastern Front in the Great Patriotic War,* Rossiiskaya Gazeta, Jan, 8 2003.

217 "I have approved": FDR to Stalin, Oct. 30, 1941, in *MDMS,* 48–49.

218 "With respect to your": Stalin to FDR, Nov. 4, 1941, in ibid., 52.

218 "[It] may be dangerous": Vyshinsky Diary, Nov. 6, 1941, fond 558, op. 11, file 363, Stalin Papers.

218 "the mental and physical strain": Paraphrase of Steinhardt to Hull, telegram, Nov. 3, 1941, Steinhardt Papers.

218 "someone who is fully": FDR to Steinhardt, cable, Nov. 5, 1941, *MDMS,* 53.

218 "They seriously counted": Speech at Celebration Meeting, Nov. 6, 1941, http://www.marx2mao.com/Stalin/GPW46.html#s7.

219 "must be quickly removed": Volkogonov, *Stalin,* 436.

219 Andrei Sakharov, then twenty: Sakharov, *Memoirs,* 44.

219 "The war is won": *Look,* June 27, 1944.

220 "Men of the Red Army": Speech at Red Army Parade, Nov. 7, 1941, http://www.marx2mao.com/Stalin/GPW46.html#s7.

220 Vyshinsky informed Ambassador Cripps: Gorodetsky, *Stafford Cripps in Moscow, 1940–42,* 210.

221 By December 18, Stalin was discussing: Ibid., 223.

221 On the previous evening: Elsey, *Unplanned Life,* 98.

221 "Thank God!": Litvinov, 1943 memo, fond 05, Litvinov Papers, AVP RF.

221 "It was a terrible thing": *FRUS, 1941,* 4:730.

221 "He began," wrote Stimson: Stimson Diary, Dec. 7, 1941.

222 "In spite of the horror": Perkins, *Roosevelt I Knew,* 379–80.

222 "Our planes were destroyed": Reston, *Deadline,* 106.

222 America was readier: Isador Lubin to Hopkins, Dec. 8, 1941, Hopkins Papers.

223 "The Chief Soviet Military Advisor": *FRUS, 1941,* 4:746.

223 "proceeded to say": Ibid., 742.

223 "First, I am suggesting": FDR to Stalin, Dec. 14, 1941, in *MDMS,* 55–56.

224 "Roosevelt has just summoned": Vyshinsky Diary.

224 "As there was no mention": Stalin to FDR, Dec. 17, 1941, in *MDMS,* 56.

224 "Russia today": *FRUS, 1941,* 4:747.

225 "was most encouraging": Gorodetsky, *Stafford Cripps in Moscow, 1940–1942,* 223.

9 : ROOSEVELT, STALIN, AND THE SECOND FRONT

226 "We've got to": Greenfield, *American Strategy in World War II*, 29.

227 "divert sizable portions": Rzheshevsky, *War and Diplomacy*, 182.

227 "involving the utilization": FDR to Stalin, April 11, 1942, in *MDMS*, 64.

227 "Your people and mine": FDR to Churchill, April 3, 1942, in Loewenheim, Langley, and Jonas, *Roosevelt and Churchill*, 202.

228 "Strike in Europe Now": *Sunday Express*, March 29, 1942, in Hastings, *Winston's War*, 233.

228 "sympathetic. It seemed": Sherwood, *Roosevelt and Hopkins*, 523–24.

228 "momentous proposal": Winston S. Churchill, *Hinge of Fate*, 317.

228 "At long meeting": Hopkins to FDR, April 15, 1942, Hopkins Papers.

228 "The British Government": Sherwood, *Roosevelt and Hopkins*, 528.

228-9 "He had no real confidantes": Ward, *Before the Trumpet*, 9.

229 "bringing his hand": King Diary, April 15, 1942.

229 "Let me thank you": Stalin to FDR, April 20, 1942, in *MDMS*, 65.

230 "eventually more or less": Cripps Diary, Dec. 18, 1941, in Gorodetsky, *Stafford Cripps in Moscow*.

230 "urging him": Churchill to Stalin, March 12, 1942, in *Stalin's Correspondence with Churchill and Attlee*, 40.

230 "an overall statement": Kimball, *Churchill and Roosevelt*, 1:222.

231 he thought Göring "attractive" and Goebbels "likable": Lukacs, *Five Days*, 62.

231 "only one word": Feb. 20, 1942, *FRUS, 1942*, 3:521.

232 "I know you": FDR to Churchill, March 18, 1942, in Kimball, *Churchill and Roosevelt*, 1:421.

232 "Every promise": Dallek, *Franklin D. Roosevelt and American Foreign Policy*, 338.

232 "Civilization is being completely": MacMillan, *Paris 1919*, 67.

233 "a rabble from the gutters": Reston, *Deadline*, 118.

233 "a callous": Winston S. Churchill, *Their Finest Hour*, 579.

233 "If Hitler invaded": Goodwin, *No Ordinary Time*, 255.

233 "listened attentively": Hull, *Memoirs*, 2:1173.

234 "had us in a swivet": Reilly, *Reilly of the White House*, 39–40.

234 "Straight from the aerodrome": Rzheshevsky, *War and Diplomacy*, 224.

234 "eyes would dart": Goodwin, *No Ordinary Time*, 344.

234 A large chunk: Eleanor Roosevelt, *This I Remember*, 254.

234 "he is *not* very pleasant": *CC*, 159.

234 "It was pretty difficult": Sherwood, *Roosevelt and Hopkins*, 558–59.

235 roly-poly, voluble: Acheson, *Present at the Creation*, 68.

235 Cross would never again: Robert Meiklejohn, conversation with Hopkins, June 5, 1945, Hopkins Papers.

235 "It had been difficult": *FRUS, 1942, Europe,* 3:567.

235 twenty-six prisoners: Hopkins Papers.

236 "if any nation": *FRUS, 1942, Europe,* 3:569.

236 "If you cannot beat": King Diary, Dec. 5, 1942.

237 "It is necessary": Rzheshevsky, *War and Diplomacy,* 177.

238 "Roosevelt's considerations": Ibid., doc. 82, sent June 1, 1942, 204.

238 "do not see an acute need": Ibid., 179.

239 "which it was assumed": William Phillips, notes, Oct. 6, 1942, Phillips Papers.

239 "about social reforms": Eleanor Roosevelt, *This I Remember,* 250.

239 "Hitler's strength would be": *FRUS, 1942, Europe,* 3:576.

239 "the war would be decided": Ibid.

239 "Could we say": Ibid., 577.

240 "Ships could not be": Ibid., 582.

240 Hitler and Ribbentrop had exerted: Shirer, *Berlin Diary,* 564.

240 "obviously Hitler had": Sherwood, *Roosevelt and Hopkins,* 565.

240 "I am, therefore": Ibid., 569.

241 "try to get": Stalin to Molotov, n.d., in Rzheshevsky, *War and Diplomacy,* 193–94.

241 he had omitted one point: *FRUS, 1942, Europe,* 3:580.

241 "ought not to have": Ibid., 581.

242 "a palpable surge": Ibid.

242 "We expected to set up": Ibid., 582.

242 a blistering cable: Rzheshevsky, *War and Diplomacy,* 210.

243 "In the course of": Ibid., 220.

243 "We shall have to accept": Ibid., 219.

244 "You must inform": Ibid., 221.

244 "a real success": Loewenheim, Langley, and Jonas, *Roosevelt and Churchill,* 219.

244 "[I] got him": *CC,* 160.

244 "I am sure": Sherwood, *Roosevelt and Hopkins,* 577–78.

245 "Britain could 'give no promise'": Gilbert, *Road to Victory,* 119–20.

246 "Though the problem": *FRUS, 1942, Europe,* 3:576.

246 "the great satisfaction": Molotov to FDR, June 12, 1942, in *MDMS,* 70.

246 "I remained calm": Chuev, *Molotov Remembers,* 45.

246 "the speediest possible opening": Maisky, *Memoirs of a Soviet Ambassador,* 277.

246 "Our American friends": Kimball, *Churchill and Roosevelt,* 1:458.

247 "If Sledgehammer is finally": Matloff and Snell, *War Department,* 277.

247 "Hopkins, Marshall and King": FDR to Hopkins, Marshall, King, handwritten letter, FDR Papers.

248 "It may not ripen": Stimson Diary, July 26, 1942.

248 "the blackest day": Sherwood, *Roosevelt and Stalin,* 648.

248 "we make a real drive": Stimson Diary, Aug. 7, 1942.

248 "We failed to see": Persico, *Roosevelt's Secret War,* 208.

248 "The French will offer": Ibid.

249 "Stimson always considered Torch": Stimson and Bundy, *On Active Service,* 427.

249 "Please," he said: *MDMS,* 93.

249 "In their hunt for oil": *NYT,* Nov. 7, 1942.

250 "represents another step": *FRUS, 1942, Europe,* 3:477.

250 "Dear Mr. Cassidy": Stalin, "The Allied Campaign in Africa," Nov. 13, 1942, http://www.marxists.org/reference/archive/stalin/works/1942/11/13 .htm.

10: POSTWAR PLANNING

251 "the dominant issue": Stephen C. Schlesinger, *Act of Creation,* 25.

251 "the first great agency": Divine, *Second Chance,* 25.

252 "The President": Welles, *Where Are We Heading?,* 21.

252 Guarded at all times: George Elsey to author, March 6, 2004.

252 According to a Map Room officer: Elsey, *Unplanned Life,* 20.

253 went complaining to FDR: Rigdon, *White House Sailor,* 15.

254 "the army and the navy": Elsey, *Unplanned Life,* 21.

255 "I should absolutely": Stimson Diary, Aug. 29, 1941.

255 "The War Department will": Vogel, *Pentagon,* 335.

256 "The President said": King Diary, Dec. 5, 1942.

257 "On the assumption": Feis, *Churchill, Roosevelt, Stalin,* 108.

257 "It has been recommended": Ibid., 109n2a.

257 "Whatever words we might": Hull, *Memoirs,* 2: 1574.

257 "then said . . . that": King Diary, Dec. 5, 1942.

258 "We didn't feel": in Rees, *The Nazis,* 15–16.

258 "Lee's surrender": FDR to Hull, Jan. 17, 1944, in *F.D.R.: His Personal Letters,* 2:1486.

259 "He wanted no negotiated": Hopkins notes, March 22, 1943, in Sherwood, *Roosevelt and Hopkins,* 715.

259 "Frankly, I do not": *F.D.R.: His Personal Letters,* 2:1486.

259 "so far as the German surrender": Stalin to Harriman, June 10, 1944, Harriman Papers.

260 "There had been a good deal": Press conference, Honolulu, July 29, 1944.

260 "We Marxists believe": *NYT,* March 5, 1935.

260 "no more fit": Stalin to Stanisław Mikołajczyk, n.d., Harriman Papers.

261 The execution of these plans: Davies, *Mission to Moscow,* 389.

261 In 1928 the Soviet Union: Overy, *Russia's War*, 17.

263 "On the whole, the three": Acheson, *Present at the Creation*, 65–71.

263 "I couldn't get": Kathleen Harriman to Mary Harriman, April 18, 1944, Harriman Papers.

264 "Stalin," Ambassador William Standley reported: Standley, *Admiral Ambassador*, 381.

265 Litvinov was having breakfast: Fond 06, op.5, Molotov Secretariat files, AVP RF. *FRUS, 1941, Far East*, 730–31.

265 "his successor as Foreign Commissar": *FRUS, The British Commonwealth, Eastern Europe, The Far East, 1943*, 3:522.

266 "when he chose": Acheson, *Present at the Creation*, 78.

266 Molotov and Stalin believed: Gromyko, *Memories*, 401.

267 "how Litvinov was": Perlmutter, *Not So Grand Alliance*, 258.

267 "I came to the conclusion": Litvinov, fond 06, Molotov Secretariat files, AVP RF.

267 "If we wish to eliminate": Litvinov memo, June 2, 1943, in Perlmutter, *Not So Grand Alliance*, 245–46.

267 "Now, without any": Stalin to FDR, June 11, 1943, in *MDMS*, 138–39, fond 558, op. 11, file 365, Stalin Papers.

268 "Since the opening": Stalin to FDR, Aug. 8, 1943, in *MDMS*, 150–51; fond 558, op. 11, Stalin Papers.

268 "with the purpose": Stalin to FDR, Aug. 22, 1943, in *MDMS*, 155.

268 "I notice that in the Soviet Union": "Talk with the German Author Emil Ludwig, December 13, 1931," *Bolshevik*, April 30, 1932, https://www.marxists.org/reference/archive/stalin/works/1931/dec/13.htm.

270 "unrelenting pressure": Harriman and Abel, *Special Envoy*, 218.

270 "I do not underrate": Ibid.

11: PROBLEMS AND SOLUTIONS

271 "We'll organize Europe and Asia": Montefiore, *Stalin*, 348.

271–2 "Eventually she [Russia]": Deane, *Strange Alliance*, 226.

272 "With a view of shortening": *MDMS*, 190.

272 "I had just seen": Harriman and Abel, *Special Envoy*, 214.

272 "reading from a paper": Harriman to FDR, Dec. 26, 1943, Harriman Papers.

273 At their first meeting: Feb. 2, 1944, meeting in the Kremlin, Harriman Papers.

273 "When German resistance": Feb. 3, 1944, *FRUS, Europe 1944*, 4:943.

273 "Let them go": Feb. 3, 1944, meeting in the Kremlin, Harriman Papers.

273 "was anxious to know": Harriman and Stalin, conversation, June 10, 1944, Harriman Papers.

274 "when you are ready": FDR to Stalin, Aug. 19, 1944, in *MDMS,* 252.

274 "I have received": Stalin to FDR, Aug. 22, 1944, ibid., 253.

274 "Stalin inquired": Harriman to FDR, telegram, Sept. 23, 1944, FDR Papers.

275 "Sufficient supplies could be": Harriman cable, Oct. 10, 1944, Harriman Papers.

278 On December 14: Harriman to FDR, navy cable, Dec. 15, 1944, Harriman Papers.

279 "It is fair to say": Harriman to FDR, Dec. 29, 1944, Harriman Papers.

279 "No, not that island": Gunther, *Roosevelt in Retrospect,* 338.

280 "solely for the purpose": Deane, *Strange Alliance,* 51.

281 "It was my first telephone": Harriman and Abel, *Special Envoy,* 293.

281 "I have arranged": Donovan to Harriman, Jan. 5, 1944, Harriman Papers.

281 "The Attorney General": Donovan to Leahy, memo, March 7, 1944, NARA.

282 "The question presented": FDR to Harriman, March 15, 1944, FDRL.

282 "The Soviet acceptance": Harriman to FDR, March 17, 1944, Harriman Papers.

283 "an unfavorable public": Costigliola, *Roosevelt's Lost Alliances,* 283.

283 "The domestic political": For Ambassador Harriman, Personal and Secret from the President, March 30, 1944, Harriman Papers.

284 "a highly dangerous": Persico, *Roosevelt's Secret War,* 291.

284 "The Joint Chiefs of Staff": FDR to Harriman, March 15, 1944, Harriman Papers.

284 "the Soviet Government": *FRUS, Europe, 1944,* 4:950.

284 "With reference to radio": FDR to Harriman, cable, March 30, 1944, NARA. General Marshall later told Donovan that both proposals had actually been sidetracked by Admiral Leahy. "When I saw General Marshall in Washington I discussed with him the question of why the exchange of the Donovan Mission had been turned down at the White House and also the proposed reciprocal establishment of radio communication stations with the Soviet Union. He told me with the utmost frankness and as a friend (with the request that I tell nobody) that he believed Admiral Leahy was unfriendly to me personally. He did not know why, but thought that Admiral Leahy's naval loyalty to Admiral Standley was the basis of it rather than anything against me personally." Memo of Conversation, W. A. Harriman, General Marshall, Subject: Admiral Leahy, Washington, D.C., May 11, 1944, Harriman Papers.

285 "The president is my friend": *CC,* 316.

285 "At Tehran the Marshal": *NYT,* Aug. 24, 1944.

285 "We must follow": Order of the Day of the Supreme Commander-in-Chief, Moscow, May 1, 1944.

285 "They [the English] find nothing sweeter": Djilas, *Conversations with Stalin*, 73.

286 "The summer offensive": Stalin to FDR, June 7, 1944, in *MDMS*, 235–36.

286 "We are going": Harriman to FDR, cable, June 11, 1944, Harriman Papers.

286 "After seven days' fighting": Werth, *Russia at War*, 775–76.

286 "Not later than": Stalin to FDR, June 21, 1944, in *MDMS*, 238.

287 "too early": Blum, *Years of War*, 239.

287 "I consider as quite": Stalin to FDR, March 10, 1944, in *MDMS*, 216.

287 "What is the main": *Notes from the Meeting Between Comrade Stalin and Economists Concerning Questions in Political Economy*, Jan. 21, 1941, Cold War International History Project, Digital Archive, working paper 33, Wilson Center.

289 "The government of the USSR": Paraphrase of Harriman to Morgenthau, embassy cable, April 20, 1944, Harriman Papers.

289 "Yesterday I called": Blum, *Years of War*, 250.

289 "England and Russia have to": Ibid.

290 "Well done. You are": Ibid.

290 "That's good": Ibid., 251.

291 "Russia doesn't need the Fund": Ibid., 258.

291 "The proposed formula": Ibid., 261.

292 "a feeling of definite need": *NYT*, July 13, 1944.

292 Harriman, in Moscow, was instructed: *FRUS, 1944, Europe*, 4:996.

292 "the answer is": Blum, *Years of War*, 275.

293 "was very anxious": *NYT*, July 21, 1944.

293 "desire to collaborate": Blum, *Years of War*, 277.

293 "If we start": Dunlop, *Donovan*, 450–51.

295 "There are all grounds": A. A. Gromyko, "On the Issue of Soviet-American Relations, 14 July, 1944," fond 06, Office of Molotov, op. 6, p. 45, file 603 (Letters of A. A. Gromyko . . . , July 14–24, 1944), p. 22, AVP RF.

295 "Our approach was clear": Gromyko, *Memories*, 148.

296 "The work was exceptionally": Ibid.

297 "The president finally": *Diaries of Edward R. Stettinius*, 130–31.

297 "we did not have room": Gromyko, *Memories*, 150.

297 "and be sent to Miss Tully": *Diaries of Edward R. Stettinius*, 131.

298 "As the president was clearly": Gromyko, *Memories*, 150.

298 "The three delegations met": Ibid., 148.

299 "The Assembly would": FDR to Stalin, Aug. 31, 1944, in *MDMS*, 255.

299 "I hope to have": Stalin to FDR, Sept. 7, 1944, in ibid., 256.

299 "I also hope": Stalin to FDR, Sept. 14, 1944, in ibid., 257–58.

300 "almost exclusively": Interpretative Report on the Soviet Press, Oct. 17, for the period August 28–October 12, 1944, Harriman Papers.

300 "did not wish": FDR to Harriman, cable, Dec. 15, 1944, Harriman Papers.

300 "What means are available": Harriman to FDR, speech delivered at the Joint Celebration meeting of the Moscow Soviet of Working People's Deputies and Representative of Moscow Party and Public Organizations, Nov. 6, 1944.

301 "Naturally, I agree": Stalin to FDR, Dec. 25, 1944, in *MDMS*, 278.

301 "much anticipation": Curtis Roosevelt, *Too Close to the Sun*, 277.

12: THE NEW WEAPON: THE ATOMIC BOMB

304 "This letter is the last": Holloway, *Stalin and the Bomb*.

304 "We should do it": Rhodes, *Dark Sun*, 61.

305 "often visited": Sudoplatov, *Special Tasks*, 183.

305 "to let you know": Rhodes, *Making of the Atomic Bomb*, 529.

306 Kurchatov's staff in January 1944: Gordin, *Red Cloud at Dawn*, 139.

306 As he signed it: Edward Teller, *Memoirs*, 147.

307 "Some recent work": Isaacson, *Einstein*, 474.

307 "Alex, what you are after": Ibid., 476.

307 "What bright idea": Nat Finney, "How F.D.R. Planned to Use the A-Bomb," *Look*, March 14, 1950.

308 "in detail": Sherwin, *World Destroyed*, 29.

308 "a systematic mobilization": Ibid., 31.

308 "in order that": FDR to Churchill, Oct. 11, 1941.

308 "to open up discussions": Sherwin, *World Destroyed*, 78.

308 "pushed not only": FDR to Vannevar Bush, March 11, 1942; Malloy, *Atomic Tragedy*, 55.

309 "I was with the President": Rhodes, *Making of the Atomic Bomb*, 526.

309 "tell our friends": Frankfurter memo, April 18, 1945, ibid.

310 "like hell": Ferrell, *Dying President*, 34.

310 "Luckily they still": Goodwin, *No Ordinary Time*, 501.

310 "It was terrible": Rhodes, *Making of the Atomic Bomb*, 530.

311 "I did not like": Ibid., 530.

311 Bohr sent FDR a long memo: Freedman, *Roosevelt and Frankfurter*, 731–35.

311 "Roosevelt agreed that an approach": Rhodes, *Making of the Atomic Bomb*, 536–37.

312 "Even six months": Sherwin, *World Destroyed*.

313 "converting Germany into a country": Kennedy, *Freedom from Fear*, 803.

313 "He spoke of this paper": Stimson Diary, March 29, 1945.

313 "We cannot get our people": King Diary, Sept. 11, 1944.

314 "The suggestion that the world": Hyde Park aide-mémoire, Sept. 18, 1944, in Sherwin, *World Destroyed*, 184.

315 "a terrific show": Gilbert, *Road to Victory*, 971.

315 "This Conference has been": Ibid., 970.

315 "Yes, I *am* tired": Gunther, *Roosevelt in Retrospect*, 18.

315 "the question of whether": Malloy, *Atomic Tragedy*, 64.

317 "should be ready": FRUS, *The Conferences at Malta and Yalta, 1945*, 383.

317 "I told him": Stimson Diary, December 31, 1944.

318 "much to be said": Sherwin, *World Destroyed*, 111–12.

318 "the time had been reached": Stettinius, *Roosevelt and the Russians*, 33. "Whole story of my part in atomic program to be done soon. FDR called me in to tell me about the whole thing. Stimson knew about the atom project—Hull didn't." Stettinius to Walter Johnson, Oct. 9, 1948, Stettinius Papers.

318 "might ask us": Stettinius to Johnson, Oct. 10, 1948, Stettinius Papers.

318 Stettinius had actually: Conference at Yalta with General Marshall on what should be said to U.S.S.R. if they used the atomic bomb. Stettinius to Johnson, Oct. 9, 1948.

319 "on the grounds that de Gaulle": Churchill to Eden, minute, March 25, 1945, in Sherwin, *World Destroyed*, 135.

319 "Bush is so delighted": Stimson Diary, Feb. 13. 1945.

319 Bush had another idea: Ibid., Feb. 15, 1945.

320 "We are up against": Ibid., March 5, 1945.

320 "We talked steadily from 8:30": King Diary, March 9, 1945.

321 "It is approaching": Stimson Diary, March 8, 1945.

13: YALTA

323 FDR looked as if a great load: Rosenman, *Working with Roosevelt*, 509–10.

323 "If we had spent": Harriman and Abel, *Special Envoy*, 390.

323 "extremely neat and clean": Harriman to FDR, Dec. 6, 1944, Harriman Papers.

324 "We are all in agreement": FDR to Churchill, Sept. 28, 1944, in Kimball, *Churchill and Roosevelt*, 3:339.

325 "the indiscriminate killings": Sherwood, *Roosevelt and Hopkins*, 138.

326 "I truly wish": Edward Delano Diary, 1841, courtesy of Diana Delano.

326 "I reacted so strongly": Winston S. Churchill, *Hinge of Fate*, 209.

326 "To the President": Moran, *Churchill at War*, 159.

327 "Why be apologetic": Meacham, *Franklin and Winston*, 239.

327 "No great portion": Winston S. Churchill, *Hinge of Fate*, 204.

328 "what might be called": Kimball, *Churchill and Roosevelt*, 1:403.

328 "When he found that": Stimson Diary, April 22, 1942.

328 "among the most miserable": Mukerjee, *Churchill's Secret War*, 18.

328 "favoring freedom for all": Phillips, *Ventures in Diplomacy*, 343.

329 "We had no objection": Mukerjee, *Churchill's Secret War*, 20.

329 "It is alarming": *Wall Street Journal*, May 2, 2008.

329 "I am not at all attracted": Mukerjee, *Churchill's Secret War*, 10.

329 "I have not become": Ibid., 106.

329 "Bengal is rapidly": Ibid., 139.

329 "This is the way royalty": Phillips, *Ventures in Diplomacy*, 350.

329 "Bengal famine is one": Keneally, *Three Famines*, 96.

329 "Many of the rural areas": Phillips, *Ventures in Diplomacy*, 394.

330 "did not care": Mukerjee, *Churchill's Secret War*, 199.

330 "We made efforts to secure": Hull, *Memoirs*, 2:1496.

330 "Winston sent me": Mukerjee, *Churchill's Secret War*, 232.

330 "has been due to the hoarding": King Diary, Sept. 12, 1944.

330 "The PM said the Hindus": Colville Diary, Feb. 21, 1945, in Gilbert, *Road to Victory*, 1232.

330 "a preliminary flourish": Mukarjee, *Churchill's Secret War*, 205.

330 Modern estimates: Hastings, *Inferno*, 412.

330 "The Big Four—ourselves": Elliott Roosevelt, *Look*, Sept. 9, 1946.

331 "It's the most horrible thing": Kimball, *Juggler*, 144.

331 "I said that all India": Phillips Diary, April 29, 1943.

332 "The recent conduct": Stalin to FDR, April 21, 1943, in *MDMS*, 126.

332 "I can well understand": FDR to Stalin, April 26, 1943, in *MDMS*, 126.

333 "we began a tour": Kathleen Harriman letter to Pamela Harriman, Jan. 28, 1944, Harriman Papers.

333 "The evidence that made": Harriman to FDR, Jan. 25, 1944, Harriman Papers.

335 According to Lord Moran: Moran, *Churchill at War*, 271.

336 camouflaged brown and pink: C. E. Olsen, "Full House at Yalta," *American Heritage*, June 1972.

336 "The Soviets just couldn't": Harriman and Abel, *Special Envoy*, 393.

337 "Physically he is only half": Moran, *Churchill at War*, 277.

337 "absolutely charming": Harriman and Abel, *Special Envoy*, 391–92.

337 "I was horrified": Costigliola, *Roosevelt's Lost Alliances*, 234.

341 "certain to come up": Byrnes, *Speaking Frankly*, 21.

342 "thinks it will be very wearing": *CC*, 390–91.

342 "We came on board": Ibid., 393.

342 "That's where they": Asbell, *Mother and Daughter*, 187.

342 "take another nap": *CC*, 393.

342 "slept and slept": Stettinius calendar notes, Feb. 2, 1945, Stettinius Papers.

343 "he worked with his usual": Rigdon, *White House Sailor*, 139.

343 "Our chief objective": Byrnes, *Speaking Frankly*, 24.

343 "the great American Illusion": Stettinius to Walter Johnson, Feb. 2, 1945, Stettinius Papers.

344 "Pleasant but no business": Eden, *Reckoning*, 592.

344 "My father and all the British party": Sarah Churchill, *Thread in the Tapestry,* 76.

345 "No Roosevelt, then": Reilly, *Reilly of the White House,* 209.

346 "the PM walked by the side": Gilbert, *Road to Victory,* 1171.

346 "a countryside as bleak": Ibid., 1172.

347 NKVD preparation for the conference: Sudoplatov, *Special Tasks,* 222–27; "Reports to Molotov and Correspondence," Fond 06, op. 7a, p. 57, file 3, 32–33, 34, 36–42, 45–46; "Reports of NKVMF and NKVD to Comr. V. M. Molotov in Connection with Preparation for the Crimean Conference, 10–27 January 1945," fond 06, op. 7a, p. 57, file 4, 27–29, 45, 46–47, AVP RF.

348 "The president, of course": Molotov Diary, "Reception of U.S. Ambassador Harriman, January 20, 1945," fond 06, op. 7a, p. 57, file 2 (Crimean Conference, 1945), 10–11, AVP RF.

349 "that this question": *FRUS, 1943,* 3:788–89.

349 "He wanted to read it": Blum, *Years of War,* 305.

350 "the United States government": Gromyko to Vyshinsky, Jan. 26, 1945, fond 06, op. 7a, p. 57, file 5 (Crimean Conference, 1945), 10–22, AVP RF.

350 "the Americans and the British": Gusev to Molotov, fond 06, op. 7a, p. 57, file 5 (Crimean Conference, 1945), 23–27, AVP RF.

350 "The USA is not interested": Pechatnov, *Stalin, Ruzvelt, Trumen,* 47.

351 "If Mother went": Asbell, *Mother and Daughter, 182.*

351 "I had to refuse": Montefiore, *Stalin,* 446.

352 "Trying to maintain good": Churchill War Rooms, London.

352 "did not confine": Eden, *Reckoning,* 593.

352 "I doubt if Winston": King Diary, Dec. 5, 1942.

354 "very much struck": *FRUS, Conferences at Malta and Yalta, 1945, 571.*

355 "in actual fact": Ibid., 572.

14: ORGANIZING THE WORLD

357 Carlo Levi: Barbara Tuchman, "If Mao Had Come to Washington," *Foreign Affairs,* Oct. 1972.

357 "rich sense of humor": Stettinius, *Roosevelt and the Russians,* 83.

357 "We understand each other": *FRUS, Conferences at Malta and Yalta, 1945, 574.*

358 "Naturally, I agree": Stalin to FDR, Dec. 25, 1944, in *MDMS,* 278.

358 "We have no treaty": Harriman and Abel, *Special Envoy,* 381.

358 "That is what I like": Birse, *Memoirs of an Interpreter,* 177.

358 "Mutual information is": Stalin to FDR, Jan. 15, 1945, in *MDMS,* 285.

359 "What were the wishes": *FRUS, Conferences at Malta and Yalta, 1945, 587.*

360 "I have never known": Reynolds, *From World War to Cold War,* 241.

360 "the complete confidence which the president": FRUS, *Conferences at Malta and Yalta, 1945, 587.*

360 "While Roosevelt reacted": Gromyko, *Memories,* 109–10.

361 "his hand was": King Diary, Dec. 4, 1942.

361 "immediately interjected, 'Ah-ha'": Stettinius, *Roosevelt and the Russians,* 114.

361 "would give it to the president": Ibid.

362 powers "represented at this table": FRUS, *Conferences at Malta and Yalta, 1945, 589.*

362 "The eagle should permit": Ibid., 590.

363 "If Hitler surrendered unconditionally": Ibid., 611–16.

366 "this was an extremely": Stettinius, *Roosevelt and the Russians,* 128.

366 "I can get the people": Ibid., 127; FRUS, *Conferences at Malta and Yalta, 1945, 628.*

367 "either here or later": Stettinius, *Roosevelt and the Russians,* 120.

367 "and he was sure": Ibid., 130.

367 "We have a plan": FRUS, *Conferences at Malta and Yalta, 1945, 620.*

367 "Why not take all": Ibid., 634.

369 "purely a family dinner": Stettinius, *Roosevelt and the Russians,* 134.

370 "What are the main social elements": Gromyko, *Memories,* 111.

370 "We sat with him": Ibid.

370 "Quite agreeable and amusing": Gilbert, *Road to Victory,* 1182–83.

370 "Where are you": Chuikov, *End of the Third Reich,* 117.

371 "Great Britain alone": Stettinius, *Roosevelt and the Russians,* 139.

371 "on the basis of": Ibid.

372 "as to believe": FRUS, *Conferences at Malta and Yalta, 1945, 661.*

372 "It is our earnest": Ibid., 662.

372 "I have, to my regret": Stalin to FDR, Dec. 26, 1944, in *MDMS,* 279.

373 realized what the question: *Diaries of Edward R. Stettinius,* 242.

374 "What powers had Mr. Churchill": FRUS, *Conferences at Malta and Yalta, 1945, 665.*

375 "Mr. Churchill had said": Ibid., 669.

376 "They are terrified of Germany": Harriman, press conference, Claridge's hotel, May 4, 1944, Harriman Papers.

376 "Privately they say": Sherwood, *Roosevelt and Hopkins,* 710.

377 "is played by hostile": Stalin to FDR, Feb. 16, 1944, in *MDMS,* 205; original in fond 558, op. 11, file 367, Stalin Papers.

377 "Cooperation and understanding": Professor Lange, Mr. Hamilton, and Stalin, conversation, May 18, 1944, Harriman Papers.

377 "He [Mikołajczyk] is fully": FDR to Stalin, June 17, 1944, in *MDMS,* 237.

377 "During the visit": Report dated June 21, 1944, in Vladimir Lota, "The Secrets of the Polish 'Tempest,'" *Russian Military Review,* no. 12 (2009).

378 "and especially democratic": Stalin to FDR, June 24, 1944, in *MDMS*, 239–40.

378 "Both the Polish National Committee": Stalin to FDR, Aug. 9, 1944, in ibid., 249.

378 "Wasn't the Warsaw rising justified": Werth, *Russia at War*, 795.

379 In September, after agreeing: King Diary, Sept. 14, 1944.

379 "was the London Poles": Isaacson and Thomas, *Wise Men*, 231.

379 "made the situation even worse": Stalin to FDR, Dec. 27, 1944, in *MDMS*, 281.

379 "The British government could not agree": *FRUS, Conferences at Malta and Yalta, 1945*, 671.

380 "The old gentleman": Kimball, *Churchill and Roosevelt*, 2:591.

380 "My dear Marshal Stalin": FDR to Stalin, Feb. 6, 1945, in *MDMS*, 292.

382 He was "unconvinced": *FRUS, Conferences at Malta and Yalta, 1945*, 710.

383 these proposals fully guaranteed: Ibid., 712.

383 the dominions of the British: Ibid.

383 "This is not good": Stettinius, *Roosevelt and the Russians*, 174.

385 "All of the below": Sherwood, *Roosevelt and Hopkins*, 862.

386 "Now we are in for": Stettinius, *Roosevelt and the Russians*, 184.

386 "and then get them": Ibid.

387 "none of these places": ERS to WJ, interview, Oct. 10, 1948, Stettinius Papers.

387 "Somehow or other": Stettinius, *Roosevelt and the Russians*, 196.

387 "We have had good": Hiss's account, given to Bohlen shortly after the incident took place. Stettinius Papers; *Diaries of Edward R. Stettinius*, 252–53.

389 General MacArthur estimated: William Manchester, *Best American Essays*, 498.

389 "I will not consider": Halberstam, *Coldest Winter*, 596.

390 "The Chiefs of Staff suggest": Joint Chiefs of Staff report, Jan. 18, 1945, Stettinius Papers.

390 "working towards": Rosenman, *Working with Roosevelt*, 536.

390 "We desire Russian entry": Undated memo to the Joint Chiefs, Recommendation to FDR to present to Stalin, Stettinius Papers.

390 "the man who will": Bullitt, *For the President*, 67.

390 "Japan should be stripped": Pogue, *Organizer of Victory*, 526.

392 "The Russians wished again": From Harriman. Personal for the President. Paraphrase of Navy cable dated Dec. 14, 1944, Harriman Papers.

395 "margarine Communists": Meiklejohn Diary, June 9, 1944, Harriman Papers.

395 "We've just saved": Meacham, *Franklin and Winston*, 317.

15: SETTLING ISSUES

397 The Catholic Church was a thorn: Rose, *Dubious Victory*, 51.

397 "I am not for the Argentines": Byrnes, *Speaking Frankly*, 39.

398 FDR's proposal in essence: *FRUS, Conferences at Malta and Yalta, 1945*, 793.

400 "We would be found": Ibid., 778–93.

401 "As we were having": Stettinius undated interview, ERS to WJ, Stettinius Papers.

401 "Great quantities of food": Leahy, *Diary*, Feb. 8, 1945.

402 "He enjoyed himself": Kathleen Harriman, Harriman Papers.

402 "He toasted Churchill": Kathleen Harriman, Harriman Papers.

403 "Who's that in the pince-nez": Montefiore, *Stalin*, 483.

403 "Stettinius remembered": Oct. 10, 1948, interview, ERS to WJ, Stettinius Papers.

403 "Interpreters of the world": Bohlen, *Witness to History*, 182.

403 he left his seat: McIntire, *White House Physician*, 215.

403 "History has recorded many meetings": Gromyko, *Memories*, 112.

403 "to the people": Byrnes, *Speaking Frankly*, 45.

404 "would be unlikely": *FRUS, Conferences at Malta and Yalta, 1945*, 826.

404 "Stalin was so pleased": Gromyko, *Memories*, 116.

407 "at the free": *FRUS, Conferences at Malta and Yalta, 1945*, 836.

407 "The present Polish Provisional Government": Stettinius, *Roosevelt and the Russians*, 224.

407 "The present Provisional Government of Poland": *FRUS, Conferences at Malta and Yalta, 1945*, 842.

408 He closed, according to Hopkins: Sherwood, *Roosevelt and Hopkins*, 865.

408 Churchill's outburst so amused: Eden, *Reckoning*, 595.

408 "I find that it": *FRUS, Conferences at Malta and Yalta, 1945*, 852.

409 "Mikolajczyk is a representative": Ibid., 853.

409 "to create democratic institutions": Ibid., 853–54.

412 should not extend past five: Ibid., 832.

412 "If we agree": Stettinius, *Roosevelt and the Russians*, 251–52.

413 "on the understanding": *FRUS, Conferences at Malta and Yalta, 1945*, 872.

413 "strong support": Ibid., 873.

417 "One cannot help noticing": Moran, *Churchill at War*, 279–80.

417 "Very good": *FRUS, Conferences at Malta and Yalta, 1945*, 907.

417 "I have rather changed": Ibid., 908.

418 "since this was the president's": Sherwood, *Roosevelt and Hopkins*, 859.

418 "Stalin rose and gripped": Moran, *Churchill at War*, 280.

418 "Stalin . . . spoke with great": Stettinius, *Roosevelt and the Russians*, 263–64.

419 "The answer is simple": Stettinius, *Roosevelt and the Russians*, 266.

419 "What should I make": Gromyko, *Memories*, 113.

420 "The Marshal thinks": Stettinius, *Roosevelt and the Russians*, 265.

420 "Mr. President: You get into trouble": Sherwood, *Roosevelt and Hopkins*, 860.

420 "suddenly looked up": Stettinius, *Roosevelt and the Russians*, 270–71.

420 Stalin now suggested: *FRUS, Conferences at Malta and Yalta, 1945*, 905.

420 asked how long ago: Stettinius notes, Yalta, Feb. 10, 1945. This conversation was heard slightly differently by note takers Charles Bohlen, H. Freeman Matthews, and Stettinius. Each recorded slightly different versions of the interchange; this is Stettinius's.

422 hoped the Marshal: Stettinius, *Roosevelt and the Russians*, 274.

422 thus illustrating: Ibid., 275.

422 "and it was difficult": Ibid., 276.

422 "extremely powerful": Ibid., 278.

424 "For those who attributed": Eden, *Reckoning*, 594.

424 "extremely anxious": Hopkins to Byrnes, Feb. 12, 1945, Hopkins Papers.

425 "It will occupy a place": Stettinius to Molotov, Feb. 14. 1945, from Cairo, Stettinius Papers.

425 "If a room has three walls": Salisbury, *Russia on the Way*, 318.

425 "undoubtedly with the purpose": Leahy Diary, Feb. 14, 1945.

16: POST-YALTA PROBLEMS

426 *Time* magazine wrote: Byrnes, *Speaking Frankly*, 45.

426 "The conference has produced": Bishop, *FDR's Last Year*, 438.

427 "It was plain to all of us": Rosenman, *Working with Roosevelt*, 524.

427 "Do you conscientiously": Franklin D. Roosevelt, "Excerpts from the Press Conference Aboard the U.S.S. Quincy En Route from Yalta," Feb. 23, 1945, APP, http://www.presidency.ucsb.edu.

428 "None too soon": Rosenman, *Working with Roosevelt*, 527.

429 "He made it so promptly": *NYT*, March 2, 1945.

429 "The Crimea Conference": APP, http://www.presidency.ucsb.edu.

429 "the conference turned out: *CC*, 397.

429 "not only its historical yesterday": U.S. embassy memo, Harriman Papers.

430 "very pleased": Beevor, *Berlin*, 137.

430 "The general atmosphere": Levering, *Debating the Origins of the Cold War*, 99.

431 the Moscow press announced: Cable, U.S. embassy memo, Feb. 19, 1945, Harriman Papers.

431 "There should be no rush": April 12, 1945, *Diary of Georgi Dimitrov*, 368.

431 "Do not worry": Chuev, *Molotov Remembers*, 51.

432 "The Red Army completely": Order of the Day, Feb. 23, 1945, http://www.marx2mao.com/Stalin/GPW46.html#s7.

432 "Each ally will provide": *FRUS, Conferences at Malta and Yalta, 1945,* 946.

433 Harriman seemed to think it "unbelievable": *FRUS, 1945,* 5:1085.

433 Also, as Molotov told: Molotov to Harriman, March 13, 1945, Harriman Papers.

434 "the difficulties which are being": FDR to Stalin, March 3, 1945, in *MDMS,* 298–99; Stimson Diary, March 3, 1945.

434 "our local representatives": Stalin to FDR, March 5, 1945, in *MDMS,* 299.

434 "With reference to the question": FDR to Stalin, March 17, 1945, in ibid., 300.

435 On March 20, American fighter planes: U.S. Military Mission, Moscow, March 20, 1945, Harriman Papers.

435 "In regard to the information": Stalin to FDR, March 22, 1945, fond 558, op. 11, file 370, Stalin Papers, in *MDMS,* 301.

435 "The war prisoners say": Harriman Papers.

436 "sleeping on the floor": Harriman to FDR, March 24 and 26, 1945, Harriman Papers.

436 "two boys he had talked with": Stimson Diary, April 2, 1945.

438 According to Stimson, it was precipitated: Ibid., March 13, 1945.

438 Alexander explained: Telegram to the Combined Chiefs of Staff, March 11, 1945, Harriman Papers.

439 "Apparently Churchill . . . overruled": Stimson Diary, March 12 and 13, 1945.

440 "The President was agreeable": King Diary, March 13, 1945.

440 "Germany will try": Montefiore, *Stalin,* 475.

441 "Recalling the friendly": FDR to Stalin, March 24, 1945, in *MDMS,* 302–03.

441 "The facts are as follows": FDR to Stalin, March 24, 1945, in *MDMS,* 304.

441 "I and Mr. Molotov regret": Stalin to FDR, March 27, 1945, in *MDMS,* 305.

442 "The Soviet Government": Stalin to FDR, March 29, 1945, in *MDMS,* 305–07.

442 "It was one of the few times": Bohlen, *Witness to History,* 209.

443 "There is no question": FDR to Stalin, March 31, 1945, in *MDMS,* 308.

443 "I have received": Stalin to FDR, April 3, 1945, in *MDMS,* 312, fond 558, op. 11, file 370, Stalin Papers.

444 "I have received with astonishment": FDR to Stalin, April 4, 1945, in *MDMS.*

445 "Molotov as usual": Frank, *Downfall*, 111.

445 "Japan, an ally of Germany": *NYT*, April 6, 1945.

446 "He was cheerful": Leahy, *I Was There*, 342.

446 "We Russians believe": Stalin to FDR, April 7, 1945, in *MDMS*, 315–17.

447 if the Red Army triumphed: Evans, *Third Reich at War*, 683; *NYT*, Feb. 25, 1945.

447 "the old men": Evans, *Third Reich at War*, 685.

447 "You have, of course": Djilas, *Conversations with Stalin*, 110.

448 Soldiers of the Red Second Guards: Axell, *Marshal Zhukov*, 138.

448 "The Germans had concentrated their forces": Khrushchev, *Khrushchev Remembers*, 221.

448 A force of 2.5 million men: Beevor, *Berlin*, 147.

448 On the evening of March 31: Meiklejohn Diary, March 31, 1945, Harriman Papers.

449 "Berlin has lost": Stalin to Eisenhower, telegram, April 1, 1945, Harriman Papers.

449 the Berlin siege: D'Este, *Eisenhower*, 691–92; Report to the Combined Chiefs of Staff, reprinted in *NYT*, June 24, 1946.

449 "no longer a particularly": D'Este, *Eisenhower*, 695.

449 "The German people as a whole": Neumann, *After Victory*, 133.

449 "Personally, and aside from": Greenfield, *American Strategy in World War II*, 19.

449 "In conversations with his inner circle": Khrushchev, *Khrushchev Remembers*, 220–21.

450 "The fall of Berlin": Churchill to FDR, April 1, 1945, in Kimball, *Churchill and Roosevelt*, 3:605.

450 "sent an explanation": *CC*, 414.

450 "Where in the hell did": Beevor, *Berlin*, 204.

17: ROOSEVELT DIES

451 "Russia was going to be": King Diary, Dec. 5, 1942.

451 "We have learned": Inaugural address, Jan. 20, 1945, APP, http://www.presidency.ucsb.edu.

452 "Let the horses go back": King Diary, Dec. 5, 1942.

453 "he would welcome": King Diary, March 13, 1945.

453 "We are the new": Roberts, *Stalin's Wars*, 243.

454 "The Warsaw government cannot under": FDR to Stalin, March 31, 1945, in *MDMS*, 311.

454 "Matters on the Polish question have really": Stalin to FDR, April 7, 1945, in ibid., 320.

454 "means not its liquidation": Ibid., 319–20.

455 "If you deem": *Stalin's Correspondence with Churchill and Attlee, 1941–1945*, 313.

455 "I very much hope": Kimball, *Churchill and Roosevelt*, 3:562.

455 "The Yalta agreements": Ibid., 563.

455 "I cannot agree": Ibid., 568–69.

455 "You will recall": Ibid., 593.

456 "If Marshal Stalin agrees": Ibid., 583.

456 "This would look": Ibid., 618.

456 "We simply cannot allow": Stimson Diary, April 2, 1945.

456 "There has been growing": Ibid., April 3, 1945.

457 "We've taken a great risk": FDR to Chester Bowles, March 20, 1945, Chester Bowles interview, Columbia Oral History Project, Columbia University.

458 "Stalin said to me": "Excerpts from the Last Press Conference in Warm Springs, Georgia," April 5, 1945, http://www.presidency.ucsb.edu.

460 Dr. Bruenn had noted: Costigliola, "Broken Circle," *Diplomatic History* 32, Nov. 2008, 712.

460 "after he gets the peace organization": *CC*, 411.

460 "He is very slowly": Ibid., 412.

460 "Thomas Jefferson, himself": Sherwood, *Roosevelt and Hopkins*, 879.

461 "You may send it": Kimball, *Churchill and Roosevelt*, 3:631.

461 "I would minimize": Ibid., 630.

462 "I was terribly shocked": Blum, *Years of War*, 17.

462 "I must confess": Harriman and Abel, *Special Envoy*, 439.

462 "I have replied": *MDMS*, 322.

463 At 1:06 the Map Room received: FDRL.

463 "I have a terrific pain": *CC*, 418.

463 "I thought that once": Costigliola, *Roosevelt's Lost Alliances*, 421.

463 high blood pressure: Costigliola, "Broken Circle," 712–13.

464 "The ambassador was obviously not quite": Pechatnov, *Stalin, Ruzvelt, Trumen*, 314.

464 "immediately, if this is convenient": Ibid., 313.

464 "he seemed deeply moved": Harriman and Abel, *Special Envoy*, 440.

464 "deeply shaken": Harriman, *America and Russia in a Changing World*, 39.

465 "The President knew": Harriman memo, April 13, 1945, Harriman Papers.

465 "Marshal Stalin then stated": Harriman and Abel, *Special Envoy*, 442–43.

465 "Our policy regarding Japan": Harriman to Truman, navy cable, April 14, 1945, Harriman Papers.

466 "the great organizer": Pechatnov, *Stalin, Ruzvelt, Trumen*, 317.

467 "I want you to know": Hopkins to Stalin, cable, April 13, 1945, Hopkins Papers.

467 "I agree completely": Stalin to Hopkins, April 15, 1945, fond 06, Office of Molotov, AVP RF.

467 "The news of the death": Pechatnov, *Stalin, Ruzvelt, Trumen,* 34, 35.

18: HOPKINS TURNS BACK THE CLOCK

469 "FDR's one really great": *CC,* 403.

470 "to be very careful": Stimson Diary, April 23, 1945.

470 Leahy, who, in fact, was: Elsey, *Unplanned Life,* 82.

470 "a strong American": Leahy, *I Was There,* 351.

471 "I have never been" McCullough, *Truman,* 376.

471 "a perfectly normal": Miscamble, *From Roosevelt to Truman,* 120.

471 "Quite unexpectedly": Gromyko, *Memories,* 122.

471 "Almost at once": Ibid.

471 "I was a little taken": Harriman and Abel, *Special Envoy,* 453–54.

471 "was more than pleasing": Leahy, *I Was There,* 352.

471 "been influenced from a sense": Costigliola, *Roosevelt's Lost Alliances,* 311.

472 "It is a very nice thing": Blum, *Years of War,* 402.

473 "untimely and incredible": Herring, *Aid to Russia,* 208.

473 "Do not barge in with pitiful": Zubok and Pleshakov, *Inside the Kremlin's Cold War,* 15.

474 "Of course once we get on": Churchill to Eden, Jan. 4, 1944, Foreign Office, London.

474 "got steamed up": Reynolds, *From World War to Cold War,* 251–52.

475 "Britain only wanted to": Truman to Acheson, March 15, 1957, in *Affection and Trust,* 162.

475 "This was consistent": Feis, *Between War and Peace,* 126.

475 "I advised not starting": Roberts, *Stalin's Wars,* 221.

476 "I remind the Conference": Stephen C. Schlesinger, *Act of Creation,* 134.

476 "had suffered so much": Press conference, April 29, 1945, in ibid., 135.

477 "It would not be an unreasonable": *NYT,* April 30, 1945.

477 "Czechoslovakia must vote": Bohlen, *Witness to History,* 214.

479 "If the Soviet Union": Stettinius, *Roosevelt and the Russians,* 320.

479 "too ill even": Sherwood, *Roosevelt and Hopkins,* 887.

479 "volunteer troublemakers": *NYT,* June 29, 1945.

480 "Ike said he felt": Feis, *Between War and Peace,* 80–81n.

481 The next evening, at the second: FRUS, *The Conference of Berlin (The Potsdam Conference), 1945,* 1:32.

481 "anyone with commonsense": Ibid., 32.

481 "If the refusal to continue": Ibid., 33.

482 "It would be a great tragedy": Ibid., 35.

482 "If Mr. Molotov": Ibid.

483 "It is my earnest hope": FDR to Stalin, Feb. 7, 1944, in *MDMS,* 202.

484 The third meeting was even more reassuring: *FRUS, The Conference of Berlin (The Potsdam Conference), 1945,* 1:42.

486 Hopkins danced one dance: Maisky, *Memoirs of a Soviet Ambassador,* 183.

487 "whether he realizes": From the Secretary of State to the Acting Secretary of State for his eyes only, undated, Stettinius Papers.

488 "sure Hitler was still alive": Sherwood, *Roosevelt and Hopkins,* 912.

488 "I feel I owe it": Stephen C. Schlesinger, *Act of Creation,* 219.

488 "can alone prevent": "Forty-Fourth Day," June 7, 1945, Stettinius Papers.

488 "if they so desire": Stettinius Papers.

489 "Well, it's all done": Transcript of conversation, June 7, 1945, Stettinius Papers.

489 "Moscow wanted to make sure": Gromyko, *Memories,* 68.

489 "his personal and official": Stephen C. Schlesinger, *Act of Creation,* 232.

490 "Mr. Hopkins had made good": Stettinius to Acting Secretary, June 5, 1945, Stettinius Papers.

490 "Stalin knows Poland well": Salisbury, *Russia on the Way,* 260.

491 By war's end it was supplying: Kennedy, *Freedom from Fear,* 857.

491 "The foundation for the alliance": Roberts, *Stalin's Wars,* 195.

491 "will become the soul": Quoted in *NYT,* June 27, 1945.

492 "It is certainly": Harry S. Truman Papers, Harry S. Truman Presidential Library, Independence, Mo.

492 "Stalin had no respect": Khrushchev, *Khrushchev Remembers,* 221.

492 "The only suggestion": Stimson Diary, June 6, 1945.

493 Marshall, in fact, went on record as saying: Costigliola, *Roosevelt's Lost Alliances,* 357.

493 "We were busy": Stimson Diary, July 3, 1945.

493 "a cosmic phenomenon": Gordin, *Five Days in August,* 46.

494 "his doctor had insisted": Rigdon, *White House Sailor,* 195–96.

494 To guard the 1,195-mile route: Montefiore, *Stalin,* 496.

494 At a break in the conference: Reston, *Deadline,* 165.

494 "a new bomb": Gordin, *Red Cloud at Dawn,* 8.

494 "no muscle moved": Montefiore, *Stalin,* 499.

494 "I was sure": Feis, *Between War and Peace,* 177.

494 "making notes on a sheet": Montefiore, *Stalin,* 501.

494 "Ask for anything": Rhodes, *Dark Sun,* 178.

495 "O.K. to release": Elsey, *Unplanned Life,* 90.

495 "Roosevelt clearly felt": Levering, *Debating the Origins of the Cold War,* 93–94.

495 "has shaken the whole world": Costigliola, *Roosevelt's Lost Alliances,* 366.

495 "They're jumping the gun": Elsey, *Unplanned Life,* 92.

496 "The bombs dropped on Japan": Chuev, *Molotov Remembers,* 58.

496 "as atomic blackmail": Zubok and Pleshakov, *Inside the Kremlin's Cold War,* 27.

496 "Glory to the armed forces": *NYT,* Sept. 3, 1945.

EPILOGUE

497 "I believe that": Stimson and Bundy, *On Active Service,* 643–45.

498 "I consider the problem": Ibid. I am indebted to Frank Costigliola for bringing to my attention, in his book *Roosevelt's Lost Alliances* and in conversations with me, the discussion that took place at the September 21 cabinet meeting and its misrepresentation in the press.

498 "We do not have a secret": Notes on cabinet meeting, Sept. 21, 1945, Matthew J. Connelly Papers, Truman Library.

499 Stimson had no intention: *FRUS, 1945,* 2:55.

499 "we are now in": Forrestal Diary, Sept. 21, 1945, Mudd Library, Princeton University.

499 "conceive of a world": Matthew J. Connelly Papers, Truman Library.

499 "If we give": Forrestal Diary, Sept. 21, 1945, Mudd Library.

499 "We should continue": Matthew J. Connelly Papers, Truman Library.

499 "We are only": Ibid.

499 "relationships are improving": Ibid.

500 "Trust had to be": Forrestal Diary, Sept. 21, 1945, Mudd Library.

500 "If we protect": Matthew J. Connelly Papers, Truman Library.

500 "as to whether": Ibid.

500 "completely, everlastingly": Forrestal Diary, Sept. 21, 1945, Mudd Library

500 "but in this case": Matthew J. Connelly Papers, Truman Library.

501 "Plea to Give": *NYT,* Sept. 22, 1945.

502 "At a U.S. Cabinet meeting": *Time,* Oct. 1, 1945.

502 "atomic carriers": Millis, *Forrestal Diaries,* 538.

502 "The Russians cannot possibly": Sept. 24, 1948, diary entry, in ibid., 495.

502 "The underlying attitude": Ibid., 95.

503 Fifty-five out of sixty-one: Isaacson and Thomas, *Wise Men,* 326.

503 "felt himself in closest agreement": *FRUS, 1945,* 2:56.

503 "undue emphasis was being given": Millis, *Forrestal Diaries,* 102.

503 At an impromptu press conference: *NYT,* Oct. 9, 1945.

504 "Both were concerned": Elsey, *Unplanned Life,* 42.

504 "I fail to see": Bohlen, *Witness to History,* 175.

504 "better give them gracefully": Doenecke and Stoler, *Debating Franklin D. Roosevelt's Foreign Policies,* 73.

505 "He knows American production figures better": Salisbury, *Russia on the Way,* 260.

506 Loan negotiations had stalled: Thomas Paterson, "The Abortive American Loan to Russia and the Origins of the Cold War, 1943–1946," *Journal of American History* 56, no. 1 (1969): 70.

506 "would give it to the president": Stettinius, *Roosevelt and the Russians,* 114.

507 "It would be suicide": *Time,* Oct. 1, 1945.

507 "going along nicely": *NYT,* March 3, 1946.

507 "This was impossible": Arthur M. Schlesinger Jr., *Cycles of American History,* 1.

507 "I had it placed": Williams, *Tragedy of American Diplomacy,* 239.

507 "Do you believe": Sept. 24, 1946, "J. V. Stalin on Post-war International Relations," *Soviet News* (1947), http://www.marx2mao.com/Stalin/GPW46.html#s7.

509 On April 12, 1946: *NYT,* April 13, 1946.

509 "Had Roosevelt lived": Robert Sherwood interview with Anthony Eden, Aug. 27, 1946, in Frank Costigliola, "Broken Circle: The Isolation of Franklin D. Roosevelt in World War II," *Diplomatic History* 32, (Nov. 2008): 716.

509 "Whether Russia gets control": Stimson and Bundy, *On Active Service,* 642.

509 "Roosevelt was a great statesman": Montefiore, *Stalin,* 486.

BIBLIOGRAPHY

BOOKS

Abramson, Rudy. *Spanning the Century: The Life of Averell Harriman, 1891–1986.* New York: William Morrow, 1992.

Acheson, Dean. *Present at the Creation: My Years in the State Department.* New York: W. W. Norton, 1969.

Adams, Henry H. *Harry Hopkins.* New York: G. P. Putnam's Sons, 1977.

Affection and Trust: The Personal Correspondence of Harry S. Truman and Dean Acheson. New York: Alfred A. Knopf, 2010.

Aid, Matthew M., and Cees Wiebes, eds. *Secrets of Signals Intelligence During the Cold War and Beyond.* London: Frank Cass, 2001.

Aldritt, Keith, *The Greatest of Friends.* London: Robert Hale, 1995.

Alliluyeva, Svetlana. *Only One Year.* New York: Harper & Row, 1969.

———. *20 Letters to a Friend.* London: Hutchinson, 1967.

Asbell, Bernard, ed. *Mother and Daughter: The Letters of Eleanor and Anna Roosevelt.* New York: Fromm International, 1988.

Axell, Albert. *Marshal Zhukov: The Man Who Beat Hitler.* London: Pearson Longman, 2003.

Beard, Charles A. *President Roosevelt and the Coming of the War, 1941.* New Haven, Conn.: Yale University Press, 1948.

Beevor, Antony. *Berlin: The Downfall, 1945.* London: Penguin, 2003.

Bellush, Bernard. *He Walked Alone.* The Hague: Mouton, 1968.

Bennett, Edward M. *Franklin D. Roosevelt and the Search for Victory.* Wilmington, Del.: SR Books, 1990.

Berezhkov, Valentin. *At Stalin's Side: His Interpreter's Memoirs from the October Revolution to the Fall of the Dictator's Empire.* Translated by Sergei V. Mikheyev. New York: Carol, 1984.

———. *History in the Making: Memoirs of World War II Diplomacy.* Moscow: Progress, 1982.

Beria, Sergo. *Beria, My Father: Inside Stalin's Kremlin.* London: Duckworth, 2001.

Birse, A. H. *Memoirs of an Interpreter.* New York: Coward-McCann, 1967.

Bishop, Jim. *FDR's Last Year, April 1944–April 1945.* New York: William Morrow, 1974.

Blum, John Morton. *From the Morgenthau Diaries:Years of Crisis,1921–1945*. Boston: Houghton Mifflin, 1959.

———. *From the Morgenthau Diaries: Years of War, 1941–1945*. Boston: Houghton Mifflin, 1967.

Bohlen, Charles E. *Witness to History, 1929–1969*. New York: W. W. Norton, 1973.

Boyd, Carl. *Hitler's Japanese Confidant*. Lawrence: University Press of Kansas, 1993.

Braithwaite, Rodric. *Moscow, 1941: A City and Its People at War*. New York: Alfred A. Knopf, 2006.

Brands, H. W. *The Reckless Decade: America in the 1890s*. New York: St. Martin's Press, 1995.

Brent, Jonathan. *Inside the Stalin Archives: Discovering the New Russia*. New York: Atlas, 2008.

British Security Coordination. *The Secret History of British Intelligence in the Americas, 1940–45*. New York: Fromm International, 1999.

Bullitt, Orville H., ed. *For the President, Personal and Secret: Correspondence Between Franklin D. Roosevelt and William C. Bullitt*. Boston: Houghton Mifflin, 1972.

Bullock, Alan. *Hitler and Stalin: Parallel Lives*. New York: Alfred A. Knopf, 1992.

Butler, Susan, ed. *My Dear Mr. Stalin: The Complete Correspondence Between Franklin D. Roosevelt and Joseph V. Stalin*. New Haven, Conn.: Yale University Press, 2005.

Byrnes, James F. *Speaking Frankly*. New York: Harper & Brothers, 1947.

Chuev, Felix. *Molotov Remembers: Inside Kremlin Politics: Conversations with Felix Chuev*. Edited by Albert Resis. Chicago: Ivan R. Dee, 1993.

Chuikov, Vasili I. *The End of the Third Reich*. Manchester, England: MacGibbon and Kee Limited, 1967.

Churchill, Sarah. *A Thread in the Tapestry*. London: Andre Deutsch, 1967.

Churchill, Winston S. *Closing the Ring*. Boston: Houghton Mifflin, 1951.

———. *The Second World War: The Gathering Storm*. Cambridge, Mass.: Riverside Press, 1948.

———. *Their Finest Hour*. Boston: Houghton Mifflin, 1949.

———. *The Hinge of Fate*. Boston: Houghton Mifflin, 1950.

Cold War International History Project. Digital Archive. Working paper 33. Wilson Center.

Conquest, Robert. *Stalin: Breaker of Nations*. New York: Viking, 1991.

Conversino, Mark J. *Fighting with the Soviets: The Failure of Operation Frantic, 1944–1945*. Lawrence: University Press of Kansas, 1997.

Cook, Blanche Wiesen. *Eleanor Roosevelt*. Vol. 1. New York: Penguin Books, 1992.

Costigliola, Frank. *Roosevelt's Lost Alliances: How Personal Politics Helped Start the Cold War.* Princeton, N.J.: Princeton University Press, 2012.

Craig, Campbell, and Sergey Radchenko. *The Atomic Bomb and the Origins of the Cold War.* New Haven, Conn.: Yale University Press, 2008.

Craven, Wesley Frank, and James Lea Cate, eds. *Europe: Argument to V-E Day, January 1944 to May 1945.* Vol. 3 of *The Army Air Forces in World War II.* Chicago: University of Chicago Press, 1951.

Dallek, Robert. *Franklin D. Roosevelt and American Foreign Policy, 1932–1945.* New York: Oxford University Press, 1979.

Davies, Joseph E. *Mission to Moscow.* New York: Simon & Schuster, 1941.

Deane, John R. *The Strange Alliance: The Story of Our Efforts at Wartime Co-operation with Russia.* New York: Viking Press, 1950.

De Santis, Hugh. *The Diplomacy of Silence: The American Foreign Service, the Soviet Union, and the Cold War, 1933–1947.* Chicago: University of Chicago Press, 1983.

D'Este, Carlo. *Eisenhower: A Soldier's Life.* New York: Henry Holt, 2002.

Deutscher, Isaac. *Stalin: A Political Biography.* New York: Vintage Books, 1960.

Dilks, David, ed. *Retreat from Power.* Vol. 2. London: Macmillan, 1981.

Dimitrov, Georgi. *The Diary of Georgi Dimitrov, 1933–1949.* New Haven, Conn.: Yale University Press, 2003.

Divine, Robert A. *Second Chance: The Triumph of Internationalism in America During World War II.* New York: Atheneum, 1967.

Djilas, Milovan. *Conversations with Stalin.* New York: Harcourt Brace Jovanovich, 1962.

Dobbs, Michael. *Six Months in 1945: From World War to Cold War.* New York: Alfred A. Knopf, 2012.

Doenecke, Justus D., and Mark A. Stoler. *Debating Franklin D. Roosevelt's Foreign Policies, 1933–1945.* New York: Rowman & Littlefield, 2005.

Dunlop, Richard. *Donovan: America's Master Spy.* Chicago: Rand McNally, 1982.

Dunn, Dennis J. *Caught Between Roosevelt and Stalin: America's Ambassadors to Moscow.* Lexington: University Press of Kentucky, 1998.

Duranty, Walter. *I Write as I Please.* New York: Simon & Schuster, 1935.

Eden, Anthony. *The Reckoning.* Boston: Houghton Mifflin, 1965.

Edmonds, Robin. *The Big Three: Churchill, Roosevelt, and Stalin in Peace and War.* London: W. W. Norton, 1991.

Elsey, George McKee. *An Unplanned Life.* Columbia: University of Missouri Press, 2005.

Eubank, Keith. *Summit at Teheran.* New York: William Morrow, 1985.

Evans, Richard J. *The Third Reich at War.* New York: Penguin Press, 2009.

Farnsworth, Beatrice, *William C. Bullitt and the Soviet Union.* Bloomington: Indiana University Press, 1967.

Feis, Herbert. *Between War and Peace: The Potsdam Conference.* Princeton, N.J.: Princeton University Press, 1960.

———. *Churchill, Roosevelt, Stalin: The War They Waged and the Peace They Sought.* Princeton, N.J.: Princeton University Press, 1967.

Ferrell, Robert H. *The Dying President: Franklin D. Roosevelt, 1944–1945.* Columbia: University of Missouri Press, 1998.

———. *Off the Record: The Private Papers of Harry S. Truman.* New York: Harper & Row, 1980.

Flagel, Thomas R. *The History Buff's Guide to World War II.* Naperville, Ill.: Source Books, 2012.

Foreign Relations of the United States. The Conferences at Cairo and Tehran, 1943. Washington, D.C.: Government Printing Office, 1961.

———. *Conference of Berlin (the Potsdam Conference) 1945,* Vol. 1. Washington, D.C.: Government Printing Office, 1960.

———. *Conferences at Malta and Yalta, 1945.* Washington, D.C.: Government Printing Office, 1945.

———. *1945, Europe,* Vol. 5. Washington, D.C.: Government Printing Office, 1967.

———. *1944, Europe,* Vol. 4. Washington, D.C.: Government Printing Office, 1966.

———. *1943, The British Commonwealth, Eastern Europe, The Far East,* Vol. 3. Washington, D.C.: Government Printing Office, 1963.

———. *1941, The Far East,* Vol. 4. Washington, D.C.: Government Printing Office, 1956.

———. *1941, General, The Soviet Union,* Vol. 1. Washington, D.C.: Government Printing Office, 1958.

———. *1942, Europe,* Vol. 3. Washington, D.C.: Government Printing Office, 1961.

———. *1939, General,* Vol. 1. Washington, D.C.: Government Printing Office, 1956.

———. *1933, Soviet Union.* Washington, D.C.: Government Printing Office, 1952.

———. *1933–1939, Soviet Union,* Washington, D.C.: Government Printing Office, 1952.

Francis, David R. *Russia from the American Embassy, April, 1916–November, 1918.* New York: C. Scribner's Sons, 1921.

Frank, Richard B. *Downfall: The End of the Imperial Japanese Empire.* New York: Penguin Books, 2001.

Freidel, Frank. *Franklin D. Roosevelt: A Rendezvous with Destiny.* Boston: Little, Brown, 1990.

Gannon, Robert I. *The Cardinal Spellman Story.* London: Robert Hale, 1963.

Gilbert, Martin. *Road to Victory: Winston S. Churchill, 1941–1945*. London: Mandarin Paperback, 1986.

Goodwin, Doris Kearns. *No Ordinary Time*. New York: Simon & Schuster, 1994.

Gordin, Michael D. *Five Days in August*. Princeton, N.J.: Princeton University Press, 2007.

———. *Red Cloud at Dawn*. New York: Farrar, Straus and Giroux, 2009.

Gorodetsky, Gabriel. *Stafford Cripps in Moscow, 1940–1942*. Portland, Ore.: Vallentine Mitchell, 2007.

———. *Grand Delusion. Stalin and the German Invasion of Russia*. New Haven, Conn.: Yale University Press, 1999.

Gray, Ian. *Stalin: Man of History*. Garden City, N.Y.: Doubleday, 1979.

Greenfield, Kent Roberts. *American Strategy in World War II: A Reconsideration*. Baltimore: Johns Hopkins University Press, 1963.

Gromyko, Andrei. *Memories: From Stalin to Gorbachev*. Translated by Harold Shukman. London: Arrow Books, 1989.

Gunther, John. *Roosevelt in Retrospect: A Profile in History*. New York: Harper & Brothers, 1950.

Halberstam, David. *The Best and the Brightest*. New York: Random House, 1972.

———. *The Coldest Winter: America and the Korean War*. New York: Hyperion, 2007.

Harriman, W. Averell, and Elie Abel. *Special Envoy to Churchill and Stalin, 1941–1946*. New York: Random House, 1975.

———. *America and Russia in a Changing World: A Half Century of Personal Observation*. Garden City, N.Y.: Doubleday, 1971.

Hassett, William D. *Off the Record with FDR, 1942–1945*. New Brunswick, N.J.: Rutgers University Press, 1958.

Hastings, Max. *Inferno: The World at War, 1939–1945*. New York: Alfred A. Knopf, 2011.

———. *Winston's War: Churchill, 1940–1945*. New York: Alfred A. Knopf, 2010.

Hathaway, Robert M. *Ambiguous Partnership*. New York: Columbia University Press, 1981.

Henderson, Loy. *A Question of Trust: The Origins of U.S.-Soviet Diplomatic Relations*. Stanford, Calif.: Hoover Institution Press, 1986.

Herring, George C. *Aid to Russia, 1941–1946*. New York: Columbia University Press, 1973.

Herzen, Alexander. *My Past and Thoughts: The Memoirs of Alexander Herzen*. New York: Alfred A. Knopf, 1968.

Hitler, Adolf. *Mein Kampf*. New York: Reynal and Hitchcock, 1939.

Holloway, David. *Stalin and the Bomb: The Soviet Union and Atomic Energy, 1939–1956.* New Haven, Conn.: Yale University Press, 1994.

Hull, Cordell. *The Memoirs of Cordell Hull.* New York: Macmillan, 1948.

Ickes, Harold. *The First Thousand Days, 1933–1936.* Vol. 1 of *The Secret Diary of Harold L. Ickes.* New York: Simon & Schuster, 1954.

———. *The Lowering Clouds, 1939–1941.* Vol. 3 of *The Secret Diary of Harold L. Ickes.* New York: Simon & Schuster, 1954.

Isaacson, Walter, and Evan Thomas. *The Wise Men: Six Friends and the World They Made.* New York: Simon & Schuster, 1986.

Ismay, Lord. *The Memoirs of General Lord Ismay.* New York: Viking Press, 1960.

Isaacson, Walter. *Einstein: His Life and Universe.* New York: Simon & Schuster, 2007.

Iurchenko, S. V. *Ialtinskaia Konferentsiia. 1945 goda: Khronika sozdaniia novogo mira.* Simferopol, Ukraine: Krym, 2005.

Jackson, Robert H. *That Man: An Insider's Portrait of Franklin D. Roosevelt.* New York: Oxford University Press, 2003.

Jones, Robert Hugh. *The Roads to Russia: United States Lend-Lease to the Soviet Union.* Norman: University of Oklahoma Press, 1969.

Josephson, Paul R. *Red Atom: Russia's Nuclear Power Program from Stalin to Today.* Pittsburgh: University of Pittsburgh Press, 2005.

Kahan, Stuart. *The Wolf of the Kremlin.* New York: William Morrow, 1987.

Keneally, Thomas. *Three Famines: Starvation and Politics.* New York: PublicAffairs, 2011.

Kennan, George F. *Memoirs, 1925–1950.* Vol. 1. Boston: Little, Brown, 1967.

Kennedy, David M. *Freedom from Fear: The American People in Depression and War, 1929–1945.* New York: Oxford University Press, 1999.

Khrushchev, Nikita. *Khrushchev Remembers.* Boston: Little, Brown, 1970.

Kimball, Warren F., ed. *Churchill and Roosevelt: The Complete Correspondence.* 3 vols. Princeton, N.J.: Princeton University Press, 1984.

———. *The Juggler: Franklin Roosevelt as Wartime Statesman.* Princeton, N.J.: Princeton University Press, 1991.

Kleeman, Rita Hale. *Gracious Lady: The Life of Sara Delano Roosevelt.* New York: D. Appleton–Century, 1935.

Kuby, Erich. *The Russians and Berlin, 1945.* London: Heinemann, 1968.

Lash, Joseph P. *Roosevelt and Churchill, 1939–1941: The Partnership That Saved the West.* New York: W. W. Norton, 1976.

———. *Love, Eleanor: Eleanor Roosevelt and Her Friends.* Garden City, N.Y.: Doubleday, 1982.

Leahy, William D. *I Was There.* New York: Arno Press, 1979.

Le Tissier, Tony. *Zhukov at the Oder: The Decisive Battle for Berlin.* Westport, Conn.: Praeger, 1996.

Levering, Ralph B. *Debating the Origins of the Cold War: American and Russian Perspectives.* Lanham, Md.: Rowman & Littlefield, 2001.

Lih, Lars T., Oleg V. Naumov, and Oleg V. Khlevniuk. *Stalin's Letters to Molotov, 1925–1936.* New Haven, Conn.: Yale University Press, 1995.

Loewenheim, Francis L., Harold D. Langley, and Manfred Jonas, eds. *Roosevelt and Churchill: Their Secret Wartime Correspondence.* New York: Da Capo, 1990.

Lukacs, John. *Churchill: Visionary, Statesman, Historian.* New Haven, Conn.: Yale University Press, 2002.

———. *Five Days in London, May 1940.* New Haven, Conn.: Yale University Press, 1999.

———. *June, 1941: Hitler and Stalin.* New Haven, Conn.: Yale University Press, 2006.

MacLean, Elizabeth Kimball. *Joseph E. Davies: Envoy to the Soviets.* Westport, Conn.: Praeger, 1992.

MacMillan, Margaret Owen. *Paris 1919: Six Months That Changed the World.* New York: Random House, 2002.

Mahan, Alfred Thayer. *The Influence of Sea Power upon History, 1660–1783.* New York: Dover, 1987.

Maisky, Ivan. *Memoirs of a Soviet Ambassador: The War, 1939–43.* New York: Charles Scribner's Sons, 1968.

Malloy, Sean. *Atomic Tragedy: Henry L. Stimson and the Decision to Use the Bomb Against Japan.* Ithaca, N.Y.: Cornell University Press, 2008.

Manchester, William. *American Caesar.* Boston: Little, Brown, 1978.

Matloff, Maurice, and Edwin M. Snell. *The War Department: Strategic Planning for Coalition Warfare, 1941–1942.* Washington, D.C.: Center of Military History, 1999.

McIntire, Ross T. *White House Physician.* New York: G. P. Putnam's Sons, 1946.

Meacham, Jon. *Franklin and Winston: An Intimate Portrait of an Epic Friendship.* New York: Random House, 2003.

Millis, Walter, ed. *The Forrestal Diaries.* New York: Viking Press, 1951.

Miscamble, Wilson D. *From Roosevelt to Truman: Potsdam, Hiroshima, and the Cold War.* Cambridge, U.K.: Cambridge University Press, 2007.

Mommen, André. *Stalin's Economist: The Economic Contributions of Jeno Varga.* London: Routledge, 2011.

Montefiore, Simon Sebag. *Stalin: The Court of the Red Tsar.* New York: Alfred A. Knopf, 2004.

———. *Young Stalin.* London: Weidenfeld & Nicolson, 2007.

Moran, Lord. *Churchill at War, 1940–45.* New York: Carroll & Graf, 2002.

Morgan, Kay Summersby. *Past Forgetting.* New York: Simon & Schuster, 1976.

Mukerjee, Madhusree. *Churchill's Secret War: The British Empire and the Ravaging of India During World War II.* New York: Basic Books, 2010.

Murphy, David E. *What Stalin Knew: The Enigma of Barbarossa.* New Haven, Conn.: Yale University Press, 2005.

Neumann, William L. *After Victory: Churchill, Roosevelt, Stalin, and the Making of the Peace.* New York: Harper & Row, 1967.

Neville, Peter. *A Traveller's History of Russia.* Brooklyn: Interlink Books, 2001.

Nisbet, Robert. *Roosevelt and Stalin: The Failed Courtship.* Washington, D.C.: Regnery Gateway, 1988.

Sovetsko-amerikanskie otnosheniia, 1939–1945 [Soviet-American relations, 1939–1945]. Moscow, 2004.

Olson, Lynne. *Citizens of London: The Americans Who Stood with Britain in Its Blackest and Finest Hour.* New York: Random House, 2010.

Olson, Lynne, and Stanley Cloud. *A Question of Honor.* New York: Alfred A. Knopf, 2003.

O'Sullivan, Christopher D. *Sumner Welles, Postwar Planning, and the Quest for a New World Order, 1937–1943.* New York: Columbia University Press, 2008.

Overy, Richard. *Russia's War.* New York: Penguin Books, 1997.

Pechatnov, Vladimir. *Stalin, Ruzvelt, Trumen: SSSR i SShA v 1940-kh gg.* [Stalin, Roosevelt, Truman: The U.S.S.R. and the U.S.A. in the 1940s]. Moscow: TERRA-Knizhnyi Klub, 2006.

Persico, Joseph E. *Roosevelt's Secret War: FDR and World War II Espionage.* New York: Random House, 2001.

Perkins, Frances. *The Roosevelt I Knew.* New York: Viking Press, 1946.

Perlmutter, Amos. *FDR and Stalin: A Not So Grand Alliance.* Columbia: University of Missouri Press, 1993.

Phillips, William. *Ventures in Diplomacy.* Boston: Beacon Press, 1952.

Plesch, Dan. *America, Hitler, and the UN.* London: I. B. Tauris, 2011.

Plokhy, S. M. *Yalta: The Price of Peace.* New York: Viking, 2010.

Pogue, Forrest C. *Ordeal and Hope, 1939–1942.* Vol. 2 of *George C. Marshall.* New York: Viking Press, 1966.

———. *Organizer of Victory, 1943–1945.* Vol. 3 of *George C. Marshall.* New York: Viking Press, 1973.

Polonsky, Rachel. *Molotov's Magic Lantern.* New York: Farrar, Straus and Giroux, 2011.

Radzinsky, Edvard. *Stalin.* New York: Anchor Books, 1996.

Rauch, Basil, ed. *The Roosevelt Reader: Selected Speeches, Messages, Press Conferences, and Letters of Franklin D. Roosevelt.* New York: Rinehart, 1957.

Rees, Laurence. *The Nazis: A Warning from History.* New York: New Press, 1997.

Reilly, Michael F. *Reilly of the White House.* New York: Simon & Schuster, 1947.

Reston, James. *Deadline: A Memoir.* New York: Random House, 1991.

Reynolds, David. *From World War to Cold War: Churchill, Roosevelt, and the International History of the 1940s.* Oxford: Oxford University Press, 2006.

Rhodes, Richard. *Dark Sun: The Making of the Hydrogen Bomb.* New York: Simon & Schuster, 1995.

———. *The Making of the Atomic Bomb.* New York: Simon & Schuster, 1986.

Rigdon, William M. *White House Sailor.* Garden City, N.Y.: Doubleday, 1962.

Roberts, Geoffrey. *Stalin's Wars: From World War to Cold War, 1939–1953.* New Haven, Conn.: Yale University Press, 2006.

———. *Molotov: Stalin's Cold Warrior.* Washington, D.C.: Potomac Books, 2012.

Roosevelt, Curtis. *Too Close to the Sun.* New York: Perseus Books, 2008.

Roosevelt, Eleanor. *This I Remember.* New York: Harper & Brothers, 1949.

Roosevelt, Elliott. *As He Saw It.* New York: Duell, Sloan and Pearce, 1946.

Roosevelt, Franklin D. *F.D.R.: His Personal Letters.* Edited by Elliott Roosevelt. With a foreword by Eleanor Roosevelt. New York: Duell, Sloan and Pearce, 1947–1950.

———. *F.D.R.: His Personal Letters, 1928–1945.* Edited by Elliott Roosevelt. New York: Duell, Sloan and Pearce, 1950.

———. *On Our Way.* New York: John Day, 1934.

Roosevelt, Franklin D. and Felix Frankfurter. *Roosevelt and Frankfurter: Their Correspondence, 1928–1945.* Annotated by Max Freedman. Boston: Little, Brown, 1968.

Roosevelt, James. *My Parents: A Differing View.* Chicago: Playboy Press, 1976.

Roosevelt, Sara. *My Boy Franklin.* New York: J. J. Little & Ives, 1933.

Rose, Lisle A. *Dubious Victory: The United States and the End of World War II.* Kent, Ohio: Kent State University Press, 1973.

Rosenman, Samuel Irving. *Working with Roosevelt.* New York: Harper & Brothers, 1952.

Rzheshevsky, Oleg A. *War and Diplomacy: The Making of the Grand Alliance.* Translated by T. Sorokina. Oxford: Harwood Academic, 1996.

Sakharov, Andrei. *Memoirs.* London: Hutchinson, 1990.

Salisbury, Harrison. *Russia on the Way.* New York: Macmillan, 1946.

Salzman, Neil Z. *Reform and Revolution: The Life and Times of Raymond Robbins.* Kent, Ohio: Kent State University Press, 1991.

Schlesinger, Arthur M., Jr. *The Coming of the New Deal.* Vol. 2 of *The Age of Roosevelt.* Boston: Riverside, 1959.

———. *The Cycles of American History.* Boston: Houghton Mifflin, 1986.

Schlesinger, Stephen C. *Act of Creation: The Founding of the United Nations.* Boulder, Colo.: Westview, 2003.

Schmitz, David. *The Triumph of Internationalism: Franklin D. Roosevelt and a World in Crisis, 1933–1941.* Washington, D.C.: Potomac Books, 2007.

Shepilov, Dmitrii. *The Kremlin's Scholar: A Memoir of Soviet Politics Under Stalin and Khrushchev.* New Haven, Conn.: Yale University Press, 2007.

Sherwin, Martin J. *A World Destroyed: Hiroshima and the Origins of the Arms Race.* New York: Vintage Books, 1987.

Sherwood, Robert E. *Roosevelt and Hopkins: An Intimate History.* New York: Harper & Brothers, 1948.

Shirer, William L. *Berlin Diary: The Journal of a Foreign Correspondent, 1934–1941.* Little, Brown, 1940.

———. *The Rise and Fall of the Third Reich.* New York: Simon & Schuster, 1960.

Skidelsky, Robert. *John Maynard Keynes: Fighting for Freedom, 1937–46.* New York: Viking, 2001.

Smelser, Ronald M., and Edward J. Davies II. *The Myth of the Eastern Front: The Nazi-Soviet War in American Popular Culture.* Cambridge, U.K.: Cambridge University Press, 2007.

Smith, Bradley F. *Sharing Secrets with Stalin: How the Allies Traded Intelligence, 1941–1945.* Lawrence: University Press of Kansas, 1996.

Smith, Jean Edward. *FDR.* New York: Random House, 2008.

Smith, R. Elberton. *The Army and Economic Mobilization.* Washington, D.C.: Office of the Chief of Military History, 1959.

Snyder, Timothy. *Bloodlands.* New York: Basic Books, 2010.

Soviet-American Relations, 1934–1939. Moscow: International Foundation "Democracy," 2003.

Soviet-American Relations, 1939–1945. Moscow: International Foundation "Democracy," 2004.

Stafford, David. *Roosevelt and Churchill: Men of Secrets.* Woodstock, N.Y.: Overlook, 2.

Stalin, Joseph. *Stalin's Correspondence with Churchill and Attlee, 1941–1945.* New York: Capricorn, 1965.

———. *On the Great Patriotic War of the Soviet Union.* Moscow: Foreign Languages Publishing House, 1946. Prepared for the Internet by David J. Romagnolo. http://www.marxists.org.

Standley, W. H. *Admiral Ambassador to Russia.* Chicago: Regnery, 1955.

Stettinius, Edward R. *The Diaries of Edward R. Stettinius Jr., 1943–1946.* Edited by Thomas M. Campbell and George C. Herring. New York: New Viewpoints, 1975.

———. *Roosevelt and the Russians: The Yalta Conference.* New York: Doubleday, 1949.

Stimson, Henry L., and McGeorge Bundy. *On Active Service in Peace and War.* New York: Harper & Brothers, 1948.

Strong, Anna Louise. *The Soviets Expected It.* New York: Dial Press, 1941.

Sudoplatov, Pavel, and Anatoli Sudoplatov. *Special Tasks: The Memoirs of an*

Unwanted Witness—a Soviet Spymaster. With Jerrold L. Schecter and Leona P. Schecter. Boston: Little, Brown, 1995.

Svanidze, Budu. *My Uncle Joseph Stalin.* New York: G. P. Putnam's Sons, 1953.

Teller, Edward. *Memoirs: A Twentieth-Century Journey in Science and Politics.* Cambridge, Mass.: Perseus Publishing, 2001.

Thayer, Charles. *Bears in the Caviar.* London: Michael Joseph Ltd., 1952.

Thomas, Evan. *Sea of Thunder: Four Commanders and the Last Great Naval Campaign, 1941–1945.* New York: Simon & Schuster, 2006.

Tully, Grace. *F.D.R.: My Boss.* Chicago: People's Book Club, 1949.

Van Ree, Erik. *The Political Thought of Joseph Stalin: A Study in Twentieth-Century Revolutionary Patriotism.* London: Routledge Curzon, 2002.

Vogel, Steve. *The Pentagon: A History.* New York: Random House, 2007.

Volkogonov, Dmitri. *Stalin: Triumph and Tragedy.* New York: Grove Press, 1988.

Ward, Geoffrey C. *Before the Trumpet: Young Franklin Roosevelt, 1882–1905.* New York: Harper & Row, 1985.

———. *A First-Class Temperament: The Emergence of Franklin Roosevelt.* New York: Harper & Row, 1989.

———, ed. *Closest Companion: The Unknown Story of the Intimate Relationship Between Franklin Roosevelt and Margaret Suckley.* Boston: Houghton Mifflin, 1995.

Wehle, Louis B. *Hidden Threads of History: Wilson Through Roosevelt.* New York: Macmillan, 1953.

Welles, Sumner. *Where Are We Heading?* New York: Harper and Brothers, 1946.

Werth, Alexander. *Russia at War, 1941–1945.* New York: Avon, 1965.

Williams, William Appleman. *The Tragedy of American Diplomacy.* New York: W. W. Norton, 1988.

———. *American-Russian Relations 1781–1947.* New York: Rinehart and Co., 1952.

Wright, Patrick. *Iron Curtain: From Stage to Cold War.* New York: Oxford University Press, 2007.

Yurchenko, Sergey. *Yalta Conference of 1945: The Story of the Creation of the New World.* Simferopol: Crimea Publishers, 2005.

Zhukov, Georgi. *The Memoirs of Marshal Zhukov.* New York: Delacorte Press, 1971.

Zubok, Vladislav, and Constantine Pleshakov. *Inside the Kremlin's Cold War.* Cambridge, Mass.: Harvard University Press, 1996.

MANUSCRIPT COLLECTIONS

Connelly, Matthew J., Papers. Harry S. Truman Library, Independence, Mo.

Forrestall, James, Papers. Seeley Mudd Manuscript Library, Princeton, N.J.

Harriman, Averell, Papers. Manuscript Division, Library of Congress, Washington, D.C.

Hopkins, Harry, Papers. Franklin D. Roosevelt Library, Hyde Park, N.Y.

King, William Lyon Mackenzie, Diaries. Library and Archives Canada, www .collectionscanada.gc.ca.

Leahy, William D., Diaries. Manuscript Division, Microfilm, Library of Congress, Washington, D.C.

Molotov, V. M. The Papers of V. M. Molotov. Fond 82, Russian State Archive of Social and Political History (RGASPI) (Lichnyi arkhiv V. M. Molotova), Moscow.

Nazi-Soviet Relations, 1939–1941. Avalon Project: 20th Century Documents. Lillian Goldman Law Library, Yale Law School, http://avalon.law.yale .edu.

Phillips, William, Papers. Houghton Library, Harvard University.

Roosevelt, Franklin D., Papers. Franklin D. Roosevelt Presidential Library, Hyde Park, N.Y.

Stalin, Joseph. The Papers of I. V. Stalin. Fond 558, Russian State Archive of Social and Political History (RGASPI) (Lichnyi arkhiv I. V. Stalina), Moscow.

Steinhardt, Laurence, Papers. Manuscript Division, Library of Congress, Washington, D.C.

Stettinius, Edward R., Jr., Papers. Albert and Shirley Small Special Collections, University of Virginia.

Stimson, Henry Lewis, Diaries. Sterling Memorial Library, Yale University.

INDEX

Page numbers beginning with 513 refer to endnotes.

ILLUSTRATION CREDITS

FDR signing UNRRA document: Franklin D. Roosevelt Library
Chiang Kai-shek, FDR, and Churchill: Franklin D. Roosevelt Library
FDR, Mackenzie King, and Churchill: Franklin D. Roosevelt Library
RAF officer with the sword of Stalingrad: Franklin D. Roosevelt Library
UNO sketch concept: Public Domain
Marshall, Clark-Kerr, Hopkins, Bohlen, Stalin, and Voroshilov: Public Domain
Svetlana Alliluyeva sitting on the lap of Beria: Public Domain
FDR and Stalin at Tehran: Franklin D. Roosevelt Library
Stalin, Lenin, and Kalinen: Public Domain
Troyanovsky, Whalen, and Oumansky: © New York Public Library
Von Ribbentrop and Stalin look on as Molotov examines the Nonaggression Pact:
    © New York Public Library
Von Ribbentrop, Stalin, and Molotov at signing of the Nonaggression Pact: © New
    York Public Library
Von Ribbentrop shaking hands: © New York Public Library
FDR at Norfolk Navy Yard: Franklin D. Roosevelt Library
Georgi Zhukov: Franklin D. Roosevelt Library
Destroyed Stalingrad: Courtesy of Library of Congress
Churchill arriving aboard the USS *Augusta*: Franklin D. Roosevelt Library
The USS *Arizona* sinking at Pearl Harbor: Franklin D. Roosevelt Library
Hull and Litvinov greet Molotov: Public Domain
U.S. A-20 attack bombers: Franklin D. Roosevelt Library
FDR press conference in Casablanca: Franklin D. Roosevelt Library
Churchill and his military staff: Public Domain
Churchill, Harriman, Stalin, and Molotov: Courtesy of Library of Congress
Stalin smoking a pipe: Courtesy of Library of Congress
Conant, Bush, and Groves: Public Domain
Kurchatov and Sakharov: Public Domain
Winant, FDR, Stettinius, and Hopkins: Public Domain
Stettinius and Molotov at Saki airfield: Franklin D. Roosevelt Library
FDR meets privately with Stalin: Signal Corps, U.S. Army
FDR meets privately with Churchill: Signal Corps, U.S. Army
FDR waiting for first plenary session to begin: Franklin D. Roosevelt Library
First plenary session under way: Franklin D. Roosevelt Library
Stettinius, FDR, and Stalin: Franklin D. Roosevelt Library
The Big Three posing for the cameras: Public Domain
The closing lunch, February 11: Franklin D. Roosevelt Library
FDR addressing Congress: Franklin D. Roosevelt Library
FDR and his cabinet: Franklin D. Roosevelt Library

Eisenhower and Marshall: Public Domain
Eisenhower viewing death camp: Franklin D. Roosevelt Library
FDR at work at his cottage: Courtesy of Library of Congress
Last photograph of FDR: Franklin D. Roosevelt Library
The train carrying FDR's body: Franklin D. Roosevelt Library
Truman, Churchill, and Stalin: Franklin D. Roosevelt Library
Stimson, Stettinius, and Forrestal: © Harry S. Truman Library
Eisenhower and Stimson: © Harry S. Truman Library
Stimson and Truman: © Harry S. Truman Library
Wallace arriving at the White House: © Harry S. Truman Library
Truman and his cabinet: © Harry S. Truman Library